MICROSOFT® VISUAL C#® 2017

AN INTRODUCTION TO OBJECT-ORIENTED PROGRAMMING, SEVENTH EDITION

SEVENTH EDITION

MICROSOFT® VISUAL C#® 2017

AN INTRODUCTION TO OBJECT-ORIENTED PROGRAMMING

JOYCE FARRELL

Australia • Brazil • Canada • Mexico • Singapore • United Kingdom • United States

Microsoft® Visual C#® 2017: An Introduction to Object-Oriented Programming, Seventh Edition
Joyce Farrell

SVP, GM Science, Technology & Math: Balraj S. Kalsi

Senior Product Director: Kathleen McMahon

Product Team Manager: Kristin McNary

Associate Product Manager: Kate Mason

Senior Director, Development: Julia Caballero

Senior Content Development Manager: Leigh Hefferon

Senior Content Developer: Alyssa Pratt

Product Assistant: Jake Toth

Marketing Director: Michele McTighe

Marketing Manager: Jeffrey A. Tousignant

Senior Content Project Manager: Jennifer Feltri-George

Senior Designer/Art Director: Diana Graham

Production Service/Composition: SPi Global

Cover image: Colormos/Photodisc/Getty Images

© 2018, 2016 Cengage Learning, Inc. ALL RIGHTS RESERVED.

No part of this work covered by the copyright herein may be reproduced or distributed in any form or by any means, except as permitted by U.S. copyright law, without the prior written permission of the copyright owner.

Unless otherwise noted all screenshots are courtesy of Microsoft Corporation

> For product information and technology assistance, contact us at
> **Cengage Customer & Sales Support, 1-800-354-9706**
> **or support.cengage.com.**
>
> For permission to use material from this text or product, submit all requests online at **www.copyright.com**.

Library of Congress Control Number: 2017941097

Softbound ISBN: 978-1-337-10210-0
Loose Leaf ISBN: 978-1-337-68577-1

Cengage
200 Pier 4 Boulevard
Boston, MA 02210
USA

Cengage is a leading provider of customized learning solutions with employees residing in nearly 40 different countries and sales in more than 125 countries around the world. Find your local representative at: **www.cengage.com**.

To learn more about Cengage platforms and services, register or access your online learning solution, or purchase materials for your course, visit **www.cengage.com**.

Notice to the Reader
Publisher does not warrant or guarantee any of the products described herein or perform any independent analysis in connection with any of the product information contained herein. Publisher does not assume, and expressly disclaims, any obligation to obtain and include information other than that provided to it by the manufacturer. The reader is expressly warned to consider and adopt all safety precautions that might be indicated by the activities described herein and to avoid all potential hazards. By following the instructions contained herein, the reader willingly assumes all risks in connection with such instructions. The publisher makes no representations or warranties of any kind, including but not limited to, the warranties of fitness for particular purpose or merchantability, nor are any such representations implied with respect to the material set forth herein, and the publisher takes no responsibility with respect to such material. The publisher shall not be liable for any special, consequential, or exemplary damages resulting, in whole or part, from the readers' use of, or reliance upon, this material.

Printed in the United States of America
Print Number: 08   Print Year: 2022

Brief Contents

	Preface	xv
CHAPTER 1	A First Program Using C#	1
CHAPTER 2	Using Data	47
CHAPTER 3	Using GUI Objects and the Visual Studio IDE	99
CHAPTER 4	Making Decisions	133
CHAPTER 5	Looping	185
CHAPTER 6	Using Arrays	223
CHAPTER 7	Using Methods	265
CHAPTER 8	Advanced Method Concepts	307
CHAPTER 9	Using Classes and Objects	351
CHAPTER 10	Introduction to Inheritance	421
CHAPTER 11	Exception Handling	483
CHAPTER 12	Using Controls	535
CHAPTER 13	Handling Events	597
CHAPTER 14	Files and Streams	645
APPENDIX A	Operator Precedence and Associativity	695
APPENDIX B	Understanding Numbering Systems and Computer Codes	697
APPENDIX C	Using the IDE Editor	707
	Glossary	711
	Index	729

Contents

Preface xv

CHAPTER 1 A First Program Using C# 1
   The Programming Process 2
   Procedural and Object-Oriented Programming 4
   Features of Object-Oriented Programming Languages. 7
   The C# Programming Language. 9
   Writing a C# Program that Produces Output 11
   Selecting Identifiers 14
   Improving Programs by Adding Comments
     and Using the `System` Namespace 18
     Adding Program Comments. 18
     Using the `System` Namespace 19
   Compiling and Executing a C# Program 23
     Compiling Code from the Command Prompt 24
     Compiling Code Using the Visual Studio IDE 26
     Noticing the Differences Between the Programs
       in the Text Editor and the IDE 29
     Deciding Which Environment to Use 30
   Chapter Summary 38
   Key Terms 38
   Review Questions 42
   Exercises. 44

CHAPTER 2 Using Data. **47**
   Declaring Variables 48
   Displaying Variable Values 52
     Variable Alignment 55
   Using the Integral Data Types. 56
   Using Floating-Point Data Types 59
     Formatting Floating-Point Values. 60
   Using Arithmetic Operators. 63
     Using Shortcut Arithmetic Operators. 64

Using the `bool` Data Type 68
Understanding Numeric Type Conversion. 71
Using the `char` Data Type 74
Using the `string` Data Type. 76
Defining Named Constants 80
   Working with Enumerations 81
Accepting Console Input 84
   Using the `Convert` Class 84
   Using the `Parse()` Methods 86
Chapter Summary 89
Key Terms 90
Review Questions 93
Exercises. 96

CHAPTER 3   Using GUI Objects and the Visual Studio IDE . . . **99**

Creating a Form in the IDE 100
Using the Toolbox to Add a `Button` to a `Form`. 105
Adding Functionality to a `Button` on a `Form` 107
Adding `Labels` and `TextBoxes` to a `Form`. 109
   Understanding Focus and Tab Control 112
   Formatting Data in GUI Applications 113
   Changing a `Label`'s Font. 114
Naming `Forms` and `Controls` 114
Correcting Errors 116
   Deleting an Unwanted Event-Handling Method. 117
   Failing to Close a `Form` Before Attempting
     to Reexecute a Program 118
   Using Visual Studio Help 118
Deciding Which Interface to Use 119
Chapter Summary 125
Key Terms 126
Review Questions 127
Exercises. 130

CHAPTER 4   Making Decisions **133**

Understanding Logic-Planning Tools and Decision Making . . .134
Making Decisions Using the `if` Statement 137
   A Note on Equivalency Comparisons. 143
Making Decisions Using the `if-else` Statement. 145

CONTENTS

Using Compound Expressions in `if` Statements 150
   Using the Conditional AND Operator 150
   Using the Conditional OR Operator. 152
   Using the Logical AND and OR Operators. 153
   Combining AND and OR Operators. 154
Making Decisions Using the `switch` Statement 159
   Using an Enumeration with a switch Statement 162
Using the Conditional Operator 164
Using the NOT Operator 165
Avoiding Common Errors When Making Decisions. 167
   Performing Accurate and Efficient Range Checks 167
   Using && and || Appropriately. 169
   Using the ! Operator Correctly 169
Decision-Making Issues in GUI Programs 171
Chapter Summary 175
Key Terms 175
Review Questions 177
Exercises. 181

CHAPTER 5   Looping 185

Creating Loops with the `while` Statement. 186
Creating Loops with the `for` Statement 195
Creating Loops with the `do` Statement. 198
Using Nested Loops 200
Accumulating Totals 206
Improving Loop Performance .208
   Avoiding Unnecessary Operations 208
   Considering the Order of Evaluation
     of Short-Circuit Operators. 209
   Employing Loop Fusion 210
   Using Prefix Incrementing Rather
     Than Postfix Incrementing. 210
Looping Issues in GUI Programs 212
Chapter Summary 215
Key Terms 216
Review Questions 217
Exercises. 220

CHAPTER 6   Using Arrays 223

Declaring an Array and Assigning Values. 224
   Initializing an Array. 226

Accessing Array Elements 228
   Using the `Length` Property. 229
   Using `foreach` 230
Searching an Array Using a Loop 233
   Using a `for` Loop to Search an Array 234
   Improving a Loop's Efficiency 236
   Using a `while` Loop to Search an Array 237
   Searching an Array for a Range Match 239
Using the `BinarySearch()`, `Sort()`,
  and `Reverse()` Methods 241
   Using the `BinarySearch()` Method 241
   Using the `Sort()` Method 243
   Using the `Reverse()` Method 244
Using Multidimensional Arrays 247
   Using Jagged Arrays .251
Array Issues in GUI Programs 253
Chapter Summary 255
Key Terms 255
Review Questions 256
Exercises 259

CHAPTER 7   Using Methods **265**

Understanding Methods and Implementation Hiding 266
   Understanding Implementation Hiding 267
Writing Methods with No Parameters
  and No Return Value .268
   An Introduction to Accessibility 269
   An Introduction to the Optional `static` Modifier 270
   An Introduction to Return Types 271
   Understanding the Method Identifier 271
   Placing a Method in a Class 272
   Declaring Variables and Constants in a Method 273
Writing Methods That Require a Single Argument 276
Writing Methods That Require Multiple Arguments 280
Writing Methods That Return a Value 282
   Writing a Method That Returns a Boolean Value 284
   Analyzing a Built-In Method 285
Passing Array Values to a Method 289
   Passing a Single Array Element to a Method 289
   Passing an Array to a Method 290

CONTENTS

Alternate Ways to Write a `Main()` Method Header 293
   Writing a `Main()` Method with a Parameter List 293
   Writing a `Main()` Method with an Integer Return Type . . .294
   Writing a `Main()` Method with `public` Access 294
Issues Using Methods in GUI Programs 295
   Understanding Methods That Are Generated
     Automatically in the Visual Environment. 295
   Appreciating Scope in a GUI Program 296
   Creating Methods to be Nonstatic When Associated
     with a `Form` .296
Chapter Summary .297
Key Terms 298
Review Questions 300
Exercises 303

CHAPTER 8   **Advanced Method Concepts** **307**

An Overview of C#'s Parameter Types 308
   Using Mandatory Value Parameters 308
Passing Parameters by Reference 310
   Using a `ref` Parameter 311
   Using an `out` Parameter 312
   Using an `out` Variable 313
   Deciding Between `out` and `ref` 313
   Using a Built-in Method That Has an `out` Parameter 314
   Using Parameter Arrays 316
Returning a Reference from a Method 319
Overloading Methods 322
   Understanding Overload Resolution 326
   Discovering Built-In Overloaded Methods 327
Avoiding Ambiguous Methods 330
Using Optional Parameters 332
   Leaving Out Unnamed Arguments 334
   Using Named Arguments 335
   Advantages to Using Named Arguments 336
   Disadvantages to Using Named Arguments 337
   Overload Resolution with Named
     and Optional Arguments 339
Chapter Summary .341
Key Terms 341
Review Questions .342
Exercises 346

CHAPTER 9	Using Classes and Objects **351**
	Understanding Class Concepts 352
	Creating a Class from Which Objects Can Be Instantiated . . .354
	Creating Instance Variables and Methods. 355
	Creating Objects 357
	Passing Objects to Methods 360
	Creating Properties 361
	Using Auto-Implemented Properties 365
	More About `public` and `private` Access Modifiers. 371
	Understanding the `this` Reference 375
	Understanding Constructors 378
	Passing Parameters to Constructors. 379
	Overloading Constructors. 380
	Using Constructor Initializers 382
	Using the `readonly` Modifier in a Constructor. 384
	Using Object Initializers 386
	Overloading Operators. .390
	Declaring an Array of Objects. 395
	Using the `Sort()` and `BinarySearch()`
	Methods with Arrays of Objects 396
	Understanding Destructors. 403
	Understanding GUI Application Objects 405
	Chapter Summary 407
	Key Terms 409
	Review Questions 411
	Exercises. 414
CHAPTER 10	Introduction to Inheritance **421**
	Understanding Inheritance 422
	Understanding Inheritance Terminology 424
	Extending Classes. 426
	Using the `protected` Access Specifier. 432
	Overriding Base Class Members 436
	Accessing Base Class Methods and Properties
	from a Derived Class 439
	Understanding Implicit Reference Conversions 445
	Using the `Object` Class. 446
	Using the `Object` Class's `GetType()` Method 448
	Using the `Object` Class's `ToString()` Method 448
	Using the `Object` Class's `Equals()` Method 449
	Using the `Object` Class's `GetHashCode()` Method 450

CONTENTS

Working with Base Class Constructors. 452
   Using Base Class Constructors That Require Arguments. . .453
Creating and Using Abstract Classes 456
Creating and Using Interfaces. 460
Using Extension Methods. 465
Recognizing Inheritance in GUI Applications 467
Chapter Summary. 470
Key Terms 471
Review Questions 473
Exercises. 476

CHAPTER 11   Exception Handling **483**

Understanding Exceptions 484
Purposely Generating a `SystemException` 486
Comparing Traditional and Object-Oriented
   Error-Handling Methods. 491
     Understanding Object-Oriented
       Exception-Handling Methods. 492
Using the `Exception` Class's `ToString()` Method
   and `Message` Property. 496
Catching Multiple Exceptions 501
Examining the Structure of the `TryParse()` Methods 506
Using the `finally` Block 508
Handling Exceptions Thrown from Outside Methods. 511
Tracing `Exception` Objects Through the Call Stack 514
A Case Study: Using `StackTrace` 515
Creating Your Own `Exception` Classes. 519
Rethrowing an `Exception`. 523
Chapter Summary. 525
Key Terms 526
Review Questions 527
Exercises. 531

CHAPTER 12   Using Controls **535**

Understanding `Controls` 536
Examining the IDE's Automatically Generated Code 541
Setting a `Control`'s Font. 545
Using a `LinkLabel`. 548
Adding Color to a `Form` 552
Using `CheckBox` and `RadioButton` Objects 559
Adding a `PictureBox` to a `Form` 563

Adding `ListBox`, `CheckedListBox`,
and `ComboBox` Controls to a Form 566
Adding `MonthCalendar` and `DateTimePicker`
Controls to a `Form` 571
Working with a `Form`'s Layout 575
   Understanding `GroupBoxes` and `Panels` 577
Adding a `MenuStrip` to a `Form` 578
Using Other `Controls` 580
Chapter Summary 590
Key Terms 591
Review Questions 591
Exercises 594

CHAPTER 13   Handling Events 597

Event Handling 598
Understanding Delegates 602
   Creating Composed Delegates 605
Declaring and Using Both Custom
and Built-in Event Handlers 611
   Using the Built-in `EventHandler` 614
Handling `Control` Component Events 621
Handling Mouse and Keyboard Events 626
   Handling Mouse Events 626
   Handling Keyboard Events 628
Managing Multiple `Controls` 631
   Defining Focus 631
   Handling Multiple Events with a Single Handler 632
Continuing to Learn about `Controls` and Events 633
Chapter Summary 636
Key Terms 637
Review Questions 638
Exercises 641

CHAPTER 14   Files and Streams 645

Files and the `File` and `Directory` Classes 646
   Using the `File` and `Directory` Classes 648
Understanding File Data Organization 652
Understanding Streams 654
Writing and Reading a Sequential Access File 658
   Writing Data to a Sequential Access Text File 658
   Reading from a Sequential Access Text File 661

CONTENTS

Searching a Sequential Text File 667
Understanding Serialization and Deserialization. 673
Chapter Summary. 686
Key Terms 687
Review Questions 689
Exercises. 692

APPENDIX A Operator Precedence and Associativity . . . **695**

Key Terms 696

APPENDIX B Understanding Numbering Systems and Computer Codes **697**

The Hexadecimal System. 703
Measuring Storage 704
Key Terms 706

APPENDIX C Using the IDE Editor. **707**

IntelliSense. 707
Providing Completion Lists 707
Providing Quick Information. 708
Providing Parameter Information 709
Adding using Statements. 709
Code Snippets 709
Squiggles and Lightbulbs. 709
Readability Aids 710
Key Terms 710

Glossary **711**

Index **729**

Preface

Microsoft Visual C# 2017, Seventh Edition provides the beginning programmer with a guide to developing programs in C#. C# is a language developed by the Microsoft Corporation as part of the .NET Framework and Visual Studio platform. The .NET Framework contains a wealth of libraries for developing applications for the Windows family of operating systems.

With C#, you can build small, reusable components that are well-suited to Web-based programming applications. Although similar to Java and C++, many features of C# make it easier to learn and ideal for the beginning programmer. You can program in C# using a simple text editor and the command prompt, or you can manipulate program components using Visual Studio's sophisticated Integrated Development Environment. This book provides you with the tools to use both techniques.

This textbook assumes that you have little or no programming experience. The writing is nontechnical and emphasizes good programming practices. The examples are business examples; they do not assume mathematical background beyond high school business math. In addition, the examples illustrate one or two major points; they do not contain so many features that you become lost following irrelevant and extraneous details. This book provides you with a solid background in good object-oriented programming techniques and introduces you to object-oriented terminology using clear, familiar language.

Organization and Coverage

Microsoft Visual C# 2017 presents C# programming concepts, enforcing good style, logical thinking, and the object-oriented paradigm. Chapter 1 introduces you to the language by letting you create working C# programs using both the simple command line and the Visual Studio environment. In Chapter 2, you learn about data and how to input, store, and output data in C#. Chapter 3 provides a quick start to creating GUI applications. You can take two approaches:

- You can cover Chapter 3 and learn about GUI objects so that you can create more visually interesting applications in the subsequent chapters on decision making, looping, and array manipulation. These subsequent chapters confine GUI examples to the end of the chapters, so you can postpone GUI manipulation if you want.

- You can skip Chapter 3 until you have learned the fundamentals of decision making, looping, and array manipulation, and until you study object-oriented concepts such as classes, objects, polymorphism, inheritance, and exception handling. Then, after Chapter 11, you can return to Chapter 3 and use the built-in GUI component classes with a deeper understanding of how they work.

PREFACE — Organization and Coverage

In Chapters 4, 5, and 6, you learn about the classic programming structures—making decisions, looping, and manipulating arrays—and how to implement them in C#. Chapters 7 and 8 provide a thorough study of methods, including passing parameters into and out of methods and overloading them.

Chapter 9 introduces the object-oriented concepts of classes, objects, data hiding, constructors, and destructors. After completing Chapters 10 and 11, you will be thoroughly grounded in the object-oriented concepts of inheritance and exception handling, and will be able to take advantage of both features in your C# programs. Chapter 12 continues the discussion of GUI objects from Chapter 3. You will learn about controls, how to set their properties, and how to make attractive, useful, graphical, and interactive programs. Chapter 13 takes you further into the intricacies of handling events in your interactive GUI programs. In Chapter 14, you learn to save data to and retrieve data from files.

Features

This text focuses on helping students become better programmers and understand C# program development through a variety of key features. In addition to chapter Objectives, Summaries, and Key Terms, these useful features will help students regardless of their learning styles.

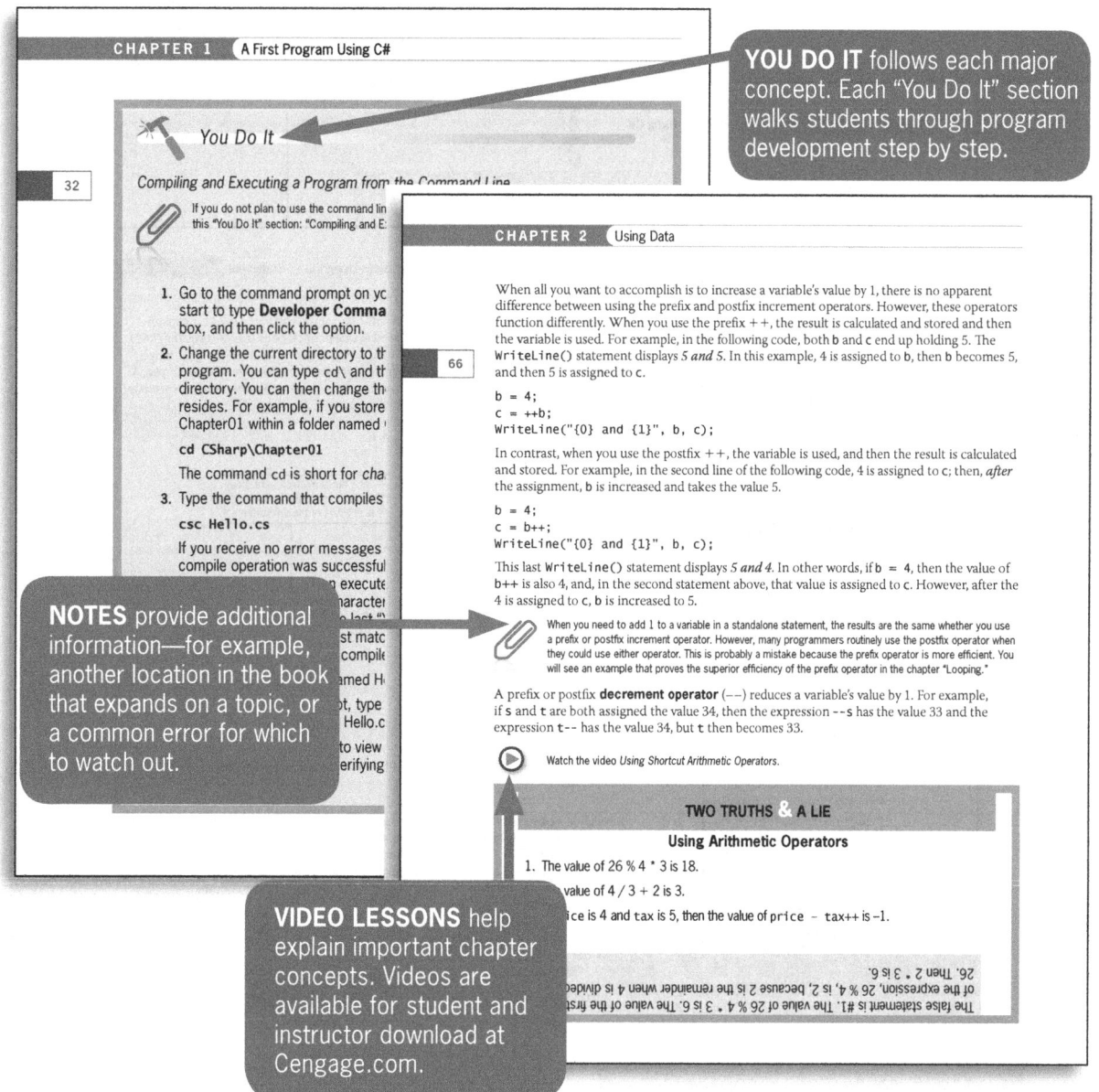

FEATURES

TWO TRUTHS & A LIE quizzes appear after each chapter section, with answers provided. The quiz contains three statements based on the preceding section of text—two statements are true and one is false. Answers give immediate feedback without "giving away" answers to the multiple-choice questions and programming problems later in the chapter.

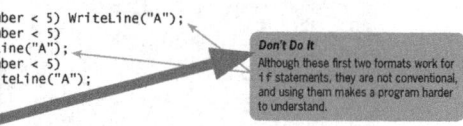

THE DON'T DO IT ICON illustrates how NOT to do something—for example, having a dead code path in a program. This icon provides a visual jolt to the student, emphasizing that particular figures are NOT to be emulated and making students more careful to recognize problems in existing code.

Assessment

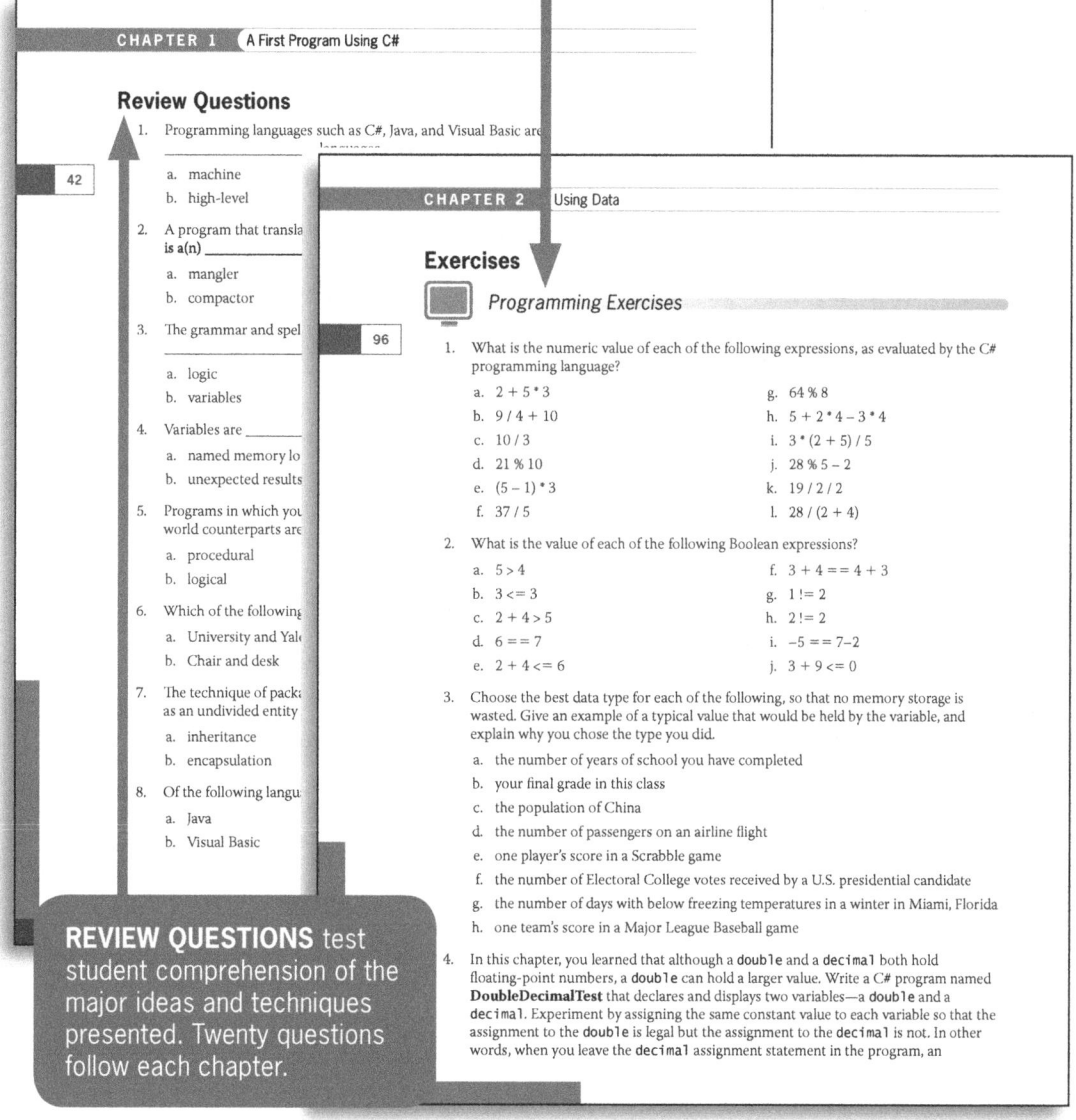

PROGRAMMING EXERCISES provide opportunities to practice concepts. These exercises increase in difficulty and allow students to explore each major programming concept presented in the chapter. Additional programming exercises are available to instructors on the Companion Site.

REVIEW QUESTIONS test student comprehension of the major ideas and techniques presented. Twenty questions follow each chapter.

ASSESSMENT

DEBUGGING EXERCISES are included with each chapter because examining programs critically and closely is a crucial programming skill. Students can download these exercises at Cengage.com. These files are also available to instructors through *sso.cengage.com*

You'll soon see 'em
On a shelf
In some museum
Burma Shave

Find a classic Burma Shave rhyme on the Web and write a program named **BurmaShave** that displays the rhyme.

Debugging Exercises

1. Each of the following files in the Chapter.01 folder of your has syntax and/or logical errors. In each case, determine the program. After you correct the errors, save each file using with *Fixed*. For example, DebugOne1.cs can become Fixed

   a. DebugOne1.cs   c. Debug
   b. DebugOne2.cs   d. Debug

CASE PROBLEMS provide opportunities to build more detailed programs that continue to incorporate increasing functionality throughout the book.

Case Problems

The case problems in this section introduce two fictional businesses. Throughout this book, you will create increasingly complex classes for these businesses that use the newest concepts you have mastered in each chapter.

1. Greenville County hosts the Greenville Idol competition each summer during the county fair. The talent competition takes place over a three-day period during which contestants are eliminated following rounds of performances until the year's ultimate winner is chosen. Write a program named **GreenvilleMotto** that displays the competition's motto, which is "The stars shine in Greenville." Create a second program named **GreenvilleMotto2** that displays the motto surrounded by a border composed of asterisks.

2. Marshall's Murals is a company that paints interior and exterior murals for both business and residential customers. Write a program named **MarshallsMotto** that displays the company motto, which is "Make your vision your view." Create a second program named **MarshallsMotto2** that displays the motto surrounded by a border composed of repeated *M*s.

Features

Microsoft Visual C# 2017 is a superior textbook because it also includes the following new features:

- *C# 7.0 in Visual Studio 2017*—This edition is written and tested using the latest edition of C#.

- *Conventional method names*—All methods have been rewritten to follow the C# naming convention of starting with an uppercase letter.

- *Splitting strings*—The new version of C# automatically splits long strings into multiple concatenated strings.

- *Returning values by reference*—A new feature in C# allows methods to return a reference.

- *Exercises*—Each chapter concludes with meaningful programming exercises that provide additional practice of the skills and concepts you learned in the chapter. Several new exercises appear in each chapter of this edition, and all the replaced exercises and solutions are available to instructors to provide as additional student assignments or to use as the basis for lectures.

Microsoft Visual C# 2017 also includes the following features:

- *Early GUI applications*—Students can begin to create GUI applications in Chapter 3. The earlier introduction helps engage students who have used GUI applications their entire lives. In subsequent chapters on selections, loops, arrays, and methods, students apply concepts to applications in both console and GUI environments. This approach keeps some examples simple while increasing the understanding that input, processing, and output are programming universals, no matter what interface is used. The book is structured so that students who want to skip Chapter 3 until they understand object-oriented programming can do so with no loss of continuity.

- *Objectives*—Each chapter begins with a list of objectives so you know the topics that will be presented in the chapter.

- *Notes*—These tips provide additional information—for example, an alternative method of performing a procedure, another term for a concept, background information on a technique, or a common error to avoid.

- *Figures*—Each chapter contains many figures. Code figures are most frequently 25 lines or shorter, illustrating one concept at a time. Frequently placed screen shots show exactly how program output appears. In this edition, all C# keywords that appear in figures are bold to help them stand out from programmer-created identifiers.

- *Summaries*—Following each chapter is a summary that recaps the programming concepts and techniques covered in the chapter. This feature helps you to check your understanding of the main points in each chapter.

Features

- *Key Terms*—Each chapter includes a list of newly introduced vocabulary, shown in the order of appearance in the text. The list of key terms provides a review of the major concepts in the chapter.

- *Two Truths & a Lie*—This short quiz appears after each main chapter section, with answers provided. This quiz contains three statements—two true and one false—and the student must identify the false one. These quizzes provide students with immediate feedback as they read, without "giving away" answers to the existing multiple-choice and programming problem questions.

- *Review Questions*—Each chapter contains 20 multiple-choice review questions that provide a review of the key concepts in the chapter.

- *Debugging Exercises*—Each chapter contains four programs that have syntax and/or logical errors for you to fix. Completing these exercises provides valuable experience in locating errors, interpreting code written by others, and observing how another programmer has approached a problem.

- *Cases*—Each chapter contains two running case problems. These cases represent projects that continue to grow throughout a semester using concepts learned in each new chapter. Two cases allow instructors to assign different cases in alternate semesters, or to divide students in a class into two case teams.

- *Program Code*—The downloadable student files provide code for each full program presented in the chapter figures. Providing the code allows students to run it, view the results for themselves, and experiment with multiple input values and changes to the code.

- *Glossary*—A glossary contains definitions for all key terms in the book, presented in alphabetical order.

- *Video lessons*—Each chapter includes three or more video lessons produced by the author. These short videos provide instruction, further explanation, or background about a topic covered in the corresponding chapter. These videos are especially useful for online classes, for student review before exams, and for students who are audio learners.

- *Quality*—Every program example in the book, as well as every exercise, case project, and game solution, was tested by the author and again by a Quality Assurance team using Visual Studio 2017.

Instructor Resources

MindTap

MindTap activities for Farrell's Microsoft Visual C# 2017: An Introduction to Object-Oriented Programming, Seventh Edition, are designed to help students master the skills they need in today's workforce. Research shows employers need critical thinkers, troubleshooters, and creative problem-solvers to stay relevant in our fast-paced, technology-driven world. MinTap < MindTap >helps you achieve this with assignments and activities that provide hands-on practice and real-life relevance. Students are guided through assignments that help them master basic knowledge and understanding before moving on to more challenging problems.

All MindTap activities and assignments are tied to defined unit learning objectives. Hands-on coding labs provide real-life application and practice. Readings and dynamic visualizations support the lecture, while a post-course assessment measures exactly how much a student has learned. MindTap provides the analytics and reporting to easily see where the class stands in terms of progress, engagement, and completion rates. Use the content and learning path as-is or pick-and-choose how our materials will wrap around yours. You control what the students see and when they see it. Learn more at http://www.cengage.com/mindtap/.

Instructor Companion Site

The following teaching tools are available for download at the Companion Site for this text. Simply search for this text at *www.cengage.com* and choose "Instructor Downloads." An instructor login is required.

- **Instructor's Manual:** The Instructor's Manual that accompanies this textbook includes additional instructional material to assist in class preparation, including items such as Overviews, Chapter Objectives, Teaching Tips, Quick Quizzes, Class Discussion Topics, Additional Projects, Additional Resources, and Key Terms. A sample syllabus is also available.

- **Test Bank:** Cengage Testing Powered by Cognero is a flexible, online system that allows you to:
    - author, edit, and manage test bank content from multiple Cengage Learning solutions
    - create multiple test versions in an instant
    - deliver tests from your LMS, your classroom, or wherever you want

- **PowerPoint Presentations:** This text provides PowerPoint slides to accompany each chapter. Slides can be used to guide classroom presentations, to make available to students for chapter review, or to print as classroom handouts. Files are provided for every figure in the text. Instructors can use the files to customize PowerPoint slides, illustrate quizzes, or create handouts.

- **Solutions:** Solutions to "You Do It" exercises and all end-of-chapter exercises are available.

Acknowledgments

Thank you to all of the people who make this book a success, including Alyssa Pratt, Senior Content Developer; and Jennifer Feltri-George, Content Project Manager. I want to acknowledge every Cengage Learning Consultant who travels the country guiding instructors in their choices of educational materials.

Thanks, too, to my husband, Geoff, for his constant support and encouragement. Finally, this book is dedicated to the newest member of our family arriving in June, 2017, after this book goes to print. We don't yet know your first name, Baby Farrell-Peterson, but I am excited and filled with love awaiting your arrival.

Joyce Farrell

Read This Before You Begin

To the User of the Data Files

To complete the steps and projects in this book, you need data files that have been created specifically for this book. Your instructor will provide the data files to you. You also can obtain the files electronically from Cengage.com. Find the ISBN of your title on the back cover of your book, then enter the ISBN in the search box at the top of the Cengage home page. You can find the data files on the product page that opens. Note that you can use a computer in your school lab or your own computer to complete the exercises in this book.

Using Your Own Computer

To use your own computer to complete the steps and exercises, you will need the following:

- *Software*—Microsoft Visual C# 2017, including the Microsoft .NET Framework.

- *Hardware*—Minimum requirements identified by Microsoft are a 1.8 GHz CPU, 2 GB of RAM, 1GB to 40GB of hard disk space, depending on features installed, and a display with a resolution of 1280 by 720.

- *Operating system*—Windows 10, or, with updates, 7 or 8.

CHAPTER 1

A First Program Using C#

Upon completion of this chapter, you will be able to:

◎ Describe the programming process

◎ Differentiate between procedural and object-oriented programming

◎ Describe the features of object-oriented programming languages

◎ Describe the C# programming language

◎ Write a C# program that produces output

◎ Select identifiers to use within your programs

◎ Improve programs by adding comments and using the `System` namespace

◎ Compile and execute a C# program using the command prompt and using Visual Studio

CHAPTER 1: A First Program Using C#

Programming a computer is an interesting, challenging, fun, and sometimes frustrating task. As you learn a programming language, you must be precise and careful as well as creative. Computer programmers must learn to plan a program's logic, and can choose from a variety of programming languages, such as Visual Basic, Java, and C++, in which to implement their logic. C# (pronounced "C Sharp") is a relatively-new programming language that offers a wide range of options and features. As you work through this book, you will master many of them, one step at a time. If this is your first programming experience, you will learn new ways to approach and solve problems and to think logically. If you know how to program but are new to C#, you will be impressed by its capabilities.

In this chapter, you will learn about the background of programming that led to the development of C#, and you will write and execute your first C# programs.

The Programming Process

A computer **program** is a set of instructions that tells a computer what to do. Programs are also called **software**; software comes in two broad categories:

- **System software** describes the programs that operate the computer. Examples include operating systems such as Microsoft Windows, Mac OSX, and Linux.

- **Application software** describes the programs that allow users to complete tasks such as creating documents, calculating paychecks, and playing games. (Application software programs are often called *apps*.)

The physical devices that make up a computer system are called **hardware**. Internally, computer hardware is constructed from circuitry that consists of small on/off switches; the most basic circuitry-level language that computers use to control the operation of those switches is called **machine language**. Machine language is expressed as a series of *1*s and *0*s—*1*s represent switches that are on, and *0*s represent switches that are off. If programmers had to write computer programs using machine language, they would have to keep track of the hundreds of thousands of *1*s and *0*s involved in programming any worthwhile task. Not only would writing a program be a time-consuming and difficult task, but modifying programs, understanding others' programs, and locating errors within programs all would be cumbersome. Additionally, the number and location of switches vary from computer to computer, which means you would need to customize a machine-language program for every type of machine on which the program had to run.

Fortunately, programming has become easier because of the development of high-level programming languages. A **high-level programming language** allows you to use a limited vocabulary of reasonable keywords. **Keywords** are predefined and reserved identifiers that have special meaning in a language. High-level language programs contain keywords such as *read*, *write*, and *add* that you use instead of the sequence of on/off switches that perform these tasks. High-level languages also allow you to assign reasonable names to areas of computer memory; you can use names without spaces, such as `hoursWorked` or `payRate`, rather than having to remember the memory locations (switch numbers) of those values.

The Programming Process

 Camel casing, or **lower camel casing**, describes the style of identifiers such as hoursWorked and payRate that appear to have a hump in the middle because they start with a lowercase letter but contain uppercase letters to identify new words. By convention in C#, data item names use camel casing. The C# programming language is case sensitive. Therefore, if you create an identifier named payRate, you cannot refer to it later using identifiers such as PayRate or payrate.

Each high-level language has its own **syntax**, or rules of the language. For example, to produce output, you might use the verb *print* in one language and *write* in another. All languages have a specific, limited vocabulary, along with a set of rules for using that vocabulary. Programmers use a computer program called a **compiler** to translate their high-level language statements into machine code. The compiler issues an error message each time a programmer commits a **syntax error**—that is, each time the programmer uses the language incorrectly. Subsequently, the programmer can correct the error and attempt another translation by compiling the program again. The program can be completely translated to machine language only when all syntax errors have been corrected. When you learn a computer programming language such as C#, C++, Visual Basic, or Java, you must learn both the vocabulary and syntax rules for that language.

 In some languages, such as BASIC, the language translator is called an *interpreter*. In others, such as assembly language, it is called an *assembler*. The various language translators operate differently, but the ultimate goal of each is to translate the higher-level language into machine language.

In addition to learning the correct syntax for a particular language, a programmer must understand computer programming logic. The **logic** behind any program involves executing the various statements and procedures in the correct order to produce the desired results. For example, you might be able to execute perfect individual notes on a musical instrument, but if you do not execute them in the proper order (or execute a B-flat when an F-sharp was expected), no one will enjoy your performance. Similarly, you might be able to use a computer language's syntax correctly but be unable to obtain correct results because the program is not constructed logically. Examples of logical errors include multiplying two values when you should divide them, or attempting to calculate a paycheck before obtaining the appropriate payroll data. The logic used to solve a problem might be identical in two programs, but the programs can be written in different languages, each using different syntax.

 Since the early days of computer programming, program errors have been called **bugs**. The term is often said to have originated from an actual moth that was discovered trapped in the circuitry of a computer at Harvard University in 1945. Actually, the term *bug* was in use prior to 1945 to mean trouble with any electrical apparatus; even during Thomas Edison's life, it meant an "industrial defect." In any case, the process of finding and correcting program errors has come to be known as **debugging** the program.

> ### TWO TRUTHS & A LIE
>
> **Programming**
>
> Two of the following statements are true, and one is false. Identify the false statement, and explain why it is false.
>
> 1. A high-level programming language allows you to use a vocabulary of reasonable terms such as *read*, *write*, or *add* instead of the sequence of on/off switches that perform these tasks.
>
> 2. Each high-level programming language has its own syntax.
>
> 3. Programmers use a computer program called a *compiler* to translate machine code into a high-level language they can understand.
>
> The false statement is #3. Programmers use a compiler to translate their high-level language statements into machine code.

Procedural and Object-Oriented Programming

Two popular approaches to writing computer programs are procedural programming and object-oriented programming.

When you write a **procedural program**, you use your knowledge about a programming language to create and name computer memory locations that can hold values, and you write a series of steps or operations to manipulate those values. For example, a simple payroll program might contain instructions similar to the following:

```
get hoursWorked
pay = hoursWorked * 10.00
output pay
```

Named computer memory locations that hold data, such as hoursWorked and pay, are called **variables** because they hold values that might vary. In programming languages, a variable is referenced by using a one-word name (an **identifier**) with no embedded spaces. For example, the memory location referenced by the name hoursWorked might contain different values at different times for different employees. During the execution of the payroll program, each value stored under the name hoursWorked might have many operations performed on it—for example, reading it from an input device, multiplying it by a pay rate, and printing it on paper.

Examples of procedural programming languages include C and Logo.

Procedural and Object-Oriented Programming

For convenience, the individual operations used in a procedural program often are grouped into logical units called **methods**. For example, a series of four or five comparisons and calculations that together determine an employee's withholding tax value might be grouped as a method named `CalculateWithholdingTax()`.

Capitalizing the first letter of all new words in an identifier, even the first one, as in `CalculateWithholdingTax()`, is a style called **Pascal casing** or **upper camel casing**. Although it is legal to start a method name with a lowercase letter, the convention used in C# is for methods to be named using Pascal casing. This helps distinguish them from variables, which conventionally use lower camel casing. Additionally, in C# all method names are followed by a set of parentheses. When this book refers to a method, the name will be followed with parentheses.

A procedural program divides a problem solution into multiple methods, each with a unique name. The program then **calls** or **invokes** the methods to input, manipulate, and output the values stored in those locations. A single procedural program often contains hundreds of variables and thousands of method calls.

Depending on the programming language, methods are sometimes called *procedures*, *subroutines*, or *functions*. In C#, the preferred term is *methods*.

Paycheck
payee hoursWorked grossPay
calculateAmount() writeCheck() cashCheck()

Figure 1-1 A diagram for a Paycheck

Object-oriented programming (OOP) is an extension of procedural programming. OOP uses variables and methods like procedural programs do, but it focuses on objects that contain the variables and methods. An **object** is a concrete entity that has attributes and behaviors. The **attributes of an object** are the features it "has"; the values of an object's attributes constitute the **state of the object**. For example, attributes of a paycheck include its payee and monetary value, and the state of those attributes might be *Alice Nelson* and *$400*. The **behaviors of an object** are the things it "does," or its methods; for example, a paycheck object can be written and cashed, and contains a method to calculate the check amount. Figure 1-1 shows how a programmer might start to visualize a paycheck—thinking about its name, attributes, and behaviors. Beyond a paycheck, object-oriented programmers might design a payroll system by thinking about all the additional objects needed to produce a paycheck, such as employees, time cards, and bank accounts.

Programmers use the term *OO*, pronounced "oh oh," as an abbreviation for *object oriented*. When discussing object-oriented programming, they use *OOP*, which rhymes with *soup*. Examples of OO languages include C#, Java, Visual Basic, and C++. You can write procedural programs in OO languages, but you cannot write OO programs in procedural languages.

With either approach, procedural or object-oriented, you can produce a correct paycheck, and both techniques employ reusable program modules. The major difference lies in the focus the programmer takes during the earliest planning stages of a project. Taking an **object-oriented approach** to a problem means defining the objects needed to accomplish a task and developing classes that describe the objects so that each object maintains its own data and carries out tasks when another object requests them. The object-oriented approach is said to be "natural"—it is more common to think of a world of objects and the ways they interact than to consider a world of systems, data items, and the logic required to manipulate them.

Object-oriented programming employs a large vocabulary; you can learn much of this terminology in the chapter called "Using Classes and Objects."

Originally, object-oriented programming was used most frequently for two major types of applications:

- **Computer simulations** are programs that attempt to mimic real-world activities so that their processes can be improved or so that users can better understand how the real-world processes operate.

- **Graphical user interfaces, or GUIs** (pronounced *gooeys*) are programs that allow users to interact with a program in a graphical environment, such as by clicking with a mouse or using a touch screen.

Thinking about objects in these two types of applications makes sense. For example, a city might want to develop a program that simulates traffic patterns to better prevent congestion. By creating a model with objects such as cars and pedestrians that contain their own data and rules for behavior, the simulation can be set in motion. For example, each car object has a specific current speed and a procedure for changing that speed. By creating a model of city traffic using objects, a computer can create a simulation of a real city at rush hour. Creating a GUI environment for users also is a natural use for object orientation. It is easy to think of the components a user manipulates on a computer screen, such as buttons and scroll bars, as similar to real-world objects. Each GUI object contains data—for example, a button on a screen has a specific size and color. Each object also contains behaviors—for example, each button can be clicked and reacts in a specific way when clicked. Some people consider the term *object-oriented programming* to be synonymous with GUI programming, but object-oriented programming means more. Although many GUI programs are object oriented, one does not imply the other. Modern businesses use object-oriented design techniques when developing all sorts of business applications, regardless of whether they are GUI applications.

Features of Object-Oriented Programming Languages

> **TWO TRUTHS & A LIE**
>
> **Procedural and Object-Oriented Programming**
>
> 1. Procedural programs use variables and tasks that are grouped into methods or procedures.
> 2. Object-oriented programming languages do not support variables or methods; instead they focus on objects.
> 3. Object-oriented programs were first used for simulations and GUI programs.
>
> The false statement is #2. Object-oriented programs contain variables and methods just as procedural programs do.

Features of Object-Oriented Programming Languages

For a language to be considered object-oriented, it must support the following features:

- Classes
- Objects
- Encapsulation and interfaces
- Inheritance
- Polymorphism

A **class** describes potential objects, including their attributes and behaviors. A class is similar to a recipe or a blueprint in that it describes what features objects will have and what they will be able to do after they are created. An object is an **instance of a class**; it is one tangible example of a class.

For example, you might create a class named Automobile. Some of an Automobile's attributes are its make, model, year, and purchase price. All Automobiles possess the same attributes, but not the same values, or states, for those attributes. (Programmers also call the values of an object's attributes the **properties** of the object.) When you create specific Automobile objects, each object can hold unique values for the attributes, such as *Ford, Taurus, 2018*, and *$27,000*. Similarly, a Dog has attributes that include its breed, name, age, and vaccination status; the attributes for a particular dog might be *Labrador retriever, Murphy, 7*, and *current*.

When you understand that an object belongs to a specific class, you know a lot about the object. If your friend purchases an Automobile, you know it has *some* model name; if your friend gets a Dog, you know it has *some* breed. You probably don't know the current state of the Automobile's speed or of the Dog's shots, but you do know that those attributes exist for the Automobile and Dog classes. Similarly, in a GUI operating environment, you expect each window you open to have specific, consistent attributes, such as a menu bar and a title bar, because each window includes these attributes as a member of the general class of GUI windows.

By convention, programmers using C# begin their class names with an uppercase letter and use a singular noun. Thus, the class that defines the attributes and methods of an automobile would probably be named Automobile, and the class that contains dogs would probably be named Dog. If the class requires two words, programmers conventionally use upper camel casing, as in BankAccount.

Besides attributes, objects possess methods that they use to accomplish tasks, including changing attributes and discovering the values of attributes. Automobiles, for example, have methods for moving forward and backward. They also can be filled with gasoline or be washed; both are methods that change some of an Automobile's attributes. Methods also exist for determining the status of certain attributes, such as the current speed of an Automobile and the number of gallons of gas in its tank. Similarly, a Dog can walk or run, eat, and get a bath, and there are methods for determining whether it needs a walk, food, or a bath. GUI operating system components, such as windows, can be maximized, minimized, and dragged; depending on the component, they also can have their color or font style altered.

Like procedural programs, object-oriented programs have variables (attributes) and procedures (methods), but the attributes and methods are encapsulated into objects that then are used much like real-world objects. **Encapsulation** is the technique of packaging an object's attributes and methods into a cohesive unit that can be used as an undivided entity. Programmers sometimes refer to encapsulation as using a **black box**, a device you use without regard for the internal mechanisms. If an object's methods are well written, the user is unaware of the low-level details about how the methods are executed; in such a case, the user must understand only the **interface** or interaction between the method and object. For example, if you can fill your Automobile with gasoline, it is because you understand the interface between the gas pump nozzle and the vehicle's gas tank opening. You don't need to understand how the pump works or where the gas tank is located inside your vehicle. If you can read your speedometer, it does not matter how the display value is calculated. In fact, if someone produces a new, more accurate speedometer and inserts it into your Automobile, you don't have to know or care how it operates, as long as the interface remains the same as the previous one. The same principles apply to well-constructed objects used in object-oriented programs.

Object-oriented programming languages support two other distinguishing features in addition to organizing objects as members of classes. One feature, **inheritance**, provides the ability to extend a class so as to create a more specific class. The more specific class contains all the attributes and methods of the more general class and usually contains new attributes or methods as well. For example, if you have created a Dog class, you might then create a more specific class named ShowDog. Each instance of the ShowDog class would contain, or inherit, all the attributes and methods of a Dog, along with additional methods or attributes. For example, a ShowDog might require an attribute to hold the number of ribbons won and a method for entering a dog show. The advantage of inheritance is that when you need a class such as ShowDog, you often can extend an existing class, thereby saving a lot of time and work.

Object-oriented languages also support **polymorphism**, which is the ability to create methods that act appropriately depending on the context. That is, programs written in object-oriented languages can distinguish between methods with the same name based on the type of object that uses them. For example, you are able to "fill" both a Dog and an Automobile, but you do so by very different means. Similarly, the procedure to "fill" a ShowDog might require different food than that for a "plain" Dog. Older, non-object-oriented languages could not make such distinctions, but object-oriented languages can.

The chapters "Using Classes and Objects" and "Introduction to Inheritance" contain much more information about the features of object-oriented programs.

Watch the video *Object-Oriented Programming*.

TWO TRUTHS & A LIE

Features of Object-Oriented Programming Languages

1. Object-oriented programs contain classes that describe the attributes and methods of objects.

2. Object-oriented programming languages support inheritance, which refers to the packaging of attributes and methods into logical units.

3. Object-oriented programming languages support polymorphism, which is the ability of a method to act appropriately based on the context.

The false statement is #2. Inheritance is the ability to extend classes to make more specific ones. Encapsulation refers to the packaging of attributes and methods.

The C# Programming Language

The **C# programming language** was developed as an object-oriented and component-oriented language. It is part of Microsoft Visual Studio, a package designed for developing applications that run on Windows computers. (The newest version of C# is C# 7.0; the version number tells you there were six major versions prior to the most recent release.) Unlike other programming languages, C# allows every piece of data to be treated as an object and to consistently employ the principles of object-oriented programming. C# provides constructs for creating components with properties, methods, and events, making it an ideal language for modern programming, where building small, reusable components is more important than building huge, stand-alone applications. You can find Microsoft's C# specifications at *msdn.microsoft.com*. Search for C# *specifications*.

If you have not programmed before, the differences between C# and other languages mean little to you. However, experienced programmers will appreciate the thought that was put into C# features. For example:

- C# contains a GUI interface that makes it similar to Visual Basic, but C# is considered more concise than Visual Basic.
- C# is modeled after the C++ programming language, but is considered easier to learn. Some of the most difficult features to understand in C++ have been eliminated in C#.

Some differences between C# and C++ are that pointers (variables that hold memory addresses) are not used in C# (except in a mode called unsafe, which is rarely used), object destructors and forward declarations are not needed, and using #include files is not necessary. Multiple inheritance, which causes many C++ programming errors, is not allowed in C#.

- C# is very similar to Java, because Java was also based on C++. However, C# is more truly object oriented. Unlike in Java, every piece of data in C# is an object, providing all data with increased functionality.

In Java, simple data types are not objects; therefore, they do not work with built-in methods. Additionally, in Java, data can only be passed to and from methods using a copy; C# omits this limitation. You will learn more in two later chapters: "Using Methods" and "Advanced Method Concepts."

The C# programming language was standardized in 2002 by Ecma International. You can read or download this set of standards at www.ecma-international.org/publications/standards/Ecma-334.htm.

TWO TRUTHS & A LIE

The C# Programming Language

1. The C# programming language was developed as an object-oriented and component-oriented language.
2. C# contains several features that make it similar to other languages such as Java and Visual Basic.
3. C# contains many advanced features, so the C++ programming language was created as a simpler version of the language.

The false statement is 3. C# is modeled after the C++ programming language, but some of the most difficult features to understand in C++ have been eliminated in C#.

Writing a C# Program that Produces Output

At first glance, even the simplest C# program involves a fair amount of confusing syntax. Consider the simple program in Figure 1-2. This program is written on seven lines, and its only task is to display *This is my first C# program* on the screen.

```
class FirstClass
{
   static void Main()
   {
      System.Console.WriteLine("This is my first C# program");
   }
}
```

Figure 1-2 `FirstClass` console application

The statement that does the actual work in this program is in the middle of the figure:

`System.Console.WriteLine("This is my first C# program");`

The statement ends with a semicolon because all C# statements do.

The text `"This is my first C# program"` is a **literal string** of characters—that is, a series of characters that will be used exactly as entered. Any literal string in C# appears between double quotation marks.

The string `"This is my first C# program"` appears within parentheses because the string is an argument to a method, and arguments to methods always appear within parentheses. **Arguments** represent information that a method needs to perform its task. For example, if making an appointment with a dentist's office was a C# method, you would write the following:

`MakeAppointment("September 10", "2 p.m.");`

Accepting and processing a dental appointment is a method that consists of a set of standard procedures. However, each appointment requires different information—the date and time— and this information can be considered the arguments of the `MakeAppointment()` method. If you make an appointment for September 10 at 2 p.m., you expect different results than if you make one for September 9 at 8 a.m. or December 25 at midnight. Likewise, if you pass the argument `"Happy Holidays"` to a method, you will expect different results than if you pass the argument `"This is my first C# program"`.

Although an argument to a method might be a string, not all arguments are strings. In this book, you will see and write methods that accept many other types of data.

CHAPTER 1 A First Program Using C#

Within the following statement, the method to which you are passing the argument string is named `WriteLine()`:

`System.Console.WriteLine("This is my first C# program");`

The `WriteLine()` method is a built-in method that is part of the C# language, and it displays output on the screen and positions the cursor on the next line, where additional output might subsequently be displayed. The `Write()` method is very similar to the `WriteLine()` method.

With `WriteLine()`, the cursor moves to the following line after the message is displayed. With `Write()`, the cursor does not advance to a new line; it remains on the same line as the output. Within the following statement `Console` is a class that contains the `WriteLine()` method:

`System.Console.WriteLine("This is my first C# program");`

Of course, not all classes have a `WriteLine()` method (for instance, you can't write a line to a computer's mouse, an `Automobile`, or a `Dog`), but the creators of C# assumed that you frequently would want to display output on the screen at your terminal. For this reason, the `Console` class was created and endowed with the method named `WriteLine()`. When you use the `WriteLine()` method, programmers say that you *call* it or *invoke* it. Soon, you will create your own C# classes and endow them with your own callable methods. Within the following statement, `System` is a namespace:

`System.Console.WriteLine("This is my first C# program");`

A **namespace** is a construct that acts like a container to provide a way to group similar classes. To organize your classes, you can (and will) create your own namespaces. The `System` namespace, which is built into your C# compiler, holds commonly used classes.

An advantage to using Visual Studio is that all of its languages use the same namespaces. In other words, everything you learn about any namespace in C# is knowledge you can transfer to Visual C++ and Visual Basic.

The dots (periods) in the phrase `System.Console.WriteLine` are used to separate the names of the namespace, class, and method. You will use this same namespace-dot-class-dot-method format repeatedly in your C# programs.

In the `FirstClass` class in Figure 1-2, the `WriteLine()` statement appears within a method named `Main()`. Every executable C# application must contain a `Main()` method because that is the starting point for every program. As you continue to learn C# from this book, you will write applications that contain additional methods. You also will create classes that are not programs, and so do not need a `Main()` method. For example, a `Dog` or `Automobile` class would not be a program. Rather they would be classes from which objects are created, and, in turn, those objects would be used in programs with a `Main()` method.

Writing a C# Program that Produces Output

Every method in C# contains a header and a body. A **method header** includes the method name and information about what will pass into and be returned from a method. A **method body** is contained within a pair of curly braces ({ }) and includes all the instructions executed by the method. The program in Figure 1-2 includes only one statement between the curly braces of the Main() method. Soon, you will write methods with many more statements.

In Figure 1-2, the WriteLine() statement within the Main() method is indented within the curly braces. Although the C# compiler does not require such indentation, it is conventional and clearly shows that the WriteLine() statement lies within the Main() method.

Do not confuse curly braces with parentheses. Curly braces have a small bump in the middle while parentheses are smooth. The left and right curly braces are located on most PC keyboards to the right of the letter p above the brackets, and the left and right parentheses are located on the number keys at the top of the keyboard above the 9 and 0. The curly braces and parentheses have separate, specific uses in C#, and a syntax error is created if you use the incorrect pair.

For every opening curly brace ({) that encloses a method's statements in a C# program, there must be a corresponding closing curly brace (}). The precise position of the opening and closing curly braces is not important to the compiler. In general, whitespace is optional in C#. **Whitespace** is any combination of spaces, tabs, and carriage returns (blank lines). You use whitespace to organize your program code and make it easier to read; it does not affect your program's execution. Usually, you vertically align each pair of opening and closing curly braces and indent the contents between them, as shown in Figure 1-2.

The method header for the Main() method in Figure 1-2 contains three words. Two of these words (**static** and **void**) are keywords. In this book, C# keywords appear in bold. A complete list of keywords appears in Table 1-1 later in this chapter. In the method header static void Main(), the keyword **static** indicates that the Main() method will be executed through a class—not by a variety of objects. It means that you do not need to create an object of type FirstClass to use the Main() method defined within FirstClass. Later in this book, you will create other methods that are nonstatic methods and that are executed by objects.

The second word in the method header in Figure 1-2 is void. In English, the word *void* means empty or having no effect. When the keyword **void** is used in the Main() method header, it does not indicate that the Main() method is empty, or that it has no effect, but rather that the method does not return any value when called. You will learn more about methods that return values (and do affect other methods) when you study methods in greater detail. In the method header, the name of the method is Main(). Main() is not a C# keyword, but all C# applications must include a method named Main(), and most C# applications will have additional methods with other names. Recall that when you execute a C# application, the Main() method always executes first. Classes that contain a Main() method are **application classes**. Applications are executable or **runnable**. Classes that do not contain a Main() method are **non-application classes**, and are not runnable. Non-application classes provide support for other classes.

Watch the video *The Parts of a C# Program*.

> **TWO TRUTHS & A LIE**
>
> **Writing a C# Program that Produces Output**
>
> 1. Strings are information that methods need to perform their tasks.
>
> 2. The `WriteLine()` method displays output on the screen and positions the cursor on the next line, where additional output might be displayed.
>
> 3. Many methods such as `WriteLine()` have been created for you because the creators of C# assumed you would need them frequently.
>
> The false statement is #1. Strings are literal values represented between quotation marks. Arguments represent information that a method needs to perform its task. Although an argument might be a string, not all arguments are strings.

Selecting Identifiers

Every method that you use within a C# program must be part of a class. To create a class, you use a class header and curly braces in much the same way you use a header and braces for a method within a class. When you write `class FirstClass`, you are defining a class named `FirstClass`. A class name does not have to contain the word *Class* as `FirstClass` does; as a matter of fact, most class names you create will not contain *Class*. You can define a C# class using any identifier you need, as long as it meets the following requirements:

- An identifier must begin with an underscore, the "at" sign (@), or a letter. Letters include foreign-alphabet letters such as Π and Ω, which are contained in the set of characters known as Unicode. You will learn more about Unicode in the next chapter.

- An identifier can contain only letters, digits, underscores, and the @ sign. An identifier cannot contain spaces or any other punctuation or special characters such as #, $, or &.

- An identifier cannot be a C# reserved keyword, such as `class` or `void`. Table 1-1 provides a complete list of reserved keywords. Actually, you can use a keyword as an identifier if you precede it with an @ sign, as in `@class`. An identifier with an @ prefix is a **verbatim identifier**. This feature allows you to use code written in other languages that do not have the same set of reserved keywords. However, when you write original C# programs, you should not use the keywords as identifiers.

Selecting Identifiers

abstract	float	return
as	for	sbyte
base	foreach	sealed
bool	goto	short
break	if	sizeof
byte	implicit	stackalloc
case	in	static
catch	int	string
char	interface	struct
checked	internal	switch
class	is	this
const	lock	throw
continue	long	true
decimal	namespace	try
default	new	typeof
delegate	null	uint
do	object	ulong
double	operator	unchecked
else	out	unsafe
enum	override	ushort
event	params	using
explicit	private	virtual
extern	protected	void
false	public	volatile
finally	readonly	while
fixed	ref	

Table 1-1 C# reserved keywords

The following identifiers have special meaning in C# but are not keywords: `add`, `alias`, `get`, `global`, `partial`, `remove`, `set`, `value`, `where`, and `yield`. For clarity, you should avoid using these words as your own identifiers.

Table 1-2 lists some valid and conventional class names you might use when creating classes in C#. You should follow established conventions for C# so that other programmers can interpret and follow your programs. Table 1-3 lists some class names that are valid, but unconventional; Table 1-4 lists some illegal class names.

Class Name	Description
Employee	Begins with an uppercase letter
FirstClass	Begins with an uppercase letter, contains no spaces, and has an initial uppercase letter that indicates the start of the second word
PushButtonControl	Begins with an uppercase letter, contains no spaces, and has an initial uppercase letter that indicates the start of all subsequent words
Budget2016	Begins with an uppercase letter and contains no spaces

Table 1-2 Some valid and conventional class names in C#

Class Name	Description
employee	Unconventional as a class name because it begins with a lowercase letter
First_Class	Although legal, the underscore is not commonly used to indicate new words in class names
Pushbuttoncontrol	No uppercase characters are used to indicate the start of a new word, making the name difficult to read
BUDGET2016	Unconventional as a class name because it contains all uppercase letters
Void	Although this identifier is legal because it is different from the keyword void, which begins with a lowercase v, the similarity could cause confusion

Table 1-3 Some unconventional (though legal) class names in C#

Class Name	Description
an employee	Space character is illegal
Push Button Control	Space characters are illegal
class	class is a reserved word
2016Budget	Class names cannot begin with a digit
phone#	The # symbol is not allowed; identifiers consist of letters, digits, underscores, or @

Table 1-4 Some illegal class names in C#

Selecting Identifiers

In Figure 1-2, the line `class FirstClass` contains the keyword `class`, which identifies `FirstClass` as a class.

The simple program shown in Figure 1-2 has many pieces to remember. For now, you can use the program shown in Figure 1-3 as a shell, where you replace the identifier `AnyLegalClassName` with any legal class name, and the line `/*********/` with any statements that you want to execute.

```
class AnyLegalClassName
{
    static void Main()
    {
        /*********/;
    }
}
```

Figure 1-3 Shell program

 Watch the video *C# Identifiers*.

TWO TRUTHS & A LIE

Selecting Identifiers

1. In C#, an identifier must begin with an underscore, the at sign (@), or an uppercase letter.

2. An identifier can contain only letters, digits, underscores, and the @ sign, not special characters such as #, $, or &.

3. An identifier cannot be a C# reserved keyword.

The false statement is #1. In C#, an identifier must begin with an underscore, the @ sign, or a letter. There is no requirement that the initial letter be capitalized, although in C#, it is a convention that the initial letter of a class name is capitalized.

Improving Programs by Adding Comments and Using the System Namespace

As you can see, even the simplest C# program takes several lines of code and contains somewhat perplexing syntax. Large programs that perform many tasks include much more code. As you work through this book, you will discover many ways to improve your ability to handle large programs. Two things you can do immediately are to add program comments and use the System namespace.

Adding Program Comments

As you write longer programs, it becomes increasingly difficult to remember why you included steps and how you intended to use particular variables. **Program comments** are nonexecuting statements that you add to document a program. Programmers use comments to leave notes for themselves and for others who might read their programs.

As you work through this book, you should add comments as the first few lines of every program file. The comments should contain your name, the date, and the name of the program. Your instructor might want you to include additional comments.

Comments also can be useful when you are developing a program. If a program is not performing as expected, you can **comment out** various statements and subsequently run the program to observe the effect. When you comment out a statement, you turn it into a comment so the compiler will ignore it. This approach helps you pinpoint the location of errant statements in malfunctioning programs.

C# offers three types of comments:

- **Line comments** start with two forward slashes (//) and continue to the end of the current line. Line comments can appear on a line by themselves, or they can occupy part of a line following executable code.

- **Block comments** start with a forward slash and an asterisk (/*) and end with an asterisk and a forward slash (*/). Block comments can appear on a line by themselves, on a line before executable code, or after executable code. When a comment is long, block comments can extend across as many lines as needed.

- C# also supports a special type of comment used to create documentation within a program: **XML-documentation format comments** use a special set of tags within angle brackets (< >). (XML stands for *Extensible Markup Language*.) You will learn more about this type of comment as you continue your study of C#.

The forward slash (/) and the backslash (\ ) characters often are confused, but they are distinct characters. You cannot use them interchangeably.

Figure 1-4 shows how comments can be used in code. The program covers 10 lines, yet only seven are part of the executable C# program, including the last two lines, which contain curly braces and are followed by partial-line comments. The only line that actually *does* anything visible when the program runs is the shaded one that displays *Message*.

```
/* This program is written to demonstrate using comments
*/
class ClassWithOneExecutingLine
{
   static void Main()
   {
      // The next line writes the message
      System.Console.WriteLine("Message");
   } // End of Main
} // End of ClassWithOneExecutingLine
```

Figure 1-4 Using comments within a program

Using the System Namespace

A program can contain as many statements as you need. For example, the program in Figure 1-5 produces the three lines of output shown in Figure 1-6. (To get the output, you have to know how to compile and execute the program, which you will learn in the next part of this chapter.) A semicolon separates each program statement.

```
class ThreeLinesOutput
{
   static void Main()
   {
      System.Console.WriteLine("Line one");
      System.Console.WriteLine("Line two");
      System.Console.WriteLine("Line three");
   }
}
```

Figure 1-5 A program that produces three lines of output

Figure 1-6 Output of the ThreeLinesOutput program

CHAPTER 1 A First Program Using C#

Figure 1-6 shows the output of the ThreeLinesOutput program when it is run in Visual Studio. The prompt to *Press any key to continue* is not part of the program; it is added by Visual Studio, but it does not appear if you run the program from the command prompt.

The program in Figure 1-5 shows a lot of repeated code—the phrase System.Console.WriteLine appears three times. When you need to repeatedly use a class from the same namespace, you can shorten the statements you type by adding a clause that indicates a namespace containing the class. You indicate a namespace with a **using clause**, or **using directive**, as shown in the shaded statement in the program in Figure 1-7. If you type using System; prior to the class definition, the compiler knows to use the System namespace when it encounters the Console class. The output of the program in Figure 1-7 is identical to that in Figure 1-5, in which System was repeated with each WriteLine() statement.

```
using System;
class ThreeLinesOutput
{
   static void Main()
   {
      Console.WriteLine("Line one");
      Console.WriteLine("Line two");
      Console.WriteLine("Line three");
   }
}
```

Figure 1-7 A program that produces three lines of output with a using System; clause

Although it was not an option in older versions of C#, now you can reduce typing in programs even further by inserting using static System.Console; at the top of a program. So, the program in Figure 1-8 uses only the method name WriteLine() in its output statements, and the program works correctly. (You have already seen the word static in the Main() method header. Recall that static means a method is used without creating an object. In Chapter 7, you will learn more about the use of the keyword static.) The simpler style shown in Figure 1-8 is the style used for programs in the rest of this book.

```
using static System.Console;
class ThreeLinesOutput
{
   static void Main()
   {
      WriteLine("Line one");
      WriteLine("Line two");
      WriteLine("Line three");
   }
}
```

Figure 1-8 A program that produces three lines of output with a using static System.Console; clause

TWO TRUTHS & A LIE

Improving Programs by Adding Comments and Using the `System` Namespace

1. Line comments start with two forward slashes (//) and end with two backslashes (\\ ).

2. Block comments can extend across as many lines as needed.

3. You use a namespace with a `using` clause, or `using` directive, to shorten statements when you need to repeatedly use a class from the same namespace.

The false statement is #1. Line comments start with two forward slashes (//) and continue to the end of the current line.

 You Do It

Now that you understand the basic framework of a program written in C#, you are ready to enter your first C# program into a text editor. It is a tradition among programmers that the first program you write in any language produces *Hello, world!* as its output. To create a C# program, you can use any simple text editor, such as Notepad, or the editor that is included as part of Microsoft Visual Studio. There are advantages to using the C# editor to write your programs, but using a plain text editor is simpler when you are getting started.

Entering a Program into an Editor

1. Start any text editor, such as Notepad, and open a new document, if necessary.

2. Type the `using` statement and the header for the class:

   using static System.Console;
   class Hello

3. On the next two lines, type the class-opening and class-closing curly braces: {}. Some programmers type a closing brace as soon as they type the opening one to guarantee that they always type complete pairs.

(continues)

(continued)

4. Between the class braces, insert a new line, type three spaces to indent, and write the Main() method header:

   static void Main()

5. On the next two lines, type the opening and closing braces for the Main() method, indenting them about three spaces.

6. Between the Main() method's braces, insert a new line and type six spaces so the next statement will be indented within the braces. Type the one executing statement in this program:

   WriteLine("Hello, world!");

   Your code should look like Figure 1-9.

   ```
   using static System.Console;
   class Hello
   {
      static void Main()
      {
         WriteLine("Hello, world!");
      }
   }
   ```

   Figure 1-9 The Hello class

7. Choose a location that is meaningful to you to save your program. For example, you might create a folder named CSharp on your hard drive. Within that folder, you might create a folder named Chapter01 in which you will store all the examples and exercises in this chapter. If you are working in a school lab, you might be assigned a storage location on your school's server. Save the program as **Hello.cs**. It is important that the file extension be *.cs*, which stands for *C Sharp*. If the file has a different extension, the compiler for C# will not recognize the program as a C# program.

Many text editors attach their own filename extension (such as *.txt* or *.doc*) to a saved file. Double-check your saved file to ensure that it does not have a double extension (as in *Hello.cs.txt*). If the file has a double extension, rename it. If you use a word-processing program as your editor, select the option to save the file as a plain text file.

Compiling and Executing a C# Program

After you write and save a program, two more steps must be performed before you can view the program output:

1. You must compile the program you wrote (the **source code**) into **intermediate language (IL)**.
2. The C# **just in time (JIT)** compiler must translate the intermediate code into executable code.

When you compile a C# program, your source code is translated into intermediate language. The JIT compiler converts IL instructions into native code at the last moment, and appropriately for each type of operating system on which the code eventually might be executed. In other words, the same set of IL can be JIT compiled and executed on any supported architecture.

Some developers say that languages such as C# are "semi-compiled." That is, instead of being translated immediately from source code to their final executable versions, programs are compiled into an intermediate version that is later translated into the correct executable statements for the environment in which the program is running.

You can write a program using a simple editor such as Notepad and then perform these steps from the command prompt in your system. You also can write a program within the Integrated Development Environment that comes with Visual Studio. Both methods can produce the same output; the one you use is a matter of preference.

- The **command line** is the line on which you type a command in a system that uses a text interface. The **command prompt** is a request for input that appears at the beginning of the command line. In DOS, the command prompt indicates the disk drive and optional path, and ends with >. When you install Microsoft Visual Studio on a computer, you get access to the **Developer Command Prompt** which is a special version of the command prompt for which specific settings have been enabled so that you can easily compile and run C# programs. (You could enact these settings yourself from the command prompt built-in with Windows; it just would be more work.) You might prefer the simplicity of the developer command prompt because you do not work with multiple menus and views as you do when you use the Integrated Development Environment. (Additionally, as you continue to study advanced features of C#, you might want to pass command-line arguments to a program. If so, you must compile from the command line.)

- The **Integrated Development Environment (IDE)** is a programming environment that allows you to issue commands by selecting choices from menus and clicking buttons. The IDE operates more like other software you may have used, such as a word processing program or spreadsheet. Many programmers prefer using the IDE because it provides features such as color-coded keywords and automatic statement completion.

Compiling Code from the Command Prompt

 If you will be using the IDE to write all your programs, you can read this section quickly, and then concentrate on the section titled "Compiling Code Using the Visual Studio IDE."

To compile your source code from the command line, you first locate the developer command prompt. In a Windows 10 operating system, you can type the first few characters of Developer Command Prompt in the Cortana "Ask me anything" search box in the lower left corner of the screen, and then select the option. If you don't find the developer command prompt window, you need to obtain and install a copy of Visual Studio. For more information, visit *msdn2.microsoft.com/en-us/vcsharp*.

In the developer command prompt window, you change the path to the location of your file (more about this shortly), and then type **csc**, followed by the name of the file that contains the source code. The command **csc** stands for *C Sharp compiler*. For example, to compile a file named ThreeLinesOutput.cs, you would type the following and then press **Enter**:

```
csc ThreeLinesOutput.cs
```

One of three outcomes is possible:

- You receive an operating system error message such as *Bad command or file name or csc is not recognized as an internal or external command, operable program or batch file*. You can recognize operating system messages because they do not start with the name of the program you are trying to compile.

- You receive one or more program language error messages. You can recognize program language error messages because they start with the name of the program followed by a line number and the position where the error was first noticed.

- You receive no error messages (only a copyright statement from Microsoft), indicating that the program has compiled successfully.

What to Do If You Receive an Operating System Error Message at the Command Prompt

If you receive an operating system message such as *csc is not recognized . . .* , or *Source file . . . could not be found*, it may mean that:

- You misspelled the command **csc**.

- You misspelled the filename.

- You forgot to include the extension .cs with the filename.

- You are not within the correct subdirectory or folder on your command line. For example, Figure 1-10 shows the **csc** command typed in the root directory of the C: drive. If the ThreeLinesOutput.cs file is stored in a folder on the C: drive rather than in the root

Compiling and Executing a C# Program

directory, then the command shown will not work because the C# file cannot be found. (Note that the compiler version referenced in the figure most likely will be different from the version used when this book was created.)

- The C# compiler was not installed properly. If you are working on your own computer, you might need to reinstall C#; if you are working in a school laboratory, you need to notify the system administrator.

```
C:\>csc ThreeLinesOutput.cs
Microsoft (R) Visual C# Compiler version 2.0.0.61104
Copyright (C) Microsoft Corporation. All rights reserved.

error CS2001: Source file 'C:\ThreeLinesOutput.cs' could not be found.

C:\>
```

Figure 1-10 Attempt to compile a program from the root directory at the command prompt, and error message received

What to Do If You Receive a Programming Language Error Message at the Command Prompt

If you receive a programming language error message, it means that the compiler was installed correctly, but that the source code contains one or more syntax errors. A syntax error occurs when you introduce typing errors into your program. Program error messages start with the program name, followed by parentheses that hold the line number and the position in the line where the compiler noticed the error. For example, in Figure 1-11, an error is found in ThreeLinesOutput.cs in line 8, position 7. In this case, the message is generated because `WriteLine` is typed as *writeLine* (with a lowercase *w*). The error message is *The name 'writeLine' does not exist in the current context*. If a problem like this occurs, you must reopen the text file that contains the source code, make the necessary corrections, save the file, and compile it again.

```
C:\CSharp\Chapter01>csc ThreeLinesOutput.cs
Microsoft (R) Visual C# Compiler version 2.0.0.61104
Copyright (C) Microsoft Corporation. All rights reserved.

ThreeLinesOutput.cs(8,7): error CS0103: The name 'writeLine' does not exist in the current context

C:\CSharp\Chapter01>
```

Figure 1-11 Error message generated when `WriteLine` is mistyped in the ThreeLinesOutput program compiled from the command prompt

The C# compiler issues warnings as well as errors. A warning is less serious than an error; it means that the compiler has determined you have done something unusual, but not illegal. If you have purposely introduced a warning situation to test a program, then you can ignore the warning. Usually, however, you should treat a warning message just as you would an error message and attempt to remedy the situation.

What to Do When the Program Compiles Successfully at the Command Prompt

If you receive no error messages after compiling the code, then the program compiled successfully, and a file with the same name as the source code—but with an .exe extension—is created and saved in the same folder as the program text file. For example, if ThreeLinesOutput.cs compiles successfully, then a file named ThreeLinesOutput.exe is created.

To run the program from the command line, you simply type the program name—for example, *ThreeLinesOutput*. You can also type the full filename, *ThreeLinesOutput.exe*, but it is not necessary to include the extension. The three lines of output, *Line one*, *Line two*, and *Line three*, appear in the command prompt window, and the command prompt is displayed again, awaiting a new command.

Compiling Code Using the Visual Studio IDE

As an alternative to using the command line, you can compile and write your program within the Visual Studio IDE. This approach has several advantages:

- Some of the code you need is already created for you.
- The code is displayed in color, so you can more easily identify parts of your program. Reserved words appear in blue, comments in green, and identifiers in black.
- If error messages appear when you compile your program, you can double-click an error message and the cursor will move to the line of code that contains the error.
- Other debugging tools are available. You will become more familiar with these tools as you develop more sophisticated programs.

If Visual Studio has been installed on your Windows 10 system, you can open it by starting to type *Visual Studio* in the "Ask me anything" search box and then selecting it. When the application opens, select *File* from the **menu bar** which, in the Visual Studio IDE, is the list of choices that runs horizontally across the top of the screen. Then select *New* and *Project* to start a new project. You designate it to be a *Console App*, give the project a name, and select *OK*. Then you type your program in the editor. Figure 1-12 shows a program named ThreeLinesOutput written in the editor of the Visual Studio IDE.

 When you install Visual Studio, you can select a color scheme, so your installed version might look slightly different from the screen images in this book.

Compiling and Executing a C# Program

Figure 1-12 The ThreeLinesOutput program as it appears in Visual Studio

Everything in Figure 1-12 was generated automatically by Visual Studio except for the following:

- The programmer selected the project name.
- The programmer added a `using static System.Console;` statement so that `WriteLine()` could be used without adding `System` and `Console` each time.
- The programmer added the three lines coded in the `Main()` method to produce output.

You can see that the Visual Studio environment looks like a word processor, containing menu options such as File, Edit, and Help, and buttons with icons representing options such as Save Selected Items and Undo. Selecting many of the menu options displays a drop-down list of additional options. Many of the options have shortcut keys that you can use instead of accessing the menus. For example, if you select *File* from the menu bar, you can see that a shortcut for Save Program.cs is *Ctrl + S*. You will learn about some of these options later in this chapter and continue to learn about more of them as you work with C# in the IDE.

In Figure 1-12, you can see a small lightbulb to the left of the `using` statement that was added by the programmer. A lightbulb indicates a place where you might be able to improve your program. In this case, if you click the lightbulb, you will see a message that indicates that you could remove the first five unnecessary `using` statements, retaining only the `using static System.Console;` `using` statement. You also can leave the extra `using` statement in place, and the program will still work correctly.

In Figure 1-12 you also can see vertical bars to the left of some of the code. These indicate changes that have been made since you opened the file. On your monitor, the bars will be green if the code has been saved, and yellow if it has not yet been saved.

CHAPTER 1 A First Program Using C#

One way to compile a program from Visual Studio is to select **Build** from the menu bar and then select **Build Solution** from the drop-down menu. As an alternative, you can press *Ctrl + Shift + B*. You can also select **Debug** from the menu bar, and then click **Start Without Debugging**. The advantage of the latter option is that the program will be compiled if there are no syntax errors and then execute so you can see the output.

What to Do If You Receive a Programming Language Error Message in the IDE

If you introduce a syntax error into a program in the IDE, you receive a programming language error message. For example, in Figure 1-13, `WriteLine` is spelled incorrectly because it uses a lowercase *w*. The error message displayed at the bottom is: *The name 'writeLine' does not exist in the current context.* (If you cannot read the entire message on your screen, you can adjust the size of the window.) The position is given (project, file, and line number), and as additional visual aids, a lightbulb appears to the left of the line containing the error, and a wavy underline emphasizes the unrecognized definition. When you fix the problem and compile the program again, the error message, wavy line, and lightbulb are eliminated.

Figure 1-13 Error message generated when `WriteLine` is mistyped in the ThreeLinesOutput program compiled in the IDE

Compiling and Executing a C# Program

In the lower left corner of Figure 1-13 you can see a code CS0103 next to the generated error message. You can search the Web for this code and discover its general meaning. However, usually sufficient explanation is provided in Visual Studio, and a Web search is unnecessary.

What to Do When the Program Compiles Successfully in the IDE

If you receive no error messages after compiling the code, then the program compiled successfully, and you can run the program. Select **Debug** from the menu bar, and then select **Start Without Debugging**. The output appears, as you saw it in Figure 1-6 earlier in this chapter.

Noticing the Differences Between the Programs in the Text Editor and the IDE

There are a few differences between the ThreeLinesOutput programs in Figures 1-8 and 1-12. Specifically, the Visual Studio version in Figure 1-12 contains the extra components that are highlighted in Figure 1-14.

- *Five* using *statements at the top of the file.* Visual Studio automatically provides you with several commonly needed using statements. In this case, you could delete all five statements from the Visual Studio version of the program, and the program would still run correctly. (The only using statement you need to retain is the using static System.Console; statement that allows you to use WriteLine() without qualification.) Conversely, you could add all five additional using statements to the command-line version of the program, and it would also run correctly.

- *A namespace declaration and its opening and closing curly braces.* You already know that C# uses built-in namespaces such as System and others that are automatically listed at the top of the Visual Studio version of programs. C# also allows you to create your own namespaces; Visual Studio assumes that you will want to create one using the name you have assigned to the project. In this case, you could remove the namespace declaration from the Visual Studio version of the program, or you could add one to the command-line version of the program. In both cases, the programs would still run correctly.

- *The class name* **Program**. Visual Studio assumes that you want to avoid confusion by having different names for your namespace and the class contained within it, so it assigns the generic name Program to the class that contains the Main() method. You could change this name to match the namespace identifier, ThreeLinesOutput, or use any other legal identifier, and the program would still work correctly. In the Notepad version of the program, you could change the class name to Program or any other legal identifier, and the program would also work.

- *The words* string[] args *between the parentheses of the* Main() *method header.* C# allows a program's Main() method header to be written in several ways. For example, you can include the words string[] args between the method's parentheses, or you can omit the words. The square brackets indicate an array, as you will learn when studying arrays later in this book. In this example, you could write the Main() method header with or without the extra code in either the Notepad or Visual Studio version of the program, and the Main() method would still work correctly.

In summary, the Visual Studio version of the ThreeLinesOutput program provides everything you need to run the program and saves you as much typing as possible in case you want to include additional options. The command-line and Visual Studio versions of the program function identically.

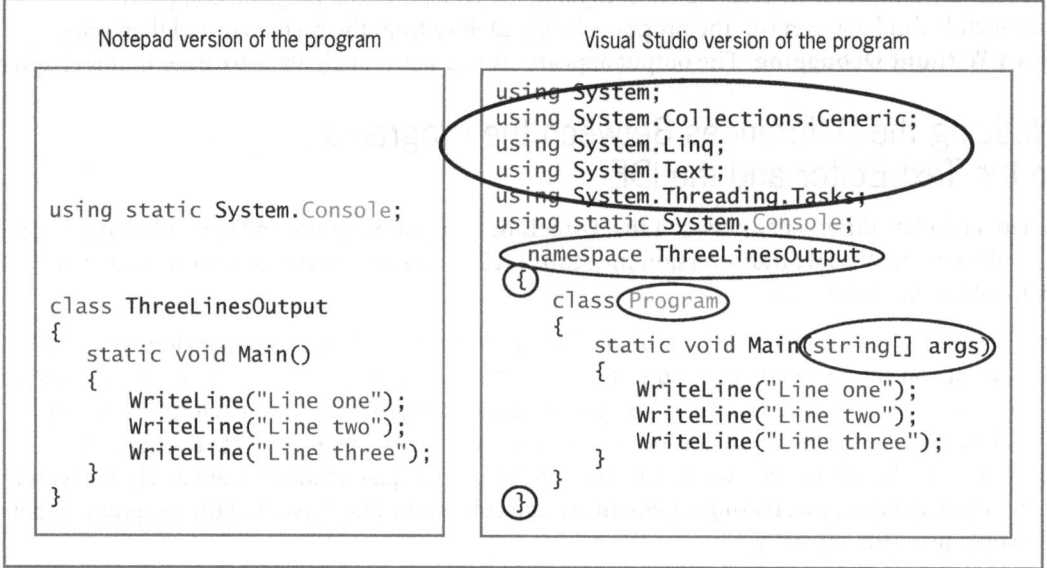

Figure 1-14 Comparing the command line and Visual Studio versions of the ThreeLinesOutput program

Deciding Which Environment to Use

When you write, compile, and execute a C# program, you can use either a text editor and the command line, or you can use the Visual Studio IDE. You would never need to use both. You might prefer using an editor with which you are already familiar (such as Notepad) and compiling from the command line because only two files are generated, saving disk space.

On the other hand, the IDE provides many useful features, such as automatic statement completion. For example, if you type *u*, then a list of choices including using is displayed and you can click using instead of typing it. Similarly, if you type *using s*, then a list of choices including static is displayed.

Additionally, in the IDE, words are displayed using different colors based on their category; for example, one color is used for C#-reserved words and a different color for literal strings. It is also easier to correct many errors using the IDE. When compiler errors or warnings are issued, you can double-click the message, and the cursor jumps to the location in the code where the error was detected. Another advantage to learning the IDE is that if you use another programming language in Visual Studio (C++ or Visual Basic), the environment will already be familiar to you. The C# language works the same way no matter which method you use to compile your programs. Everything you learn in the next chapters about input, output, decision making, loops, and arrays is correct in both environments. You can use just one technique or compile some programs in each environment as the mood strikes you. You also can mix and match techniques if you prefer. For example, you can use an editor you like to compose your programs, then paste them into the IDE to execute them. Although any program can be written using either compilation technique, when you write GUI applications that use existing objects such as buttons and labels, you will find that the extensive amount of code automatically generated by the IDE is very helpful.

 Watch the video *Writing and Compiling a Program*.

TWO TRUTHS & A LIE

Compiling and Executing a C# Program

1. After you write and save a program, you must compile it into intermediate language, and then the C# just in time (JIT) compiler must translate the intermediate code into executable code.

2. You can compile and execute a C# program from the command line or within the Integrated Development Environment (IDE) that comes with Visual Studio.

3. Many programmers prefer to compile their programs from the command line because it provides features such as color-coded keywords and automatic statement completion.

The false statement is #3. Programmers who prefer the command line prefer its simplicity. Programmers who prefer the Visual Studio IDE prefer the color-coded keywords and automatic statement completion.

You Do It

Compiling and Executing a Program from the Command Line

If you do not plan to use the command line to execute programs, you can skip to the next part of this "You Do It" section: "Compiling and Executing a Program Using the Visual Studio IDE."

1. Go to the command prompt on your system. For example, in Windows 10, start to type **Developer Command Prompt** in the "Ask me anything" search box, and then click the option.

2. Change the current directory to the name of the folder that holds your program. You can type cd\ and then press Enter to return to the root directory. You can then change the path to the one where your program resides. For example, if you stored your program file in a folder named Chapter01 within a folder named CSharp, then you can type the following:

   `cd CSharp\Chapter01`

   The command cd is short for *change directory*.

3. Type the command that compiles your program:

   `csc Hello.cs`

   If you receive no error messages and the prompt returns, it means that the compile operation was successful, that a file named Hello.exe has been created, and that you can execute the program. If you do receive error messages, check every character of the program you typed to make sure it matches Figure 1-9 in the last "You Do It" section. Remember, C# is case sensitive, so all casing must match exactly. When you have corrected the errors, repeat this step to compile the program again.

4. You can verify that a file named Hello.exe was created in these ways:
   - At the command prompt, type **dir** to view a directory of the files stored in the current folder. Both Hello.cs and Hello.exe should appear in the list.
   - Use Windows Explorer to view the contents of the folder in which you stored your program, verifying that two Hello files are listed.

(continues)

(continued)

5. At the command prompt, type **Hello**, which is the name of the program (the name of the executable file), and then press **Enter**. Alternatively, you can type the full filename **Hello.exe**, but typing the .exe extension isn't necessary. The output should look like Figure 1-15.

Figure 1-15 Output of the Hello application

Compiling and Executing a Program Using the Visual Studio IDE

Next, you use the C# compiler environment to compile and execute the same Hello program you ran from the command line.

1. Open **Visual Studio**. If there is a shortcut icon on your desktop, you can double-click it. Alternatively, in Windows 10, you can start to type **Visual Studio** in the Cortana "Ask me anything" search box, and then select it. When you see the Start Page, click **File** on the main menu, then click **New** and **Project**.

2. In the New Project window, click **Visual C#**, and then click **Console App**. By default, the name for the project is set to *ConsoleApp1*. (If you keep the name *ConsoleApp1*, the next project will be named *ConsoleApp2* by default.)

   Change the project name to **Hello**, and select the path where you want to save the project (see Figure 1-16). Click **OK**. Visual C# creates a new folder for your project named after the project title.

 Students might like to walk through these "You Do It" exercises multiple times for practice. Note that Visual Studio does not allow you to create a project with the same name as one already stored in a folder. When you perform these steps additional times, either delete the first version of the project before you start the next one, store the new version in a different folder, or give the new project a different name.

(continues)

CHAPTER 1 A First Program Using C#

(continued)

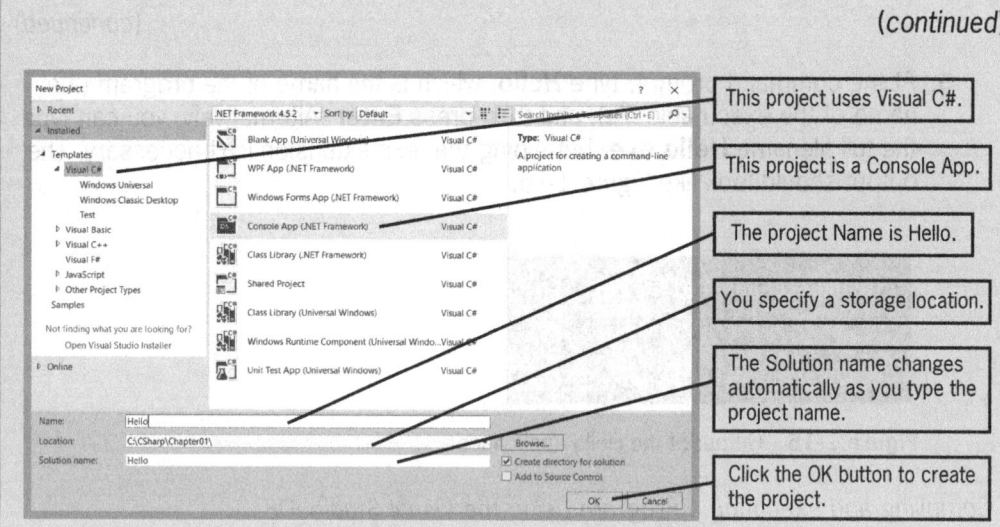

Figure 1-16 Starting a new project

3. The Hello application editing window appears. A lot of code is already written for you in this window, including some `using` statements, a namespace named `Hello`, a class named `Program`, and a `Main()` method. To create the Hello program, you need to add only two statements to the prewritten code. Place your cursor after the last using statement, press **Enter** to start a new line, and add an additional using statement:

   `using static System.Console;`

   After the opening brace of the `Main()` method, press **Enter** to start a new line, and add the following statement:

   `WriteLine("Hello, world!");`

   Figure 1-17 shows the editing window after the `using` and `WriteLine()` statements have been added.

(continues)

(continued)

```
1   using System;
2   using System.Collections.Generic;
3   using System.Linq;
4   using System.Text;
5   using System.Threading.Tasks;
6   using static System.Console;
7   namespace Hello
8   {
9       class Program
10      {
11          static void Main(string[] args)
12          {
13              WriteLine("Hello, world!");
14          }
15      }
16  }
17
```

These two lines were added by the programmer.

Figure 1-17 The Hello application editing window after the code has been added

4. Save the project by clicking **File** on the menu bar and then clicking **Save All**, or by clicking the **Save All** button (which shows two disks) on the toolbar, or by typing *Ctrl + Shift + S*.

5. To compile the program, click **Build** on the menu bar, and then click **Build Solution**. You should receive no error messages, and the words *Build succeeded* should appear near the lower-left edge of the window.

6. Click **Debug** on the menu bar, and then click **Start Without Debugging**. Figure 1-18 shows the output; you see *Hello, world!* followed by the message *Press any key to continue*. Press any key to close the output screen.

Figure 1-18 Output of the Hello application in Visual Studio

(continues)

(continued)

7. Close Visual Studio by clicking **File** on the menu bar and then clicking **Exit**, or by clicking the **Close** box in the upper-right corner of the Visual Studio window.

8. When you create a C# program using an editor such as Notepad and compile it with the `csc` command, only two files are created—Hello.cs and Hello.exe. When you create a C# program using the Visual Studio editor, many additional files are created. You can view their filenames from the command prompt or visually:

   - At the command prompt, type **dir** to view a directory of the files stored in the folder where you saved the project (for example, your Chapter01 folder). Within the folder, a new folder named Hello has been created. Type the command **cd Hello** to change the current path to include this new folder, then type **dir** again. You see another folder named Hello. Type **cd Hello** again, and **dir** again. You should see several folders and files. (Depending on the version of Visual Studio you use, your folder configuration might be slightly different.)

   - Use File Explorer to view the contents of the Hello folders within the Chapter01 folder.

   Regardless of the technique you use to examine the folders, you will find that the innermost Hello folder contains a bin folder, an obj folder, a Properties folder, and additional files. If you explore further, you will find that the bin folder contains a Debug folder, which includes several additional files. Using the Visual Studio editor to compile your programs creates a significant amount of overhead. These additional files become important as you create more sophisticated C# projects.

If you followed the earlier instructions about compiling a program from the command line, and you used the same folder when using the IDE, you will see the additional Hello.cs and Hello.exe files in your folder. These files will have an earlier time stamp than the files you just created. If you were to execute a new program within Visual Studio without saving and executing it from the command line first, you would not see these two additional files.

(continues)

(continued)

Adding Comments to a Program

Comments are nonexecuting statements that help to document a program. In the following steps, you add some comments to the program you just created.

1. If you prefer compiling programs from the command line, then open the **Hello.cs** file in your text editor. If you prefer compiling programs from Visual Studio, then open Visual Studio, click **File**, point to **Open**, click **Project/Solution**, browse for the correct folder, double-click the **Hello** folder, and then double-click the **Hello** file.

2. Position your cursor at the top of the file, press **Enter** to insert a new line, press the **up** arrow to go to that line, and then type the following comments at the top of the file. Press **Enter** after typing each line. Insert your name and today's date where indicated.

   ```
   //Filename Hello.cs
   //Written by <your name>
   //Written on <today's date>
   ```

3. Scroll to the line that reads `static void Main()`, and press **Enter** to start a new line. Then press the **up** arrow; in the new blank line, aligned with the start of the `Main()` method header, type the following block comment in the program:

   ```
   /* This program demonstrates the use of the WriteLine() method
   to display the message Hello, world! */
   ```

4. Save the file, replacing the old Hello.cs file with this new, commented version.

5. If you prefer to compile programs from the command line, type `csc Hello.cs` at the command line. When the program compiles successfully, execute it with the command **Hello**. If you prefer compiling and executing programs from Visual Studio, click **Debug**, and then click **Start Without Debugging**. Adding program comments makes no difference in the execution of the program.

6. If you are working from the command line, you can close the command-line window. If you are working from Visual Studio, you can close the output screen and then close Visual Studio.

CHAPTER 1　A First Program Using C#

Chapter Summary

- A computer program is a set of instructions that tells a computer what to do. Programmers use a compiler to translate their high-level language statements into intermediate language and machine code. A program works correctly when both its syntax and logic are correct.

- Procedural programming involves creating variables and methods. In object-oriented programming, the focus is on objects that encapsulate variables and methods. OOP techniques were first used for simulations and GUIs.

- Objects are instances of classes and are made up of attributes and methods. Object-oriented programming languages support encapsulation, inheritance, and polymorphism.

- The C# programming language was developed as an object-oriented and component-oriented language. It contains many features similar to those in Visual Basic, Java, and C++.

- To produce a line of console output in a C# program, you must pass a literal string as an argument to the `System.Console.WriteLine()` method. `System` is a namespace and `Console` is a class. Calls to the `WriteLine()` method can appear within the `Main()` method of a class you create.

- You can define a C# class or variable by using any name or identifier that begins with an underscore, a letter, or an @ sign. These names can contain only letters, digits, underscores, and the @ sign, and cannot be C#-reserved keywords.

- You can improve programs by adding comments, which are nonexecuting statements that you add to document a program or to disable statements when you test a program. The three types of comments in C# are line comments, block comments, and XML-documentation comments. You also can improve programs and shorten the statements you type by using a clause that indicates a namespace where your classes can be found.

- To create a C# program, you can use the Microsoft Visual Studio IDE or any text editor, such as Notepad. After you write and save a program, you must compile the source code into intermediate and machine language.

Key Terms

A computer **program** is a set of instructions that tell a computer what to do.

Software is computer programs.

System software describes the programs that operate the computer.

Application software is the programs that allow users to complete tasks.

Hardware comprises all the physical devices associated with a computer.

Key Terms

Machine language is the most basic circuitry-level language.

A **high-level programming language** allows you to use a vocabulary of keywords instead of the sequence of on/off switches that perform these tasks.

Keywords are predefined and reserved identifiers that have special meaning to the compiler.

Camel casing, also called **lower camel casing**, is a style of creating identifiers in which the first letter is not capitalized, but each new word is.

A language's **syntax** is its set of rules.

A **compiler** is a computer program that translates high-level language statements into machine code.

A **syntax error** is an error that occurs when a programming language is used incorrectly.

The **logic** behind any program involves executing the various statements and methods in the correct order to produce the desired results.

A **bug** is an error in a computer program.

Debugging a program is the process of removing all syntax and logical errors from the program.

A **procedural program** is created by writing a series of steps or operations to manipulate values.

Variables are named computer memory locations that hold values that might vary during program execution.

An **identifier** is the name of a program component such as a variable, class, or method.

Methods are compartmentalized, named program units containing instructions that accomplish tasks.

Pascal casing, also called **upper camel casing**, is a style of creating identifiers in which the first letter of all new words in a name, even the first one, is capitalized.

A program **calls** or **invokes** methods.

Object-oriented programming (OOP) is a programming technique that features objects, classes, encapsulation, interfaces, polymorphism, and inheritance.

An **object** is a concrete entity that has attributes and behaviors; an object is an instance of a class.

The **attributes of an object** represent its characteristics.

The **state of an object** is the collective value of all its attributes at any point in time.

The **behaviors of an object** are its methods.

Taking an **object-oriented approach** to a problem means defining the objects needed to accomplish a task and developing classes that describe the objects so each maintains its own data and carries out tasks when another object requests them.

Computer simulations Computer simulations are programs that attempt to mimic real-world activities to foster a better understanding of them.

CHAPTER 1 A First Program Using C#

Graphical user interfaces Graphical User Interfaces, or GUIs (pronounced *gooeys*), are program elements that allow users to interact with a program in a graphical environment.

A **class** is a category of objects or a type of object.

An **instance of a class** is an object.

The **properties** of an object are its values.

Encapsulation is the technique of packaging an object's attributes and methods into a cohesive unit that can be used as an undivided entity.

A **black box** is a device you use without regard for the internal mechanisms.

An **interface** is the interaction between a method and an object.

Inheritance is the ability to extend a class so as to create a more specific class that contains all the attributes and methods of a more general class; the extended class usually contains new attributes or methods as well.

Polymorphism is the ability to create methods that act appropriately depending on the context.

The **C# programming language** was developed as an object-oriented and component-oriented language. It exists as part of Visual Studio, a package used for developing applications for the Windows family of operating systems.

A **literal string** of characters is a series of characters enclosed in double quotes that is used exactly as entered.

An **argument** to a method represents information that a method needs to perform its task; it is used between parentheses when you call a method.

A **namespace** is a construct that acts like a container to provide a way to group similar classes.

A **method header** includes the method name and information about what will pass into and be returned from a method.

The **method body** of every method is contained within a pair of curly braces ({}) and includes all the instructions executed by the method.

Whitespace is any combination of spaces, tabs, and carriage returns (blank lines). You use whitespace to organize your program code and make it easier to read.

The keyword `static`, when used in a method header, indicates that a method will be executed through a class and not by an object.

The keyword `void`, when used in a method header, indicates that the method does not return any value.

Key Terms

Application classes contain a Main() method and are executable programs.

Runnable describes files that are executable.

Non-application classes do not contain a Main() method; they provide support for other classes.

A **verbatim identifier** is an identifier with an @ prefix.

Program comments are nonexecuting statements that you add to document a program.

To **comment out** a statement is to make a statement nonexecuting.

Line comments start with two forward slashes (//) and continue to the end of the current line. Line comments can appear on a line by themselves or at the end of a line following executable code.

Block comments start with a forward slash and an asterisk (/*) and end with an asterisk and a forward slash (*/). Block comments can appear on a line by themselves, on a line before executable code, or after executable code. They also can extend across as many lines as needed.

XML-documentation format comments use a special set of tags within angle brackets to create documentation within a program.

A **using clause** or **using directive** declares a namespace.

Source code is the statements you write when you create a program.

Intermediate language (IL) is the language into which source code statements are compiled.

The C# **Just in time (JIT)** compiler translates intermediate code into executable code.

The **command line** is the line on which you type a command in a system that uses a text interface.

The **command prompt** is a request for input that appears at the beginning of the command line.

The **Developer Command Prompt** is a special version of the command prompt for which specific settings have been enabled so that you can easily compile and run C# programs.

An **Integrated Development Environment (IDE)** is a program development environment that allows you to select options from menus or by clicking buttons. An IDE provides such helpful features as color coding and automatic statement completion.

The **menu bar** in the IDE lies horizontally across the top of the window, and includes submenus that list additional options.

CHAPTER 1 A First Program Using C#

Review Questions

1. Programming languages such as C#, Java, and Visual Basic are _____ languages.

   a. machine
   b. high-level
   c. low-level
   d. uninterpreted

2. A program that translates high-level programs into intermediate or machine code is a(n) _____.

   a. mangler
   b. compactor
   c. analyst
   d. compiler

3. The grammar and spelling rules of a programming language constitute its _____.

   a. logic
   b. variables
   c. class
   d. syntax

4. Variables are _____.

   a. named memory locations
   b. unexpected results
   c. grammar rules
   d. operations

5. Programs in which you create and use objects that have attributes similar to their real-world counterparts are known as _____ programs.

   a. procedural
   b. logical
   c. object-oriented
   d. authentic

6. Which of the following pairs is an example of a class and an object, in that order?

   a. University and Yale
   b. Chair and desk
   c. Clydesdale and horse
   d. Maple and tree

7. The technique of packaging an object's attributes into a cohesive unit that can be used as an undivided entity is _____.

   a. inheritance
   b. encapsulation
   c. polymorphism
   d. interfacing

8. Of the following languages, which is least similar to C#?

   a. Java
   b. Visual Basic
   c. C++
   d. machine language

Review Questions

9. A series of characters that appears within double quotation marks is a(n) _____ .

   a. method
   b. interface
   c. argument
   d. literal string

10. The C# method that produces a line of output on the screen and then positions the cursor on the next line is _____ .

    a. `WriteLine()`
    b. `PrintLine()`
    c. `DisplayLine()`
    d. `OutLine()`

11. Which of the following is a class?

    a. `System`
    b. `Console`
    c. `void`
    d. `WriteLine()`

12. In C#, a container that groups similar classes is a(n) _____ .

    a. superclass
    b. method
    c. namespace
    d. identifier

13. Every method in C# contains a _____ .

    a. header and a body
    b. header and a footer
    c. variable and a class
    d. class and an object

14. Which of the following is a method?

    a. `namespace`
    b. `class`
    c. `Main()`
    d. `static`

15. In C#, an identifier _____ .

    a. must begin with an underscore
    b. can contain digits
    c. must be no more than 16 characters
    d. can contain only lowercase letters

16. Which of the following identifiers is not legal in C#?

    a. `per cent increase`
    b. `annualReview`
    c. `HTML`
    d. `alternativetaxcredit`

17. The text of a program you write is called _____.

    a. object code
    b. source code
    c. machine language
    d. executable documentation

18. Programming errors such as using incorrect punctuation or misspelling words are collectively known as _____ errors.

    a. syntax
    b. logical
    c. executable
    d. fatal

19. A comment in the form `/*this is a comment */` is a(n) _____.

    a. XML comment
    b. block comment
    c. executable comment
    d. line comment

20. If a programmer inserts `using static System.Console;` at the top of a C# program, which of the following can the programmer use as an alternative to `System.Console.WriteLine("Hello");`?

    a. `System("Hello");`
    b. `WriteLine("Hello");`
    c. `Console.WriteLine("Hello");`
    d. `Console("Hello");`

Exercises

Programming Exercises

1. Indicate whether each of the following C# programming language identifiers is legal or illegal. If it is legal, indicate whether it is a conventional identifier for a class.

    a. `electricBill`
    b. `ElectricBill`
    c. `Electric bill`
    d. `Static`
    e. `void`
    f. `#ssn`
    g. `Ay56we`
    h. `Theater_Tickets`
    i. `212AreaCode`
    j. `heightInCentimeters`
    k. `Zip23891`
    l. `Void`

2. Name at least three attributes that might be appropriate for each of the following classes:

    a. `TVShow`
    b. `Party`
    c. `JobApplication`
    d. `CheckingAccount`

3. Name at least two classes to which each of these objects might belong:

   a. your cousin
   b. Macys
   c. Egypt
   d. Thomas Jefferson

4. Write, compile, and test a program named **PersonalInfo** that displays a person's name, birthdate, work phone number, and cell phone number.

5. Write, compile, and test a program named **Lyrics** that displays at least four lines of your favorite song.

6. Write, compile, and test a program named **Comments** that displays a statement that defines program comments. Include at least one block comment and one line comment in the program.

7. Write, compile, and test a program named **StopSign** that displays a pattern similar to the image shown in Figure 1-19.

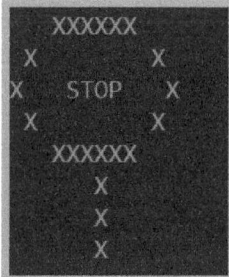

Figure 1-19 Output of StopSign program

8. Write a program named **BigLetter** that displays a large letter composed of smaller letters. For example, if you choose H, then the output should look similar to the image shown in Figure 1-20.

Figure 1-20 Typical output of BigLetter program

9. From 1925 through 1963, Burma Shave advertising signs appeared next to highways all across the United States. There were always four or five signs in a row containing pieces of a rhyme, followed by a final sign that read "Burma Shave." For example, one set of signs that has been preserved by the Smithsonian Institution reads as follows:

Shaving brushes
You'll soon see 'em
On a shelf
In some museum
Burma Shave

Find a classic Burma Shave rhyme on the Web and write a program named **BurmaShave** that displays the rhyme.

Debugging Exercises

1. Each of the following files in the Chapter.01 folder of your downloadable student files has syntax and/or logical errors. In each case, determine the problem and fix the program. After you correct the errors, save each file using the same filename preceded with *Fixed*. For example, DebugOne1.cs will become FixedDebugOne1.cs.

   a. DebugOne1.cs
   b. DebugOne2.cs
   c. DebugOne3.cs
   d. DebugOne4.cs

Case Problems

The case problems in this section introduce two fictional businesses. Throughout this book, you will create increasingly complex classes for these businesses that use the newest concepts you have mastered in each chapter.

1. Greenville County hosts the Greenville Idol competition each summer during the county fair. The talent competition takes place over a three-day period during which contestants are eliminated following rounds of performances until the year's ultimate winner is chosen. Write a program named **GreenvilleMotto** that displays the competition's motto, which is "The stars shine in Greenville." Create a second program named **GreenvilleMotto2** that displays the motto surrounded by a border composed of asterisks.

2. Marshall's Murals is a company that paints interior and exterior murals for both business and residential customers. Write a program named **MarshallsMotto** that displays the company motto, which is "Make your vision your view." Create a second program named **MarshallsMotto2** that displays the motto surrounded by a border composed of repeated *Ms*.

CHAPTER 2

Using Data

Upon completion of this chapter, you will be able to:

- ◎ Declare variables
- ◎ Display variable values
- ◎ Use integral data types
- ◎ Use floating-point data types
- ◎ Use arithmetic operators
- ◎ Use the `bool` data type
- ◎ Describe numeric type conversion
- ◎ Use the `char` data type
- ◎ Use the `string` data type
- ◎ Define named constants and enumerations
- ◎ Accept console input

CHAPTER 2 — Using Data

In Chapter 1, you learned about programming in general and the C# programming language in particular. You wrote, compiled, and ran a C# program that produced output. In this chapter, you build on your basic C# programming skills by learning how to manipulate data and use data types, variables, and constants. As you will see, using variables to hold data makes computer programs flexible.

Declaring Variables

A data item is **constant** when it cannot be changed after a program is compiled—in other words, when it cannot vary. For example, if you use the number 347 within a C# program, then 347 is a constant, and every time you execute the program, the value 347 will be used. You can refer to the number 347 as a **literal constant**, because its value is taken literally at each use. (A number like 347 is also called an *unnamed constant* because no name is associated with it. Later in this chapter you will learn about named constants.)

On the other hand, when you want a data item's value to be able to change, you can create a variable. As you learned in Chapter 1, a variable is a named location in computer memory that can hold different values at different points in time. For example, if you create a variable named heatingBill and include it in a C# program, heatingBill might contain the value 347, or it might contain 200. Different values might be used when the program is executed multiple times, or different values might be used at different times during a single program execution. Because you can use a variable to hold heatingBill within a program used by a utility company's automated billing system, you can write one set of instructions to compute heatingBill, yet use different heatingBill values for thousands of utility customers.

Whether it is a constant or a variable, each data item you use in a C# program has a data type. A **data type** describes the format and size of (amount of memory occupied by) a data item and defines what types of operations can be performed with the item. C# provides for 15 basic, or **intrinsic types**, of data, as shown in Table 2-1. Of these built-in data types, the ones most commonly used are int, double, decimal, char, string, and bool. Each C# intrinsic type is an **alias**, or other name, for a class in the System namespace. (You learned about the System namespace in Chapter 1.) All of the built-in types except object and string are called **simple types**.

The meaning of the largest and smallest values for the numeric types in Table 2-1 is probably clear to you, but some of the other values require explanation.

- The highest char value, 0xFFFF, represents the character in which every bit is turned on. The lowest value, 0x0000, represents the character in which every bit is turned off. Any value that begins with *0x* represents a hexadecimal, or base 16, value.

- For any two strings, the one with the higher Unicode character value in an earlier position is considered higher. (**Unicode** is the system that provides a numeric value for every character. You will learn more about Unicode later in this chapter, and Appendix B contains further information.) For example, "AAB" is higher than "AAA". The string type has no true minimum; however, you can think of the empty string "" as being the lowest.

- Although the bool type has no true maximum or minimum, you can think of true as the highest and false as the lowest.

Type	System Type	Bytes	Description	Largest Value	Smallest Value
Types that hold numbers with no decimal places					
byte	Byte	1	Unsigned byte	255	0
sbyte	Sbyte	1	Signed byte	127	−128
short	Int16	2	Signed short	32,767	−32,768
ushort	UInt16	2	Unsigned short	65,535	0
int	Int32	4	Signed integer	2,147,483,647	−2,147,483,648
uint	UInt32	4	Unsigned integer	4,294,967,295	0
long	Int64	8	Signed long integer	Approximately 9×10^{18}	Approximately -9×10^{18}
ulong	UInt64	8	Unsigned long interger	Approximately 18×10^{18}	0
Types that hold numbers with decimal places					
float	Single	4	Floating-point	Approximately 3.4×10^{38}	Approximately -3.4×10^{38}
double	Double	8	Double-precision floating-point	Approximately 1.8×10^{308}	Approximately -1.8×10^{308}
decimal	Decimal	16	Fixed-precision number	Approximately 7.9×10^{28}	Approximately -7.9×10^{28}
Types that hold other values					
char	Char	2	Unicode character	0xFFFF	0x0000
bool	Boolean	1	Boolean value (true or false)	NA	NA
string	String	NA	Unicode string	NA	NA
object	Object	NA	Any object	NA	NA

Table 2-1 C# data types

Variable names follow the same rules as class identifiers: A variable name must start with a letter, cannot include embedded spaces, and cannot be a reserved keyword. (Table 1-1 in Chapter 1 lists all the C# keywords.) By convention, each C# variable name starts with a lowercase letter and uses camel casing if it contains multiple words.

You must declare all variables you want to use in a program. A **variable declaration** is the statement that names a variable and reserves storage for it. A declaration includes the following:

- The data type that the variable will store
- The variable's name (its identifier)
- An optional assignment operator and assigned value when you want a variable to contain an initial value
- An ending semicolon.

For example, the following statement declares a variable of type `int` named `myAge` and assigns it an initial value of 25:

```
int myAge = 25;
```

The **int** data type represents an **integer**; which is a whole number. Complete discussion of this data type appears in the section "Using the Integral Data Types" later in this chapter. The equal sign (=) is the **assignment operator**; any value to the right of the assignment operator is assigned to the identifier to the left. An assignment made when a variable is declared is an **initialization**; an assignment made later is simply an **assignment**. Thus, the following statement initializes `myAge` to 25:

```
int myAge = 25;
```

A statement such as the following assigns a new value to the variable:

```
myAge = 42;
```

Notice that the data type is not used again when an assignment is made; it is used only in a declaration.

Also note that the expression `25 = myAge;` is illegal because assignment always takes place from right to left. By definition, a literal constant cannot be altered, so it is illegal to place one (such as 25) on the left side of an assignment operator. The assignment operator means "is assigned the value of the following expression." In other words, the statement `myAge = 25;` can be read as "`myAge` is assigned the value of the expression 25."

Instead of using a type name from the *Type* column of Table 2-1, you could use the fully qualified type name from the `System` namespace that is listed in the *System Type* column. For example, instead of using the type name `int`, you can use the full name `System.Int32`. (The number 32 in the name `System.Int32` represents the number of bits of storage allowed for the data type. There are eight bits in a byte, and an `int` occupies four bytes.) It's better to use the shorter alias `int`, however, for the following reasons:

- The shorter alias is easier to type and read.
- The shorter alias resembles type names used in other languages such as Java and C++.
- Other C# programmers expect the shorter type names.

You can declare a variable without an initialization value, as in the following statement:

`int myAge;`

You can make an assignment to an uninitialized variable later in the program, but you cannot use the variable in a calculation or display it until a value has been assigned to it.

You can declare multiple variables of the same type in separate statements. For example, the following statements declare two integer variables:

```
int myAge = 25;
int yourAge = 19;
```

If variables have different types, each must be declared in its own statement, but you can declare multiple variables of the same type in a single statement by using the type once and separating the variable declarations with a comma, as shown in the following statement:

`int myAge = 25, yourAge = 19;`

Some programmers prefer to break declarations across multiple lines, as in the following example:

```
int myAge = 25,
   yourAge = 19;
```

When a statement occupies more than one line, it is easier to read if lines after the first one are indented a few spaces. This book follows that convention.

 Watch the video *Declaring Variables*.

TWO TRUTHS & A LIE

Declaring Variables

1. A constant value cannot be changed after a program is compiled, but a variable can be changed.

2. A data type describes the format and size of a data item and the types of operations that can be performed with it.

3. A variable declaration requires a data type, name, and assigned value.

The false statement is #3. A variable declaration names a variable and reserves storage for it; it includes the data type that the variable will store and an identifier. An assignment operator and assigned value can be included, but they are not required.

CHAPTER 2 Using Data

Displaying Variable Values

You can display variable values by using the variable name within a `Write()` or `WriteLine()` method call. For example, Figure 2-1 shows a C# program that displays the value of the variable someMoney. Figure 2-2 shows the output of the program when executed at the command prompt.

```
using static System.Console;
class DisplaySomeMoney
{
    static void Main()
    {
        double someMoney = 39.45;
        WriteLine(someMoney);
    }
}
```

Figure 2-1 Program that displays a variable value

Figure 2-2 Output of the DisplaySomeMoney program

The output shown in Figure 2-2 is rather stark—just a number with no explanation. The program in Figure 2-3 adds some explanation to the output; the result is shown in Figure 2-4. This program uses the `Write()` method to display the string "The money is $" before displaying the value of someMoney. Because the program uses `Write()` instead of `WriteLine()` for the first output, the second output appears on the same line as the first.

```
using static System.Console;
class DisplaySomeMoney2
{
    static void Main()
    {
        double someMoney = 39.45;
        Write("The money is $");
        WriteLine(someMoney);
    }
}
```

Figure 2-3 Program that displays a string and a variable value

Figure 2-4 Output of the DisplaySomeMoney2 program

Displaying Variable Values

If you want to display several strings and several variables, you can end up with quite a few `Write()` and `WriteLine()` statements. To make producing output easier, you can combine strings and variable values into a single `Write()` or `WriteLine()` statement by concatenating them or by using a format string.

When you **concatenate** a string with another value, you join the values with a plus sign. For example, the following statement produces the same output as shown in Figure 2-4 but uses only one `WriteLine()` statement:

```
WriteLine("The money is $" + someMoney);
```

A **format string** is a string of characters that controls the appearance of output. It optionally contains fixed text and contains one or more format items or *placeholders* for variable values. A **placeholder** holds a position for a variable value within a string. It consists of a pair of curly braces containing a number that indicates the desired variable's position in a list that follows the string. The first position is always position 0.

You can create a formatted string using the `String.Format()` method that is built into C#. For example, the following statements create a formatted string and then display it:

```
double someMoney = 39.45;
string mySentence =
    String.Format("The money is ${0} exactly", someMoney);
WriteLine(mySentence);
```

The curly braces that contain a digit create a placeholder {0} into which the value of someMoney is inserted. Because someMoney is the first variable after the format string (as well as the only variable in this example), its position is 0. The process of replacing string place holders with values is often called **string interpolation** or *variable substitution*.

C# also includes a string interpolation feature that allows you to use a dollar sign in place of the `String.Format()` method call, as in the following:

```
string yourSentence = $"The money is ${someMoney} exactly";
WriteLine(yourSentence);
```

C# also allows you to use a shortcut with the `Write()` and `WriteLine()` methods. You can format a string and output it in one step without declaring a temporary string variable and without explicitly naming the `String.Format()` method, as in either of the following examples:

```
WriteLine("The money is ${0} exactly", someMoney);
WriteLine($"The money is ${someMoney} exactly");
```

For example, the program in Figure 2-5 produces the output shown in Figure 2-6.

```
using static System.Console;
class DisplaySomeMoney3
{
   static void Main()
   {
      double someMoney = 39.45;
      WriteLine("The money is ${0} exactly", someMoney);
   }
}
```

Figure 2-5 Using a format string

```
The money is $39.45 exactly
```

Figure 2-6 Output produced using format string

To display two variables within a single call to `Write()` or `WriteLine()`, you can use a statement like either of the following:

```
WriteLine("The money is {0} and my age is {1}", someMoney, myAge);
WriteLine($"The Money is {someMoney} and age is {myAge}");
```

The two examples above produce the same output. In the first example, the value of `someMoney` will appear at position 0, and `myAge` will appear at position 1. The number within any pair of curly braces in a format string must be less than the number of values you list after the format string. In other words, if you list six values to be displayed, valid format position numbers are 0 through 5. You do not have to use the positions in order. You also can display a specific value multiple times. For example, if `someMoney` has been assigned the value 39.45, the following code produces the output shown in Figure 2-7:

```
WriteLine("I have ${0}. ${0}!! ${0}!!", someMoney);
```

```
I have $39.45. $39.45!! $39.45!!
```

Figure 2-7 Displaying the same value multiple times

The output in Figure 2-7 could be displayed without using a format string, but you would have to name the `someMoney` variable three separate times as in either of the following examples:

```
WriteLine("I have $" + someMoney + ". $" + someMoney +
   "!! $" + someMoney + "!!");
WriteLine($"I have ${someMoney}. ${someMoney}!! ${someMoney}!!");
```

Variable Alignment

When you use a series of `WriteLine()` statements to display a list of variable values, the values are not automatically right-aligned as you normally expect numbers to be. For example, the following code produces the unaligned output shown in Figure 2-8:

```
WriteLine("{0}", 4);
WriteLine("{0}", 56);
WriteLine("{0}", 789);
```

If you use a second number within the curly braces in a format string, you can specify alignment and field size. By default, numbers are right-aligned in their fields. If you use a negative value for the field size in a `Write()` or `WriteLine()` statement, the displayed value will be left-aligned in the field. Most often, you want numbers to be right-aligned and string values to be left-aligned. For example, the following code produces the output shown in Figure 2-9. The output created by each of the first three `WriteLine()` statements is a right-aligned number in a field that is five characters wide, and the output created by each of the last three statements is two left-aligned strings in a field that is eight characters wide.

```
WriteLine("{0, 5}", 4);
WriteLine("{0, 5}", 56);
WriteLine("{0, 5}", 789);
WriteLine("{0, -8}{1, -8}", "Richard", "Lee");
WriteLine("{0, -8}{1, -8}", "Marcia", "Parker");
WriteLine("{0, -8}{1, -8}", "Ed", "Tompkins");
```

Figure 2-8 Displaying values with different numbers of digits without using field sizes

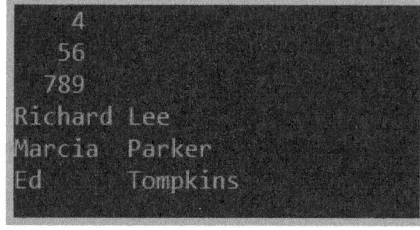

Figure 2-9 Displaying values with different numbers of digits using field sizes

Format strings can become very long. However, when you include any string value in a program, you cannot extend it across multiple lines by pressing Enter. If you do, you will receive an error message: *Newline in constant*. Instead, if you want to break a long string into multiple lines of code, you can concatenate multiple strings into a single entity, as in the following:

```
WriteLine("I have ${0}. " +
   "${0} is a lot. ", someMoney);
```

In the concatenated example, the + could go at the end of the first code line or the beginning of the second one. If the + is placed at the end of the first line, someone reading your code is more likely to notice that the statement is not yet complete. Because of the limitations of this book's page width, you will see examples of concatenation frequently in program code.

CHAPTER 2 Using Data

 A new feature when you use the IDE for Visual Studio 2017 allows you to place your cursor inside a string, press Enter, and the string is concatenated for you. That is, an ending quotation mark and a plus sign are inserted where you press Enter, and an opening quotation mark is inserted at the start of the last part of the string on the new, next line.

> ## TWO TRUTHS & A LIE
> ### Displaying Variable Values
>
> 1. Assuming number and answer are legally declared variables with assigned values, then the following statement is valid:
>
>   WriteLine("{1}{2}", number, answer);
>
> 2. Assuming number and answer are legally declared variables with assigned values, then the following statement is valid:
>
>   WriteLine("{1}{1}{0}", number, answer);
>
> 3. Assuming number and answer are legally declared variables with assigned values, then the following statement is valid:
>
>   WriteLine("{0}{1}{1}{0}", number, answer);
>
> The false statement is #1. When two values are available for display, the position number between any pair of curly braces in the format string must be 0 or 1. If three values were listed after the format string, the position numbers could be any combination of 0, 1, and 2.

Using the Integral Data Types

In C#, nine data types are considered **integral data types**—that is, types that store whole numbers. The nine types are **byte**, **sbyte**, **short**, **ushort**, **int**, **uint**, **long**, **ulong**, and **char**. The first eight always represent whole numbers, and the ninth type, char, is used for characters such as *A* or *a*. Actually, you can think of all nine types as numbers because every Unicode character, including the letters of the alphabet and punctuation marks, can be represented as a number. For example, the character *A* is stored within your computer as a 65. Because you more commonly think of the char type as holding alphabetic characters instead of their numeric equivalents, the char type will be discussed in its own section later in this chapter.

The most basic of the other eight integral types is int. You use variables of type int to store (or hold) integers, or whole numbers without any fractional part. An int uses four bytes of memory and can hold any whole number value ranging from 2,147,483,647 down to −2,147,483,648. When you type a whole-number constant such as 3 or 589 into a C# program, by default it is an int.

If you want to save memory and know you need only a small value, you can use one of the shorter integer types—**byte**, **sbyte** (which stands for signed byte), **short** (short int), or

Using the Integral Data Types

`ushort` (unsigned short `int`). For example, a payroll program might contain a variable named `numberOfDependents` that is declared as type `byte`, because `numberOfDependents` will never need to hold a value exceeding 255; for that reason, you can allocate just one byte of storage to hold the value. When you declare variables, you always make a judgment about which type to use. If you use a type that is too large, you waste storage. If you use a type that is too small, your program won't compile. Many programmers simply use `int` for most whole numbers.

Saving memory is seldom an issue for an application that runs on a PC. However, when you write applications for small devices with limited memory, such as smartphones, conserving memory becomes more important.

The word *integer* has only one *r*—at the end. Pronouncing it as "in-ter-ger," with an r in the middle, would mark you as unprofessional.

When you assign a value to any numeric variable, you do not use any commas or other nonnumeric characters such as dollar or percent signs; you type only digits. The exception is that, starting with C# 7.0, you can insert underscores as **digit separators** for readability. For example, the two declarations are identical, but you might find one easier to read:

```
int aLotOfMoney = 23456789;
int aLotOfMoney = 23_456_789;
```

You can also type a plus or minus sign to indicate a positive or negative integer; a value without a sign is assumed to be positive. For example, to initialize a variable named `annualSalary`, you might write the following without a dollar sign or comma:

```
int annualSalary = 20000;
```

TWO TRUTHS & A LIE

Using the Integral Data Types

1. C# supports nine integral data types, including the most basic one, `int`.
2. Every Unicode character, including the letters of the alphabet and punctuation marks, can be represented as a number.
3. When you assign a value to any numeric variable, it is optional to use commas for values in the thousands.

The false statement is #3. When you assign a value to a numeric variable, you do not use commas, but you can type a plus or minus sign to indicate a positive or negative integer.

You Do It

Declaring and Using Variables

In the following steps, you write a program that declares several integral variables, assigns values to them, and displays the results.

1. Open a new file. If you are using a simple text editor to write your C# programs, you will save the file as **DemoVariables.cs**. If you are using Visual Studio, select **Console Application**, name the project **DemoVariables**, and delete all the code in the program-editing window before starting.

2. Create the beginning of a program that will demonstrate variable use. Name the class `DemoVariables`, and type the class-opening curly brace.

   ```
   using static System.Console;
   class DemoVariables
   {
   ```

3. In the `Main()` method, declare two variables (an integer and an unsigned integer), and assign values to them.

   ```
   static void Main()
   {
       int anInt = -123;
       uint anUnsignedInt = 567;
   ```

4. Add a statement to display the two values.

   ```
   WriteLine("The int is {0} and the unsigned int is {1}.",
       anInt, anUnsignedInt);
   ```

5. Add two closing curly braces—one that closes the `Main()` method and one that closes the `DemoVariables` class. Align each closing curly brace vertically with the opening brace that is its partner. In other words, the first closing brace aligns with the brace that opens `Main()`, and the second aligns with the brace that opens `DemoVariables`.

6. Save the program, and compile it. If you receive any error messages, correct the errors and compile the program again. When the file is error-free, execute the program. The output should look like Figure 2-10.

```
The int is -123 and the unsigned int is 567.
```

Figure 2-10 Output of the `DemoVariables` program

(continues)

(continued)

7. Experiment with the program by introducing invalid values for the named variables. For example, change the value of anUnsignedInt to **−567** by typing a minus sign in front of the constant value. Compile the program. You receive the following error message: *Constant value '−567' cannot be converted to a 'uint'*.

8. Correct the error either by removing the minus sign or by changing the data type of the variable to **int**, and compile the program again. You should not receive any error messages. Remember to save your program file after you make each change and before you compile.

9. Change the value of anInt from **−123** to **−123456789000**. When you compile the program, the following error message appears: *Cannot implicitly convert type 'long' to 'int'*.

    The value is a long because it is greater than the highest allowed int value. Correct the error either by using a lower value or by changing the variable type to long, and compile the program again. You should not receive any error messages.

10. Experiment with other changes to the variables. Include some variables of type short, ushort, byte, and sbyte, and experiment with their values.

Using Floating-Point Data Types

A **floating-point** number is one that contains decimal positions. Floating-point numbers are described as having varying numbers of significant digits. A value's number of **significant digits** specifies the mathematical accuracy of the value. The concept is often used in rounding. For example, in the statement "The population of New York City is 8,000,000," there is just one significant digit—the 8. The zeros serve as placeholders and are meant to approximate the actual value.

When numbers are stored in computer memory, using a decimal point that can "float" provides a wider possible range of values. As a very simple example, suppose that the largest number you could store had only two digits with a fixed decimal point between them. Then the positive numbers that could be stored would range from 0.0 to 9.9. However, if the decimal point can float to be first, middle, or last, then the range becomes .00 through 99.

C# supports three floating-point data types: float, double, and decimal.

- A **float** data type can hold as many as seven significant digits of accuracy. For example, a float assigned the value 1234.56789 will appear as 1234.568 because it is accurate only to the seventh digit (the third digit to the right of the decimal point).

- A **double** data type can hold 15 or 16 significant digits of accuracy. For example, a double given the value 123456789.987654321 will appear as 123456789.987654 because it is accurate to only the fifteenth digit (the sixth digit to the right of the decimal point).

- Compared to floats and doubles, the **decimal** type has a greater precision and a smaller range, which makes it suitable for financial and monetary calculations. A decimal is significant to 28 or 29 digits. As Table 2-1 shows, a decimal cannot hold as large a value as a double can (the highest value is about 10^{28}; the highest value of a double is 10^{308}, but the decimal will be more accurate to more decimal places.

Just as an integer constant is an int by default, a floating-point number constant is a double by default. To explicitly store a constant as a float, you place an *F* (either lowercase or uppercase) after the number, as in the following:

```
float pocketChange = 4.87F;
```

You can also place a *D* (or *d*) after a floating-point value to indicate that it is a double; even without the *D*, however, it will be stored as a double by default. To explicitly store a value as a decimal, use an *M* (or *m*) after the number. (*M* stands for monetary; *D* can't be used for a decimal because it indicates double.)

Because monetary values are extremely important in business applications, many C# developers frequently use the decimal data type. This book most often uses the double type for floating-point values because floating-point numbers are double by default and do not require a modifying letter after the value. However, you should use the data type preferred by your instructor or manager or the type that is most appropriate to your application. Some programmers prefer to use the decimal type for any measurement created by humans (for example, money or test scores) and double for measurements of naturally occurring phenomena (for example, half-lives of elements).

If you store a value that is too large (or too small) in a floating-point variable, you will see output expressed in **scientific notation**. Values expressed in scientific notation include an *E* (for exponent). For example, if you declare float f = 1234567890f;, the value is output as 1.234568E9, meaning that the numeric constant you used is approximately 1.234568 times 10 to the ninth power, or 1.234568 with the decimal point moved nine positions to the right. When the value that follows the *E* is negative, it means the value is very small and the decimal point should move to the left. For example, the value 1.234E-07 represents 0.0000001234.

Formatting Floating-Point Values

By default, C# always displays floating-point numbers in the most concise way possible that maintains the correct value. For example, if you declare a variable and display it as in the following statements, the output will appear as *The amount is 14*.

```
double myMoney = 14.00;
WriteLine("The amount is {0}", myMoney);
```

Using Floating-Point Data Types

The two zeros to the right of the decimal point in the assigned value will not appear in the output because they add no mathematical information. To see the decimal places in the output, you can convert the floating-point value to a string using a standard numeric format string.

Standard numeric format strings are strings of characters expressed within double quotation marks that indicate a format for output. They take the form *X0*, where *X* is the format specifier and *0* is the precision specifier. The **format specifier** can be one of nine built-in format characters that define the most commonly used numeric format types. The **precision specifier** controls the number of significant digits or zeros to the right of the decimal point. Table 2-2 lists the nine format specifiers.

Format Character	Description	Default Format (if no precision is given)
C or c	Currency	$XX,XXX.XX ($XX,XXX.XX)
D or d	Decimal	[−]XXXXXXX
E or e	Scientific (exponential)	[−]X.XXXXXXE+xxx [−]X.XXXXXXe+xxx [−]X.XXXXXXE-xxx [−]X.XXXXXXe-xxx
F or f	Fixed point	[−]XXXXXXX.XX
G or g	General	Variable; either with decimal places or scientific
N or n	Number	[−]XX,XXX.XX
P or p	Percent	Represents a numeric value as a percentage
R or r	Round trip	Ensure that numbers converted to strings will have the same values when they are converted back into numbers
X or x	Hexadecimal	Minimum hexadecimal (base 16) representation

Table 2-2 Format specifiers

You can use a format specifier with the `ToString()` method to convert a number into a string that has the desired format. For example, you can use the *F* format specifier to insert a decimal point to the right of a number that does not contain digits to the right of the decimal point, followed by the number of zeros indicated by the precision specifier. (If no precision specifier is supplied, two zeros are inserted.) For example, the first `WriteLine()` statement in the following code produces 123.00, and the second produces 123.000:

```
double someMoney = 123;
string moneyString;
moneyString = someMoney.ToString("F");
WriteLine(moneyString);
moneyString = someMoney.ToString("F3");
WriteLine(moneyString);
```

You will learn more about creating and using methods in the chapters "Introduction to Methods" and "Advanced Method Concepts."

You use *C* as the format specifier when you want to represent a number as a currency value. Currency values appear with a dollar sign, appropriate commas, and the desired number of decimal places; negative values appear within parentheses. The integer you use following the *C* indicates the number of decimal places. If you do not provide a value for the number of decimal places, then two digits are shown after the decimal separator by default. For example, the following `WriteLine()` statement produces $456,789.00:

```
double moneyValue = 456789;
string conversion;
conversion = moneyValue.ToString("C");
WriteLine(conversion);
```

Currency appears with a dollar sign and commas in the English culture, but not in some other cultures. A **culture** is a set of rules that determines how culturally dependent values such as money and dates are formatted. You can change a program's culture by using the `CultureInfoClass`. The .NET framework supports more than 200 culture settings, such as Japanese, French, Urdu, and Sanskrit.

To display a numeric value as a formatted string, you do not have to create a separate string object. You also can make the conversion in a single statement; for example, the following code displays $12,345.00:

```
double payAmount = 12345;
WriteLine(payAmount.ToString("C"));
```

TWO TRUTHS & A LIE

Using Floating-Point Data Types

1. A floating-point number is one in which the decimal point varies each time you reference it.
2. C# supports three floating-point data types: `float`, `double`, and `decimal`.
3. To explicitly store a constant as a `float`, you may place an *F* after the number, but to store a constant as a `double` you need no special designation.

The false statement is #1. A floating-point number is one that contains decimal positions.

Using Arithmetic Operators

Table 2-3 describes the five most commonly used **arithmetic operators**. You use these operators to manipulate values in your programs. The values that operators use in expressions are called **operands**. These arithmetic operators are called **binary operators** because you use two operands with each—one value to the left of the operator and another value to the right of it.

Operator	Description	Example
+	Addition	45 + 2: the result is 47
−	Subtraction	45 − 2: the result is 43
*	Multiplication	45 * 2: the result is 90
/	Division	45 / 2: the result is 22 (not 22.5)
%	Remainder (modulus)	45 % 2: the result is 1 (that is, 45 / 2 = 22 with a remainder of 1)

Table 2-3 Binary arithmetic operators

Unlike some other programming languages, C# does not have an exponential operator. Instead, you can use the built-in method `Math.Pow()` that you will learn about in the chapter "Introduction to Methods."

The operators / and % deserve special consideration. When you divide two numbers and at least one is a floating-point value, the answer is a floating-point value. For example, 45.0 / 2 is 22.5. However, when you divide integers using the / operator, whether they are integer constants or integer variables, the result is an integer; in other words, any fractional part of the result is lost. For example, the result of 45 / 2 is 22, not 22.5.

When you use the remainder operator with two integers, the result is an integer with the value of the remainder after division takes place—so the result of 45 % 2 is 1 because 2 "goes into" 45 twenty-two times with a remainder of 1. Remainder operations should not be performed with floating-point numbers. The results are unpredictable because of the way floating-point numbers are stored in computer memory.

In older languages, such as assembly languages, you had to perform division before you could take a remainder. In C#, performing a division operation is not necessary before using a remainder operation. In other words, a remainder operation can stand alone.

You might hear programmers refer to the remainder operator as the *modulus operator*. Although modulus has a similar meaning to remainder, there are differences.

Even though you define a result variable as a floating-point type, integer division still results in an integer. For example, the statement `double d = 7 / 2;` results in d holding 3, not 3.5, because the expression on the right is evaluated as integer-by-integer division before the assignment takes place. If you want the result to hold 3.5, at least one of the operands in the calculation must be a floating-point number, or else you must perform a cast. You will learn about casting later in this chapter.

When you combine mathematical operations in a single statement, you must understand **operator precedence**, or the rules that determine the order in which parts of a mathematical expression are evaluated. Multiplication, division, and remainder always take place prior to addition or subtraction in an expression. For example, the following expression results in 14:

```
int result = 2 + 3 * 4;
```

The result is 14 because the multiplication operation (3 * 4) occurs before adding 2. You can override normal operator precedence by putting the operation that should be performed first in parentheses. The following statement results in 20 because the addition within parentheses takes place first:

```
int result = (2 + 3) * 4;
```

In this statement, an intermediate result (5) is calculated before it is multiplied by 4.

Operator precedence is also called **order of operation**. A closely linked term is **associativity**, which specifies the order in which a sequence of operations with the same precedence are evaluated. Appendix A describes the precedence and associativity of every C# operator.

You can use parentheses in an arithmetic expression, even if they do not alter the default order of operation. For example, even though multiplication takes place before addition without parentheses, it is perfectly acceptable to add them as follows:

```
weeklyPay = (hours * rate) + bonus;
```

You can use parentheses to make your intentions clear to other programmers who read your programs, which means they do not have to rely on their memory of operator precedence. In summary, the order of operations for arithmetic operators is:

- *Parentheses*. Evaluate expressions within parentheses first.
- *Multiplication, division, remainder*. Evaluate these operations next from left to right.
- *Addition, subtraction*. Evaluate these operations next from left to right.

Using Shortcut Arithmetic Operators

Increasing the value held in a variable is a common programming task. Assume that you have declared a variable named counter that counts the number of times an event has occurred. Each time the event occurs, you want to execute a statement such as the following:

```
counter = counter + 1;
```

This type of statement looks incorrect to an algebra student, but the equal sign (=) is not used to compare values in C#; it is used to assign values. The statement counter = counter + 1; says "Take the value of counter, add 1 to it, and assign the result to counter."

Because increasing the value of a variable is such a common task, C# provides several shortcut ways to count and accumulate. The following two statements are identical in meaning:

```
counter += 1;
counter = counter + 1;
```

The += operator is the **add and assign operator**; it adds the operand on the right to the operand on the left and assigns the result to the operand on the left in one step. For example, if payRate is 20, then payRate += 5 results in payRate holding the value 25. Similarly, the following statements both increase bankBal by a rate stored in interestRate:

```
bankBal += bankBal * interestRate;
bankBal = bankBal + bankBal * interestRate;
```

For example, if bankBal is 100.00 and interestRate is 0.02, then both of the previous statements result in bankBal holding 102.00.

Additional shortcut operators in C# are -=, *=, and /=. Each of these operators is used to perform an operation and assign the result in one step. You cannot place spaces between the two characters that compose these operators; spaces preceding or following the operators are optional. Examples in which the shortcut operators are useful follow:

- balanceDue -= payment subtracts a payment from balanceDue and assigns the result to balanceDue.
- rate *= 100 multiplies rate by 100 and assigns the result to rate. For example, it converts a fractional value stored in rate, such as 0.27, to a whole number, such as 27.
- payment /= 12 changes a payment value from an annual amount to a monthly amount.

When you want to increase a variable's value by exactly 1, you can use either of two other shortcut operators—the **prefix increment operator** and the **postfix increment operator**. To use a prefix increment operator, you type two plus signs before the variable name. For example, these statements result in someValue holding 7:

```
int someValue = 6;
++someValue;
```

The variable someValue holds 1 more than it held before the ++ operator was applied. To use a postfix ++, you type two plus signs just after a variable name. Executing the following statements results in anotherValue holding 57:

```
int anotherValue = 56;
anotherValue++;
```

You can use the prefix ++ and postfix ++ with variables but not with constants. An expression such as ++84 is illegal because 84 is constant and must always remain 84. However, you can create a variable as in int val = 84;, and then write either ++val or val++ to increase the variable's value to 85.

The prefix and postfix increment operators are **unary operators** because you use them with one operand. Most arithmetic operators, such as those used for addition and multiplication, are binary operators that operate on two operands.

When all you want to accomplish is to increase a variable's value by 1, there is no apparent difference between using the prefix and postfix increment operators. However, these operators function differently. When you use the prefix ++, the result is calculated and stored and then the variable is used. For example, in the following code, both b and c end up holding 5. The WriteLine() statement displays *5 and 5*. In this example, 4 is assigned to b, then b becomes 5, and then 5 is assigned to c.

```
b = 4;
c = ++b;
WriteLine("{0} and {1}", b, c);
```

In contrast, when you use the postfix ++, the variable is used, and then the result is calculated and stored. For example, in the second line of the following code, 4 is assigned to c; then, *after* the assignment, b is increased and takes the value 5.

```
b = 4;
c = b++;
WriteLine("{0} and {1}", b, c);
```

This last WriteLine() statement displays *5 and 4*. In other words, if b = 4, then the value of b++ is also 4, and, in the second statement above, that value is assigned to c. However, after the 4 is assigned to c, b is increased to 5.

When you need to add 1 to a variable in a standalone statement, the results are the same whether you use a prefix or postfix increment operator. However, many programmers routinely use the postfix operator when they could use either operator. This is probably a mistake because the prefix operator is more efficient. You will see an example that proves the superior efficiency of the prefix operator in the chapter "Looping."

A prefix or postfix **decrement operator** (--) reduces a variable's value by 1. For example, if s and t are both assigned the value 34, then the expression --s has the value 33 and the expression t-- has the value 34, but t then becomes 33.

  Watch the video *Using Shortcut Arithmetic Operators*.

TWO TRUTHS & A LIE

Using Arithmetic Operators

1. The value of 26 % 4 * 3 is 18.

2. The value of 4 / 3 + 2 is 3.

3. If price is 4 and tax is 5, then the value of price - tax++ is -1.

The false statement is #1. The value of 26 % 4 * 3 is 6. The value of the first part of the expression, 26 % 4, is 2, because 2 is the remainder when 4 is divided into 26. Then 2 * 3 is 6.

You Do It

Performing Arithmetic

In the following steps, you add some arithmetic statements to a program.

1. Open a new C# program file named **DemoVariables2**, and enter the following statements to start a program that demonstrates arithmetic operations:

   ```
   using static System.Console;
   class DemoVariables2
   {
       static void Main()
       {
   ```

2. Write a statement that declares seven integer variables. Assign initial values to two of the variables; the values for the other five variables will be calculated. Because all of these variables are the same type, you can use a single statement to declare all seven integers. Recall that to do this, you insert commas between variable names and place a single semicolon at the end. You can place line breaks wherever you want for readability. (Alternatively, you could use as many as seven separate declarations.)

   ```
   int value1 = 43, value2 = 10,
       sum, diff, product, quotient, remainder;
   ```

3. Write the arithmetic statements that calculate the sum of, difference between, product of, quotient of, and remainder of the two assigned variables.

   ```
   sum = value1 + value2;
   diff = value1 - value2;
   product = value1 * value2;
   quotient = value1 / value2;
   remainder = value1 % value2;
   ```

    Instead of declaring the variables sum, diff, product, quotient, and remainder and assigning values later, you could declare and assign all of them at once, as in int sum = value1 + value2;. The only requirement is that value1 and value2 must be assigned values before you can use them in a calculation.

4. Include five WriteLine() statements to display the results.

   ```
   WriteLine("The sum of {0} and {1} is {2}",
       value1, value2, sum);
   WriteLine("The difference between {0} and {1}" +
       " is {2}", value1, value2, diff);
   ```

   (continues)

(continued)

```
WriteLine("The product of {0} and {1} is {2}",
    value1, value2, product);
WriteLine("{0} divided by {1} is {2}", value1,
    value2, quotient);
WriteLine("and the remainder is {0}", remainder);
```

5. Add two closing curly braces—one for the Main() method and the other for the DemoVariables2 class.

6. Save the file, compile the program, and execute it. The output should look like Figure 2-11.

```
The sum of 43 and 10 is 53
The difference between 43 and 10 is 33
The product of 43 and 10 is 430
43 divided by 10 is 4
and the remainder is 3
```

Figure 2-11 Output of the DemoVariables2 program

7. Change the values of the value1 and value2 variables to any values you choose, save the program, and compile and run it again. Repeat this process several times. After each execution, analyze the output to make sure you understand the results of the arithmetic operations.

Using the bool Data Type

Boolean logic is based on true-or-false comparisons. An int variable can hold millions of different values at different times, but a **Boolean variable** can hold only one of two values—true or false. You declare a Boolean variable by using the data type **bool**. The following statements declare and assign appropriate values to two bool variables:

```
bool isItMonday = false;
bool areYouTired = true;
```

Although there are no naming requirements, if you begin a bool variable name with a form of the verb "to be" or "to do," such as "is" or "are," then you can more easily recognize the identifiers as Boolean variables when you encounter them within your programs. It also frequently makes sense to start a bool variable identifier with a "question" word such as *can* or *has*.

Using the bool Data Type

 When you use *Boolean* as an adjective, as in the expressions *Boolean variable* and *Boolean logic*, you usually begin with an uppercase *B* because the data type is named for Sir George Boole, the founder of symbolic logic, who lived from 1815 to 1864. The C# data type bool, however, begins with a lowercase *b*.

You also can assign values based on the result of comparisons to Boolean variables. A **comparison operator** compares two items; an expression containing a comparison operator has a Boolean value. Table 2-4 describes the six comparison operators that C# supports.

Operator	Description	true Example	false Example
<	Less than	3 < 8	8 < 3
>	Greater than	4 > 2	2 > 4
==	Equal to	7 == 7	3 == 9
<=	Less than or equal to	5 <= 5	8 <= 6
>=	Greater than or equal to	7 >= 3	1 >= 2
!=	Not equal to	5 != 6	3 != 3

Table 2-4 Comparison operators

When using any of the operators that require two keystrokes (==, <=, >=, or !=), you cannot place any whitespace between the two symbols.

A frequent mistake among new programmers is attempting to create a Boolean expression for equivalency with a single equal sign. The equivalency operator uses two equal signs. For example, the following assigns either true or false to isDiscountProvided:

isDiscountProvided = custStatus == 1;

The second operator in the statement (==) compares custStatus to 1. The result is then assigned to the variable on the left using the assignment operator (=).

Legal (but somewhat useless) declaration statements might include the following, which compare two values directly:

```
bool isBigger = 6 > 5; // Value stored would be true
bool isSmallerOrEqual = 7 <= 4; // Value stored would be false
```

Using Boolean values is more meaningful when you use variables (that have been assigned values) rather than constants in the comparisons, as in the following examples:

```
bool doesEmployeeReceiveOvertime = hoursWorked > 40;
bool isHighTaxBracket = annualIncome > 100000;
```

In the first statement, the hoursWorked variable is compared to a constant value of 40. If the hoursWorked variable holds a value less than or equal to 40, then the expression is evaluated as false. In the second statement, the annualIncome variable value must be greater than 100000 for the expression to be true.

Boolean variables become more useful after you learn to make decisions within C# programs in Chapter 4.

When you display a bool variable's value with a call to Write() or WriteLine(), the displayed value is capitalized as True or False. However, the values within programs are lowercase: true or false.

TWO TRUTHS & A LIE

Using the bool Data Type

1. If rate is 7.5 and min is 7, then the value of rate >= min is false.
2. If rate is 7.5 and min is 7, then the value of rate < min is false.
3. If rate is 7.5 and min is 7, then the value of rate == min is false.

The false statement is #1. If rate is 7.5 and min is 7, then the value of rate >=min is true.

You Do It

Working with Boolean Variables

Next, you will write a program that demonstrates how Boolean variables operate.

1. Open a new file in your editor, and name it **DemoVariables3**.
2. Enter the following code. In the Main() method, you declare an integer value, then assign different values to a Boolean variable. Notice that when you declare value and isSixMore, you assign types. When you reassign values to these variables later in the program, you do not redeclare them by using a type name. Instead, you simply assign new values to the already declared variables.

(continues)

(continued)

```
using static System.Console;
class DemoVariables3
{
    static void Main()
    {
        int comparisonValue = 4;
        bool isSixMore = 6 > comparisonValue;
        WriteLine("When comparisonValue is {0}, isSixMore is {1}",
            comparisonValue, isSixMore);
        comparisonValue = 35;
        isSixMore = 6 > comparisonValue;
        WriteLine("When comparisonValue is {0}, isSixMore is {1}",
            comparisonValue, isSixMore);
    }
}
```

3. Save, compile, and run the program. The output looks like Figure 2-12.

```
When comparisonValue is 4, isSixMore is True
When comparisonValue is 35, isSixMore is False
```

Figure 2-12 Output of the DemoVariables3 program

4. Change the value of the variable named `comparisonValue` to any values you choose, both in the initialization statement and in the later assignment statement. Try to predict the output, and then run the program to confirm your prediction. Change `comparisonValue` to 6 in at least one location, try to predict the outcome, and run the program again.

Understanding Numeric Type Conversion

When you perform arithmetic with variables or constants of the same type, the result of the arithmetic retains that type. For example, when you divide two `int`s, the result is an `int`; when you subtract two `double`s, the result is a `double`. Often, however, you need to perform mathematical operations on different types. For example, in the following code, you multiply an `int` by a `double`:

```
int hoursWorked = 36;
double payRate = 12.35;
double grossPay = hoursWorked * payRate;
```

When you perform arithmetic operations with operands of dissimilar types, C# chooses a **unifying type** for the result and **implicitly** (or automatically) converts nonconforming operands to the unifying type, which is the type with the higher **type precedence**. The conversion is called an **implicit conversion** or an **implicit cast**—the automatic transformation that occurs when a value is assigned to a type with higher precedence.

The implicit numeric conversions are:

- From sbyte to short, int, long, float, double, or decimal
- From byte to short, ushort, int, uint, long, ulong, float, double, or decimal
- From short to int, long, float, double, or decimal
- From ushort to int, uint, long, ulong, float, double, or decimal
- From int to long, float, double, or decimal
- From uint to long, ulong, float, double, or decimal
- From long to float, double, or decimal
- From ulong to float, double, or decimal
- From char to ushort, int, uint, long, ulong, float, double, or decimal
- From float to double

Implicit conversions occur in simple assignments as well as in calculations. For example, if money is declared as a double, then the following statement implicitly converts the integer 15 to a double:

money = 15;

Conversions from int, uint, or long to float and from long to double might cause a loss of precision but will never cause a loss of magnitude.

A constant expression of type int, such as 25, can be converted to sbyte, byte, short, ushort, uint, or ulong. For example, sbyte age = 19;, which assigns an int to an sbyte, is legal. However, you must make sure that the assigned value is within the allowed range for the destination type, or the program will not compile. For example, sbyte age = 200; is illegal because the highest value allowed for an sbyte is 127.

For example, if you multiply an int and a double, the result is implicitly a double. This requirement means the result must be stored in a double; if you attempt to assign the result to an int, you will receive a compiler error message like the one shown in Figure 2-13.

Figure 2-13 Error message received when trying to compile a program that attempts to store a double in an int

Understanding Numeric Type Conversion

The error message in Figure 2-13 asks "are you missing a cast?" You can **explicitly** (or purposefully) override the unifying type imposed by C# by performing an explicit cast. An **explicit cast** involves placing the desired result type in parentheses followed by the variable or constant to be cast. For example, two explicit casts are performed in the following code:

```
double bankBalance = 191.66;
float weeklyBudget = (float) bankBalance / 4;
   // weeklyBudget is 47.915, one-fourth of bankBalance
int dollars = (int) weeklyBudget;
   // dollars is 47, the integer part of weeklyBudget
```

The value of bankBalance / 4 is implicitly a double because a double divided by an int produces a double. The explicit cast then converts the double result to a float before it is stored in weeklyBudget. Similarly, the float value weeklyBudget is cast to an int before it is stored in dollars (and the decimal-place values are lost).

It is easy to lose data when performing a cast. For example, the largest byte value is 255, and the largest int value is 2,147,483,647, so the following statements produce distorted results because some information is lost during the cast:

- int anOkayInt = 256;
- byte aBadByte = (byte)anOkayInt;

In this example, displaying aBadByte shows 0. If you stored 257 in anOkayInt, the result would appear as 1; if you stored 258, the result would appear as 2; and so on.

 Watch the video *Numeric Type Conversion*.

TWO TRUTHS & A LIE

Understanding Numeric Type Conversion

1. If deptNum is an int with a value of 10, then the following is valid:
   double answer = deptNum;

2. If answer is a double with a value of 10.0, then the following is valid:
   int deptNum = answer;

3. If value is a double with a value of 12.2, then the following is valid:
   double answer = (int)value;

The false statement is #2. A double cannot be implicitly converted to an int.

Using the char Data Type

You use the **char** data type to hold any single character. You place constant character values within single quotation marks because the computer stores characters and integers differently. For example, the following statement assigns *D* to initial:

```
char initial = 'D';
```

A number can be a character, in which case it must be enclosed in single quotation marks and declared as a char type, as in the following:

```
char aCharValue = '9';
```

When you store a digit such as '9' as a character, you cannot use it in ordinary arithmetic statements. If the value of 9 is needed for use in arithmetic, you should store it without quotes as a numeric type, such as int.

A variable of type char can hold only one character, and a literal character is written using single quotation marks. To store a string of characters, such as a person's name, you must use a string; a literal string is written using double quotation marks. You will learn about strings later in this chapter.

You can store any character—including nonprinting characters such as a backspace or a tab—in a char variable. To store these characters, you use two symbols in an **escape sequence**, which always begins with a backslash. The pair of symbols represents a single character. For example, the following code stores a backspace character and a tab character in the char variables aBackspaceChar and aTabChar, respectively:

```
char aBackspaceChar = '\b';
char aTabChar = '\t';
```

In the preceding code, the escape sequence indicates a unique value for each character—a backspace or tab instead of the letter *b* or *t*. Table 2-5 describes some common escape sequences that are used in C#.

The characters used in C# are represented in Unicode, which is a 16-bit coding scheme for characters. For example, the letter *A* actually is stored in computer memory as a set of 16 zeros and ones—namely, 0000 0000 0100 0001. (The spaces are inserted here after every set of four digits for readability.) Because 16-bit numbers are difficult to read, programmers often use a shorthand notation called **hexadecimal**, or **base 16**. In hexadecimal shorthand, 0000 becomes 0, 0100 becomes 4, and 0001 becomes 1. Thus, the letter *A* is represented in hexadecimal as 0041. You tell the compiler to treat the four-digit hexadecimal 0041 as a single character by preceding it with the \u escape sequence. Therefore, there are two ways to store the character *A*:

```
char letter = 'A';
char letter = '\u0041';
```

For more information about Unicode, see Appendix B.

Using the char Data Type

Escape Sequence	Character Name
\'	Single quotation mark
\''	Double quotation mark
\\	Backslash
\0	Null
\a	Alert
\b	Backspace
\f	Form feed
\n	Newline
\r	Carriage return
\t	Horizontal tab
\v	Vertical tab

Table 2-5 Common escape sequences

The second option, using hexadecimal, obviously is more difficult and confusing than the first option, so it is not recommended that you store letters of the alphabet using the hexadecimal method. However, you can produce some interesting values using the Unicode format. For example, letters from foreign alphabets that are not on a standard keyboard (such as letters from Greek, Hebrew, and Chinese alphabets) and other special symbols (foreign currency symbols, mathematical symbols, geometric shapes, and so on) are available in Unicode. You can even output the sound of a beep by displaying the hexadecimal character '\u0007'.

TWO TRUTHS & A LIE

Using the char Data Type

1. The following statement is legal in C#:
   char department = '5';

2. The following statement is legal in C#:
   char department = '\f';

3. The following statement is legal in C#:
   char department = '32';

The false statement is #3. Only a single character can appear between single quotation marks, with the exception of escape sequence characters such as '\t' and '\f'. In these cases, a single character is created using two symbols.

You Do It

Using Escape Sequences

Next, you will write a short program to demonstrate the use of escape sequences.

1. Open a new file, and name it **DemoEscapeSequences**.
2. Enter the following code. The three `WriteLine()` statements demonstrate using escape sequences for tabs, a newline, and an alert.

   ```
   using static System.Console;
   class DemoEscapeSequences
   {
      static void Main()
      {
         WriteLine("This line\tcontains two\ttabs");
         WriteLine("This statement\ncontains a new line");
         WriteLine("This statement sounds an alert \a");
      }
   }
   ```

3. Save, compile, and execute the program. Your output should look like Figure 2-14. The two instances of \t produce a tab character, the \n sequence forces a new line, and, if your system has speakers and they are on, you should hear a musical sound generated by the alert character: \a.

   ```
   This line       contains two    tabs
   This statement
   contains a new line
   This statement sounds an alert
   ```

   Figure 2-14 Output of the DemoEscapeSequences program

Using the `string` Data Type

In C#, you use the **string** data type to hold a series of characters. The value of a `string` is expressed within double quotation marks. For example, the following statement declares a `string` named `firstName` and assigns *Jane* to it:

```
string firstName = "Jane";
```

Using the string Data Type

 You can also initialize a string with a character array. The "Using Arrays" chapter explains more.

You can compare the value of one string to another using the == and != operators in the same ways that you compare numeric or character variables. For example, the program in Figure 2-15 declares three string variables. Figure 2-16 shows the results: strings that contain *Amy* and *Amy* are considered equal, but strings that contain *Amy* and *Matthew* are not.

```
using static System.Console;
class CompareNames1
{
   static void Main()
   {
      string name1 = "Amy";
      string name2 = "Amy";
      string name3 = "Matthew";
      WriteLine("compare {0} to {1}: {2}",
         name1, name2, name1 == name2);
      WriteLine("compare {0} to {1}: {2}",
         name1, name3, name1 == name3);
   }
}
```

Figure 2-15 CompareNames1 program that compares two strings using == operator

```
compare Amy to Amy: True
compare Amy to Matthew: False
```

Figure 2-16 Output of the program in Figure 2-15

In addition to the == comparison operator, you can use several prewritten methods to compare strings, including whether one is greater than the other. A string is considered equal to, greater than, or less than another string **lexically**, which in the case of letter values means alphabetically. That is, when you compare two strings, you compare each character in turn from left to right. If each Unicode value is the same, then the strings are equivalent. If any corresponding character values are different, the string that has the greater Unicode value earlier in the string is considered greater.

The advantage to using the comparison methods instead of the == operator is that they have standard names; when you use most other C# classes written by others, they will use methods with the same names to compare their objects. You can compare strings with any of the following methods:

- An Equals() method call takes the format name1.Equals(name2); its value is true or false.

- A CompareTo() method call takes the format name1.CompareTo(name2); and its value is integer—0 when the compared strings are equal, a negative number if the first string is less, and a positive number if the second string (the one in parentheses) is less.

- A Compare() method call takes the format Compare(name1, name2); and its value is an integer—like CompareTo(), 0 when the compared strings are equal, a negative number if the first string is less, and a positive number if the second string is less. When you use the Compare() method you must include the following statement at the top of the using static System.String; statement.

The value of a method such as Equals() or CompareTo() is the value the method *returns*. You first learned about this term in Chapter 1, and you will learn more about it in Chapter 7.

Figure 2-17 shows a program that makes several comparisons using the three methods; in each case the method call is shaded. Figure 2-18 shows the program's output.

Methods like Compare() that are not preceded with an object and a dot when they are called are *static methods*. Methods like CompareTo() that are preceded with an object and a dot are nonstatic and are *instance methods*. The "Advanced Method Concepts" chapter explains more.

```
using System;
using static System.Console;
using static System.String;
class CompareNames2
{
   static void Main()
   {
      string name1 = "Amy";
      string name2 = "Amy";
      string name3 = "Matthew";
      WriteLine("{0} and {1}; Equals() method gives {2}",
         name1, name2, name1.Equals(name2));
      WriteLine("{0} and {1}; Equals() method gives {2}",
         name1, name3, name1.Equals(name3));
      WriteLine("{0} and {1}; CompareTo() method gives {2}",
         name1, name2, name1.CompareTo(name2));
      WriteLine("{0} and {1}; CompareTo() method gives {2}",
         name1, name3, name1.CompareTo(name3));
      WriteLine("{0} and {1}; Compare() method gives {2}",
         name1, name2, Compare(name1, name2));
      WriteLine("{0} and {1}; Compare() method gives {2}",
         name1, name3, Compare(name1, name3));
   }
}
```

Figure 2-17 CompareNames2 program that compares two strings using three methods

Using the string Data Type

```
Amy and Amy; Equals() method gives True
Amy and Matthew; Equals() method gives False
Amy and Amy; CompareTo() method gives 0
Amy and Matthew; CompareTo() method gives -1
Amy and Amy; Compare() method gives 0
Amy and Matthew; Compare() method gives -1
```

Figure 2-18 Output of the program in Figure 2-17

In C#, a string is **immutable**. That is, a string's value is not actually modified when you assign a new value to it. For example, when you write name = "Amy"; followed by name = "Donald";, the first literal string of characters, *Amy*, still exists in computer memory, but the name variable no longer refers to that string's memory address. Instead, name refers to a new address where the characters in *Donald* are stored. Programmers might say that name now *points* to the new address. The situation is different from that with numbers; when you assign a new value to a numeric variable, the value at the named memory address actually changes, replacing and erasing the original value.

The comparisons made by the Equals(), Compare(), and CompareTo() methods are case sensitive. In other words, *Amy* does not equal *amy*. In Unicode, the decimal value of each uppercase letter is exactly 32 less than its lowercase equivalent. For example, the decimal value of a Unicode *a* is 97 and the value of *A* is 65.

You can use the Length property of a string to determine its length. For example, suppose you declare a string as follows:

string word = "water";

The value of word.Length is 5. Notice that Length is not a method and that it is not followed with parentheses.

The Substring() method can be used to extract a portion of a string from a starting point for a specific length. For example, Figure 2-19 shows a string that contains the word *water*. The first character in a string is at position 0, and the last character is at position Length - 1.

Therefore, after you declare string word = "water";, each of the first five expressions in the figure is true. The last expression produces an error message because the combination of the starting position and length attempt to access values outside the range of the string.

The StartsWith() method determines whether a string starts with the characters in the string that is used as an argument. For example, if word is "water", the expression word.StartsWith("wa") is true, and the expression word.StartsWith("waet") is false.

CHAPTER 2 Using Data

```
string word = "water";
Position:  0   1   2   3   4
          ┌───┬───┬───┬───┬───┐
          │ w │ a │ t │ e │ r │
          └───┴───┴───┴───┴───┘
         Start position    Length
                ⬇           ⬇
word.Substring(0, 1) is "w"
word.Substring(0, 2) is "wa"
word.Substring(1, 2) is "at"
word.Substring(2, 3) is "ter"
word.Substring(0, word.Length) is "water"
word.Substring(3, 4) produces an error message
```

Figure 2-19 Using the Substring() method

TWO TRUTHS & A LIE

Using the string Data Type

1. If creature1 = "dog" and creature2 = "cat", then the value of String.Equals(creature1, creature2) is false.

2. If creature1 = "dog" and creature2 = "cat", then the value of String.Compare(creature1, creature2) is false.

3. If creature1 = "dog" and creature2 = "cat", then the value of creature1.CompareTo(creature2) is a positive number.

The false statement is #2. If creature1 = "dog" and creature2 = "cat", then the value of String.Compare(creature1, creature2) is a positive number.

Defining Named Constants

By definition, a variable's value can vary or change. Sometimes you want to create a **named constant**, an identifier for a memory location whose contents cannot change. You create a named constant by adding the keyword `const` before the data type in a declaration. Programmers sometimes follow the convention of naming constants using all uppercase letters, inserting underscores for readability. This convention makes constant names stand out so that a reader is less likely to confuse them with variable names. For example, the following declares a constant named TAX_RATE that is initialized to 0.06:

```
const double TAX_RATE = 0.06;
```

Other programmers object to this style and call it **screaming caps**. You should use whatever style is recommended by your organization.

You must assign a value to a constant when you create it. You can use a constant just as you would use a variable of the same type—for example, display it or use it in a mathematical equation—but you cannot assign any new value to it.

It's good programming practice to use named constants for any values that should never change; doing so makes your programs clearer. For example, when you declare a constant const int INCHES_IN_A_FOOT = 12; within a program, then you can use a statement such as the following:

lengthInInches = lengthInFeet * INCHES_IN_A_FOOT;

This statement is **self-documenting**; that is, even without a program comment, it is easy for someone reading your program to tell why you performed the calculation in the way you did.

Working with Enumerations

An **enumeration** is a set of constants represented by identifiers. You place an enumeration in a class outside of any methods. Frequently, programmers place enumerations at the top of a file before the Main() method. You create an enumeration using the keyword enum and an identifier, followed by a comma-separated list of constants between curly braces. By convention, the enumerator identifier begins with an uppercase letter. For example, the following is an enumeration called DayOfWeek:

```
enum DayOfWeek
{
    SUNDAY, MONDAY, TUESDAY, WEDNESDAY,
       THURSDAY, FRIDAY, SATURDAY
}
```

By default, enumeration values are integers. You could also declare an enum's type to be byte, sbyte, short, ushort, uint, long, or ulong by including a colon and the type after the enumeration name and before the opening curly brace of the assignment list.

Frequently, the identifiers in an enumeration are meant to hold consecutive values. When you do not supply values for the items in an enum list, they start with 0 and are automatically increased by 1. For example, in the DayOfWeek enumeration, SUNDAY is 0, MONDAY is 1, and so on.

As is the convention with other constants, you might prefer to name enum constants using all uppercase letters and underscores for readability, as shown in the DayOfWeek enumeration here. This helps distinguish enumeration names from variables. However, the developers of C# frequently violate this convention in both their online documentation and in built-in enumerations in the language. For example, the built-in FontStyle enumeration contains constants with mixed-case names such as Bold and Italic. When you create enumerations, you should follow the convention your instructor or supervisor prefers. Another convention is to use a singular noun or noun phrase as the enum identifier. In other words, DayOfWeek is better than DaysOfWeek.

If you want the first enum constant in the list to have a value other than 0, you can assign one, as in the following:

```
enum DayOfWeek
{
    SUNDAY = 1, MONDAY, TUESDAY, WEDNESDAY,
        THURSDAY, FRIDAY, SATURDAY
}
```

In this case, SUNDAY is 1, MONDAY is 2, TUESDAY is 3, and so on.

As another option, you can assign values to each enumeration, as in the following:

```
enum SpeedLimit
{
    SCHOOL_ZONE_SPEED = 20,
    CITY_STREET_SPEED = 30,
    HIGHWAY_SPEED = 55
}
```

The names used within an enum must be unique, but the values assigned don't have to be. When you create an enumeration, you clearly identify what values are valid for an item. You also make your code more self-documenting. You should consider creating an enumeration any time you have a fixed number of integral values allowed for a variable.

As a side benefit, when you use an enum in Visual Studio, Intellisense lists the defined values. Appendix C provides more information on Intellisense.

After you have created an enumeration, you can declare variables of the enumeration type, and you can assign enumeration values to them. For example, you can use the following statements to declare payrollDay as data type DayOfWeek, and assign a value to it:

```
DayOfWeek payrollDay;
payrollDay = DayOfWeek.TUESDAY;
```

In the chapter "Using Classes and Objects," you will learn to create many additional data types that are more complex than the built-in data types.

You can convert an enum value to another data type or an integral type to an enum value by using a cast. For example, the following are valid statements:

```
int shipDay;
DayOfWeek deliverDay;
shipDay = (int)DayOfWeek.THURSDAY;
deliverDay = (DayOfWeek)shipDay;
```

Defining Named Constants

Using the preceding example, you can display 5 and *THURSDAY* with the following statements:

```
WriteLine(shipDay);
WriteLine(deliverDay);
```

Creating an enumeration type provides you with several advantages. For example, the `DayOfWeek` enumeration improves your programs in the following ways:

- If you did not create an enumerated type, you could use another type—for example, `int` or `string`. The problem is that any value could be assigned to an `int` or `string` variable, but only the seven allowed values can be assigned to a `DayOfWeek` object.

- If you did not create an enumerated type, you could create another type to represent days, but invalid behavior could be applied to the values. For example, if you used integers to represent days, you could multiply or divide two days, which is not logical. Programmers say using `enums` makes the values type-safe. **Type-safe** describes a data type for which only appropriate behaviors are allowed.

- The `enum` constants provide a form of self-documentation. Someone reading your program might misinterpret what 3 means as a day value, but there is less confusion when you use the identifier WEDNESDAY.

This discussion is meant to be a brief introduction to enumerations. At this point in your study of C#, the advantages to using enumerations are limited. Enumerations are particularly useful with `switch` statements, which you will learn about in the "Making Decisions" chapter.

TWO TRUTHS & A LIE

Defining Named Constants

1. The following is a valid and conventional C# constant declaration:

   `const string FIRST_HEADING = "Progress Report";`

2. The following is a valid and conventional C# constant declaration:

   `const double COMMISSION_RATE;`

3. By default, enumeration values are integers.

The false statement is #2. A constant must be assigned a value when it is declared.

Accepting Console Input

A program that allows user input is an **interactive program**. You can use the ReadLine() method to create an interactive program that accepts user input from the keyboard. This method accepts all of the characters entered by a user until the user presses Enter. The characters can be assigned to a string. For example, the following statement accepts a user's input and stores it in the variable myString:

myString = ReadLine();

The Read() method is similar to the ReadLine() method. Read() reads just one character from the input stream, whereas ReadLine() reads every character in the input stream until the user presses Enter.

Prior to the release of C# 6.0, the qualified names Console.ReadLine() and Console.Read() were required. However, just like with WriteLine() and Write(), you can now include using static System.Console; at the top of a file allowing you to use the shorter method names ReadLine() and Read().

If you want to use the input value as a type other than string, then you must use a conversion method to change the input string to the proper type. Two methods are available for converting strings—the Convert class and Parse() methods.

Using the Convert Class

Figure 2-20 shows an interactive program that prompts the user for a price and calculates a 6 percent sales tax. The program displays *Enter the price of an item* on the screen. Such an instruction to the user is a **prompt**. Notice that two using statements appear at the top of the

- using System; to include the Convert class
- using static System.Console; to include the ReadLine() and WriteLine() methods

Notice that the program in Figure 2-20 uses a Write() statement for the prompt instead of a WriteLine() statement so that the user's input appears on the screen on the same line as the prompt. Also, notice that the prompt contains a space just before the closing quote so that the prompt does not crowd the user's input on the screen.

After the prompt appears, the ReadLine() statement accepts a string of characters and assigns them to the variable itemPriceAsString. Before the tax can be calculated, this value must be converted to a number. This conversion is accomplished using the Convert class ToDouble() method in the shaded statement. Figure 2-21 shows a typical execution of the program in which the user typed 28.77 as the input value.

Accepting Console Input

```
using System;
using static System.Console;
class InteractiveSalesTax
{
   static void Main()
   {
      const double TAX_RATE = 0.06;
      string itemPriceAsString;
      double itemPrice;
      double total;
      Write("Enter the price of an item >> ");
      itemPriceAsString = ReadLine();
      itemPrice = Convert.ToDouble(itemPriceAsString);
      total = itemPrice * TAX_RATE;
      WriteLine("With a tax rate of {0}, a {1} item " +
         "costs {2} more.", TAX_RATE, itemPrice.ToString("C"),
         total.ToString("C"));
   }
}
```

Figure 2-20 The InteractiveSalesTax program

In the program in Figure 2-20, the angle brackets at the end of the prompt are not required; they are merely cosmetic. You might prefer other punctuation such as a colon, ellipsis, or hyphen to help indicate that input is required.

```
Enter the price of an item >> 28.77
With a tax rate of 0.06, a $28.77 item costs $1.73 more.
```

Figure 2-21 Typical execution of the InteractiveSalesTax program

As a shortcut, you can avoid declaring and using the extra string variable itemPriceAsString in the program in Figure 2-20. Instead, you can accept and convert the input string in one step by nesting the ReadLine() and ToDouble() method calls, as in the following:

itemPrice = Convert.ToDouble(ReadLine());

Table 2-6 shows Convert class methods you can use to change strings into additional useful data types. The methods use the system types (also called runtime types) in their names. For example, recall from Table 2-1 that the "formal" name for an int is Int32, so the method you use to convert a string to an int is named Convert.ToInt32().

Method	Description
ToBoolean()	Converts a specified value to an equivalent Boolean value
ToByte()	Converts a specified value to an 8-bit unsigned integer
ToChar()	Converts a specified value to a Unicode character
ToDecimal()	Converts a specified value to a decimal number
ToDouble()	Converts a specified value to a double-precision floating-point number
ToInt16()	Converts a specified value to a 16-bit signed integer (a short)
ToInt32()	Converts a specified value to a 32-bit signed integer (an int)
ToInt64()	Converts a specified value to a 64-bit signed integer (a long)
ToSByte()	Converts a specified value to an 8-bit signed integer
ToSingle()	Converts a specified value to a single-precision floating-point number
ToString()	Converts a specified value to its equivalent String representation
ToUInt16()	Converts a specified value to a 16-bit unsigned integer
ToUInt32()	Converts a specified value to a 32-bit unsigned integer
ToUInt64()	Converts a specified value to a 64-bit unsigned integer

Table 2-6 Selected Convert class methods

Using the Parse() Methods

As an alternative to the Convert class methods, you can use a Parse() method to convert a string to a number. For example, to convert a string to a double in the InteractiveSalesTax program in Figure 2-20, you can replace the Convert.ToDouble() statement with either of the following Parse() method statements:

```
itemPrice = double.Parse(itemPriceAsString);
itemPrice = Double.Parse(itemPriceAsString);
```

Each of the previous two statements uses a Parse() method defined in the Double class. You can use the system type name Double or its simple type name double. Either version converts the string argument within the parentheses to the correct data type.

Similar methods exist for other data types, such as int.Parse() and boolean.Parse(). For example, either of the following two statements reads an integer and stores it in a variable named score without using a temporary string to hold the input value:

```
score = int.Parse(ReadLine());
score = Int32.Parse(ReadLine());
```

There are some performance differences between the Convert and Parse() techniques, but they are minor and relatively technical. Until you learn more about C#, you should use the method preferred by your instructor or organization.

Accepting Console Input

 The term **parse** means to break into component parts. Grammarians talk about "parsing a sentence"—deconstructing it so as to describe its grammatical components. Parsing a `string` converts it to its numeric equivalent.

TWO TRUTHS & A LIE
Accepting Console Input

1. The following is valid:

   `int age = Convert.ToInt(ReadLine());`

2. The following is valid:

   `double payRate = Convert.ToDouble(ReadLine());`

3. The following is valid:

   `int dependents = int.Parse(ReadLine());`

The false statement is #1. The Convert class method to convert a string to an integer is ToInt32(), not ToInt().

You Do It

Writing a Program that Accepts User Input

In the next steps, you will write an interactive program that allows the user to enter two integer values. The program then calculates and displays their sum.

1. Open a new file named **InteractiveAddition**, and type the first few lines needed for the Main() method:

```
using System;
using static System.Console;
class InteractiveAddition
{
   static void Main()
   {
```

(continues)

(continued)

2. Add variable declarations for two **string**s that will accept the user's input values. Also, declare three integers for the numeric equivalents of the **string** input values and their sum.

   ```
   string name, firstString, secondString;
   int first, second, sum;
   ```

3. Prompt the user for his or her name, accept it into the **name string**, and then display a personalized greeting to the user, along with the prompt for the first integer value.

   ```
   Write("Enter your name... ");
   name = ReadLine();
   Write("Hello {0}! Enter the first integer... ", name);
   ```

4. Accept the user's input as a **string**, and then convert the input **string** to an integer.

   ```
   firstString = ReadLine();
   first = Convert.ToInt32(firstString);
   ```

5. Add statements that prompt for and accept the second **string** and convert it to an integer.

   ```
   Write("Enter the second integer... ");
   secondString = ReadLine();
   second = Convert.ToInt32(secondString);
   ```

6. Assign the sum of the two integers to the **sum** variable and display all of the values. Add the closing curly brace for the **Main()** method and the closing curly brace for the class.

   ```
         sum = first + second;
         WriteLine("{0}, the sum of {1} and {2} is {3}",
            name, first, second, sum);
      }
   }
   ```

7. Save, compile, and run the program. When prompted, supply your name and any integers you want, and confirm that the result appears correctly. Figure 2-22 shows a typical run of the program.

   ```
   Enter your name... Emily
   Hello Emily! Enter the first integer... 12
   Enter the second integer... 399
   Emily, the sum of 12 and 399 is 411
   ```

   Figure 2-22 Typical execution of the InteractiveAddition program

Chapter Summary

- A constant is a data value that cannot be changed after a program is compiled; a value in a variable can change. C# provides for 15 basic built-in types of data. A variable declaration includes a data type, an identifier, an optional assigned value, and a semicolon.

- You can display variable values by using the variable name within a `WriteLine()` or `Write()` method call. To make producing output easier, you can combine strings and variable values into a single `Write()` or `WriteLine()` statement by using a format string.

- C# supports nine integral data types: `byte`, `sbyte`, `short`, `ushort`, `int`, `uint`, `long`, `ulong`, and `char`.

- C# supports three floating-point data types: `float`, `double`, and `decimal`. You can use format and precision specifiers to display floating-point data to a specified number of decimal places.

- You use the binary arithmetic operators +, -, *, /, and % to manipulate values in your programs. Multiplication, division, and remainder always take place prior to addition or subtraction in an expression, unless you use parentheses to override the normal precedence. C# provides several shortcut arithmetic operators, including the binary operators +=, -=, *=, /=, and the unary prefix and postfix increment (++) and decrement (--) operators.

- A `bool` variable can hold only one of two values—true or false. C# supports six comparison operators: >, <, >=, <=, ==, and !=. An expression containing a comparison operator has a Boolean value.

- When you perform arithmetic with variables or constants of the same type, the result of the arithmetic retains that type. When you perform arithmetic operations with operands of different types, C# chooses a unifying type for the result and implicitly converts nonconforming operands to the unifying type. You can explicitly override the unifying type imposed by C# by performing a cast.

- You use the `char` data type to hold any single character. You place constant character values within single quotation marks. You can store any character—including nonprinting characters such as a backspace or a tab—in a `char` variable. To store these characters, you must use an escape sequence, which always begins with a backslash.

- In C#, you use the `string` data type to hold a series of characters. The value of a `string` is expressed within double quotation marks. Although the == and != comparison operators can be used with `strings` that are assigned literal values, you also can use the `Equals()`, `Compare()`, `CompareTo()`, and `Substring()` methods and the `Length` property that belong to the `String` class.

- Named constants are program identifiers whose values cannot change. Conventionally, their identifiers are all uppercase, with underscores inserted for readability. Enumerations are lists of named constants that are integers by default, and frequently the lists hold consecutive values.
- You can use the `ReadLine()` method to accept user input. Often you must use a `Convert` class method to change the input string into a usable data type.

Key Terms

Constant describes data items whose values are fixed.

A **literal constant** is a value that is taken literally at each use.

A **data type** describes the format and size of a data item and defines what types of operations can be performed with the item.

Intrinsic types of data are basic types; C# provides 15 intrinsic types.

An **alias** is another name for something.

A **simple type** is one of the following in C#: `byte`, `sbyte`, `short`, `ushort`, `int`, `uint`, `long`, `ulong`, `float`, `double`, `decimal`, `char`, and `bool`.

Unicode is a 16-bit coding scheme for characters.

A **variable declaration** is the statement that names a variable; it includes a data type, an identifier, an optional assignment operator and assigned value, and an ending semicolon.

The **assignment operator** is the equal sign (=); any value to the right of the assignment operator is assigned to, or taken on by, the variable to the left.

An **initialization** is an assignment made when a variable is declared.

An `int` data type holds an integer.

An **integer** is a whole number.

An **assignment** is a statement that provides a variable with a value.

To **concatenate** a string with another value is to join the two values end to end using a plus sign.

A **format string** is a string of characters that controls the appearance of output.

A **place holder** holds a position for a variable value within a string; it consists of a pair of curly braces containing a number that indicates the desired variable's position in a list that follows the string.

String interpolation is the process of replacing string place holders with values; also called *variable substitution*.

Key Terms

Integral data types are those that store whole numbers. The nine integral types are byte, sbyte, short, ushort, int, uint, long, ulong, and char. The first eight always represent whole numbers, and the ninth type, char, is used for characters such as 'A' or 'a'.

Digit separators are symbols used to separate the digits in a long number for readability; in C# the underscore (_) is the digit separator.

A **floating-point** number is one that contains decimal positions.

Significant digits provide a measure of the mathematical accuracy of a value.

A **float** data type can hold a floating-point number with as many as seven significant digits of accuracy.

A **double** data type can hold a floating-point number with 15 or 16 significant digits of accuracy.

The **decimal** data type is a floating-point type that has a greater precision and a smaller range than a float or double, which makes it suitable for financial and monetary calculations.

Scientific notation is a means of expressing very large and small numbers using an exponent.

Standard numeric format strings are strings of characters expressed within double quotation marks that indicate a format for output.

The **format specifier** in a format string can be one of nine built-in format characters that define the most commonly used numeric format types.

The **precision specifier** in a format string controls the number of significant digits or zeros to the right of the decimal point.

A C# **culture** is a set of rules that determines how culturally dependent values such as money and dates are formatted.

Arithmetic operators are used to perform arithmetic; they include +, -, *, /, and %.

Operands are the values that operators use in expressions.

Binary operators use two operands—one value to the left of the operator and another value to the right of it.

Operator precedence determines the order in which parts of a mathematical expression are evaluated.

Order of operation is another term for operator precedence.

Associativity specifies the order in which a sequence of operations with the same precedence are evaluated.

The **add and assign operator** (+=) adds the operand on the right to the operand on the left and assigns the result to the operand on the left in one step.

CHAPTER 2 Using Data

The **prefix increment operator** (++ before a variable) increases the variable's value by 1 and then evaluates it.

The **postfix increment operator** (++ after a variable) evaluates a variable and then adds 1 to it.

Unary operators are operators used with one operand.

The **decrement operator** (--) reduces a variable's value by 1. There is a prefix and a postfix version.

A **Boolean variable** can hold only one of two values—true or false.

The `bool` data type holds a Boolean value.

A **comparison operator** compares two items; an expression containing a comparison operator has a Boolean value.

A **unifying type** is the type chosen for an arithmetic result when operands are of dissimilar types.

Implicitly means automatically.

Type precedence is a hierarchy of data types used to determine the unifying type in arithmetic expressions containing dissimilar data types.

An **implicit conversion** or **implicit cast** is the automatic transformation that occurs when a value is assigned to a type with higher precedence.

Explicitly means purposefully.

An **explicit cast** purposefully assigns a value to a different data type; it involves placing the desired result type in parentheses followed by the variable or constant to be cast.

The `char` data type can hold any single character; a literal character is contained between single quotation marks.

An **escape sequence** is two symbols beginning with a backslash that represent a nonprinting character such as a tab.

Hexadecimal, or **base 16**, is a mathematical system that uses 16 symbols to represent numbers.

The `string` data type is used to hold a series of characters; a literal string is contained between double quotation marks.

Lexically means alphabetically.

Immutable describes unchangeable objects such as `strings` that refer to a new memory location when a new value is assigned.

A **named constant** is an identifier whose value must be assigned upon declaration and whose contents cannot change.

Screaming caps is a style that uses all uppercase letters and underscores to name a program component—often a named constant.

A **self-documenting** program element is one that is self-explanatory.

An **enumeration** is a set of constants represented by identifiers.

Type-safe describes a data type for which only appropriate behaviors are allowed.

An **interactive program** is one that allows user input.

A **prompt** is an instruction to the user to enter data.

To **parse** an item is to break it into component parts.

Review Questions

1. When you use a number such as 45 in a C# program, the number is a _____.

    a. figurative constant
    b. literal constant
    c. literal variable
    d. figurative variable

2. A variable declaration must contain all of the following *except* a(n) _____.

    a. data type
    b. identifier
    c. assigned value
    d. ending semicolon

3. Which of the following is true of variable declarations?

    a. Two variables of different types can be declared in the same statement.
    b. Two variables of the same type can be declared in the same statement.
    c. Two variables of the same type must be declared in the same statement.
    d. Two variables of the same type cannot coexist in a program.

4. Assume that you have two variables declared as `int var1 = 3;` and `int var2 = 8;`. Which of the following would display 838?

    a. `WriteLine("{0}{1}{2}", var1, var2);`
    b. `WriteLine("{0}{1}{0}", var2, var1);`
    c. `WriteLine("{0}{1}{2}", var2, var1);`
    d. `WriteLine("{0}{1}{0}", var1, var2);`

5. Assume that you have a variable declared as `int var1 = 3;`. Which of the following would display *X 3X*?

    a. `WriteLine("X{0}X", var1);`
    b. `WriteLine("X{0,2}X", var1);`
    c. `WriteLine("X{2,0}X", var1);`
    d. `WriteLine("X{0}{2}", var1);`

CHAPTER 2   Using Data

6. Assume that you have a variable declared as `int var1 = 3;`. What is the value of `22 % var1`?

   a. 21

   b. 7

   c. 1

   d. 0

7. Assume that you have a variable declared as `int var1 = 3;`. What is the value of `22 / var1`?

   a. 21

   b. 7.333

   c. 7

   d. 1

8. What is the value of the expression `4 + 2 * 3`?

   a. 0

   b. 10

   c. 18

   d. 36

9. Assume that you have a variable declared as `int var1 = 3;`. If `var2 = ++var1`, what is the value of `var2`?

   a. 2

   b. 3

   c. 4

   d. 5

10. Assume that you have a variable declared as `int var1 = 3;`. If `var2 = var1++`, what is the value of `var2`?

    a. 2

    b. 3

    c. 4

    d. 5

11. A variable that can hold the two values `true` and `false` is of type _____.

    a. `char`

    b. `it`

    c. `bool`

    d. `double`

12. Which of the following is *not* a C# comparison operator?

    a. `=>`

    b. `!=`

    c. `==`

    d. `<`

13. What is the value of the expression `6 >= 7`?

    a. 0

    b. 1

    c. `true`

    d. `false`

14. Which of the following C# types *cannot* contain floating-point numbers?

    a. `float`

    b. `double`

    c. `decimal`

    d. `int`

Review Questions

15. Assume that you have declared a variable as double hourly = 13.00;. What will the statement WriteLine(hourly); display?

    a. 13
    b. 13.0
    c. 13.00
    d. 13.000000

16. Assume that you have declared a variable as double salary = 45000.00;. Which of the following will display *$45,000*?

    a. WriteLine(salary.ToString("c"));
    b. WriteLine(salary.ToString("c0"));
    c. WriteLine(salary);
    d. two of these

17. When you perform arithmetic operations with operands of different types, such as adding an int and a float, _____.

    a. C# chooses a unifying type for the result
    b. you must choose a unifying type for the result
    c. you must provide a cast
    d. you receive an error message

18. Unicode is _____.

    a. an object-oriented language
    b. a subset of the C# language
    c. a 16-bit coding scheme
    d. another term for hexadecimal

19. Which of the following declares a variable that can hold the word *computer*?

    a. string device = 'computer';
    b. string device = "computer";
    c. char device = 'computer';
    d. char device = "computer";

20. Which of the following compares two string variables named string1 and string2 to determine if their contents are equal?

    a. string1 = string2
    b. string1 == string2
    c. Equals.String(string1, string2)
    d. two of the above

CHAPTER 2 Using Data

Exercises

 Programming Exercises

1. What is the numeric value of each of the following expressions, as evaluated by the C# programming language?

   a. 2 + 5 * 3
   b. 9 / 4 + 10
   c. 10 / 3
   d. 21 % 10
   e. (5 – 1) * 3
   f. 37 / 5

   g. 64 % 8
   h. 5 + 2 * 4 – 3 * 4
   i. 3 * (2 + 5) / 5
   j. 28 % 5 – 2
   k. 19 / 2 / 2
   l. 28 / (2 + 4)

2. What is the value of each of the following Boolean expressions?

   a. 5 > 4
   b. 3 <= 3
   c. 2 + 4 > 5
   d. 6 == 7
   e. 2 + 4 <= 6

   f. 3 + 4 == 4 + 3
   g. 1 != 2
   h. 2 != 2
   i. –5 == 7–2
   j. 3 + 9 <= 0

3. Choose the best data type for each of the following, so that no memory storage is wasted. Give an example of a typical value that would be held by the variable, and explain why you chose the type you did.

   a. the number of years of school you have completed
   b. your final grade in this class
   c. the population of China
   d. the number of passengers on an airline flight
   e. one player's score in a Scrabble game
   f. the number of Electoral College votes received by a U.S. presidential candidate
   g. the number of days with below freezing temperatures in a winter in Miami, Florida
   h. one team's score in a Major League Baseball game

4. In this chapter, you learned that although a **double** and a **decimal** both hold floating-point numbers, a **double** can hold a larger value. Write a C# program named **DoubleDecimalTest** that declares and displays two variables—a **double** and a **decimal**. Experiment by assigning the same constant value to each variable so that the assignment to the **double** is legal but the assignment to the **decimal** is not. In other words, when you leave the **decimal** assignment statement in the program, an

error message should be generated that indicates the value is outside the range of the type decimal, but when you comment out the decimal assignment and its output statement, the program should compile correctly.

5. Write a C# program named **InchesToCentmeters** that declares a named constant that holds the number of centimeters in an inch: 2.54. Also declare a variable to represent a measurement in inches, and assign a value. Display the measurement in both inches and centimeters—for example, *3 inches is 7.62 centimeters.*

6. Convert the InchesToCentimeters program to an interactive application named **InchesToCentimetersInteractive**. Instead of assigning a value to the inches variable, accept the value from the user as input.

7. Write a C# program named **ProjectedRaises** that includes a named constant representing next year's anticipated 4 percent raise for each employee in a company. Also declare variables to represent the current salaries for three employees. Assign values to the variables, and display, with explanatory text, next year's salary for each employee.

8. Convert the ProjectedRaises class to an interactive application named **ProjectedRaisesInteractive**. Instead of assigning values to the salaries, accept them from the user as input.

9. Malcolm Movers charges a base rate of $200 per move plus $150 per hour and $2 per mile. Write a program named **MoveEstimator** that prompts a user for and accepts estimates for the number of hours for a job and the number of miles involved in the move and displays the total moving fee.

10. Write a program named **HoursAndMinutes** that declares a minutes variable to represent minutes worked on a job, and assign a value to it. Display the value in hours and minutes. For example, 197 minutes becomes 3 hours and 17 minutes.

11. Write a program named **Eggs** that declares four variables to hold the number of eggs produced in a month by each of four chickens, and assign a value to each variable. Sum the eggs, then display the total in dozens and eggs. For example, a total of 127 eggs is 10 dozen and 7 eggs.

12. Modify the Eggs program to create a new one named **EggsInteractive** that prompts the user for and accepts a number of eggs for each chicken.

13. Write a program named **MakeChange** that calculates and displays the conversion of an entered number of dollars into currency denominations—twenties, tens, fives, and ones. For example, $113 is 5 twenties, 1 ten, 0 fives, and 3 ones.

14. Write a program named **TestsInteractive** that prompts a user for eight test scores and displays the average of the test scores to two decimal places.

15. Write a program named **FahrenheitToCelsius** that accepts a temperature in Fahrenheit from a user and converts it to Celsius by subtracting 32 from the Fahrenheit value and multiplying the result by 5/9. Display both values to one decimal place.

16. Create an enumeration named Month that holds values for the months of the year, starting with JANUARY equal to 1. Write a program named **MonthNames** that prompts the user for a month integer. Convert the user's entry to a Month value, and display it.

17. Create an enumeration named Planet that holds the names for the eight planets in our solar system, starting with MERCURY and ending with NEPTUNE. Write a program named **Planets** that prompts the user for a numeric position, and display the name of the planet that is in the requested position.

18. Pig Latin is a nonsense language. To create a word in pig Latin, you remove the first letter and then add the first letter and "ay" at the end of the word. For example, "dog" becomes "ogday" and "cat" becomes "atcay." Write a program named **PigLatin** that allows the user to enter a word and displays the pig Latin version.

Debugging Exercises

1. Each of the following files in the Chapter.02 folder of your downloadable student files has syntax and/or logical errors. In each case, determine the problem and fix the program. After you correct the errors, save each file using the same filename preceded with *Fixed*. For example, DebugTwo1.cs will become FixedDebugTwo1.cs.

   a. DebugTwo1.cs   c. DebugTwo3.cs
   b. DebugTwo2.cs   d. DebugTwo4.cs

Case Problems

1. In Chapter 1, you created two programs to display the motto for the Greenville Idol competition that is held each summer during the Greenville County Fair. Now write a program named **GreenvilleRevenue** that prompts a user for the number of contestants entered in last year's competition and in this year's competition. Display all the input data. Compute and display the revenue expected for this year's competition if each contestant pays a $25 entrance fee. Also display a statement that indicates whether this year's competition has more contestants than last year's.

2. In Chapter 1, you created two programs to display the motto for Marshall's Murals. Now write a program named **MarshallsRevenue** that prompts a user for the number of interior and exterior murals scheduled to be painted during the next month. Compute the expected revenue for each type of mural. Interior murals cost $500 each, and exterior murals cost $750 each. Also display the total expected revenue and a statement that indicates whether more interior murals are scheduled than exterior ones.

CHAPTER 3

Using GUI Objects and the Visual Studio IDE

Upon completion of this chapter, you will be able to:

◎ Create a `Form` in the Visual Studio IDE

◎ Use the `Toolbox` to add a `Button` to a `Form`

◎ Add `Labels` and `TextBoxes` to a `Form`

◎ Name `Forms` and controls

◎ Correct errors

◎ Decide which interface to use

CHAPTER 3 Using GUI Objects and the Visual Studio IDE

You have learned to write simple C# programs that accept input from a user at the console and produce output at the command line. The environment the user sees is a program's **interface**; unfortunately, the interfaces in the applications you have written so far look dull. Most modern applications use visually pleasing graphic objects to interact with users. These graphical user interface (GUI) objects include the labels, buttons, and text boxes you manipulate or control with a mouse, touch screen, or keyboard when interacting with Windows-type programs.

In Chapter 1, you learned that when you write a console application, you can use a simple text editor such as Notepad or you can use the Visual Studio integrated development environment (IDE). Technically, you have the same options when you write a GUI program. However, so much code is needed to create even the simplest of GUI programs that it is far more practical to develop the user interface visually in the IDE. This approach allows the IDE to automatically generate much of the code you need to develop appealing GUI programs that are easy to use.

In Visual Studio versions before .NET, C#, C++, and Visual Basic each had its own IDE, so you had to learn about a new environment with each programming language you studied. Now, you can use one IDE to create projects in all the supported languages.

Creating a Form in the IDE

Forms are rectangular GUI objects that provide an interface for collecting, displaying, and delivering information. Although they are not required, forms almost always include **controls**, which are devices such as labels, text boxes, and buttons that users can manipulate to interact with a program. The C# class that creates a form is Form. To create a Form visually using the IDE, you start Visual Studio, select **File** from the main menu, then **New** and **Project**, and then choose **Windows Forms App**, as shown in Figure 3-1. By default, Visual Studio names your first Forms application *WindowsFormsApp1*. You can change the name if you want, and you can browse to choose a location to save the application. You should almost always provide a more meaningful name for applications than the default name suggested. Most of the examples in this chapter retain the default names to minimize the number of changes required if you want to replicate the steps on your computer.

After you click **OK** in the New Project window, you see the IDE main window, as shown in Figure 3-2. The main window contains several smaller windows, each of which can be resized, relocated, or closed. If a window is not currently visible, you can select it from the View menu in the menu bar. Some key features in the IDE follow:

- The *name of the project* shown in three places: on the title bar, and in two locations in the Solution Explorer. In Figure 3-2, the application has the default name *WindowsFormsApp1*.

- The *menu bar*, which lies horizontally across the top of the window and includes a File menu from which you open, close, and save projects. It also contains submenus for editing, debugging, and help tasks, among others.

Figure 3-1 Choosing Windows Forms App in the New Project window

 As you work through any project, you should choose **Save All** frequently. You can select this action from the File menu or click the **Save All** button, which has an icon that looks like two overlapping disks.

- The *Toolbox tab*, which, when opened, provides lists of controls you can drag onto a Form so that you can develop programs visually, using a mouse or touch pad.
- The *Form Designer*, which appears in the center of the screen. This is where you design applications visually.
- The *Solution Explorer*, for viewing and managing project files and settings.
- The *Properties window*, for configuring properties and events on controls in your user interface. For example, you can use this window to set the Size property of a Button or the Text property of a Form.
- The *Error list*, which displays any warnings and errors that occur when you build or execute a program.

If some of these features are not visible after you start a project in the IDE, you can select them from the View menu.

The Solution Explorer file list shows the files that are part of the current project. The *Program.cs* file contains the automatically generated Main() method of the application, and the *Form1.cs* file contains other automatically generated code and is where you write code describing the tasks you will assign to controls in your application.

CHAPTER 3 Using GUI Objects and the Visual Studio IDE

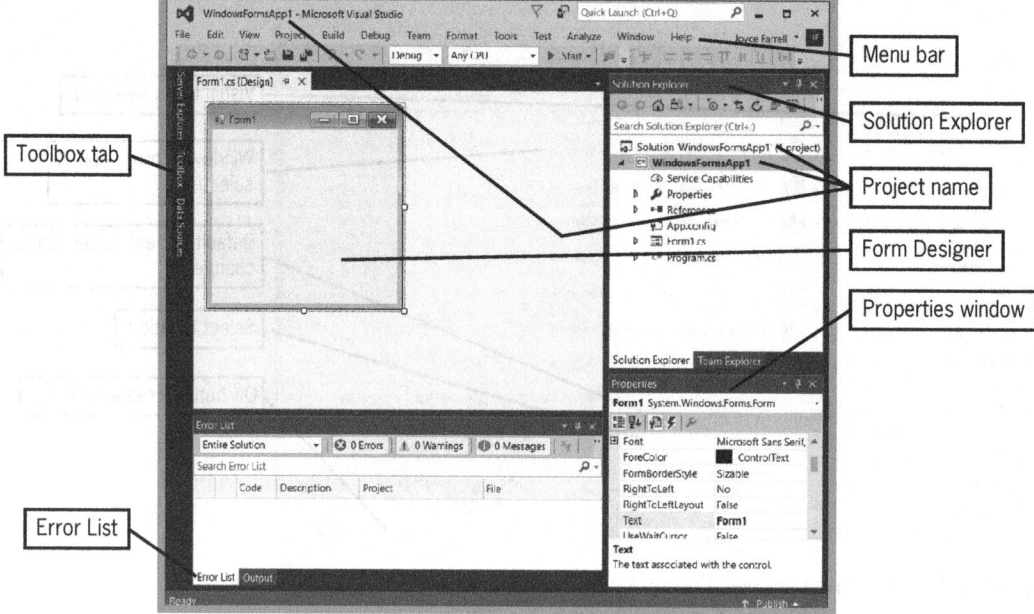

Figure 3-2 The IDE main window

 To the left of some of the items in the Solution Explorer, you see a small triangle node. A **node** is an icon that can be used to expand or condense a list or a section of code. (In Visual Studio, some nodes appear as triangles, and others appear as small plus or minus signs.) When a triangle-shaped node points straight to the right, you see a condensed view. Clicking the triangle reveals hidden items or code—the triangle will point diagonally down and to the right, and you see all the items in the list (or all the hidden code). Clicking the triangle again collapses the list so you can work with a condensed view.

If you expand the Form1.cs node by clicking it, you see a file named *Form1.Designer.cs*. The Windows Form Designer automatically writes code in the *Designer.cs* file; the code created there implements all the actions that are performed when you drag and drop controls from the Toolbox. You should avoid making manual changes to this file because you could easily corrupt a program.

When you create a Windows Forms project, Visual C# adds a form to the project and calls it `Form1`. After you click the Form in the Form Designer area, you can see the name of the form in the following locations as shown in Figure 3-3:

- On the folder tab at the top of the Form Designer area (followed by *[Design]*)
- In the title bar of the form in the Form Designer area
- In the Solution Explorer file list (with a .cs extension)
- At the top of the Properties window indicating that the properties listed are for `Form1`
- As the contents of the `Text` property listed within the Properties window

Creating a Form in the IDE

Figure 3-3 Displaying the properties of `Form1`

You can scroll through a list of properties in the Properties window. For example, `Size`, `Text`, and `Font` are listed. If you click a property, a brief description of it appears at the bottom of the Properties window. For example, Figure 3-3 displays a description of the `Text` property of `Form1`.

You can change the appearance, size, color, and window-management features of a `Form` by setting its properties. The `Form` class contains approximately 100 properties; Table 3-1 lists a few of the `Form` features you can change. For example, setting the `Text` property allows you to specify the caption of the `Form` in the title bar, and setting the `Size`, `BackColor`, and `ForeColor` allows you to further customize the `Form`. The two left buttons at the top of the Properties list allow you to organize properties by category or alphabetically. Not every property that can be used with a `Form` appears in the Properties window in the Visual Studio IDE—only the most frequently used properties are listed.

Property Name	Description
AcceptButton	Gets or sets the button on the form that is clicked when the user presses the Enter key
BackColor	Gets or sets the background color of the Form
CancelButton	Gets or sets the button control that is clicked when the user presses the Esc key
ForeColor	Gets or sets the foreground color of the Form
Name	Gets or sets the name of the Form
Size	Gets or sets the size of the Form
Text	Gets or sets the text associated with the control
Visible	Gets or sets a value indicating whether the control is visible

Table 3-1 Selected properties of `Forms`

Some of the properties listed in the Properties window have a small plus sign that appears to the left of the property name. This is a node that you can click to expand or condense a property. For example, if you click the Size node, you will see an expanded list that displays the two parts of Size (Width and Height) separately. When the list is expanded, the node changes to a minus sign, which you can then click to condense the expanded list.

When you sort Properties in alphabetical order in the Properties window, the Name entry is not in alphabetical order—it appears near the top of the list. Name appears in parentheses because the opening parenthesis has a lower value than an *A*, so when the Properties list is sorted in alphabetical order, Name is near the top and easy to find. (An opening parenthesis has a lower Unicode value than any alphabetic letter; Appendix B contains information about Unicode.) For most professional applications, you will want to provide a Form with a reasonable identifier that is more descriptive than Form1.

Do not confuse a Form's Name with its Text property. If you change a Form's Name, you don't notice any difference in the visual design, but all references to the form are changed in the code. Therefore, a Form's Name property is an identifier, and it must follow the rules for variable names. This means, for example, that a Form's Name cannot contain spaces and cannot start with a digit. However, a Form's Text is what appears in its title bar, and it can be any string. For example, in an accounting application, you might name a form BudgetForm but assign *2018 Budget Calculator* as its Text.

In Chapter 2, you learned to enclose a string's contents in quotation marks. Although a Form's Text is a string, you do not type containing quotes when you enter a value for the Text property in the Properties list. However, when you view C# code, you will see quotation marks around the Text value.

 Watch the video *The Visual Studio IDE*.

TWO TRUTHS & A LIE

Creating a Form in the IDE

1. The Visual Studio IDE allows you to use a visual environment for designing Forms.

2. Some key features in Visual C# include the Toolbox, Form Designer, and Solution Explorer.

3. When you create a first Windows Forms project in any folder, Visual C# names the project MyFirstForm by default.

The false statement is #3. When you create a first Windows Forms project in any folder, Visual C# names the project WindowsFormsApp1 by default.

Using the Toolbox to Add a Button to a Form

When you open the IDE, the left border displays a Toolbox tab. (If you don't see the tab, you can select **View** and then **Toolbox** from the IDE's menu bar.) When you open the Toolbox, a list of tool groups is displayed. The list automatically closes when you move your mouse off the list and click elsewhere, or you can pin the Toolbox to the screen to keep it open by clicking the pushpin icon at the top of the list. When you pin the Toolbox, the Form moves to the right to remain as visible as possible, depending on how you have sized the windows in the IDE. Selecting **All Windows Forms** at the top of the Toolbox displays a complete list of available tools; selecting **Common Controls** displays a smaller list that is a subset of the original one. As shown in Figure 3-4, the Common Controls list contains many controls: the GUI objects a user can click or manipulate. The list includes controls you probably have seen when using Windows applications—for example, Button and CheckBox. You can drag these controls onto the Form. This chapter features only three controls from the Toolbox—Label, Button, and TextBox. You will learn about many of the other controls in the chapter called "Using Controls."

All windows in Visual C# can be made dockable or floating, hidden or visible, or can be moved to new locations. To change the behavior of a window, click the down arrow or pushpin icon on the title bar, and select from the available options. You can customize many aspects of the IDE by clicking the **Tools** menu, then clicking **Options**. To reset the windows to their original states, click **Window** on the main Visual Studio menu bar, and then click **Reset Window Layout**.

Figure 3-4 The open Toolbox in the IDE

You can drag controls onto a Form where you think they will be most useful or contribute to a pleasing design. After a control is on a Form, you can relocate it by dragging it, or delete the control by selecting it and pressing the **Del** key on your keyboard. You also can delete a control by right-clicking it and selecting the **Delete** option from the menu that appears. In Figure 3-5, the programmer has dragged a button onto the Form. By default, its Name is button1. (You might guess that if you drag a second Button onto a Form, its Name automatically becomes button2.) In a professional application, you would probably want to change the Name property of the Button to a unique and memorable identifier.

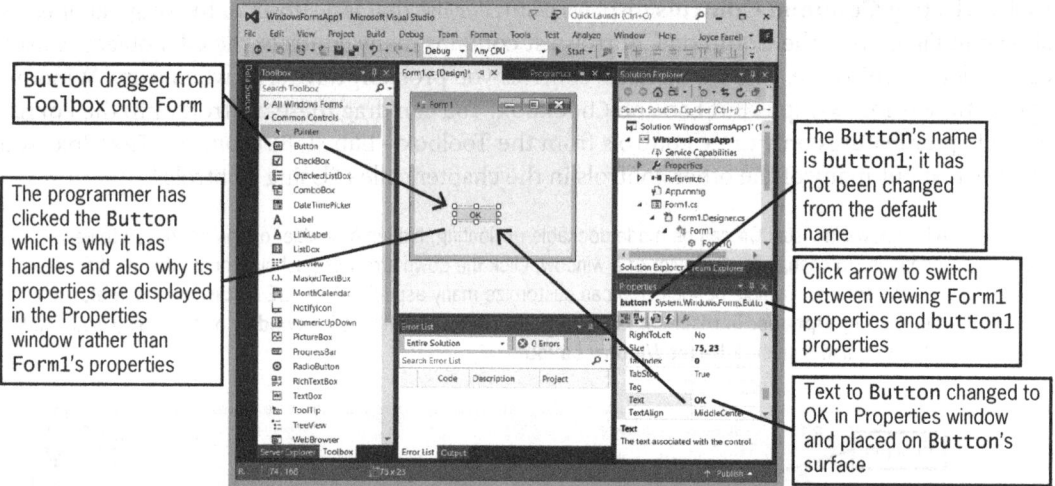

Figure 3-5 A Button dragged onto a Form

In Figure 3-5, the programmer has clicked button1, so the Properties window shows the properties for button1. (If you click the Form, the Properties window changes to show Form properties instead of Button properties.) The Text property of button1 has been changed to *OK*, and the button on the Form has handles that can be used to resize it. You can scroll through the Properties list and examine other properties that can be modified for the Button. For example, you can change its BackColor, ForeColor, Font, and Size. Table 3-2 describes a few

Property Name	Description
BackColor	Gets or sets the background color of the control
Enabled	Gets or sets whether the control is enabled
Font	Gets or sets the current font for the control
ForeColor	Gets or sets the foreground color of the control
Name	Gets or sets the name of the control
Size	Gets or sets the size of the control
Text	Gets or sets the text associated with the control
Visible	Gets or sets a value indicating whether the control is visible

Table 3-2 Selected properties of Buttons

Using the Toolbox to Add a Button to a Form

of the properties available for Button objects. This chapter discusses only a few properties of each control. You can learn about other properties in the chapter "Using Controls."

 You can click a control on a Form to display its Properties list in the Properties window. Alternatively, you can click the arrow next to the current control name shown at the top of the Properties list and select the desired control to view from a drop-down list. See Figure 3-5.

Adding Functionality to a Button on a Form

Adding functionality to a Button is easy when you use the IDE. After you have dragged a Button onto a Form, you can double-click it to create a method that executes when the user clicks the Button. For example, if you have dragged a Button onto a Form and have not changed its default name from button1, code is automatically generated when you double-click the button, as shown in Figure 3-6. (The viewing windows in the figure have been resized by dragging their borders so that you can see more of the code.) You can view the Form Designer again by selecting **View** and then **Designer** from the menu bar. Then, you can revert to the code window by selecting **View** and **Code**. As you create GUI applications, you frequently will switch back and forth between the visual environment and the code. Alternatively, you can use the tabs or press one of the shortcut keys displayed on the drop-down menu to switch the view.

 When you double-click a button to generate a click method, you generate code for the button's default event. Clicking is a button's default event because users typically expect to click a button. As you learn more about C#, you will find that you can write other events for a button. For example, perhaps you want to take a specific action if a user double-clicks or right-clicks a button.

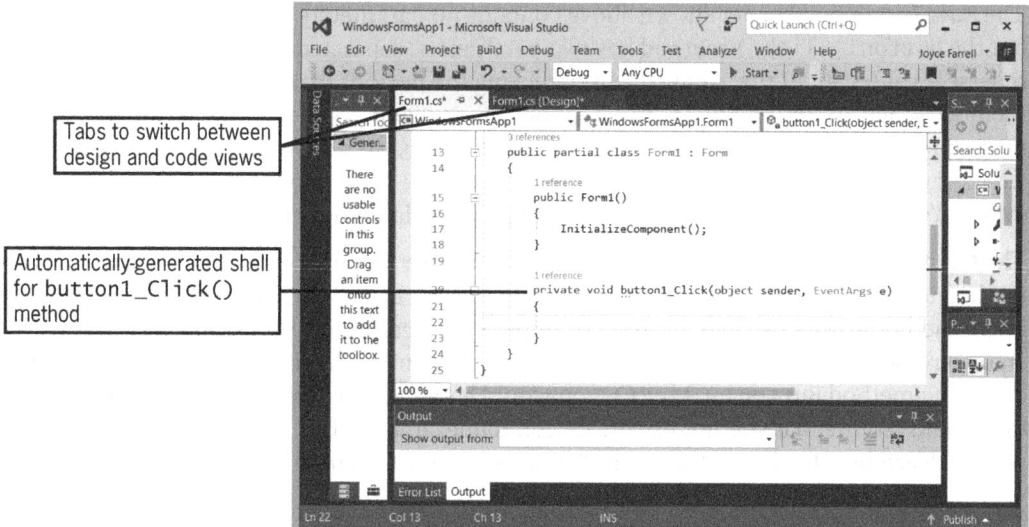

Figure 3-6 The automatically generated code after double-clicking button1

If you scroll through the exposed code, you see many generated statements, some of which are confusing. However, to make a `Button` perform an action, you can ignore most of the statements. You only need to write code between the curly braces of the method with the following header:

```
private void button1_Click(object sender, EventArgs e)
```

Instead of automatically generating the method header that executes when a user clicks a `Button`, you could write it yourself. However, you would have to know more about both methods and event handlers because other code is also automatically written elsewhere in the project that links the `Form`'s button to the method. You will learn about these topics in later chapters.

You have seen the following method header used in console applications:

```
static void Main()
```

The GUI application also contains a `Main()` method that is created automatically; you can see it by opening the *Program.cs* file that is part of the application.

The `button1_Click()` method and the `Main()` method headers both use the `void` return type, but the methods differ in the following ways:

- The `button1_Click()` method has a `private` access specifier. An **access specifier** is a keyword that dictates which types of outside classes can use a method. By default, Visual Studio makes the `button1_Click()` method `private`, which limits the ability of other classes to use the method, but you could remove the word `private` and notice no difference in how the button works. You will learn more about access specifiers later in this book.

- The `Main()` method is `static`, whereas the `button1_Click()` method is not. A `static` method executes without an object. The `button1_Click()` method cannot be `static` because it needs an object, which is the `Form` in which it is running. The chapter called "Using Classes and Objects" provides more detail about the keyword `static`.

- The `Main()` method header shown above contains no parameters between its parentheses, but the `button1_Click()` method has two parameters, separated with a comma. These represent values about the event (the user clicking the button) that causes execution of the method. When a user interacts with a GUI object, an **event** is generated that causes the program to perform a task. When a user clicks a `Button`, the action fires a **click event**, which causes the `Button`'s `Click()` method to execute. This chapter discusses only click events. You can learn about other events in the "Event Handling" chapter.

- The `Main()` method identifier begins with an uppercase *M*, but the `button1_Click()` method identifier begins with a lowercase *b*. In Chapter 1, you learned that by convention in C#, method names use Pascal casing or upper camel casing, which means they start with an uppercase letter, so `button1_Click()` defies that convention. However, to automatically create the method `Button1_Click()`, you would have to name the `Button` `Button1`, and that would require that you not use the default name supplied by C#. Later in this chapter, you will learn how to change the method name to follow C#'s method-naming convention.

If you change a `Button`'s `Name` from `button1` and then place a second button on the `Form`, the new `Button` is named `button1`. If you leave the first `Button`'s default name as `button1`, then the second `Button` you place on the `Form` is named `button2`, and its default `Click()` method is named `button2_Click()`. C# automatically creates a method name for each `Button` based on its associated object's name.

You are not required to create a `Click()` method for a `Button`. If, for some reason, you did not want to take any action when a user clicked a `Button`, you simply would not include the method in your program. Alternatively, you could create an empty method that contains no statements between its curly braces and thus does nothing. However, these choices would be unusual and a poor programming practice—you usually place a `Button` on a `Form` because you expect it to be clicked at some point. You will frustrate users if you do not allow your controls to act in expected ways.

You can write any statements you want between the curly braces of the `button1_Click()` method. For example, you can declare variables, perform arithmetic statements, and produce output. You also can include block or line comments. The next sections of this chapter include several statements added to a `Click()` method.

 Watch the video *Creating a Functional Button*.

TWO TRUTHS & A LIE

Using the Toolbox to Add a Button to a Form

1. When a user clicks a `Button`, the action fires a click event that causes the `Button`'s `Click()` method to execute.

2. If a `Button`'s identifier is `reportButton`, then the name of its `Click()` method is `reportButton.Click()`.

3. You can write any statements you want between the curly braces of a `Button`'s `Click()` method.

The false statement is #2. If a `Button`'s identifier is `reportButton`, then the name of its `Click()` method is `reportButton_Click()` using an underscore and not a dot.

Adding Labels and TextBoxes to a Form

Suppose that you want to create an interactive GUI program that accepts two numbers from a user and outputs their sum when the user clicks a `Button`. To provide prompts for the user and to display output, you can add `Label`s to a `Form`, and to get input from a user, you can provide `TextBox`es.

A **label** is a control that you use to display text to communicate with an application's user; the C# class that creates a label is `Label`. Just like a `Button`, you can drag a `Label` onto a `Form`, as shown in Figure 3-7. By default, the first `Label` you drag onto a `Form` is named `label1`, and the text that appears on the `Label` also is `label1`. You can change its `Text` property to display any

CHAPTER 3 Using GUI Objects and the Visual Studio IDE

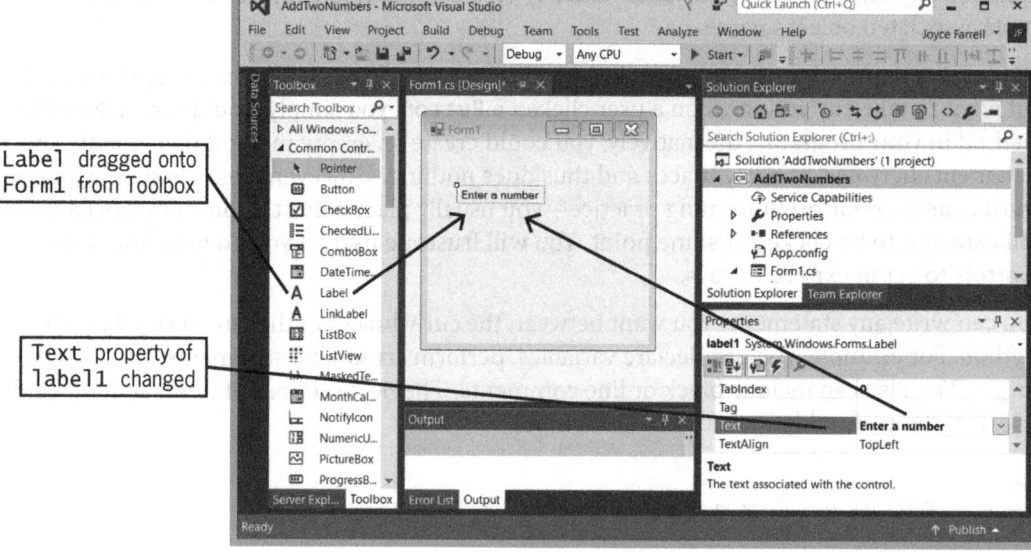

Figure 3-7 A Label on a Form

string of text; depending on the amount of text you enter, you might need to change the size of the Label by dragging its resizing handles or altering its Size property.

In Figure 3-7, *Enter a number* has been assigned to label1's Text property. If you want to create multiple lines of text on a Label, click the small, downward-pointing arrow to the right of the Text property value to open an editor, and type the needed text in separate lines. You might want a program to start with no text appearing on a label. If so, just delete the entry from the Text property in the Properties list. If you execute a program that starts with a blank label and don't make any changes to its color, the label will be invisible to the user. Note that a label's Text property can be blank, but a Label's Name property cannot.

A **text box** is a GUI control through which a user can enter input data; the C# class is TextBox. Figure 3-8 shows a TextBox on a Form. If the intention is for a user to enter data in a TextBox, you might want to start with its Text property empty, but you are allowed to add text to its Text property if desired.

Figure 3-9 shows a Form with three Labels, two TextBoxes, and a Button. The third Label has not yet been provided with new text, so it still contains *label3*. You can delete the Text value in the Properties window if you want the Label to be empty at first.

When a user runs the program that displays the Form in Figure 3-9, the intention is for the user to enter a number in each TextBox. When the user clicks the Button, the sum of the two numbers will be displayed in label3. To sum the numbers, you must write code for the Button. In the Form Designer, you can double-click the Button to expose the prewritten shell of the button1_Click() method.

Figure 3-10 shows the code you can write within the button1_Click() method. The method contains declarations for three integers. When a user types a value into a TextBox in an executing

Adding Labels and TextBoxes to a Form

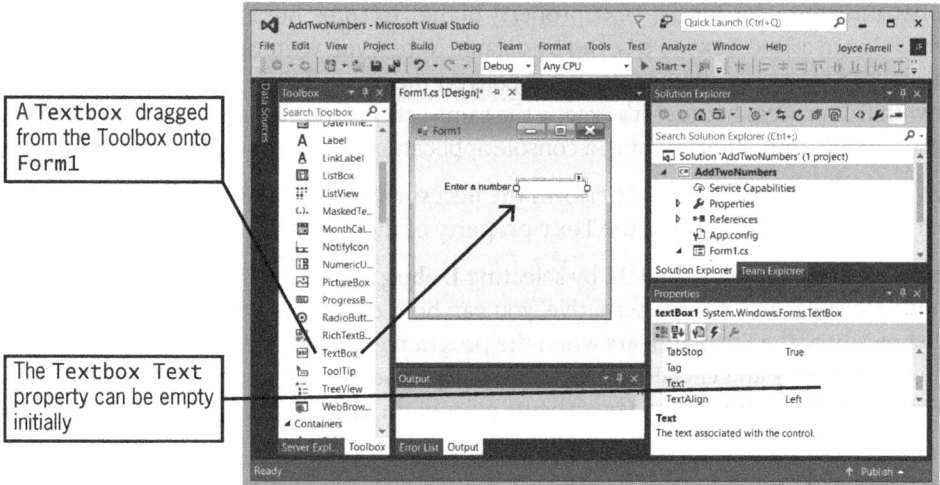

Figure 3-8　A Label and TextBox on a form

Figure 3-9　A Form with several controls

```
private void button1_Click(object sender, EventArgs e)
{
   int num1;
   int num2;
   int sum;
   num1 = Convert.ToInt32(textBox1.Text);
   num2 = Convert.ToInt32(textBox2.Text);
   sum = num1 + num2;
   label3.Text = "Sum is " + sum;
}
```

Figure 3-10　The button1_Click() method that calculates the sum of the entries in two TextBoxes program, it becomes the value for the Text property of the TextBox. Because a user might type any value, the value in a TextBox is a string by default. When you write an application in which the user is supposed to enter a number, you must convert the entered string into a number. You are familiar with this process because it's exactly the same action required when a user enters data in response to a ReadLine() statement in a console application.

The last two statements in the method perform the necessary addition operation and assign a string with the concatenated sum to the Text property of the Label that displays the output.

You can execute a program from the IDE by selecting **Debug** from the menu bar and then **Start Without Debugging**. (As an alternative, you can hold down the **Ctrl** key and press **F5**.) Figure 3-11 shows how the Form appears when the program executes and the result after the user has entered numbers and clicked the Button. The period during which you design a program is called **design time**. When you execute a program, the stage is called **runtime**.

You can change the values in either or both of the TextBoxes in the Form and click the Button to see a new result. When you finish using the application, you can close it by clicking the **Close** button in the upper-right corner of the Form.

Figure 3-11 The Form when it first appears and after a user has entered two integers and clicked the Button

Understanding Focus and Tab Control

When a GUI program displays a Form, one of the components on the Form has focus. The control with **focus** is the one that can receive keyboard input. When a Button has focus, a thin, bright line appears around it to draw your attention, and the Button's associated event executes when you click the button or press the **Enter** key on the keyboard. When a TextBox has focus, a blinking cursor appears inside it.

When an application is running, the user can give focus to a component by clicking it or can switch focus from one component to another using the Tab key. The order in which controls receive focus from successive Tab key presses is their **tab order**. By default, controls are assigned a tab order based on the order in which you place them on a Form when designing a program. The first control you place on a Form has TabIndex 0, the next control has TabIndex 1, and so on. When you start a program, the control with TabIndex 0 automatically has focus. You can check a control's tab order by viewing its TabIndex property in the Properties list of the IDE. If you do not want a control to be part of the tabbing sequence for a Form, you can change its TabStop property from true to false in the Properties list.

You can change a control's TabIndex value by changing the entry next to TabIndex in the Properties list of the IDE. Alternatively, you can select **View** from the menu bar and then select **Tab Order**. You see a representation of the Form with a small blue number next to each control to represent the tab values. To change the focus order for the controls, simply click each control in the desired order. Select **View** and then **Tab Order** again to remove the blue numbers.

 Watch the video *Visual Studio's Automatically Generated Code.*

Formatting Data in GUI Applications

In Chapter 2, you learned about format strings that can be used to make numeric data align appropriately, display the desired number of decimal places, and display dollar signs. For example, the following displays *Total is $4.55* because the double variable myMoney is converted to currency format and placed in position 0 in a string:

```
double myMoney = 4.558;
string mySentence = String.Format("Total is {0}",
   myMoney.ToString("C"));
WriteLine(mySentence);
```

You can use the same String.Format() method to create formatted strings in your GUI applications. For example, suppose you have retrieved a double from a TextBox with a statement similar to the following:

```
double money = Convert.ToDouble(textBox1.Text);
```

You can display the value on a label with explanatory text and as currency with two decimal places with a statement similar to the following:

```
label1.Text = String.Format("The money value is {0}",
   money.ToString("C2"));
```

If necessary, you also can use escape characters in strings that are assigned to controls such as labels. For example, a two-line label might be created using the following code:

```
label1.Text = "Hello\nthere";
```

Changing a Label's Font

The Font property for controls was described briefly in Table 3-2 earlier in this chapter. You will learn more about this property in Chapter 12, but you might want to experiment with it now to align numbers.

When you click any control on a Form and examine its Properties list, you discover that the default font for controls is Microsoft Sans Serif. This font is a **proportional font**, which means that different characters have different pitches or widths. For example, a *w* is wider than an *i*. The opposite of a proportional font is a **fixed-pitch font**, or a **monospaced font**, in which each character has the same width. You might want to use a fixed-pitch font to help align text values on controls. For example, when you stack $11.11 and $88.88 on a Label, you typically want the characters to be an equal width so that the values align.

To change the font for a Label, select the small box with an ellipsis (three dots) to the right of the existing Font name in the Properties list, and select a new Font from the dialog box that opens. For example, Courier New and Consolas are popular fixed-pitch fonts. (You can also change the font style and size if desired.)

TWO TRUTHS & A LIE

Adding Labels and TextBoxes to a Form

1. A Label and a TextBox both have a Text property.
2. When a user types a value on a Label in an executing program, it becomes the value for the Text property of the Label.
3. You can display the value on a Label using a format string.

The false statement is #2. A user does not type on a Label. When a user types a value into a TextBox in an executing program, it becomes the value for the Text property of the TextBox.

Naming Forms and Controls

Usually, you want to provide reasonable Name property values for all the controls you place on a Form. Although any identifier that starts with a letter is legal, note the following conventions that are used in some organizations:

- Start control names with a lowercase letter, and use camel casing as appropriate.
- Start Form names with an uppercase letter, and use camel casing as appropriate.
- Use the type of object in the name. For example, use names such as okButton, firstValueTextBox, or ArithmeticForm.

Naming Forms and Controls

 Professional programmers usually do not retain the default names for `Forms` and controls. An exception is sometimes made for `Labels` that never change. For example, if three labels provide directions or explanations to the user and are never altered during a program's execution, many programmers would approve of retaining their names as `label1`, `label2`, and `label3`.

Most often, you will want to name controls as soon as you add them to a `Form`. If you rename a control after you have created an event for it, the program still works, but the name of the control no longer corresponds to its associated method, making the code harder to understand. If you simply change the method name to match the control name, the event code will generate errors. For example, assume that you have placed a button named `button1` on a `Form` and that you have double-clicked it, creating a method named `button1_Click()`.

You might want to change this method name for one or both of these reasons:

- Method names conventionally start with an uppercase letter.
- If you change the name of the `Button`, you might want its `Click()` method name to match the new control name.

To rename a method, you must refactor the code. **Code refactoring** is the process of changing a program's internal structure without changing the way the program works. To refactor the code after changing the button's name, do the following:

- View the code and right-click the name of the method `button1_Click()`.
- From the menu that appears, click **Rename**, as shown on the left side of Figure 3-12.
- When you click **Rename**, the `button1_Click` method name is highlighted and a box appears with the heading *Rename button1_Click*, as shown on the right side of Figure 3-12.

Figure 3-12 Choosing the Rename option for a method

- Type the new method name (for example, SumButton_Click to replace button1_Click in the code.
- When you finish, you can check the **Preview Changes** checkbox if you want to view all the changes before they are applied, although at this point, the changes will not have much meaning for you. Click **Apply** or press **Enter**. A Preview Changes dialog box will highlight the change. You can confirm the change by clicking **Apply**.

TWO TRUTHS & A LIE

Naming Forms and Controls

1. Label and TextBox names usually start with an uppercase letter, but Form names usually start with a lowercase letter.
2. Professional programmers usually do not retain the default names for Forms and controls.
3. If you rename an event method, you must refactor the code.

The false statement is #1. Label and TextBox names usually start with a lowercase letter, but Form names usually start with an uppercase letter.

Correcting Errors

Just like in console-based programs, you will often generate syntax errors when you use the visual developer to create GUI applications. If you build or run a program that contains a syntax error, you see *Build failed* in the lower-left corner of the IDE. You also see an error dialog box like the one shown in Figure 3-13. When you are developing a program, you should always click **No** in response to "Would you like to continue and run the last successful build?" Clicking **Yes** will run the previous version of the program you created before inserting the mistake that caused the dialog box to appear. Instead, click **No**, examine the error messages and code, and correct the mistake.

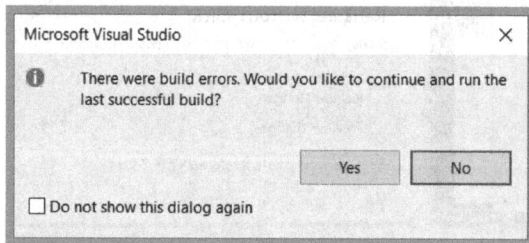

Figure 3-13 Dialog box that appears when an error occurs during compilation

Correcting Errors

 When you select **Build** from the menu bar, two options are Build Solution and Rebuild Solution. The Build Solution option uses only files that have changed since the most recent build, whereas Rebuild Solution works with all the files in a project, regardless of whether they have changed. The Build Solution option is usually sufficient and faster, but if you have made many changes to several parts of a project, you might choose Rebuild Solution to make sure that all files are currently coordinated.

When errors occur, they are shown in the error list at the bottom of the screen. If you do not see error messages, you can click **View** from the IDE's menu bar and then click **Error List**. If the list is partially or completely hidden, you can drag up the divider between the development window and the error list and then click the **Error List** tab. Figure 3-14 shows a single error message, *; expected*, which means *semicolon expected*. The error list also shows the file and line number in which the error occurred. If you double-click the error message, the cursor is placed at the location in the code where the error was found. A wiggly red underline will help you locate the error in the code window. In this case, a semicolon is missing at the end of a statement. You can fix the error and attempt another compilation.

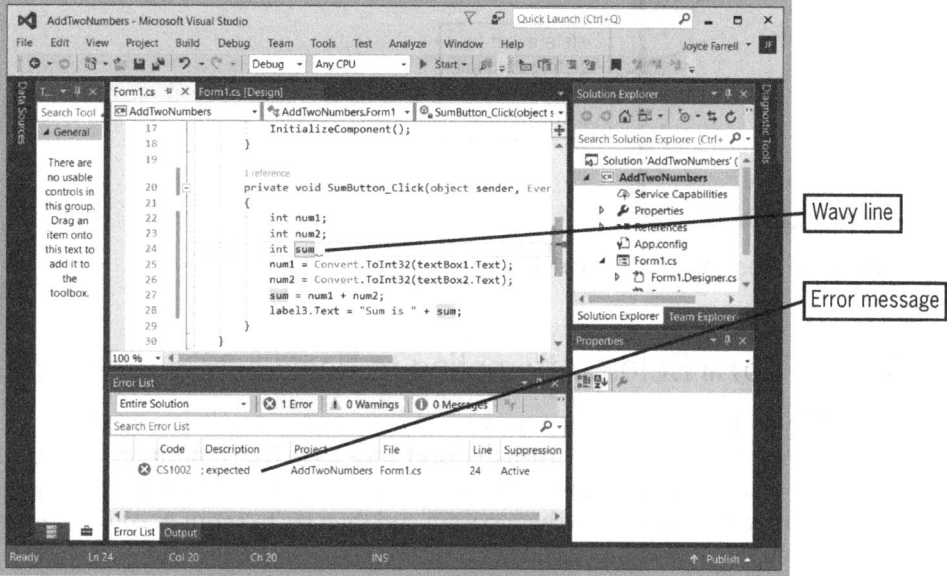

Figure 3-14 The error list

As with console-based programs, GUI applications might compile successfully but contain logical errors. For example, you might type a minus sign instead of a plus sign in the statement that is intended to calculate the sum of two input numbers. You should be prepared to execute a program multiple times and carefully examine the output to discover any logical errors.

Deleting an Unwanted Event-Handling Method

When you are working in the Form Designer in the IDE, it is easy to inadvertently double-click a control and automatically create an event-handling method that you do not want.

For example, you might double-click a `Label` named `label1` by mistake and generate a method named `label1_Click()`. You can leave the automatically created method empty so that no actions result, but in a professional program you typically would not include empty methods. Such empty methods that never execute are known as **orphaned methods**. You should not just delete an orphaned method because, behind the scenes, other code might have been created that refers to the method; if so, the program will not compile. Instead of deleting the method code, you should click the control with the unwanted method so it appears in the Properties window, then click the Events button, which looks like a lightning bolt. Select the event you want to eliminate, and delete the name of the method (see Figure 3-15). This eliminates all the references to the method, and your program can again run successfully.

Figure 3-15 Deleting an event from the Properties window

Failing to Close a `Form` Before Attempting to Reexecute a Program

Often you will execute a GUI application and notice something you want to correct in the program. For example, you might want to reword the `Text` on a `Label`, or reposition a `Button` on the `Form`. In your haste to make the improvement, you might forget to close the application that is still running. If you make a change to the program and then try to rerun it, you get an error message that indicates that changes are not allowed while the program is running. The solution is simply to close the previous execution of the application and then try again.

Using Visual Studio Help

When working with a class that is new to you, such as `Button` or `Form`, no book can answer all your questions. The ultimate authority on C# classes is the Visual Studio Help documentation. You should use this tool often as you continue to learn about C# in particular and the Visual Studio products in general. The Help documentation for Visual Studio is in the MSDN Library, which you can install locally on your own computer. It is also available at *http://msdn.microsoft.com*.

TWO TRUTHS & A LIE

Correcting Errors

1. When a program in Visual Studio has a syntax error, you see an error dialog box that asks if you want to continue with the last successful build. You should always respond No.

2. Program errors are harder to locate in the Visual Studio IDE than they are in applications written using a plain text editor.

3. If you inadvertently create a `Click()` method in Visual Studio, you should not delete its code. You should select the event in the Properties window and delete it there.

The false statement is #2. In the Visual Studio IDE, any displayed syntax errors include the filename, line, position in the line, and project in which the error occurred.

Deciding Which Interface to Use

You have learned to create console applications in which most of the action occurs in a `Main()` method and the `WriteLine()` and `ReadLine()` methods are used for input and output. You also have learned to create GUI applications in which most of the action occurs within an event-handling method such as a `Click()` method and `Label`s and `TextBox`es are used for input and output. Both types of applications can use declared variables and constants, and, as you will learn in the next few chapters, both types of programs can contain the basic building blocks of applications—decisions, loops, arrays, and calls to other methods. When you want to write a program that displays a greeting or sums some integers, you can do so using either type of interface and employing the same logic to get the same results. So, should you develop programs using a GUI interface or a console interface?

- GUI applications look "snazzier." It is easy to add colors and fonts to them, and they contain controls that a user can manipulate with a mouse or touch screen. Also, users are accustomed to GUI applications from their experiences on the Web. However, GUI programs usually take longer to develop than their console counterparts because you can spend a lot of time setting up the controls, placing them on a `Form`, and adjusting their sizes and relative positions before you write the code that does the actual work of the program. GUI applications created in the IDE also require much more disk space to store.

 Designing aesthetically pleasing, functional, and user-friendly `Form`s is an art; entire books are devoted to the topic.

- Console applications look dull in comparison to GUIs, but they can often be developed more quickly because you do not spend much time setting up objects for a user to manipulate. When you are learning programming concepts such as the ones you will read about in the next two chapters (decision making and looping), you might prefer to keep the interface simple so that you can better concentrate on the new logical constructs being presented.

In short, it doesn't matter which interface you use to develop programs while learning the intricacies of the C# programming language. In the following "You Do It" section, you develop an application that is similar to the one you developed at the console in Chapter 1. In the programming exercises at the end of this chapter, you will develop programs that are identical in purpose to programs written using the console in the chapter called "Using Data." Throughout the next several chapters, many concepts will be illustrated in console applications, because the programs are shorter and development is simpler. However, you also will occasionally see the same concept illustrated in a program that uses a GUI interface, to remind you that the program logic is the same no matter which interface is used. After you complete the chapters "Using Classes and Objects," "Using Controls," and "Handling Events," you will be able to write even more sophisticated GUI applications.

When writing your own programs, you will use the interface you prefer or one that your instructor or boss requires. If time permits, you might even want to develop programs both ways in future chapter exercises.

TWO TRUTHS & A LIE

Deciding Which Interface to Use

1. Console applications are used for declaring variables and constants and performing arithmetic, but GUI applications are not.

2. GUI programs usually take longer to develop than their console counterparts because you can spend a lot of time setting up and arranging the controls.

3. Console applications look dull compared to GUI applications, but they can often be developed more quickly because you do not spend much time setting up objects for a user to manipulate.

The false statement is #1. Both console and GUI applications can use declared variables and constants and perform arithmetic.

Deciding Which Interface to Use

You Do It

Working with the Visual Studio IDE

In the next steps, you use the IDE to create a Form with a Button and a Label. Your first console application in Chapter 1's "You Do It" section displayed "Hello, world!" at the command prompt. This application displays "Hello, Visual World!" on a Form.

1. Open Microsoft Visual Studio. You might have a desktop shortcut you can double-click, or in Windows 10 you can type the first few letters of **Visual Studio** in the "Ask me anything" search box, and then select it from the list of choices. Your steps might differ slightly from the ones listed here if you are using a different version of Visual Studio or a different operating system. If you are using a school network, you might be able to select **Visual Studio** from the school's computing menu.

2. Within Visual Studio, select **File** from the main menu, then **New** and **Project**. Then, in the New Project window, select **Visual C#** and **Windows Forms App**. (Refer to Figure 3-1.) Instead of using the default project name, use **HelloVisualWorld**, and select a location to store the project. Then click **OK**.

3. The HelloVisualWorld development environment opens, as shown in Figure 3-16. The text in the title bar of the blank Form contains the default text

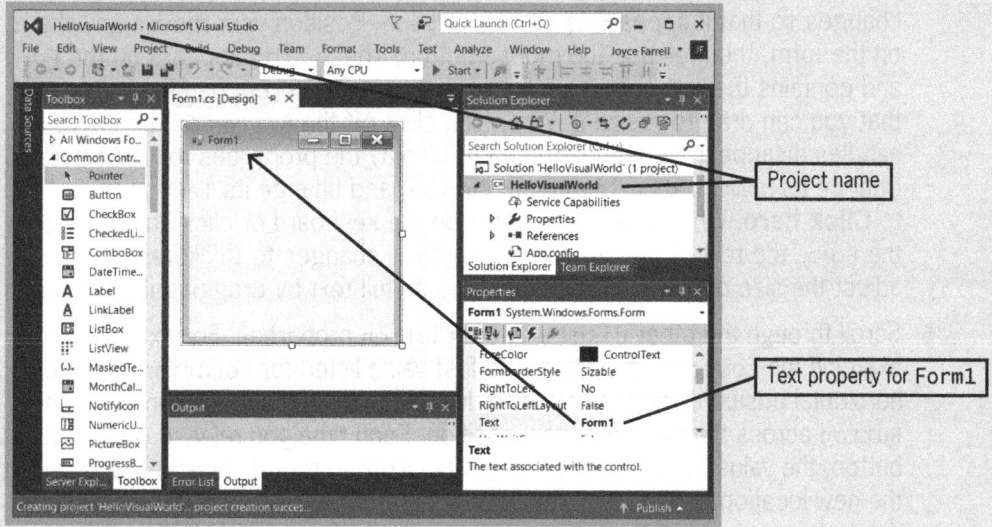

Figure 3-16 The HelloVisualWorld project development environment

(continues)

(continued)

Form1. If you click the Form, its Properties window appears in the lower-right portion of the screen, and you can see that the Text property for the Form is set to Form1. Take a moment to scroll through the list in the Properties window, examining the values of other properties of the Form. For example, the value of the Size property is 300, 300 by default.

If you do not see the Properties window in the lower-right corner of your screen, click the title bar on the Form. Alternatively, press **F4** or click **View** in the menu bar and then click **Properties Window**. If you do not see the Toolbox shown in Figure 3-16, click the **Toolbox tab** at the left side of the screen, and then click the pushpin near the top to pin the Toolbox to the screen. Alternatively, click **View** from the menu bar and then click **Toolbox**. If you do not see the error list at the bottom of the screen, as in Figure 3-16, you can select **View** from the menu bar and then select **Error List**. You might have to drag up the divider that separates the error list from the window above it.

4. In the Properties window, change the Name of the Form to **HelloForm**. (The Name property is under Design if you choose to have the list categorized; if you choose to display it alphabetically, then Name is near the top.) Then change the Text of the Form to **Hello Visual World**. Press **Enter**; the title of the Form in the center of the screen changes to *Hello Visual World*.

5. Examine the Toolbox on the left side of the screen. Select **Common Controls** if it is not already selected. In the Toolbox, click and hold **Button**. As you move your mouse off the Toolbox and onto the Form, the mouse pointer changes so that it appears to carry a Button. Position your mouse anywhere on the form, then release the mouse button. The Button appears on the Form and contains the text *button1*. When you click the Button, handles appear that you can drag to resize it. When you click off the Button on the Form, the handles disappear. Click the Button to display the properties for button1. Change its Name to **displayOutputButton**, and change its Text property to **Click here**. When you press **Enter** on the keyboard or click anywhere on the Form, the text of the Button on the Form changes to *Click here*. You can adjust the size of the Button so you see its full text by dragging its handles.

6. Scroll through the other displayOutputButton properties. For example, examine the Location property. The first value listed for Location indicates horizontal position, and the second value indicates vertical position. Drag the Button across the Form to a new position. Each time you release your mouse button, the value of the Form Button's Location property is updated to reflect the new location. Try to drag the Button to Location 80, 50. Alternatively, delete the contents of the Location property field and type **80**, **50**. The Button moves to the requested location on the Form. See Figure 3-17.

(continues)

Deciding Which Interface to Use

(continued)

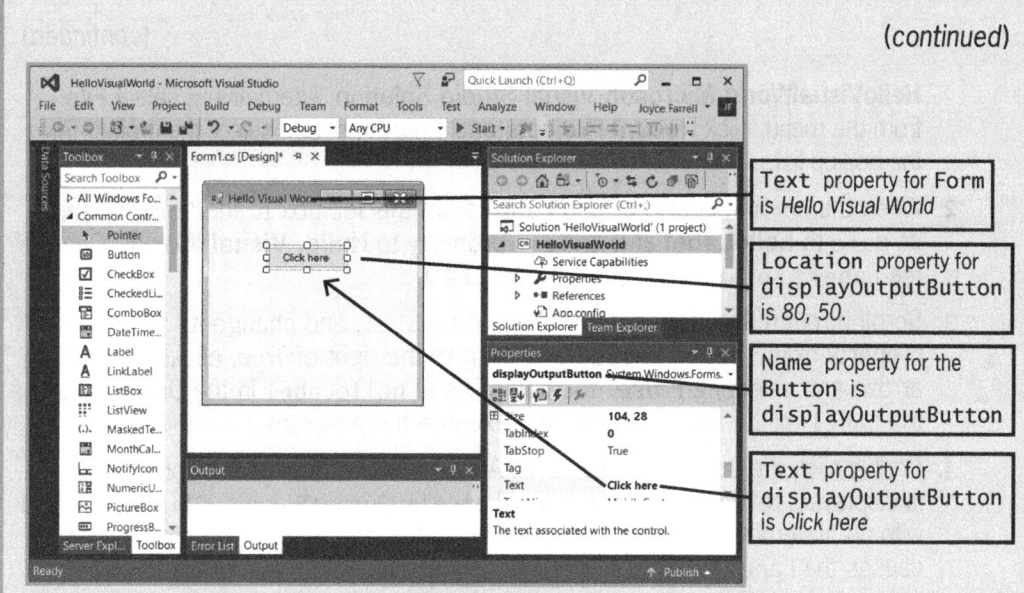

Figure 3-17 Changes to the HelloVisualWorld project

7. Save your form by clicking **File** on the menu bar, then clicking **Save All**. Alternatively, you can click the **Save All** button on the toolbar; its icon is two overlapping disks.

8. Although your Form doesn't do much yet, you can execute the program anyway. Click **Debug** on the menu bar, and then click **Start Without Debugging**. The Form appears. You can drag, minimize, and restore it, and you can click its Button. The Button has not yet been programmed to do anything, but it appears to be pressed when you click it. Click the Form's **Close** button to dismiss the Form.

9. You can close a project at any time and come back to it later. Exit Visual Studio now by clicking the **Close** button in the upper-right corner of the screen, or by clicking **File** on the menu bar and then clicking **Exit**. If you have made more changes since the last time you saved, you will be prompted to save again. When you choose **Yes**, the program closes.

Providing Functionality for a Button

In the next steps, you make the Button on the HelloVisualWorld Form functional; it will display a message when the user clicks it.

1. Start Visual Studio. Select **File** from the menu, click **Open**, click **Project/Solution**, and browse for the **HelloVisualWorld** folder. Double-click it, and select the

(continues)

(continued)

HelloVisualWorld Microsoft Visual Studio Solution. Alternatively, select **File** from the menu, click **Recent Projects and Solutions**, and select the project from the pop-up list.

2. When the Form appears, drag a Label from the Toolbox to the Form. Change its Name to **helloLabel** and its Text property to **Hello, Visual World!**. Change the Label's Location property to **80, 140**.

3. Scroll through the Properties list for helloLabel, and change its Visible property from True to False by clicking to the right of *True*, clicking the down arrow, and selecting *False*. You can still see helloLabel in the Designer, but the Label will be invisible when you execute the program.

4. Double-click the Button on the Form. A new window that contains program code is displayed, revealing a newly created displayOutputButton_Click() method with no statements. Between the curly braces, type the following statement that causes the Label to appear when the user clicks the Button on the Form:

   `helloLabel.Visible = true;`

5. Change the name of the displayOutputButton_Click() method to use conventional Pascal casing by right-clicking the method name, selecting **Rename**, and changing the highlighted name to start with an uppercase **D**. Click **Apply**.

6. Save the file, then run the program by clicking **Debug** on the menu bar and clicking **Start Without Debugging**, or by pressing **Ctrl+F5**. When the Form appears, click the **Click here** button to reveal the greeting. If you want, experiment with values for some of the Label properties, such as Font, BackColor, and ForeColor.

Adding a Second Button to a Form

In the next steps, you add a second Button to the Form in the HelloVisualWorld project.

1. In the IDE, switch to Design View. Drag a second button onto the Form. Make its Location property **80, 195**. Change the new Button's Name property to **changeOutputButton** and change its Text to **Click me last**. Drag the button's handles to adjust the size so all the text is visible.

2. Double-click the changeOutputButton to expose the changeOutputButton_Click() method. Rename the method to use Pascal casing.

3. Between the curly braces of the method, add the following code:

   `helloLabel.Text = "Goodbye";`

(continues)

(continued)

4. Save the project, then execute the program. Click the `displayOutputButton` to reveal *Hello, Visual World!*. Then click the `changeOutputButton` to reveal *Goodbye*.

5. Execute the program again. This time, click the second `Button` first. No message appears because the `Label` with the message has not been made visible. When you click the `displayOutputButton`, the `Label` becomes visible, but it displays *Goodbye* because the `changeOutputButton`'s `Click()` method has already changed the `Label`'s Text.

6. Return to the Form1.cs [Design] tab. Click the `changeOutputButton`, and change its `Enabled` property to `False`. Now, when the program executes, the user will not be immediately able to click the second `Button`.

7. Double-click the `displayOutputButton`. Add the following statement to the `Click()` method so that the `changeOutputButton` becomes enabled when the `displayOutputButton` is clicked:

    `changeOutputButton.Enabled = true;`

8. Save the project, then execute the program. When the `Form` appears, the `changeOutputButton` is dimmed and not clickable because it is not enabled. Click the enabled `displayOutputButton` to reveal the *Hello, Visual World!* message and to enable the second `Button`. Then click the `changeOutputButton` to expose the *Goodbye* message.

9. Dismiss the `Form`, and close Visual Studio.

Chapter Summary

- `Forms` are GUI objects that provide an interface for collecting, displaying, and delivering information. They almost always include controls such as labels, text boxes, and buttons that users can manipulate to interact with a program. Every `Form` and control on a `Form` has multiple properties you can set using the IDE.

- The Toolbox displays a list of available controls you can add to a `Form` including controls such as `Button`, `CheckBox`, and `Label`. You can drag controls onto a `Form`. After you have dragged a `Button` onto a `Form`, you can double-click it to create the method that executes when a user clicks the `Button`, and you can write any statements you want between the curly braces of the `Click()` method.

- `Label`s are controls that you use to display text to communicate with an application's user. `TextBox`es are controls through which a user can enter input data in a GUI application. Both have a `Text` property; frequently an application starts with the `Text` empty for `TextBox`es. Because a user might type any value, the value in a `TextBox` is a `string` by default.
- Usually, you want to provide reasonable `Name` property values for all the controls you place on a `Form`. Although any identifier that starts with a letter is legal, by convention you should start control names with a lowercase letter and use camel casing as appropriate, start `Form` names with an uppercase letter and use camel casing as appropriate, and use the type of object in the name.
- If you build or run a program that contains a syntax error, you see *Build failed* in the lower-left corner of the IDE and an error dialog box. An error list shows the filename, line, position in the line, and project for each error. If you double-click an error message, the cursor is placed at the location in the code where the error was found. If you inadvertently create an event-handling method that you do not want, you should eliminate the event using the Properties window in the IDE. To rename an event method, you must refactor the code. Both console and GUI applications can contain variable declarations and similar statements. GUI applications look "snazzier," and they contain controls that a user can manipulate with a mouse. However, GUI programs usually take longer to develop than their console counterparts. When writing your own programs, you will use the interface you prefer or one that your instructor or boss requires.

Key Terms

The **interface** is the environment a user sees when a program executes.

Forms are GUI objects that provide an interface for collecting, displaying, and delivering information.

Controls are devices such as labels, text boxes, and buttons that users can manipulate to communicate with a GUI program.

A **node** is an icon that appears beside a list or a section of code and that can be expanded or condensed.

An **access specifier** is a keyword that dictates what outside classes can use a method.

An **event** causes a program to perform a task.

A **click event** is the event generated when a user clicks a control in a GUI program.

A **label** is a control that you use to display text to communicate with an application's user.

A **text box** is a control through which a user can enter input data in a GUI application.

Design time is the period during which a programmer designs the interface and writes the code.

Runtime is the period during which a program executes.

Focus describes the attribute of a Form control that stands out visually from the others and that reacts to keyboard input.

Tab order describes the sequence of controls selected when the user presses the Tab key.

A **proportional font** is one in which different characters have different pitches or widths.

A **fixed-pitch font** is one in which each character occupies the same width.

A **monospaced font** is one in which each character occupies the same width.

Code refactoring is the process of changing a program's internal structure without changing the way the program works.

An **orphaned method** is one that never executes in an application and thus serves no purpose.

Review Questions

1. Which of the following is a GUI object that provides an interface for collecting, displaying, and delivering information and that contains other controls?

    a. Button
    b. Form
    c. TextBox
    d. Label

2. In the Visual Studio IDE main window, where does the menu bar lie?

    a. vertically along the left border
    b. vertically along the right border
    c. horizontally across the bottom of the window
    d. horizontally across the top of the window

3. In the IDE, the area where you visually construct a Form is the _____.

    a. Toolbox
    b. Form Designer
    c. Easel
    d. Sandbox

4. When you create a new Windows Forms project, by default the first Form you see is named _____.

    a. Form
    b. FormA
    c. Form1
    d. FormAlpha

5. The Form class has _____ properties.

    a. three
    b. ten
    c. about 100
    d. about 1000

CHAPTER 3 — Using GUI Objects and the Visual Studio IDE

6. Which of the following is not a Form property?
   a. BackColor
   b. Size
   c. Text
   d. ProjectName

7. Which of the following is a legal Form Name property value?
   a. PayrollForm
   b. Payroll Form
   c. either of the above
   d. none of the above

8. Which of the following is a legal Form Text property value?
   a. PayrollForm
   b. Payroll Form
   c. either of the above
   d. none of the above

9. Which of the following does not appear in the IDE's Toolbox list?
   a. Label
   b. Button
   c. Text
   d. TextBox

10. After you have dragged a Button onto a Form in the IDE, you can double-click it to _____.
    a. delete it
    b. view its properties
    c. create a method that executes when a user clicks the Button
    d. increase its size

11. The button1_Click() method that is generated by the IDE _____.
    a. has a private access specifier
    b. is nonstatic
    c. contains parameters between its parentheses
    d. all of the above

12. A(n) _____ is generated when a user interacts with a GUI object.
    a. error
    b. occasion
    c. method
    d. event

13. If you create a Button named yesButton, the default name of the method that responds to clicks on it is _____.
    a. button1_Click()
    b. yesButton_Method()
    c. click_YesButton()
    d. yesButton_Click()

Review Questions

14. Statements allowed in a `Click()` method include _____ .
    a. variable declarations
    b. arithmetic statements
    c. both of the above
    d. none of the above

15. _____ are controls through which a user can enter input data in a GUI application.
    a. `Labels`
    b. `Tags`
    c. `Tickets`
    d. `TextBox`es

16. The value in a `TextBox` is _____ .
    a. an `int`
    b. a `double`
    c. a `string`
    d. It might be any of the above.

17. Which of the following is a legal and conventional name for a `TextBox`?
    a. `Salary TextBox`
    b. `salaryTextBox`
    c. both of the above
    d. none of the above

18. The process of changing a program's internal structure without changing the way the program works is _____ .
    a. compiling
    b. debugging
    c. code refactoring
    d. systems analysis

19. If you inadvertently create a `Click()` method for a control that should not generate a click event, you can successfully eliminate the method by _____ .
    a. deleting the method code from the *Form1.cs* file
    b. eliminating the method from the Events list in the Properties window
    c. adding the method to the Discard window
    d. making the method a comment by placing two forward slashes at the start of each line

20. Of the following, the most significant difference between many console applications and GUI applications is _____ .
    a. their appearance
    b. their ability to accept input
    c. their ability to perform calculations
    d. their ability to be created using C#

Exercises

Programming Exercises

The exercises in this section should look familiar to you. Each is similar to an exercise in Chapter 2, where you created solutions using console input and output.

1. Write a GUI program named **InchesToCentimetersGUI** that allows the user to input a measurement in inches, click a `Button`, and output the value in centimeters. There are 2.54 centimeters in an inch.

2. Write a GUI program named **ProjectedRaisesGUI** that allows a user to enter an employee's salary. Then display, with explanatory text, next year's salary, which reflects a 4 percent increase.

3. Write a program named **MoveEstimatorGUI** that prompts a user for the number of hours for a moving job and the number of miles involved in the move. After the user clicks a `Button`, display the moving fee which includes a base rate of $200 plus $150 per hour and $2 per mile.

4. Write a GUI program named **EggsInteractiveGUI** that allows a user to input the number of eggs produced in a month by each of five chickens. Sum the eggs, then display the total in dozens and eggs. For example, a total of 127 eggs is 10 dozen and 7 eggs.

5. Write a GUI program named **MakeChangeGUI** that calculates and displays the conversion of an entered number of dollars into currency denominations—twenties, tens, fives, and ones. For example, $113 is 5 twenties, 1 ten, 0 fives, and 3 ones.

6. Write a GUI program named **TestsInteractiveGUI** that allows a user to enter scores for five tests he has taken. Display the average of the test scores to two decimal places.

7. Create an enumeration named `Month` that holds values for the months of the year, starting with JANUARY equal to 1. (Recall that an enumeration must be placed within a class but outside of any method.) Write a GUI program named **MonthNamesGUI** that prompts the user for a month integer. Convert the user's entry to a `Month` value, and display it.

8. Pig Latin is a nonsense language. To create a word in pig Latin, you remove the first letter and then add the first letter and *ay* at the end of the word. For example, *dog* becomes *ogday*, and *cat* becomes *atcay*. Write a GUI program named **PigLatinGUI** that allows the user to enter a word and displays the pig Latin version.

Exercises

Debugging Exercises

1. Each of the following projects in the Chapter.03 folder of your downloadable student files has syntax and/or logical errors. In each case, immediately save a copy of the project folder with a new name that begins with *Fixed* before you open the project in Visual Studio. For example, the project folder for DebugThree1 will become FixedDebugThree1. All the files within the folders have already been named with the *Fixed* prefix, so you do not need to provide new filenames for any of the files in the top-level folder. After naming the new folder, open the project, determine the problems, and fix them.

   a. DebugThree1
   b. DebugThree2
   c. DebugThree3
   d. DebugThree4

Case Problems

1. In Chapter 2, you created a program for the Greenville Idol competition that prompts a user for the number of contestants entered in last year's competition and in this year's competition. The program displays the revenue expected for this year's competition if each contestant pays a $25 entrance fee. The application also displays a statement that indicates whether this year's competition has more contestants than last year's. Now, create an interactive GUI program named **GreenvilleRevenueGUI** that performs all the same tasks.

2. In Chapter 2, you created a program for Marshall's Murals that prompts a user for the number of interior and exterior murals scheduled to be painted during the next month. The program computes the expected revenue for each type of mural when interior murals cost $500 each and exterior murals cost $750 each. The application should display, by mural type, the number of murals ordered, the cost for each type, and a subtotal. The application also displays the total expected revenue and a statement that indicates whether more interior murals are scheduled than exterior ones. Now create an interactive GUI program named **MarshallsRevenueGUI** that performs all the same tasks.

CHAPTER 4

Making Decisions

Upon completion of this chapter, you will be able to:

◎ Understand logic-planning tools and decision making

◎ Make decisions using `if` statements

◎ Make decisions using `if-else` statements

◎ Use compound expressions in `if` statements

◎ Make decisions using `switch` statements

◎ Use the conditional operator

◎ Use the NOT operator

◎ Avoid common errors when making decisions

◎ Appreciate decision-making issues in GUI programs

CHAPTER 4 Making Decisions

Computer programs are powerful because of their ability to make decisions. Programs that decide which travel route will offer the best weather conditions, which website will provide the closest match to search criteria, or which recommended medical treatment has the highest probability of success all rely on a program's decision making. In this chapter, you will learn to make decisions in C# programs.

Understanding Logic-Planning Tools and Decision Making

When computer programmers write programs, they rarely just sit down at a keyboard and begin typing. Programmers must plan the complex portions of programs. Programmers often use **pseudocode**, a tool that helps them plan a program's logic by writing plain English statements. Using pseudocode requires that you write down the logic of a given task in everyday language and not the syntax used in a programming language. (You learned the difference between *logic* and *syntax* in Chapter 1.) In fact, a task you write in pseudocode does not have to be computer-related. If you have ever written a list of directions to your house—for example, (1) go west on Algonquin Road, (2) turn left on Roselle Road, (3) enter expressway heading east, and so on—you have written pseudocode. A **flowchart** is similar to pseudocode, but you write the steps in diagram form, as a series of shapes connected by arrows or *flowlines*.

Some programmers use a variety of shapes to represent different tasks in their flowcharts, but you can draw simple flowcharts that express very complex situations using just rectangles, diamonds, and connecting flowlines. You can use a rectangle to represent any process or step and a diamond to represent any decision. For example, Figure 4-1 shows a flowchart and pseudocode describing driving directions to a friend's house.

Notice how the actions illustrated in the flowchart and the pseudocode statements in Figure 4-1 correspond. Figure 4-1 illustrates a logical structure called a **sequence structure**—one step follows another unconditionally. A sequence structure might contain any number of steps, but one task follows another with no chance to branch away or skip a step.

Figure 4-1 Flowchart and pseudocode of a sequence structure

Sometimes, logical steps do not follow in an unconditional sequence. Instead, some tasks might or might not occur based on the outcome of some decisions. To represent a decision, flowchart creators use a diamond shape to hold a question, and they draw paths to alternative courses of action emerging from the corner of the diamond. Figure 4-2 shows a flowchart describing directions in which the execution of some steps depends on a decision. Figure 4-2 shows a **decision structure**—one that involves choosing between alternative courses of action based on a value.

CHAPTER 4 Making Decisions

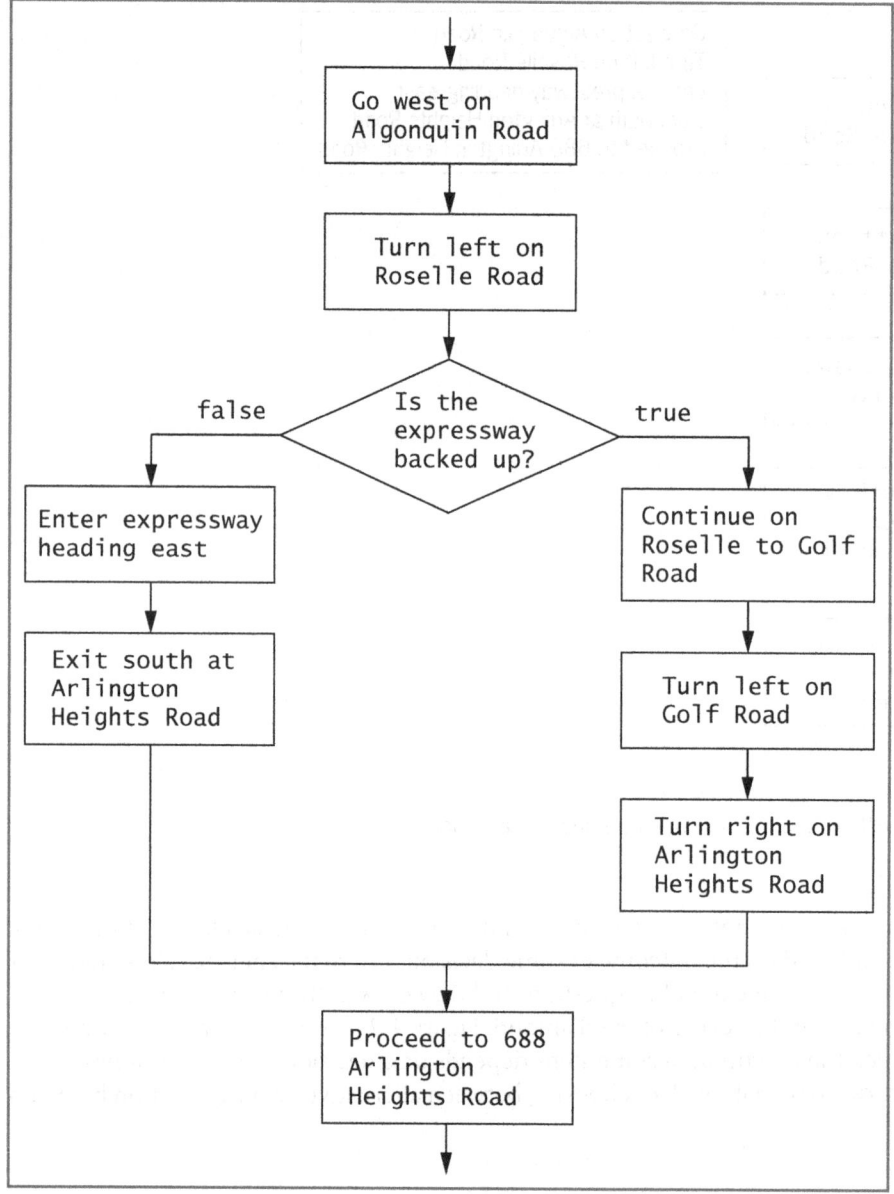

Figure 4-2 Flowchart including a decision structure

When reduced to their most basic form, all computer decisions are true-or-false decisions. This is because computer circuitry consists of millions of tiny switches that are either "on" or "off," and the result of every decision sets one of these switches in memory. The values `true` and `false` are Boolean values; every computer decision results in a Boolean value. For example, program code that you write never includes a question like "What number did the user enter?" Instead, the decisions might be: "Did the user enter a 1?" "If not, did the user enter a 2?" "If not, did the user enter a 3?"

> **TWO TRUTHS & A LIE**
>
> **Understanding Logic-Planning Tools and Decision Making**
>
> 1. A sequence structure has three or more alternative logical paths.
> 2. A decision structure involves choosing between alternative courses of action based on some value within a program.
> 3. When reduced to their most basic form, all computer decisions are yes-or-no decisions.
>
> The false statement is #1. In a sequence structure, one step follows another unconditionally.

Making Decisions Using the if Statement

The if and if-else statements are the two most commonly used decision-making statements in C#. You use an **if statement** to make a single-alternative decision. In other words, you use an if statement to determine whether an action will occur. The if statement takes the following form:

```
if(testedExpression)
   statement;
```

In this statement, *testedExpression* represents any C# expression that can be evaluated as true or false, and *statement* represents the action that will take place if the expression evaluates as true. You must place the if statement's evaluated expression between parentheses. You can leave a space between the keyword if and the opening parenthesis if you think that format is easier to read.

Usable expressions in an if statement include Boolean expressions such as amount > 5 and month == "May" as well as the value of bool variables such as isValidIDNumber. If the expression evaluates as true, then the statement in the expression executes; otherwise it does not. Whether the expression evaluates as true or false, the program continues with the next statement following the complete if statement.

CHAPTER 4 Making Decisions

You learned about Boolean expressions and the `bool` data type in Chapter 2. Table 2-4 summarizes how comparison operators are used.

In the chapter "Introduction to Methods," you will learn to write methods that return values. A method call that returns a Boolean value also can be used as the tested expression in an `if` statement.

In some programming languages, such as C++, nonzero numbers evaluate as `true` and 0 evaluates as `false`. However, in C#, only Boolean expressions evaluate as `true` and `false`.

For example, the code segment written and diagrammed in Figure 4-3 displays A and B when `number` holds a value less than 5, but when `number` is 5 or greater, only B is displayed. When the tested Boolean expression `number < 5` is `false`, the statement that displays A never executes.

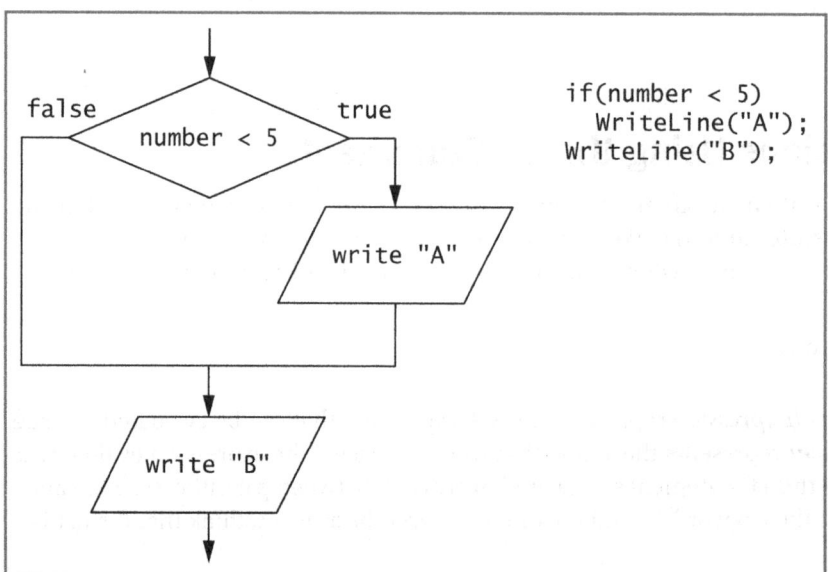

Figure 4-3 Flowchart and code including a typical `if` statement followed by a separate statement

Although you can create a meaningful flowchart using only rectangles, diamonds, and flowlines, parallelograms have traditionally been used to represent input and output statements, so they are used in Figure 4-3 and in other figures in this chapter.

Making Decisions Using the if Statement

In the code in Figure 4-3, notice there is no semicolon at the end of the line that contains if(number < 5). The statement does not end at that point; it ends after WriteLine("A");. If you incorrectly insert a semicolon at the end of if(number < 5), then the code means, "If number is less than 5, do nothing; then, no matter what the value of number is, display *A*." Figure 4-4 shows the flowchart logic that matches the code when a semicolon is incorrectly placed at the end of the if expression.

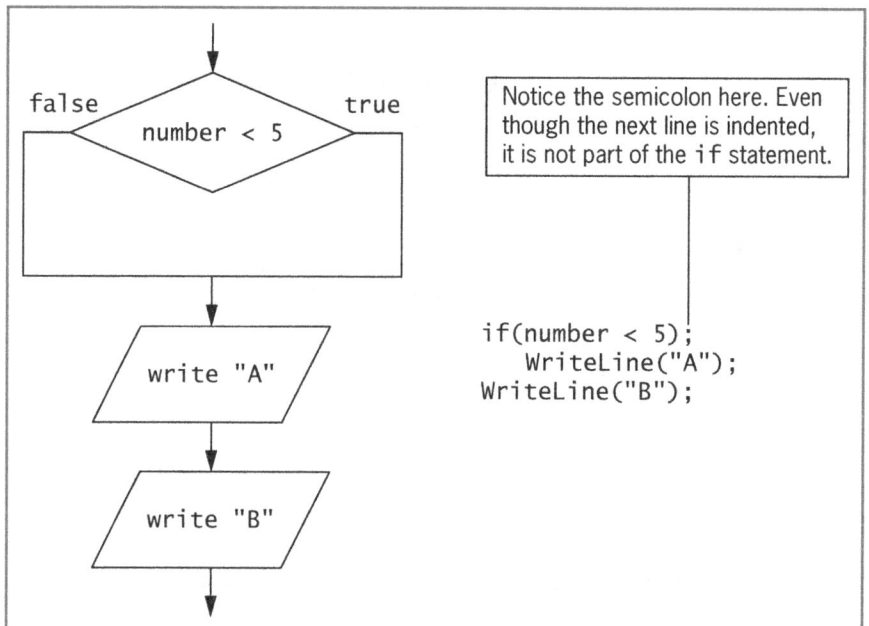

Figure 4-4 Flowchart and code including an if statement with a semicolon following the if expression

Although it is customary, and good style, to indent any statement that executes when an if Boolean expression evaluates as true, the C# compiler does not pay any attention to the indentation. Each of the following if statements displays *A* when number is less than 5. The first shows an if statement written on a single line; the second shows an if statement on two lines but with no indentation. The third uses conventional indentation. All three examples execute identically.

```
if(number < 5) WriteLine("A");
if(number < 5)
WriteLine("A");
if(number < 5)
   WriteLine("A");
```

Don't Do It
Although these first two formats work for if statements, they are not conventional, and using them makes a program harder to understand.

When you want to execute two or more statements conditionally, you place the statements within a block. A **block** is a collection of one or more statements contained within a pair of curly braces. For example, the code segment written and diagrammed in Figure 4-5 displays both *C* and *D* when number is less than 5, and it displays neither when number is not less than 5. The if expression that precedes the block is the **control statement** for the decision structure.

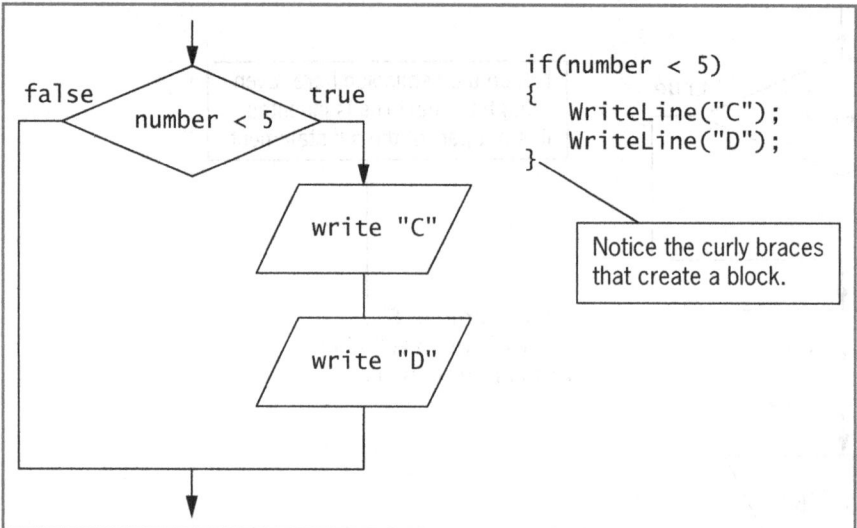

Figure 4-5   Flowchart and code including a typical if statement containing a block

Indenting alone does not cause multiple statements to depend on the evaluation of a Boolean expression following an if control statement. For multiple statements to depend on an if, they must be blocked with braces. For example, Figure 4-6 shows two statements that are indented below an if expression. When you glance at the code, it might first appear that both statements depend on the if; however, only the first one does, as shown in the flowchart, because the statements are not blocked.

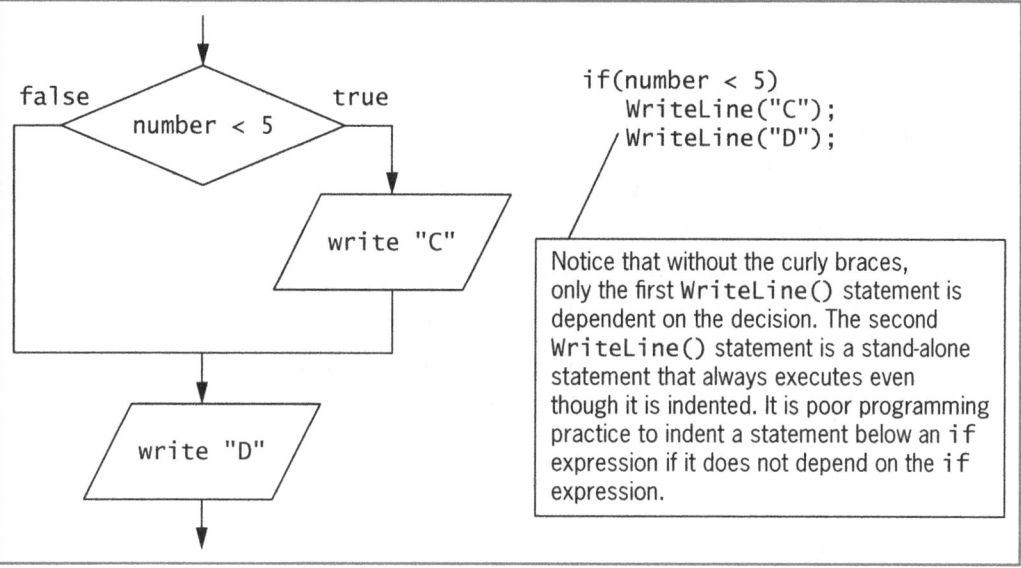

Figure 4-6 Flowchart and code including an if statement that is missing curly braces or that has inappropriate indenting

When you create a block using curly braces, you do not have to place multiple statements within it. It is perfectly legal to block a single statement. Blocking a single statement can be a useful technique to help prevent future errors because when a program later is modified to include multiple statements that depend on the if, the braces serve as a reminder to use a block. Creating a block that contains no statements also is legal in C#. You usually do so only when starting to write a program, as a reminder to yourself to add statements later.

In C#, it is customary to align a block's opening and closing braces. Some programmers prefer to place the opening brace on the same line as the if expression instead of giving the brace its own line. This style is called the *K & R style*, named for Brian Kernighan and Dennis Ritchie, who wrote the first book on the C programming language.

You can place any number of statements within a block, including other if statements. If a second if statement is the only statement that depends on the first if, then no braces are required. Figure 4-7 shows the logic for a **nested if** statement in which one decision structure is contained within another. With a nested if statement, a second if's Boolean expression is tested only when the first if's Boolean expression evaluates as true.

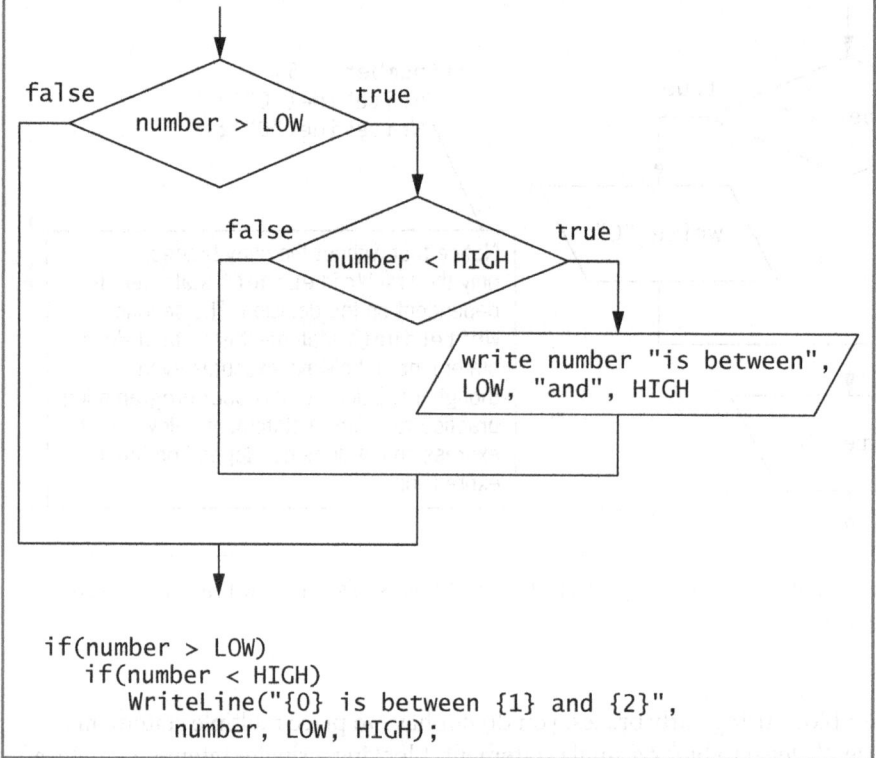

Figure 4-7 Flowchart and code showing the logic of a nested if

Figure 4-8 shows a program that contains the logic in Figure 4-7. When a user enters a number greater than 5, the first tested expression is true and the if statement that tests whether the number is less than 10 executes. When the second tested expression also is true, the WriteLine() statement executes. If either the first or second tested expression is false, no output occurs. Figure 4-9 shows the output after the program is executed three times using three different input values. Notice that when the value input by the user is not between 5 and 10, this program produces no output message.

Making Decisions Using the if Statement

```
using System;
using static System.Console;
class NestedDecision
{
   static void Main()
   {
      const int HIGH = 10, LOW = 5;
      string numberString;
      int number;
      Write("Enter an integer ");
      numberString = ReadLine();
      number = Convert.ToInt32(numberString);
      if(number > LOW)
         if(number < HIGH)
            WriteLine("{0} is between {1} and {2}",
               number, LOW, HIGH);
   }
}
```

Figure 4-8 Program using nested if

Figure 4-9 Output of three executions of the NestedDecision program

A Note on Equivalency Comparisons

Often, programmers mistakenly use a single equal sign rather than the double equal sign when testing for equivalency. For example, the expression number = HIGH does not compare number to HIGH. Instead, it attempts to assign the value HIGH to the variable number. When an assignment is used between the parentheses in an if statement, as in if(number = HIGH), the assignment is illegal, and the program will not compile.

CHAPTER 4 Making Decisions

The only condition under which the assignment operator would work as part of the tested expression in an `if` statement is when the assignment is made to a `bool` variable. For example, suppose that a payroll program contains a `bool` variable named `doesEmployeeHaveDependents`, and then uses the following statement:

`if(doesEmployeeHaveDependents = numDependents > 0)...`

In this case, `numDependents` would be compared to 0, and the result, `true` or `false`, would be assigned to `doesEmployeeHaveDependents`. Then the decision would be made based on the assigned value. This is not a recommended way to make a comparison because it looks confusing. If your intention was to assign a value to `doesEmployeeHaveDependents` and to make a decision based on the value, then your intentions would be clearer with the following code:

```
doesEmployeeHaveDependents = numDependents > 0;
if(doesEmployeeHaveDependents)...
```

Notice the difference in the following statement that uses two equal signs within the parentheses in the `if` statement:

`if(doesEmployeeHaveDependents == numDependents > 0)...`

This statement compares `doesEmployeeHaveDependents` to the result of comparing `numDependents` to 0 but does not change the value of `doesEmployeeHaveDependents`.

One of the many advantages of using the Visual Studio IDE to write programs is that if you use an assignment operator in place of an equivalency operator in a Boolean expression, your mistake will be flagged as an error immediately.

TWO TRUTHS & A LIE

Making Decisions Using the `if` Statement

1. In C#, you must place an `if` statement's evaluated expression between parentheses.
2. In C#, for multiple statements to depend on an `if`, they must be indented.
3. In C#, you can place one `if` statement within a block that depends on another `if` statement.

The false statement is #2. Indenting alone does not cause multiple statements to depend on the evaluation of a Boolean expression in an `if`. For multiple statements to depend on an `if`, they must be blocked with braces.

Making Decisions Using the `if-else` Statement

Some decisions are **dual-alternative decisions**; they have two possible resulting actions. If you want to perform one action when a Boolean expression evaluates as `true` and an alternate action when it evaluates as `false`, you can use an **if-else statement**. The `if-else` statement takes the following form:

```
if(expression)
   statement1;
else
   statement2;
```

You can code an `if` without an `else`, but it is illegal to code an `else` without an `if`.

Just as you can block several statements so they all execute when an expression within an `if` is `true`, you can block multiple statements after an `else` so that they will all execute when the evaluated expression is `false`. For example, the following code assigns 0 to bonus and also produces a line of output when the Boolean variable `isProjectUnderBudget` is `false`:

```
if(isProjectUnderBudget)
   bonus = 200;
else
{
   bonus = 0;
   WriteLine("Notify contractor");
}
```

Figure 4-10 shows the logic for an `if-else` statement, and Figure 4-11 shows a program that contains the statement. With every execution of the program, one or the other of the two `WriteLine()` statements executes. The indentation shown in the `if-else` example in Figure 4-11 is not required, but it is standard. You vertically align the keyword `if` with the keyword `else`, and then indent the action statements that depend on the evaluation. Figure 4-12 shows two executions of the program.

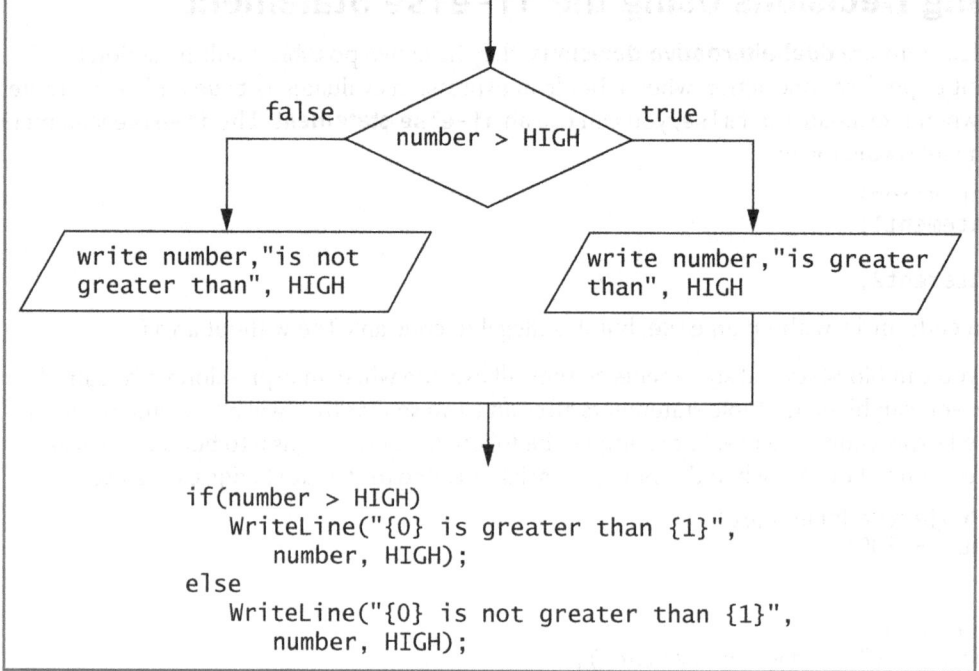

Figure 4-10 Flowchart and code showing the logic of a dual-alternative `if-else` statement

```
using System;
using static System.Console;
class IfElseDecision
{
   static void Main()
   {
      const int HIGH = 10;
      string numberString;
      int number;
      Write("Enter an integer ");
      numberString = ReadLine();
      number = Convert.ToInt32(numberString);
      if(number > HIGH)
         WriteLine("{0} is greater  than {1}",
            number, HIGH);
      else
         WriteLine("{0} is not greater than {1}",
            number, HIGH);
   }
}
```

Figure 4-11 Program with a dual-alternative `if-else` statement

Making Decisions Using the if-else Statement

```
Enter an integer 8
8 is not greater than 10

Enter an integer 32
32 is greater than 10
```

Figure 4-12 Output of two executions of the IfElseDecision program

When if-else statements are nested, each else always is paired with the most recent unpaired if. For example, in the following code, the else is paired with the second if. Correct indentation helps to make this clear.

```
if(saleAmount > 1000)
   if(saleAmount < 2000)
      bonus = 100;
   else
      bonus = 500;
```

In this example, the following bonuses are assigned:

- If saleAmount is between $1000 and $2000, bonus is $100 because both evaluated expressions are true.

- If saleAmount is $2000 or more, bonus is $500 because the first evaluated expression is true and the second one is false.

- If saleAmount is $1000 or less, bonus is unassigned because the first evaluated expression is false and there is no corresponding else.

TWO TRUTHS & A LIE

Making Decisions Using the if-else Statement

1. Dual-alternative decisions have two possible outcomes.

2. In an if-else statement, a semicolon might be the last character typed before the else.

3. When if-else statements are nested, the first if always is paired with the first else.

The false statement is #3. When if-else statements are nested, each else always is paired with the most recent unpaired if.

You Do It

Using if-else Statements

In the next steps, you write a program that requires using multiple, nested if-else statements to accomplish its goal—determining whether any of the three integers entered by a user are equal.

1. Open a new file or project named **CompareThreeNumbers**, and write the first lines necessary for the class:

```
using System;
using static System.Console;
class CompareThreeNumbers
{
```

2. Begin a Main() method by declaring a string for input and three integers that will hold the input values.

```
static void Main()
{
    string numberString;
    int num1, num2, num3;
```

3. Add the statements that retrieve the three integers from the user and assign them to the appropriate variables.

```
Write("Enter an integer ");
numberString = ReadLine();
num1 = Convert.ToInt32(numberString);
Write("Enter an integer ");
numberString = ReadLine();
num2 = Convert.ToInt32(numberString);
Write("Enter an integer ");
numberString = ReadLine();
num3 = Convert.ToInt32(numberString);
```

 In the chapter "Introduction to Methods," you will learn to write methods, which will allow you to avoid repetitive code like that shown here.

(continues)

Making Decisions Using the if-else Statement

(continued)

4. If the first number and the second number are equal, there are two possibilities: either the first is also equal to the third, in which case all three numbers are equal, or the first is not equal to the third, in which case only the first two numbers are equal. Insert the following code:

```
if(num1 == num2)
    if(num1 == num3)
        WriteLine("All three numbers are equal");
    else
        WriteLine("First two are equal");
```

5. If the first two numbers are not equal, but the first and third are equal, display an appropriate message. For clarity, the else should vertically align under the first if statement that compares num1 and num2.

```
else
    if(num1 == num3)
        WriteLine("First and last are equal");
```

6. When num1 and num2 are not equal, and num1 and num3 are not equal, but num2 and num3 are equal, display an appropriate message. For clarity, the else should vertically align under the statement that compares num1 and num3.

```
else
    if(num2 == num3)
        WriteLine("Last two are equal");
```

7. Finally, if none of the pairs (num1 and num2, num1 and num3, or num2 and num3) is equal, display an appropriate message. For clarity, the else should vertically align under the statement that compares num2 and num3.

```
else
    WriteLine("No two numbers are equal");
```

8. Add a closing curly brace for the Main() method and a closing curly brace for the class.

9. Save and compile the program, and then execute it several times, providing different combinations of equal and nonequal integers when prompted. Figure 4-13 shows several executions of the program.

(continues)

(continued)

Figure 4-13   Several executions of the CompareThreeNumbers program

Using Compound Expressions in if Statements

In many programming situations, you need to make multiple decisions before taking action. No matter how many decisions must be made, you can produce the correct results by using a series of if statements. For convenience and clarity, however, you can combine multiple decisions into a single, compound Boolean expression using a combination of conditional AND and OR operators.

Using the Conditional AND Operator

As an alternative to nested if statements, you can use the **conditional AND operator** (or simply the **AND operator**) to create a compound Boolean expression. The conditional AND operator is written as two ampersands (&&).

A tool that can help you understand the && operator is a truth table. **Truth tables** are diagrams used in mathematics and logic to help describe the truth of an entire expression based on the truth of its parts. Table 4-1 shows a truth table that lists all the possibilities with compound expressions that use && and two operands. For any two expressions x and y, the expression x && y is true only if both x and y are true individually. If either x or y alone is false, or if both are false, then the expression x && y is false.

Using Compound Expressions in if Statements

x	y	x && y
True	True	True
True	False	False
False	True	False
False	False	False

Table 4-1 Truth table for the conditional && operator

For example, the two code samples shown in Figure 4-14 work exactly the same way. The age variable is tested, and if it is greater than or equal to 0 and less than 120, a message is displayed to explain that the value is valid.

```
// using the && operator
if(age >= 0 && age < 120)
   WriteLine("Age is valid");

// using nested ifs
if(age >= 0)
   if(age < 120)
      WriteLine("Age is valid");
```

Figure 4-14 Comparison of the && operator and nested if statements

Using the && operator is never required, because nested if statements achieve the same result, but using the && operator often makes your code more concise, less error-prone, and easier to understand.

It is important to note that when you use the && operator, you must include a complete Boolean expression on each side of the operator. If you want to set a bonus to $400 when saleAmount is both greater than $1000 and less than $5000, the correct statement is as follows:

```
if(saleAmount > 1000 && saleAmount < 5000)
   bonus = 400;
```

The following statement is incorrect and will not compile:

```
if(saleAmount > 1000 && < 5000)
   bonus = 400;
```

Don't Do It
< 5000 is not a Boolean expression because the < operator requires two operands, so this statement is invalid.

For clarity, many programmers prefer to surround each Boolean expression that is part of a compound Boolean expression with its own set of parentheses. For example:

```
if((saleAmount > 1000) && (saleAmount < 5000))
   bonus = 400;
```

In this example, the if clause has a set of parentheses (the first opening parenthesis and the last closing parenthesis), and each Boolean expression that is part of the compound condition has its own set of parentheses. Use this format if it is clearer to you.

The expressions in each part of a compound, conditional Boolean expression are evaluated only as much as necessary to determine whether the entire expression is true or false. This feature is called **short-circuit evaluation**. With the && operator, both Boolean expressions must be true before the action in the statement can occur. If the first expression is false, the second expression is never evaluated, because its value does not matter. For example, if a is not greater than LIMIT in the following if statement, then the evaluation is complete because there is no need to evaluate whether b is greater than LIMIT.

```
if(a > LIMIT && b > LIMIT)
   WriteLine("Both are greater than the limit.");
```

Using the Conditional OR Operator

You can use the **conditional OR operator** (or simply the **OR operator**) when you want some action to occur even if only one of two conditions is true. The OR operator is written as ||. When you use the || operator, only one of the listed conditions must be met for the resulting action to take place. Table 4-2 shows the truth table for the || operator. As you can see, the entire expression x||y is false *only* when x and y each is false individually.

x	y	x||y
True	True	True
True	False	True
False	True	True
False	False	False

Table 4-2 Truth table for the || operator

For example, if you want to display a message indicating an invalid age when the value of an age variable is less than 0 or more than 120, you can use either code sample in Figure 4-15.

You create the conditional OR operator by using two vertical pipes. On most keyboards, the pipe is found above the backslash key; typing it requires that you also hold down the Shift key.

Using Compound Expressions in if Statements

```
// using the || operator
if(age < 0 || age > 120)
   WriteLine("Age is not valid");

// using nested ifs
if(age < 0)
   WriteLine("Age is not valid");
else
   if(age > 120)
      WriteLine("Age is not valid");
```

Figure 4-15 Comparison of the || operator and nested if statements

When the || operator is used in an if statement, only one of the two Boolean expressions in the tested expression needs to be true for the resulting action to occur. When the first Boolean expression is true, the second expression is never evaluated because it doesn't matter whether the second expression is true or false. As with the && operator, this feature is called *short-circuit evaluation*.

 Watch the video *Using the AND and OR Operators*.

Using the Logical AND and OR Operators

C# provides two logical operators that you generally do *not* want to use when making comparisons. However, you should learn about them because they might be used in programs written by others, and because you might use one by mistake when you intend to use a conditional operator.

The **Boolean logical AND operator** (&) and **Boolean logical inclusive OR operator** (|) work just like their && and || (*conditional* AND and OR) counterparts, except they do not support short-circuit evaluation. That is, they always evaluate both sides of the expression, no matter what the first evaluation is. This can lead to a **side effect**, or unintended consequence. For example, in the following statement that uses &&, if salesAmountForYear is not at least 10,000, the first half of the expression is false, so the second half of the Boolean expression is never evaluated and yearsOfService is not increased.

```
if(salesAmountForYear >= 10000 && ++yearsOfService > 10)
   bonus = 200;
```

On the other hand, when a single & is used and salesAmountForYear is not at least 10,000, then even though the first half of the expression is false, and bonus is not set to 200, the second half of the expression is still evaluated, and yearsOfService is always increased whether it is more than 10 or not:

```
if(salesAmountForYear >= 10000 & ++yearsOfService > 10)
   bonus = 200;
```

In general, you should avoid writing expressions that contain side effects. If you want yearsOfService to increase no matter what the value of salesAmountForYear is, then you should increase it in a stand-alone statement. If you want it increased only when the sales amount exceeds 10,000, then you should increase it in a statement that depends on that decision.

The & and | operators are Boolean logical operators when they are placed between Boolean expressions. When the same operators are used between integer expressions, they are **bitwise operators** that are used to manipulate the individual bits of values.

Combining AND and OR Operators

You can combine as many AND and OR operators in an expression as you need. For example, when three conditions must be true before performing an action, you can use multiple AND or OR operators in the same expression. For example, in the following statement, all three Boolean variables must be true to produce the output:

```
if(isWeekendDay && isOver80Degrees && isSunny)
   WriteLine("Good day for the beach");
```

In the following statement, only one of the three Boolean variables needs to be true to produce the output:

```
if(isWeekendDay || isHoliday || amSick)
   WriteLine("No work today");
```

When you use a series of only && or only || operators in an expression, they are evaluated from left to right as far as is necessary to determine the value of the entire expression. However, when you combine && and || operators within the same Boolean expression, they are not necessarily evaluated from left to right. Instead, the && operators take precedence, meaning they are evaluated first. For example, consider a program that determines whether a movie theater patron can purchase a discounted ticket. Assume that discounts are allowed for children (age 12 and younger) and for senior citizens (age 65 and older) who attend G-rated movies. (To keep the comparisons simple, this example assumes that movie ratings are always a single character.) The following code looks reasonable, but it produces incorrect results because the && evaluates before the ||.

```
if(age <= 12 || age >= 65 && rating == 'G')
   WriteLine("Discount applies");
```

For example, suppose that a movie patron is 10 years old and the movie rating is *R*. The patron should not receive a discount (or be allowed to see the movie!). However, within the if statement above, the compound expression age >= 65 && rating == 'G' evaluates first. It is false, so the if becomes the equivalent of if(age <= 12 || false). Because age <= 12 is true, the if becomes the equivalent of if(true || false), which evaluates as true, and the statement *Discount applies* is displayed, which is not the intention for a 10-year-old seeing an R-rated movie.

Using Compound Expressions in if Statements

You can use parentheses to correct the logic and force the expression age <= 12 || age >= 65 to evaluate first, as shown in the following code:

```
if((age <= 12 || age >= 65) && rating == 'G')
   WriteLine("Discount applies");
```

With the added parentheses, both age comparisons are made first. If the age value qualifies a patron for a discount, the expression is evaluated as if(true && rating == 'G'). Then the rating value must also be acceptable for the message to be displayed. Figure 4-16 shows the if statement within a complete program; note that the discount age limits are represented as named constants in the complete program. Figure 4-17 shows the execution before the parentheses were added to the if statement, and Figure 4-18 shows the output after the inclusion of the parentheses.

```
using static System.Console;
class MovieDiscount
{
   static void Main()
   {
      int age = 10;
      char rating = 'R';
      const int CHILD_AGE = 12;
      const int SENIOR_AGE = 65;
      WriteLine("When age is {0} and rating is {1}",
         age, rating);
      if((age <= CHILD_AGE || age >= SENIOR_AGE) && rating == 'G')
         WriteLine("Discount applies");
      else
         WriteLine("Full price");
   }
}
```

Figure 4-16 Movie ticket discount program using parentheses to alter precedence of Boolean evaluations

```
When age is 10 and rating is R
Discount applies
```

Figure 4-17 Incorrect results when MovieDiscount program is executed without added parentheses

CHAPTER 4 Making Decisions

```
When age is 10 and rating is R
Full price
```

Figure 4-18 Correct results when parentheses are added to MovieDiscount program as shown in Figure 4-16

You can use parentheses for clarity in a Boolean expression, even when they are not required. For example, the following expressions both evaluate a && b first:

```
a && b || c
(a && b) || c
```

If the version with parentheses makes your intentions clearer, you should use it.

In Chapter 2, you learned that parentheses also control arithmetic operator precedence. Appendix A describes the precedence of every C# operator, which is important to understand in complicated expressions. For example, in Appendix A you can see that the arithmetic and relational operators have higher precedence than && and ||.

 Watch the video *Combining AND and OR Operations*.

TWO TRUTHS & A LIE

Using Compound Expressions in if Statements

1. If a is true and b and c are false, then the value of b && c || a is true.
2. If d is true and e and f are false, then the value of e || d && f is true.
3. If g is true and h and i are false, then the value of g || h && i is true.

The false statement is #2. If d is true and e and f are false, then the value of e || d && f is false. Because you evaluate && before ||, first d && f is evaluated and found to be false, then e || false is evaluated and found to be false.

Using Compound Expressions in if Statements

 You Do It

Using AND and OR Logic

In the next steps, you create an interactive program that allows you to test AND and OR logic for yourself. The program decides whether a delivery charge applies to a shipment. If the customer lives in Zone 1 or Zone 2, then shipping is free, as long as the order contains fewer than 10 boxes. If the customer lives in another zone or if the order is too large, then a delivery charge applies.

1. Open a new file named **DemoORAndAND**, and then enter the first few lines of the program. Define constants for ZONE1, ZONE2, and the LOW_QUANTITY limit as well as variables to hold the customer's input strings, which will be converted to the zone and number of boxes in the shipment.

```
using System;
using static System.Console;
class DemoORAndAND
{
   static void Main()
   {
      const int ZONE1 = 1, ZONE2 = 2;
      const int LOW_QUANTITY = 10;
      string inputString;
      int quantity;
      int deliveryZone;
```

2. Enter statements that describe the delivery charge criteria to the user and accept keyboard values for the customer's delivery zone and shipment size.

```
WriteLine("Delivery is free for zone {0} or {1}",
   ZONE1, ZONE2);
WriteLine("when the number of boxes is less than {0}",
   LOW_QUANTITY);
WriteLine("Enter delivery zone ");
inputString = ReadLine();
deliveryZone = Convert.ToInt32(inputString);
WriteLine("Enter the number of boxes in the shipment");
inputString = ReadLine();
quantity = Convert.ToInt32(inputString);
```

(continues)

(continued)

3. Write a compound `if` statement that tests whether the customer lives in Zone 1 or 2 and has a shipment consisting of fewer than 10 boxes. Notice that the first two comparisons joined with the `||` operator are contained in their own set of nested parentheses.

   ```
   if((deliveryZone == ZONE1 || deliveryZone == ZONE2) &&
      quantity < LOW_QUANTITY)
         WriteLine("Delivery is free");
   else
      WriteLine("A delivery charge applies");
   ```

4. Add closing curly braces for the `Main()` method and for the class, and save the program. Compile and execute the program. Enter values for the zone and shipment size. Figure 4-19 shows the output.

   ```
   Delivery is free for zone 1 or 2
   when the number of boxes is less than 10
   Enter delivery zone
   1
   Enter the number of boxes in the shipment
   20
   A delivery charge applies
   ```

   Figure 4-19 Sample execution of DemoORAndAND program

5. To demonstrate the importance of the nested parentheses in the `if` statement, remove the inner set of parentheses that surround the expression `deliveryZone == ZONE1 || deliveryZone == ZONE2` in the `Main()` method. Save the new version of the program, and compile it. When you execute this version of the program, the output indicates that any delivery to `ZONE1` is free, but it should not be. The way the `if` statement is currently constructed, as soon as `deliveryZone == zone1` is `true`, the rest of the Boolean expression is not even evaluated. Reinstate the parentheses, and then save and compile the program. Execute it, and confirm that the output is again correct.

Making Decisions Using the `switch` Statement

By nesting a series of `if` and `else` statements, you can choose from any number of alternatives. For example, suppose that you want to display different strings based on a student's class year. Figure 4-20 shows the logic using nested `if` statements. The program segment tests the `year` variable four times and executes one of four statements, or displays an error message.

```
if(year == 1)
   WriteLine("Freshman");
else
   if(year == 2)
      WriteLine("Sophomore");
   else
      if(year == 3)
         WriteLine("Junior");
      else
         if(year == 4)
            WriteLine("Senior");
         else
            WriteLine("Invalid year");
```

Figure 4-20 Executing multiple alternatives using a series of `if` statements

An alternative to the series of nested `if` statements in Figure 4-20 is to use the `switch` structure (see Figure 4-21). The **switch structure** tests a single variable against a series of exact matches. The `switch` structure is sometimes called the *case structure* or the *switch-case structure*. The `switch` structure in Figure 4-21 is easier to read and interpret than the series of nested `if` statements in Figure 4-20. The `if` statements would become harder to read if additional choices were required and if multiple statements had to execute in each case. These additional choices and statements might also increase the potential to make mistakes.

```
switch(year)
{
   case 1:
      WriteLine("Freshman");
      break;
   case 2:
      WriteLine("Sophomore");
      break;
   case 3:
      WriteLine("Junior");
      break;
   case 4:
      WriteLine("Senior");
      break;
   default:
      WriteLine("Invalid year");
      break;
}
```

Figure 4-21 Executing multiple alternatives using a switch statement

The switch structure uses four new keywords:

- The keyword switch starts the structure and is followed immediately by a test expression (called the switch *expression*) enclosed in parentheses.

- The keyword case is followed by one of the possible values that might equal the switch expression. A colon follows the value. The entire expression—for example, case 1:—is a case label. A **case label** identifies a course of action in a switch structure. Most switch structures contain several case labels. The value that follows case is the **governing type** of the switch statement. Prior to C# 7.0, there were restrictions on the governing type in a switch statement, but with the newest version, the governing type can be any data type.

- The keyword break usually terminates a switch structure at the end of each case. Although other statements can end a case, break is the most commonly used.

- The keyword default optionally is used prior to any action that should occur if the test expression does not match any case.

 Instead of break, you can use a return statement or a throw statement to end a case. You learn about return statements in the chapter "Introduction to Methods" and throw statements in the chapter "Exception Handling."

Making Decisions Using the `switch` Statement

The `switch` structure shown in Figure 4-21 begins by evaluating the `year` variable. If `year` is equal to any `case` label value, then the output statement for that case executes. The `break` statements that follow each output statement cause a bypass of other cases. If `year` does not contain the same value as any of the `case` label expressions, then the `default` statement or statements execute.

You are not required to list the `case` label values in ascending order, as shown in Figure 4-21, but doing so can make the statement easier for a reader to follow. You can even list the `default` case first, although usually it is listed last. You receive a compiler error if two or more `case` label values are the same in a `switch` statement.

In C#, an error occurs if you reach the end point of the statement list of a `case` section. For example, the following code is not allowed because when the `year` value is 1, *Freshman* is displayed, and the code reaches the end of the `case`. The problem could be fixed by inserting a `break` statement before `case 2`.

```
switch(year)
{
   case 1:
      WriteLine("Freshman");
   case 2:
      WriteLine("Sophomore");
      break;
}
```

Dont' Do It
This code is invalid because the end of the case is reached after *Freshman* is displayed.

Not allowing code to reach the end of a `case` is known as the "no fall-through rule." In several other programming languages, such as Java and C++, if you write a `case` without a `break` statement, the subsequent `cases` execute until a `break` is encountered. For example, in some languages, with the code above, both *Freshman* and *Sophomore* would be displayed when `year` is 1. However, falling through to the next `case` is not allowed in C#.

A `switch` structure does not need to contain a `default` case. If the test expression in a `switch` does not match any of the `case` label values, and there is no `default` value, then the program simply continues with the next executable statement. However, it is good programming practice to include a `default` label in a `switch` structure; that way, you provide for actions when your data does not match any case.

In C#, it is legal for a `case` to contain no list of statements. This feature allows you to use multiple labels to govern a list of actions. For example, in the code in Figure 4-22, *Upperclass* is displayed whether the `year` value is 3 or 4.

```
switch(year)
{
   case 1:
      WriteLine("Freshman");
      break;
   case 2:
      WriteLine("Sophomore");
      break;
   case 3:                        ┐ Cases 3 and 4 are
   case 4:                        ┘ both "Upperclass".
      WriteLine("Upperclass");
      break;
   default:
      WriteLine("Invalidyear");
      break;
}
```

Figure 4-22   Example `switch` structure using multiple labels to execute a single statement block

Using a `switch` structure is never required; you can always achieve the same results with `if` statements. The `switch` statement is not as flexible as the `if` statement because you can test only one variable, and it must be tested for equality. The `switch` structure is simply a convenience you can use when there are several alternative courses of action depending on a match with a variable. Additionally, it makes sense to use a `switch` only when there are a reasonable number of specific matching values to be tested. For example, if every sale amount from $1 to $500 requires a 5 percent commission, it is not reasonable to test every possible dollar amount using the following code:

```
switch(saleAmount)
{
   case 1:
   case 2:
   case 3:
   // ...and so on for several hundred more cases
      commRate = .05;
   break;
```

With 500 different dollar values resulting in the same commission, one test—`if(saleAmount <= 500)`—is far more reasonable than listing 500 separate cases.

Using an Enumeration with a `switch` Statement

Using an enumeration with a `switch` structure can often be convenient. Recall from Chapter 2 that an enumeration allows you to apply values to a list of constants. For example, Figure 4-23 shows a program that uses an enumeration to represent major courses of study at a college. In the enumeration list in Figure 4-23, ACCOUNTING is assigned 1, so the other values in the list are 2, 3, 4, and 5 in order. Suppose that students who are accounting, CIS, or marketing majors

Making Decisions Using the switch Statement

are in the business division of the college, and English and math majors are in the humanities division. The program shows how the enumeration values can be used in a `switch` structure. In the program, the user enters an integer. Next, in the shaded `switch` control statement, the input integer is cast to an enumeration value. Then, enumeration values become the governing types for each case. For someone reading the code, the purposes of `enum` values such as ACCOUNTING and CIS are clearer than their integer equivalents would be. Figure 4-24 shows a typical execution of the program.

```csharp
using System;
using static System.Console;
class DivisionBasedOnMajor
{
   enum Major
   {
      ACCOUNTING = 1, CIS, ENGLISH, MATH, MARKETING
   }
   static void Main()
   {
      int major;
      string message;
      Write("Enter major code >> ");
      major = Convert.ToInt32(ReadLine());
      switch((Major)major)
      {
         case Major.ACCOUNTING:
         case Major.CIS:
         case Major.MARKETING:
            message = "Major is in the business division";
            break;
         case Major.ENGLISH:
         case Major.MATH:
            message = "Major is in the humanities division";
            break;
         default:
            message = "Department number is invalid";
            break;
      }
      WriteLine(message);
   }
}
```

Figure 4-23 The DivisionBasedOnMajor class

```
Enter major code >> 2
Major is in the business division
```

Figure 4-24 Typical execution of the DivisionBasedOnMajor program

CHAPTER 4 Making Decisions

> **TWO TRUTHS & A LIE**
>
> **Making Decisions Using the `switch` Statement**
>
> 1. In a `switch` statement, the keyword `case` is followed by one of the possible values that might equal the `switch` expression, and a colon follows the value.
> 2. The keyword `break` always terminates a `switch` structure at the end of each case.
> 3. A `switch` statement does not need to contain a `default` case.
>
> The false statement is #2. The keyword `break` typically is used to terminate a `switch` structure at the end of each case, but other statements can end a case.

Using the Conditional Operator

The **conditional operator** is used as an abbreviated version of the `if-else` statement; it requires three expressions separated with a question mark and a colon. Like the `switch` structure, using the conditional operator is never required. Rather, it is simply a convenient shortcut, especially when you want to use the result immediately as an expression. The syntax of the conditional operator is:

`testExpression ? trueResult : falseResult;`

Unary operators use one operand; binary operators use two. The conditional operator `?:` is **ternary** because it requires three arguments: a test expression and `true` and `false` result expressions. The conditional operator is the only ternary operator in C#.

The first expression, `testExpression`, is evaluated as `true` or `false`. If it is `true`, then the entire conditional expression takes on the value of the expression before the colon (`trueResult`). If the value of the `testExpression` is `false`, then the entire expression takes on the value of the expression following the colon (`falseResult`). For example, consider the following statement:

`biggerNum = (a > b) ? a : b;`

This statement evaluates `a > b`. If `a` is greater than `b`, then the entire conditional expression takes the value of `a`, which then is assigned to `biggerNum`. If `a` is not greater than `b`, then the expression assumes the value of `b`, and `b` is assigned to `biggerNum`.

The conditional operator is most often applied when you want to use the result as an expression without creating an intermediate variable. For example, a conditional operator can be used directly in an output statement using either of the following formats:

```
WriteLine((testScore >= 60) ? "Pass" : "Fail");
WriteLine($"{(testScore >= 60 ? "Pass" : "Fail")}");
```

In these examples, no variable was created to hold *Pass* or *Fail*. Instead one of the strings was output directly based on the `testScore` comparison. The second example used string interpolation, which you learned about in Chapter 2. This format makes it easy to include other variables in the same string. For example:

`WriteLine($"{name}'s status is {(testScore >= 60 ? "Pass" : "Fail"}");`

If `name` is *Sally* and `testScore` is 62, the output would be *Sally's status is Pass*.

Conditional expressions can be more difficult to read than `if-else` statements, but they can be used in places where `if-else` statements cannot, such as in method calls.

TWO TRUTHS & A LIE

Using the Conditional Operator

1. If j = 2 and k = 3, then the value of the following expression is 2:

   `int m = j < k ? j : k;`

2. If j = 2 and k = 3, then the value of the following expression is 4:

   `int n = j < k ? j + j : k + k;`

3. If j = 2 and k = 3, then the value of the following expression is 5:

   `int p = j > k ? j + k : j * k;`

The false statement is #3. If j = 2 and k = 3, then the value of the expression j > k is false. Therefore 6 (j * k) is assigned to p.

Using the NOT Operator

You use the **NOT operator**, which is written as an exclamation point (!), to negate the result of any Boolean expression. Any expression that evaluates as `true` becomes `false` when preceded by the ! operator, and any `false` expression preceded by the ! operator becomes `true`.

In Chapter 2 you learned that an exclamation point and equal sign together form the "not equal to" operator. The != operator is a binary operator; it compares two operands. The ! operator is a unary operator; it reverses the meaning of a single Boolean expression.

For example, suppose that a monthly car insurance premium is $200 if the driver is younger than age 26 and $125 if the driver is age 26 or older. Each of the following `if` statements (which have been placed on single lines for convenience) correctly assigns the premium values:

```
if(age < 26) premium = 200; else premium = 125;
if(!(age < 26)) premium = 125; else premium = 200;
if(age >= 26) premium = 125; else premium = 200;
if(!(age>= 26)) premium = 200; else premium = 125;
```

CHAPTER 4 Making Decisions

The statements with the ! operator are somewhat more difficult to read, particularly because they require the double set of parentheses, but the result is the same in each case. Using the ! operator is clearer when the value of a Boolean variable is tested. For example, a variable initialized as `bool oldEnough = (age >= 25);` can become part of the relatively easy-to-read expression `if(!oldEnough)`....

The ! operator has higher precedence than the && and || operators. For example, suppose that you have declared two Boolean variables named `ageOverMinimum` and `ticketsUnderMinimum`. The following expressions are evaluated in the same way:

```
ageOverMinimum && !ticketsUnderMinimum
ageOverMinimum && (!ticketsUnderMinimum)
```

Augustus de Morgan was a 19th-century mathematician who originally observed the following:

- !(a && b) is equivalent to !a || !b
- !(a || b) is equivalent to !(a && b)

TWO TRUTHS & A LIE

Using the NOT Operator

1. Assume that p, q, and r are all Boolean variables that have been assigned the value true. After the following statement executes, the value of p is still true.

   `p = !q || r;`

2. Assume that p, q, and r are all Boolean variables that have been assigned the value true. After the following statement executes, the value of p is still true.

   `p = !(!q && !r);`

3. Assume that p, q and r are all Boolean variables that have been assigned the value true. After the following statement executes, the value of p is still true.

   `p = !(q || !r);`

The false statement is #3. If p, q, and r are all Boolean variables that have been assigned the value true, then after p = !(q || !r); executes, the value of p is false. First q is evaluated as true, so the entire expression within the parentheses is true. The leading NOT operator reverses that result to false and assigns it to p.

Avoiding Common Errors When Making Decisions

New programmers frequently make errors when they first learn to make decisions. As you have seen, the most frequent errors include the following:

- Using the assignment operator (=) instead of the comparison operator (==) when testing for equality
- Inserting a semicolon after the Boolean expression in an `if` statement instead of using it after the entire statement is completed
- Failing to block a set of statements with curly braces when several statements depend on the `if` or the `else` statement
- Failing to include a complete Boolean expression on each side of an **&&** or **||** operator in an `if` statement

In this section, you will learn to avoid other types of errors with `if` statements. Programmers often make errors at the following times:

- When performing a range check incorrectly or inefficiently
- When using the wrong operator
- When using ! incorrectly

Performing Accurate and Efficient Range Checks

When new programmers must make a range check, they often introduce incorrect or inefficient code into their programs. A **range check** is a series of `if` statements that determine whether a value falls within a specified range. Consider a situation in which salespeople can receive one of three possible commission rates based on an integer named `saleAmount`. For example, a sale totaling $1000 or more earns the salesperson an 8 percent commission, a sale totaling $500 through $999 earns 6 percent of the sale amount, and any sale totaling $499 or less earns 5 percent. Using three separate `if` statements to test single Boolean expressions might result in some incorrect commission assignments. For example, examine the following code:

```
if(saleAmount >= 1000)
    commissionRate = 0.08;
if(saleAmount >= 500)
    commissionRate = 0.06;
if(saleAmount <= 499)
    commissionRate = 0.05;
```

Don't Do It
Although it was not the programmer's intention, both of the first two if statements are true for any `saleAmount` greater than or equal to 1000.

Using this code, if `saleAmount` is $5000, the first `if` statement executes. The Boolean expression (`saleAmount >= 1000`) evaluates as `true`, and 0.08 is correctly assigned to `commissionRate`. However, the next `if` expression, (`saleAmount >= 500`), also evaluates as `true`, so the `commissionRate`, which was 0.08, is incorrectly reset to 0.06.

A partial solution to this problem is to add an `else` clause to the statement:

```
if(saleAmount >= 1000)
    commissionRate = 0.08;
else if(saleAmount >= 500)
    commissionRate = 0.06;
else if(saleAmount <= 499)
    commissionRate = 0.05;
```

Don't Do It
If the logic reaches this point, the expression must be true, so it is a waste of time to test this condition.

The last two logical tests in this code are sometimes called `else-if` statements because each `else` and its subsequent `if` are placed on the same line. When the `else-if` format is used to test multiple cases, programmers frequently forego the traditional indentation and align each `else-if` with the others.

With this code, when `saleAmount` is $5000, the expression (`saleAmount >= 1000`) is `true` and `commissionRate` becomes 0.08; then the entire `if` structure ends. When `saleAmount` is not greater than or equal to $1000 (for example, $800), the first `if` expression is `false` and the `else` statement executes and correctly sets `commissionRate` to 0.06.

This version of the code works, but it is somewhat inefficient because it executes as follows:

- When `saleAmount` is at least $1000, the first Boolean test is `true`, so `commissionRate` is assigned .08 and the `if` structure ends.

- When `saleAmount` is less than $1000 but at least $500, the first Boolean test is `false`, but the second one is `true`, so `commissionRate` is assigned .06 and the `if` structure ends.

- The only `saleAmount` values that reach the third Boolean test are less than $500, so the next Boolean test, `if(saleAmount <= 499)`, is always `true`. When an expression is always `true`, there is no need to evaluate it. In other words, if `saleAmount` is not at least $1000 and is also not at least $500, it must by default be less than or equal to $499.

The improved code is as follows:

```
if(saleAmount >= 1000)
    commissionRate = 0.08;
else if(saleAmount >= 500)
    commissionRate = 0.06;
else
    commissionRate = 0.05;
```

In other words, because this example uses three commission rates, two boundaries should be checked. If there were four rates, there would be three boundaries to check, and so on.

Within a nested `if-else`, processing is most efficient when the first question asked is the one that is most likely to be `true`. In other words, if you know that a large number of `saleAmount` values are greater than $1000, compare `saleAmount` to that value first. That way, the logic bypasses the rest of the decisions. If, however, you know that most `saleAmounts` are small, processing is most efficient when the first decision is `if(saleAmount < 500)`.

Using && and || Appropriately

Beginning programmers often use the **&&** operator when they mean to use **||**, and often use **||** when they should use **&&**. Part of the problem lies in the way we use the English language. For example, your boss might request, "Display an error message when an employee's hourly pay rate is less than $5.65 and when an employee's hourly pay rate is greater than $60." Because your boss used the word *and* in the request, you might be tempted to write a program statement like the following:

```
if(payRate < 5.65 && payRate > 60)
   WriteLine("Error in pay rate");
```
Don't Do It
This expression can never be true.

However, as a single variable, no **payRate** value can ever be both less than 5.65 and greater than 60 at the same time, so the output statement can never execute, no matter what value **payRate** has. In this case, you must write the following statement to display the error message under the correct circumstances:

```
if(payRate < 5.65 || payRate > 60)
   WriteLine("Error in pay rate");
```

Similarly, your boss might request, "Output the names of those employees in departments 1 and 2." Because the boss used the word *and* in the request, you might be tempted to write the following:

```
if(department == 1 && department == 2)
   WriteLine("Name is: {0}", name);
```
Don't Do It
This expression can never be true.

However, the variable **department** can never contain both a 1 and a 2 at the same time, so no employee name will ever be output, no matter what department the employee is in.

The correct statement is:

```
if(department == 1 || department == 2)
   WriteLine("Name is: {0}", name);
```

Using the ! Operator Correctly

Whenever you use negatives, it is easy to make logical mistakes. For example, suppose that your boss says, "Make sure that if the sales code is not *A* or *B*, the customer gets a 10 percent discount." You might be tempted to code the following:

```
if(salesCode != 'A' || salesCode != 'B')
   discount = 0.10;
```
Don't Do it
This expression can never be true.

However, this logic will result in every customer receiving the 10 percent discount because every **salesCode** is either not *A* or not *B*. For example, if **salesCode** is *A*, then it is not *B*. The expression **salesCode != 'A' || salesCode != 'B'** is always **true**. The correct statement is either one of the following:

```
if(salesCode != 'A' && salesCode != 'B')
   discount = 0.10;
```

CHAPTER 4 Making Decisions

```
if(!(salesCode == 'A' || salesCode == 'B'))
   discount = 0.10;
```

In the first example, if `salesCode` is not `'A'` and it also is not `'B'`, then the discount is applied correctly. In the second example, if `salesCode` is `'A'` or `'B'`, the inner Boolean expression is `true`, and the NOT operator (!) changes the evaluation to `false`, not applying the discount for *A* or *B* sales. You also could avoid the confusing negative situation by asking questions in a positive way, as in the following:

```
if(salesCode == 'A' || salesCode == 'B')
   discount = 0;
else
   discount = 0.10;
```

 Watch the video *Avoiding Common Decision Errors*.

TWO TRUTHS & A LIE

Avoiding Common Errors When Making Decisions

1. If you want to display *OK* when `userEntry` is 12 and when it is 13, then the following is a usable C# statement:

   ```
   if(userEntry == 12 && userEntry == 13)
      WriteLine("OK");
   ```

2. If you want to display *OK* when `userEntry` is 20 or when `highestScore` is at least 70, then the following is a usable C# statement:

   ```
   if(userEntry == 20 || highestScore >= 70)
      WriteLine("OK");
   ```

3. If you want to display *OK* when `userEntry` is anything other than 99 or 100, then the following is a usable C# statement:

   ```
   if(userEntry != 99 && userEntry != 100)
      WriteLine("OK");
   ```

The false statement is #1. If you want to display *OK* when `userEntry` is 12 and when it is 13, then you want to display it when it is either 12 or 13 because it cannot be both simultaneously. The expression `userEntry == 12 && userEntry == 13` can never be true. The correct Boolean expression is `userEntry == 12 || userEntry == 13`.

Decision-Making Issues in GUI Programs

Making a decision within a method in a GUI application is no different from making one in a console application; you can use if, if...else, and switch statements in the same ways. For example, Figure 4-25 shows a GUI Form that determines a movie patron discount as described in a program earlier in this chapter. Patrons who are 12 or younger or 65 or older and are seeing a G-rated movie receive a discount, and any other combination pays full price. Figure 4-26 contains the Click() method that makes the discount determination based on age and rating after a user clicks the *Discount?* button. The Boolean expression tested in the if statement in this method is identical to the one in the console version of the program in Figure 4-16.

Figure 4-25 The Movie Discount Form

```
private void DiscountButton_Click(object sender,
   EventArgs e)
{
   int age;
   char rating;
   const int CHILD_AGE = 12;
   const int SENIOR_AGE = 65;
   age = Convert.ToInt32(textBox1.Text);
   rating = Convert.ToChar(textBox2.Text);
   outputLabel.Text = String.Format
      ("When age is {0} and rating is {1}", age, rating);
   if ((age <= CHILD_AGE || age >= SENIOR_AGE) && rating == 'G')
      outputLabel.Text += "\nDiscount applies";
   else
      outputLabel.Text += "\nFull price";
}
```

Figure 4-26 The DiscountButton_Click() method for the Form in Figure 4-25

CHAPTER 4 Making Decisions

Event-driven programs often require fewer coded decisions than console applications. That's because in event-driven programs, some events are determined by the user's actions when the program is running (also called **at runtime**), rather than by the programmer's coding beforehand. You might say that in many situations, a console-based application must act, but an event-driven application has to *react*.

Suppose that you want to write a program in which the user must select whether to receive instructions in English or Spanish. In a console application, you would issue a prompt such as the following:

Which language do you prefer? Enter 1 for English or 2 for Spanish >>

The program would accept the user's entry, make a decision about it, and take appropriate action. However, in a GUI application, you are more likely to place controls on a `Form` to get a user's response. For example, you might use two `Button`s—one for English and one for Spanish. The user clicks a `Button`, and an appropriate method executes. No decision is written in the program because a different event is fired from each `Button`, causing execution of a different `Click()` method. The interactive environment decides which method is called, so the programmer does not have to code a decision. (Of course, you might alternately place a `TextBox` on a `Form` and ask a user to enter a 1 or a 2. In that case, the decision-making process would be identical to that in the console-based program.)

An additional benefit to having the user click a button to select an option is that the user cannot enter an invalid value. For example, if the user enters a letter in response to a prompt for an integer, the program will fail unless you write additional code to handle the mistake. However, if the user has a limited selection of buttons to click, no invalid entry can be made.

TWO TRUTHS & A LIE

Decision-Making Issues in GUI Programs

1. Event-driven programs can contain `if`, `if...else`, and `switch` statements.
2. Event-driven programs often require fewer coded decisions than console applications.
3. Event-driven programs usually contain more coded decisions than corresponding console-based applications.

The false statement is #3. Event-driven programs often require fewer coded decisions because user actions, such as clicking a button, are often used to trigger different methods.

Decision-Making Issues in GUI Programs

 You Do It

Creating a GUI Application That Uses an Enumeration and a switch Structure

In these steps, you create a GUI application for the Chatterbox Diner that allows a user to enter a day and see the special meal offered that day. Creating the program provides experience using an enumeration in a switch structure.

1. Open a new project in Visual Studio, and name it **DailySpecial**.
2. Design a Form like the one in Figure 4-27 that prompts the user for a day number and allows the user to enter it in a TextBox. Name the TextBox **dayBox** and the Button **specialButton**.

Figure 4-27 The Daily Special form

3. Below the Button, add a Label named **outputLabel** and delete its text.
4. Double-click **specialButton** to create a specialButton_Click() method shell. Rename the method to start with an uppercase letter:

   SpecialButton_Click()

(continues)

(continued)

5. Above the method, add an enumeration for the days of the week as follows:

   ```
   enum Day
   {
       SUNDAY = 1, MONDAY, TUESDAY, WEDNESDAY,
           THURSDAY, FRIDAY, SATURDAY
   }
   ```

6. Within the method, declare an integer and accept a value from the **TextBox**, and then declare a **string** to hold the daily special.

   ```
   int day = Convert.ToInt32(dayBox.Text);
   string special;
   ```

7. Add a **switch** structure that lists the daily specials as follows:

   ```
   switch ((Day)day)
   {
       case Day.SUNDAY:
           special = "fried chicken";
           break;
       case Day.MONDAY:
           special = "Sorry - closed";
           break;
       case Day.TUESDAY:
       case Day.WEDNESDAY:
       case Day.THURSDAY:
           special = "meat loaf";
           break;
       case Day.FRIDAY:
           special = "fish fry";
           break;
       case Day.SATURDAY:
           special = "liver and onions";
           break;
       default:
           special = "Invalid day";
           break;
   }
   ```

8. Following the completed **case** structure, assign the result to the **Text** property of **outputLabel**:

   ```
   outputLabel.Text = "Today's special is " + special;
   ```

9. Save, compile, and execute the application. The appropriate special is displayed for each day of the week.

Chapter Summary

- A flowchart is a pictorial tool that helps you understand a program's logic. A decision structure is one that involves choosing between alternative courses of action based on some value within a program.

- The `if` statement makes a single-alternative decision using the keyword `if`, followed by parentheses that contain a Boolean expression. When the expression is true, the statement body executes. The body can be a single statement or a block of statements.

- When you make a dual-alternative decision, you can use an `if-else` statement. You can block multiple statements after an `else` so they all execute when the evaluated expression is `false`.

- The conditional AND operator (`&&`) takes action when two operand Boolean expressions are both `true`. The conditional OR operator (`||`) takes action when at least one of two operand Boolean expressions is `true`. When `&&` and `||` operators are combined within the same Boolean expression without parentheses, the `&&` operators take precedence, meaning their Boolean values are evaluated first.

- The `switch` statement tests a single variable against a series of exact matches.

- The conditional operator is used as an abbreviated version of the `if-else` statement. It requires three expressions separated with a question mark and a colon.

- The NOT operator, which is written as an exclamation point (`!`), negates the result of any Boolean expression.

- Common errors when making decisions include using the assignment operator instead of the comparison operator, inserting a semicolon after the Boolean expression in an `if` statement, failing to block a set of statements when they should be blocked, and performing a range check incorrectly or inefficiently.

- Making a decision within a method in a GUI application is no different from making one in a console application; you can use `if`, `if...else`, and `switch` statements in the same ways. However, event-driven programs often require fewer coded decisions than console applications because some events are determined by the user's actions when the program is running, rather than by the programmer's coding beforehand.

Key Terms

Pseudocode is a tool that helps programmers plan a program's logic by writing plain English statements.

A **flowchart** is a tool that helps programmers plan a program's logic by writing program steps in diagram form, as a series of shapes connected by arrows.

A **sequence structure** is a unit of program logic in which one step follows another unconditionally.

A **decision structure** is a unit of program logic that involves choosing between alternative courses of action based on some value.

An **if statement** is used to make a single-alternative decision.

A **block** is a collection of one or more statements contained within a pair of curly braces.

A **control statement** is the part of a structure that determines whether the subsequent block of statements executes.

A **nested if** statement is one in which one decision structure is contained within another.

Dual-alternative decisions have two possible outcomes.

An **if-else statement** performs a dual-alternative decision.

The **conditional AND operator** (or simply the **AND operator**) determines whether two expressions are both `true`; it is written using two ampersands (&&).

Truth tables are diagrams used in mathematics and logic to help describe the truth of an entire expression based on the truth of its parts.

Short-circuit evaluation is the C# feature in which parts of an AND or OR expression are evaluated only as far as necessary to determine whether the entire expression is `true` or `false`.

The **conditional OR operator** (or simply the **OR operator**) determines whether at least one of two conditions is **true**; it is written using two pipes (||).

The **Boolean logical AND operator** determines whether two expressions are both `true`; it is written using a single ampersand (&), but, unlike the conditional AND operator, it does not use short-circuit evaluation.

The **Boolean logical inclusive OR operator** determines whether at least one of two conditions is `true`; it is written using a single pipe (|), but, unlike the conditional OR operator, it does not use short-circuit evaluation.

A **side effect** is an unintended consequence.

Bitwise operators are used to manipulate the individual bits of values.

The **switch structure** tests a single variable against a series of exact matches.

A **case label** identifies a course of action in a `switch` structure.

The **governing type** of a `switch` statement is established by the `switch` expression and can be any data type.

The **conditional operator** is used as an abbreviated version of the `if-else` statement; it requires three expressions separated by a question mark and a colon.

A **ternary** operator requires three arguments.

The **NOT operator** (!) negates the result of any Boolean expression.

A **range check** is a series of if statements that determine whether a value falls within a specified range.

At runtime is a phrase that means *during the time a program is running*.

Review Questions

1. What is the output of the following code segment?

    ```
    int a = 3, b = 4;
    if(a == b)
       Write("X");
       WriteLine("Y");
    ```

    a. X
    b. Y
    c. XY
    d. nothing

2. What is the output of the following code segment?

    ```
    int a = 3, b = 4;
    if(a < b)
    {
       Write("Y");
       WriteLine("Z");
    }
    ```

    a. Y
    b. Z
    c. YZ
    d. nothing

3. What is the output of the following code segment?

    ```
    int a = 3, b = 4;
    if(a > b)
       Write("Up");
    else
       WriteLine("Down");
    ```

    a. Up
    b. Down
    c. UpDown
    d. nothing

4. If the following code segment compiles correctly, what do you know about the variable x?

    ```
    if(x) WriteLine("OK");
    ```

    a. x is an integer variable.
    b. x is a Boolean variable.
    c. x is greater than 0.
    d. none of these

CHAPTER 4　Making Decisions

5. What is the output of the following code segment?

   ```
   int c = 6, d = 12;
   if(c > d);
       Write("Green");
       WriteLine("Yellow");
   ```

   a. Green
   b. Yellow
   c. GreenYellow
   d. nothing

6. What is the output of the following code segment?

   ```
   int c = 6, d = 12;
   if(c < d)
       if(c > 8)
           Write("Blue");
       else
           Write("Red");
   else
       Write("Green");
   ```

   a. Blue
   b. Red
   c. Green
   d. nothing

7. What is the output of the following code segment?

   ```
   int e = 5, f = 10;
   if(e < f && f < 0)
       Write("Red");
   else
       Write("Orange");
   ```

   a. Red
   b. Orange
   c. RedOrange
   d. nothing

8. What is the output of the following code segment?

   ```
   int e = 5, f = 10;
   if(e < f || f < 0)
       Write("Purple");
   else
       Write("Gold");
   ```

   a. Purple
   b. Gold
   c. PurpleGold
   d. nothing

Review Questions

9. Which of the following expressions is equivalent to the following code segment?

   ```
   if(g > h)
      if(g < k)
         Write("Brown");
   ```

   a. `if(g > h && g < k) Write("Brown");`
   b. `if(g > h && < k) Write("Brown");`
   c. `if(g > h || g < k) Write("Brown");`
   d. two of these

10. Which of the following expressions assigns true to a Boolean variable named isIDValid when idNumber is both greater than 1000 and less than or equal to 9999, or else is equal to 123456?

    a. `isIDValid = (idNumber > 1000 && idNumber <= 9999 && idNumber == 123456)`
    b. `isIDValid = (idNumber > 1000 && idNumber <= 9999 || idNumber == 123456)`
    c. `isIDValid = ((idNumber > 1000 && idNumber <= 9999) || idNumber == 123456)`
    d. two of these

11. Which of the following expressions is equivalent to a || b && c || d?

    a. `a && b || c && d`
    b. `(a || b) && (c || d)`
    c. `a || (b && c) || d`
    d. two of these

12. How many case labels would a switch statement require to be equivalent to the following if statement?

    ```
    if(v == 1)
       WriteLine("one");
    else
       WriteLine("two");
    ```

    a. zero
    b. one
    c. two
    d. impossible to tell

13. In C#, falling through a switch case is most often prevented by using the _____ statement.

    a. break
    b. default
    c. case
    d. end

CHAPTER 4 Making Decisions

14. If the test expression in a `switch` does not match any of the `case` values, and there is no `default` value, then _____.

    a. a compiler error occurs

    b. a runtime error occurs

    c. the program continues with the next executable statement

    d. the expression is incremented and the `case` values are tested again

15. Which of the following is equivalent to the following statement?

    ```
    if(m == 0)
        d = 0;
    else
        d = 1;
    ```

    a. `d = (m == 0) : d = 0, d = 1;`

    b. `m ? (d = 0); (d = 1);`

    c. `m == 0; d = 0; d = 1?`

    d. `d = (m == 0) ? 0 : 1;`

16. Which of the following C# expressions is equivalent to `a < b && b < c`?

    a. `c > b > a`

    b. `a < b && c >= b`

    c. `!(b <= a) && b < c`

    d. two of these

17. Which of the following C# expressions means, "If `itemNumber` is not 8 or 9, add TAX to `price`"?

    a. `if(itemNumber != 8 || itemNumber != 9)`
       `price = price + TAX;`

    b. `if(itemNumber != 8 && itemNumber != 9)`
       `price = price + TAX;`

    c. `if(itemNumber != 8 && != 9)`
       `price = price + TAX;`

    d. two of these

18. Which of the following C# expressions means, "If `itemNumber` is 1 or 2 and `quantity` is 12 or more, add TAX to `price`"?

    a. `if(itemNumber = 1 || itemNumber = 2 && quantity >=12)`
       `price = price + TAX;`

    b. `if(itemNumber == 1 || itemNumber == 2 || quantity >=12)`
       `price = price + TAX;`

    c. `if(itemNumber == 1 && itemNumber == 2 && quantity >=12)`
       `price = price + TAX;`

    d. none of these

19. Which of the following C# expressions means, "If itemNumber is 5 and zone is 1 or 3, add TAX to price"?

    a. if(itemNumber == 5 && zone == 1 || zone == 3)
          price = price + TAX;
    b. if(itemNumber == 5 && (zone == 1 || zone == 3))
          price = price + TAX;
    c. if(itemNumber == 5 && (zone ==1 || 3))
          price = price + TAX;
    d. two of these

20. Which of the following C# expressions results in TAX being added to price if the integer itemNumber is not 100?

    a. if(itemNumber != 100)
          price = price + TAX;
    b. if(!(itemNumber == 100))
          price = price + TAX;
    c. if(itemNumber <100 || itemNumber > 100)
          price = price + TAX;
    d. all of these

Exercises

Programming Exercises

1. Write a program named **CheckCredit** that prompts users to enter a purchase price for an item. If the value entered is greater than a credit limit of $8,000, display an error message; otherwise, display *Approved*.

2. Write a program named **Twitter** that accepts a user's message and determines whether it is short enough for a social networking service that does not accept messages of more than 140 characters.

3. Write a program named **Admission** for a college's admissions office. The user enters a numeric high school grade point average (for example, 3.2) and an admission test score. Display the message *Accept* if the student meets either of the following requirements:

    - A grade point average of 3.0 or higher, and an admission test score of at least 60
    - A grade point average of less than 3.0, and an admission test score of at least 80
    - If the student does not meet either of the qualification criteria, display *Reject*.

4. The Saffir-Simpson Hurricane Scale classifies hurricanes into five categories numbered 1 through 5. Write an application named **Hurricane** that outputs a hurricane's category based on the user's input of the wind speed. Category 5 hurricanes have sustained winds of at least 157 miles per hour. The minimum sustained wind speeds for categories 4 through 1 are 130, 111, 96, and 74 miles per hour, respectively. Any storm with winds of less than 74 miles per hour is not a hurricane.

5. a. Write a program named **CheckMonth** that prompts a user to enter a birth month. If the value entered is greater than 12 or less than 1, display an error message; otherwise, display the valid month with a message such as *3 is a valid month*.

   b. Write a program named **CheckMonth2** that prompts a user to enter a birth month and day. Display an error message if the month is invalid (not 1 through 12) or the day is invalid for the month (for example, not between 1 and 31 for January or between 1 and 29 for February). If the month and day are valid, display them with a message.

6. Account numbers sometimes contain a check digit that is the result of a mathematical calculation. The inclusion of the digit in an account number helps ascertain whether the number is a valid one. Write an application named **CheckDigit** that asks a user to enter a four-digit account number and determines whether it is a valid number. The number is valid if the fourth digit is the remainder when the number represented by the first three digits of the four-digit number is divided by 7. For example, 7770 is valid, because 0 is the remainder when 777 is divided by 7.

> The next problems rely on the generation of a random number. You can create a random number that is at least min but less than max using the following statements:
>
> ```
> Random ranNumberGenerator = new Random();
> int randomNumber;
> randomNumber = ranNumberGenerator.Next(min, max);
> ```

7. Write a program named **GuessingGame** that generates a random number between 1 and 10. (In other words, in the example above, min is 1 and max is 11.) Ask a user to guess the random number, then display the random number and a message indicating whether the user's guess was too high, too low, or correct.

8. In the game Rock Paper Scissors, two players simultaneously choose one of three options: rock, paper, or scissors. If both players choose the same option, then the result is a tie. However, if they choose differently, the winner is determined as follows:

   - Rock beats scissors, because a rock can break a pair of scissors.
   - Scissors beats paper, because scissors can cut paper.
   - Paper beats rock, because a piece of paper can cover a rock.

Create a game in which the computer randomly chooses rock, paper, or scissors. Let the user enter a character, *r*, *p*, or *s*, each representing one of the three choices. Then, determine the winner. Save the application as **RockPaperScissors.cs**.

9. Create a lottery game application named **Lottery**. Generate three random numbers, each between 1 and 4. Allow the user to guess three numbers. Compare each of the user's guesses to the three random numbers, and display a message that includes the user's guess, the randomly determined three-digit number, and the amount of money the user has won as follows:

Matching Numbers	Award ($)
Any one matching	10
Two matching	100
Three matching, not in order	1000
Three matching in exact order	10,000
No matches	0

Make certain that your application accommodates repeating digits. For example, if a user guesses 1, 2, and 3, and the randomly generated digits are 1, 1, and 1, do not give the user credit for three correct guesses—just one.

Debugging Exercises

1. Each of the following files in the Chapter.04 folder of your downloadable student files has syntax and/or logical errors. In each case, determine the problem, and fix the program. After you correct the errors, save each file using the same filename preceded with *Fixed*. For example, save DebugFour1.cs as **FixedDebugFour1.cs**.

    a. DebugFour1.cs
    b. DebugFour2.cs
    c. DebugFour3.cs
    d. DebugFour4.cs

Case Problems

1. In Chapter 2, you created an interactive application named **GreenvilleRevenue**, and in Chapter 3 you created a GUI version of the application named **GreenvilleRevenueGUI**. The programs prompt a user for the number of contestants entered in this year's and last year's Greenville Idol competition, and then they display

the revenue expected for this year's competition if each contestant pays a $25 entrance fee. The programs also display a statement that compares the number of contestants each year. Now, replace that statement with one of the following messages:

- If the competition has more than twice as many contestants as last year, display *The competition is more than twice as big this year!*
- If the competition is bigger than last year's but not more than twice as big, display *The competition is bigger than ever!*
- If the competition is smaller than last year's, display, *A tighter race this year! Come out and cast your vote!*

2. In Chapter 2, you created an interactive application named **MarshallsRevenue**, and in Chapter 3 you created a GUI version of the application named **MarshallsRevenueGUI**. The programs prompt a user for the number of interior and exterior murals scheduled to be painted during the next month by Marshall's Murals. Next, the programs compute the expected revenue for each type of mural when interior murals cost $500 each and exterior murals cost $750 each. The applications also display the total expected revenue and a statement that indicates whether more interior murals are scheduled than exterior ones. Now, modify one or both of the applications to accept a numeric value for the month being scheduled and to modify the pricing as follows:

- Because of uncertain weather conditions, exterior murals cannot be painted in December through February, so change the number of exterior murals to 0 for those months.
- Marshall prefers to paint exterior murals in April, May, September, and October. To encourage business, he charges only $699 for an exterior mural during those months. Murals in other months continue to cost $750.
- Marshall prefers to paint interior murals in July and August, so he charges only $450 for an interior mural during those months. Murals in other months continue to cost $500.

CHAPTER 5

Looping

Upon completion of this chapter, you will be able to:

- ◎ Create loops using the `while` statement
- ◎ Create loops using the `for` statement
- ◎ Create loops using the `do` statement
- ◎ Use nested loops
- ◎ Accumulate totals
- ◎ Understand how to improve loop performance
- ◎ Appreciate looping issues in GUI programs

CHAPTER 5 Looping

In the previous chapter, you learned how computers make decisions by evaluating Boolean expressions. Looping allows a program to repeat tasks based on the value of a Boolean expression. For example, programs that produce thousands of paychecks or invoices rely on the ability to loop to repeat instructions. Likewise, programs that repeatedly prompt users for a valid credit card number or for the correct answer to a tutorial question run more efficiently with loop structures. In this chapter, you will learn to create loops in C# programs. Computer programs seem smart because of their ability to make decisions; looping makes programs seem powerful.

Creating Loops with the `while` Statement

A **loop** is a structure that allows repeated execution of a block of statements. Within a looping structure, a Boolean expression is evaluated. If it is `true`, a block of statements called the **loop body** executes and the Boolean expression is evaluated again. As long as the expression is `true`, the statements in the loop body continue to execute and the loop-controlling Boolean expression continues to be reevaluated. When the Boolean evaluation is `false`, the loop ends. Figure 5-1 shows a diagram of the logic of a loop. One execution of any loop is called an **iteration**.

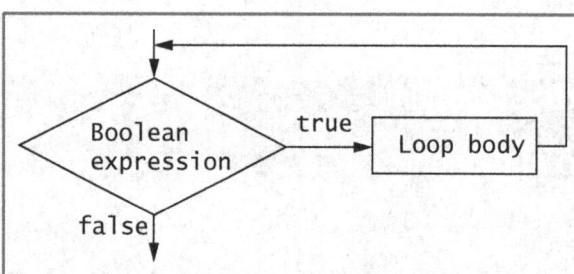

Figure 5-1 Flowchart of a loop structure

You can use a **while loop** to execute a body of statements continuously as long as the loop's test condition continues to be `true`. A `while` loop consists of the following:

- the keyword `while`
- a Boolean expression within parentheses
- the loop body

The evaluated Boolean expression in a `while` statement can be either a single Boolean expression or a compound expression that uses ANDs and ORs. The body can be a single statement or any number of statements surrounded by curly braces.

Creating Loops with the `while` Statement

For example, the following code shows an integer declaration followed by a loop that causes the message *Hello* to display (theoretically) forever because there is no code to end the loop:

```
int number = 1;
while(number > 0)
   WriteLine("Hello");
```

A loop that never ends is called an **infinite loop**. An infinite loop might not actually execute infinitely. All programs run with the help of computer memory and hardware, both of which have finite capacities, so a program with an infinite loop might eventually fail and end. However, any loop that potentially runs forever is called infinite.

Because `number` is set to 1 in the code sample above, when this loop starts, the expression `number > 0` evaluates as `true`, and *Hello* is displayed. The expression `number > 0` evaluates as `true` again, and *Hello* is displayed again. Because the value of `number` is never altered, the loop runs forever, evaluating the same Boolean expression and repeatedly displaying *Hello* as long as computer memory and hardware allow.

Writing an infinite loop is always a bad idea, although even experienced programmers write them by accident. If you ever find yourself in the midst of an infinite loop in a console application, you can break out by holding down the Ctrl key and pressing the C key or the Break (Pause) key. In a GUI program, you can simply close the `Frame` that is hosting the application.

To make a `while` loop end correctly, three separate actions should occur:

- A variable, the **loop control variable**, is initialized (before entering the loop).
- The loop control variable is tested in the `while` expression.
- The body of the loop must take some action that alters the value of the loop control variable (so that the `while` expression eventually evaluates as `false`).

For example, Figure 5-2 shows the logic for a loop that displays *Hello* four times. The variable `number` is initialized to 1, and a constant, `LIMIT`, is initialized to 5. The variable is less than `LIMIT`, and so the loop body executes. The loop body shown in Figure 5-2 contains two statements. The first displays *Hello*, and the second adds 1 to `number`. The next time `number` is evaluated, its value is 2, which is still less than `LIMIT`, so the loop body executes again. *Hello* displays a third time, and `number` becomes 4; then *Hello* displays a fourth time, and `number` becomes 5. Now, when the expression `number < LIMIT` is evaluated, it is `false`, so the loop ends. If there were any subsequent statements following the `while` loop's closing curly brace, they would execute after the loop was finished.

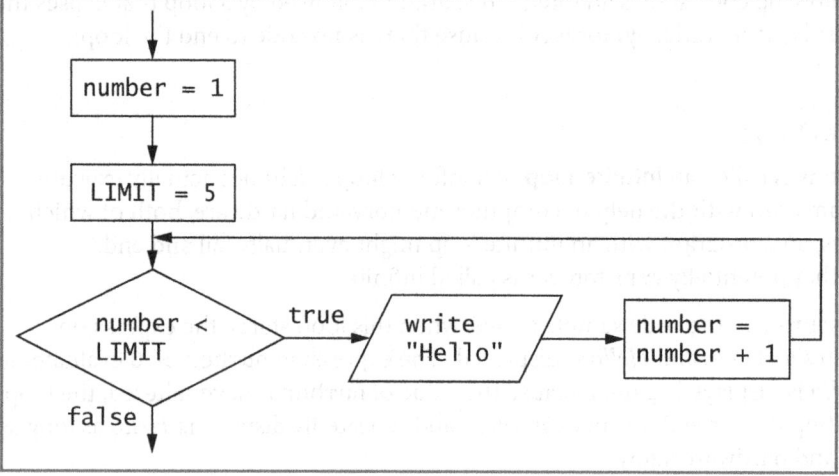

Figure 5-2 Flowchart for the logic of a while loop whose body executes four times

Figure 5-3 shows a C# program that uses the same logic as diagrammed in Figure 5-2. After the declarations, the shaded while expression compares number to LIMIT. The two statements that execute each time the Boolean expression is true are blocked using a pair of curly braces. Figure 5-4 shows the output.

```
using static System.Console;
class FourHellos
{
    static void Main()
    {
        int number = 1;
        const int LIMIT = 5;
        while(number < LIMIT)
        {
            WriteLine("Hello");
            number = number + 1;
        }
    }
}
```

Figure 5-3 A program that contains a while loop whose body executes four times

Creating Loops with the while Statement

Figure 5-4 Output of the FourHellos program

 Recall from Chapter 2 that you also can use a shortcut operator to increase the value of a variable by 1. Instead of number = number + 1, you could achieve the same final result by writing number++, ++number, or number += 1. Because counting is such a common feature of loops, you might want to review the difference between the prefix and postfix increment operators.

The curly braces surrounding the body of the while loop in Figure 5-3 are important. If they are omitted, the while loop ends at the end of the statement that displays *Hello*. Without the braces, adding 1 to number would no longer be part of the loop body, so an infinite loop would be created. Even if the statement that increases number was indented under the while statement, it would not be part of the loop without the surrounding curly braces. Figure 5-5 shows the incorrect logic that would result from omitting the curly braces. For clarity, many programmers recommend surrounding a loop body with curly braces even when there is only one statement in the body.

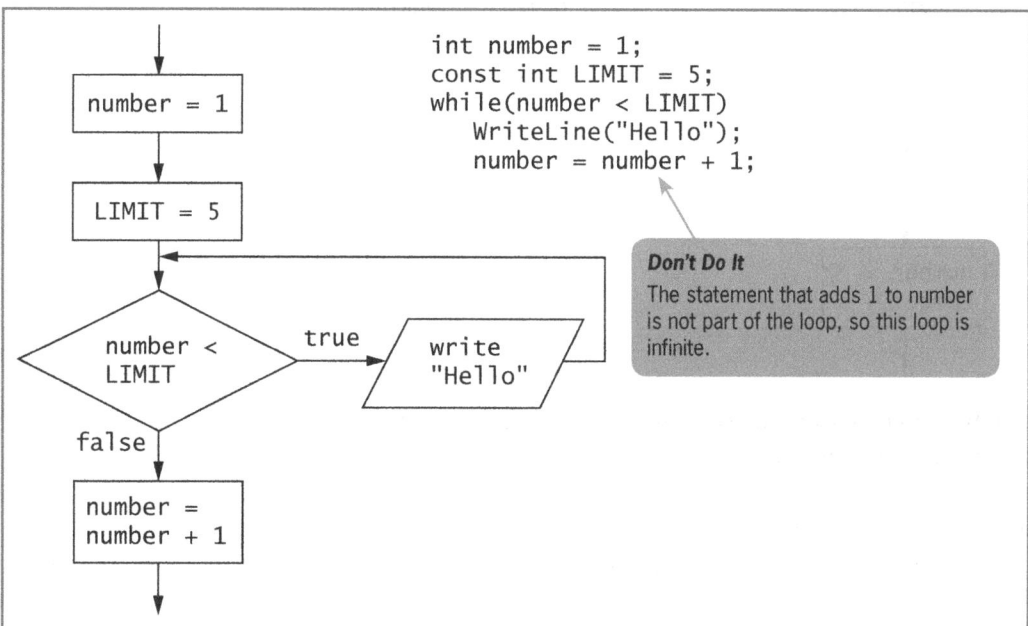

Figure 5-5 Incorrect logic when curly braces are omitted from the loop in the FourHellos program

CHAPTER 5 Looping

Because the code in Figure 5-5 contains no curly braces, the while statement ends with the first semicolon, and an infinite loop is created.

Also, if a semicolon is mistakenly placed at the end of the partial statement, as in Figure 5-6, then the loop is also infinite. This loop has an **empty body**, or a body with no statements. In this case, number is initialized to 1, the Boolean expression number < LIMIT evaluates, and because it is true, the loop body is entered. Because the loop body is empty, ending at the semicolon, no action takes place, and the Boolean expression evaluates again. It is still true (nothing has changed), so the empty body is entered again, and the infinite loop continues. The program can never progress to either the statement that displays *Hello* or the statement that increases the value of number. The fact that these two statements are blocked using curly braces has no effect because of the incorrectly placed semicolon.

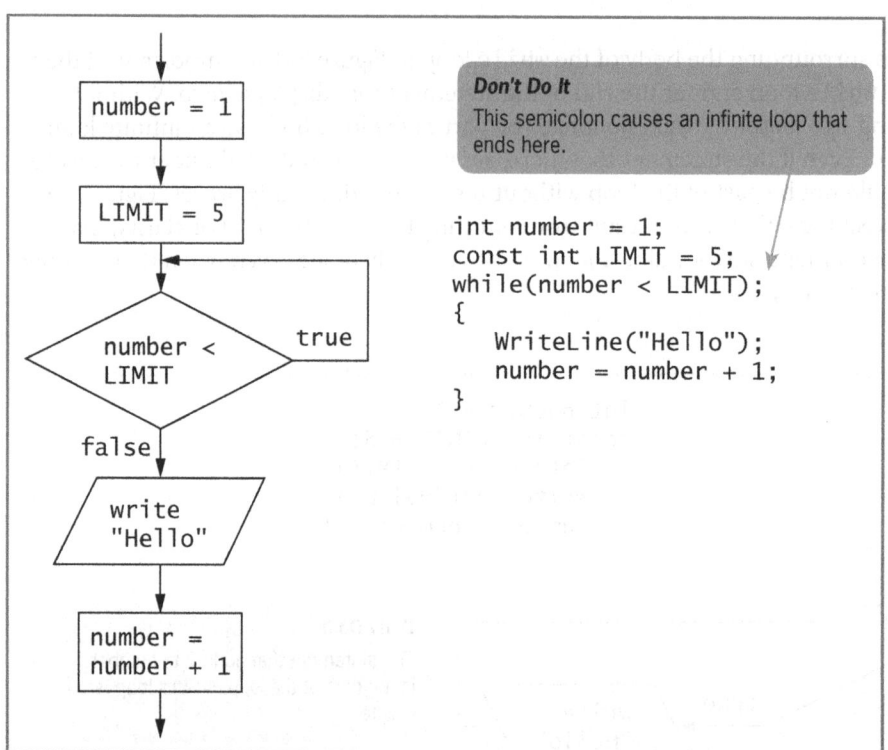

Figure 5-6 Incorrect logic when an unwanted semicolon is mistakenly added to the loop in the FourHellos program

Within a correctly functioning loop's body, you can change the value of the loop control variable in a number of ways. Many loop control variable values are altered by **incrementing**, or adding to them, as in Figures 5-2 and 5-3. Other loops are controlled by reducing, or **decrementing**, a variable and testing whether the value remains greater than some benchmark value.

Creating Loops with the `while` Statement

A loop for which the number of iterations is predetermined is called a **definite loop** or **counted loop**. Often, the value of a loop control variable is not altered by arithmetic but instead is altered by user input. For example, perhaps you want to continue performing some task while the user indicates a desire to continue. In that case, you do not know when you write the program whether the loop will be executed two times, 200 times, or not at all. This type of loop is an **indefinite loop**.

Consider a program that displays a bank balance and asks if the user wants to see what the balance will be after one year of interest has accumulated. Each time the user indicates she wants to continue, an increased balance appears. When the user finally indicates she has had enough, the program ends. The program appears in Figure 5-7, and a typical execution appears in Figure 5-8.

```
using System;
using static System.Console;
class LoopingBankBal
{
   static void Main()
   {
      double bankBal = 1000;
      const double INT_RATE = 0.04;
      string inputString;
      char response;
      Write("Do you want to see your balance? Y or N...");
      inputString = ReadLine();
      response = Convert.ToChar(inputString);
      while(response == 'Y')
      {
         WriteLine("Bank balance is {0}",
            bankBal.ToString("C"));
         bankBal = bankBal + bankBal * INT_RATE;
         Write("Do you want to see next year's balance? Y or N...");
         inputString = ReadLine();
         response = Convert.ToChar(inputString);
      }
      WriteLine("Have a nice day!");
   }
}
```

Figure 5-7 The LoopingBankBal program

CHAPTER 5 Looping

```
Do you want to see your balance? Y or N ...Y
Bank balance is $1,000.00
Do you want to see next year's balance? Y or N ...Y
Bank balance is $1,040.00
Do you want to see next year's balance? Y or N ...Y
Bank balance is $1,081.60
Do you want to see next year's balance? Y or N ...N
Have a nice day!
```

Figure 5-8 Typical execution of the `LoopingBankBal` program

 The program shown in Figure 5-7 continues to display bank balances while the response is *Y*. It could also be written to display while the response is not *N*, as in `while(response != 'N')`.... A value such as `'Y'` or `'N'` that a user must supply to stop a loop is a **sentinel value**.

In the program shown in Figure 5-7, the loop control variable is `response`. It is initialized by the first input and tested with the Boolean expression `response == 'Y'`. If the user types any character other than *Y*, then the loop body never executes; instead, the next statement to execute displays *Have a nice day!*. However, if the user enters *Y*, then all five statements within the loop body execute. The current balance is displayed, and the program increases the balance by the interest rate value; this value will not be displayed unless the user requests another loop repetition. Within the loop, the program prompts the user and reads in a new value for `response`. This input statement is the one that potentially alters the loop control variable. The loop ends with a closing curly brace, and program control returns to the top of the loop, where the Boolean expression is tested again. If the user typed *Y* at the last prompt, then the loop is reentered, and the increased `bankBal` value that was calculated during the last loop cycle is displayed.

 In C#, character data is case sensitive. If a program tests `response == 'Y'`, a user response of *y* will result in a `false` evaluation. Beware of the pitfall of writing a loop similar to `while(response != 'Y' || response != 'y')`... to test both for uppercase and lowercase versions of the response. Every character is either not *Y* or not *y*, even *Y* and *y*. A correct loop might begin with the following:

```
while(response != 'Y' && response != 'y')...
```

 Watch the video *Using the while Loop*.

TWO TRUTHS & A LIE

Creating Loops with the while Statement

1. To make a while loop that executes correctly, a loop control variable is initialized before entering the loop.

2. To make a while loop that executes correctly, the loop control variable is tested in the while expression.

3. To make a while loop that executes correctly, the body of the while statement must never alter the value of the loop control variable.

The false statement is #3. To make a while loop that executes correctly, the body of the while statement must take some action that alters the value of the loop control variable.

You Do It

Using a while Loop

In the next steps, you write a program that continuously prompts the user for a valid ID number until the user enters one. For this application, assume that a valid ID number must be between 1000 and 9999, inclusive.

1. Open a new project named **ValidID**, and enter the beginning of the program by declaring variables for an ID number, the user's input, and constant values for the highest and lowest acceptable ID numbers.

```
using System;
using static System.Console;
class ValidID
{
    static void Main()
    {
        int idNum;
        string input;
        const int LOW = 1000;
        const int HIGH = 9999;
```

(continues)

(continued)

2. Add code to prompt the user for an ID number, and to then convert it to an integer.

   ```
   Write("Enter an ID number: ");
   input = ReadLine();
   idNum = Convert.ToInt32(input);
   ```

3. Create a loop that continues while the entered ID number is out of range. While the number is invalid, explain valid ID parameters and reprompt the user, converting the input to an integer.

   ```
   while(idNum < LOW || idNum > HIGH)
   {
      WriteLine("{0} is an invalid ID number", idNum);
      Write("ID numbers must be ");
      WriteLine("between {0} and {1} inclusive", LOW, HIGH);
      Write("Enter an ID number: ");
      input = ReadLine();
      idNum = Convert.ToInt32(input);
   }
   ```

4. When the user eventually enters a valid ID number, the loop ends. Display a message, and add closing curly braces for the Main() method and for the class.

   ```
         WriteLine("ID number {0} is valid", idNum);
      }
   }
   ```

5. Save the file, compile the program, and execute it. A typical execution during which the user makes several invalid entries is shown in Figure 5-9.

   ```
   Enter an ID number: 34
   34 is an invalid ID number
   ID numbers must be between 1000 and 9999 inclusive
   Enter an ID number: 10000
   10000 is an invalid ID number
   ID numbers must be between 1000 and 9999 inclusive
   Enter an ID number: 999
   999 is an invalid ID number
   ID numbers must be between 1000 and 9999 inclusive
   Enter an ID number: 4170
   ID number 4170 is valid
   ```

   Figure 5-9 Typical execution of the ValidID program

Creating Loops with the for Statement

The LoopingBankBal program in Figure 5-7 contains an indefinite loop because the number of executions is not predetermined; each time the program executes, the user might continue the loop a different number of times. You can use a `while` loop for either definite or indefinite loops. To write either type of `while` loop, you initialize a loop control variable, and as long as its test expression is `true`, you continue to execute the body of the `while` loop. To avoid an infinite loop, the body of the `while` loop must contain a statement that alters the loop control variable.

Because you need definite loops (ones with a predefined number of iterations) so frequently when you write programs, C# provides a shorthand way to create such loops. With a **for loop**, you can indicate the starting value for the loop control variable, the test condition that controls loop entry, and the expression that alters the loop control variable, all in one convenient place.

You begin a `for` statement with the keyword `for` followed by a set of parentheses. Within the parentheses are three sections separated by exactly two semicolons. The three sections are usually used for:

1. Initializing the loop control variable
2. Testing the loop control variable
3. Updating the loop control variable

As with an `if` or a `while` statement, you can use a single statement as the body of a `for` loop, or you can use a block of statements enclosed in curly braces. The `while` and `for` statements shown in Figure 5-10 produce the same output—the integers 1 through 10.

```
// Declare loop control variable and limit
int x;
const int LIMIT = 10;

// Using a while loop to display 1 through 10
x = 1;
while(x <= LIMIT)
{
   WriteLine(x);
   ++x;
}

// Using a for loop to display 1 through 10
for(x = 1; x <= LIMIT; ++x)
   WriteLine(x);
```

Figure 5-10 Displaying integers 1 through 10 with `while` and `for` loops

The amount by which a loop control variable increases or decreases on each cycle through the loop is often called the **step value**. That's because in the BASIC programming language, and its descendent, the Visual Basic language, the keyword STEP is actually used in `for` loops.

Within the parentheses of the `for` statement shown in Figure 5-10, the initialization section prior to the first semicolon sets a variable named x to 1. The program executes this statement once, no matter how many times the body of the `for` loop eventually executes.

After the initialization expression executes, program control passes to the middle section, or test section, of the `for` statement. If the Boolean expression found there evaluates to `true`, then the body of the `for` loop is entered. In the program segment shown in Figure 5-10, x is initialized to 1, so when x <= LIMIT is tested, it evaluates to `true`, and the loop body outputs the value of x.

After the loop body executes, the final one-third of the `for` expression (the update section that follows the last semicolon) executes, and x increases to 2. Following the third section, program control returns to the second (test) section, where x is compared to LIMIT a second time. Because the value of x is 2, it is still less than or equal to LIMIT, so the body of the `for` loop executes, and the value of x is displayed. Then the third, altering portion of the `for` statement executes again. The variable x increases to 3, and the `for` loop continues.

Eventually, when x is *not* less than or equal to LIMIT (after 1 through 10 have been output), the `for` loop ends, and the program continues with any statements that follow the `for` loop.

Although the three sections of the `for` loop are most commonly used for initializing a variable, testing it, and incrementing it, you can also perform other tasks:

- You can initialize more than one variable by placing commas between separate initializations in the first section of the `for` statement, as in the following:

    for(g = 0, h = 1; g < 6; ++g)

- You can declare a new variable within the `for` statement, as in the following:

    for(int k = 0; k < 5; ++k)

In this example, k is declared to be an `int` and is initialized to 0. This technique is used frequently when the variable exists for no other purpose than to control the loop. When a variable is declared inside a loop, as k is in this example, it can be referenced only for the duration of the loop body. When a variable (or named constant) can be accessed, it is in **scope** or in an area where it is known and can be used. When a loop body ends, any declarations made within it are **out of scope**, which means they are not usable because they have ceased to exist.

- You can perform more than one test in the middle section of the `for` statement by evaluating compound conditions, as in the following:

    for(g = 0; g < 3 && h > 1; ++g)

- You can perform tasks other than incrementing at the end of the loop's execution, as in the following code that decrements a variable:

    for(g = 5; g >= 1; --g)

- You can perform multiple tasks at the end of the loop's execution by separating the actions with commas, as in the following:

    for(g = 0; g < 5; ++g, ++h)

- You can leave one or more portions of the for expression empty, although the two semicolons are still required as placeholders to separate the three sections. Usually, you want to use all three sections because the function of the loop is clearer to someone reading your program.

Generally, you should use the for loop in the standard manner, which is a shorthand way of initializing, testing, and altering a variable that controls a definite loop. You will learn about a similar loop, the foreach loop, when you study arrays in the next chapter.

Just as with a decision or a while loop, statements in a for loop body can be blocked. For example, the following loop displays *Hello* and *Goodbye* four times each:

```
const int TIMES = 4;
for(int x = 0; x < TIMES; ++x)
{
   WriteLine("Hello");
   WriteLine("Goodbye");
}
```

Without the curly braces in this code, the for loop would end after the statement that displays *Hello*. In other words, *Hello* would be displayed four times, but *Goodbye* would be displayed only once.

 Watch the video *Using the for Loop*.

TWO TRUTHS & A LIE

Creating Loops with the for Statement

1. The following statement displays the numbers 3 through 6:

   ```
   for(int x = 3; x <= 6; ++x)
      WriteLine(x);
   ```

2. The following statement displays the numbers 4 through 9:

   ```
   for(int x = 3; x < 9; ++x)
      WriteLine(x + 1);
   ```

3. The following statement displays the numbers 5 through 12:

   ```
   for(int x = 5; x < 12; ++x)
      WriteLine(x);
   ```

The false statement is #3. That loop displays only the numbers 5 through 11, because when x is 12, the loop body is not entered.

Creating Loops with the do Statement

With each of the loop statements you have learned about so far, the loop body might execute many times, but it is also possible that the loop will not execute at all. For example, recall the bank balance program that displays compound interest, part of which is shown in Figure 5-11. The loop begins at the shaded line by testing the value of response. If the user has not entered Y, the loop body never executes. The while loop checks a value at the "top" of the loop.

```
Write("Do you want to see your balance? Y or N...");
inputString = ReadLine();
response = Convert.ToChar(inputString);
while(response == 'Y')
{
   WriteLine("Bank balance is {0}", bankBal.ToString("C"));
   bankBal = bankBal + bankBal * INT_RATE;
   Write("Do you want to see next year's balance? Y or N...");
   inputString = ReadLine();
   response = Convert.ToChar(inputString);
}
```

Figure 5-11 Part of the bank balance program using a while loop

Sometimes you might need a loop body always to execute at least one time. If so, you can write a loop that checks at the "bottom" of the loop after the first iteration. The **do loop** (also called a **do...while loop**) checks the loop-controlling Boolean expression after one iteration. Figure 5-12 shows a diagram of the structure of a do loop.

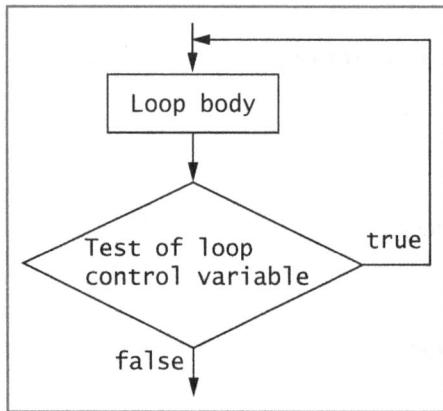

Figure 5-12 Flowchart of a do loop

Figure 5-13 shows the logic and the C# code for a do loop in a bank balance program. The loop starts with the keyword do. The body of the loop follows and is contained within curly braces.

Creating Loops with the do Statement

Within the loop, the next balance is calculated, and the user is prompted for a response. The Boolean expression that controls loop execution is written using a `while` statement, placed after the loop body. The `bankBal` variable is output the first time before the user has any option of responding. At the end of the loop, the user is prompted, *Do you want to see next year's balance? Y or N....* Now the user has the option of seeing more balances, but the first view of the balance was unavoidable.

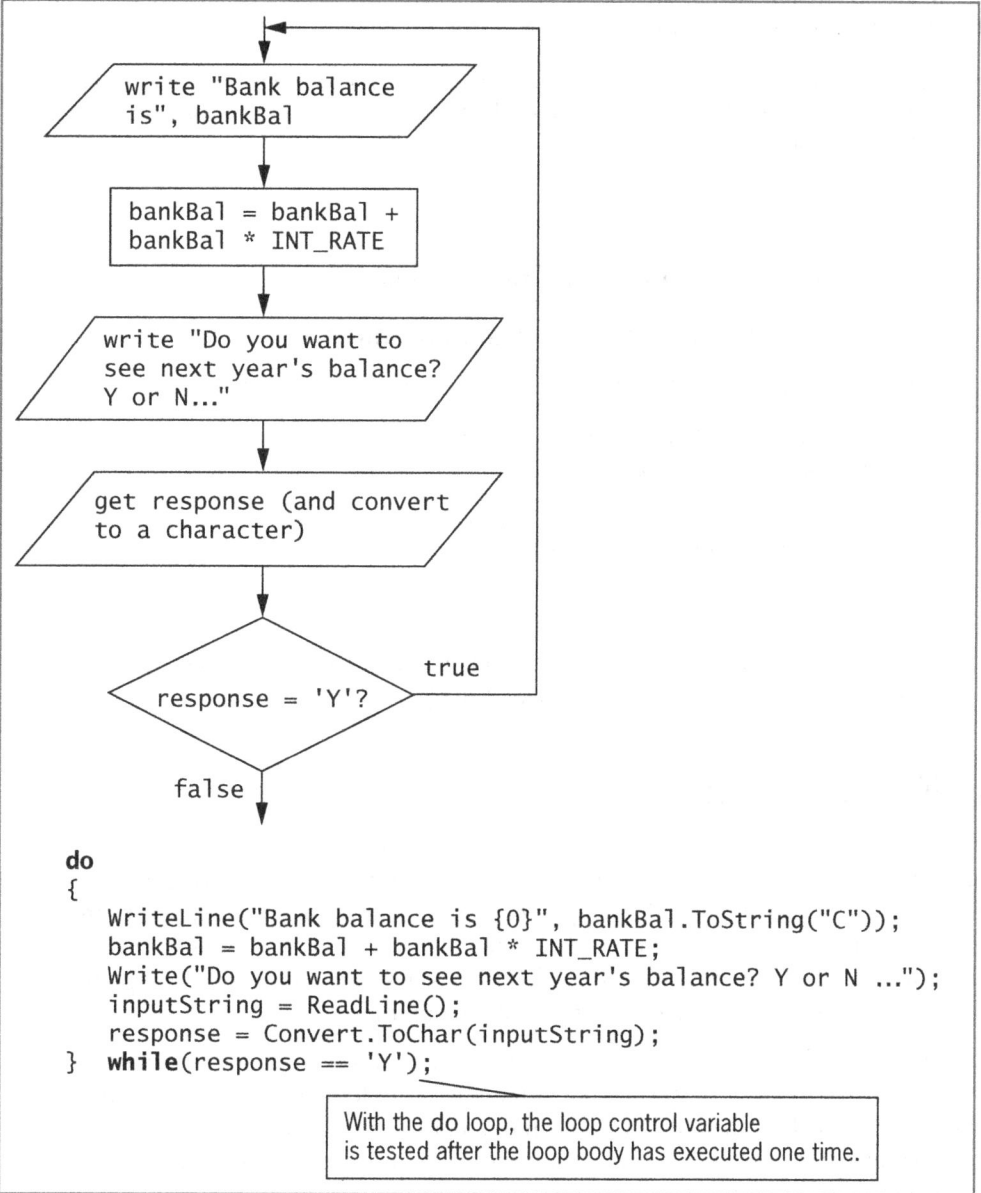

Figure 5-13 Part of the bank balance program using a do loop

In a do loop, as a matter of style, many programmers prefer to align the while expression with the do keyword that starts the loop. Others feel that placing the while expression on its own line increases the chances that readers might misinterpret the line as the start of its own while statement instead of marking the end of a do statement.

You never are required to use a do loop. Within the bank balance example, you could achieve the same results by unconditionally displaying the bank balance once, prompting the user, and then starting a while loop that might not be entered. However, when a task must be performed at least one time, the do loop is convenient.

The while loop and for loop are **pretest loops**—ones in which the loop control variable is tested before the loop body executes. The do loop is a **posttest loop**—one in which the loop control variable is tested after the loop body executes.

TWO TRUTHS & A LIE

Creating Loops with the do Statement

1. The do loop checks the bottom of the loop after one iteration has occurred.

2. The Boolean expression that controls do loop execution is written using a do statement, placed after the loop body.

3. You never are required to use a do loop; you can always substitute one execution of the body statements followed by a while loop.

The false statement is #2. The Boolean expression that controls do loop execution is written using a while statement, placed after the loop body.

Using Nested Loops

Like if statements, loop statements also can be nested. You can place a while loop within a while loop, a for loop within a for loop, a while loop within a for loop, or any other combination. When loops are nested, each pair contains an **inner loop** and an **outer loop**. The inner loop must be contained entirely within the outer loop; loops can never overlap. Figure 5-14 shows a diagram in which the shaded loop is nested within another loop; the shaded area is the inner loop as well as the body of the outer loop.

Suppose you want to display future bank balances for different years at a variety of interest rates. Figure 5-15 shows an application that contains an outer loop controlled by interest rates (starting with the first shaded statement in the figure) and an inner loop controlled by years (starting with the second shaded statement). The application displays annually compounded interest on $1000 at 4 percent, 6 percent, and 8 percent interest rates for one through five years. Figure 5-16 shows the output.

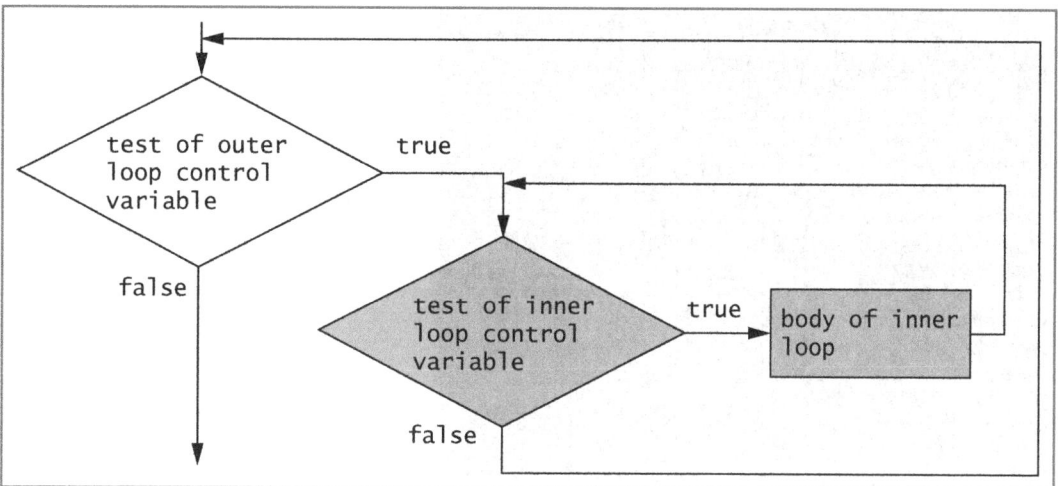

Figure 5-14 Nested loops

```
using static System.Console;
class LoopingBankBal2
{
   static void Main()
   {
      double bankBal;
      double rate;
      int year;
      const double START_BAL = 1000;
      const double START_INT = 0.04;
      const double INT_INCREASE = 0.02;
      const double LAST_INT = 0.08;
      const int END_YEAR = 5;
      for(rate = START_INT; rate <= LAST_INT; rate += INT_INCREASE)
      {
         bankBal = START_BAL;
         WriteLine("Starting bank balance is {0}",
            bankBal.ToString("C"));
         WriteLine(" Interest Rate: {0}", rate.ToString("P"));
         for(year = 1; year <= END_YEAR; ++year)
         {
            bankBal = bankBal + bankBal * rate;
            WriteLine(" After year {0}, bank balance is {1}",
               year, bankBal.ToString("C"));
         }
      }
   }
}
```

Figure 5-15 The LoopingBankBal2 program

CHAPTER 5 Looping

```
Starting bank balance is $1,000.00
  Interest Rate: 4.00 %
    After year 1, bank balance is $1,040.00
    After year 2, bank balance is $1,081.60
    After year 3, bank balance is $1,124.86
    After year 4, bank balance is $1,169.86
    After year 5, bank balance is $1,216.65
Starting bank balance is $1,000.00
  Interest Rate: 6.00 %
    After year 1, bank balance is $1,060.00
    After year 2, bank balance is $1,123.60
    After year 3, bank balance is $1,191.02
    After year 4, bank balance is $1,262.48
    After year 5, bank balance is $1,338.23
Starting bank balance is $1,000.00
  Interest Rate: 8.00 %
    After year 1, bank balance is $1,080.00
    After year 2, bank balance is $1,166.40
    After year 3, bank balance is $1,259.71
    After year 4, bank balance is $1,360.49
    After year 5, bank balance is $1,469.33
```

Figure 5-16 Output of the `LoopingBankBal2` program

When you use a loop within a loop, you should always think of the outer loop as the all-encompassing loop. When you describe the task at hand, you often use the word *each* to refer to the inner loop. For example, if you wanted to output balances for different interest rates each year for 10 years, you could appropriately initialize some constants as follows:

```
const double RATE1 = 0.03;
const double RATE2 = 0.07
const double RATE_INCREASE = 0.01
const int END_YEAR = 10;
```

Then you could use the following nested `for` loops:

```
for(rate = RATE1; rate <= RATE2; rate += RATE_INCREASE)
   for(year = 1; year <= END_YEAR; ++year)
      WriteLine(bankBal + bankBal * rate);
```

However, if you wanted to display balances for different years for each possible interest rate, you would use the following:

```
for(year = 1; year <= END_YEAR; ++year)
   for(rate = RATE1; rate <= RATE2; rate += RATE_INCREASE)
      WriteLine(bankBal + bankBal * rate);
```

In both of these examples, the same 50 values would be displayed—five different interest rates (from 0.03 through 0.07) for 10 years (1 through 10). However, in the first example, balances for years 1 through 10 would be displayed *within* each interest rate category, and in the second example, each balance for each interest rate would be displayed *within* each year category. In other words, in the first example, the first 10 amounts displayed would all use the first rate of 0.03 for 10 different years, and in the second example, the first five amounts displayed would use different interest values all in the first year.

Watch the video *Using Nested Loops*.

TWO TRUTHS & A LIE

Using Nested Loops

1. The body of the following loop executes six times:
   ```
   for(a = 1; a < 4; ++a)
      for(b = 2; b < 3; ++b)
   ```
2. The body of the following loop executes four times:
   ```
   for(c = 1; c < 3; ++c)
      for(d = 1; d < 3; ++d)
   ```
3. The body of the following loop executes 15 times:
   ```
   for(e = 1; e <= 5; ++e)
      for(f = 2; f <= 4; ++f)
   ```

The false statement is #1. That loop executes only three times. The outer loop executes when a is 1, 2, and 3. The inner loop executes just once for each of those iterations.

 You Do It

Using a Nested Loop

In the next steps, you write a program that creates a tipping table that restaurant patrons can use to approximate the correct tip for meals. Prices range from $10 to $100, and tipping percentage rates range from 10 percent to 25 percent. The program uses several loops.

1. Open a new file to start a program named **TippingTable**. It begins by declaring variables to use for the price of a dinner, a tip percentage rate, and the amount of the tip.

   ```
   using static System.Console;
   class TippingTable
   {
      static void Main()
      {
         double dinnerPrice = 10.00;
         double tipRate;
         double tip;
   ```

(continues)

(continued)

2. Next, create some constants. Every tip from 10 percent through 25 percent will be computed in 5 percent intervals, so declare those values as LOWRATE, MAXRATE, and TIPSTEP. Tips will be calculated on dinner prices up to $100.00 in $10.00 intervals, so declare those constants, too.

   ```
   const double LOWRATE = 0.10;
   const double MAXRATE = 0.25;
   const double TIPSTEP = 0.05;
   const double MAXDINNER = 100.00;
   const double DINNERSTEP = 10.00;
   ```

3. To create a heading for the table, display *Price*. (For alignment, insert three spaces after the quotes and before the *P* in *Price*.) On the same line, use a loop that displays every tip rate from LOWRATE through MAXRATE in increments of TIPSTEP. In other words, the tip rates are 0.10, 0.15, 0.20, and 0.25. Complete the heading for the table using a WriteLine() statement that advances the cursor to the next line of output and a WriteLine() statement that displays a dashed line.

   ```
   Write("   Price");
   for(tipRate = LOWRATE; tipRate <= MAXRATE; tipRate += TIPSTEP)
      Write("{0, 8}", tipRate.ToString("F"));
   WriteLine();
   WriteLine("----------------------------------------");
   ```

Recall that within a for loop, the expression before the first semicolon executes once, the middle expression is tested, the loop body executes, and then the expression to the right of the second semicolon executes. In other words, TIPSTEP is not added to tipRate until after tipRate is displayed on each cycle through the loop.

As an alternative to typing 40 dashes in the WriteLine() statement, you could use the following loop to display a single dash 40 times. When the 40 dashes were completed, you could use WriteLine() to advance the cursor to a new line.

   ```
   const int NUM_DASHES = 40;
   for(int x = 0; x < NUM_DASHES; ++x)
      Write("-");
   WriteLine();
   ```

4. Reset tipRate to 0.10. You must reset the rate because after the last loop, the rate will have been increased to greater than 0.25.

   tipRate = LOWRATE;

5. Create a nested loop that continues while the dinnerPrice remains 100.00 (MAXDINNER) or less. Each iteration of this loop displays one row of the tip table. Within this loop, display the dinnerPrice, then loop to display four tips while the tipRate varies from 0.10 through 0.25. At the end of the loop,

(continues)

(continued)

increase the dinnerPrice by 10.00, reset the tipRate to 0.10 so it is ready for the next row, and write a new line to advance the cursor.

```
while(dinnerPrice <= MAXDINNER)
{
   Write("{0, 8}", dinnerPrice.ToString("C"));
   while(tipRate <= MAXRATE)
   {
      tip = dinnerPrice * tipRate;
      Write("{0, 8}", tip.ToString("F"));
      tipRate += TIPSTEP;
   }
   dinnerPrice += DINNERSTEP;
   tipRate = LOWRATE;
   WriteLine();
}
```

Recall that the {0, 8} format string in the Write() statements displays the first argument in fields that are eight characters wide. You learned about format strings in Chapter 2.

6. Add two closing curly braces—one for the Main() method and one for the class.

7. Save the file, compile it, and execute the program. The output looks like Figure 5-17.

```
   Price     0.10     0.15     0.20     0.25

  $10.00     1.00     1.50     2.00     2.50
  $20.00     2.00     3.00     4.00     5.00
  $30.00     3.00     4.50     6.00     7.50
  $40.00     4.00     6.00     8.00    10.00
  $50.00     5.00     7.50    10.00    12.50
  $60.00     6.00     9.00    12.00    15.00
  $70.00     7.00    10.50    14.00    17.50
  $80.00     8.00    12.00    16.00    20.00
  $90.00     9.00    13.50    18.00    22.50
 $100.00    10.00    15.00    20.00    25.00
```

Figure 5-17 Output of the TippingTable program

(continues)

>
> (continued)
>
> In the exercises at the end of this chapter, you will be instructed to make an interactive version of the TippingTable program in which many of the values are input by the user instead of being coded into the program as unnamed constants.
>
> Using a *do* Loop
>
> In the next steps, you revise the TippingTable program to use a do loop in place of the `while` loop.
>
> 1. Open the **TippingTable** program, change the class name to `TippingTable2`, and save the file as **TippingTable2**.
> 2. Cut the `while` loop clause (`while(dinnerPrice <= MAXDINNER)`), and replace it with **do**.
> 3. Paste the `while` loop clause just after the closing curly brace for the loop and before the final two curly braces in the program, and then add a semicolon.
> 4. Save, compile, and execute the program. The output is identical to the output in Figure 5-17.

Accumulating Totals

Many computer programs display totals. When you receive a credit card or telephone service bill, you are usually provided with individual transaction details, but you are most interested in the total bill. Similarly, some programs total the number of credit hours generated by college students, the gross payroll for all employees of a company, or the total accounts receivable value for an organization. These totals are **accumulated**—that is, they are summed one at a time in a loop.

Figure 5-18 shows an example of an interactive program that accumulates the user's total purchases. The program prompts the user to enter a purchase price or *0* to quit. While the user continues to enter nonzero values, the amounts are added to a total. With each pass through the loop, the total is recalculated to include the new purchase amount. After the user enters the loop-terminating *0*, the accumulated total can be displayed. Figure 5-19 shows a typical program execution.

Accumulating Totals

```
using System;
using static System.Console;
class TotalPurchase
{
   static void Main()
   {
      double purchase;
      double total = 0;
      string inputString;
      const double QUIT = 0;
      Write("Enter purchase amount >> ");
      inputString = ReadLine();
      purchase = Convert.ToDouble(inputString);
      while(purchase != QUIT)
      {
         total += purchase;
         Write("Enter next purchase amount, or " +
            QUIT + " to quit >> ");
         inputString = ReadLine();
         purchase = Convert.ToDouble(inputString);
      }
      WriteLine("Your total is {0}", total.ToString("C"));
   }
}
```

Figure 5-18 An application that accumulates total purchases entered by the user

```
Enter purchase amount >> 12.55
Enter next purchase amount, or 0 to quit >> 7.00
Enter next purchase amount, or 0 to quit >> 124.50
Enter next purchase amount, or 0 to quit >> 0
Your total is $144.05
```

Figure 5-19 Typical execution of the TotalPurchase program

Recall from Chapter 2 that the expression total += purchase uses the shortcut add and assign operator, and that it is equivalent to total = total + purchase. The add and assign operator is frequently used when a running total is kept.

In the application in Figure 5-18, it is very important that the total variable used for accumulation is set to 0 before the loop begins. When it is not, the program will not compile. An unknown, unassigned value is known as **garbage**. The C# compiler prevents you from seeing an incorrect total by requiring you to provide a starting value; C# will not use the garbage value that happens to be stored at an uninitialized memory location.

In the application in Figure 5-18, the total variable must be initialized to 0, but the purchase variable is uninitialized. Many programmers would say it makes no sense to initialize this variable because no matter what starting value you provide, the value can be changed by the first input statement before the variable is ever used. As a matter of style, this book generally does not initialize variables if the initialization value is never used; doing so might mislead you into thinking the starting value had some purpose.

TWO TRUTHS & A LIE
Accumulating Totals

1. When totals are accumulated, 1 is added to a variable that represents the total.

2. A variable used to hold a total must be set to 0 before it is used to accumulate a total.

3. The C# compiler will not allow you to accumulate totals in an uninitialized variable.

The false statement is #1. When totals are accumulated, any value might be added to a variable that represents the total. For example, if you total 10 test scores, then each score is added. If you add only 1 to a total variable on each cycle through a loop, then you are counting rather than accumulating a total.

Improving Loop Performance

Whether you decide to use a while, for, or do loop in an application, you can improve loop performance by doing the following:

- Make sure the loop avoids unnecessary operations.
- Consider the order of evaluation for short-circuit operators.
- Employ loop fusion.
- Use prefix incrementing rather than postfix incrementing.

Avoiding Unnecessary Operations

You can improve loop performance by making sure the loop does not include unnecessary operations or statements. For example, suppose that a loop should execute while x is less than the sum of two integers a and b, and that neither a nor b is altered in the loop body. The loop could be written as:

```
while(x < a + b)
   // loop body
```

If this loop executes 1,000 times, then the expression a + b is calculated 1,000 times. Instead, if you use the following code, the results are the same, but the arithmetic is performed only once:

```
int sum = a + b;
while(x < sum)
   // loop body
```

Of course, if a or b is altered in the loop body, then a new sum must be calculated with every loop iteration. However, if the sum of a and b is fixed prior to the start of the loop, then writing the code the second way is far more efficient.

As another example, suppose you need a temporary variable within a loop to use for some calculation. The loop could be written as follows:

```
while(x < LIMIT)
{
   int tempTotal = a + b;
   // more statements here
}
```

When you declare a variable like tempTotal within a loop, it exists only for the duration of the loop; that is, it exists only until the loop's closing brace. Each time the loop executes, the variable is recreated. A more efficient solution is to declare the variable outside of the loop, as follows:

```
int tempTotal;
while(x < LIMIT)
{
   tempTotal = a + b;
   // more statements here
}
```

It is more efficient to declare this variable outside the loop than to redeclare it on every loop iteration.

Considering the Order of Evaluation of Short-Circuit Operators

In Chapter 4, you learned that the expressions in each part of an AND or OR expression use short-circuit evaluation; that is, they are evaluated only as much as necessary to determine whether the entire expression is true or false. When a loop might execute many times, it becomes increasingly important to consider the number of evaluations that take place.

For example, suppose that a user can request any number of printed copies of a report from 1 to 15, and you want to validate the user's input before proceeding. If you believe that users are far more likely to enter a value that is too high than to enter a negative value, then you want to start a loop that reprompts the user with the following expression:

```
while(requestedNum > 15 || requestedNum < 1)...
```

Because you believe that the first Boolean expression is more likely to be true than the second one, you can eliminate testing the second one on more occasions. The order of the expressions is not very important in a single loop, but if this loop is nested within other loops, then the difference in the number of required tests increases. Similarly, the order of the evaluations in `if` statements is more important when the `if` statements are nested within a loop.

Employing Loop Fusion

Loop fusion is the technique of combining two loops into one. For example, suppose that you want to call two methods 100 times each. You can set a constant named TIMES to 100 and use the following code:

```
for(int x = 0; x < TIMES; ++x)
    method1();
for(int x = 0; x < TIMES; ++x)
    method2();
```

However, you can also use the following code:

```
for(int x = 0; x < TIMES; ++x)
{
    method1();
    method2();
}
```

Fusing loops will not work in every situation; sometimes all the activities for each execution of `method1()` must be finished before any of those in `method2()` can begin. However, if the two methods do not depend on each other, fusing the loops can improve performance. Performance issues can be crucial when you write programs for small mobile devices such as phones. On the other hand, if saving a few milliseconds ends up making your code harder to understand, you almost always should err in favor of slower but more readable programs.

Using Prefix Incrementing Rather Than Postfix Incrementing

Probably the most common action after the second semicolon in a `for` statement is to increment the loop control variable. In most textbooks and in many professional programs, the postfix increment operator is used for this purpose, as in the following:

```
for(int x = 0; x < LIMIT; x++)
```

Because incrementing x is a stand-alone statement in the `for` loop, the result is identical whether you use x++ or ++x. However, using the prefix increment operator produces a faster loop.

One way to prove that the prefix increment operator produces a faster loop is to use C#'s `Stopwatch` class. To use the class, you include the statement `using System.Diagnostics;` at the top of the program file. You will better understand how this class works after you read Chapter 9, "Using Classes and Objects," but you can use the class now by making statements similar to the following:

```
Stopwatch sw = Stopwatch.StartNew();
    // Place statements to be timed here
sw.Stop();
```

The first statement creates and starts a `Stopwatch` object for timing events. The object's name is sw—you can use any legal C# identifier. The last statement stops the `Stopwatch`.

Subsequently, you can use a statement similar to the following to output the object's elapsed time in milliseconds:

`WriteLine("Time used: {0} ms", sw.Elapsed.TotalMilliseconds);`

Figure 5-20 contains a program that uses the `Stopwatch` class to compare loops that execute the same high number of times. One uses prefix incrementing, and the other uses postfix incrementing. Figure 5-21 shows the output of a typical execution of the program.

```
using System;
using static System.Console;
using System.Diagnostics;
class PrefixPostfixComparison
{
   static void Main()
   {
      int LOOPS = 100000000;
      Stopwatch sw = Stopwatch.StartNew();
      for(int x = 0; x < LOOPS; ++x);
      sw.Stop();
      Stopwatch sw2 = Stopwatch.StartNew();
      for(int x = 0; x < LOOPS; x++);
      sw2.Stop();
      WriteLine("Time with prefix increment: {0} ms",
         sw.Elapsed.TotalMilliseconds);
      WriteLine("Time with postfix increment: {0} ms",
         sw2.Elapsed.TotalMilliseconds);
   }
}
```

Figure 5-20 The `PrefixPostfixComparison` program

```
Time with prefix increment: 250.0484 ms
Time with postfix increment: 273.0695 ms
```

Figure 5-21 Typical execution of the `PrefixPostfixComparison` program

In Figure 5-21, you can see that the program that uses prefix incrementing runs slightly faster than the one that uses postfix incrementing. The difference in duration for the loops is very small, but it would increase if tasks were added to the loop bodies. If you run the PrefixPostfixComparison program multiple times, you will get different results, and occasionally the prefix operator loop might take longer than the postfix loop because other programs are running concurrently on your computer. However, using the prefix operator typically saves a small amount of time. As a professional, you will encounter programmers who insist on using either postfix or prefix increments in their loops. You should follow the conventions established by your organization, but now you have the tools to prove that prefix incrementing is faster.

As you continue to study programming, you will discover many situations in which you can make your programs more efficient. You should always be on the lookout for ways to improve program performance without sacrificing readability.

TWO TRUTHS & A LIE

Improving Loop Performance

1. You can improve loop performance by making sure the loop does not include unnecessary operations or statements.

2. You can improve loop performance by declaring temporary variables outside of a loop instead of continuously redeclaring them.

3. You can improve loop performance by omitting the initialization of the loop control variable.

The false statement is #3. A loop control variable must be initialized for every loop.

Looping Issues in GUI Programs

Using a loop within a method in a GUI application is no different from using one in a console application; you can use `while`, `for`, and `do` statements in the same ways in both types of programs. For example, Figure 5-22 shows a GUI Form that prompts a user to enter a number and then displays *Hello* the corresponding number of times. The image on the left shows the Form when the program starts, and the image on the right shows the output after the user enters a value and clicks the button. Figure 5-23 shows the code in the `GreetingsButton_Click()` method. When a user clicks the `greetingsButton`, an integer is extracted from the `TextBox` on the Form. Then a `for` loop appends *Hello* and a newline character to the `Text` property of the `outputLabel` the correct number of times.

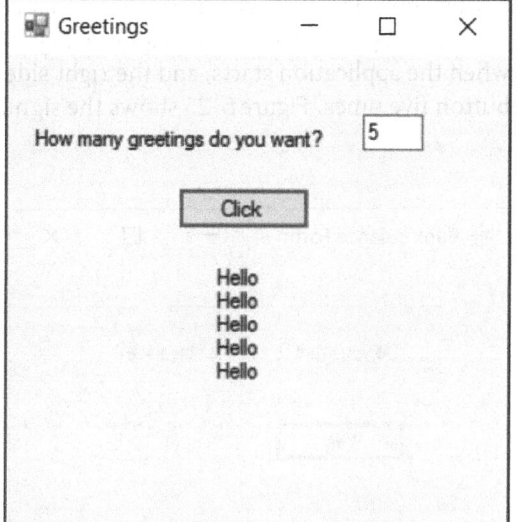

Figure 5-22 The Greetings Form when it starts and after the user enters a number and clicks the button

```
private void GreetingsButton_Click(object sender, EventArgs e)
{
   int numGreetings = Convert.ToInt32(greetingsTextBox.Text);
   int count;
   for (count = 0; count < numGreetings; ++count)
      outputLabel.Text += "Hello\n";
}
```

Figure 5-23 The GreetingsButton_Click() method in the ManyHellosGUI application

If the user clicked the button in the ManyHellosGUI program again, new instances of *Hello* would be added to the ones that are already displayed. If your intention was to show only new *Hellos* then you could clear the Label Text property by adding the statement outputLabel.Text = ""; to the GreetingsButton_Click() method before the start of the loop.

Event-driven programs sometimes require fewer coded loops than their counterpart console applications, because in these programs some events are determined by the user's actions when the program is running, rather than by the programmer's coding beforehand. You can write an event-driven program so that an action continues as long as the user continues to make an appropriate selection. Depending on the application, the sentinel value for this sort of implicit loop might occur when the user either clicks a button that indicates *quit* or clicks the close button on the Form that hosts the application.

CHAPTER 5 Looping

For example, Figure 5-24 shows a Form that controls a bank balance application similar to the one shown earlier in this chapter in Figure 5-7. The left side of the figure shows the Form when the application starts, and the right side shows the Form after the user has clicked the Yes button five times. Figure 5-25 shows the significant Form class code.

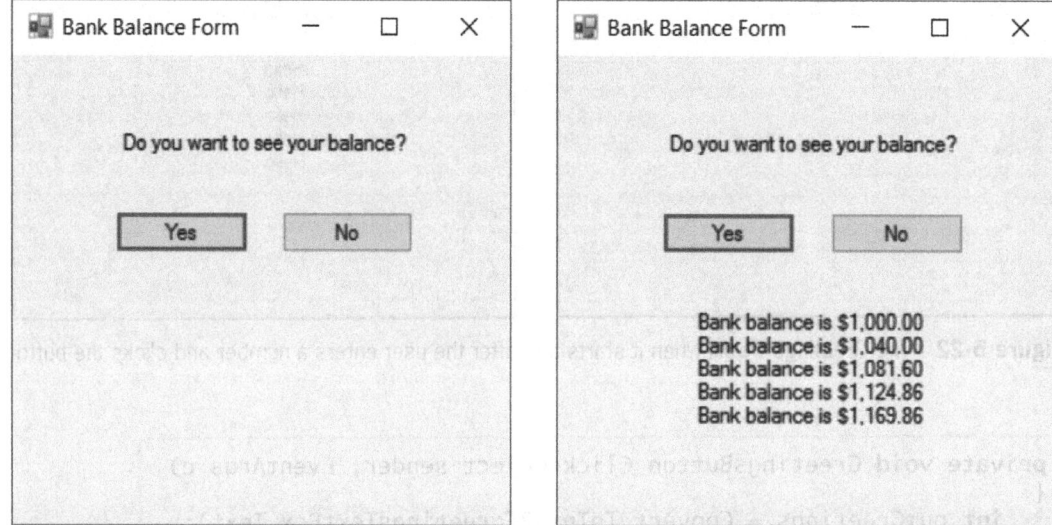

Figure 5-24 The BankBalance Form when it starts and after the user has clicked Yes five times

```
namespace LoopingBankBalGUI
{
    partial class Form1 : Form
    {
        double bankBal = 1000;
        const double INT_RATE = 0.04;
        private void YesButton_Click(object sender, EventArgs e)
        {
            outputLabel.Text += String.Format("Bank balance is {0}\n",
                bankBal.ToString ("C"));
            bankBal = bankBal + bankBal * INT_RATE;
        }
        private void NoButton_Click(object sender, EventArgs e)
        {
            outputLabel.Text = "Have a nice day!";
        }
    }
}
```

Figure 5-25 Code for the LoopingBankBalGUI program

Chapter Summary

 In the LoopingBankBalGUI program, you might also choose to disable the *Yes* button or make it invisible so that the user cannot select it again after clicking *No*.

No loop is written in the code in Figure 5-25 because a loop body execution is caused automatically each time a user clicks the *Yes* button on the Form. Whenever YesButton_Click() executes, the Text of the outputLabel is appended to include a new line that displays the bank balance, and then the bank balance is increased by the interest rate. It is important that the bankBal variable is initialized outside the YesButton_Click() method; if it was initialized within the method, the balance would be reset to the original value of $1000 with each new button click. In the application in Figure 5-25, the balances in the outputLabel are replaced with *Have a nice day!* when the user indicates no more balances are needed.

Chapter Summary

- You can use a while loop to execute a body of statements continuously while a condition continues to be true. A while loop consists of the keyword while, a Boolean expression within parentheses, and the body of the loop, which can be a single statement or a block of statements surrounded by curly braces.

- A for statement includes loop control variable initialization, the test condition that controls loop entry, and the expression that alters the loop control variable. You begin a for statement with the keyword for, followed by a set of parentheses. Within the parentheses, the initialization, test, and update sections are separated by semicolons.

- The do loop checks the loop-controlling Boolean expression at the bottom of the loop after one repetition has occurred.

- You can nest any combination of loops.

- In computer programs, totals frequently are accumulated—that is, summed one at a time in a loop.

- You can improve loop performance by making sure the loop does not include unnecessary operations or statements, considering the order of evaluation for short-circuit operators, using comparisons to zero, employing loop fusion, and using prefix incrementing.

- You can use while, for, and do statements in the same ways in console and GUI programs. However, event-driven programs sometimes require fewer coded loops than console applications because some events are determined by the user's actions when the program is running, rather than by the programmer's coding beforehand.

CHAPTER 5 Looping

Key Terms

A **loop** is a structure that allows repeated execution of a block of statements.

A **loop body** is the block of statements executed in a loop.

An **iteration** is one execution of any loop.

A `while loop` executes a body of statements continuously while a test condition continues to be true; it uses the keyword `while`.

An **infinite loop** is one that (theoretically) never ends.

A **loop control variable** determines whether loop execution will continue.

An **empty body** has no statements in it.

Incrementing a variable means adding a value to it. (Specifically, the term often means to add 1 to a variable.)

Decrementing a variable means subtracting a value from it. (Specifically, the term often means to subtract 1 from a variable.)

In a **definite loop**, the number of iterations is predetermined.

A **counted loop** is a definite loop.

An **indefinite loop** is one in which the number of iterations is not predetermined.

A **sentinel value** is one that a user must supply to stop a loop.

A `for loop` contains the starting value for the loop control variable, the test condition that controls loop entry, and the expression that alters the loop control variable, all in one statement.

A **step value** is the amount by which a loop control variable is altered, especially in a `for` loop.

Scope is the area of a program in which a variable or named constant is known and can be used.

Out of scope describes a program component that is not usable because it has ceased to exist.

The **do loop** (also called a `do...while loop`) checks the loop-controlling Boolean expression at the bottom of the loop after one repetition has occurred.

A **pretest loop** is a loop in which the loop control variable is tested before the loop body executes.

A **posttest loop** is one in which the loop control variable is tested after the loop body executes.

An **inner loop** is the loop in a pair of nested loops that is entirely contained within another loop.

An **outer loop** is the loop in a pair of nested loops that contains another loop.

Accumulated totals are computed by adding values one at a time in a loop.

Garbage is a term used to describe an unknown memory value.

Loop fusion is the technique of combining two loops into one.

Review Questions

1. A structure that allows repeated execution of a block of statements is a(n) _____.

   a. sequence
   b. selection
   c. array
   d. loop

2. The body of a while loop can consist of _____.

   a. a single statement
   b. a block of statements within curly braces
   c. either a or b
   d. neither a nor b

3. A loop that never ends is called an _____ loop.

   a. indefinite
   b. interminable
   c. infinite
   d. intermediate

4. Which of the following is not required of a loop control variable in a correctly working loop?

   a. It is reset to its initial value before the loop ends.
   b. It is initialized before the loop starts.
   c. It is tested.
   d. It is altered in the loop body.

5. A while loop with an empty body contains no _____.

   a. statements
   b. loop control variable
   c. curly braces
   d. test within the parentheses of the while statement

6. A loop for which you do not know the number of iterations when you write it is a(n) _____.

   a. indefinite loop
   b. definite loop
   c. counted loop
   d. for loop

7. What is the major advantage of using a for loop instead of a while loop?

   a. With a for loop, it is impossible to create an infinite loop.
   b. The loop control variable is initialized, tested, and altered all in one place.
   c. It is the only way to achieve an indefinite loop.
   d. Unlike with a while loop, the execution of multiple statements can depend on the test condition.

CHAPTER 5 Looping

8. A `for` loop statement must contain _____.
   a. two semicolons
   b. three commas
   c. four dots
   d. five pipes

9. In a `for` statement, the section before the first semicolon executes _____.
   a. once
   b. once prior to each loop iteration
   c. once after each loop iteration
   d. one less time than the initial loop control variable value

10. The three sections of the `for` loop are most commonly used for _____ the loop control variable.
    a. testing, outputting, and incrementing
    b. initializing, testing, and incrementing
    c. incrementing, selecting, and testing
    d. initializing, converting, and outputting

11. Which loop is most convenient to use if the loop body must always execute at least once?
    a. a `while` loop
    b. a `for` loop
    c. a `do` loop
    d. an `if` loop

12. The loop control variable is checked at the bottom of which kind of loop?
    a. a `while` loop
    b. a `for` loop
    c. a `do` loop
    d. all of the above

13. A `for` loop is an example of a(n) _____ loop.
    a. untested
    b. pretest
    c. posttest
    d. infinite

14. A `while` loop is an example of a(n) _____ loop.
    a. untested
    b. pretest
    c. posttest
    d. infinite

15. When a loop is placed within another loop, the loops are said to be _____.
    a. infinite
    b. bubbled
    c. overlapping
    d. nested

Review Questions

16. What does the following code segment display?

    ```
    a = 1;
    while (a < 5);
    {
       Write("{0} ", a);
       ++a;
    }
    ```

    a. 1 2 3 4   c. 4
    b. 1   d. nothing

17. What is the output of the following code segment?

    ```
    s=1;
    while(s < 4)
       ++s;
       Write("{0} ", s);
    ```

    a. 1   c. 1 2 3 4
    b. 4   d. 2 3 4

18. What is the output of the following code segment?

    ```
    j = 5;
    while(j > 0)
    {
       Write("{0} ", j);
       j--;
    }
    ```

    a. 0   c. 5 4 3 2 1
    b. 5   d. 5 4 3 2 1 0

19. What does the following code segment display?

    ```
    for(f = 0; f < 3; ++f);
       Write("{0} ", f);
    ```

    a. 0   c. 3
    b. 0 1 2   d. nothing

20. What does the following code segment display?

    ```
    for(t = 0; t < 3; ++t)
       Write("{0} ", t);
    ```

    a. 0   c. 0 1 2
    b. 0 1   d. 0 1 2 3

CHAPTER 5 Looping

Exercises

 Programming Exercises

1. Write an application named **SumFiveInts** that allows the user to enter five integers and displays their sum.

2. Write an application named **SumInts** that allows the user to enter any number of integers continuously until the user enters *999*. Display the sum of the values entered, not including 999.

3. Write an application named **EnterUppercaseLetters** that asks the user to type an uppercase letter from the keyboard. If the character entered is an uppercase letter, display *OK*; if it is not an uppercase letter, display an error message. The program continues until the user types an exclamation point.

4. Write an application named **DailyTemps** that continuously prompts a user for a series of daily high temperatures until the user enters a sentinel value. Valid temperatures range from −20 through 130 Fahrenheit. When the user enters a valid temperature, add it to a total; when the user enters an invalid temperature, display an error message. Before the program ends, display the number of temperatures entered and the average temperature.

5. Danielle, Edward, and Francis are three salespeople at Holiday Homes. Write an application named **HomeSales** that prompts the user for a salesperson initial (*D*, *E*, or *F*). Either uppercase or lowercase initials are valid. While the user does not type *Z*, continue by prompting for the amount of a sale. Issue an error message for any invalid initials entered. Keep a running total of the amounts sold by each salesperson. After the user types *Z* or *z* for an initial, display each salesperson's total, a grand total for all sales, and the name of the salesperson with the highest total.

6. Write an application named **DisplayMultiplicationTable** that displays a table of the products of every combination of two integers from 1 through 10.

7. Write an application named **MultiplicationTable** that prompts the user for an integer value, for example *7*. Then display the product of every integer from 1 through 10 when multiplied by the entered value. For example, the first three lines of the table might read *1 × 7 = 7, 2 × 7 = 14,* and *3 × 7 = 21*.

8. Write an application named **OddNums** that displays all the odd numbers from 1 through 99.

9. Write an application named **Sum200** that sums the integers from 1 through 200. Display the running total when the program is halfway complete (after the first 100 numbers), and at the end.

10. Write an application named **Perfect** that displays every perfect number from 1 through 10,000. A number is perfect if it equals the sum of all the smaller positive integers that divide evenly into it. For example, 6 is perfect because 1, 2, and 3 divide evenly into it and their sum is 6.

11. In a "You Do It" section of this chapter, you created a tipping table for patrons to use when analyzing their restaurant bills. Now, create a modified program named **TippingTable3** in which each of the following values is obtained from user input:

    - The lowest tipping percentage
    - The highest tipping percentage
    - The lowest possible restaurant bill
    - The highest restaurant bill

12. Write a program named **WebAddress** that asks a user for a business name. Suggest a good Web address by adding *www.* to the front of the name, removing all spaces from the name, and adding *.com* to the end of the name. For example, a good Web address for Acme Plumbing and Supply is *www.AcmePlumbingandSupply.com*.

13. Write a program named **CountVowels** that accepts a phrase from the user and counts the number of vowels in the phrase. For this exercise, count both uppercase and lowercase vowels, but do not consider *y* to be a vowel.

14. In Chapter 4, you created a program that generates a random number, allows a user to guess it, and displays a message indicating whether the guess is too low, too high, or correct. Now, create a modified program called **GuessingGame2** in which the user can continue to enter values until the correct guess is made. After the user guesses correctly, display the number of guesses made.

Recall that you can generate a random number whose value is at least min and less than max using the following statements:

```
Random ranNumber = new Random();
int randomNumber;
randomNumber = ranNumber.Next(min, max);
```

15. Modify the GuessingGame2 program to create a program called **GuessingGame3** in which the player is criticized for making a "dumb" guess. For example, if the player guesses that the random number is 4 and is told that the guess is too low, and then the player subsequently makes a guess lower than 4, display a message that the user should have known not to make such a low guess.

CHAPTER 5 Looping

 Debugging Exercises

1. Each of the following files in the Chapter.05 folder of your downloadable student files has syntax and/or logical errors. In each case, determine the problem, and fix the program. After you correct the errors, save each file using the same filename preceded with *Fixed*. For example, save DebugFive1.cs as **FixedDebugFive1.cs**.

   a. DebugFive1.cs
   b. DebugFive2.cs
   c. DebugFive3.cs
   d. DebugFive4.cs

 Case Problems

1. In Chapter 4, you created an interactive application named **GreenvilleRevenue** that prompts a user for the number of contestants entered in this year's and last year's Greenville Idol competition and displays the revenue expected for this year's competition if each contestant pays a $25 entrance fee. The program also displays one of three appropriate statements specified in the case problem in Chapter 4, based on a comparison between the number of contestants this year and last year. Now, modify the program so that the user must enter a number between 0 and 30, inclusive, for the number of contestants each year. If the user enters an incorrect number, the program prompts for a valid value.

2. In Chapter 4, you created an interactive application named **MarshallsRevenue** that prompts a user for the number of interior and exterior murals scheduled to be painted during a month and computes the expected revenue for each type of mural. The program also prompts the user for the month number and modifies the pricing based on requirements listed in Chapter 4. Now, modify the program so that the user must enter a month value from 1 through 12. If the user enters an incorrect number, the program prompts for a valid value. Also, the user must enter a number between 0 and 30 inclusive for the number of murals of each type; otherwise, the program prompts the user again.

CHAPTER 6

Using Arrays

Upon completion of this chapter, you will be able to:

◎ Declare an array and assign values to array elements

◎ Access array elements

◎ Search an array using a loop

◎ Use the `BinarySearch()`, `Sort()`, and `Reverse()` methods

◎ Use multidimensional arrays

◎ Appreciate array issues in GUI programs

CHAPTER 6 Using Arrays

Storing values in variables provides programs with flexibility; a program that uses variables to replace constants can manipulate different values each time it executes. When you add loops to your programs, the same variable can hold different values during successive cycles through the loop within the same program execution. Learning to use the data structure known as an array offers further flexibility. Arrays allow you to store multiple values in adjacent memory locations and access them by varying a value that indicates which of the stored values to use. In this chapter, you will learn to create and manage C# arrays.

Declaring an Array and Assigning Values

Sometimes, storing just one value in memory at a time isn't adequate. For example, a sales manager who supervises 20 employees might want to determine whether each employee has produced sales above or below the average amount. When you enter the first employee's sales value into a program, you can't determine whether it is above or below average because you won't know the average until you have entered all 20 values. You might plan to assign 20 sales values to 20 separate variables, each with a unique name, then sum and average them. However, that process is awkward and unwieldy: You need 20 prompts, 20 input statements using 20 separate storage locations (in other words, 20 separate variable names), and 20 addition statements. This method might work for 20 salespeople, but what if you have 30, 40, or 10,000 salespeople?

You could enter data for 20 salespeople using just one variable in 20 successive iterations through a loop that contains one prompt, one input statement, and one addition statement. Unfortunately, when you enter the sales value for the second employee, that data item replaces the value for the first employee, and the first employee's value is no longer available to compare to the average of all 20 values. With this approach, when the data-entry loop finishes, the only individual sales value left in memory is the last one entered.

The best solution to this problem is to create an array. An **array** is a list of data items that all have the same data type and the same name. Each object in an array is an **array element**. You can distinguish each element from the others in an array with a subscript. A **subscript** (also called an **index**) is an integer that indicates the position of a particular array element. In C#, a subscript is written between square brackets that follow an array name.

You declare an array variable with a data type, a pair of square brackets, and an identifier. For example, to declare an array of `double` values to hold sales values for salespeople, you write the following:

```
double[] sales;
```

In some programming languages, such as C++ and Java, you also can declare an array variable by placing the square brackets after the array name, as in `double sales[];`. This format is illegal in C#.

Declaring an Array and Assigning Values

You can provide any legal identifier you want for an array, but programmers conventionally name arrays like they name variables—starting with a lowercase letter and using uppercase letters to begin subsequent words. Additionally, many programmers observe one of the following conventions to make it more obvious that the name represents a group of items:

- Arrays are often named using a plural noun such as `sales`.
- Arrays are often named by adding a final word that implies a group, such as `salesList`, `salesTable`, or `salesArray`.

After you declare an array variable, you still need to create the actual array because declaring an array and reserving memory space for it are two distinct processes. You can declare an array variable and reserve memory locations for 20 `sales` objects using the following two statements:

```
double[] sales;
sales = new double[20];
```

The keyword **new** is also known as the ***new operator***; it is used to create objects. In this case, it creates 20 separate `sales` elements. You also can declare and create an array in one statement, such as the following:

```
double[] sales = new double[20];
```

You can change the size of an array associated with an identifier, if necessary. For example, if you declare `int[] myArray;`, you can assign five elements later with `myArray = new int[5];`; later in the program, you might alter the array size to 100 with `myArray = new int[100];`. Most other programming languages do not provide this capability. If you resize an array in C#, the same identifier refers to a new array in memory, and all the values are set to the default value for the data type.

The statement `double[] sales = new double[20];` reserves 20 memory locations. In C#, an array's elements are numbered beginning with 0, so if an array has 20 elements, you can use any subscript from 0 through 19. In other words, the first `sales` array element is `sales[0]`, and the last `sales` element is `sales[19]`.

Figure 6-1 shows how the array of 20 sales values appears in computer memory. The figure assumes that the array begins at memory address 20000. When you instantiate an array, you cannot choose its location in memory any more than you can choose the location of any other variable. However, you do know that after the first array element, the subsequent elements will follow immediately. Because a **double** takes eight bytes of storage, each element of a **double** array is stored in succession at an address that is eight bytes higher than the previous one.

CHAPTER 6   Using Arrays

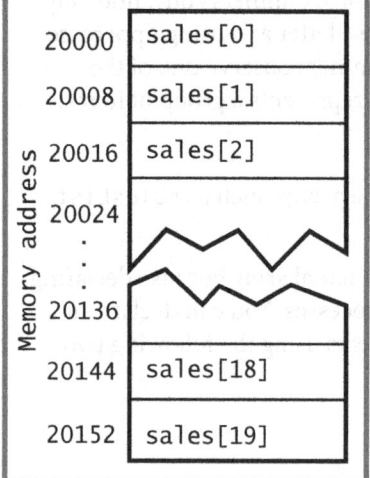

Figure 6-1 An array of 20 `sales` items in memory

In C#, an array subscript must be an integer. For example, no array contains an element with a subscript of 1.5. A subscript can be an integer constant or variable or an expression that evaluates to an integer. For example, if `x` and `y` are integers, and their sum is at least 0 but less than the size of an array named `array`, then it is legal to refer to the element `array[x + y]`.

> Some other languages, such as COBOL, BASIC, and Visual Basic, use parentheses rather than square brackets to refer to individual array elements. By using brackets, the creators of C# made it easier for you to distinguish arrays from methods. Like C#, C++ and Java also use brackets surrounding array subscripts.

A common mistake is to forget that the first element in an array is element 0 (sometimes called the *zeroth element*), especially if you know another programming language in which the first array element is element 1. Making this mistake means you will be "off by one" in your use of any array. If you are "off by one" but still using a valid subscript when accessing an array element, your program most likely will produce incorrect output. If you are "off by one" so that your subscript becomes larger than the highest value allowed, you will cause a program error.

To remember that array elements begin with element 0, it might be helpful to think of the first array element as being "zero elements away from" the beginning of the array, the second element as being "one element away from" the beginning of the array, and so on.

When you work with any individual array element, you treat it no differently than you treat a single variable of the same type. For example, to assign a value to the first element in the `sales` array, you use a simple assignment statement, such as the following:

`sales[0] = 2100.00;`

To output the value of the last `sales` in a 20-element array, you write:

`WriteLine(sales[19]);`

  Watch the video *Declaring an Array*.

Initializing an Array

In C#, arrays are objects. When you instantiate an array, you are creating a specific instance of a class that derives from, or builds upon, the built-in class named `System.Array`. (In the chapter "Introduction to Inheritance," you will learn more about deriving classes.)

Declaring an Array and Assigning Values

When you declare arrays or any other objects, the following default values are assigned to the elements:

- Numeric fields are set to 0.
- Character fields are set to '\u0000' or `null`. (You learned about escape sequences that start with '\u' in Chapter 2.)
- `bool` fields are set to `false`.

You can assign nondefault values to array elements at declaration by including a comma-separated list of values enclosed within curly braces. For example, if you want to create an array named `myScores` and store five test scores within the array, you can use any of the following declarations:

```
int[] myScores = new int[5] {100, 76, 88, 100, 90};
int[] myScores = new int[] {100, 76, 88, 100, 90};
int[] myScores = {100, 76, 88, 100, 90};
```

The list of values provided for an array is an **initializer list**. When you initialize an array by providing a size and an initializer list, as in the first example, the stated size and number of list elements must match. However, when you initialize an array with values, you are not required to give the array a size, as shown in the second example; in that case, the size is assigned based on the number of values in the initializing list. The third example shows that when you initialize an array, you do not need to use the keyword **new** and repeat the type; instead, memory is assigned based on the stated array type and the length of the list of provided values. Of these three examples, the first is most explicit, but it requires two changes if the number of elements is altered. The third example requires the least typing but might not clarify that a new object is being created. Microsoft's documentation prefers the third example because it is most concise, but you should use the form of array initialization that is clearest to you or that is conventional in your organization.

When you use curly braces at the end of a block of code, you do not follow the closing curly brace with a semicolon. However, when you use curly braces to enclose a list of array values, you must complete the statement with a semicolon.

Programmers who have used other languages such as C++ might expect that when an initialization list is shorter than the number of declared array elements, the "extra" elements will be set to default values. This is not the case in C#; if you declare a size and list any values, then you must list a value for each element.

An array of characters can be assigned to a string. For example, you can write the following:

```
char[] arrayOfLetters = {'h', 'e', 'l', 'l', 'o'};
string word = new string(arrayOfLetters);
```

You also can access a single character in a string using a subscript. For example, if you have defined `string greeting = "Hello";`, then `greeting[0]` is `'H'`. However, a string is not an array of characters, and you cannot assign a character to a portion of a string such as in the invalid assignment `word[0] = 'A';`.

TWO TRUTHS & A LIE

Declaring an Array and Assigning Values

1. To reserve memory locations for 10 testScores objects, you can use the following statement:

   int[] testScores = new int[9];

2. To assign 60 to the last element in a 10-element array named testScores, you can use the following statement:

   testScores[9] = 60;

3. The following statement creates an array named testScores and stores four values within the array:

   int[] testScores = new int[] {90, 85, 76, 92};

The false statement is #1. To reserve memory locations for 10 testScores objects, you must use 10 within the second set of square braces. The 10 elements will use the subscripts 0 through 9.

Accessing Array Elements

When you declare an array of five integers, such as the following, you often want to perform the same operation on each array element:

int[] myScores = {100, 76, 88, 100, 90};

To increase each array element by 3, for example, you can write the following five statements:

myScores[0] += 3;
myScores[1] += 3;
myScores[2] += 3;
myScores[3] += 3;
myScores[4] += 3;

If you treat each array element as an individual entity, declaring an array doesn't offer much of an advantage over declaring individual variables. The power of arrays becomes apparent when

Accessing Array Elements

you use subscripts that are variables rather than constant values. Then you can use a loop to perform arithmetic on each element in the array. For example, you can use a `while` loop, as follows:

```
int sub = 0;
while(sub < 5)
{
   myScores[sub] += 3;
   ++sub;
}
```

You also can use a `for` loop, as follows:

```
for(int sub = 0; sub < 5; ++sub)
   myScores[sub] += 3;
```

In both examples, the variable `sub` is declared and initialized to 0, then compared to 5. Because it is less than 5, the loop executes, and `myScores[0]` increases by 3. The variable `sub` is incremented and becomes 1, which is still less than 5, so when the loop executes again, `myScores[1]` increases by 3, and so on. If the array had 100 elements, individually increasing the array values by 3 would require 95 additional statements, but the only change required using either loop would be to change the limiting value for `sub` from 5 to 100.

New array users sometimes think there is a permanent connection between a variable used as a subscript and the array with which it is used, but that is not the case. For example, if you vary `sub` from 0 to 10 to fill an array, you do not need to use `sub` later when displaying the array elements—either the same variable or a different variable can be used as a subscript elsewhere in the program.

Using the Length Property

When you work with array elements, you must ensure that the subscript you use remains in the range of 0 through one less than the array's length. If you declare an array with five elements and use a subscript that is negative or more than 4, you will receive the error message *IndexOutOfRangeException* when you run the program. (You will learn about the `IndexOutOfRangeException` in the chapter "Exception Handling.") This message means the index, or subscript, does not hold a value that legally can access an array element. For example, if you declare an array of five integers, you can display them as follows:

```
int[] myScores = {100, 75, 88, 100, 90};
for(int sub = 0; sub < 5; ++sub)
   WriteLine("{0} ", myScores[sub]);
```

If you modify your program to change the size of the array, you must remember to change the comparison in the `for` loop as well as every other reference to the array size within the program. Many text editors have a "find and replace" feature that lets you change (for example) all of the 5s in a file, either simultaneously or one by one. However, you must be careful not to change 5s that have nothing to do with the array; for example, do not change the 5 in the score 75 inadvertently—it is the second listed value in the `myScores` array and has nothing to do with the array size.

A better approach is to use a value that is automatically altered when you declare an array. Because every array automatically derives from the class `System.Array`, you can use the fields and methods that are part of the `System.Array` class with any array you create. In Chapter 2, you learned that every `string` has a `Length` property. Similarly, every array has a `Length` property that is a member of the `System.Array` class and that automatically holds an array's length. The `Length` property is always updated to reflect any changes you make to an array's size. The following segment of code displays *Array size is 5* and subsequently displays the array's contents:

```
int[] myScores = {100, 76, 88, 100, 90};
WriteLine("Array size is {0}", myScores.Length);
for(int x = 0; x < myScores.Length; ++x)
    WriteLine(myScores[x]);
```

An array's `Length` is a **read-only** property—a property you can access, but to which you cannot assign a new value. It is capitalized, as is the convention with all C# property identifiers. You will create property identifiers for your own classes in the chapter "Using Classes and Objects."

When you write a program in which a large array is required, you might want to test it first with a much smaller array. For example, if a program requires interactive data entry for 50 items, you might want to test it first with only three or four items so you can work out the bugs without wasting too much time on data entry. After the program works correctly with just a few items, if you have used the `Length` property to access the array, you need only make one change to the array size at the top of the program when you are ready to test the full version.

Using foreach

You can easily navigate through arrays using a `for` or `while` loop that varies a subscript from 0 through `Array.Length` - 1. C# also supports a `foreach` statement that you can use to cycle through every array element without using a subscript. With the `foreach` statement, you provide a temporary **iteration variable** that automatically holds each array value in turn.

For example, the following code displays each element in the `payRates` array in sequence:

```
double[] payRates = {12.00, 17.35, 21.12, 27.45, 32.22};
foreach(double money in payRates)
    WriteLine("{0}", money.ToString("C"));
```

The variable money is declared as a double within the foreach statement. During the execution of the loop, money holds each payRates element value in turn—first, payRates[0], then payRates[1], and so on. As a simple variable, money does not require a subscript, making it easier to work with.

The foreach statement is used only under certain circumstances:

- You typically use foreach only when you want to access every array element. To access only selected array elements, you must manipulate subscripts using some other technique—for example, using a for loop or while loop.
- The foreach iteration variable is read-only—that is, you can access it, but you cannot assign a value to it. If you want to assign a value to array elements, you must use a different type of loop.

TWO TRUTHS & A LIE

Accessing Array Elements

1. Assume you have declared an array of six doubles named balances. The following statement displays all the elements:

   ```
   for(int index = 0; index < 6; ++index)
       WriteLine(balances[index]);
   ```

2. Assume you have declared an array of eight doubles named prices. The following statement subtracts 2 from each element:

   ```
   for(double pr = 0; pr < 8; ++pr)
       prices[pr] -= 2;
   ```

3. The following code displays 3:

   ```
   int[] array = {1, 2, 3};
   WriteLine(array.Length);
   ```

The false statement is #2. You can only use an int as the subscript to an array, and this example attempts to use a double.

You Do It

Creating and Using an Array

In the next steps, you create a small array to see how it is used. The array will hold salaries for four categories of employees.

1. Open a new file, and begin a console-based program named **ArrayDemo1** that demonstrates array use:

   ```
   using static System.Console;
   class ArrayDemo1
   {
       static void Main()
       {
   ```

2. Declare and create an array that holds four `double` values by typing:

   ```
   double[] payRate = {13.00, 17.35, 19.12, 22.45};
   ```

3. To confirm that the four values have been assigned, display them using the following code:

   ```
   for(int x = 0; x < payRate.Length; ++x)
       WriteLine("Pay rate {0} is {1}",
           x, payRate[x].ToString("C"));
   ```

4. Add the two closing curly braces that end the `Main()` method and the `ArrayDemo1` class.

5. Save the program, and then compile and run it. The output appears in Figure 6-2.

```
Pay rate 0 is $13.00
Pay rate 1 is $17.35
Pay rate 2 is $19.12
Pay rate 3 is $22.45
```

Figure 6-2 Output of the ArrayDemo1 program

Searching an Array Using a Loop

When you want to determine whether a variable holds one of many possible valid values, one option is to use `if` statements to compare the variable to valid values. For example, suppose that a company manufactures 10 items. When a customer places an order for an item, you need to determine whether the item number is valid. If valid item numbers are sequential, say 101 through 110, then the following simple `if` statement that uses an AND operator can verify the order number and set a Boolean field to `true`:

```
if(itemOrdered >= 101 && itemOrdered <= 110)
   isValidItem = true;
```

If the valid item numbers are nonsequential, however—for example, 101, 108, 201, 213, 266, 304, and so on—you must code the following deeply nested `if` statement or a lengthy OR comparison to determine the validity of an item number:

```
if(itemOrdered == 101)
   isValidItem = true;
else if(itemOrdered == 108)
   isValidItem = true;
else if(itemOrdered == 201)
   isValidItem = true;
// and so on
```

Instead of creating a long series of `if` statements, a more elegant solution to determining whether a value is valid is to compare it to a list of values in an array. For example, you can initialize an array with the valid values by using the following statement:

```
int[] validValues = {101, 108, 201, 213, 266, 304, 311,
   409, 411, 412};
```

> You might prefer to declare the `validValues` array as a constant because, presumably, the valid item numbers should not change during program execution. In C# you must use the keywords `static` and `readonly` prior to the constant declaration. To keep these examples simple, all arrays in this chapter are declared as variable arrays.

After the `validValues` array is declared, you can use either a `for` loop or a `while` loop to search whether the `itemOrdered` variable value matches any of the array entries.

Using a for Loop to Search an Array

One way to determine whether an `itemOrdered` value equals a value in the `validValues` array is to use a `for` statement to loop through the array and set a Boolean variable to `true` when a match is found:

```
for(int x = 0; x < validValues.Length; ++x)
   if(itemOrdered == validValues[x])
      isValidItem = true;
```

This type of search is called a **sequential search** because each array element is examined in sequence. This simple `for` loop replaces the long series of `if` statements. What's more, if a company carries 1000 items instead of 10, then the list of valid items in the array must be altered, but the `for` statement does not change at all. As an added bonus, if you set up another array as a **parallel array** with the same number of elements and corresponding data, you can use the same subscript to access additional information. For example, if the 10 items your company carries have 10 different prices, then you can set up an array to hold those prices as follows:

```
double[] prices = {0.89, 1.23, 3.50, 0.69...}; // and so on
```

The prices must appear in the same order as their corresponding item numbers in the `validValues` array. Now the same `for` loop that finds the valid item number also finds the price, as shown in the program in Figure 6-3. In other words, if the item number is found in the second position in the `validValues` array, then you can find the correct price in the second position in the `prices` array. In the program in Figure 6-3, the variable used as a subscript, `x`, is set to 0 and the Boolean variable `isValidItem` is `false`. In the shaded portion of the figure, while the subscript remains smaller than the length of the array of valid item numbers, the subscript is continuously increased so that subsequent array values can be tested. When a match is found between the user's item and an item in the array, `isValidItem` is set to `true` and the price of the item is stored in `itemPrice`. Figure 6-4 shows two typical program executions.

If you initialize parallel arrays, it is convenient to use spacing (as shown in Figure 6-3) so that the corresponding values visually align on the screen or printed page.

Although parallel arrays can be very useful, they also can increase the likelihood of mistakes. Any time you make a change to one array, you must remember to make the corresponding change in its parallel array. As you continue to study C#, you will learn superior ways to correlate data items. For example, in the chapter "Using Classes and Objects," you will learn that you can encapsulate corresponding data items in objects and create arrays of objects.

Searching an Array Using a Loop

```
using System;
using static System.Console;
class FindPriceWithForLoop
{
   static void Main()
   {
      int[] validValues = {101, 108, 201, 213, 266,
         304, 311, 409, 411, 412};
      double[] prices =   {0.89, 1.23, 3.50, 0.69, 5.79,
         3.19, 0.99, 0.89, 1.26, 8.00};
      int itemOrdered;
      double itemPrice = 0;
      bool isValidItem = false;
      Write("Please enter an item ");
      itemOrdered = Convert.ToInt32(ReadLine());
      for(int x = 0; x < validValues.Length; ++x)
      {
         if(itemOrdered == validValues[x])
         {
            isValidItem = true;
            itemPrice = prices[x];
         }
      }
      if(isValidItem)
         WriteLine("Price is {0}", itemPrice);
      else
         WriteLine("Sorry - item not found");
   }
}
```

Figure 6-3   The FindPriceWithForLoop program

```
Please enter an item 266
Price is 5.79
```
```
Please enter an item 267
Sorry - item not found
```

Figure 6-4   Two typical executions of the FindPriceWithForLoop program

In the fourth statement of the `Main()` method in Figure 6-3, `itemPrice` is set to 0. Setting this variable is required because its value is later altered only if an item number match is found in the `validValues` array. When C# determines that a variable's value is only set depending on an `if` statement, C# will not allow you to display the variable because the compiler assumes that the `if` statement's Boolean expression could have been `false` and the variable might not have been set to a valid value.

Improving a Loop's Efficiency

The code shown in Figure 6-3 can be made more efficient. Currently, the program compares every `itemOrdered` with each of the 10 `validValues`. Even when an `itemOrdered` is equivalent to the first value in the `validValues` array (101), you always make nine additional cycles through the array comparing all the values. On each of these nine additional iterations, the comparison between `itemOrdered` and `validValues[x]` is always `false`. As soon as a match for an `itemOrdered` is found, the most efficient action is to break out of the `for` loop early. An easy way to accomplish this task is to set `x` to a high value within the block of statements executed when a match is found. Then, after a match, the `for` loop will not execute again because the limiting comparison (`x < validValues.Length`) will have been surpassed. Figure 6-5 shows this approach.

```
for(int x = 0; x < validValues.Length; ++x)
{
   if(itemOrdered == validValues[x])
   {
      isValidItem = true;
      itemPrice = prices[x];
      x = validValues.Length;
         // Change x to force break out of loop
         // when you find a match
   }
}
```

Figure 6-5 Loop with forced early exit

Searching an Array Using a Loop

In the code segment in Figure 6-5, instead of the statement that sets x to validValues.Length when a match is found, you could remove that statement and change the comparison in the middle section of the for statement to a compound statement, as follows:

for(int x = 0; x < validValues.Length && !isValidItem; ++x)...

As another alternative, you could remove the statement that sets x to validValues.Length and place a break statement within the loop in its place. A break statement exits the current code block immediately.

If you decide to leave a loop as soon as a match is found, the most efficient strategy is to place the most common items first so they are matched sooner. For example, if item 311 is ordered most often, place 311 first in the validValues array and its price ($0.99) first in the prices array. However, it might be more convenient for people to view the item numbers in ascending numerical order. In many business applications, your first consideration is how easily users can read, understand, and modify your programs. However, in other applications, such as programming for mobile devices, speed and memory considerations are more important. You should follow the recommendations of your instructors or supervisors.

Some programmers disapprove of exiting a for loop early, whether by setting a variable's value or by using a break statement. They argue that programs are easier to debug and maintain if each program segment has only one entry and one exit point. If you (or your instructor) agree with this philosophy, then you can select an approach that uses a while statement, as described next.

Using a while Loop to Search an Array

As an alternative to using a for loop to search an array, you can use a while loop to search for a match. Using this approach, you set a subscript to 0 and, while the itemOrdered is not equal to a value in the array, increase the subscript and keep looking. You search only while the subscript remains lower than the number of elements in the array. If the subscript increases until it matches validValues.Length, then you never found a match in the array. If the loop ends before the subscript reaches validValues.Length, then you found a match, and the correct price can be assigned to the itemPrice variable. Figure 6-6 shows a program that uses this approach.

```
using System;
using static System.Console;
class FindPriceWithWhileLoop
{
   static void Main()
   {
      int x;
      string inputString;
      int itemOrdered;
      double itemPrice = 0;
      bool isValidItem = false;
      int[] validValues = {101, 108,  201,  213,  266,
         304,  311,  409,  411,  412};
      double[] prices =  {0.89, 1.23, 3.50, 0.69, 5.79,
          3.19, 0.99, 0.89, 1.26, 8.00};
      Write("Enter item number ");
      inputString = ReadLine();
      itemOrdered = Convert.ToInt32(inputString);
      x = 0;
      while(x < validValues.Length && itemOrdered != validValues[x])
         ++x;
      if(x != validValues.Length)
      {
         isValidItem = true;
         itemPrice = prices[x];
      }
      if(isValidItem)
         WriteLine("Item {0} sells for {1}",
            itemOrdered, itemPrice.ToString("C"));
      else
         WriteLine("No such item as {0}", itemOrdered);
   }
}
```

Figure 6-6 The FindPriceWithWhileLoop program that searches with a `while` loop

In the application in Figure 6-6, the variable used as a subscript, `x`, is set to 0 and the Boolean variable `isValidItem` is `false`. In the shaded portion of the figure, while the subscript remains smaller than the length of the array of valid item numbers, and while the user's requested item does not match a valid item, the subscript is increased so that subsequent array values can be tested. The `while` loop ends when a match is found or the array tests have been exhausted, whichever comes first. When the loop ends, if `x` is not equal to the size of the array, then a valid item has been found, and its price can be retrieved from the `prices` array. Figure 6-7 shows two executions of the program. In the first execution, a match is found; in the second, an invalid item number is entered, so no match is found.

Searching an Array Using a Loop

Figure 6-7 Two executions of the FindPriceWithWhileLoop application

 Watch the video *Searching an Array*.

Searching an Array for a Range Match

Searching an array for an exact match is not always practical. For example, suppose your mail-order company gives customer discounts based on the quantity of items ordered. Perhaps no discount is given for any order of up to a dozen items, but increasing discounts are available for orders of increasing quantities, as shown in Figure 6-8.

Total Quantity Ordered	Discount (%)
1 to 12	None
13 to 49	10
50 to 99	14
100 to 199	18
200 or more	20

Figure 6-8 Discount table for a mail-order company

One awkward, impractical option is to create a single array to store the discount rates. You could use a variable named `numOfItems` as a subscript to the array, but the array would need hundreds of entries, such as the following:

```
double[] discounts = {0, 0, 0, 0, 0, 0, 0, 0, 0, 0,
   0, 0, 0, 0.10, 0.10, 0.10 ...}; // and so on
```

When `numOfItems` is 3, for example, then `discounts[numOfItems]` or `discounts[3]` is 0. When `numOfItems` is 14, then `discounts[numOfItems]` or `discounts[14]` is 0.10. Because a customer might order thousands of items, the array would need to be ridiculously large.

A better option is to create parallel arrays. One array will hold the five discount rates, and the other array will hold five discount range limits. Then you can perform a **range match** by determining the pair of limiting values between which a customer's order falls. The Total Quantity Ordered column in Figure 6-8 shows five ranges. If you use only the first value in each range, then you can create an array that holds five low limits:

`int[] discountRangeLowLimits = {1, 13, 50, 100, 200};`

A parallel array will hold the five discount rates:

`double[] discounts = {0, 0.10, 0.14, 0.18, 0.20};`

Then, starting at the last `discountRangeLowLimits` array element, for any `numOfItems` greater than or equal to `discountRangeLowLimits[4]`, the appropriate discount is `discounts[4]`. In other words, for any `numOfItems` less than `discountRangeLowLimits[4]`, you should decrement the subscript and look in a lower range. Figure 6-9 shows the code.

```
// Assume numOfItems is a declared integer for which a user
// has input a value
int[] discountRangeLowLimits = {1, 13,   50,   100,  200};
double[] discounts =          {0, 0.10, 0.14, 0.18, 0.20};
double customerDiscount;
int sub = discountRangeLowLimits.Length - 1;
while(sub >= 0 && numOfItems < discountRangeLowLimits[sub])
   --sub;
customerDiscount = discounts[sub];
```

Figure 6-9 Searching an array of range limits

As an alternate approach to the range-checking logic in Figure 6-9, you can choose to create an array that contains the upper limit of each range, such as the following:

`int[] discountRangeUpperLimits = {12, 49, 99, 199, 9999999};`

Then the logic can be written to compare `numOfItems` to each range limit until the correct range is located, as follows:

```
int sub = 0;
while(sub < discountRangeUpperLimits.Length &&
   numOfItems > discountRangeUpperLimits[sub])
   ++sub;
customerDiscount = discounts[sub];
```

In this example, `sub` is initialized to 0. While it remains within array bounds, and while `numOfItems` is more than each upper-range limit, `sub` is increased. In other words, if `numOfItems` is 3, the `while` expression is `false` on the first loop iteration, the loop ends, `sub` remains 0, and the customer discount is the first discount. However, if `numOfItems` is 30, then the `while` expression is `true` on the first loop iteration, `sub` becomes 1, the `while` expression is `false` on the second iteration, and the second discount is used. In this example, the last `discountRangeUpperLimits` array value is 9999999. This very high value was used with the assumption that no `numOfItems` would ever exceed it, but, because this assumption could

Using the `BinarySearch()`, `Sort()`, and `Reverse()` Methods

possibly be wrong, many programmers prefer to use a range-checking method that uses lower range limits. As with many issues in programming, multiple correct approaches frequently exist for the same problem.

> **TWO TRUTHS & A LIE**
>
> **Searching an Array Using a Loop**
>
> 1. A parallel array has the same number of elements as another array and corresponding data.
>
> 2. When you search an array for an exact match in a parallel array, you must perform a loop as many times as there are elements in the arrays.
>
> 3. One practical solution to creating an array with which to perform a range check is to design the array to hold the lowest value in each range.
>
> The false statement is #2. When you search an array for an exact match in a parallel array, you can perform a loop as many times as there are elements in the arrays, but once a match is found, the additional loop iterations are unnecessary. Terminating the loop cycles as soon as a match is found is the most efficient approach.

Using the `BinarySearch()`, `Sort()`, and `Reverse()` Methods

You have already learned that every array in C# can use the `Length` property it gets from the `System.Array` class. Additionally, the `System.Array` class contains a variety of useful, built-in methods that you can use with arrays. This section shows you how to use the methods `Array.BinarySearch()` method to find an element in an array, the `Array.Sort()` method to sort an array's elements, and the `Array.Reverse()` method to reverse the order of elements. If you include the statement `using static System.Array();`, you can use each of these methods without using the `Array` class name and the dot.

Using the `BinarySearch()` Method

A **binary search** is one in which a sorted list of objects is split in half repeatedly as the search gets closer and closer to a match. Perhaps you have played a guessing game, trying to guess a number from 1 to 100. If you asked, "Is it less than 50?" and continued to narrow your guesses upon hearing each subsequent answer, then you have performed a binary search. In C#, the `BinarySearch()` method finds a requested value in a sorted array.

Figure 6-10 shows a program that declares an array of integer idNumbers arranged in ascending order. The program prompts a user for a value, converts it to an integer, and passes the array and the entered value to the BinarySearch() method in the shaded statement. The method returns −1 if the value is not found in the array; otherwise, it returns the array position of the sought value. Figure 6-11 shows two executions of this program.

The BinarySearch() method takes two arguments—the array name and the value for which to search. In Chapter 1 you learned that arguments represent information that a method needs to perform its task. When methods require multiple arguments, they are separated by commas. For example, when you have used the WriteLine() method, you have passed a format string and values to be displayed, all separated by commas.

```
using System;
using static System.Console;
class BinarySearchDemo
{
   static void Main()
   {
      int[] idNumbers = {122, 167, 204, 219, 345};
      int x;
      string entryString;
      int entryId;
      Write("Enter an Employee ID ");
      entryString = ReadLine();
      entryId = Convert.ToInt32(entryString);
      x = Array.BinarySearch(idNumbers, entryId);
      if(x < 0)
         WriteLine("ID {0} not found", entryId);
      else
         WriteLine("ID {0} found at position {1} ",
            entryId, x);
   }
}
```

Figure 6-10   The BinarySearchDemo program

```
Enter an Employee ID 219
ID 219 found at position 3
```
```
Enter an Employee ID 220
ID 220 not found
```

Figure 6-11   Two executions of the BinarySearchDemo program

You have sent arguments to methods, as in the following statement:

Write("Enter an Employee ID ");

You also have accepted methods' returned values, as in the following statement:

entryString = ReadLine();

Using the BinarySearch(), Sort(), and Reverse() Methods

When you use the BinarySearch() method, you both send arguments and receive returned values:

x = Array.BinarySearch(idNumbers, entryId);

The statement calls the method that performs the search, returning –1 or the position where entryId was found; that value is then stored in x. This single line of code is easier to write, less prone to error, and easier to understand than writing a loop to cycle through the idNumbers array looking for a match. Still, it is worthwhile to understand how to perform the search without the BinarySearch() method, as you learned while studying parallel arrays earlier in this chapter. You will need to use that technique under the following conditions, when the BinarySearch() method proves inadequate:

- If your array items are not arranged in ascending order, the BinarySearch() method does not work correctly.

- If your array holds duplicate values and you want to find all of them, the BinarySearch() method doesn't work—it can return only one value, so it returns the position of the first matching value it finds (which is not necessarily the first instance of the value in the array).

- If you want to find a range match rather than an exact match, you can't use the BinarySearch() method.

Using the Sort() Method

The Sort() method arranges array items in ascending order. The method works numerically for number types and alphabetically for characters and strings. To use the method, you pass the array name to Array.Sort(), and the element positions within the array are rearranged appropriately. Figure 6-12 shows a program that sorts an array of strings; Figure 6-13 shows its execution.

```
using System;
using static System.Console;
class SortArray
{
    static void Main()
    {
        string[] names = {"Olive", "Patty",
            "Richard", "Ned", "Mindy"};
        int x;
        Array.Sort(names);
        for(x = 0; x < names.Length; ++x)
            WriteLine(names[x]);
    }
}
```

Figure 6-12 The SortArray program

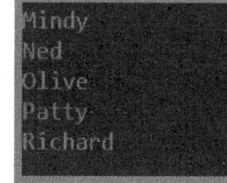

Figure 6-13 Execution of the SortArray program

CHAPTER 6 Using Arrays

Because the `BinarySearch()` method requires that array elements be sorted in order, the `Sort()` method is often used in conjunction with it.

 The `Array.Sort()` method provides a good example of encapsulation—you can use the method without understanding how it works internally. The method actually uses an algorithm named *Quicksort*. You will learn how to implement this algorithm yourself as you continue to study programming.

Using the `Reverse()` Method

The `Reverse()` method reverses the order of items in an array. In other words, for any array, the element that starts in position 0 is relocated to position `Length - 1`, the element that starts in position 1 is relocated to position `Length - 2`, and so on until the element that starts in position `Length - 1` is relocated to position 0. When you `Reverse()` an array that contains an odd number of elements, the middle element will remain in its original location. The `Reverse()` method does not sort array elements; it only rearranges their values to the opposite order.

You call the `Reverse()` method the same way you call the `Sort()` method—you simply pass the array name to the method. Figure 6-14 shows a program that uses `Reverse()` with an array of strings, and Figure 6-15 shows its execution.

```
using System;
using static System.Console;
class ReverseArray
{
   static void Main()
   {
      string[] names = {"Zach", "Rose",
         "Wendy", "Marcia"};
      int x;
      Array.Reverse(names);
      for(x = 0; x < names.Length; ++x)
         WriteLine(names[x]);
   }
}
```

Figure 6-14 The ReverseArray program

Figure 6-15 Execution of the ReverseArray program

Using the BinarySearch(), Sort(), and Reverse() Methods

TWO TRUTHS & A LIE

Using the BinarySearch(), Sort(), and Reverse() Methods

1. When you use the BinarySearch() method, the searched array items must first be organized in ascending order.

2. The Array.Sort() and Array.Reverse() methods are similar in that both require a single argument.

3. The Array.Sort() and Array.Reverse() methods are different in that one places items in ascending order and the other places them in descending order.

The false statement is #3. The Array.Sort() method places items in ascending order, but the Array.Reverse() method simply reverses the existing order of any array whether it was presorted or not.

 You Do It

Using the Sort() and Reverse() Methods

In the next steps, you create an array of integers and use the Sort() and Reverse() methods to manipulate it.

1. Open a new file and type the beginning of a program named **ArrayDemo2** that includes an array of eight integer test scores, an integer you will use as a subscript, and a string that will hold user-entered data.

   ```
   using System;
   using static System.Console;
   class ArrayDemo2
   {
      static void Main()
      {
         int[] scores = new int[8];
         int x;
         string inputString;
   ```

2. Add two more items that will be used to improve the appearance of the output: a counter to count dashes to be displayed in a line and a constant for the number of dashes:

   ```
   int count;
   const int DASHES = 50;
   ```

(continues)

(continued)

3. Add a loop that prompts the user, accepts a test score, converts the score to an integer, and stores it as the appropriate element of the scores array. When the loop is complete, execute a WriteLine() statement so that the next output appears on a new line.

   ```
   for(x = 0; x < scores.Length; ++x)
   {
      Write("Enter your score on test {0} ", x + 1);
      inputString = ReadLine();
      scores[x] = Convert.ToInt32(inputString);
   }
   WriteLine();
   ```

   The program displays x + 1 with each score[x] because, although array elements are numbered starting with 0, people usually count items starting with 1.

4. Add a loop that creates a dashed line to visually separate the input from the output.

   ```
   for(count = 0; count < DASHES; ++count)
      Write("-");
   WriteLine();
   ```

5. Display *Scores in original order:*, then use a loop to display each score in a field that is six characters wide.

   ```
   WriteLine("Scores in original order:");
   for(x = 0; x < scores.Length; ++x)
      Write("{0, 6}", scores[x]);
   WriteLine();
   ```

6. Add another dashed line for visual separation, then pass the scores array to the Array.Sort() method. Display *Scores in sorted order:*, then use a loop to display each of the newly sorted scores.

   ```
   for(count = 0; count < DASHES; ++count)
      Write("-");
   WriteLine();
   Array.Sort(scores);
   WriteLine("Scores in sorted order:");
   for(x = 0; x < scores.Length; ++x)
      Write("{0, 6}", scores[x]);
   WriteLine();
   ```

7. Add one more dashed line, reverse the array elements by passing scores to the Array.Reverse() method, display *Scores in reverse order:*, and show the rearranged scores.

(continues)

Using Multidimensional Arrays

(continued)

```
        for(count = 0; count < DASHES; ++count)
            Write("-");
        WriteLine();
        Array.Reverse(scores);
        WriteLine("Scores in reverse order:");
        for(x = 0; x < scores.Length; ++x)
            Write("{0, 6}", scores[x]);
```

8. Add two closing curly braces—one for the Main() method and one for the class.

9. Save the file, and then compile and execute the program. Figure 6-16 shows a typical execution of the program. The user-entered scores are not in order, but after the call to the Sort() method, they appear in ascending order. After the call to the Reverse() method, they appear in descending order.

```
Enter your score on test 1 75
Enter your score on test 2 88
Enter your score on test 3 62
Enter your score on test 4 100
Enter your score on test 5 95
Enter your score on test 6 90
Enter your score on test 7 89
Enter your score on test 8 91
--------------------------------------------------
Scores in original order:
    75    88    62   100    95    90    89    91
--------------------------------------------------
Scores in sorted order:
    62    75    88    89    90    91    95   100
--------------------------------------------------
Scores in reverse order:
   100    95    91    90    89    88    75    62
```

Figure 6-16 Typical execution of the ArrayDemo2 program

Using Multidimensional Arrays

When you declare an array such as `double[] sales = new double[20];`, you can envision the declared integers as a list or column of numbers in memory, as shown at the beginning of this chapter in Figure 6-1. In other words, you can picture the 20 declared numbers stacked one on top of the next. An array that you can picture as a column of values, and whose elements you can access using a single subscript, is a **one-dimensional** or **single-dimensional array**. You can think of the single dimension of a single-dimensional array as the height of the array.

C# also supports **multidimensional arrays**—those that require multiple subscripts to access the array elements. The most commonly used multidimensional arrays are two-dimensional arrays that are rectangular. **Two-dimensional arrays** have two or more columns of values for each row, as shown in Figure 6-17. You can think of the two dimensions of a two-dimensional array as height and width.

sales[0, 0]	sales[0, 1]	sales[0, 2]	sales[0, 3]
sales[1, 0]	sales[1, 1]	sales[1, 2]	sales[1, 3]
sales[2, 0]	sales[2, 1]	sales[2, 2]	sales[2, 3]

Figure 6-17 View of a rectangular, two-dimensional array in memory

The array in Figure 6-17 is a rectangular array. In a **rectangular array**, each row has the same number of columns. You must use two subscripts when you access an element in a two-dimensional array. When mathematicians use a two-dimensional array, they often call it a *matrix* or a *table*; you might have used a two-dimensional array called a spreadsheet. You might want to create a `sales` array with two dimensions, as shown in Figure 6-17, if, for example, each row represented a category of items sold, and each column represented a salesperson who sold them.

When you declare a one-dimensional array, you type a single, empty set of square brackets after the array type, and you use a single subscript in a set of square brackets when reserving memory. To declare a two-dimensional array, you type a comma in the square brackets after the array type, and you use two subscripts, separated by a comma in brackets, when reserving memory. For example, the array in Figure 6-17 can be declared as the following, creating an array named `sales` that holds three rows and four columns:

```
double[ , ] sales = new double[3, 4];
```

When you declare a two-dimensional array, spaces surrounding the comma within the square brackets are optional.

Just as with a one-dimensional array, every element in a two-dimensional array is the same data type. Also, just as with a one-dimensional array if you do not provide values for the elements in a two-dimensional array, the values are set to the default value for the data type (for example, 0 for numeric data). You can assign other values to the array elements later. For example, the following statement assigns the value 14.00 to the element of the `sales` array that is in the first column of the first row:

```
sales[0, 0] = 14.00;
```

Alternatively, you can initialize a two-dimensional array by assigning values when it is created. For example, the following code assigns values to `sales` upon declaration:

```
double[ , ] sales = {{14.00, 15.00, 16.00, 17.00},
                     {21.99, 34.55, 67.88, 31.99},
                     {12.03, 55.55, 32.89, 1.17}};
```

Using Multidimensional Arrays

The `sales` array contains three rows and four columns. You contain the entire set of values within a pair of curly braces. The first row of the array holds the four `doubles` 14.00, 15.00, 16.00, and 17.00. Notice that these four values are placed within their own inner set of curly braces to indicate that they constitute one row, or the first row, which is row 0. The row and its curly braces are separated from the next row with a comma. The next four values in their own set of braces make up the second row (row 1), which you reference with the subscript 1, and the last four values constitute the third row (row 2).

When you refer to an element in a two-dimensional array, the first value within the brackets following the array name always refers to the row; the second value, after the comma, refers to the column. As examples, the value of `sales[0, 0]` is 14.00, the value of `sales[0, 1]` is 15.00, the value of `sales[1, 0]` is 21.99, and the value of `sales[2, 3]` is 1.17. You do not need to place each row of values that initializes a two-dimensional array on its own line. However, doing so makes the positions of values easier to understand.

As an example of how useful two-dimensional arrays can be, assume that you own an apartment building with four floors—a basement, which you refer to as floor zero, and three other floors numbered one, two, and three. In addition, each of the floors has studio (with no bedroom), one-, and two-bedroom apartments. The monthly rent for each type of apartment is different, and the rent is higher for apartments with more bedrooms. Figure 6-18 shows the rental amounts.

Floor	Zero Bedrooms	One Bedroom	Two Bedrooms
0	400	450	510
1	500	560	630
2	625	676	740
3	1000	1250	1600

Figure 6-18 Rents charged (in dollars)

To determine a tenant's rent, you need to know two pieces of information about the apartment: the floor and the number of bedrooms. Within a C# program, you can declare an array of rents using the following code:

```
int[ , ] rents = { {400, 450, 510},
                   {500, 560, 630},
                   {625, 676, 740},
                   {1000, 1250, 1600} };
```

If `floor` and `bedrooms` are integers with in-range values, then any tenant's rent can be referred to as `rents[floor, bedrooms]`.

Figure 6-19 shows a complete program that uses a rectangular, two-dimensional array to hold rent values. Figure 6-20 shows a typical execution.

CHAPTER 6 Using Arrays

```
using System;
using static System.Console;
class RentFinder
{
    static void Main()
    {
        int[ , ] rents = { {400, 450, 510},
                           {500, 560, 630},
                           {625, 676, 740},
                           {1000, 1250, 1600} };
        int floor;
        int bedrooms;
        string inputString;
        Write("Enter the floor on which you want to live ");
        inputString = ReadLine();
        floor = Convert.ToInt32(inputString);
        Write("Enter the number of bedrooms you need ");
        inputString = ReadLine();
        bedrooms = Convert.ToInt32(inputString);
        WriteLine("The rent is {0}", rents[floor, bedrooms]);
    }
}
```

Figure 6-19 The RentFinder program

```
Enter the floor on which you want to live 2
Enter the number of bedrooms you need 1
The rent is 676
```

Figure 6-20 Typical execution of the RentFinder program

 Watch the video *Using a Two-Dimensional Array*.

C# supports arrays with more than two dimensions. For example, as in the program in Figure 6-19, if you own a multistory apartment building with different numbers of bedrooms available in apartments on each floor, you can use a two-dimensional array to store the rental fees. However, if you own several apartment buildings, you might want to employ a third dimension to store the building number. Suppose you want to store rents for four buildings that have three floors each and that each hold two types of apartments. Figure 6-21 shows how you might define such an array.

Using Multidimensional Arrays

```
int[ , , ] rents = { { {400, 500}, {450, 550}, {500, 550}},
                     { {510, 610}, {710, 810}, {910, 1010}},
                     { {525, 625}, {725, 825}, {925, 1025}},
                     { {850, 950}, {1050, 1150}, {1250, 1350}}};
```

Figure 6-21 A three-dimensional `array` definition

The empty brackets that follow the data type contain two commas, showing that the array supports three dimensions. A set of curly braces surrounds all the data; the inner curly braces represent the following:

- Four inner sets of braces surround the data for each building—each row of values represents a building (0 through 3).

- Within each row, the three sets of inner braces represent each floor—first a basement, then floor one, and floor two. For example, in building 0, {400, 500} are rents for floor 0, and {450, 550} are rents for floor 1.

- Within each floor, the two braced values represent the bedrooms—first a zero-bedroom apartment and then a one-bedroom apartment. For example, in building 0, floor 0, 400 is the rent for a zero-bedroom apartment, and 500 is the rent for a one-bedroom apartment.

Using the three-dimensional array in Figure 6-21, an expression such as `rents[building, floor, bedrooms]` refers to a specific rent value for a building whose number is stored in the `building` variable and whose floor and bedroom numbers are stored in the `floor` and `bedrooms` variables. Specifically, `rents[3, 1, 0]` refers to a studio (zero-bedroom) apartment on the first floor of building 3 (which is the fourth building). The value of `rents[3, 1, 0]` is $1050 in Figure 6-21. When you are programming in C#, you can use four, five, or more dimensions in an array. As long as you can keep track of the order of the variables needed as subscripts, and as long as you don't exhaust your computer's memory, C# lets you create arrays of any size.

Using Jagged Arrays

C# also supports jagged arrays. A **jagged array** is a one-dimensional array in which each element is another array. The major difference between jagged and rectangular arrays is that in jagged arrays, each row can be a different length.

For example, consider an application in which you want to store train ticket prices for each stop along five different routes. Suppose some of the routes have as many as 10 stops and others have as few as two. Each of the five routes could be represented by a row in a multidimensional array. Then you would have two logical choices for the columns:

- You could create a rectangular, two-dimensional array, allowing 10 columns for each row. In some of the rows, as many as eight of the columns would be empty, because some routes have only two stops.

- You could create a jagged array, allowing a different number of elements for each row. Figure 6-22 shows how you could implement this option.

```
double [][] tickets = {
   new double[] {5.50, 6.75, 7.95, 9.00, 12.00,
      13.00, 14.50, 17.00, 19.00, 20.25},
   new double[] {5.00, 6.00},
   new double[] {7.50, 9.00, 9.95, 12.00, 13.00, 14.00},
   new double[] {3.50, 6.45, 9.95, 10.00, 12.75},
   new double[] {15.00, 16.00} };
```

Figure 6-22 A jagged array

Two square brackets are used following the data type of the array in Figure 6-22. This notation declares a jagged array that is composed of five separate one-dimensional arrays. Within the jagged array, each row needs its own **new** operator and data type. To refer to a jagged array element, you use two sets of brackets after the array name—for example, tickets[route][stop]. In Figure 6-22, the value of tickets[0][0] is 5.50, the value of tickets[0][1] is 6.75, and the value of tickets[0][2] is 7.95. The value of tickets[1][0] is 5.00, and the value of tickets[1][1] is 6.00. Referring to tickets[1][2] is invalid because there is no column 2 in the second row (that is, there are only two stops, not three, on the second train route).

TWO TRUTHS & A LIE

Using Multidimensional Arrays

1. A rectangular array has the same number of columns as rows.

2. The following array contains two rows and three columns:
   ```
   int[ , ] departments = {{12, 54, 16},
                           {22, 44, 47}};
   ```

3. A jagged array is a one-dimensional array in which each element is another array.

The false statement is #1. In a rectangular array, each row has the same number of columns, but the numbers of rows and columns are not required to be the same.

Array Issues in GUI Programs

The major unusual consideration when using an array in a GUI program is that if the array values change based on user input, the array must be stored outside any method that reacts to the user's event. For example, consider an application that accumulates contribution totals for a fund-raising drive competition among four departments in a company. The left side of Figure 6-23 shows a Form into which a user types a department number and a contribution amount. For example, in the figure, the user is adding a $25 contribution for Department 2. The user clicks OK, then enters the next contribution amount. When the user clicks the Done button, a summary of contributions appears, as shown in the right side of Figure 6-23. For example, during program execution, in all $305 in contributions were added for Department 2.

Figure 6-23 The Form for the CountContributions program as the user enters a value and after the user clicks Done

Figure 6-24 shows the code needed to implement the application. An array named `total` is declared outside of any methods. (See shading.) The `OkButton_Click()` method accepts a department number and contribution amount from the user. It then adds the contribution into the array element that corresponds to the department and clears the text boxes so they are empty prior to the next entry. The `total` array must be declared outside of the `OkButton_Click()` method; if it was inside the method, it would be redeclared, and all its elements would be reset to 0 with each button click. The `DoneButton_Click()` method displays the array's contents.

CHAPTER 6 Using Arrays

```
double[] total = { 0, 0, 0, 0 };
private void OkButton_Click(object sender, EventArgs e)
{
    int dept;
    double contribution;
    dept = Convert.ToInt32(deptTextbox.Text);
    contribution = Convert.ToDouble(contributionTextbox.Text);
    --dept;
    total[dept] += contribution;
    deptTextbox.Text = "";
    contributionTextbox.Text = "";
}
private void DoneButton_Click(object sender, EventArgs e)
{
    outputLabel.Text = "Dept Total";
    for (int x = 0; x < total.Length; ++x)
        outputLabel.Text +=
            String.Format("\n {0}{1, 10}", x + 1, total[x]. ToString("C"));
}
```

Figure 6-24 Code that declares array and two methods needed for the CountContributions application

TWO TRUTHS & A LIE

Array Issues in GUI Programs

1. A GUI program can contain declarations for any number of arrays of any data type.

2. If a method reacts to a user-initiated event, it cannot contain an array declaration.

3. If a method reacts to a user-initiated event and the method contains an array declaration, the array will be redeclared with each event occurrence.

The false statement is #2. If a method reacts to a user-initiated event, it can contain an array. The only problem is that the array will be redeclared with each new event, so it cannot store data that must persist over a number of events.

Chapter Summary

- An array is a list of data items, all of which have the same type and the same name but are distinguished from each other using a subscript or index. You declare an array variable by inserting a pair of square brackets after the type and reserve memory for an array by using the keyword `new`. Any array's elements are numbered 0 through one less than the array's length. In C#, arrays are objects that derive from a class named `System.Array`. An array's elements are initialized to default values. To initialize an array to nondefault values, you use a list of values that are separated by commas and enclosed within curly braces.

- Arrays are most powerful when variable subscripts are used to process array elements. Any array subscript must remain in the range of 0 through `Length - 1`. The `Length` property automatically holds an array's length. You can use the `foreach` statement to cycle through every array element without using subscripts.

- When you want to determine whether a variable holds one of many possible valid values, you can compare the variable to a list of values in an array. You can set up a parallel array to access additional information.

- The `BinarySearch()` method finds a requested value in a sorted array. The method returns –1 if the value is not found in the array; otherwise, it returns the array position of the sought value. The `Sort()` method arranges array items in ascending order. The `Reverse()` method reverses the order of items in an array.

- C# supports multidimensional arrays that require multiple subscripts to access the array elements. The most commonly used multidimensional arrays are two-dimensional arrays that are rectangular. Two-dimensional arrays have two or more columns of values for each row. In a rectangular array, each row has the same number of columns. C# also supports jagged arrays, which are arrays of arrays.

- The major unusual consideration when using an array in a GUI program is that if the array values change based on user input, the array must be stored outside any method that reacts to the user's event.

Key Terms

An **array** is a list of data items that all have the same data type and the same name but are distinguished from each other by a subscript or index.

An **array element** is an individual object within an array.

A **subscript** (also called an **index**) is an integer contained within square brackets that indicates the position of one of an array's elements.

An **initializer list** is the list of values provided for an array.

Read-only describes a value that can be accessed but not altered.

An **iteration variable** is a temporary location that holds each array value in turn in a foreach statement.

A **sequential search** is conducted by examining a list in sequence.

A **parallel array** has the same number of elements as another array and corresponding data.

A **range match** determines the pair of limiting values between which a value falls.

A **binary search** is an algorithm that attempts to find an item in a list by splitting the sorted list of objects in half repeatedly as the search gets closer to a match.

A **one-dimensional** or **single-dimensional** array is an array whose elements you can access using a single subscript.

Multidimensional arrays require multiple subscripts to access the array elements.

Two-dimensional arrays have two or more columns of values for each row.

A **rectangular array** is an array in which each row has the same number of columns.

A **jagged array** is a one-dimensional array in which each element is another array.

Review Questions

1. In an array, every element has the same _____.
   a. subscript
   b. memory location
   c. data type
   d. all of the above

2. The operator used to create objects is _____.
   a. =
   b. +=
   c. new
   d. create

3. Which of the following correctly declares an array of six integers?
   a. `int array[6];`
   b. `int[] array = 6;`
   c. `int[6] array;`
   d. `int[] array = new int[6];`

4. The value placed within square brackets after an array name is _____.
   a. always a constant
   b. always a `double`
   c. called a subscript
   d. all of these

Review Questions

5. If you define an array to contain 10 elements, then the highest array subscript you can use is _____.

   a. 8
   b. 9
   c. 10
   d. 11

6. Initializing an array is _____ in C#.

   a. optional
   b. required
   c. difficult
   d. prohibited

7. When you declare an array of six `double` elements but provide no initialization values, the value of the first element is _____.

   a. 0.0
   b. 1.0
   c. 5.0
   d. unknown

8. Which of the following correctly declares an array of four integers?

   a. `int[] ages = new int[4] {20, 30, 40, 50};`
   b. `int[] ages = new int[] {20, 30, 40, 50};`
   c. `int[] ages = {20, 30, 40, 50};`
   d. all of these

9. When an `ages` array is correctly initialized using the values {20, 30, 40, 50}, then the value of `ages[1]` is _____.

   a. 0
   b. 20
   c. 30
   d. undefined

10. When an `ages` array is correctly initialized using the values {20, 30, 40, 50}, then the value of `ages[4]` is _____.

    a. 0
    b. 4
    c. 50
    d. undefined

11. When you declare an array as `int[] temperature = {0, 32, 50, 90, 212, 451};`, the value of `temperature.Length` is _____.

    a. 5
    b. 6
    c. 7
    d. unknown

12. Which of the following doubles every value in a 10-element integer array named amount?

    a. for(int x = 9; x >= 0; --x) amount[x] *= 2;
    b. foreach(int number in amount) number *= 2;
    c. both of these
    d. neither of these

13. Which of the following adds 10 to every value in a 16-element integer array named points?

    a. for(int sub = 0; sub > 16; ++sub) points[sub] += 10;
    b. foreach(int sub in points) points += 10;
    c. both of these
    d. neither of these

14. Two arrays that store related information in corresponding element positions are _____ arrays.

    a. jagged
    b. parallel
    c. relative
    d. rectangular

15. Assume an array is defined as int[] nums = {2, 3, 4, 5};. Which of the following would display the values in the array in reverse?

    a. for(int x = 4; x > 0; --x)
          Write(nums[x]);
    b. for(int x = 3; x >= 0; --x)
          Write(nums[x]);
    c. for(int x = 3; x > 0; --x)
          Write(nums[x]);
    d. for(int x = 4; x >= 0; --x)
          Write(nums[x]);

16. Assume an array is defined as int[] nums = {7, 15, 23, 5};. Which of the following would place the values in the array in descending numeric order?

    a. Array.Sort(nums);
    b. Array.Reverse(nums);
    c. Array.Sort(nums); Array.Reverse(nums);
    d. Array.Reverse(nums); Array.Sort(nums);

17. Which of the following traits do the BinarySearch() and Sort() methods have in common?

    a. Both methods take a single argument that must be an array.
    b. They both operate only arrays made up of numeric data.
    c. The array that each method uses must start in ascending order.
    d. Both methods belong to the System.Array class.

18. If you use the BinarySearch() method, and the object you seek is not found in the array, _____.

    a. an error message is displayed
    b. a zero is returned
    c. the value false is returned
    d. a negative value is returned

19. The BinarySearch() method is inadequate when _____.

    a. array items are in ascending order
    b. the array holds duplicate values and you want to find them all
    c. you want to find an exact match for a value
    d. array items are not numeric

20. Which of the following declares an integer array that contains eight rows and five columns?

    a. `int[8, 5] num = new int[ , ];`
    b. `int[8][5] num = new int[];`
    c. `int[ , ] num = new int[5, 8];`
    d. `int[ , ] num = new int[8, 5];`

Exercises

 Programming Exercises

For each of the following exercises, you may choose to write a console-based or GUI application, or both.

1. Write a program named **ArrayDemo** that stores an array of 10 integers. Until the user enters a sentinel value, allow the user four options: (1) to view the list in order from the first to last position in the stored array, (2) to view the list in order from the last to first position, (3) to choose a specific position to view, or (4) to quit the application.

2. Write a program named **TestScoreList** that accepts eight `int` values representing student test scores. Display each of the values along with a message that indicates how far it is from the average.

3. Write a program named **TemperaturesComparison** that allows a user to input five daily Fahrenheit temperatures that must range from −30 to 130; if a temperature is out of range, require the user to reenter it. If no temperature is lower than any previous one, display a message *Getting warmer*. If every temperature is lower than the previous one, display a message *Getting cooler*. If the temperatures are not entered in either ascending or descending order, display a message *It's a mixed bag*. Finally, display the temperatures in the order they were entered, and then display the average of the temperatures.

4. Write a program named **CheckZips** that is used by a package delivery service to check delivery areas. The program contains an array that holds the 10 zip codes of areas to which the company makes deliveries. Prompt a user to enter a zip code, and display a message indicating whether the zip code is in the company's delivery area.

5. Write a program called **DeliveryCharges** for the package delivery service in Exercise 4. The program should again use an array that holds the 10 zip codes of areas to which the company makes deliveries. Create a parallel array containing 10 delivery charges that differ for each zip code. Prompt a user to enter a zip code, and then display either a message indicating the price of delivery to that zip code or a message indicating that the company does not deliver to the requested zip code.

6. The Chat-A-While phone company provides service to six area codes and charges the per-minute rates for phone calls shown in Figure 6-25. Write a program named **ChatAWhile** that stores the area codes and rates in parallel arrays and allows a user to enter an area code and the length of time for a call in minutes, and then display the total cost of the call.

Area Code	Per-Minute Rate ($)
262	0.07
414	0.10
608	0.05
715	0.16
815	0.24
920	0.14

Figure 6-25 Per-minute phone call rates

7. The Nimble Fingers Typing School assigns grades based on words typed per minute, as shown in Figure 6-26. Write a program named **TypingGrades** that allows a user to enter a student's number of words typed. The output is the letter grade.

Words typed	Grade
0–15	F
16–30	D
31–50	C
51–75	B
76 and over	A

Figure 6-26 Typing grades

8. Write a program for The Carefree Resort named **ResortPrices** that prompts the user to enter the number of days for a resort stay. Then display the price per night and the total price. Nightly rates are $200 for one or two nights; $180 for three or four nights; $160 for five, six, or seven nights; and $145 for eight nights or more.

9. In Chapter 5, you wrote a **HomeSales** application for three salespeople: Danielle, Edward, and Francis. Now, modify the program to use arrays to store the salesperson names, allowed initials, and accumulated sales values.

10. Create a game similar to Hangman named **GuessAWord** in which a player guesses letters to try to replicate a hidden word. Store at least eight words in an array, and randomly select one to be the hidden word. (The statements needed to generate a random number are shown in the Exercises in the "Decision Making" and "Looping" chapters.) Initially, display the hidden word using asterisks to represent each letter. Allow the user to guess letters to replace the asterisks in the hidden word until the user completes the entire word. If the user guesses a letter that is not in the hidden word, display an appropriate message. If the user guesses a letter that appears multiple times in the hidden word, make sure that each correct letter is placed. Figure 6-27 shows typical games in progress in a console-based application and in a GUI application. In the GUI application, the user has successfully guessed *e*, and is about to guess *r*. *Hint:* If you create the GUI version of the game, you might want to include a Start button that selects the random word and performs other startup tasks before you reveal the game interface. After the startup tasks are complete, you can remove the Start button from the form.

CHAPTER 6 Using Arrays

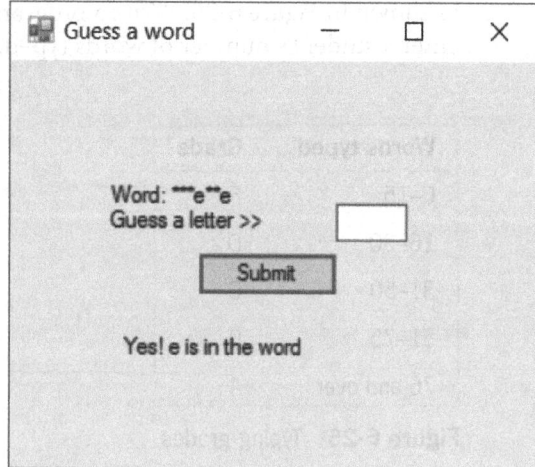

Figure 6-27 Typical executions of console-based and GUI GuessAWord programs

Debugging Exercises

1. Each of the following files in the Chapter.06 folder of your downloadable student files has syntax and/or logical errors. In each case, determine the problem, and fix the program. After you correct the errors, save each file using the same filename preceded with *Fixed*. For example, DebugSix01.cs will become FixedDebugSix01.cs.

   a. DebugSix01.cs   c. DebugSix03.cs

   b. DebugSix02.cs   d. DebugSix04.cs

Case Problems

1. In previous chapters, you created applications for the Greenville Idol competition. Now, modify the version of the **GreenvilleRevenue** program created in Chapter 5 so that after the user enters the number of contestants in this year's competition, the user is prompted for the appropriate number of contestant names and a code for each contestant that indicates the type of talent: *S* for singing, *D* for dancing, *M* for playing a musical instrument, or *O* for other. Make sure that all entered codes are valid, and if not, reprompt the user to enter a correct code. After contestant data entry is complete, display a count of each type of talent. Then, continuously prompt the user for a

talent code until the user enters a sentinel value. With each code entry, display a list of the contestants with that code, or display a message that the code is not valid and reprompt the user.

2. In previous chapters, you created applications for Marshall's Murals. Now, modify the version of the **MarshallsRevenue** program created in Chapter 5 so that after mural data entry is complete, the user is prompted for the appropriate number of customer names for both the interior and exterior murals and a code for each that indicates the mural style: *L* for landscape, *S* for seascape, *A* for abstract, *C* for children's, or *O* for other. When a code is invalid, reprompt the user for a valid code continuously. After data entry is complete, display a count of each type of mural. Then, continuously prompt the user for a mural style code until the user enters a sentinel value. With each code entry, display a list of all the customers with that code and whether their mural is interior or exterior. If the requested code is invalid, display an appropriate message and reprompt the user.

CHAPTER 7

Using Methods

Upon completion of this chapter, you will be able to:

◎ Understand methods and implementation hiding
◎ Write methods with no parameters and no return value
◎ Write methods that require a single argument
◎ Write methods that require multiple arguments
◎ Write methods that return a value
◎ Pass array values to a method
◎ Understand some alternate ways to write a `Main()` method header
◎ Appreciate issues using methods in GUI programs

CHAPTER 7 Using Methods

In the first chapters of this book, you learned to create C# programs containing `Main()` methods that can contain variable declarations, accept input, perform arithmetic, and produce output. You also learned to add decisions, loops, and arrays to your programs. As your programs grow in complexity, their `Main()` methods will contain many additional statements. Rather than creating increasingly long `Main()` methods, most programmers prefer to modularize their programs, placing instructions in smaller "packages" called methods. In this chapter, you learn to create many types of C# methods. You will understand how to send data to these methods and receive information back from them.

Understanding Methods and Implementation Hiding

A **method** is an encapsulated series of statements that carry out a task. Any class can contain an unlimited number of methods. So far, you have written console-based applications that contain a `Main()` method but no others, and you also have created GUI applications with a `Click()` method. Frequently, the methods you have written have **invoked**, or **called**, other methods; that is, your program used a method's name and the method executed to perform a task for the class. For example, you have created many programs that call the `WriteLine()` and `ReadLine()` methods, and in Chapter 6 you used `BinarySearch()`, `Sort()`, and `Reverse()` methods. These methods are prewritten; you only had to call them to have them work.

For example, consider the simple HelloClass program shown in Figure 7-1. The `Main()` method contains a statement that calls the `WriteLine()` method. You can identify method names in a program because they always are followed by a set of parentheses. Depending on the method, there might be an argument within the parentheses. You first encountered the term *argument* in Chapter 1. An argument is the data that appears between the parentheses in a method call. The call to the `WriteLine()` method within the HelloClass program in Figure 7-1 contains the string argument "Hello". Some methods you can invoke don't require any arguments.

Methods are similar to the procedures, functions, and subroutines used in other programming languages.

```
using static System.Console;
class HelloClass
{
    static void Main()
    {
        WriteLine("Hello");
    }
}
```

Figure 7-1 The HelloClass program

In the HelloClass program in Figure 7-1, `Main()` is a **calling method**—one that calls another. The `WriteLine()` method is a **called method**.

Understanding Implementation Hiding

When you call the `WriteLine()` method within the HelloClass program in Figure 7-1, you use a method that has already been created for you. Because the creators of C# knew you would often want to write a message to the output screen, they created a method you could call to accomplish that task. This method takes care of all the hardware details of producing a message on the output device; you simply call the method and pass the desired message to it. The `WriteLine()` method provides an example of **implementation hiding**, which means keeping the details of a method's operations hidden. For example, when you make a dental appointment, you do not need to know how the appointment is actually recorded at the dental office—perhaps it is written in a book, marked on a large chalkboard, or entered into a computerized database. The implementation details are of no concern to you as a client, and if the dental office changes its methods from one year to the next, the change does not affect your use of the appointment-making method. Your only concern is the way you interact with the dental office, not how the office tracks appointments. In the same way that you are a client of the dental practice, a method that uses another is a **client** of that method.

Hidden implementation methods often are said to exist in a black box. A **black box** is any device you can use without knowing how it works internally. The same is true with well-written program methods; the invoking program or method must know the name of the method it is using and what type of information to send it, but the program does not need to know how the method works. Later, you might substitute a new, improved method for the old one, and if the user's means of accessing the method does not change, you won't need to make any changes in programs that invoke the method. The creators of C# were able to anticipate many of the methods that would be necessary for your programs; you will continue to use many of these methods throughout this book. However, your programs often will require custom methods that the creators of C# could not have expected. In this chapter, you will learn to write your own custom methods.

To more easily incorporate methods into a program, it is common practice to store methods (or groups of associated methods) in their own classes and files. Then you can add the methods into any application that uses them. The resulting compound program is called a **multifile assembly**. As you learn more about C#, you might prefer to take this approach with your own programs. For simplicity, most example methods in this book are contained in the same file as any other methods that use them.

TWO TRUTHS & A LIE

Understanding Methods and Implementation Hiding

1. A method is an encapsulated series of statements that carry out a task.

2. Any class can contain an unlimited number of methods.

3. All the methods that will be used by your programs have been written for you and stored in files.

The false statement is #3. As you write programs, you will want to write many of your own custom methods.

Writing Methods with No Parameters and No Return Value

The output of the program in Figure 7-1 is simply the word *Hello*. Suppose you want to add three more lines of output to display a standard welcoming message when users execute your program. Of course, you can add three new `WriteLine()` statements to the existing program, but you also can create a method to display the three new lines.

Creating a method instead of adding three lines to the existing program is useful for two major reasons:

- If you add a method call instead of three new lines, the `Main()` method will remain short and easy to follow. The `Main()` method will contain just one new statement that calls a method rather than three separate `WriteLine()` statements.

- More importantly, a method is easily *reusable*. After you create the welcoming method, you can use it in any program, and you can allow other programmers to use it in their programs. In other words, you do the work once, and then you can use the method many times.

When you place code in a callable method instead of repeating the same code at several points in a program, you are avoiding **code bloat**—a colorful term that describes unnecessarily long or repetitive statements.

Figure 7-2 shows the parts of a C# method. A method must include:

- A **method declaration**, which is also known as a **method header** or **method definition**
- An opening curly brace
- A **method body**, which is a block of statements that carry out the method's work
- A closing curly brace

The method declaration defines the rules for using the method. It contains:

- Optional declared accessibility
- An optional `static` modifier
- The return type for the method
- The method name, or identifier
- An opening parenthesis
- An optional list of method parameters (separated with commas if there is more than one parameter)
- A closing parenthesis

> Writing Methods with No Parameters and No Return Value

```
private static void ShowWelcomeMessage()
{
    WriteLine("Welcome.");
    WriteLine("Have fun!");
    WriteLine("Enjoy the program!");
}
```

- Access modifier (If omitted, it's `private`)
- Optional `static` modifier
- Method return type
- Method name
- Method header (usually written on a single line)
- Method body between curly braces
- Optionally, method parameters could appear between these parentheses

Figure 7-2 The `ShowWelcomeMessage()` method

An Introduction to Accessibility

The optional declared **accessibility** for a method sets limits as to how other methods can use your method; accessibility can be any of the levels described in Table 7-1. The two levels you will use most frequently, `public` and `private` access, are shaded in the table. You will learn about protected access and what it means to derive types in the chapter "Introduction to Inheritance."

- **Public access** is established by including a `public` modifier in the member declaration. This modifier allows access to the method from other classes.

- **Private access** is established by including a `private` modifier in the member declaration or by omitting any accessibility modifier. This modifier limits method access to the class that contains the method.

Declared accessibility	Can methods contained in the same class access this method?	Can derived classes access this method?	Can assemblies or projects that contain this class access this method?	Can any class access this methods?
`public`	Yes	Yes	Yes	Yes
`protected internal`	Yes	Yes	Yes	No
`protected`	Yes	Yes	No	No
`internal`	Yes	No	Yes	No
`private`	Yes	No	No	No

Table 7-1 Summary of method accessibility

If you do not provide an accessibility modifier for a method, it is `private` by default. The `Main()` method headers that you have seen in all of the examples in this book have no access modifier, so they are `private`. You could explicitly add the keyword `private` to the method headers in any of the programs you have seen so far in this book, and you would notice no difference in execution: The methods still would be `private`. Actually, you also could substitute the `public` keyword in the `Main()` method headers without noticing any execution differences either—it's just that with that modification, other classes could have called the public `Main()` methods by using the appropriate class name and a dot before the method name. When you use a method's complete name, including its class, you are using its **fully qualified** name. In Chapter 1, you learned that you can use the fully qualified method call `System.Console.WriteLine()` to produce output. When you include `using static System.Console;` at the top of a program, then you do not need to use the fully qualified method name. Either way, because the classes you write can use the `Console` class method `WriteLine()`, you know the method must not be private.

In Chapter 3, you learned to create simple GUI applications, and you learned how to automatically generate a `Click()` method for a button; the generated method header started with the keyword `private`. For example, a private method named `Button1_Click()` cannot be used by any other class. If you changed the method's access specifier to `public`, it could be used by another class, but you probably would have no reason to do so. As you study C#, you will learn how to decide which access modifier to choose for each method you write. For now, unless you want a method to be accessible by outside classes, you should use the `private` access modifier with the method. This book uses no modifiers with `Main()` methods because Visual Studio does not create them in its automatically generated code, but this book uses appropriate access modifiers with other methods.

An Introduction to the Optional `static` Modifier

You can declare a method to be **static** or **nonstatic**. If you use the keyword modifier `static`, you indicate that a method can be called without referring to an object. Instead, you refer only to the class. For example, if `MethodS()` is static and `MethodN()` is nonstatic, the following statements describe typical method calls:

```
someClass.MethodS();
someObject.MethodN();
```

 You won't create objects until Chapter 9, so this chapter will use only nonstatic methods.

Writing Methods with No Parameters and No Return Value

A nonstatic method might be called with or without its class name. For example, if you have a class named `PayrollApplication` that contains a static method named `DeductUnionDues()`, you can call the method in two ways:

- If you call the method from a method in a different class (meaning it is public), you use the class name, a dot, and the method name, as in the following:

    `PayrollApplication.DeductUnionDues();`

- If you call the method from another method in the same class, you *can* use the class name as a prefix as shown above, but this approach is neither required nor conventional. Within a method in the `PayrollApplication` class, you can simply write the following abbreviated method call:

    `DeductUnionDues();`

If you do not indicate that a method is static, it is nonstatic by default and can be used only in conjunction with an object. When you begin to create your own classes in the chapter "Using Classes and Objects," you will write many nonstatic methods, and your understanding of the terms *static* and *nonstatic* will become clearer. As you work through this chapter, you will learn why each method is created to be static or nonstatic. Do not worry if you do not completely understand this chapter's references to nonstatic methods that require an object—the concept is explored in Chapter 9.

An Introduction to Return Types

Every method has a **return type**, indicating what kind of value the method will return to any other method that calls it. If a method does not return a value, its return type is `void`. A method's return type is known more succinctly as a **method's type**. Later in this chapter, you will create methods with return types such as `int` or `double` that return values of the corresponding type; such methods can be called *value-returning methods*. For now, the methods discussed are `void` methods that do not return a value.

When a method's return type is `void`, most C# programmers do not end the method with a `return` statement. However, you can end a `void` method with the following statement that indicates nothing is returned:

`return;`

Understanding the Method Identifier

Every method has a name that must be a legal C# identifier; that is, it must not contain spaces and must begin with a letter of the alphabet or an underscore. By convention, many programmers start method names with a verb because methods cause actions. Examples of conventional method names include `DeductTax()` and `DisplayNetPay()`.

Every method name is followed by a set of parentheses. Sometimes these parentheses contain parameters, but in the simplest methods, the parentheses are empty. A **parameter to a method** is a variable that holds data passed to a method when it is called. The terms *argument* and *parameter* are closely related. An argument is data in a method call, and a parameter is in the method header—it receives an argument's value when the method executes.

The parentheses that follow a method name in its header can hold one parameter or multiple parameters separated with commas. The contents within the parentheses are known as the **parameter list**.

Placing a Method in a Class

In summary, the first methods you write in console applications will be `private`, `static`, and `void` and will have empty parameter lists. That means they won't be called from other classes, they won't require an object reference, they will not return any value to their calling method, and they will not accept any data from the outside. Therefore, you can write the `ShowWelcomeMessage()` method as it is shown in Figure 7-2. According to its declaration, the method is `private` and `static`. It returns nothing, so the return type is `void`. Its identifier is `ShowWelcomeMessage`, and it receives nothing, so its parameter list is empty. The method body, consisting of three `WriteLine()` statements, appears within curly braces that follow the header.

By convention, programmers indent the statements in a method body, which makes the method header and its braces stand out. When you write a method using the Visual Studio editor, the method statements are indented for you automatically. You can place as many statements as you want within a method body.

Methods cannot overlap, and usually you want to place methods one after the other within a class. The order that methods appear in a class is not important; it is only the order in which they are called that affects how they execute.

In early versions of C#, you could not place a method within another method, however, starting with C# 7.0, you can. When a method resides entirely within another method, it is known as a **local function**, and it can be called only from its containing method and not from any other methods. (Some special rules are in place for local functions. For example, they cannot be static, and they do not use an accessibility modifier, so the rest of the methods used in this book will not be local functions.)

To make the `Main()` method call the `ShowWelcomeMessage()` method, you simply use the `ShowWelcomeMessage()` method's name as a statement within the body of the `Main()` method. Figure 7-3 shows the complete program with the method call shaded, and Figure 7-4 shows the output.

The `ShowWelcomeMessage()` method in the `HelloClass` class is `static`, and therefore it is called from the `Main()` method without an object reference (that is, without an object name and a dot before the method name. It also resides in the same class as the `Main()` method, so it can be called without using its class name.

Writing Methods with No Parameters and No Return Value

```
using static System.Console;
class HelloClass
{
    static void Main()
    {
        ShowWelcomeMessage();
        WriteLine("Hello");
    }
    private static void ShowWelcomeMessage()
    {
        WriteLine("Welcome.");
        WriteLine("Have fun!");
        WriteLine("Enjoy the program!");
    }
}
```

Figure 7-3 The HelloClass program with `Main()` method calling the `ShowWelcomeMessage()` method

Figure 7-4 Output of the HelloClass program

When the `Main()` method executes, it calls the `ShowWelcomeMessage()` method, so the three lines that make up the welcome message appear first in the output in Figure 7-4. Then, after the `ShowWelcomeMessage()` method is done, the `Main()` method displays *Hello*.

Each of two different classes can have its own method named `ShowWelcomeMessage()`. Such a method in the second class would be entirely distinct from the identically named method in the first class. The complete name of this method is `HelloClass.ShowWelcomeMessage()`, but you do not need to use the complete name when calling the method within the same class.

If another class named `SomeOtherClass` had a *public* static method with the same name, you could call the method from `HelloClass` using the following statement:

`SomeOtherClass.ShowWelcomeMessage();`

Declaring Variables and Constants in a Method

You can write any statements you need within a method, including variable and constant declarations. In Chapter 5, you learned that the term to describe the area of a program in which a variable or named constant is known is called its *scope*. Variables and constants that are declared within a method are in scope only from the point at which they are declared to the end of the method; programmers also say that the area in which an item can be used is the area in which it is **visible**. Programmers also say that the variable is a **local variable**. A locally-declared variable is not known to other methods or usable in them, and if another method contains a variable with the same name, the two variables are completely distinct.

CHAPTER 7 Using Methods

For example, Figure 7-5 shows a program containing two methods—`Main()` and `MethodWithItsOwnA()`—that each declare a variable named a. The variable in each method is completely distinct from the other and holds its own value, as shown in Figure 7-6. If you declared a variable named b in the `Main()` method and then tried to use b in `MethodWithItsOwnA()`, you would generate a compiler error. If you declared a variable named c in `MethodWithItsOwnA()` and tried to use it in `Main()`, you also would generate a compiler error.

```
using static System.Console;
class LocalVariableDemo
{
   static void Main()
   {
      int a = 12;
      WriteLine("In Main() a is {0}", a);
      MethodWithItsOwnA();
      WriteLine("In Main() a is {0}", a);
   }
   private static void MethodWithItsOwnA()
   {
      int a = 354;
      WriteLine("In method a is {0}", a);
   }
}
```

Figure 7-5 The LocalVariableDemo program

```
In Main() a is 12
In method a is 354
In Main() a is 12
```

Figure 7-6 Execution of the LocalVariableDemo program

 Watch the video *Using Methods*.

TWO TRUTHS & A LIE

Writing Methods with No Parameters and No Return Value

1. A method header must contain declared accessibility.
2. A method header must contain a return type.
3. A method header must contain an identifier.

The false statement is #1. Declaring accessibility in a method header is optional. If you do not use an access modifier, the method is private by default.

Writing Methods with No Parameters and No Return Value

You Do It

Calling a Method

In this section, you write a program in which a `Main()` method calls another method that displays a company's logo.

1. Open a new program named **DemoLogo**, and enter the statement that allows the program to use `System.Console` methods without qualifying them. Then type the class header for the `DemoLogo` class and the class-opening curly brace.

   ```
   using static System.Console;
   class DemoLogo
   {
   ```

2. Type the `Main()` method for the `DemoLogo` class. This method displays a line, then calls the `DisplayCompanyLogo()` method.

   ```
   static void Main()
   {
      Write("Our company is ");
      DisplayCompanyLogo();
   }
   ```

3. Add a method that displays a two-line logo for a company.

   ```
   private static void DisplayCompanyLogo()
   {
      WriteLine("See Sharp Optical");
      WriteLine("We prize your eyes");
   }
   ```

4. Add the closing curly brace for the class (}), and then save the file.

5. Compile and execute the program. The output should look like Figure 7-7.

   ```
   Our company is See Sharp Optical
   We prize your eyes
   ```

   Figure 7-7 Output of the DemoLogo program

(continues)

> *(continued)*
>
> 6. Remove the keyword `static` from the `DisplayCompanyLogo()` method, and then save and compile the program. An error message appears, as shown in Figure 7-8. The message indicates that an object reference is required for the nonstatic `DisplayCompanyLogo()` method. The error occurs because the `Main()` method is `static` and cannot call a nonstatic method without an object reference (that is, without using an object name and a dot before the method call). Remember that you will learn to create objects in Chapter 9, and then you can create the types of methods that do not use the keyword `static`. For now, retype the keyword `static` in the `DisplayCompanyLogo()` method header, and compile and execute the program again.
>
> ```
> DemoLogo.cs(7,7): error CS0120: An object reference is required for the
> non-static field, method, or property 'DemoLogo.DisplayCompanyLogo()'
> ```
>
> **Figure 7-8** Error message when calling a nonstatic method from a static method
>
> 7. Remove the keyword `private` from the header of the `DisplayCompanyLogo()` method. Save and compile the program, and then execute it. The execution is successful because the `private` keyword is optional. Replace the `private` keyword, and save the program.

Writing Methods That Require a Single Argument

Some methods require additional information. If a method could not receive arguments, then you would have to write an infinite number of methods to cover every possible situation. For example, when you make a dental appointment, you do not need to employ a different method for every date of the year at every possible time of day. Rather, you can supply the date and time as information to the method, and no matter what date and time you supply, the method is carried out correctly. If you design a method to compute an employee's paycheck, it makes sense that you can write a method named `ComputePaycheck()` and supply it with an hourly pay rate rather than having to develop methods with names like `ComputePaycheckAtFourteenDollarsAnHour()`, `ComputePaycheckAtFifteenDollarsAnHour()`, and so on.

You already have used methods to which you supplied a wide variety of parameters. At any call, the `WriteLine()` method can receive any one of an infinite number of strings as a parameter—"Hello", "Goodbye", and so on. No matter what message you send to the `WriteLine()` method, the message is displayed correctly.

Writing Methods That Require a Single Argument

When you write the declaration for a method that accepts a parameter, you need to include the following items within the method declaration parentheses:

- The data type of the parameter
- A local identifier (name) for the parameter.

For example, consider a method named `DisplaySalesTax()`, which computes and displays a tax as 7 percent of a selling price. The method header for a usable `DisplaySalesTax()` method could be the following:

```
static void DisplaySalesTax(double saleAmount)
```

You can think of the parentheses in a method declaration as a funnel into the method—data parameters listed there are "dropping in" to the method.

The parameter `double saleAmount` within the parentheses indicates that the `DisplaySalesTax()` method will receive a value of type `double`. Within the method, the value will be known as `saleAmount`. Figure 7-9 shows a complete method.

```
private static void DisplaySalesTax(double saleAmount)
{
   double tax;
   const double RATE = 0.07;
   tax = saleAmount * RATE;
   WriteLine("The tax on {0} is {1}",
      saleAmount, tax.ToString("C"));
}
```

Figure 7-9 The `DisplaySalesTax()` method

Within the `DisplaySalesTax()` method, you must use the format string and `ToString()` method if you want figures to display to exactly two decimal positions. You learned how to display values to a fixed number of decimal places in Chapter 2; recall that using the fixed format with no number defaults to two decimal places.

You create the `DisplaySalesTax()` method as a `void` method (one that has a `void` return type) because you do not need it to return any value to any method that uses it—its only function is to receive the `saleAmount` value, multiply it by 0.07, and then display the result. You create it as a `static` method because you do not want the `Main()` method to be required to create an object with which to use it; you want the static `Main()` method to be able to call the method directly.

Within a program, you can call the `DisplaySalesTax()` method by using the method's name and, within parentheses, an argument that is either a constant value or a variable. Thus, assuming `myPurchase` is a declared `double` variable with an assigned value, both of the following calls to the `DisplaySalesTax()` method invoke it correctly:

```
DisplaySalesTax(12.99);
DisplaySalesTax(myPurchase);
```

You can call the `DisplaySalesTax()` method any number of times, with a different constant or variable argument each time. The value of each of these arguments becomes known as `saleAmount` within the method. Interestingly, if the argument in the method call is a variable, it might possess the same identifier as `saleAmount` or a different one, such as `myPurchase`. The identifier `saleAmount` is simply the name the value "goes by" while being used within the method, no matter what name it uses in the calling program. That is, the variable `saleAmount` is a local variable to the `DisplaySalesTax()` method, as are variables and constants declared within a method.

The variable `saleAmount` declared in the method header is an example of a **formal parameter**, a parameter within a method header that accepts a value. In contrast, arguments within a method *call* often are referred to as **actual parameters**. For example, in the method calling statement `DisplaySalesTax(myPurchase);`, `myPurchase` is an actual parameter.

The formal parameter `saleAmount` also is an example of a *value parameter*, or a parameter that receives a copy of the value passed to it. You will learn more about value parameters and other types of parameters in the next chapter.

The `DisplaySalesTax()` method employs implementation hiding. That is, if a programmer changes the way in which the tax value is calculated—for example, by coding one of the following—programs that use the `DisplaySalesTax()` method will not be affected and will not need to be modified:

```
tax = saleAmount * 7 / 100;
tax = 0.07 * saleAmount;
tax = RATE * saleAmount;
```

No matter how the tax is calculated, a calling program passes a value into the `DisplaySalesTax()` method, and a calculated result appears on the screen.

Figure 7-10 shows a complete program called `UseTaxMethod`. It uses the `DisplaySalesTax()` method twice, first with a variable argument, and then with a constant argument. The program's output appears in Figure 7-11.

Writing Methods That Require a Single Argument

```
using static System.Console;
class UseTaxMethod
{
   static void Main()
   {
      double myPurchase = 12.99;
      DisplaySalesTax(myPurchase);
      DisplaySalesTax(35.67);
   }
   private static void DisplaySalesTax(double saleAmount)
   {
      double tax;
      const double RATE = 0.07;
      tax = saleAmount * RATE;
      WriteLine("The tax on {0} is {1}",
         saleAmount.ToString("C"), tax.ToString("C"));
   }
}
```

Figure 7-10 Complete program using the `DisplaySalesTax()` method two times

```
The tax on $12.99 is $0.91
The tax on $35.67 is $2.50
```

Figure 7-11 Output of the UseTaxMethod program

An argument type in a method call can match the method's parameter type exactly, but it can use a different data type if the argument can be converted automatically to the parameter type. Recall from Chapter 2 that C# supports the following automatic conversions:

- From sbyte to short, int, long, float, double, or decimal
- From byte to short, ushort, int, uint, long, ulong, float, double, or decimal
- From short to int, long, float, double, or decimal
- From ushort to int, uint, long, ulong, float, double, or decimal
- From int to long, float, double, or decimal
- From uint to long, ulong, float, double, or decimal
- From long to float, double, or decimal
- From ulong to float, double, or decimal
- From char to ushort, int, uint, long, ulong, float, double, or decimal
- From float to double

CHAPTER 7 Using Methods

As an example, a method with the header `private static void DisplaySalesTax(double saleAmount)` can work with the following method call that uses an integer argument because integers are promoted automatically to `double`s:

`DisplaySalesTax(100);`

Now that you have seen how to write methods that accept an argument, you might guess that when you write `WriteLine("Hello");`, the header for the called method is similar to `public static void WriteLine(string s)`. You might not know the parameter name the creators of C# have chosen, but you do know the method's return type, name, and parameter type. (If you use the IntelliSense feature of Visual Studio, you can discover the parameter name. See Appendix C for more details.)

Watch the video *Arguments and Parameters*.

TWO TRUTHS & A LIE

Writing Methods That Require a Single Argument

1. When you write the declaration for a method that accepts a parameter, you need to include the parameter's data type within the method header.

2. When you write the declaration for a method that accepts a parameter, you need to include the identifier of the argument that will be sent to the method within the method header.

3. When you write the declaration for a method that accepts a parameter, you need to include a local identifier for the parameter within the method header.

The false statement is #2. When you write the definition for a method, you include the data type and a local parameter name within the parentheses of the method header, but you do not include the name of any argument that will be sent from a calling method. After all, the method might be invoked any number of times with any number of different arguments.

Writing Methods That Require Multiple Arguments

You can pass multiple arguments to a method by listing the arguments within the call to the method and separating them with commas. For example, rather than creating a `DisplaySalesTax()` method that multiplies an amount by 0.07, you might prefer to create a more flexible method to which you can pass two values—the value on which the tax is calculated and the tax percentage by which it should be multiplied. Figure 7-12 shows a method that uses two parameters.

Writing Methods That Require Multiple Arguments

```
private static void DisplaySalesTax(double saleAmount, double taxRate)
{
   double tax;
   tax = saleAmount * taxRate;
   WriteLine("The tax on {0} at {1} is {2}",
      saleAmount.ToString("C"), taxRate.ToString("P"),
      tax.ToString("C"));
}
```

Figure 7-12 The `DisplaySalesTax()` method that accepts two parameters

In Figure 7-12, two parameters (`saleAmount` and `taxRate`) appear within the parentheses in the method header. A comma separates the parameters, and each parameter requires its own named type (in this case, both parameters are of type `double`) and an identifier. A declaration for a method that receives two or more arguments must list the type for each parameter separately, even if the parameters have the *same* type.

When you pass values to the method in a statement such as `DisplaySalesTax(myPurchase, localRate);`, the first value passed will be referenced as `saleAmount` within the method, and the second value passed will be referenced as `taxRate`. Therefore, it is very important that arguments be passed to a method in the correct order. The following call results in output stating that *The tax on $200.00 at 10.00% is $20.00*:

`DisplaySalesTax(200.00, 0.10);`

However, the following call results in output stating that *The tax on $0.10 at 200.00% is $20.00*. Although the arithmetic is the same, the explanation is wrong (unless there is an extremely high local tax rate).

`DisplaySalesTax(0.10, 200.00);`

You can write a method to take any number of parameters in any order. When you call the method, however, the arguments you send to it must match (in both number and type) the parameters listed in the method declaration, with the following exceptions:

- The type of an argument does not need to match the parameter list exactly if the argument can be promoted to the parameter type. For example, an `int` argument can be passed to a `double` parameter.

- The number of arguments does not need to match the number in the parameter list when you use *default arguments*. You will learn about default arguments in Chapter 8.

Thus, a method to compute and display an automobile salesperson's commission might require arguments such as a string for the salesperson's name, an integer value of a sold car, a `double` percentage commission rate, and a character code for the vehicle type. The correct method will execute only when all arguments of the correct types are sent in the correct order.

> **TWO TRUTHS & A LIE**
>
> **Writing Methods That Require Multiple Arguments**
>
> 1. The following is a usable C# method header:
>
>   `private static void MyMethod(double amt, sum)`
>
> 2. The following is a usable C# method header:
>
>   `private static void MyMethod2(int x, double y)`
>
> 3. The following is a usable C# method header:
>
>   `static void MyMethod3(int id, string name, double rate)`
>
> The false statement is #1. In a method header, each parameter must have a data type, even if the data types for all the parameters are the same. The header in #3 does not contain an accessibility indicator, but that is optional.

Writing Methods That Return a Value

A method can return, at most, one value to a method that calls it. The return type for a method can be any type used in the C# programming language, which includes the basic built-in types `int`, `double`, `char`, and so on. You can also use a class type as the return type for a method, including any type built into the C# language. For example, you have used a return value from the `ReadLine()` method when writing a statement such as `inputString = ReadLine();`. Because the `ReadLine()` method call can be assigned to a `string`, its return type is `string`. In Chapter 3 you learned about some control types, such as `Button` and `Label`. Objects of these types could be returned from a method. You also will learn to create your own types in Chapter 9, and these can be returned from a method too. Of course, a method also can return nothing, in which case the return type is `void`.

For example, suppose that you want to create a method to accept the hours an employee worked and the hourly pay rate, and to return a calculated gross pay value. The header for this method could be:

`private static double CalcPay(double hours, double rate)`

Figure 7-13 shows this method.

```
private static double CalcPay(double hours, double rate)
{
   double gross;
   gross = hours * rate;
   return gross;
}
```

Figure 7-13 The `CalcPay()` method

Writing Methods That Return a Value

Notice the `return` statement, which is the last statement within the `CalcPay()` method. A **return statement** causes a value to be sent back to the calling method; in the `CalcPay()` method, the value stored in `gross` is sent back to any method that calls the `CalcPay()` method. Also notice the type `double` that precedes the method name in the method header. The data type used in a method's `return` statement must be the same as the return type declared in the method's header, or the program will not compile.

If a method returns a value and you call the method, you typically will want to use the returned value, although you are not required to use it. For example, when you invoke the `CalcPay()` method, you might want to assign the value to a `double` variable named `grossPay`, as in the following statement:

`grossPay = CalcPay(myHours, myRate);`

The `CalcPay()` method returns a `double`, so it is appropriate to assign the returned value to a `double` variable. Figure 7-14 shows a program that uses the `CalcPay()` method in the shaded statement, and Figure 7-15 shows the output.

```
using static System.Console;
class UseCalcPay
{
    static void Main()
    {
        double myHours = 37.5;
        double myRate = 12.75;
        double grossPay;
        grossPay = CalcPay(myHours, myRate);
        WriteLine("I worked {0} hours at {1} per hour",
            myHours, myRate);
        WriteLine("My gross pay is {0}", grossPay.ToString("C"));
    }
    private static double CalcPay(double hours, double rate)
    {
        double gross;
        gross = hours * rate;
        return gross;
    }
}
```

Figure 7-14 Program using the `CalcPay()` method

```
I worked 37.5 hours at 12.75 per hour
My gross pay is $478.13
```

Figure 7-15 Output of the `UseCalcPay` program

Instead of storing a method's returned value in a variable, you can use it directly, as in statements that produce output or perform arithmetic such as the following:

```
WriteLine("My gross pay is {0}",
    CalcPay(myHours, myRate).ToString("C"));
double tax = CalcPay(myHours, myRate) * TAX_RATE;
```

In the first statement, the call to the `CalcPay()` method is made within the `WriteLine()` method call. In the second, `CalcPay()`'s returned value is used in an arithmetic statement. Because `CalcPay()` returns a `double`, you can use the method call `CalcPay()` in the same way you would use any `double` value. The method call `CalcPay()` has a `double` data type in the same way a `double` variable does.

As an additional example, suppose that you have a method named `GetPrice()` that accepts an item number and returns its price. The header is as follows:

```
private static double GetPrice(int itemNumber)
```

Further suppose that you want to ask the user to enter an item number from the keyboard so you can pass it to the `GetPrice()` method. You can get the value from the user, store it in a string, convert the string to an integer, pass the integer to the `GetPrice()` method, and store the returned value in a variable named `price` in four or five separate statements. Or you can write the following:

```
price = GetPrice(Convert.ToInt32(ReadLine()));
```

This statement contains a method call to `ReadLine()` within a method call to `Convert.ToInt32()`, within a method call to `GetPrice()`. When method calls are placed inside other method calls, the calls are **nested method calls**. When you write a statement with three nested method calls as in the previous statement, the innermost method executes first. Its return value is then used as an argument to the intermediate method, and its return value is used as an argument to the outer method. There is no limit to how "deep" you can go with nested method calls.

The system keeps track of where to return after a method call in an area of memory called the *stack*. Another area of memory called the *heap* is where memory can be allocated while a program is executing.

Writing a Method That Returns a Boolean Value

When a method returns a value that is type `bool`, the method call can be used anywhere you can use a Boolean expression. For example, suppose you have written a method named `isPreferredCustomer()` that returns a Boolean value indicating whether a customer is a preferred customer who qualifies for a discount. Then you can write an `if` statement such as the following:

```
if(isPreferredCustomer())
    price = price - DISCOUNT;
```

Writing Methods That Return a Value

In Chapter 4 you learned about side effects and how they affect compound Boolean expressions. When you use Boolean methods, you must be especially careful not to cause unintended side effects. For example, consider the following `if` statement, in which the intention is to set a delivery fee to 0 if both the `isPreferredCustomer()` and `isLocalCustomer()` methods return true:

```
if(isPreferredCustomer() && isLocalCustomer())
   deliveryFee = 0;
```

If the `isLocalCustomer()` method should perform some desired task—for example, displaying a message about the customer's status or applying a local customer discount to the price—then you might not achieve the desired results. Because of short-circuit evaluation, if the `isPreferredCustomer()` method returns `false`, the `isLocalCustomer()` method never executes. If that is your intention, then using methods in this way is fine, but always consider any unintended side effects.

Analyzing a Built-In Method

C# provides you with many prewritten methods such as `WriteLine()` and `ReadLine()`. In Chapter 2, you learned about C#'s arithmetic operators, such as + and *, and you learned that C# provides no exponential operator. Instead, to raise a number to a power, you can use the built-in `Pow()` method. For example, to raise 2 to the third power (2 * 2 * 2) and store the answer in the variable `result`, you can write a program that includes the following statement:

```
double result = Math.Pow(2.0, 3.0);
```

From this statement, you know the following about the `Pow()` method:

- It is in the `Math` class because the class name and a dot precede the method call.
- It is `public` because you can write a program that uses it.
- It is `static` because it is used with its class name and a dot, without any object.
- It accepts two `double` parameters.
- It returns a `double` or a type that can be promoted automatically to a `double` (such as an `int`) because its answer is stored in a `double`.

Although you know many facts about the `Pow()` method, you do not know how its instructions are carried out internally. In good object-oriented style, its implementation is hidden.

CHAPTER 7 Using Methods

TWO TRUTHS & A LIE

Writing a Method That Returns a Value

1. A method can return, at most, one value to a method that calls it.

2. The data type used in a method's `return` statement must be the same as the return type declared in the method's header.

3. If a method returns a value and you call the method, you must store the value in a variable that has the same data type as the method's parameter.

> The false statement is #3. If a method returns a value and you call the method, you typically will want to use the returned value, but you are not required to use it. Furthermore, if you do assign the returned value to a storage variable, that variable does not have to match any parameter's value. Instead, the storage variable needs to be capable of accepting the method's returned type.

You Do It

Writing a Method That Receives Parameters and Returns a Value

Next, you write a method named `CalcPhoneCallPrice()` that both receives parameters and returns a value. The purpose of the method is to accept the length of a phone call in minutes and the rate charged per minute and then to calculate the price of a call, assuming each call includes a 25-cent connection charge in addition to the per-minute charge. After writing the `CalcPhoneCallPrice()` method, you write a `Main()` method that calls the `CalcPhoneCallPrice()` method using four different sets of data as arguments.

1. Start a program named **PhoneCall** by typing a `using` statement, class header, and opening brace:

   ```
   using static System.Console;
   class PhoneCall
   {
   ```

(continues)

(continued)

2. Type the following `CalcPhoneCallPrice()` method. The method is declared as `static` because it will be called by a `static` `Main()` method without creating an object. The method receives an integer and a `double` as parameters. The fee for a call is calculated as 0.25 plus the minutes times the rate per minute. The method returns the phone call fee to the calling method.

   ```
   private static double CalcPhoneCallPrice(int minutes,
      double rate)
   {
      const double BASE_FEE = 0.25;
      double callFee;
      callFee = BASE_FEE + minutes * rate;
      return callFee;
   }
   ```

3. Add the `Main()` method header for the `PhoneCall` class. Begin the method by declaring two arrays; one contains two call lengths, and the other contains two rates. You will use all the possible combinations of call lengths and rates to test the `CalcPhoneCallPrice()` method. Also, declare a `double` named `priceOfCall` that will hold the result of a calculated call price.

   ```
   static void Main()
   {
      int[] callLengths = {2, 5};
      double[] rates = {0.03, 0.12};
      double priceOfCall;
   ```

4. Add a statement that displays column headings under which you can list combinations of call lengths, rates, and prices. The three column headings are right-aligned, each in a field 10 characters wide.

   ```
   WriteLine("{0, 10}{1, 10}{2, 10}",
      "Minutes", "Rate", "Price");
   ```

(continues)

(continued)

5. Add a pair of nested loops that pass each callLength and each rate to the CalcPhoneCallPrice() method in turn. As each pair is passed, the result is stored in the priceOfCall variable, and the details are displayed. Using the nested loops allows you to pass each combination of call time and rate so that multiple possibilities for the values can be tested conveniently.

```
for(int x = 0; x < callLengths.Length; ++x)
   for(int y = 0; y < rates.Length; ++y)
   {
       priceOfCall = CalcPhoneCallPrice(callLengths[x],
           rates[y]);
       WriteLine("{0, 10}{1, 10}{2, 10}",
           callLengths[x], rates[y], priceOfCall.ToString("C"));
   }
```

6. Add a closing curly brace for the Main() method and another for the PhoneCall class.

7. Save the file, and then compile and run the program. The output looks like Figure 7-16. It shows how a single method can produce a variety of results when you use different values for the arguments.

```
Minutes      Rate      Price
      2      0.03     $0.31
      2      0.12     $0.49
      5      0.03     $0.40
      5      0.12     $0.85
```

Figure 7-16 Output of the PhoneCall program

Passing Array Values to a Method

Passing an array element to a method and passing an array to a method require different approaches.

Passing a Single Array Element to a Method

In the chapter "Using Arrays," you learned that you can declare an array to create a list of elements, and that you can use any individual array element in the same manner as you would use any single variable of the same type. That is, suppose you declare an integer array as follows:

`int[] someNums = new int[12];`

You can subsequently output `someNums[0]` or add 1 to `someNums[1]`, just as you would for any integer. Similarly, you can pass a single array element to a method in exactly the same manner as you would pass a variable.

Consider the program shown in Figure 7-17. This program creates and uses an array of four integers. Figure 7-18 shows the program's execution.

```
using static System.Console;
class PassArrayElement
{
   static void Main()
   {
      int[] someNums = {10, 12, 22, 35};
      int x;
      Write("\nAt beginning of Main() method...");
      for(x = 0; x < someNums.Length; ++x)
         Write("{0,6}", someNums[x]);
      WriteLine();
      for(x = 0; x < someNums.Length; ++x)
         MethodGetsOneInt(someNums[x]);
      Write("At end of Main() method.........");
      for(x = 0; x < someNums.Length; ++x)
         Write("{0,6}", someNums[x]);
   }
   private static void MethodGetsOneInt(int oneVal)
   {
      Write("In MethodGetsOneInt() {0}", oneVal);
      oneVal = 999;
      WriteLine("    After change {0}", oneVal);
   }
}
```

Figure 7-17 The PassArrayElement program

```
At beginning of Main() method...    10      12      22      35
In MethodGetsOneInt() 10      After change 999
In MethodGetsOneInt() 12      After change 999
In MethodGetsOneInt() 22      After change 999
In MethodGetsOneInt() 35      After change 999
At end of Main() method.........    10      12      22      35
```

Figure 7-18 Output of the PassArrayElement program

As you can see in Figure 7-18, the program displays the four original values, then passes each to the `MethodGetsOneInt()` method, where it is displayed and then changed to 999. After the method executes four times, the `Main()` method displays the four values again, showing that they are unchanged by the assignments within `MethodGetsOneInt()`. The `oneVal` variable is local to the `MethodGetsOneInt()` method; therefore, any changes to variables passed into the method are not permanent and are not reflected in the array declared in the `Main()` program. Each time the `MethodGetsOneInt()` method executes, its `oneVal` parameter holds only a copy of the array element passed into the method, and the `oneVal` variable exists only while the `MethodGetsOneInt()` method is executing.

Passing an Array to a Method

Instead of passing a single array element to a method, you can pass an entire array. You indicate that a method parameter must be an array by placing square brackets after the data type in the method's parameter list. When you pass an array to a method, changes you make to array elements within the method are reflected in the original array that was sent to the method. A memory address is also known as a **reference**. Arrays, like all objects but unlike built-in types such as `double` and `int`, are **passed by reference**. That is, when a simple built-in type is passed to a method, it is **passed by value**. That is, the method receives a copy of the value at a new memory address. However, when an array is passed to a method, the method receives the actual memory address of the array and has access to the actual values in the array elements. You already have seen that methods can alter arrays passed to them. When you used the `Sort()` and `Reverse()` methods in Chapter 6, you saw that the methods changed their array parameter contents.

The program shown in Figure 7-19 creates an array of four integers. After the integers are displayed, the entire array is passed to a method named `MethodGetsArray()` in the shaded statement. Within the method header, the parameter is declared as an array by using square brackets after the parameter data type. Within the method, the numbers are output, which shows that they retain their values from `Main()` upon entering the method, but then the value 888 is assigned to each number. Even though `MethodGetsArray()` is a `void` method (meaning that nothing is returned to the `Main()` method), when the program displays the array for the second time within the `Main()` method, all of the values have been changed to 888, as you can see in Figure 7-20. Because arrays are passed by reference, the `MethodGetsArray()` method "knows" the address of the array declared in `Main()` and makes its changes directly to the original array that was declared in the `Main()` method.

Passing Array Values to a Method

```
using static System.Console;
class PassEntireArray
{
   static void Main()
   {
      int[] someNums = {10, 12, 22, 35};
      int x;
      Write("\nAt beginning of Main() method...");
      for(x = 0; x < someNums.Length; ++x)
         Write("{0, 6}", someNums[x]);
      WriteLine();
      MethodGetsArray(someNums);
      Write("At end of Main() method..........");
      for(x = 0; x < someNums.Length; ++x)
         Write("{0, 6}", someNums[x]);
   }
   private static void MethodGetsArray(int[] vals)
   {
      int x;
      Write("In MethodGetsArray() ");
      for(x = 0; x < vals.Length; ++x)
         Write(" {0}", vals[x]);
      WriteLine();
      for(x = 0; x < vals.Length; ++x)
         vals[x] = 888;
      Write("After change");
      for(x = 0; x < vals.Length; ++x)
         Write(" {0}", vals[x]);
      WriteLine();
   }
}
```

Figure 7-19 The PassEntireArray program

```
At beginning of Main() method...    10    12    22    35
In MethodGetsArray()  10 12 22 35
After change 888 888 888 888
At end of Main() method..........   888   888   888   888
```

Figure 7-20 Output of the PassEntireArray program

Notice that you do not insert a number within the square brackets of the array definition in the method parameter list. Inserting a number causes a compiler error. It makes sense that the brackets are empty because a method that receives an array gets its starting address, not a number of elements.

You can create and pass an unnamed array to a method in a single step. For example, you can write the following:

```
MethodThatAcceptsArray(new int[] {45, 67, 89});
```

You can pass a multidimensional array to a method by indicating the appropriate number of dimensions after the data type in the method header. For example, the following method headers accept two-dimensional arrays of `ints` and `doubles`, respectively:

```
private static void displayScores(int[ , ] scoresArray)
private static bool areAllPricesHigh(double[ , ] prices)
```

With jagged arrays, you can insert the appropriate number of square brackets after the data type in the method header. For example, the following method headers accept jagged arrays of `ints` and `doubles`, respectively:

```
private static void displayIDs(int[][] idArray)
private static double computeTotal(double[][] prices)
```

With methods that accept multidimensional arrays as parameters (whether jagged or not), notice that the brackets that define the array in each method header are empty. Like any other array passed to a method, inserting numbers into the brackets for a jagged array is not necessary because each passed array name is a starting memory address. The way you manipulate subscripts within the method determines how rows and columns are accessed.

The size of each dimension of a multidimensional array can be accessed using the `GetLength()` method. For example, `scoresArray.GetLength(0)` returns the value of the first dimension of `scoresArray`.

Watch the video *Passing Arrays to Methods*.

TWO TRUTHS & A LIE

Passing Array Values to a Method

1. You indicate that a method parameter can be an array element by placing a data type and identifier in the method's parameter list.

2. You indicate that a method parameter must be an array by placing parentheses after the data type in the method's parameter list.

3. Arrays are passed by reference; that is, the method receives the actual memory address of the array and has access to the actual values in the array elements.

The false statement is #2. You indicate that a method parameter must be an array by placing square brackets after the data type in the method's parameter list.

Alternate Ways to Write a `Main()` Method Header

Throughout this book, you have written `Main()` methods with the following header:

`static void Main()`

Using the return type `void` and listing nothing between the parentheses that follow `Main` is just one way to write a `Main()` method header in a program. However, it is the first way listed in the C# documentation, and it is the convention used in this book. This section describes alternatives because you might see different `Main()` method headers in other books or in programs written by others.

Writing a `Main()` Method with a Parameter List

An alternate way to write a `Main()` method header is as follows:

`static void Main(string[] args)`

The phrase `string[] args` is a parameter to the `Main()` method. The variable `args` represents an array of strings that you can pass to `Main()`. Although you can use any identifier, `args` is conventional. In particular, Java programmers might prefer the C# version of `Main()` that includes the `string[] args` parameter because their convention is to write main methods with the same parameter.

Use this format for the `Main()` method header if you need to access command-line arguments passed in to your application. For example, the program in Figure 7-21 displays an `args` array that is a parameter to its `Main()` method. Figure 7-22 shows how a program might be executed from the command line using arguments to `Main()`.

```
using static System.Console;
class DisplayArgs
{
   static void Main(string[] args)
   {
      for(int x = 0; x < args.Length; ++x)
         WriteLine("Argument {0} is {1}", x, args[x]);
   }
}
```

Figure 7-21 A `Main()` method with a `string[] args` parameter

```
C:\CSharp>DisplayArgs Alpha Beta Gamma Delta
Argument 0 is Alpha
Argument 1 is Beta
Argument 2 is Gamma
Argument 3 is Delta

C:\CSharp>
```

Figure 7-22 Executing the DisplayArgs program with arguments

CHAPTER 7 Using Methods

Even if you do not need access to command-line arguments, you can still use the version of the `Main()` method header that references them. You should use this version if your instructor or supervisor indicates you should follow this convention.

Writing a `Main()` Method with an Integer Return Type

Some programmers prefer to write `Main()` method headers that have a return type of `int` instead of `void`. If you use this form, the last statement in the `Main()` method must be a `return` statement that returns an integer. By convention, a return value of 0 means that an application ended without error. The value might be used by your operating system or another program that uses your program. In particular, C++ programmers might prefer the version of `Main()` that returns an `int` because conventionally they write their main methods with an `int` return type.

Even if you do not need to use a return value from a `Main()` method, you can still use the version of the `Main()` method header that includes a return value. You should use this version if your instructor or supervisor indicates you should follow this convention.

Writing a `Main()` Method with `public` Access

Some programmers prefer to write `Main()` method headers with `public` access rather than `private`, which is the default access when no specifier is listed. In particular, Java programmers might prefer using `public` because the style is conventional for them. If a class's `Main()` method is `public`, it can be called from another class by using its fully qualified name. Because you rarely want to do this, C# programmers often omit the `Main()` method's access specifier, making it `private` by default.

TWO TRUTHS & A LIE

Alternate Ways to Write a `Main()` Method Header

1. In C#, a `Main()` method header can be written `public static void Main()`.
2. In C#, a `Main()` method header can be written `static void Main(string[] args)`.
3. In C#, a `Main()` method header can be written `static int main(string args)`.

The false statement is #3. In C#, a `Main()` method header can be written as shown in either of the first two examples. Statement #3 is wrong because `main()` must be capitalized, and `string` must be followed by a pair of square brackets.

Issues Using Methods in GUI Programs

You can call methods from other methods in a GUI application in the same way you can in a console application. Some special considerations when creating GUI applications include the following:

- Understanding methods that are automatically generated in the visual environment
- Appreciating scope in a GUI program
- Creating methods to be nonstatic when associated with a Form

Understanding Methods That Are Generated Automatically in the Visual Environment

When you create GUI applications using the IDE, many methods are generated automatically. For example, when you place a Button named okButton on a Form in the IDE and double-click it, a method is generated with the following header:

`private void okButton_Click(object sender, EventArgs e)`

The method is private, which means it can be used only within its class, and it is void, meaning it does not return a value. You could change the access specifier to public and the method still would work, but usually you would have no reason to make such a change. If you change the return type (void), the program will not compile.

The format of the method name okButton_Click() is conventional for event-handling methods that are created automatically. The name includes the control name, an underscore, and the event that causes the method to execute—in this case, a Click event. Because the C# convention is to begin method names with an uppercase letter, you usually want to change the automatically-generated method names as you saw in the examples in Chapter 3. For example, you might change okButton_Click() to OkButton_Click().

The parameters received by a Click() method arrive automatically when a user clicks the corresponding Button. The parameter sender is the object that generated the event that caused the method to execute, and the parameter e contains information about the type of event. Figure 7-23 shows a Click() method in a GUI application that displays the ToString() values of these two parameters.

```
private void OkButton_Click(object sender, EventArgs e)
{
   label1.Text = "object sender is: " + sender.ToString();
   label2.Text = "EventArgs e is: " + e.ToString();
}
```

Figure 7-23 The OkButton_Click() method in the ClickParameterInfo program

Figure 7-24 shows the output after the button is clicked. The object that generated the event is the button that contains the text *OK*, and the type of event was generated by a mouse. You have seen many `Click()` methods in earlier chapters that had the same parameters, but you did not use them. As with any other method, you never are required to use the parameters passed in.

Figure 7-24 Output generated by the `OkButton_Click()` method in Figure 7-23

Appreciating Scope in a GUI Program

When you create event-handling methods in a GUI application, you must constantly be aware of which variables and constants are needed by multiple methods. When you declare a variable or constant within a method, it is local to that method. If a variable or constant is needed by multiple event-handling methods—for example, by two different `Click()` methods—then the variables or constants in question must be defined outside the methods (but within the `Form` class) so that both `Click()` methods have access to them. When you write other methods, you can decide what arguments to pass in, but event-handling methods that are generated automatically have predefined sets of parameters, so you cannot be as flexible in using them as you can with other methods you write. In Chapter 9, "Using Classes and Objects," you see many examples of variables declared within a class but outside methods; such variables are called *fields*.

Creating Methods to be Nonstatic When Associated with a `Form`

In Chapter 1, you learned that the keyword `static` is used with `Main()` methods in console applications because the method is associated with its containing class and not with an object. When you create a GUI application and generate a method, such as a `Click()` method associated with a `Button` on a `Form`, the keyword `static` does not appear in the method header because the method is associated with an object—the `Form` from which the method-invoking events are sent. When you execute a GUI program using a `Form`, the program creates a `Form` object, and the methods associated with it are nonstatic. In the chapter "Using Classes and Objects," you will learn much more about the differences between static and nonstatic methods. For now, omit the word `static` when you create methods that are intended to be called by other nonstatic methods in your GUI applications. For example, if you create a `Click()` method that responds to button clicks, it will be nonstatic by default because it is associated with an object that is a `Form`.

TWO TRUTHS & A LIE

Issues Using Methods in GUI Programs

1. An advantage to using the IDE to create GUI programs is that many methods you need are generated automatically.

2. As with any other methods, when you create a Click() method associated with a button in a GUI application, you do not need to reference the parameters within the method body.

3. If you want a Click() method to add two variables, you must pass them in as parameters.

The false statement is #3. Event-handling methods that are generated automatically have predefined sets of parameters, so you cannot be as flexible in using them as you can with other methods you write. Typically, the variables used in a Click() method would be defined outside the method but inside the Form class where the Click() method resides.

Chapter Summary

- A method is a series of statements that carry out a task. Any class can contain an unlimited number of methods. Object-oriented programs hide their methods' implementations.

- You write methods to make programs easier to understand and so that you can easily reuse them. In C#, a method must include a method declaration, an opening curly brace, a method body, and a closing curly brace. The method declaration defines the rules for using the method; it contains an optional declared accessibility, an optional `static` modifier, a return type for the method, an identifier, and an optional list of method parameters between parentheses.

- Some method calls require arguments. The items received by a method are parameters. When you write the declaration for a method that can receive a parameter, you need to include the type of parameter and a local identifier for it within the method declaration parentheses. A variable declared in a method header is a formal parameter, and an argument within a method call is an actual parameter.

- You can pass multiple arguments to a method by listing the arguments within the parentheses in the call to the method and separating them with commas. You can write a method to take any number of parameters. When you call the method, the arguments you send to it must match in both number and type (allowing for type conversion) with the nondefault parameters listed in the method declaration.

- The return type for a method defines the type of value sent back to the calling method. It can be any type used in the C# programming language, which includes the basic built-in types int, double, char, and so on, as well as class types (including class types you create). A method also can return nothing, in which case the return type is void.

- You can pass an array as a parameter to a method. You indicate that a method parameter is an array by placing square brackets after the data type in the method's parameter list. Arrays, like all objects but unlike built-in types, are passed by reference; that is, the method receives the actual memory address of the array and has access to the actual values in the array elements.

- You might see different Main() method headers in other books or in programs written by others. Some programmers include an array of strings as a parameter to Main(), some programmers return an int from the Main() method, and some programmers give Main() methods public access.

- Special considerations exist for methods when you create GUI applications. You must understand the automatically generated methods in the visual environment, appreciate the differences in scope in GUI programs, and understand that many methods must be nonstatic when associated with a Form.

Key Terms

A **method** is an encapsulated series of statements that carry out a task.

Invoked and **called** describe what one method has done to execute another.

A **calling method** calls another method.

A **called method** is invoked by another method.

Implementation hiding means keeping the details of a method's operations hidden.

A **client** is a method that uses another method.

A **black box** is any device you can use without knowing how it works internally.

A **multifile assembly** is a group of files containing methods that work together to create an application.

Code bloat describes unnecessarily long or repetitive program statements.

A **method declaration** is a **method header** or **method definition**.

A **method body** is a block of statements that carry out a method's work.

Key Terms

Accessibility for a method is a declaration that sets limits as to whether and how other methods can use it.

Public access is a level of method accessibility that allows unlimited access to a method by any class.

Private access is a level of method accessibility that limits method access to the containing class.

A **fully qualified** name is one that includes the class name.

A **static** method is called without an object reference. It can be called from any class using its class name, a dot, and the method name, as well as any required arguments. Within its own class, a static method can be called by using just its name and any needed arguments.

A **nonstatic** method call requires an object reference.

A **return type** indicates what kind of value a method will return to any other method that calls it.

A **method's type** is its return type.

A **parameter to a method** is a variable that holds data passed to a method when it is called.

A **parameter list** consists of the data types and parameter names that appear between parentheses in a method header; the list might hold only one item or multiple items separated with commas.

A **local function** is a method that resides within another method and can be called only from the containing method.

Visible describes a program element that is in scope.

A **local variable** is one that is declared in the current method and is known only to that method.

A **formal parameter** is a parameter within a method header that accepts a value.

Actual parameters are arguments within a method call.

A **return statement** causes a value to be sent back from a method to its calling method.

Nested method calls are method calls placed inside other method calls.

A **reference** is a memory address.

Passed by reference describes the state of an argument passed to a method when the method receives its memory address.

Passed by value describes the state of an argument passed to a method when the method receives a copy of the argument.

CHAPTER 7 Using Methods

Review Questions

1. At most, a class can contain _____ method(s).
   a. 0
   b. 1
   c. 2
   d. any number of

2. Which of the following is a good reason for creating methods within a program?
   a. Methods are easily reusable.
   b. Because all methods must be stored in the same class, they are easy to find.
   c. The `Main()` method becomes more detailed.
   d. All of these are true.

3. In C#, a method must include all of the following *except* _____.
   a. a return type
   b. an access modifier
   c. curly braces
   d. a closing curly brace

4. If a method does not contain a declared accessibility, then the method is _____.
   a. illegal
   b. nonstatic
   c. `private`
   d. `void`

5. Every method declaration must contain _____.
   a. a statement of purpose
   b. a return type
   c. the `static` modifier
   d. declared accessibility

6. If you want to create a method that other methods in other classes can access without limitations, you declare the method to be _____.
   a. unlimited
   b. shared
   c. public
   d. unrestricted

7. If you use the keyword modifier `static` in a method header, you indicate that the method _____.
   a. cannot be copied
   b. is called without an object reference
   c. cannot require parameters
   d. can be called only once

Review Questions

8. A method's type is also its _____.
   a. return type
   b. accessibility
   c. parameter type
   d. scope

9. When you use a method, you do not need to know how it operates internally. This feature is called _____.
   a. scope management
   b. selective ignorance
   c. implementation hiding
   d. privacy

10. When you write the method declaration for a method that can receive a parameter, you need to include all of the following items *except* _____.
    a. a pair of parentheses
    b. the type of the parameter
    c. a local name for the parameter
    d. an initial value for the parameter

11. Suppose you have declared a variable as `int myAge = 21;`. Which of the following is a legal call to a method with the following declaration?

    `private static void AMethod(int num)`

    a. `AMethod(int 55);`
    b. `AMethod(myAge);`
    c. `AMethod(int myAge);`
    d. `AMethod();`

12. Suppose you have declared a method named `private static void CalculatePay(double rate)`. When a method calls the `CalculatePay()` method, the calling method _____.
    a. must contain a declared `double` named `rate`
    b. might contain a declared `double` named `rate`
    c. cannot contain a declared `double` named `rate`
    d. cannot contain any declared `double` variables

13. In the method call `PrintTheData(double salary);`, `salary` is the _____ parameter.
    a. actual
    b. formal
    c. proposed
    d. preferred

14. A program contains the method call `PrintTheData(salary);`. In the method definition, the name of the formal parameter must be _____.
    a. `salary`
    b. any legal identifier other than `salary`
    c. any legal identifier
    d. omitted

15. What is a correct declaration for a method that receives two `double` arguments, calculates and displays the difference between them, and returns nothing?

    a. `private static void CalcDifference(double price1, price2)`

    b. `private static void CalcDifference(double price1, double price2)`

    c. Both of these are correct.

    d. None of these are correct.

16. What is a correct declaration for a method that receives two `double` arguments and sums them but does not return anything?

    a. `private static void CalcSum(double firstValue, double secondValue)`

    b. `private static void CalcSum(double price1, double price2)`

    c. Both of these are correct.

    d. None of these are correct.

17. A method is declared as `private static double CalcPay(int hoursWorked)`. Suppose you write a `Main()` method in the same class and that it contains the declarations `int hours = 35;` and `double pay;`. Which of the following represents a correct way to call the `CalcPay()` method from the `Main()` method?

    a. `hours = CalcPay();`

    b. `hours = Main.CalcPay();`

    c. `pay = CalcPay(hoursWorked);`

    d. `pay = CalcPay(hours);`

18. Suppose the value of `IsRateOK()` is `true`, and the value of `IsQuantityOK()` is `false`. When you evaluate the expression `IsRateOK() || IsQuantityOK()`, which of the following is true?

    a. Only the method `IsRateOK()` executes.

    b. Only the method `IsQuantityOK()` executes.

    c. Both methods execute.

    d. Neither method executes.

19. Suppose the value of `isRateOK()` is `true`, and the value of `IsQuantityOK()` is `false`. When you evaluate the expression `IsRateOK() && IsQuantityOK()`, which of the following is true?

    a. Only the method `IsRateOK()` executes.

    b. Only the method `IsQuantityOK()` executes.

    c. Both methods execute.

    d. Neither method executes.

Exercises

20. When an array is passed to a method, the method has access to the array's memory address. This means an array is passed by _____.

   a. reference
   b. value
   c. alias
   d. orientation

Exercises

 Programming Exercises

1. Create a C# statement that uses each of the following built-in methods you have used in previous chapters, then make an intelligent guess about the return type and parameter list for the method used in each statement you created.

   a. `Console.WriteLine()`
   b. `String.Equals()`
   c. `String.Compare()`
   d. `Convert.ToInt32()`
   e. `Convert.ToChar()`
   f. `Array.Sort()`

2. Create a program named **SalesLetter** whose `Main()` method uses several `WriteLine()` calls to display a sales letter to prospective clients for a business of your choice. Display your contact information at least three times in the letter. The contact information should contain at least three lines with data such as land line phone number, cellphone number, email address, and so on. Each time you want to display the contact information, call a method named `DisplayContactInfo()`.

3. Create a program named **PaintingEstimate** whose `Main()` method prompts a user for length and width of a room in feet. Create a method that accepts the values and then computes the cost of painting the room, assuming the room is rectangular and has four full walls and 9-foot ceilings. The price of the job is $6 per square foot. Return the price to the `Main()` method, and display it.

4. Create an application named **ConvertMilesToKilometers** whose `Main()` method prompts a user for a number of miles, passes the value to a method that converts the value to kilometers, and then returns the value to the `Main()` method where it is displayed. A mile is 1.60934 kilometers.

5. Create a program named **FortuneTeller** whose `Main()` method contains an array of at least six strings with fortune-telling phrases such as *I see a tall, dark stranger in your future*. The program randomly selects two different fortunes and passes them to a method that displays them.

6. Create an application for a library and name it **FineForOverdueBooks**. The `Main()` method asks the user to input the number of books checked out and the number of days they are overdue. Pass those values to a method that displays the library fine, which is 10 cents per book per day for the first seven days a book is overdue, then 20 cents per book per day for each additional day.

7. In Chapter 4, you wrote a program named **Admission** for a college admissions office in which the user enters a numeric high school grade point average and an admission test score. The program displays *Accept* or *Reject* based on those values. Now, create a modified program named **AdmissionModularized** in which the grade point average and test score are passed to a method that returns a string containing *Accept* or *Reject*.

8. In Chapter 4, you wrote a program named **Hurricane** that classified hurricanes into five categories using the Saffir-Simpson Hurricane Scale. Now, create a modified version named **HurricaneModularized** that passes a user's input wind speed to a method that returns the hurricane category.

9. Write a program named **CountVowelsModularized** that passes a string to a method that returns the number of vowels in the string.

10. Create a program named **FlexibleArrayMethod** that declares at least three integer arrays of different sizes. In turn, pass each array to a method that displays all the integers in each array and their sum.

Debugging Exercises

1. Each of the following files in the Chapter.07 folder of your downloadable student files has syntax and/or logical errors. In each case, determine the problem, and fix the program. After you correct the errors, save each file using the same filename preceded with *Fixed*. For example, DebugSeven1.cs will become FixedDebugSeven1.cs.

    a. DebugSeven1.cs
    b. DebugSeven2.cs
    c. DebugSeven3.cs
    d. DebugSeven4.cs

Exercises

 Case Problems

1. In Chapter 6, you continued to modify the **GreenvilleRevenue** program. Now, modify the program so that the major functions appear in the following individual methods:

    - A method that gets and returns a valid number of contestants and is called twice—once for last year's number of contestants and once for this year's value

    - A method that accepts the number of contestants this year and last year and displays one of the three messages that describes the relationship between the two contestant values

    - A method that fills the array of competitors and their talent codes

    - A method that continuously prompts for talent codes and displays contestants with the corresponding talent until a sentinel value is entered

2. In previous chapters, you continued to modify the **MarshallsRevenue** program. Now, modify the program so that the major functions appear in the following individual methods:

    - A method that prompts for and returns the month

    - A method that prompts for and returns the number of murals scheduled and is called twice—once for interior murals and once for exterior murals

    - A method that accepts the number of interior and exterior murals scheduled, accepts the month they are scheduled, displays the interior and exterior prices, and then returns the total expected revenue

    - A method that fills an array with customer names and mural codes and is called twice—once to fill the array of interior murals and once to fill the array of exterior murals

    - A method that continuously prompts for mural codes and displays jobs of the corresponding type until a sentinel value is entered.

CHAPTER 8

Advanced Method Concepts

Upon completion of this chapter, you will be able to:

- ◎ Describe C#'s parameter types
- ◎ Pass parameters by reference
- ◎ Return a reference from a method
- ◎ Overload methods
- ◎ Recognize and avoid ambiguous methods
- ◎ Use optional parameters

CHAPTER 8 Advanced Method Concepts

In the last chapter, you learned to call methods, pass arguments to them, and receive values returned from them. In this chapter, you will expand your method-handling skills to include more sophisticated techniques, including using reference, output, and optional parameters and overloading methods. Understanding how to manipulate methods is crucial when you are working on large, professional, real-world projects. With methods, you can more easily coordinate your work with that of other programmers.

An Overview of C#'s Parameter Types

In Chapter 7, you learned that a memory address is a *reference* and you passed arguments of simple data types (like `int` and `double`) by value, and you passed arrays by reference. In this chapter, you will review how to pass simple data types by value, and you will learn to pass simple data types by reference.

- When a value is passed by value, the method receives a copy of the value and cannot alter the original.

- When a value is passed by reference, the method receives the memory address and can alter the original.

Parameters also can be classified as mandatory or optional.

- A **mandatory parameter** to a method is one that is required in every method call.

- An **optional parameter** to a method is one for which a default value is automatically supplied if you do not explicitly send one as an argument.

All the methods that you saw in Chapter 7 used mandatory parameters.

Mandatory parameters include:

- Value parameters, when they are declared without default values (like all the parameters you saw in Chapter 7)
- Reference parameters
- Output parameters
- Parameter arrays

C# includes only one type of optional parameter:

- Value parameters, when they are declared *with* default values

Using Mandatory Value Parameters

So far, all of the method parameters you have created have been mandatory, and all except arrays have been value parameters. When you use a **value parameter** in a method header, you indicate the parameter's type and name, and the method receives a copy of the value passed to it. A variable that is used as an argument to a method with a value parameter must have a value assigned to it. If it does not, the program will not compile.

An Overview of C#'s Parameter Types

The value of a method's value parameter is stored at a different memory address than the variable used as the argument in the method call. In other words, the actual parameter (the argument in the calling method) and the formal parameter (the parameter in the method header) refer to two separate memory locations, and the called method receives a copy of the sent value. Changes to value parameters never affect the original arguments in calling methods.

 A popular advertising campaign declares, "What happens in Vegas, stays in Vegas." The same is true of value parameters within a method—changes to them do not persist outside the method.

Figure 8-1 shows a program that declares a variable named x; the figure assumes that x is stored at memory address 2000. The value 4 is assigned to x and then displayed. Then x is passed to a method that accepts a value parameter. The method declares its own local parameter named x, which receives the value 4. This local variable is at a different memory address; for example, assume that it is 8800. The method assigns a new value, 777, to the local variable and displays it. When control returns to the Main() method, the value of x is accessed from memory location 2000 and remains 4.

```
using static System.Console;
class ParameterDemo1
{
    static void Main()
    {
        int x = 4;
        WriteLine("In Main x is {0}", x);
        DisplayValueParameter(x);
        WriteLine("In Main x is {0}", x);
    }
    private static void DisplayValueParameter(int x)
    {
        x = 777;
        WriteLine("In  method, x is {0}", x);
    }
}
```

During this program's execution, memory address 2000 is named x and holds 4.

During this program's execution, memory address 8800 is also called x. It holds 4 at first, then is changed to 777.

Figure 8-1 Program calling a method with a value parameter

Changing the value of x within the DisplayValueParameter() method has no effect on x in the Main() method. Even though both methods contain a variable named x, they represent two separate variables, each with its own memory location. Programmers say that a value parameter is used for "in" parameter passing—values for "in" parameters go into a method,

CHAPTER 8 Advanced Method Concepts

```
In Main x is 4
In method, x is 777
In Main x is 4
```

Figure 8-2 Output of the ParameterDemo1 program

but modifications to them do not come "out." In the program in Figure 8-1, it makes no difference whether you use the name x as the Main() method's actual parameter or use some other name. In either case, the parameter received by the DisplayValueParameter() method occupies a separate memory location. Figure 8-2 shows the output of the program in Figure 8-1.

TWO TRUTHS & A LIE

An Overview of C#'s Parameter Types

1. When you call a method that has a mandatory parameter, you must send an argument.

2. When you call a method that has an optional parameter, you do not have to send an argument, but you can.

3. When you call a method with a mandatory value parameter, you must pass an argument, but if it is a variable, you do not have to have initialized it.

The false statement is #3. A mandatory value parameter must receive an initialized argument.

Passing Parameters by Reference

On occasion, you might want a method to be able to alter a value you pass to it. In that case, you can pass a reference to a value. When you use a **reference parameter**, **output parameter**, or **parameter array**, you pass a memory address to a method, allowing the method to alter the original variable. Reference parameters, output parameters, and parameter arrays differ as follows:

- When you declare a reference parameter in a method header, the argument used to call the method must have been assigned a value.

- When you declare an output parameter, the argument used in the call need not contain an original, assigned value. However, an output parameter must be assigned a value before the method ends.

- When you declare a parameter array, the argument used in the call need not contain any original, assigned values, and the parameter array need not be assigned any values within the method.

Reference parameters, output parameters, and parameter arrays do not occupy their own memory locations. Rather, they act as aliases, or pseudonyms (other names), for the same memory location occupied by the values passed to them. You use the keyword ref as

Passing Parameters by Reference

a modifier to indicate a reference parameter, the keyword **out** as a modifier to indicate an output parameter, and the keyword **params** to indicate a parameter array.

 Using an alias for a variable is similar to using an alias for a person. Jane Doe might be known as "Ms. Doe" at work but "Sissy" at home. Both names refer to the same person.

Using a ref Parameter

Figure 8-3 shows a `Main()` method that calls a `DisplayReferenceParameter()` method. The `Main()` method declares and initializes a variable, displays its value, and then passes the variable to the method. The modifier **ref** precedes both the variable name in the method call and the parameter declaration in the method header. The method's parameter **number** refers to the memory address of **x**, making **number** an alias for **x**. When `DisplayReferenceParameter()` changes the value of **number**, the change persists in the **x** variable within `Main()`. Figure 8-4 shows the output of the program.

```
using static System.Console;
public class ParameterDemo2
{
    static void Main()
    {
        int x = 4;                                  ──(4)       (4)
        WriteLine("In Main x is {0}", x);
        DisplayReferenceParameter (ref x);          ────────(4)
        WriteLine("In Main x is {0}", x);──(888)
    }                                                          (4)
    private static void DisplayReferenceParameter(ref int number)
    {
        number = 888;                               ──────(888)
        WriteLine("In method, number is {0}", number);──(888)
    }
}
```

During this program's execution, memory location 2000 is called x, then number, and then x again, and holds different values as the program progresses.

Figure 8-3 Program calling a method with a reference parameter

```
In Main x is 4
In method, number is 888
In Main x is 888
```

Figure 8-4 Output of the ParameterDemo2 program

In the header for the DisplayReferenceParameter() method, it makes no difference whether you use the same name as the Main() method's passed variable (x) or some other name, such as number. In either case, the passed and received variables occupy the same memory location—the address of one is the address of the other.

Using an out Parameter

When you use a reference parameter, any passed variable must have an assigned value. Using an output parameter is convenient when the passed variable doesn't have a value yet. For example, the program in Figure 8-5 uses InputMethod() to obtain values for two parameters. The arguments that are sent in the shaded statement get their values from the called method, so it makes sense to provide them with no values going in. Instead, they acquire values in the method and retain the values coming out. Figure 8-6 shows a typical execution of the program.

```
using System;
using static System.Console;
class InputMethodDemo
{
    static void Main()
    {
        int first, second;
        InputMethod(out first, out second);
        WriteLine("After InputMethod first is {0}", first);
        WriteLine("and second is {0}", second);
    }
    private static void InputMethod(out int one, out int two)
    {
        string s1, s2;
        Write("Enter first integer ");
        s1 = ReadLine();
        Write("Enter second integer ");
        s2 = ReadLine();
        one = Convert.ToInt32(s1);
        two = Convert.ToInt32(s2);
    }
}
```

Notice the keyword out.

Figure 8-5 The InputMethodDemo program

```
Enter first integer 23
Enter second integer 45
After InputMethod first is 23
and second is 45
```

Figure 8-6 Output of the InputMethodDemo program

Using an out Variable

A new feature of C# 7.0 allows you to declare a variable at the point where it is passed as an out argument. The variable is known as an **out variable**. For example, in the InputMethodDemo program in Figure 8-5, you could remove the line with the declarations `int first, second;` and change the method call to the following:

`InputMethod(out int first, out int second);`

Deciding Between out and ref

It might be helpful to remember:

- If you will always have an initial value, use `ref`.

- If you do not have an initial value or you do not know whether you will have an initial value, use `out`. (For example, in an interactive program, a user might not provide a value for a variable, so you don't know whether the variable has an initial value.)

In summary, when you need a method to share a single value from a calling method, you have two options:

- Use a return type. You can send an argument to a method that accepts a value parameter, alter the local version of the variable within the method, return the altered value, and assign the return value to the original variable back in the calling method. The drawback to this approach is that a method can have only a single return type and can return, at most, only one value.

- Pass by reference. You can send an argument to a method that accepts a reference or output parameter and alter the value at the original memory location within the method. A major advantage to using reference or output parameters exists when you want a method to change multiple variables. A method can have only a single return type and can return, at most, only one value, but by using reference or output parameters to a method, you can change multiple values. However, a major disadvantage to using reference and output parameters is that they allow multiple methods to have access to the same data, weakening the "black box" paradigm that is so important to object-oriented methodology. You should never use `ref` or `out` parameters to avoid having to return a value, but you should understand them so you can use them if required.

 Watch the video *Using ref and out Parameters*.

 As with simple parameters, you can use `out` or `ref` when passing an array to a method. You do so when you want to declare the array in the calling method, but use the `new` operator to allocate memory for it in the called method.

CHAPTER 8 Advanced Method Concepts

Using a Built-in Method That Has an out Parameter

In Chapter 2, you learned two ways to convert a string to a number—you can use a `Convert` class method or a `Parse()` method. For example, each of the following statements accepts a string and converts it to an integer named `score`:

```
int score = Convert.ToInt32(ReadLine());
int score = int.Parse(ReadLine());
```

With either of these statements, if the value accepted by `ReadLine()` cannot be converted to an integer (for example, because it contains a decimal point or an alphabetic character), the program abruptly stops running. Consider the simple program in Figure 8-7. The program prompts the user for a score and displays it. Figure 8-8 shows two executions of the program. In the first execution, the user enters a valid integer and everything goes smoothly. In the second execution, the user enters alphabetic characters, the program stops, and a series of error messages is displayed.

```
using static System.Console;
class ConversionWithParse
{
   static void Main()
   {
      string entryString;
      int score;
      Write("Enter your test score >> ");
      entryString = ReadLine();
      score = int.Parse(entryString);
      WriteLine("You entered {0}", score);
   }
}
```

Figure 8-7 The ConversionWithParse program

```
Enter your test score >> 100
You entered 100
```

```
Enter your test score >> perfect
Unhandled Exception: System.FormatException: Input string was not in a correct format.
   at System.Number.StringToNumber(String str, NumberStyles options, NumberBuffer& number, NumberFormatInfo info, Boolean parseDecimal)
   at System.Number.ParseInt32(String s, NumberStyles style, NumberFormatInfo info)
   at ConversionWithParse.Main()
```

Figure 8-8 Two typical executions of the `ConversionWithParse` program

The messages in Figure 8-8 indicate that the program contains an unhandled exception because *Input string was not in a correct format*. An *exception* is a program error; you will learn much more about exceptions in Chapter 11, "Exception Handling." For now, however, you can handle data conversion exceptions by the `TryParse()` method. Unlike the `Parse()`

Passing Parameters by Reference

method, `TryParse()` accepts an `out` parameter. The `TryParse()` method converts a string to the correct data type and stores the result in a passed variable if possible. If conversion is not possible, the method assigns 0 to the variable.

Figure 8-9 contains a program that uses the `int.TryParse()` method to convert `entryString` to an integer that is assigned to `score`. The only differences from the program in Figure 8-7 are the shaded change to the class name and the shaded call to the `int.TryParse()` method. The `TryParse()` method accepts two parameters: the string to be converted and the variable where the result is stored. The keyword `out` is required with the second parameter because the method receives its address and changes the value. Figure 8-10 shows two typical executions of the ConversionWithTryParse program. When the user's input cannot be converted correctly, the `out` parameter is assigned 0. Whether or not the user's input is in the correct format, the program continues and displays output instead of error messages.

```
using static System.Console;
class ConversionWithTryParse
{
   static void Main()
   {
      string entryString;
      int score;
      Write("Enter your test score >> ");
      entryString = ReadLine();
      int.TryParse(entryString, out score);
      WriteLine("You entered {0}", score);
   }
}
```

Figure 8-9 The ConversionWithTryParse program

```
Enter your test score >> 100
You entered 100
```
```
Enter your test score >> perfect
You entered 0
```

Figure 8-10 Two typical executions of the ConversionWithTryParse program

The `TryParse()` method requires the receiving variable to be an `out` parameter for two reasons:

- The argument does not have an assigned value in the calling method.
- The method returns a Boolean value that indicates whether the conversion was successful and, so, it cannot return the `score` value too.

Suppose that you do not want a score to be assigned 0 if the conversion fails, because 0 is a legitimate score. Instead, you want to assign a −1 if the conversion fails. In that case you can use a statement similar to the following:

```
if(!int.TryParse(entryString, out score))
   score = -1;
```

In this example, if `entryString`'s conversion is successful, `score` holds the converted value; otherwise, `score` holds –1.

As another example, you might consider code that includes a loop that continues until the entered value is in the correct format, such as the following:

```
Write("Enter your test score >> ");
entryString = ReadLine();
while(!int.TryParse(entryString, out score))
{
   WriteLine("Input data was not formatted correctly");
   Write("Please enter score again >> ");
   entryString = ReadLine();
}
```

In this example, the loop continues until the `TryParse()` method returns `true`.

C# also provides `char.TryParse()`, `double.TryParse()`, and `decimal.TryParse()` methods that work in the same way—each converts a first parameter string and assigns its value to the second parameter variable, returning `true` or `false` based on the success of the conversion.

Using Parameter Arrays

When you don't know how many arguments of the same data type might eventually be sent to a method, you can declare a parameter array—a local array declared within the method header using the keyword `params`. Such a method accepts any number of elements that are all the same data type.

For example, a method with the following header accepts an array of strings:

```
private static void DisplayStrings(params string[] people)
```

In the call to this method, you can use any number of strings as actual parameters; within the method, they will be treated as an array.

When a method header uses the `params` keyword, two restrictions apply:

- Only one `params` keyword is permitted in a method declaration.

- If a method declares multiple parameters, the `params`-qualified parameter must be the last one in the list.

Figure 8-11 shows a program that calls `DisplayStrings()` three times—once with one string argument, once with three string arguments, and once with an array of strings. In each case, the method works correctly, treating the passed strings as an array and displaying them appropriately. Figure 8-12 shows the output.

Passing Parameters by Reference

```
using static System.Console;
class ParamsDemo
{
   static void Main()
   {
      string[] names = {"Mark", "Paulette", "Carol", "James"};
      DisplayStrings("Ginger");
      DisplayStrings("George", "Maria", "Thomas");
      DisplayStrings(names);
   }
   private static void DisplayStrings(params string[] people)
   {
      foreach(string person in people)
         Write("{0} ", person);
      WriteLine("\n--------------");
   }
}
```

Figure 8-11   The ParamsDemo program

Figure 8-12   Output of the ParamsDemo program

You could create an even more flexible method by using a method header such as Display(params Object[] things). Then the passed parameters could be any type—strings, integers, other classes, and so on. The method could be implemented as follows:

```
private static void Display(params Object[] things)
{
   foreach(Object obj in things)
      Write("{0} ", obj);
   WriteLine("\n--------------");
}
```

All data types are Objects; you will learn more about the Object class in the chapters "Using Classes and Objects" and "Introduction to Inheritance."

CHAPTER 8 Advanced Method Concepts

TWO TRUTHS & A LIE

Passing Parameters by Reference

1. Both reference and output parameters represent memory addresses that are passed to a method, allowing the method to alter the original variables.

2. When you declare a reference parameter in a method header, the parameter must not have been assigned a value.

3. When you use an output parameter, it need not contain an original, assigned value when the method is called, but it must receive a value before the method ends.

The false statement is #2. When you declare a reference parameter in a method header, the parameter must have been assigned a value.

You Do It

Using Reference Parameters

You use reference parameters when you want a method to have access to the memory address of arguments in a calling method. For example, suppose that you have two values and you want to exchange them (or swap them), making each equal to the value of the other. Because you want to change two values, a method that accepts copies of arguments will not work—a method can return, at most, only one value. Therefore, you can use reference parameters to provide your method with the actual addresses of the values you want to change.

1. Open your editor and begin a program named **SwapProgram** as follows:

   ```
   using static System.Console;
   class SwapProgram
   {
       static void Main()
       {
   ```

2. Declare two integers, and display their values. Call the Swap() method, and pass in the addresses of the two variables to swap. Because the parameters already have assigned values, and because you want to alter those values

(continues)

(continued)

in Main(), you can use reference parameters. After the method call, display the two values again. Add the closing curly brace for the Main() method.

```
int first = 34, second = 712;
Write("Before swap first is {0}", first);
WriteLine(" and second is {0}", second);
Swap(ref first, ref second);
Write("After swap first is {0}", first);
WriteLine(" and second is {0}", second);
}
```

3. Create the Swap() method as shown. You can swap two values by storing the first value in a temporary variable, then assigning the second value to the first variable. At this point, both variables hold the value originally held by the second variable. When you assign the temporary variable's value to the second variable, the two values are reversed.

```
private static void Swap(ref int one, ref int two)
{
    int temp;
    temp = one;
    one = two;
    two = temp;
}
```

4. Add the closing curly brace for the class. Save the program, and then compile and execute it. Figure 8-13 shows the output.

```
Before swap first is 34 and second is 712
After swap first is 712 and second is 34
```

Figure 8-13 Output of the SwapProgram program

You might want to use a method like Swap() as part of a larger program in which you verify, for example, that a higher value is displayed before a lower one; you would include the call to Swap() as part of a decision whose body executes only when a first value is less than a second one.

Returning a Reference from a Method

A new feature in C# 7.0 called **ref return** allows you to return a reference from a method. Using a ref return has some restrictions; you can only return references that C# considers "safe to return." For example, you can return a reference from a method if the reference was passed into the method, but cannot if the value was passed into the method. Consider the program in Figure 8-14. It declares an array of five inventory item numbers and displays them. The program then prompts the user for an item to find and accepts it from the keyboard. In the shaded statement, a reference named `soldItem` is declared and assigned the value returned from a method named `FindItem()`.

```
using System;
using static System.Console;
class ReturnRefDemo
{
   static void Main()
   {
      int itemToFind;
      int x;
      int[] items = {123, 241, 375, 410, 555};
      WriteLine("Before replacement: ");
      for(x = 0; x < items.Length; ++x)
         Write("   " + items[x]);
      Write("\n   Enter the value to find >> ");
      itemToFind = Convert.ToInt32(ReadLine());
      ref int soldItem = ref FindItem(itemToFind, items);
      soldItem = 0;
      WriteLine("After replacement: ");
      for(x = 0; x < items.Length; ++x)
         Write("   " + items[x]);
      WriteLine();
   }
   public static ref int FindItem(int findValue, int[] elements)
   {
      int x;
      int position = -1;
      for(x = 0; x < elements.Length; ++x)
      {
         if(findValue == elements[x])
            position = x;
      }
      return ref elements[position];
   }
}
```

Figure 8-14 The ReturnRefDemo program

You can see in the shaded method call in Figure 8-14 that the `FindItem()` method accepts an integer to find in the array of valid item numbers. As you learned in Chapter 7, when an array is passed to a method, its address is received by the method.

The `FindItem()` method in Figure 8-14 uses a `for` loop to search the passed `elements` array for a match to the `findValue` parameter. When a match is found, the position is saved, and, in the `return` statement, the memory address of the found array element is returned. (Note that in this example, if the `findValue` parameter is not matched in the array, then the address of an invalid element that uses a negative subscript (−1) is returned from the method. You need to learn about exception handling in Chapter 11 before you can handle this mistake.)

In the Main() method, following the call to FindItem(), soldItem, which represents the memory address of the matching element, is set to 0 to indicate the item is no longer available. When the items array is displayed again, the correct element has been changed to 0. Figure 8-15 shows two separate executions of the program in which a different items element is removed each time.

```
Before replacement:
   123   241   375   410   555
        Enter the value to find >> 410
After replacement:
   123   241   375    0    555
```

```
Before replacement:
   123   241   375   410   555
        Enter the value to find >> 123
After replacement:
     0   241   375   410   555
```

Figure 8-15 Two typical executions of the ReturnRefDemo program

You could accomplish the removal of an item from the items array in the ReturnRefDemo program without returning a reference. For example, you could create the FindItem() method to return an integer subscript that is not a reference and then use it to access the desired element in the Main() method. So, for now, returning a reference from a method will be of limited value to you. However, you should understand that you can now return a reference in C#, and you might someday use the technique in a large program where it might be impractical to pass large amounts of data into and out of methods and much more practical to pass references.

TWO TRUTHS & A LIE

Returning a Reference from a Method

1. A reference can be returned from any method.
2. When a reference is returned from a method, the calling method receives a memory address.
3. When a method returns a reference, it cannot also return a value.

The false statement is #1. There are some restrictions on the uses of ref returns. For example, you can return a reference from a method if the reference was passed into the method, but cannot if the value was passed into the method.

Overloading Methods

Overloading involves the ability to write multiple versions of a method using the same method name. When you make a purchase at a store, you might use one of a variety of "pay" methods they accept, for example, cash, a credit card, or a check. The "pay" method works differently depending on the type of currency sent to it, but all of the transactions are called "pay." When you overload a C# method, you write multiple method implementations with the same name but different parameter lists. A method's name and parameter list constitute the method's **signature**.

In this book, you have seen the WriteLine() method used with a string parameter and a numeric parameter. You can use it with no parameter to output a blank line. You also have seen the method used with several parameters when you have used a format string along with several variables. Therefore, you know WriteLine() is an overloaded method.

Some C# operators are overloaded. For example, a + between two numeric values indicates addition, but a single + to the left of a value means the value is positive. The + sign has different meanings based on the operands used with it. In the chapter "Using Classes and Objects," you will learn how to overload operators to make them mean what you want with your own classes.

The compiler understands which method to use based on the arguments you use in a method call. For example, suppose that you create a method to display a `string` surrounded by a border. The method receives a `string` and uses the `string Length` property to determine how many asterisks to use to construct a border around the `string`. Figure 8-16 shows a program that contains the method.

```
using static System.Console;
class BorderDemo1
{
   static void Main()
   {
      DisplayWithBorder("Ed");
      DisplayWithBorder("Theodore");
      DisplayWithBorder("Jennifer Ann");
   }
   private static void DisplayWithBorder(string word)
   {
      const int EXTRA_STARS = 4;
      const string SYMBOL = "*";
      int size = word.Length + EXTRA_STARS;
      int x;
      for(x = 0; x < size; ++x)
         Write(SYMBOL);
      WriteLine();
      WriteLine(SYMBOL + " " + word + " " + SYMBOL);
      for(x = 0; x < size; ++x)
         Write(SYMBOL);
      WriteLine("\n\n");
   }
}
```

Figure 8-16 The BorderDemo1 program

Overloading Methods

When the Main() method calls the DisplayWithBorder() method in the program in Figure 8-16 and passes a string value, the method calculates a size as the length of the string plus 4, and then draws that many symbols on a single line. The method then displays a symbol, a space, the string, another space, and another symbol on the next line. Figure 8-17 shows the output.

Suppose that you are so pleased with the output of the DisplayWithBorder() method that you want to use something similar to display your company's weekly sales goal figure. The problem is that the weekly sales goal amount is stored as an integer, and so it cannot be passed to the existing method. You can take one of several approaches:

- You can convert the integer sales goal to a string and use the existing method. This is an acceptable approach, but it requires that you remember to write an extra step in any program in which you display an integer using the border.

- You can create a new method with a unique name such as DisplayWithBorderUsingInt() and use it to accept an integer parameter. The drawback to this approach is that you must remember different method names when you use different data types.

Figure 8-17 Output of the BorderDemo1 program

- You can overload the DisplayWithBorder() method. Overloading methods involves writing multiple methods with the same name but with different parameter types. For example, in addition to the DisplayWithBorder() method shown in Figure 8-16, you could use the method shown in Figure 8-18.

```
private static void DisplayWithBorder(int number)
{
   const int EXTRA_STARS = 4;
   const string SYMBOL = "*";
   int size = EXTRA_STARS + 1;
   int leftOver = number;
   int x;
   while(leftOver >= 10)
   {
      leftOver = leftOver / 10;
      ++size;
   }
   for(x = 0; x < size; ++x)
      Write(SYMBOL);
   WriteLine();
   WriteLine(SYMBOL + " " + number + " " + SYMBOL);
   for(x = 0; x < size; ++x)
      Write(SYMBOL);
   WriteLine("\n\n");
}
```

Figure 8-18 The DisplayWithBorder() method with an integer parameter

CHAPTER 8 Advanced Method Concepts

In the version of the DisplayWithBorder() method in Figure 8-18, the parameter is an int. To determine how many asterisks to display, the method initializes size to the number of extra stars in the display (in this case 4), plus one more. It then determines the number of asterisks to display in the border by repeatedly dividing the parameter by 10 and adding the result to size. For example, when the argument to the method is 456, leftOver is initialized to 456. Because it is at least 10, it is divided by 10, giving 45, and size is increased from 5 to 6. Then 45 is divided by 10, giving 4, and size is increased to 7. Because 4 is not at least 10, the loop ends, and the program has determined that the top and bottom borders of the box surrounding 456 require seven stars each. The rest of the method executes like the original version that accepts a string parameter.

The DisplayWithBorder() method does not quite work correctly if a negative integer is passed to it because the negative sign occupies an additional display space. To rectify the problem, you could modify the method to add an extra symbol to the border when a negative argument is passed in, or you could force all negative numbers to be their positive equivalent.

If both versions of DisplayWithBorder() are included in a program and you call the method using a string, as in DisplayWithBorder("Ed"), the first version of the method shown in Figure 8-16 executes. If you use an integer as the argument in the call to DisplayWithBorder(), as in DisplayWithBorder(456), then the method shown in Figure 8-18 executes. Figure 8-19 shows a program that demonstrates several method calls, and Figure 8-20 shows the output.

Methods are overloaded correctly when they have the same identifier but their parameter lists are different. Parameter lists differ when the number and order of types within the lists are unique. For example, you could write several methods with the same identifier, and one method could accept an int, another two ints, and another three ints. A fourth method could accept an int followed by a double, and another could accept a double followed by an int. Yet another version could accept no parameters. The parameter identifiers in overloaded methods do not matter, nor do the return types of the methods. The only two requirements to overload methods are the same identifier and different parameter lists.

Instead of overloading methods, you can choose to use methods with different names to accept the diverse data types, and you can place a decision within your program to determine which version of the method to call. However, it is more convenient to use one method name and then let the compiler determine which method to use. Overloading a method also makes it more convenient for other programmers to use your method in the future. Usually you do not create overloaded methods so that a single program can use all the versions. More often, you create overloaded methods so different programs can use the version most appropriate to the task at hand. Frequently, you create overloaded methods in your classes not because you need them immediately, but because you know client programs might need multiple versions in the future, and it is easier for programmers to remember one reasonable name for tasks that are functionally identical except for parameter types.

```
using static System.Console;
class BorderDemo2
{
   static void Main()
   {
      DisplayWithBorder("Ed");
      DisplayWithBorder(3);
      DisplayWithBorder(456);
      DisplayWithBorder(897654);
      DisplayWithBorder("Veronica");
   }
   private static void DisplayWithBorder(string word)
   {
      const int EXTRA_STARS = 4;
      const string SYMBOL = '*';
      int size = word.Length + EXTRA_STARS;
      int x;
      for(x = 0; x < size; ++x)
         Write(SYMBOL);
      WriteLine();
      WriteLine(SYMBOL + " " + word + " " + SYMBOL);
      for(x = 0; x < size; ++x)
         Write(SYMBOL);
      WriteLine("\n\n");
   }
   private static void DisplayWithBorder(int number)
   {
      const int EXTRA_STARS = 4;
      const string SYMBOL = "*";
      int size = EXTRA_STARS + 1;
      int leftOver = number;
      int x;
      while(leftOver >= 10)
      {
         leftOver = leftOver / 10;
         ++size;
      }
      for(x = 0; x < size; ++x)
         Write(SYMBOL);
      WriteLine();
      WriteLine(SYMBOL + " " + number + " " + SYMBOL);
      for(x = 0; x < size; ++x)
         Write(SYMBOL);
      WriteLine("\n\n");
   }
}
```

Figure 8-19 The BorderDemo2 program

Figure 8-20 Output of the BorderDemo2 program

Understanding Overload Resolution

When a method call *could* execute multiple overloaded method versions, C# determines which method to execute using a process called **overload resolution**. For example, suppose that you create a method with the following declaration:

private static void MyMethod(double d)

You can call this method using a double argument, as in the following:

MyMethod(2.5);

You can also call this method using an int argument, as in the following:

MyMethod(4);

The call that uses the int argument works because an int can automatically be promoted to a double. In Chapter 2 you learned that when an int is promoted to a double, the process is called an *implicit conversion* or *implicit cast*.

Suppose that you create overloaded methods with the following declarations:

private static void MyMethod(double d)
private static void MyMethod(int i)

If you then call MyMethod() using an integer argument, both methods are **applicable methods**. That means either method on its own could accept a call that uses an int. However, if both methods exist in the same class (making them overloaded), the second version will execute because it is a better match for the method call. The rules that determine which method version to call are known as **betterness rules**.

Betterness rules are similar to the implicit conversion rules you learned in Chapter 2. For example, although an int could be accepted by a method that accepts an int, a float, or a double, an int is the best match. If no method version with an int parameter exists, then a float is a better match than a double. Table 8-1 shows the betterness rules for several data types.

Data Type	Conversions Are Better in This Order
byte	short, ushort, int, uint, long, ulong, float, double, decimal
sbyte	short, int, long, float, double, decimal
short	int, long, float, double, decimal
ushort	int, uint, long, ulong, float, double, decimal
int	long, float, double, decimal
uint	long, ulong, float, double, decimal
long	float, double, decimal
ulong	float, double, decimal
float	double
char	ushort, int, uint, long, ulong, float, double, decimal

Table 8-1 Betterness rules for data type conversion

Discovering Built-In Overloaded Methods

When you use the IDE to create programs, Visual Studio's IntelliSense features provide information about methods you are using. For example, Figure 8-21 shows the IDE just after the programmer has typed the opening parenthesis to the `Convert.ToInt32()` method. Notice the drop-down list that indicates `Convert.ToInt32(bool value)` is just 1 of 19 overloaded versions of the method. You can click the nodes to scroll through the rest of the list and see that other versions accept `bool`, `byte`, `char`, and so on. When retrieving an entry from a `TextBox` on a `Form`, your intention is to use the `Convert.ToInt32(string value)` version of the method, but many overloaded versions are available for your convenience. C# could have included multiple methods with different names such as `ConvertBool.ToInt32()` and `ConvertString.ToInt32()`, but having a single method with the name `Convert.ToInt32()` that takes many different argument types makes it easier for you to remember the method name and to use it. As you work with the IDE, you will examine many such methods.

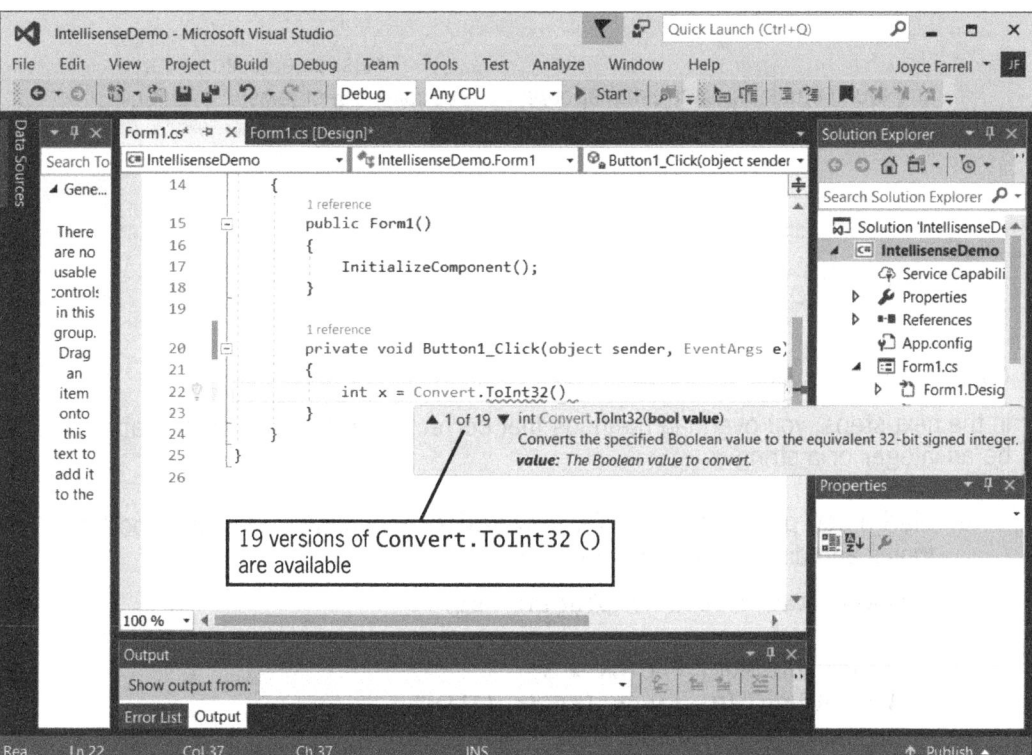

Figure 8-21 Examining the overloaded versions of `Convert.ToInt32()`

CHAPTER 8 Advanced Method Concepts

TWO TRUTHS & A LIE

Overloading Methods

1. The following methods are overloaded:

   ```
   private static void MethodA(int a)
   private static void MethodA(double b)
   ```

2. The following methods are overloaded:

   ```
   private static void MethodC(int c)
   private static void MethodD(int c)
   ```

3. The following methods are overloaded:

   ```
   private static void MethodE(int e)
   private static void MethodE(int e, int f)
   ```

The false answer is #2. Overloaded methods must have the same name but different parameter lists.

 You Do It

Overloading Methods

In the next steps, you overload methods that correctly triple a parameter that might be an integer or a string.

1. Start a new program named **OverloadedTriples**, and create a method that triples and displays an integer parameter as follows:

   ```
   private static void Triple(int num)
   {
       const int MULT_FACTOR = 3;
       WriteLine("{0} times {1} is {2}\n",
           num, MULT_FACTOR, num * MULT_FACTOR);
   }
   ```

(continues)

(continued)

2. Create a second method with the same name that takes a string parameter. Assume you want to define tripling a message as displaying it three times, separated by tabs.

```
private static void Triple(string message)
{
   WriteLine("{0}\t{0}\t{0}\n", message);
}
```

3. Position your cursor at the top of the file, and add a using statement, class header, and opening curly brace so the overloaded Triple() methods will be contained in a class named OverloadedTriples.

```
using static System.Console;
class OverloadedTriples
{
```

4. Position your cursor at the bottom of the file, and add the closing curly brace for the OverloadedTriples class.

5. Position your cursor after the opening curly brace for the class. On a new line, insert a Main() method that declares an integer and a string and, in turn, passes each to the appropriate Triple() method. Notice that as you type the parenthesis after the Triple() method, the IDE displays your two overloaded Triple() methods.

```
static void Main()
{
   int num = 20;
   string message = "Go team!";
   Triple(num);
   Triple(message);
}
```

6. Save the file, and then compile and execute the program. Figure 8-22 shows the output. Even though the same method name is used in the two method calls, the appropriate overloaded method executes each time.

```
20 times 3 is 60

Go team!        Go team!        Go team!
```

Figure 8-22 Output of the OverloadedTriples program

Avoiding Ambiguous Methods

When you overload a method, you run the risk of creating **ambiguous** methods—a situation in which the compiler cannot determine which method to use. Every time you call a method, the compiler decides whether a suitable method exists; if so, the method executes, and if not, you receive an error message.

For example, suppose that you write two versions of a simple method, as in the program in Figure 8-23. The class contains two versions of a method named `SimpleMethod()`—one that takes a `double` and an `int`, and one that takes an `int` and a `double`.

```
using static System.Console;
class AmbiguousMethods
{
   static void Main()
   {
      int iNum = 20;
      double dNum = 4.5;
      SimpleMethod(iNum, dNum); // calls first version
      SimpleMethod(dNum, iNum); // calls second version
      SimpleMethod(iNum, iNum); // error! Call is ambiguous.
   }
   private static void SimpleMethod(int i, double d)
   {
      WriteLine("Method receives int and double");
   }
   private static void SimpleMethod(double d, int i)
   {
      WriteLine("Method receives double and int");
   }
}
```

Figure 8-23 Program containing an ambiguous method call

In the `Main()` method in Figure 8-23, a call to `SimpleMethod()` with an integer argument first and a `double` argument second executes the first version of the method, and a call to `SimpleMethod()` with a `double` argument first and an integer argument second executes the second version of the method. With each of these calls, the compiler can find an exact match for the arguments you send. However, if you call `SimpleMethod()` using two integer arguments, as in the shaded statement, an ambiguous situation arises because there is no exact match for the method call. Because the first integer could be promoted to a `double` (matching the second version of the overloaded method), or the second integer could be

Avoiding Ambiguous Methods

promoted to a `double` (matching the first version), the compiler does not know which version of `SimpleMethod()` to use, and the program will not compile or execute. Figure 8-24 shows the error message that is generated.

```
AmbiguousMethods.cs(10,7): error CS0121: The call is ambiguous
between the following methods or properties: 'AmbiguousMethods.
SimpleMethod(int, double)' and 'AmbiguousMethods.SimpleMethod(d
ouble, int)'
```

Figure 8-24 Error message generated by an ambiguous method call

An overloaded method is not ambiguous on its own—it becomes ambiguous only if you create an ambiguous situation. A program with potentially ambiguous methods will run without problems if you make no ambiguous method calls. For example, if you remove the shaded statement from Figure 8-23 that calls `SimpleMethod()` using two integer arguments, the program compiles and executes.

If you remove one of the versions of `SimpleMethod()` from the program in Figure 8-23, then the method call that uses two integer arguments would work, because one of the integers could be promoted to a `double`. However, then one of the other method calls would fail.

Methods can be overloaded correctly by providing different parameter lists for methods with the same name. Methods with identical names that have identical parameter lists but different return types are not overloaded—they are illegal. For example, the following two methods cannot coexist within a class:

```
private static int AMethod(int x)
private static void AMethod(int x)
```

The compiler determines which of several versions of a method to call based on parameter lists. When the method call `AMethod(17);` is made, the compiler will not know which method to execute because both possibilities take an integer argument. Similarly, the following method could not coexist with either of the previous versions:

```
private static void AMethod(int someNumber)
```

Even though this method uses a different local identifier for the parameter, its parameter list—a single integer—is still the same to the compiler.

 Watch the video *Overloading Methods*.

> ### TWO TRUTHS & A LIE
>
> **Avoiding Ambiguous Methods**
>
> 1. The following methods are potentially ambiguous:
>
>    ```
>    private static int Method1(int g)
>    private static int Method1(int g, int h)
>    ```
>
> 2. The following methods are potentially ambiguous:
>
>    ```
>    private static double Method2(int j)
>    private static void Method2(int k)
>    ```
>
> 3. The following methods are potentially ambiguous:
>
>    ```
>    private static void Method3(string m)
>    private static string Method3(string n)
>    ```
>
> The false answer is #1. Those methods are not ambiguous because they have different parameter lists. Their matching return types do not cause ambiguity.

Using Optional Parameters

Sometimes it is useful to create a method that allows one or more arguments to be omitted from the method call. An optional parameter is not required; if you don't send a value as an argument, a default value is automatically supplied. You make a parameter optional by providing a value for it in the method declaration. Only value parameters can be given default values; those that use `ref`, `out`, and `params` cannot have default values. Any optional parameters in a parameter list must appear to the right of the mandatory parameters.

For example, suppose that you write a method that calculates either the area of a square or the volume of a cube, depending on whether two or three arguments are sent to it. Figure 8-25 shows such a method; notice the shaded default value provided for the third parameter. When you want a cube's volume, you can pass three arguments to the method: length, width, and height. When you want a square's area, you pass only two parameters, and a default value of 1 is used for the height. In this example, the height is a default parameter and is optional; the length and width, which are not provided with default values, are mandatory parameters. That is, at least two arguments must be sent to the `DisplaySize()` method, but three *can* be sent. In the program in Figure 8-25, calling `DisplaySize(4, 6)` has the same effect as calling `DisplaySize(4, 6, 1)`. Figure 8-26 shows the execution of the OptionalParameterDemo program.

```csharp
using static System.Console;
class OptionalParameterDemo
{
   static void Main()
   {
      Write("Using 2 arguments: ");
      DisplaySize(4, 6);
      Write("Using 3 arguments: ");
      DisplaySize(4, 6, 8);
   }
   private static void DisplaySize(int length, int width, int height = 1)
   {
      int area = length * width * height;
      WriteLine("Size is {0}", area);
   }
}
```

Figure 8-25 The OptionalParameterDemo program

```
Using 2 arguments: Size is 24
Using 3 arguments: Size is 192
```

Figure 8-26 Execution of the OptionalParameterDemo program

If you assign a default value to any variable in a method's parameter list, then all parameters to the right of that parameter must also have default values. Table 8-2 shows some examples of valid and invalid method declarations.

CHAPTER 8 Advanced Method Concepts

Method Declaration	Explanation
`private static void M1(int a, int b, int c, int d = 10)`	Valid. The first three parameters are mandatory and the last one is optional.
`private static void M2(int a, int b = 3, int c)`	Invalid. Because b has a default value, c must also have one.
`private static void M3(int a = 3, int b = 4, int c = 5)`	Valid. All parameters are optional.
`private static void M4(int a, int b, int c)`	Valid. All parameters are mandatory.
`private static void M5(int a = 4, int b, int c = 8)`	Invalid. Because a has a default value, both b and c must have default values.

Table 8-2 Examples of valid and invalid optional parameter method declarations

When you call a method that contains default parameters, you can always choose to provide a value for every parameter. However, if you omit an argument when you call a method that has default parameters, then you must do one of the following:

- You must leave out all unnamed arguments to the right of the last argument you use.
- You can name arguments.

Leaving Out Unnamed Arguments

When calling a method with optional parameters (and using unnamed arguments), you must leave out any arguments to the right of the last one used. In other words, once an argument is left out, you must leave out all the arguments that would otherwise follow.

For example, assume you have declared a method as follows:

`private static void Method1(int a, char b, int c = 22, double d = 33.2)`

Table 8-3 shows some legal and illegal calls to this method.

Call to Method1()	Explanation
Method1(1, 'A', 3, 4.4);	Valid. The four arguments are assigned to the four parameters.
Method1(1, 'K', 9);	Valid. The three arguments are assigned to a, b, and c in the method, and the default value of 33.2 is used for d.
Method1(5, 'D');	Valid. The two arguments are assigned to a and b in the method, and the default values of 22 and 33.2 are used for c and d, respectively.
Method1(1);	Invalid. Method1() requires at least two arguments for the first two parameters.
Method1();	Invalid. Method1() requires at least two arguments for the first two parameters.
Method1(3, 18.5);	Invalid. The first argument, 3, can be assigned to a, but the second argument must be type char.
Method1(4, 'R', 55.5);	Invalid. The first argument, 4, can be assigned to a, and the second argument, 'R', can be assigned to b, but the third argument must be type int. When arguments are unnamed, you cannot "skip" parameter c, use its default value, and assign 55.5 to parameter d.

Table 8-3 Examples of legal and illegal calls to Method1()

Using Named Arguments

You can leave out optional arguments in a method call if you pass the remaining arguments by name. A **named argument** is a method argument that is preceded with the name of the called method's parameter to which it will be assigned. Named arguments can appear in any order, but they must appear after all the unnamed arguments have been listed. Each unnamed argument is also known as a **positional argument**. You name an argument using its parameter name and a colon before the value.

In Chapter 7, you learned that if you use the IntelliSense feature of Visual Studio, you can discover a method's parameter names. See Appendix C for more details.

CHAPTER 8　Advanced Method Concepts

For example, assume you have declared a method as follows:

`private static void Method2(int a, char b, int c = 22, double d = 33.2)`

Table 8-4 shows some legal and illegal calls to this method.

Call to Method2()	Explanation
`Method2(1, 'A');`	Valid. The two arguments are assigned to a and b in the method, and the default values of 22 and 33.2 are used for c and d, respectively.
`Method2(2, 'E', 3);`	Valid. The three arguments are assigned to a, b, and c. The default value 33.2 is used for d.
`Method2(2, 'E', c : 3);`	Valid. This call is identical to the one above.
`Method2(1, 'K', d : 88.8);`	Valid. The first two arguments are assigned to a and b. The default value 22 is used for c. The named value 88.8 is used for d.
`Method2(d : 2.1, b : 'A', c : 88, a: 12);`	Valid. All the arguments are assigned to parameters whether they are listed in order or not.
`Method2(5, 'S', d : 7.4, c: 9);`	Valid. The first two arguments are assigned to a and b. Even though the values for c and d are not listed in order, they are assigned correctly.
`Method2(d : 11.1, 6, 'P');`	Invalid. This call contains an unnamed argument after the first named argument. Named arguments must appear after all unnamed arguments.

Table 8-4　Examples of legal and illegal calls to `Method2()`

Advantages to Using Named Arguments

Optional parameters can provide a convenient shortcut to writing multiple overloaded versions of a method. For example, suppose that you want to create a method that adds your signature to business letters. Usually, you want the signature to be *Sincerely, James O'Hara*. However, occasionally you want to change the name to a more casual *Jim*. You could write two method versions, as shown on the top in Figure 8-27, or you could write one version, as shown on the bottom. With both versions, you can call `Closing()` with or without an argument. The version with the optional parameter is less work when you write the method. It is also less work if you later want to modify the method—for example, to change *Sincerely* to *Best wishes* or some other closing.

```
// Overloaded implementations of Closing()
private static void Closing()
{
   WriteLine("Sincerely,");
   WriteLine("James O'Hara");
}
private static void Closing(string name)
{
   WriteLine("Sincerely,");
   WriteLine(name);
}

// Single implementation of Closing() with optional parameter
private static void Closing(string name = "James O'Hara")
{
   WriteLine("Sincerely,");
   WriteLine(name);
}
```

Figure 8-27 Two ways to implement `Closing()` to accept a name parameter or not

Another advantage to using named parameters is to make your programs more self-documenting. Programs that are **self-documenting** provide built-in explanations that make the code clearer to readers and therefore easier for others to modify in the future. For example, suppose that you encounter the following method call:

`DisplayEmployeeData(empNumber, true);`

From the method call, it is not clear what `true` means. Perhaps it means that only certain parts of the record should be displayed, or that the employee is a current employee, or that the employee's salary should be hidden from view. The following method call makes your intentions clearer:

`DisplayEmployeeData(empNumber, shouldHideSalary : true);`

Of course, a program comment adjacent to the statement could also provide clarity.

Disadvantages to Using Named Arguments

A major disadvantage to using named arguments is that the calling method becomes linked to details within the method. When the calling method must know parameter names within the called method, an important principle of programming—method implementation hiding—is compromised. If the parameter name in the called method is changed in the future, the client method also will have to change.

CHAPTER 8 Advanced Method Concepts

Suppose that a payroll program contains two methods used in paycheck calculations. The first method, shown in Figure 8-28, accepts three parameters—hours, rate, and bonus. A gross pay value is calculated by multiplying hours by rate, and a bonus value is assigned based on the number of hours worked. The second method sums its gross and bonus parameters. The intention is that an employee who works 40 hours at $10 per hour receives $400 gross pay, plus a $100 bonus, for a total of $500.

```
private static double ComputeGross(double hours, double rate,
   out double bonus)
{
   double gross = hours * rate;
   if (hours >= 40)
      bonus = 100;
   else
      bonus = 50;
   return gross;
}
private static double ComputeTotalPay(double gross, double bonus)
{
   double total = gross + bonus;
   return total;
}
```

Figure 8-28 Two payroll program methods

Figure 8-29 shows the Main() method of a program that assigns 40 to hours and 10.00 to rate. Then, the method calls the ComputeTotalPay() method by passing it the result of ComputeGross() and the value of bonus that is set within ComputeGross(). Figure 8-30 shows that the employee's total pay is correctly calculated as $500.

```
static void Main()
{
   double hours = 40;
   double rate = 10.00;
   double bonus = 0;
   double totalPay;
   totalPay = ComputeTotalPay(ComputeGross(hours, rate, out bonus),
      bonus);
   WriteLine("Total pay is {0}", totalPay);
}
```

Figure 8-29 A Main() method that calls ComputeTotalPay() using positional arguments

Using Optional Parameters

Figure 8-30 Execution of the Main() method in Figure 8-29

A possible disadvantage to using named arguments occurs when a named parameter value is an expression instead of a constant. Figure 8-31 shows a Main() method that calls ComputeTotalPay() using named arguments. The only difference from the program in Figure 8-29 is the shaded method call that uses named arguments. In this case, when ComputeTotalPay() is called, first 0 is sent to bonus, and then ComputeGross() is called to assign a value to gross. However, the bonus alteration in ComputeGross() is too late because bonus has already been assigned. The program output is incorrect, as shown in Figure 8-32.

```
static void Main()
{
   double hours = 40;
   double rate = 10.00;
   double bonus = 0;
   double totalPay;
   totalPay = ComputeTotalPay(bonus: bonus,
         gross: ComputeGross(hours, rate, out bonus));
   WriteLine("Total pay is {0}", totalPay);
}
```

Figure 8-31 A Main() method that calls ComputeTotalPay() using named arguments

Figure 8-32 Execution of the Main() method in Figure 8-31

In Chapter 4, you learned that when you combine operands in a Boolean expression using && or ||, you risk side effects because of short-circuit evaluation. The situation with named arguments is similar. When a named argument is an expression, there can be unintended consequences.

Overload Resolution with Named and Optional Arguments

Named and optional arguments affect overload resolution. The rules for betterness on argument conversions are applied only for arguments that are given explicitly; in other words, omitted optional arguments are ignored for betterness purposes. For example, suppose that you have the following methods:

```
private static void AMethod(int a, double b = 2.2)
private static void AMethod(int a, char b = 'H')
```

Both are applicable methods when a call is made using an integer argument; in other words, if either method existed alone, the call AMethod(12) would work. When the two methods coexist, however, neither is "better." Because C# cannot determine which one is better, the code will not compile.

If two signatures are equally good, the one that does not omit optional parameters is considered better. For example, suppose that you have two methods as follows:

```
private static void BMethod(int a)
private static void BMethod(int a, char b = 'B')
```

If either method existed alone, the call BMethod(12) would work, but when the two coexist, the first version is better because no optional parameters are omitted in the call.

 Watch the video *Using Optional Method Parameters*.

TWO TRUTHS & A LIE

Using Optional Parameters

1. An optional parameter to a method is one for which an argument can be a value parameter, a ref parameter, or an out parameter.

2. You make a parameter optional by providing a value for it in the method declaration.

3. If you assign a default value to any variable in a method's parameter list, then all parameters to the right of that parameter must also have default values.

The false statement is #1. An optional parameter to a method is one for which a default value is automatically supplied if you do not explicitly send one as an argument. Only value parameters can be optional.

Chapter Summary

- Method parameters can be mandatory or optional. Mandatory parameters include value parameters without default values, reference parameters, output parameters, and parameter arrays. A value parameter can be optional if it is supplied with a default value.
- When you use a reference parameter, output parameter, or parameter array, you pass a memory address to a method, allowing the method to alter the original variable.
- You can use a `ref` return to return a reference from a method.
- When you overload a C# method, you write multiple methods with a shared name but different parameter lists. When a method call could execute multiple overloaded method versions, C# determines which method to execute using a process called *overload resolution*.
- Methods must not be ambiguous; they can be overloaded correctly by providing different parameter lists for methods with the same name.
- An optional parameter to a method is a value parameter for which a default value is automatically supplied if you do not explicitly send one as an argument. You make a parameter optional by providing a value for it in the method declaration. When calling a method with optional parameters, you must leave out all unnamed arguments to the right of the last one used, or you can name arguments.

Key Terms

Mandatory parameters are method parameters for which an argument is required in every method call.

An **optional parameter** to a method is one for which a default value is supplied automatically if you do not explicitly send one as an argument; a parameter is optional when it is given a value in the method declaration.

A **value parameter** in a method header receives a copy of the value passed to it.

A **reference parameter** in a method header receives the parameter's address; a variable sent to a reference parameter is required to have been assigned a value before it is used in the method call.

An **output parameter** in a method header receives the parameter's address; a variable sent to an output parameter is not required to have been assigned a value before it is used in the method call.

A **parameter array** is a local array declared within a method header that can accept any number of elements of the same data type.

CHAPTER 8 Advanced Method Concepts

An **out variable** is a variable declared at the point where it is passed to a method as an out argument.

Overloading involves the ability to write multiple versions of a method using the same method name but different parameter lists.

A method's **signature** is composed of its name and parameter list.

Overload resolution is the process of determining which of multiple applicable methods is the best match for a method call.

Applicable methods are all the methods that could be used by a method call.

Betterness rules are the rules that determine the best overloaded method to execute based on the arguments in a method call.

Ambiguous methods are overloaded methods from which the compiler cannot determine which one to use.

A **named argument** is a method argument that is preceded with the name of the called method's parameter to which it will be assigned.

A **positional argument** is an unnamed method argument that is assigned to a parameter list based on its position in the method call.

Self-documenting describes programs that provide built-in explanations to make the code clearer to readers and therefore easier for others to modify in the future.

Review Questions

1. A mandatory parameter _____.

    a. requires an argument to be sent from a method call

    b. is any argument sent to a method

    c. is preceded by the keyword man

    d. All of the above are true.

2. Which is *not* a type of method parameter in C#?

    a. value   c. reference

    b. forensic   d. output

3. Which type of method parameter receives the address of the variable passed in?

    a. a value parameter   c. an output parameter

    b. a reference parameter   d. two of the above

Review Questions

4. When you declare a value parameter, you precede its name with _____.

   a. nothing
   b. a data type
   c. the keyword val and a data type
   d. the keyword ref and its data type

5. Assume that you declare a variable as `int x = 100;` and correctly pass it to a method with the declaration `private static void IncreaseValue(ref int x)`. There is a single statement within the `IncreaseValue()` method: `x = x + 25;`. Back in the `Main()` method, after the method call, what is the value of x?

   a. 100
   b. 125
   c. It is impossible to tell.
   d. The program will not run.

6. Assume that you declare a variable as `int x = 100;` and correctly pass it to a method with the declaration `private static void IncreaseValue(int x)`. There is a single statement within the `IncreaseValue()` method: `x = x + 25;`. Back in the `Main()` method, after the method call, what is the value of x?

   a. 100
   b. 125
   c. It is impossible to tell.
   d. The program will not run.

7. A reference parameter differs from an output parameter in that a reference parameter _____ but an output parameter does not.

   a. receives a memory address
   b. occupies a unique memory address
   c. requires an initial value
   d. must be a simple data type

8. A parameter array _____.

   a. is declared using the keyword params
   b. can accept any number of arguments of the same data type
   c. Both of these are true.
   d. Neither of these is true.

9. Assume that you have declared a method with the following header:
   `private static void DisplayScores(params int[] scores)`
   Which of the following method calls is valid?

   a. `DisplayScores(20);`
   b. `DisplayScores(20, 33);`
   c. `DisplayScores(20, 30, 90);`
   d. All of the above are valid.

CHAPTER 8 Advanced Method Concepts

10. Correctly overloaded methods must have the same _____.

    a. return type
    b. identifier
    c. parameter list
    d. All of the above.

11. Methods are ambiguous when they _____.

    a. are overloaded
    b. are written in a confusing manner
    c. are indistinguishable to the compiler
    d. have the same parameter type as their return type

12. Which of the following pairs of method declarations represent correctly overloaded methods?

    a. `private static void MethodA(int a)`
       `private static void MethodA(int b, double c)`
    b. `private static void MethodB(double d)`
       `private static void MethodB()`
    c. `private static double MethodC(int e)`
       `private static double MethodD(int f)`
    d. Two of these are correctly overloaded methods.

13. Which of the following pairs of method declarations represent correctly overloaded methods?

    a. `private static void Method(int a)`
       `private static void Method(int b)`
    b. `private static void Method(double d)`
       `private static int Method()`
    c. `private static double Method(int e)`
       `private static int Method(int f)`
    d. Two of these are correctly overloaded methods.

14. The process of determining which overloaded version of a method to execute is overload _____.

    a. confusion
    b. infusion
    c. revolution
    d. resolution

15. When one of a method's parameters is optional, it means that _____.

   a. no arguments are required in a call to the method
   b. a default value will be assigned to the parameter if no argument is sent for it
   c. a default value will override any argument value sent to it
   d. you are not required to use the parameter within the method body

16. Which of the following is an illegal method declaration?

   a. `private static void CreateStatement(int acctNum, double balance = 0.0)`
   b. `private static void CreateStatement(int acctNum = 0, double balance)`
   c. `private static void CreateStatement(int acctNum = 0, double balance = 0)`
   d. All of these are legal.

17. Assume you have declared a method as follows:
    `private static double ComputeBill(int acct, double price, double discount = 0)`
    Which of the following is a legal method call?

   a. `ComputeBill();`
   b. `ComputeBill(1001);`
   c. `ComputeBill(1001, 200.00);`
   d. None of the above is legal.

18. Assume you have declared a method as follows:
    `private static double CalculateDiscount(int acct = 0, double price = 0, double discount = 0)`
    Which of the following is a legal method call?

   a. `CalculateDiscount();`
   b. `CalculateDiscount(200.00);`
   c. `CalculateDiscount(3000.00, 0.02);`
   d. None of the above is legal.

19. Assume you have declared a method as follows:
    `private static double DisplayData(string name = "XX", double amount = 10.0)`
    Which of the following is an illegal method call?

   a. `DisplayData(name : "Albert");`
   b. `DisplayData(amount : 200, name : "Albert");`
   c. `DisplayData(amount : 900.00);`
   d. All of these are legal.

20. Suppose that you have declared an integer array named scores, and you make the following method call:
TotalScores(scores, num : 1);
Of the following overloaded method definitions, which would execute?

a. private static void TotalScores(int[] scores)

b. private static void TotalScores(int[] scores, int num)

c. private static void TotalScores(int[] scores, int num = 10, int code = 10)

d. The program would not compile.

Exercises

Programming Exercises

1. a. Create a program named **Reverse3** whose Main() method declares three integers named firstInt, middleInt, and lastInt. Assign values to the variables, display them, and then pass them to a method that accepts them as reference variables, places the first value in the lastInt variable, and places the last value in the firstInt variable. In the Main() method, display the three variables again, demonstrating that their positions have been reversed.

   b. Create a new program named **Reverse4**, which contains a method that reverses the positions of four variables. Write a Main() method that demonstrates the method works correctly.

2. Create a program named **IntegerFacts** whose Main() method declares an array of 10 integers. Call a method to interactively fill the array with any number of values up to 10 or until a sentinel value is entered. If an entry is not an integer, reprompt the user. Call a second method that accepts out parameters for the highest value in the array, lowest value in the array, sum of the values in the array, and arithmetic average. In the Main() method, display all the statistics.

3. Create a program for Smalltown Regional Airport **Flights** that accepts either an integer flight number or string airport code from the options in Figure 8-33. Pass the

Flight number	Airport code	Airport name	Time
201	AUS	Austin	0710
321	CRP	Corpus Christi	0830
510	DFW	Dallas Fort Worth	0915
633	HOU	Houston	1140

Figure 8-33 Flight information for Smalltown Regional Airport

user's entry to one of two overloaded `GetFlightInfo()` methods, and then display a returned string with all the flight details. The method version that accepts an integer looks up the airport code, name, and time of flight; the version that accepts a string description looks up the flight number, airport name, and time. The methods return an appropriate message if the flight is not found.

4. Create a program named **Auction** that allows a user to enter an amount bid on an online auction item. Include three overloaded methods that accept an `int`, `double`, or `string` bid. Each method should display the bid and indicate whether it is over the minimum acceptable bid of $10. If the bid is a `string`, accept it only if one of the following is true: it is numeric and preceded with a dollar sign, or it is numeric and followed by the word *dollars*. Otherwise, display a message that indicates the format was incorrect.

5. Create a program named **TipCalculation** that includes two overloaded methods—one that accepts a meal price and a tip as `doubles` (for example, 30.00 and 0.20, where 0.20 represents a 20 percent tip), and one that accepts a meal price as a `double` and a tip amount as an integer (for example, 30.00 and 5, where 5 represents a $5 tip). Each method displays the meal price, the tip as a percentage of the meal price, the tip in dollars, and the total of the meal plus the tip. Include a `Main()` method that demonstrates each method.

6. Write a program named **InputMethodDemo2** that eliminates the repetitive code in the `InputMethod()` in the `InputMethodDemo` program in Figure 8-5. Rewrite the program so the `InputMethod()` contains only two statements:
   ```
   one = DataEntry("first");
   two = DataEntry("second");
   ```

7. Write a program named **Averages** that includes a method that accepts any number of numeric parameters, displays them, and displays their average. Demonstrate that the method works correctly when passed one, two, or three numbers, or an array of numbers.

8. Write a program named **SortWords** that includes a method that accepts any number of words and sorts them in alphabetical order. Demonstrate that the program works correctly when the method is called with one, two, five, and ten words.

9. Write a program named **Movie** that contains a method that accepts and displays two parameters: a string name of a movie and an integer running time in minutes. Provide a default value for the minutes so that if you call the method without an integer argument, `minutes` is set to 90. Write a `Main()` method that proves you can call the movie method with only a `string` argument as well as with a `string` and an integer.

10. In the card game War, a deck of playing cards is divided between two players. Each player exposes a card; the player whose card has the higher value wins possession of both exposed cards. Create a console-based computerized game of War named **WarCardGame** in which a standard 52-card deck is randomly divided between two

players, one of which is the computer. Reveal one card for the computer and one card for the player at a time. Award two points for the player whose card has the higher value. (For this game, the king is the highest card, followed by the queen and jack, then the numbers 10 down to 2, and finally the ace.) If the computer and player expose cards with equal values in the same turn, award one point to each. At the end of the game, all 52 cards should have been played only once, and the sum of the player's and computer's score will be 52.

a. Use an array of 52 integers to store unique values for each card. Write a method named `FillDeck()` that places 52 unique values into this array. Write another method named `SelectCard()` that you call twice on each deal to select a unique card for each player, with no repetition of cards in 26 deals. (To pause the play between each dealt hand, use a call to `ReadLine()`.)

The first part of Figure 8-34 shows the start of a typical program execution. (*Caution*: This is a difficult exercise!)

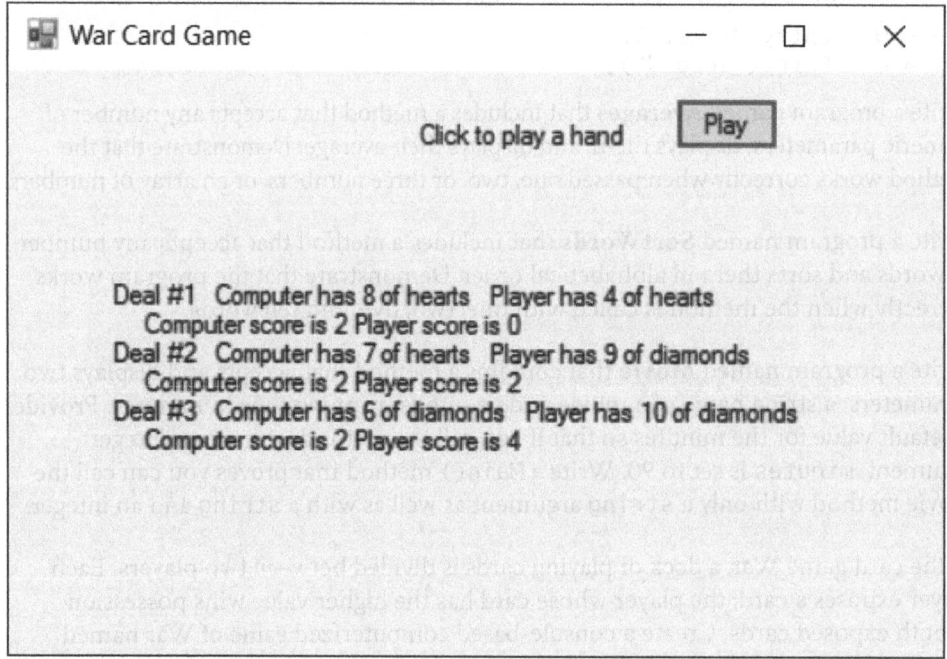

Figure 8-34 Start of typical execution of console-based and GUI WarCardGame programs

b. Create a GUI version of the War card game described in Exercise 11a, and name it **WarCardGameGUI**. Let the user click a button to deal the cards, then make that button invisible and expose a Play button. Each time the user clicks Play, a pair of cards is revealed. To keep the Frame size reasonable, you might want to erase the output label's contents every four hands or so. The second part of Figure 8-34 shows a typical game in progress.

Debugging Exercises

1. Each of the following files in the Chapter.08 folder of your downloadable student files has syntax and/or logical errors. In each case, determine the problem, and fix the program. After you correct the errors, save each file using the same filename preceded with *Fixed*. For example, DebugEight1.cs will become FixedDebugEight1.cs.

    a. DebugEight1.cs
    b. DebugEight2.cs
    c. DebugEight3.cs
    d. DebugEight4.cs

Case Problems

1. In Chapter 7, you modified the **GreenvilleRevenue** program to include a number of methods. Now modify every data entry statement to use a `TryParse()` method to ensure that each piece of data is the correct type. Any invalid user entries should generate an appropriate message, and the user should be required to reenter the data.

2. In Chapter 7, you modified the **MarshallsRevenue** program to include a number of methods. Now modify every data entry statement to use a `TryParse()` method to ensure that each piece of data is the correct type. Any invalid user entries should generate an appropriate message, and the user should be required to reenter the data.

CHAPTER 9

Using Classes and Objects

Upon completion of this chapter, you will be able to:

- ◎ Describe class concepts
- ◎ Create classes from which objects can be instantiated
- ◎ Create objects
- ◎ Create properties, including auto-implemented properties
- ◎ Use `public` and `private` access modifiers
- ◎ Use the `this` reference
- ◎ Write and use constructors
- ◎ Use object initializers
- ◎ Overload operators
- ◎ Declare object arrays and use methods with them
- ◎ Write destructors
- ◎ Understand GUI application objects

CHAPTER 9: Using Classes and Objects

Much of your understanding of the world comes from your ability to categorize objects and events into classes. As a young child, you learned the concept of *animal* long before you knew the word. Your first encounter with an animal might have been with the family dog, a neighbor's cat, or a goat at a petting zoo. As you developed speech, you might have used the same term for all of these creatures, gleefully shouting, "Doggie!" as your parents pointed out cows, horses, and sheep in picture books or along the roadside on drives in the country. As you grew more sophisticated, you learned to distinguish dogs from cows; still later, you learned to distinguish breeds. Your understanding of the class *animal* helps you see the similarities between dogs and cows, and your understanding of the class *dog* helps you see the similarities between a Great Dane and a Chihuahua. Understanding classes gives you a framework for categorizing new experiences. You might not know the term *okapi*, but when you learn it's an animal rather than a food or piece of clothing, you begin to develop a concept of what an okapi might be like.

Classes are also the basic building blocks of object-oriented programming. You already understand that differences exist among the `Double`, `Int32`, and `Float` classes, yet you also know that items belonging to these classes possess similarities—they are all data types, you can perform arithmetic with all of them, they all can be converted to strings, and so on. Understanding classes enables you to see similarities in objects and increases your understanding of the programming process. In this chapter, you will discover how C# handles classes, learn to create your own classes, and learn to construct objects that are members of those classes.

Understanding Class Concepts

When you write programs in C#, you create two types of classes:

- *Classes that are just application programs with a `Main()` method.* These classes can contain other methods that the `Main()` method calls, but these classes are not used as blueprints for objects. You have been creating these classes throughout this book.

- *Classes from which you instantiate objects.* To **instantiate** an object is to create a tangible example. An object is an **instantiation** of a class or an **instance** of a class. A class that is created to be a model for object instantiations can contain a `Main()` method, but it is not required. This chapter explores the nuances of such classes.

When you think in an object-oriented manner, things are objects, and every object is an instance or example of a class. You can think of any inanimate physical item as an object—your desk, your computer, and your house are all called *objects* in everyday conversation. You can think of living things as objects, too—your houseplant, your pet fish, and your sister are objects. Events also are objects—for example, the stock purchase you made, the mortgage closing you attended, or a graduation party in your honor.

Every object is an instance of a more general class. Your desk is a specific instance of the class that includes all desks, and your pet fish is an instance of the class that contains all fish. In part, the concept of a class is useful because it provides you with knowledge about objects.

Objects receive their attributes from classes; so, for example, if you invite me to a graduation party, I automatically know many things about the object. I assume that there will be a starting time, a number of guests, and some refreshments. I understand your party because of my previous knowledge of the `Party` class. I don't necessarily know the number of guests or the date or time of this particular party, but I understand that because all parties have a date and time, then this one must as well. Similarly, even though every stock purchase is unique, each must have a dollar amount and a number of shares. All objects have predictable attributes because they are instances of certain classes.

The data components of a class that differ for each object are stored in **instance variables**. Instance variables also are called **fields** to help distinguish them from other variables you might use. In Chapter 1, you learned that the data field values of an object are also called its *attributes* and that the set of attributes is known as an object's *state*. For example, the current state of a specific party is 8 p.m. and Friday; the state of a specific stock purchase is $10 and five shares.

In addition to their attributes, objects have methods associated with them, and every object that is an instance of the same class possesses the same methods. Methods associated with objects are **instance methods**. For example, two `Party` objects might possess the identifiers myGraduationParty and yourAnniversaryParty that both have access to an `IssueInvitations()` method. The method might operate in the same way for both `Party` objects, but use data appropriate to the specific object. When you program in C#, you frequently create classes from which objects will be instantiated. You also write applications to use the objects, along with their data and methods. Often, you will write programs that use classes created by others; similarly, you might create a class that other programmers will use to instantiate objects within their own programs. A program or class that instantiates objects of another prewritten class is a **class client** or **class user**.

TWO TRUTHS & A LIE

Understanding Class Concepts

1. C# classes always contain a `Main()` method.
2. An object is an instantiation of a class.
3. The data components of a class often are its instance variables.

The false statement is #1. C# applications always contain a Main() method, but some classes do not if they are not meant to be run as programs.

Creating a Class from Which Objects Can Be Instantiated

When you create a class, you must assign a name to it and determine what data and methods will be part of the class. For example, suppose that you decide to create a class named `Employee`. One instance variable of `Employee` might be an employee number, and one necessary method might display a welcome message to new employees. To begin, you create a **class header** or **class definition** that starts the class. It contains three parts:

1. an optional access modifier
2. the keyword `class`
3. any legal identifier you choose for the name of your class; because each class represents a type of object, class names are usually singular nouns

You will learn about other optional components that can be added to a class definition as you continue to study C#.

For example, one usable header for an `Employee` class is `internal class Employee`. The keyword internal is an example of a **class access modifier**. You can declare a class using any of the modifiers in Table 9-1.

Class Access Modifier	Description
`public`	Access to the class is not limited.
`protected`	Access to the class is limited to the class and to any classes derived from the class. (You will learn about deriving classes in the chapter *Introduction to Inheritance*.)
`internal`	Access is limited to the assembly to which the class belongs. (An **assembly** is a group of code modules compiled together to create an executable program. The .exe files you create after compiling a C# program are assemblies.)
`private`	Access is limited to another class to which the class belongs. In other words, a class should be private if it is contained within another class, and the containing class is the only one that should have access to it.

Table 9-1 Class access modifiers

If you do not explicitly include an access specifier, class access is `internal` by default. Because most classes you create will have `internal` access, typing an access specifier is often unnecessary. (When you declare a class using a namespace, you must declare it to be `public` or `internal`.)

In addition to the class header, classes you create must have a class body enclosed between curly braces. Figure 9-1 shows a shell for an `Employee` class.

Creating a Class from Which Objects Can Be Instantiated

```
class Employee
{
    // Instance variables and methods go here
}
```

Figure 9-1 `Employee` class shell

Creating Instance Variables and Methods

When you create a class, you define both its attributes and its methods. You declare the class's instance variables within the curly braces using the same syntax you use to declare other variables—you provide a type and an identifier. For example, within the `Employee` class, you can declare an integer ID number, and when you create `Employee` objects, each will have its own `idNumber`. You can define the ID number simply as `int idNumber;`. However, programmers frequently include an access modifier for each field in a class and declare the `idNumber` as `private int idNumber;`. Figure 9-2 shows an `Employee` class that contains the private `idNumber` field.

```
class Employee
{
    private int idNumber;
}
```

Figure 9-2 `Employee` class containing `idNumber` field

The allowable field modifiers are `new`, `public`, `protected`, `internal`, `private`, `static`, `readonly`, and `volatile`. If you do not provide an access specifier for a field, its access is `private` and nonstatic by default, which means that no other class can access the field's values, and only nonstatic methods of the same class will be allowed to use the private field directly. Using private fields within classes is an example of **information hiding**, a feature found in all object-oriented languages.

You see cases of information hiding in real-life objects every day. For instance, you cannot see into your automobile's gas tank to determine how full it is. Instead, you use a gauge on the dashboard to provide you with the necessary information. Similarly, data fields are frequently `private` in object-oriented programming, but their contents are accessed through `public` methods. The `private` data of a class should be changed or manipulated only by its own methods, not by methods that belong to other classes. A benefit of making data items `private` is the ability to control their values. A method that sets a variable's value can use decisions to ensure that the value falls within a specified range. For example, perhaps an `Employee`'s salary should not be below the federal minimum wage, or perhaps a department number should not be negative or greater than 10.

In contrast to a class's `private` data fields, most instance methods are not usually `private`; they are `public`. The resulting `private` data/`public` method arrangement provides a means to control outside access to your data—only a class's nonprivate methods can be used to access a class's `private` data. The situation is similar to having a "public" receptionist who controls the messages passed in and out of your private office. The way in which the nonprivate methods are written controls how you will use the `private` data.

For example, an `Employee` class that contains an `idNumber` might need a method to display the employee's welcoming message to company clients. A reasonable name for this method is `WelcomeMessage()`, and its declaration is `public void WelcomeMessage()`, because it will have `public` access and return nothing. Figure 9-3 shows the `Employee` class with the addition of the `WelcomeMessage()` method.

```
class Employee
{
    private int idNumber;
    public void WelcomeMessage()
    {
        WriteLine("Welcome from Employee #{0}", idNumber);
        WriteLine("How can I help you?");
    }
}
```

Figure 9-3 `Employee` class with `idNumber` field and `WelcomeMessage()` method

Notice that the `WelcomeMessage()` method does not employ the `static` modifier, unlike many other methods you have created. The keyword `static` is used for classwide methods but not for instance methods that "belong" to objects. If you are creating a program with a `Main()` method that you will execute to perform some task, then many of your methods will be `static`. You call `static` methods from `Main()` without creating an object. (If the method is in a different class, you use the class name, a dot, and the method call.) However, if you are creating a class from which objects will be instantiated, most methods will probably be nonstatic, as you will be associating the methods with individual objects and their data. (You use an object name, a dot, and the method call.) Each time the `WelcomeMessage()` instance method is used in the class in Figure 9-3, it will display an `idNumber` for a specific object. In other words, the method will work appropriately for each object instance, so it is not static.

In Chapter 7, you learned that when you create a `Form`, you sometimes include nonstatic variable declarations outside of any methods—for example, if two `Click()` methods must access the same data. Now you can understand that such variables are nonstatic because they are associated with an object—the `Form` that is being defined.

The `Employee` class in Figure 9-3 is not a program that will run; it contains no `Main()` method. Rather, it simply describes what `Employee` objects will have (an `idNumber`) and be able to do (display a greeting) when you write a program that contains one or more `Employee` objects.

A class can contain fields that are objects of other classes. For example, you might create a class named Date that contains a month, day, and year and add two Date fields to an Employee class to hold the Employee's birth date and hire date. You might also create a BusinessOffice class and declare Employee objects within it. Using an object within another object is known as **composition**. The relationship created is also called a **has-a relationship** because one object "has an" instance of another.

Watch the video *Creating a Class*.

TWO TRUTHS & A LIE
Creating a Class from Which Objects Can Be Instantiated

1. A class header always contains the keyword class.
2. When you create a class, you define both its attributes and its methods.
3. Most fields and methods defined in a class are private.

The false statement is #3. Most fields in a class are private, but most methods are public.

Creating Objects

Declaring a class does not create any actual objects. A class is just an abstract description of what an object will be like if any objects are ever actually instantiated. Just as you might understand all the characteristics of an item you intend to manufacture long before the first item rolls off the assembly line, you can create a class with fields and methods before you instantiate any objects that are occurrences of that class. You can think of a class declaration as similar to a blueprint for building a new house or a recipe for baking a cake. In other words, it is a plan that exists before any objects are created.

Defining an object is similar to defining a simple variable that is a built-in data type; in each case, you use a data type and an identifier. For example, you might define an integer as `int someValue;`, and you might define an Employee as `Employee myAssistant;`, where `myAssistant` could be any legal identifier you choose to represent an Employee.

Every object name is a reference—that is, it holds a computer memory location where the fields for the object reside. The memory location holds the values for the object.

When you declare an integer as `int myInteger;`, you notify the compiler that an integer named `myInteger` will exist, and computer memory automatically is reserved for it at the same time—the exact amount of computer memory depends on the declared data type. When you declare the `myAssistant` instance of the `Employee` class, you are notifying the compiler that you will use the identifier `myAssistant`. However, you are not yet setting aside computer memory in which the `Employee` named `myAssistant` can be stored—that is done only for the built-in, predefined types. To allocate the needed memory for the object, you must use the new operator. You used the new operator earlier in this book when you learned to set aside memory for an array.

Defining an `Employee` object named `myAssistant` requires two steps—you must declare a reference to the object and then you must use the statement that actually sets aside enough memory to hold `myAssistant`:

```
Employee myAssistant;
myAssistant = new Employee();
```

You also can declare and reserve memory for `myAssistant` in one statement, as in the following:

```
Employee myAssistant = new Employee();
```

In this statement, `Employee` is the object's type (as well as its class), and `myAssistant` is the name of the object. The equal sign is the assignment operator, so a value is being assigned to `myAssistant`. The new operator is allocating a new, unused portion of computer memory for `myAssistant`. The value being assigned to `myAssistant` is a memory address at which the object created by the `Employee()` constructor will be located. You need not be concerned with the actual memory address—when you refer to `myAssistant`, the compiler will locate it at the appropriate address for you.

Because the identifiers for objects are references to their memory addresses, you can call any class a **reference type**—in other words, a type that refers to a specific memory location. A reference type is a type that holds an address, as opposed to the predefined types such as `int`, `double`, and `char`, which are **value types** and hold a value as opposed to its address. (In Chapter 2, you learned about enumerations; they are value types, too.)

In programming circles, you might hear debate about whether everything in C# is an object. Although some disagree, the general consensus is that value types like `int` and `double` are not objects; only reference types are. Further confusing the issue, a value type can easily be converted to an `Object` with a statement such as `Object myObject = myInteger;`. The action that takes place in such an implicit conversion is known as *boxing*.

In C#, you can create a `struct` which is similar to a class in that it can contain fields and methods but is a value type rather than a reference type. See the C# documentation for further details.

You also can use the new operator for simple data types. For example, to declare an integer variable x, you can write the following:

```
int x = new int();
```

However, programmers usually use the simpler form:

```
int x;
```

With the first form, x is initialized to 0. With the second form, x holds no usable starting value.

In the statement Employee myAssistant = new Employee();, the last portion of the statement after the new operator, Employee(), looks suspiciously like a method name with its parentheses. In fact, it is the name of a method that constructs an Employee object. Employee() is a *constructor*. You will write your own constructors later in this chapter. For now, note that when you don't write a constructor for a class, C# writes one for you, and the name of the constructor is always the same as the name of the class whose objects it constructs.

Later in this chapter you will learn that the automatically-generated constructor for a class is a *default constructor*, which means it takes no parameters. Programmers sometimes erroneously equate the terms *automatically-generated* and *default*. The automatically created constructor for a class is an *example* of a default constructor, but you also can explicitly create your own default constructor.

After an object has been instantiated, its nonstatic public members can be accessed using the object's identifier, a dot, and the nonstatic public member's identifier. For example, if you declare an Employee named myAssistant, you can access myAssistant's WelcomeMessage() method with the following statement:

myAssistant.WelcomeMessage();

An object such as myAssistant that uses an instance method is an **invoking object**. The statement myAssistant.WelcomeMessage(); would be illegal if WelcomeMessage() was a static method. The method can be used appropriately with each unique Employee object only because it is nonstatic.

A program that declares myAssistant cannot access myAssistant's idNumber directly; the only way a program can access the private data is by using one of the object's public methods. Because the WelcomeMessage() method is part of the same class as idNumber, and because WelcomeMessage() is public, a client method (for example, a Main() method in a program) can use the method. Figure 9-4 shows a class named CreateEmployee whose Main() method declares an Employee and displays the Employee's welcome message. Figure 9-5 shows the execution of the program.

```
using static System.Console;
class CreateEmployee
{
   static void Main()
   {
      Employee myAssistant = new Employee();
      myAssistant.WelcomeMessage();
   }
}
```

Figure 9-4 The CreateEmployee program

CHAPTER 9 Using Classes and Objects

```
Welcome from Employee #0
How can I help you?
```

Figure 9-5 Output of the CreateEmployee program

In the output in Figure 9-5, the Employee's ID number is 0. By default, all unassigned numeric fields in an object are initialized to 0. When you compile the program in Figure 9-4, you receive a warning message:

```
Field 'Employee.idNumber' is never assigned to, and will always have its
default value 0.
```

Of course, usually you want to provide a different value for each `Employee`'s `idNumber` field. One way to provide values for object fields is to create *properties*, which you will do later in this chapter.

Passing Objects to Methods

A class represents a data type, and you can pass objects to methods just as you can pass variables that are simple data types. For example, the program in Figure 9-6 shows how string and `Employee` objects can be passed to a `DisplayEmployeeData()` method. Each `Employee` is assigned to the emp parameter within the method. Figure 9-7 shows the program's output.

```
using static System.Console;
class CreateTwoEmployees
{
   static void Main()
   {
      Employee aWorker = new Employee();
      Employee anotherWorker = new Employee();
      DisplayEmployeeData("First", aWorker);
      DisplayEmployeeData("Second", anotherWorker);
   }
   static void DisplayEmployeeData(string order, Employee emp)
   {
      WriteLine("\n{0} employee's message:", order);
      emp.WelcomeMessage();
   }
}
```

Figure 9-6 The CreateTwoEmployees program

```
First employee's message:
Welcome from Employee #0
How can I help you?

Second employee's message:
Welcome from Employee #0
How can I help you?
```

Figure 9-7 Output of the CreateTwoEmployees program

When you pass an object to a method, you pass a reference. Therefore, any change made to an object parameter in a method also affects the object used as an argument in the calling method.

In Figure 9-6, the `DisplayEmployeeData()` method is `internal` by default. Because the method accepts an `Employee` parameter, it must be no more accessible than the `Employee` class, which is also `internal`. This restriction preserves the security provided for the `Employee` class's nonpublic members. The program would also work if you made both the `DisplayEmployeeData()` method and the `Employee` class `public`.

TWO TRUTHS & A LIE

Creating Objects

1. Declaring a class creates one object of a new data type.

2. After you declare a class, you must use the new operator to allocate memory for an object of that class and to instantiate it.

3. After an object has been instantiated, its public members can be accessed using the object's identifier, a dot, and a method call.

The false statement is #1. Declaring a class does not create any actual objects; the declaration describes only what an object of that class will be.

Creating Properties

Frequently, methods you call with an object are used to alter the states of its fields. For example, you might want to set or change the date or time of a party. In the Employee class, you could write a method such as `SetIdNumber()` to set an employee's `idNumber` field as follows:

```
public void SetIdNumber(int number)
{
   idNumber = number;
}
```

Then, after you instantiate an `Employee` object named `myAssistant`, you could call the method with a statement like the following:

`myAssistant.SetIdNumber(785);`

Although this technique would work, and might be used in other programming languages, C# programmers more often create properties to perform similar tasks. A **property** is a member of a class that provides access to a field of a class; properties define how fields will be set and retrieved. C# programmers refer to properties as *smart fields* because they provide a combination of the best features of `private` fields and `public` methods:

- Like public methods, properties protect `private` data from outside access.
- Like fields, property names are used in the same way simple variable names are used. When you create properties, the syntax in your client programs becomes more natural and easier to understand.

Properties have **accessors** that specify the statements that execute when a class's fields are accessed. Specifically, properties contain **set accessors** for setting an object's fields and **get accessors** for retrieving the stored values. Figure 9-8 shows an `Employee` class in which a property named `IdNumber` has been defined in the shaded area.

```
class Employee
{
    private int idNumber;
    public int IdNumber
    {
        get
        {
            return idNumber;
        }
        set
        {
            idNumber = value;
        }
    }
    public void WelcomeMessage()
    {
        WriteLine("Welcome from Employee #{0}", IdNumber);
        WriteLine("How can I help you?");
    }
}
```

Notice that this statement uses the property `IdNumber` instead of the field `idNumber`.

Figure 9-8 `Employee` class with defined property

A property declaration resembles a variable declaration; it contains an access modifier, a data type, and an identifier. It also resembles a method in that it is followed by curly braces that contain statements. By convention, a property identifier is the same as the field it manipulates, except the first letter is capitalized. The field that supports a property is its **backing field**. Be careful with capitalization of properties. For example, within a get accessor for IdNumber, if you return the property (IdNumber) instead of the backing field (idNumber), you initiate an infinite loop—the property continuously accesses itself.

The IdNumber property in Figure 9-8 contains both get and set accessors defined between curly braces; a property declaration can contain a get accessor, a set accessor, or both. When a property has a set accessor, programmers say the property can be *written to*. When it has a get accessor, programmers say the property can be *read from*. When a property has only a get accessor (and not a set accessor), it is a **readonly property**. In C#, the get and set accessors often are called the **getter** and the **setter**, respectively.

In the WelcomeMessage() method in Figure 9-8, the IdNumber property is displayed. Alternatively, this method could continue to use the idNumber field (as in Figure 9-3) because the method is a member of the same class as the field. Programmers are divided on whether a method of a class should use a field or a property to access its own methods. One popular position is that if get and set accessors are well designed, they should be used everywhere, even within the class. Sometimes, you want a field to be readonly, so you do not create a set accessor. In such a case, you can use the field (with the lowercase initial by convention) within class methods.

Throughout this book you have seen keywords displayed in boldface in the program figures. The words get, set, and value are not C# keywords—for example, you could declare a variable named get within a C# program. However, within a property, get, set, and value have special meanings and are not allowed to be declared as identifiers there. In the Visual Studio Integrated Development Environment, these three words appear in blue within properties, but in black elsewhere. Identifiers that act like keywords in specific circumstances are **contextual keywords**. C# has 13 contextual keywords: add, async, await, dynamic, get, global, partial, remove, set, value, var, where, and yield.

Each accessor in a property looks like a method, except no parentheses are included in the identifier. A set accessor acts like a method that accepts a parameter and assigns it to a variable. However, it is not a method and you do not use parentheses with it. A get accessor returns the value of the field associated with the property, but you do not code a return type; the return type of a get accessor is implicitly the type of the property in which it is contained.

When you use set and get accessors in a method, you do not use the words *set* or *get*. Instead, to set a value, you use the assignment operator (=), and to get a value, you simply use the property name. For example, if you declare an Employee named myChef, you can assign an IdNumber as simply as you would a variable, as in the following:

```
Employee myChef = new Employee();
myChef.IdNumber = 2345;
```

In the second statement, the `IdNumber` property is set to 2345. The value to the right of the equal sign is sent to the `set` accessor as an implicit parameter named value. (An **implicit parameter** is one that is undeclared and that gets its value automatically.) In the statement `myChef.IdNumber = 2345;`, the constant 2345 is sent to the `set` accessor, where it becomes the value of `value`. Within the `set` accessor, value is assigned to the field `idNumber`. The `idNumber` field could not have been set directly from `Main()` because it is `private`; however, the `IdNumber` property can be set through its `set` accessor because the property is `public`.

Writing a `get` accessor allows you to use a property as you would a simple variable. For example, a declared `Employee`'s ID number can be displayed with the following:

`WriteLine("ID number is {0}", myChef.IdNumber);`

The expression myChef.idNumber (using the field name that starts with a lowercase *i*) would not be allowed in a client program because `idNumber` is `private`; however, the `public get` accessor of the property allows myChef.IdNumber to be displayed. Figure 9-9 shows a complete application that uses the `Employee` class with accessors defined in Figure 9-8. Figure 9-10 shows the output.

```
using static System.Console;
class CreateEmployee2
{
    static void Main()
    {
        Employee myChef = new Employee();
        myChef.IdNumber = 2345;
        WriteLine("ID number is {0}"), myChef.IdNumber);
        myChef.WelcomeMessage();
    }
}
```

Figure 9-9 The CreateEmployee2 application that uses the `Employee` class containing a property

```
ID number is 2345
Welcome from Employee #2345
How can I help you?
```

Figure 9-10 Output of the CreateEmployee2 application

At this point, declaring `get` and `set` accessors that do nothing except retrieve a value from a field or assign a value to one might seem like a lot of work for very little payoff. After all, if a field was `public` instead of `private`, you would just use it directly and avoid the work of creating the property. However, it is conventional (and consistent with object-oriented principles) to make a class's fields `private` and allow accessors to manipulate them only as you deem appropriate. Keeping data hidden is an important feature of object-oriented programming, as is controlling how data values are set and used. Additionally, you can customize accessors to suit the restrictions you want to impose on how some fields are retrieved and accessed. For example, you could write a `set` accessor that restricts ID numbers within the `Employee` class as follows:

```
set
{
   if(value < 500)
      idNumber = value;
   else
      idNumber = 500;
}
```

This `set` accessor would ensure that an `Employee idNumber` would never be greater than 500. If clients had direct access to a `private idNumber` field, you could not control what values could be assigned there, but when you write a custom `set` accessor for your class, you gain full control over the allowed data values.

A minor inconvenience when using properties is that a property cannot be passed to a method as a `ref` or `out` parameter. For example, if `IdNumber` is an `Employee` property and `myChef` is an `Employee` object, the following statement does not compile:

```
int.TryParse(ReadLine(), out myChef.IdNumber);
```

Instead, to use `TryParse()` to interactively get an `IdNumber` value, you must use a temporary variable, as in the following example:

```
int temp;
int.TryParse(ReadLine(), out temp);
myChef.IdNumber = temp;
```

Using Auto-Implemented Properties

Although you can include any number of custom statements within the `get` and `set` accessors in a property, the most frequent scenario is that a `set` accessor simply assigns a value to the appropriate field, and the `get` accessor simply returns the field value. Because the code in `get` and `set` accessors frequently is standard as well as brief, programmers sometimes take one of several shorthand approaches to writing properties.

For example, instead of writing an `IdNumber` property using 11 code lines as in Figure 9-8, a programmer might write the property on five lines, as follows:

```
public int IdNumber
{
    get {return idNumber;}
    set {idNumber = value;}
}
```

This format does not eliminate any of the characters in the original version of the property; it eliminates only some of the white space, placing each accessor on a single line.

Other programmers choose an even more condensed form and write the entire property on one line as:

```
public int IdNumber {get {return idNumber;} set {idNumber = value;}}
```

An even more concise format was introduced in C# 3.0. In this and newer versions of C#, you can write a property as follows:

```
public int IdNumber {get; set;}
```

A property written in this format is an **auto-implemented property**. The property's implementation (its set of working statements) is created for you automatically with the assumptions that the `set` accessor should simply assign a value to the appropriate field, and the `get` accessor should simply return the field. You cannot use an auto-implemented property if you need to include customized statements within one of your accessors (such as placing restrictions on an assigned value), and you can declare an auto-implemented property only when you use both `get` and `set`. Auto-implemented properties are sometimes called **automatic properties**.

When you create an auto-implemented property, you should not declare the backing field that corresponds to the property. The corresponding backing field is generated by the compiler and has an internal name that would not match the field's name if you had coded the field yourself. If you also declare a field for the property and do not refer to it explicitly, you will receive a warning that your field is never used because your field and the property's field refer to separate memory addresses. You can avoid the warning by using the declared field, but that can lead to potential confusion and errors. For example, Figure 9-11 shows an `Employee` class in which no specialized code is needed for the properties associated with the ID number and salary. In this class, the fields are not declared explicitly; only auto-implemented properties are declared.

Following the `Employee` class, Figure 9-11 also contains a short program that uses the class; Figure 9-12 shows the output. Auto-implemented properties provide a convenient shortcut when you need both `get` and `set` abilities without specialized statements.

```
using static System.Console;
class CreateEmployee3
{
   static void Main()
   {
      Employee aWorker = new Employee();
      aWorker.IdNumber = 3872;
      aWorker.Salary = 22.11;
      WriteLine("Employee #{0} makes {1}",
         aWorker.IdNumber, aWorker.Salary.ToString("C"));
   }
}
class Employee
{
   public int IdNumber {get; set;}
   public double Salary {get; set;}
}
```

Figure 9-11 An Employee class with no declared fields and auto-implemented properties, and a program that uses them

```
Employee #3872 makes $22.11
```

Figure 9-12 Output of the CreateEmployee3 application

If you want to create a read-only property using auto-implemented accessors, you can make the set accessor private, as in the following:

`public int IdNumber {get; private set;}`

Using this technique, the `IdNumber` property cannot be set by any statement in another class. However, it could be assigned a value by methods within its own class. You also might want to create a property that outside classes could set but not retrieve, as follows:

`public int IdNumber {private get; set;}`

 Watch the video *Creating Properties*.

TWO TRUTHS & A LIE

Creating Properties

1. A property is a member of a class that defines how fields will be set and retrieved.

2. Properties contain set accessors for retrieving an object's fields and get accessors for setting the stored values.

3. You can create auto-implemented properties when you want a field's set accessor simply to assign a value to the appropriate field, and a field's get accessor simply to return the field value.

The false statement is #2. Properties contain set accessors for setting an object's fields and get accessors for retrieving the stored values.

You Do It

Creating a Class and Objects

In this section, you create a Student class and instantiate objects from it. This class contains an ID number, last name, and grade point average for the Student. It also contains properties that get and set each of these fields. You also pass each Student object to a method.

1. Start a new project by declaring a Student class. Insert an opening curly brace, and declare three private fields that will hold an ID number, last name, and grade point average, as follows:

```
class Student
{
    private int idNumber;
    private string lastName;
    private double gradePointAverage;
```

2. Add two constants that represent the highest and lowest possible values for a grade point average.

```
public const double HIGHEST_GPA = 4.0;
public const double LOWEST_GPA = 0.0;
```

(continues)

(continued)

3. Add two properties that get and set `idNumber` and `lastName`. By convention, properties have an identifier that is the same as the field they service, except they start with a capital letter.

```
public int IdNumber
{
   get
   {
      return idNumber;
   }
   set
   {
      idNumber = value;
   }
}
public string LastName
{
   get
   {
      return lastName;
   }
   set
   {
      lastName = value;
   }
}
```

4. Add the following `set` accessor in the property for the `gradePointAverage` field. It sets limits on the value assigned, assigning 0 if the value is out of range.

```
public double GradePointAverage
{
   get
   {
      return gradePointAverage;
   }
   set
   {
      if(value >= LOWEST_GPA && value <= HIGHEST_GPA)
         gradePointAverage = value;
      else
         gradePointAverage = LOWEST_GPA;
   }
}
```

(continues)

(continued)

5. Add a closing curly brace for the class. Save the file as **CreateStudents.cs**.

6. At the top of the file, begin a program that creates two Student objects, assigns some values, and displays the Students.

   ```
   using System;
   using static System.Console;
   class CreateStudents
   {
   ```

7. Add a Main() method that declares two Students. Assign field values, including one "illegal" value—a grade point average that is too high.

   ```
   static void Main()
   {
      Student first = new Student();
      Student second = new Student();
      first.IdNumber = 123;
      first.LastName = "Anderson";
      first.GradePointAverage = 3.5;
      second.IdNumber = 789;
      second.LastName = "Daniels";
      second.GradePointAverage = 4.1;
   ```

8. Instead of creating similar WriteLine() statements to display the two Students, call a method with each Student. You will create the method to accept a Student argument in the next step. Add a closing curly brace for the Main() method.

   ```
      Display(first);
      Display(second);
   }
   ```

9. Write the Display() method so that the passed-in Student's IdNumber, LastName, and GradePointAverage are displayed and aligned. Add a closing curly brace for the class.

   ```
   static void Display(Student stu)
   {
      WriteLine("{0, 5} {1, -10}{2, 6}", stu.IdNumber,
         stu.LastName, stu.GradePointAverage.ToString("F1"));
   }
   }
   ```

Recall that field contents are left-aligned when you use a minus sign before the field size. Also recall that the "F1" argument to the ToString() method causes the value to be displayed to one decimal place.

(continues)

More About public and private Access Modifiers

(continued)

10. Save the file, and then compile and execute the program. Figure 9-13 shows the output. Each Student has unique data values and uses the same Display() method. Notice how the second Student's grade point average was forced to 0 by the set accessor in the property for the field.

Figure 9-13 Output of the CreateStudents program

Using Auto-Implemented Properties

When a property's get accessor simply returns the corresponding field's value, and its set accessor simply assigns a value to the appropriate field, you can reduce the code in your classes by using auto-implemented properties. In the Student class, both IdNumber and LastName are candidates for this shortcut, so you can replace the full versions of these properties with their auto-implemented versions. The GradePointAverage property cannot take advantage of auto-implementation because additional code is required for the property to fulfill its intended function.

1. Open the file that contains the Student class if it is not still open on your screen. Remove the properties for IdNumber and LastName and replace them with these auto-implemented versions:

   ```
   public int IdNumber {get; set;}
   public string LastName {get; set;}
   ```

2. Remove the declarations for the fields idNumber and lastName.

3. Save the file, and then recompile and execute it. The output is the same as when the program used the original version of the Student class in Figure 9-13.

More About public and private Access Modifiers

Most of the time, a class's data fields are private and its methods are public. This technique ensures that data will be used and changed only in the ways provided in your accessors. Novice programmers might make a data field public to avoid having to create a property containing get and set accessors. However, doing so violates a basic principle of object-oriented programming. Data should be hidden when at all possible, and access to it should be controlled by well-designed accessors.

CHAPTER 9 Using Classes and Objects

Although `private` fields and `public` methods and accessors are the norm, occasionally you need to create `public` fields or `private` methods. Consider the `Carpet` class shown in Figure 9-14. Although it contains several `private` data fields, this class also contains one `public` constant field (shaded). Following the three `public` property declarations, one `private` method is defined (also shaded).

```
class Carpet
{
   public const string MOTTO ="Our carpets are quality-made";
   private int length;
   private int width;
   private int area;
   public int Length
   {
      get
      {
         return length;
      }
      set
      {
         length = value;
         CalcArea();
      }
   }
   public int Width
   {
      get
      {
         return width;
      }
      set
      {
         width = value;
         CalcArea();
      }
   }
   public int Area
   {
      get
      {
         return area;
      }
   }
   private void CalcArea()
   {
      area = Length * Width;
   }
}
```

Figure 9-14 The Carpet class

More About public and private Access Modifiers

When you create `Carpet` objects from the class in Figure 9-14, each `Carpet` will have its own `length`, `width`, and `area`, but all `Carpet` objects will have the same `MOTTO`. The field `MOTTO` is preceded by the keyword `const`, meaning `MOTTO` is constant. That is, no program can change its value. Making a constant `public` does not violate information hiding in the way that making an object's data fields `public` would, because programs that use this class cannot change the constant's value.

When you define a named constant within a class, it is always `static`, even though you cannot use the keyword `static` as a modifier. In other words, the field belongs to the entire class, not to any particular instance of the class. When you create a `static` field, only one copy is stored for the entire class, no matter how many objects you instantiate. When you use a constant field in a client class, you use the class name and a dot rather than an object name, as in `Carpet.MOTTO`. Some built-in C# classes contain useful named constants, such as `Math.PI`, which contains the value of pi. You do not create a `Math` object to use `PI`; therefore, you know it is `static`.

 Throughout this book, you have been using `static` to describe the `Main()` method of a class. You do not need to create an object of any class that contains a `Main()` method to be able to use `Main()`.

Figure 9-15 shows a program that instantiates and uses a `Carpet` object, and Figure 9-16 shows the results when the program executes. Notice that, although the output statements require an object to use the `Width`, `Length`, and `Area` properties, `MOTTO` is referenced using the class name only.

```
using static System.Console;
class TestCarpet
{
   static void Main()
   {
      Carpet aRug = new Carpet();
      aRug.Width = 12;
      aRug.Length = 14;
      Write("The {0} X {1} carpet ", aRug.Width, aRug.Length);
      WriteLine("has an area of {0}", aRug.Area);
      WriteLine("Our motto is: {0}", Carpet.MOTTO);
   }
}
```

Figure 9-15 The TestCarpet program

```
The 12 X 14 carpet has an area of 168
Our motto is: Our carpets are quality-made
```

Figure 9-16 Output of the TestCarpet program

The `Carpet` class contains one private method named `CalcArea()`. As you examine the code in the `TestCarpet` class in Figure 9-15, notice that `Width` and `Length` are set using an assignment operator but `Area` is not. The `TestCarpet` class can make assignments to `Width` and `Length` because these properties are `public`. However, you would not want a client program to assign a value to `Area` because the assigned value might not agree with the `Width` and `Length` values. Therefore, the `Area` property is a read-only property—it does not contain a `set` accessor, and no assignments by clients are allowed. Instead, whenever the `Width` or `Length` properties are changed, the `private CalcArea()` method is called from the accessor. The `CalcArea()` method is defined as `private` because there is no reason for a client class like `TestCarpet` to call `CalcArea()`. Programmers probably create `private` methods more frequently than they create `public` data fields. Some programmers feel that the best style is to use `public` methods that are nothing but a list of method calls with descriptive names. Then, the methods that actually do the work are all `private`.

TWO TRUTHS & A LIE

More About `public` and `private` Access Modifiers

1. Good object-oriented techniques require that data should usually be hidden and access to it should be controlled by well-designed accessors.

2. Although `private` fields, methods, and accessors are the norm, occasionally you need to create `public` versions of them.

3. When you define a named constant within a class, it is always `static`; that is, the field belongs to the entire class, not to any particular instance of the class.

The false statement is #2. Although private fields and public methods and accessors are the norm, occasionally you need to create public fields or private methods.

Understanding the this Reference

When you create a class, only one copy of the class code is stored in computer memory. However, you might eventually create thousands of objects from the class. When you create each object, you provide storage for each of the object's instance variables. For example, Figure 9-17 shows part of a Book class that contains three fields, a property for the title field, and an advertising message method. When you declare several Book objects, as in the following statements, each Book object requires separate memory locations for its title, numPages, and price:

```
Book myBook = new Book();
Book yourBook = new Book();
```

```
class Book
{
    private string title;
    private int numPages;
    private double price;
    public string Title
    {
        get
        {
            return title;
        }
        set
        {
            title = value;
        }
    }
    public void AdvertisingMessage()
    {
        WriteLine("Buy it now: {0}", Title);
    }
}
```

Figure 9-17 Partially developed Book class

 When you compile the Book class, you receive warnings that the numPages and price fields are never used. The omission was purposeful for this demonstration program.

In this example, storing a single Book object requires allocating storage space for three separate fields; the storage requirements for Book objects used by a library or retail bookstore would be far more considerable, but necessary—each Book must be able to "hold" its own data, including publisher, date published, author, ISBN, and so on. Each nonstatic field is called an *instance variable* precisely because separate values are stored for each instance. In addition to its fields, if each Book object also required its own copy of each property and method contained in the class, the storage requirements would multiply. It makes sense that each Book needs space to store its unique title and other data, but because every Book uses the same methods, storing multiple copies of methods is wasteful and unnecessary.

Fortunately, each Book object does not need to store its own copy of each property and method. Whether you make the method call myBook.AdvertisingMessage() or yourBook.AdvertisingMessage(), you access the same AdvertisingMessage() method. However, there must be a difference between the two method calls, because each displays a different title in its message. The difference lies in an implicit, or invisible, reference that is passed to every instance method and property accessor. The implicitly passed reference is the **this reference**, which is the address of the invoking object. When you call the method myBook.AdvertisingMessage(), you automatically pass the this reference to the method so that it knows which instance of Book to use. Only nonstatic methods receive a this reference. The this reference is aptly named. When you execute a nonstatic method such as myBook.AdvertisingMessage(), you might ask yourself which object's data will be used in the method. The answer is "*This* object's (myBook's) data."

You can explicitly refer to the this reference within an instance method or property, as shown in Figure 9-18. When you refer to Title (or title) within a Book class method or accessor, you are referring to the title field of "this" Book—the Book whose name you used in the method call, perhaps myBook or yourBook. Using the shaded keywords in Figure 9-18 is not required; the version of the methods shown in Figure 9-17 (where this was implied but not written explicitly) works just as well. Figure 9-19 shows an application that uses the Book class, and Figure 9-20 shows the output.

```
class Book
{
    private string title;
    private int numPages;
    private double price;
    public string Title
    {
        get
        {
            return this.title;
        }
        set
        {
            this.title = value;
        }
    }
    public void AdvertisingMessage()
    {
        WriteLine("Buy it now: {0}", this.Title);
    }
}
```

Figure 9-18 The Book class with methods explicitly using this references

Understanding the this Reference

```
using static System.Console;
class CreateTwoBooks
{
    static void Main()
    {
        Book myBook = new Book();
        Book yourBook = new Book();
        myBook.Title = "Silas Marner";
        yourBook.Title = "The Time Traveler's Wife";
        myBook.AdvertisingMessage();
        yourBook.AdvertisingMessage();
    }
}
```

Figure 9-19 Program that declares two Book objects

```
Buy it now: Silas Marner
Buy it now: The Time Traveler's Wife
```

Figure 9-20 Output of the CreateTwoBooks program

The Book class in Figure 9-18 worked without adding the explicit references to this. However, you should be aware that the this reference is always there, working behind the scenes, even if you do not code it. Sometimes, you might want to include the this reference within a method for clarity, so the reader has no doubt when you are referring to an instance variable.

On occasion, you might need to explicitly code the this reference. For example, consider the abbreviated Book class in Figure 9-21. The programmer has chosen the same identifier for a field and a parameter to a method that uses the field. To distinguish between the two, the field must be referenced as this.price within the method that has a parameter with the same name. All references to price (without using this) in the SetPriceAndTax() method in Figure 9-21 are references to the local parameter. If the method included the statement price = price;, the parameter's value would be assigned to itself and the class's field would never be set.

CHAPTER 9 Using Classes and Objects

```
class Book
{
    private double tax;
    private double price;
    public void SetPriceAndTax(double price)
    {
        const double TAX_RATE = 0.07;
        this.price = price;
        tax = price * TAX_RATE;
    }
}
```

The field price is this.price within the method.

The parameter price is just price within the method.

Figure 9-21 Book class that must explicitly use the `this` reference

 Watch the video Understanding the *this* Reference.

TWO TRUTHS & A LIE

Understanding the `this` Reference

1. An implicit, or invisible, `this` reference is passed to every instance method and property accessor in a class; instance methods and properties are nonstatic.

2. You can explicitly refer to the `this` reference within an instance method or property.

3. Although the `this` reference exists in every instance method, it is invisible, so you can never refer to it within a method.

The false statement is #3. Sometimes, you might want to include the `this` reference within a method for clarity, so the reader has no doubt when you are referring to an instance variable.

Understanding Constructors

When you create a class such as Employee and instantiate an object with a statement such as `Employee aWorker = new Employee();`, you are actually calling a method named `Employee()` that is provided by C#. A **constructor** is a method that instantiates (creates an instance of) an object. If you do not write a constructor for a class, then each class you create is automatically supplied with a `public` constructor with no parameters. A constructor without

Understanding Constructors

parameters is a class's **default constructor**. (The term *default constructor* is not just used for a class's automatically supplied constructor; it is used for any constructor that takes no parameters. You will learn to create constructors with parameters in the next section.)

The automatically created constructor named `Employee()` establishes one `Employee` with the identifier `aWorker`, and provides the following initial values to the `Employee`'s data fields:

- Numeric fields are set to 0 (zero).
- Character fields are set to '\0'.
- Boolean fields are set to `false`.
- References, such as `string` fields or any other object fields, are set to `null` (or empty).

The value of an object initialized with a default constructor is known as the **default value of the object**. If you do not want all of an `Employee`'s fields to hold default values, or if you want to perform additional tasks when you create an `Employee`, you can write your own constructor to replace the automatically supplied version. Any constructor you write must have the same name as its class, and constructors cannot have a return type. For example, if you create an `Employee` class that contains a `Salary` property, and you want every new `Employee` object to have a `salary` of 300.00, you could write the constructor for the `Employee` class as follows:

```
Employee()
{
    Salary = 300.00;
}
```

Assuming a `Salary` property has been defined for the `salary` field, any instantiated `Employee` will have a default `salary` value of 300.00.

You can write any statement in a constructor. For example, you can perform arithmetic or display a message. However, the most common constructor task is to initialize fields. If you create a class in which one or more fields are never assigned a value, the compiler will issue a warning that the fields in question will hold default values.

Passing Parameters to Constructors

You can create a constructor to ensure that all objects of a class are initialized with the same values in their data fields. Alternatively, you might create objects initialized with unique field values by writing constructors to which you pass one or more parameters. You then can use the parameter values to set properties or fields for individual object instantiations.

For example, consider an `Employee` class with two data fields, a constructor, and an auto-implemented property, as shown in Figure 9-22. Its constructor assigns 9.99 to each potentially instantiated `Employee`'s `PayRate`. Any time an `Employee` object is created using a statement such as `Employee partTimeWorker = new Employee();`, even if no other data-assigning methods are ever used, you are ensured that the `Employee's PayRate` holds a default value.

```
class Employee
{
   private int idNumber;
   private string name;
   public Employee()
   {
      PayRate = 9.99;
   }
   public double PayRate {get; set;}
   // Other class members can go here
}
```

Figure 9-22 Employee class with a parameterless constructor

The constructor in Figure 9-22 is a **parameterless constructor**—one that takes no arguments. In other words, it is a default constructor. As an alternative, you might choose to create Employees with a different initial pay rate value for each Employee. To accomplish this task, you can pass a pay rate to the constructor. Figure 9-23 shows an Employee constructor that receives a parameter. A value is passed to the constructor using a statement such as the following:

`Employee partTimeWorker = new Employee(12.50);`

When the constructor executes, the double used as the actual parameter within the method call is passed to Employee() and assigned to the Employee's PayRate.

```
public Employee(double rate)
{
   PayRate = rate;
}
```

Figure 9-23 Employee constructor with parameter

Overloading Constructors

C# automatically provides a default constructor for your classes. As soon as you create your own constructor, whether it has parameters or not, you no longer have access to the automatically-created version. However, if you want a class to have both parameter and parameterless versions of a constructor, you can create them. Like any other C# methods, constructors can be overloaded. You can write as many constructors for a class as you want,

Understanding Constructors

as long as their parameter lists do not cause ambiguity. A class can contain only one parameterless constructor: the default constructor, which can be the automatically-provided one or one that you write. If you wrote multiple parameterless constructors, they would be ambiguous. If you create any number of constructors but do not create a parameterless version, then the class does not have a default constructor.

For example, the `Employee` class in Figure 9-24 contains four constructors. The `Main()` method within the `CreateSomeEmployees` class in Figure 9-25 shows how different types of `Employees` might be instantiated. Notice that one version of the `Employee` constructor—the one that supports a character parameter—doesn't even use the parameter; sometimes you might create a constructor with a specific parameter type simply to force that constructor to be the version that executes. The output of the `CreateSomeEmployees` program is shown in Figure 9-26.

```
class Employee
{
    public int IdNumber {get; set;}

    public double Salary {get; set;}
    public Employee()    ⎯⎯⎯  This parameterless constructor is
    {                          the class's default constructor.
        IdNumber = 999;
        Salary = 0;
    }
    public Employee(int empId)
    {
        IdNumber = empId;
        Salary = 0;
    }
    public Employee(int empId, double sal)
    {
        IdNumber = empId;
        Salary = sal;
    }
    public Employee(char code)
    {
        IdNumber = 111;
        Salary = 100000;
    }
}
```

Figure 9-24 Employee class with four constructors

```
using static System.Console;
class CreateSomeEmployees
{
   static void Main()
   {
      Employee aWorker = new Employee();
      Employee anotherWorker = new Employee(234);
      Employee theBoss = new Employee('A');
      WriteLine("{0, 4}{1, 14}", aWorker.IdNumber,
         aWorker.Salary.ToString("C"));
      WriteLine("{0, 4}{1, 14}",
         anotherWorker.IdNumber,
         anotherWorker.Salary.ToString("C"));
      WriteLine("{0, 4}{1, 14}", theBoss.IdNumber,
         theBoss.Salary.ToString("C"));
   }
}
```

Figure 9-25 The CreateSomeEmployees program

```
999         $0.00
234         $0.00
111   $100,000.00
```

Figure 9-26 Output of the CreateSomeEmployees program

Most likely, a single application would not use all four constructors of the Employee class. More likely, each application that uses the class would use only one or two constructors. You create a class with multiple constructors to provide flexibility for your clients. For example, some clients might choose to construct Employee objects with just ID numbers, and others might prefer to construct them with ID numbers and salaries.

Using Constructor Initializers

The Employee class in Figure 9-24 contains four constructors, and each constructor initializes the same two fields. In a fully developed class used by a company, many more fields would be initialized, creating a lot of duplicated code. Besides the original extra work of writing the repetitive statements in these constructors, even more work will be required when the class is modified in the future. For example, if your organization institutes a new employee ID number format that requires a specific number of digits, then each constructor will have to be modified, requiring extra work. In addition, one or more of the constructor versions that must be modified might be overlooked, introducing errors into the programs that are clients of the class.

Understanding Constructors

As an alternative to repeating code in the constructors, you can use a constructor initializer. A **constructor initializer** is a clause that indicates another instance of a class constructor should be executed before any statements in the current constructor body. Figure 9-27 shows a new version of the Employee class using constructor initializers in three of the four overloaded constructor versions.

```
class Employee
{
    public int IdNumber {get; set;}
    public double Salary {get; set;}
    public Employee() : this(999, 0)
    {
    }
    public Employee(int empId) : this(empId, 0)
    {
    }
    public Employee(int empId, double sal)
    {
        IdNumber = empId;
        Salary = sal;
    }
    public Employee(char code) : this(111, 100000)
    {
    }
}
```

Figure 9-27 Employee class with constructor initializers

In the three shaded clauses in Figure 9-27, the this reference is used to mean "the constructor for this object being constructed." For example, when a client calls the parameterless Employee constructor, 999 and 0 are passed to the two-parameter constructor. There, they become empId and sal, parameters that are assigned to the IdNumber and Salary properties. If statements were written within the parameterless constructor, they would then execute; however, in this class, additional statements are not necessary. Similarly, if a client uses the constructor version that accepts only an ID number, that parameter and a 0 for salary are passed to the two-parameter constructor. The only time just one version of the constructor executes is when a client uses both an ID number and a salary as constructor arguments. In the future, if additional statements need to be added to the class (for example, a decision that ensures an ID number was at least five digits at construction), the decision would be added only to the two-parameter version of the constructor, and all the other versions could use it.

Using the `readonly` Modifier in a Constructor

You have already learned that when you use the `const` modifier with a variable, you must assign a value at declaration and the value cannot be changed. The `readonly` modifier is similar to `const` in that it is used to assign a constant value that cannot be changed, but when you use `readonly` with a field you can assign a value either at declaration or within a constructor. This means that different constructor versions can assign different values to a `readonly` field. A `const` field must be assigned its value when a program is compiled, but a `readonly` field can be assigned a value when initialized or at runtime. For example, a `readonly` field's value might be retrieved from user input or from the operating system.

Figure 9-28 shows a program with an `Employee` class with an `idNumber` field that has been declared `readonly`. (See the first shaded statement.) The `Main()` program can send different values to the constructor to assign to `idNumber`, but after construction, `idNumber` cannot be changed. The second shaded statement causes a compiler error.

```
class EmployeesReadOnlyDemo
{
    static void Main()
    {
        Employee myAssistant = new Employee(1234);
        Employee myDriver = new Employee(2345);
        myAssistant.IdNumber = 3456;
    }
}
class Employee
{
    private readonly int idNumber;
    public Employee(int id)
    {
        idNumber = id;
    }
    public int IdNumber
    {
        get
        {
            return idNumber;
        }
        set
        {
            idNumber = value;
        }
    }
}
```

Don't Do It
The `idNumber` field cannot be assigned a value after construction. This statement generates an error.

Figure 9-28 Employee class with a `readonly` field

TWO TRUTHS & A LIE

Understanding Constructors

1. Every class you create is automatically supplied with a public constructor with no parameters.

2. If you write a constructor for a class, you do not have a default constructor for the class.

3. Any constructor you write must have the same name as its class, and constructors cannot have a return type.

The false statement is #2. If you write a parameterless constructor for a class, it becomes the default constructor, and you lose the automatically supplied version. If you write only constructors that require parameters, then the class no longer contains a default constructor.

 You Do It

Adding Overloaded Constructors to a Class

In these steps, you add overloaded constructors to the Student class.

1. Open the file that contains the Student class if it is not still open on your screen. Just before the closing curly brace for the Student class, add the following constructor. It takes three parameters and assigns them to the appropriate fields:

   ```
   public Student(int id, string name, double gpa)
   {
       IdNumber = id;
       LastName = name;
       GradePointAverage = gpa;
   }
   ```

2. Add a second parameterless constructor. It calls the first constructor, passing 0 for the ID number, "XXX" for the name, and 0.0 for the grade point average. Its body is empty.

   ```
   public Student() : this(0, "XXX", 0.0)
   {
   }
   ```

(continues)

> *(continued)*
>
> 3. Change the name of the CreateStudents class to **CreateStudents2**.
> 4. After the existing declarations of the Student objects, add two more declarations. With one, use three arguments, but with the other, do not use any.
>
>    ```
>    Student third = new Student(456, "Marco", 2.4);
>    Student fourth = new Student();
>    ```
>
> 5. At the end of the Main() method, just after the two existing calls to the Display() method, add two more calls using the new objects:
>
>    ```
>    Display(third);
>    Display(fourth);
>    ```
>
> 6. Save the file, and then compile and execute it. The output looks like Figure 9-29. All four objects are displayed. The first two have had values assigned to them after declaration, but the third and fourth ones obtained their values from their constructors.
>
> ```
> 123  Anderson   3.5
> 789  Daniels    0.0
> 456  Marco      2.4
>   0  XXX        0.0
> ```
>
> **Figure 9-29** Output of the CreateStudents2 program

Using Object Initializers

An **object initializer** allows you to assign values to any accessible members or properties of a class at the time of instantiation without calling a constructor with parameters. For example, assuming an Employee class has been created with a `public IdNumber` property and a parameterless constructor, you can write an object initializer in either of the following ways, with or without parentheses:

```
Employee aWorker = new Employee{IdNumber = 101};
Employee aWorker = new Employee(){IdNumber = 101};
```

Using Object Initializers

In either of these statements, 101 is assigned to the aWorker object's IdNumber property. The assignment is made within a pair of curly braces; using parentheses with the constructor name is optional. When either of these statements execute, the parameterless, default constructor for the class is executed first, and then the object initializer assignment is made.

For example, Figure 9-30 shows an Employee class that contains properties for IdNumber and Salary and a default constructor that assigns a value to Salary. For demonstration purposes, the constructor displays the current object's ID number and salary. The figure also shows a program that instantiates one Employee object and displays its value, and Figure 9-31 shows the output. When the object is created in the shaded statement, the constructor executes, assigns 99.99 to Salary, and displays the first line of output, showing IdNumber is still 0. After the object is constructed in the Main() method, the next output line is displayed, showing that the assignment of the ID number occurred after construction.

```
using static System.Console;
class DemoObjectInitializer
{
   static void Main()
   {
      Employee aWorker = new Employee {IdNumber = 101};
      WriteLine("Employee #{0} exists. Salary is {1}.",
         aWorker.IdNumber, aWorker.Salary);
   }
}
class Employee
{
   public int IdNumber {get; set;}
   public double Salary {get; set;}
   public Employee()
   {
      Salary = 99.99;
      WriteLine("Employee #{0} created. Salary is {1}.",
         IdNumber, Salary);
   }
}
```

Figure 9-30 The DemoObjectInitializer program

```
Employee #0 created. Salary is 99.99.
Employee #101 exists. Salary is 99.99.
```

Figure 9-31 Output of the DemoObjectInitializer program

To use object initializers, a class must have a default constructor. That is, you either must not create any constructors or you must create one that requires no parameters.

Multiple assignments can be made with an object initializer by separating them with commas, as in the following:

```
Employee myAssistant = new Employee {IdNumber = 202, Salary = 25.00};
```

This single code line has the same results as the following three statements:

```
Employee myAssistant = new Employee();
myAssistant.IdNumber = 202;
myAssistant.Salary = 25.00;
```

Using object initializers allows you to create multiple objects with different initial assignments without having to provide multiple constructors to cover every possible situation. Additionally, using object initializers allows you to create objects with different starting values for different properties of the same data type. For example, consider a class like the Box class in Figure 9-32 that contains multiple properties of the same type. The constructor sets the Height, Width, and Depth properties to 1. You could write a constructor that accepts a single integer parameter to be assigned to Height (using the default value 1 for the other dimensions), but then you could not write an additional overloaded constructor that accepts a single integer parameter to be assigned to Width because the constructors would be ambiguous. However, by using object initializers, you can create objects to which you assign the properties you want. Figure 9-33 shows a program that declares three Box objects, each with a different assigned dimension, and Figure 9-34 shows the output, which demonstrates that each property was assigned appropriately.

```
class Box
{
    public int Height {get; set;}
    public int Width {get; set;}
    public int Depth {get; set;}
    public Box()
    {
        Height = 1;
        Width = 1;
        Depth = 1;
    }
}
```

Figure 9-32 The Box class

Using Object Initializers

```
using static System.Console;
class DemoObjectInitializer2
{
   static void Main()
   {
      Box box1 = new Box {Height = 3};
      Box box2 = new Box {Width = 15};
      Box box3 = new Box {Depth = 268};
      DisplayDimensions(1, box1);
      DisplayDimensions(2, box2);
      DisplayDimensions(3, box3);
   }
   static void DisplayDimensions(int num, Box box)
   {
      WriteLine("Box {0}: Height: {1} Width: {2} Depth: {3}",
         num, box.Height, box.Width, box.Depth);
   }
}
```

Figure 9-33 The DemoObjectInitializer2 program

```
Box 1: Height: 3 Width: 1 Depth: 1
Box 2: Height: 1 Width: 15 Depth: 1
Box 3: Height: 1 Width: 1 Depth: 268
```

Figure 9-34 Output of the DemoObjectInitializer2 program

TWO TRUTHS & A LIE

Using Object Initializers

Assume that a working program contains the following object initializer:

Invoice oneBill = new Invoice{Amount = 0};

1. You know that the Invoice class contains a default constructor.

2. You know that an Invoice object could be constructed without using a parameter.

3. You know that the Invoice class contains a single property.

The false statement is #3. The Invoice class might have any number of properties. However, only one is being initialized in this statement.

Overloading Operators

C# operators are the symbols you use to perform operations on objects. You have used many operators, including arithmetic operators (such as + and -) and logical operators (such as == and <). Separate actions can result from what seems to be the same operation or command. This occurs frequently in all computer programming languages, not just object-oriented languages. For example, in most programming languages and applications such as spreadsheets and databases, the + operator has a variety of meanings. A few of them include:

- Alone before a value (called *unary form*), + indicates a positive value, as in the expression +7.

- Between two integers (called *binary form*), + indicates integer addition, as in the expression 5 + 9.

- Between two floating-point numbers (also called binary form), + indicates floating-point addition, as in the expression 6.4 + 2.1.

- Between two strings, + indicates concatenation, as in the expression "Hello," + "there".

Expressing a value as positive is a different operation from using the + operator to perform arithmetic or concatenate strings, so + is overloaded several times, in that it can take one or two arguments and have a different meaning in each case. It also can take different operand types—you use a + to add two ints, two doubles, an int and a double, and a variety of other combinations. Each use results in different actions behind the scenes.

Just as it is convenient to use a + between both integers and doubles to add them, it also can be convenient to use a + between objects, such as Employees or Books, to add them. To be able to use arithmetic symbols with your own objects, you must overload the symbols.

C# operators are classified as unary or binary, depending on whether they take one or two arguments, respectively. The rules for overloading are shown in the following list.

- The overloadable unary operators are:

    + - ! ~ ++ -- true false

- The overloadable binary operators are:

    + - * / % & | ^ == != > < >= <=

- You cannot overload the following operators:

    = && || ?? ?: checked unchecked new typeof as is

- You cannot overload an operator for a built-in data type. For example, you cannot change the meaning of + between two ints.

Overloading Operators

- When a binary operator is overloaded and it has a corresponding assignment operator, it is also overloaded. For example, if you overload +, then += is automatically overloaded, too.

- Some operators must be overloaded in pairs. For example, when you overload ==, you also must overload !=, and when you overload >, you also must overload <.

When you overload ==, you also receive warnings about methods in the Object class. You will learn about this class in the chapter "Introduction to Inheritance"; you should not attempt to overload == until you have studied that chapter.

You have used many, but not all, of the operators listed above. If you want to include an overloaded operator in a class, you must decide what the operator will mean in your class. When you do, you write statements in a method to carry out your meaning. The method has a return type and arguments just like other methods, but its identifier is required to be named operator followed by the operator being overloaded—for example, operator+() or operator*().

For example, suppose that you create a Book class in which each object has a title, number of pages, and a price. Further assume that, as a publisher, you have decided to "add" Books together. That is, you want to take two existing Books and combine them into one. Assume that you want the new Book to have the following characteristics:

- The new title is a combination of the old titles, joined by the word *and*.

- The number of pages in the new book is equal to the sum of the pages in the original Books.

- Instead of charging twice as much for a new Book, you have decided to charge the price of the more expensive of the two original Books, plus $10.

A different publisher might have decided that "adding Books" means something different—for example, an added Book might have a fixed new price of $29.99. The statements you write in your operator+() method depend on how you define adding for your class. You could write an ordinary method to perform these tasks, but you could also overload the + operator to mean "add two Books." Figure 9-35 shows a Book class that has properties for each field and a shaded operator+() method.

CHAPTER 9 Using Classes and Objects

```
class Book
{
   public Book(string title, int pages, double price)
   {
      Title = title;
      NumPages = pages;
      Price = price;
   }
   public static Book operator+(Book first, Book second)
   {
      const double EXTRA = 10.00;
      string newTitle = first.Title + " and " + second.Title;
      int newPages = first.NumPages + second.NumPages;
      double newPrice;
      if(first.Price > second.Price)
         newPrice = first.Price + EXTRA;
      else
         newPrice = second.Price + EXTRA;
      return(new Book(newTitle, newPages, newPrice));
   }
   public string Title {get; set;}
   public int NumPages {get; set;}
   public double Price {get; set;}
}
```

Figure 9-35 Book class with overloaded + operator

The `operator+()` method in Figure 9-35 is declared to be `public` (so that class clients can use it) and `static` (which is required). The method is `static` because it does not receive a `this` reference to any object; instead, the two objects to be added are both parameters to the method.

The return type is `Book` because the addition of two `Book`s is defined to be a new `Book` with values different from either of the originals. You could overload the + operator so that when two `Book`s are added they return some other type, but it is most common to make the addition of two objects result in an "answer" of the same type.

The two parameters in the `operator+()` method in the `Book` class are both `Book`s. Therefore, when you eventually call this method, the data types on both sides of the + sign will be `Book`s. For example, you could write other methods that add a `Book` and an `Employee`, or a `Book` and a `double`.

Within the `operator+()` method, the statements perform the following tasks:

- A constant is declared to hold the extra price used in creating a new `Book` from two existing ones.

- A new string is created and assigned the first parameter `Book`'s title, plus the `string` " and ", plus the second parameter `Book`'s title.

- A new integer is declared and assigned the sum of the number of pages in each of the parameter Books.
- A new double is declared and assigned the value of the more expensive original Book plus $10.00.
- Within the return statement, a new anonymous Book is created (an anonymous object is one without an identifier) using the new title, page number, and price and is returned to the calling method. (Instead of an anonymous Book, it would have been perfectly acceptable to use two statements—the first one creating a named Book with the same arguments, and the second one returning the named Book.)

Figure 9-36 shows a client program that can use the + operator in the Book class. It first declares three Books; then, in the shaded statement, it adds two Books together and assigns the result to the third. When book1 and book2 are added, the operator+() method is called. The returned Book is assigned to book3, which is then displayed. Figure 9-37 shows the results.

```
using static System.Console;
class AddBooks
{
   static void Main()
   {
      Book book1 = new Book("Silas Marner", 350, 15.95);
      Book book2 = new Book("Moby Dick", 250, 16.00);
      Book book3;
      book3 = book1 + book2;
      WriteLine("The new book is \"{0}\"", book3.Title);
      WriteLine("It has {0} pages and costs {1}",
         book3.NumPages, book3.Price.ToString("C"));
   }
}
```

Figure 9-36 The AddBooks program

```
The new book is "Silas Marner and Moby Dick"
It has 600 pages and costs $26.00
```

Figure 9-37 Output of the AddBooks program

In the Book class, it took many statements to overload the operator; however, in the client class, just typing a + between objects allows a programmer to use the objects and operator intuitively. You could write any statements you wanted within the operator method. However, for clarity, you should write statements that intuitively have the same meaning as the common use of the operator. For example, although you could overload the operator*() method to display a Book's title and price instead of performing multiplication, it would be a bad programming technique.

Because each addition operation returns a Book, it is possible to chain addition in a statement such as collection = book1 + book2 + book3;, assuming that all the variables have been declared to be Book objects. In this example, book1 and book2 would be added, returning a temporary Book. Then the temporary Book and book3 would be added, returning a different temporary Book that would be assigned to collection.

When you overload an operator, at least one argument to the method must be a member of the containing class. In other words, within the Book class, you can overload operator*() to multiply a Book by an integer, but you cannot overload operator*() to multiply a double by an integer.

When you overload a unary operator, the method takes a single argument. For example, suppose that you want to use a negative sign with a Book to make its price negative. You could use the operator in a statement such as the following:

returnedBook = -purchasedBook;

The operator-() method header might appear as follows:

public static Book operator-(Book aBook)

In this example, the minus sign is understood to cause unary negation instead of binary subtraction because the method accepts only one parameter, which is a Book. The method also returns a Book, which is an altered version of the parameter. Figure 9-38 shows a method that overloads the minus sign for a Book object. The method accepts a Book parameter, changes the price to its negative value, and returns the altered Book object to the calling method.

```
public static Book operator-(Book aBook)
{
    aBook.Price = -aBook.Price;
    return aBook;
}
```

Figure 9-38 An operator-() method for a Book

In some other languages, notably C++, you can write two methods to overload ++ and -- differently as prefix and postfix operators. However, when you overload either the ++ or -- operator in C#, the operator can be used either before or after the object, but the same method executes either way.

Watch the video *Overloading Operators*.

> **TWO TRUTHS & A LIE**
>
> **Overloading Operators**
>
> 1. All C# operators can be overloaded.
> 2. You cannot overload an operator for a built-in data type.
> 3. Some operators must be overloaded in pairs.
>
> The false statement is #1. You cannot overload the following operators: = && ||
> ?? ?: checked unchecked new typeof as is

Declaring an Array of Objects

Just as you can declare arrays of integers or `doubles`, you can declare arrays that hold elements of any type, including objects. Remember that object names are references. When you create an array from a value type, such as `int` or `char`, the array holds the actual values. When you create an array from a reference type, such as a class you create, the array holds the memory addresses of the objects. In other words, the array "refers to" the objects instead of containing the objects.

You can create an array of references to seven `Employee` objects as follows:

```
Employee[] empArray = new Employee[7];
```

This statement reserves enough computer memory for the references to seven `Employee` objects named `empArray[0]` through `empArray[6]`. It does not actually construct those `Employees`; all the references are initialized to `null`. To create objects to fill the array, you must call the `Employee()` constructor seven times.

If the `Employee` class contains a default constructor, you can use the following loop to call the constructor seven times:

```
for(int x = 0; x < empArray.Length; ++x)
   empArray[x] = new Employee();
```

As `x` varies from 0 through 6, each of the seven `empArray` objects is constructed.

If you want to use a nondefault constructor, you must provide appropriate arguments. For example, if the `Employee` class contains a constructor with an `int` parameter, you can write the following to fill three of the seven array elements:

```
Employee[] empArray = {new Employee(123),
   new Employee(234), new Employee(345)};
```

To use a method that belongs to an object that is part of an array, you insert the appropriate subscript notation after the array name and before the dot-method. For example, to set all seven `Employee IdNumber` properties to 999, you can write the following:

```
for(int x = 0; x < empArray.Length; ++x)
   empArray[x].IdNumber = 999;
```

Using the Sort() and BinarySearch() Methods with Arrays of Objects

In the chapter "Using Arrays," you learned about using the `System.Array` class's built-in `BinarySearch()` and `Sort()` methods with simple data types such as `int`, `double`, and `string`. The `Sort()` method accepts an array parameter and arranges its elements in descending order. The `BinarySearch()` method accepts a sorted array and a value that it attempts to match in the array.

A complication arises when you consider searching or sorting arrays of objects you create. When you create and sort an array of simple data items like `int`s or `double`s, there is only one type of value to consider. Each of the classes that support simple data items contain a method named `CompareTo()`, which provides the details about how the basic data types compare to each other. In other words, they define comparisons such as *2 is more than 1* and *B is more than A*. The `Sort()` and `BinarySearch()` methods use the `CompareTo()` method for the current type of data being sorted. In other words, `Sort()` uses the `Int32` version of `CompareTo()` when sorting integers and the `Char` version of `CompareTo()` when sorting characters.

You have been using the `String` class (and its `string` alias) throughout this book. The class also contains a `CompareTo()` method that you first used in Chapter 2.

When you create a class in which comparisons will be made between objects, you must tell the compiler which field to use when making those comparisons. For example, you logically might sort an organization's `Employee` objects by ID number, salary, department number, last name, hire date, or any field contained in the class. To tell C# which field to use for placing `Employee` objects in order, you must create an interface.

An **abstract method** has no method statements; an interface contains abstract methods. In the next chapter, you learn more about abstract methods. For now, understand that an **interface** is

Declaring an Array of Objects

a data type, like a class, except it is a collection of empty, abstract methods (and perhaps other members) that can be used by any class, as long as the class provides definitions to override the interface's do-nothing method definitions. Unlike a class, an interface cannot contain instance fields, and you cannot create objects from it.

A class that implements an interface must override the interface's methods. When a method **overrides** another, it takes precedence over the method, and is used instead of the original version. In other words, the methods in an interface are empty, and any class that uses them must contain a new version that provides the details and is used instead. Interfaces define named behaviors that classes must implement, so that all classes can use the same method names but use them appropriately for the class. In this way, interfaces provide for polymorphism—the ability of different objects to use the same method names but act appropriately based on the context.

When a method overrides another, it has the same signature as the method it overrides. When methods are overloaded, they have different signatures. You will learn more about overriding methods and abstract methods and classes in the next chapter.

C# supports many interfaces. You can identify an interface name by its initial letter *I*. For example, C# contains an `IComparable` interface, which contains the definition for the `CompareTo()` method that compares one object to another and returns an integer. Figure 9-39 shows the definition of `IComparable`. The `CompareTo()` method accepts a parameter `Object` but does not contain any statements; you must provide an implementation for this method in classes you create if you want the objects to be comparable. That is, the `CompareTo()` method is abstract, and you must determine the meanings of *greater than*, *less than*, and *equal to* for the class.

```
interface IComparable
{
    int CompareTo(Object o);
}
```

Figure 9-39 The `IComparable` interface

When you create a class whose instances will likely be compared by clients:

- You must include a single colon and the interface name `IComparable` after the class name.
- You must write a method that contains the following header:

  `int IComparable.CompareTo(Object o)`

Object is a class—the most generic of all classes. Every Employee object you create is not only an Employee but also an Object. By using the type Object as a parameter, the CompareTo() method can accept anything. You will learn more about the Object class in the next chapter.

CHAPTER 9 Using Classes and Objects

To work correctly in methods such as BinarySearch() and Sort(), the CompareTo() method you create for your class must return an integer value. Table 9-2 shows the return values that every version of CompareTo() should provide.

Return Value	Meaning
Negative	This instance is less than the compared object.
Zero	This instance is equal to the compared object.
Positive	This instance is greater than the compared object.

Table 9-2 Return values of IComparable.CompareTo() method

When you create a class that contains an IComparable.CompareTo() method, the method is an instance method and receives a this reference to the object used to call it. A second object is passed to the method; within the method, you first must convert, or cast, the passed object to the same type as the calling object's class and then compare the corresponding fields you want from the this object and the passed object. For example, Figure 9-40 shows an Employee class that contains a shaded CompareTo() method and compares Employee objects based on the contents of their idNumber fields.

```
class Employee : IComparable
{
    public int IdNumber {get;set;}
    public double Salary {get;set;}
    int IComparable.CompareTo(Object o)
    {
        int returnVal;
        Employee temp = (Employee)o;
        if(this.IdNumber > temp.IdNumber)
            returnVal = 1;
        else
            if(this.IdNumber < temp.IdNumber)
                returnVal = -1;
            else
                returnVal = 0;
        return returnVal;
    }
}
```

Figure 9-40 Employee class using IComparable interface

The Employee class in Figure 9-40 uses a colon and IComparable in its class header to indicate an interface. The shaded method is an instance method; that is, it "belongs" to an Employee object. When another `Employee` is passed in as `Object o`, it is cast as an `Employee` and stored in the `temp` variable. The `idNumber` values of the `this Employee` and the passed `Employee` are compared, and one of three integer values is returned. For example, if you declare two `Employee` objects named `worker1` and `worker2`, you can use the following statement:

```
int answer = worker1.CompareTo(worker2);
```

Within the `CompareTo()` method in the `Employee` class, `worker1` would be "this" `Employee`—the controlling `Employee` in the method (the invoking `Employee` object). The `temp Employee` would be `worker2`. If, for example, `worker1` had a higher ID number than `worker2`, the value of `answer` would be 1.

Figure 9-41 shows a program that uses the `Employee` class. The program declares an array of five `Employee` objects with different ID numbers and all with salaries of 0; the ID numbers are purposely out of order to demonstrate that the `Sort()` method works correctly. The program also declares a `seekEmp` object with an ID number of 222. The program sorts the array, displays the sorted elements, then finds the array element that matches the `seekEmp` object. Figure 9-42 shows the program execution.

```
using System;
using static System.Console;
class ComparableEmployeeArray
{
   static void Main()
   {
      Employee[] empArray = new Employee[5];
      int x;
      for(x = 0; x < empArray.Length; ++x)
         empArray[x] = new Employee();
      empArray[0].IdNumber = 333;
      empArray[1].IdNumber = 444;
      empArray[2].IdNumber = 555;
      empArray[3].IdNumber = 111;
      empArray[4].IdNumber = 222;
      Employee seekEmp = new Employee();
      seekEmp.IdNumber = 222;
      Array.Sort(empArray);
      WriteLine("Sorted employees:");
      for(x = 0; x < empArray.Length; ++x)
         WriteLine("Employee #{0}: {1} {2}", x,
            empArray[x].IdNumber, empArray[x].Salary.ToString("C"));
      x = Array.BinarySearch(empArray, seekEmp);
      WriteLine("Employee #{0} was found at position {1}",
         seekEmp.IdNumber, x);
   }
}
```

Figure 9-41 The ComparableEmployeeArray program

CHAPTER 9 Using Classes and Objects

```
Sorted employees:
Employee #0: 111 $0.00
Employee #1: 222 $0.00
Employee #2: 333 $0.00
Employee #3: 444 $0.00
Employee #4: 555 $0.00
Employee #222 was found at position 1
```

Figure 9-42 Output of the ComparableEmployeeArray program

Notice that the seekEmp object matches the Employee in the second array position based on the idNumber only—not the salary—because the CompareTo() method in the Employee class uses only idNumber values and not salaries to make comparisons. You *could* have written code that requires both the idNumber and salary values to match before returning a positive number.

TWO TRUTHS & A LIE

Declaring an Array of Objects

Assume that a working program contains the following array declaration:

BankAccount[] acctArray = new BankAccount[500];

1. This statement reserves enough computer memory for 500 BankAccount objects.
2. This statement constructs 500 BankAccount objects.
3. The valid subscripts for acctArray are 0 through 499.

The false statement is #2. This statement reserves space for 500 BankAccount objects but does not actually construct those objects; to do so, you must call the constructor 500 times.

You Do It

Creating an Array of Objects

In the next steps, you create an array of Student objects. You prompt the user for data to fill the array, and you sort the array by student ID number before displaying all the data.

1. Open the **CreateStudents2** program and immediately save it as **CreateStudents3**. Change the class name to **CreateStudents3**.

2. Delete all the existing statements in the Main() method, leaving the opening and closing curly braces. Between the braces, declare an array of eight Student objects. Also declare a variable to use as an array subscript and declare three variables that will temporarily hold a user's input data before Student objects are constructed.

   ```
   Student[] students = new Student[8];
   int x;
   int id;
   string name;
   double gpa;
   ```

3. In a loop, call a GetData() method (which you will write shortly). Send the method out arguments so that you can retrieve values for variables that will hold an ID number, name, and grade point average. Then, in turn, send these three values to the Student constructor for each of the eight Student objects.

   ```
   for(x = 0; x < students.Length; ++x)
   {
      GetData(out id, out name, out gpa);
      students[x] = new Student(id, name, gpa);
   }
   ```

4. Call the Array.Sort() method, sending it the students array. Then, one object at a time in a loop, call the Display() method that you wrote in the last set of steps.

   ```
   Array.Sort(students);
   WriteLine("Sorted List:");
   for(x = 0; x < students.Length; ++x)
      Display(students[x]);
   ```

(continues)

(continued)

5. Write the `GetData()` method. Its parameters are `out` parameters so that their values will be known to the calling method. The method simply prompts the user for each data item, reads it, and converts it to the appropriate type, if necessary.

```
static void GetData(out int id, out string name,
   out double gpa)
{
   string inString;
   Write("Please enter student ID number >> ");
   inString = ReadLine();
   int.TryParse(inString, out id);
   Write("Please enter last name for student {0} >> ",
      id);
   name = ReadLine();
   Write("Please enter grade point average >> ");
   inString = ReadLine();
   double.TryParse(inString, out gpa);
}
```

6. After the header for the `Student` class, add a colon and **IComparable** so that objects of the class can be sorted:

   `class Student : IComparable`

7. Just before the closing curly brace for the `Student` class, add the `IComparable.CompareTo()` method that is required for the objects of the class to be sortable. The method will sort `Student` objects based on their ID numbers, so it returns 1, −1, or 0 based on `IdNumber` property comparisons. The method accepts an object that is cast to a `Student` object. If the `IdNumber` of the controlling `Student` object is greater than the argument's `IdNumber`, then the return value is set to 1. If the `IdNumber` of the controlling `Student` object is less than the argument's `IdNumber`, then the return value is −1. Otherwise, the return value is 0.

```
int IComparable.CompareTo(Object o)
{
   int returnVal;
   Student temp = (Student)o;
   if(this.IdNumber > temp.IdNumber)
      returnVal = 1;
   else
      if(this.IdNumber < temp.IdNumber)
         returnVal = -1;
      else
         returnVal = 0;
   return returnVal;
}
```

(continues)

(continued)

8. Save the file, and then compile and execute it. When prompted, enter any student IDs, names, and grade point averages you choose. The objects will be sorted and displayed in `idNumber` order. Figure 9-43 shows a typical execution.

```
Please enter student ID number >> 477
Please enter last name for student 477 >> Patton
Please enter grade point average >> 3.4
Please enter student ID number >> 891
Please enter last name for student 891 >> Daniels
Please enter grade point average >> 2.5
Please enter student ID number >> 210
Please enter last name for student 210 >> Giardino
Please enter grade point average >> 3.0
Please enter student ID number >> 300
Please enter last name for student 300 >> Kaplan
Please enter grade point average >> 3.9
Please enter student ID number >> 111
Please enter last name for student 111 >> Renard
Please enter grade point average >> 2.1
Please enter student ID number >> 738
Please enter last name for student 738 >> Williams
Please enter grade point average >> 3.1
Please enter student ID number >> 639
Please enter last name for student 639 >> Adams
Please enter grade point average >> 2.8
Please enter student ID number >> 475
Please enter last name for student 475 >> Quincy
Please enter grade point average >> 3.8
Sorted List:
   111   Renard      2.1
   210   Giardino    3.0
   300   Kaplan      3.9
   475   Quincy      3.8
   477   Patton      3.4
   639   Adams       2.8
   738   Williams    3.1
   891   Daniels     2.5
```

Figure 9-43 Typical execution of the `CreateStudents3` program

Understanding Destructors

A **destructor** contains the actions you require when an instance of a class is destroyed. Most often, an instance of a class is destroyed when it goes out of scope. As with constructors, if you do not explicitly create a destructor for a class, C# automatically provides one.

To explicitly declare a destructor, you use an identifier that consists of a tilde (~) followed by the class name. You cannot provide any arguments when you call a destructor; it must have an empty parameter list. As a consequence, destructors cannot be overloaded; a class can have one destructor at most. Like a constructor, a destructor has no return type.

Figure 9-44 shows an `Employee` class that contains only one field (`idNumber`), a property, a constructor, and a (shaded) destructor. When you execute the `Main()` method in the `DemoEmployeeDestructor` class in Figure 9-45, you instantiate two `Employee` objects, each with its own `idNumber` value. When the `Main()` method ends, the two `Employee` objects go out of scope, and the destructor for each object is called. Figure 9-46 shows the output.

```
class Employee
{
    public int idNumber {get; set;}
    public Employee(int empID)
    {
        IdNumber = empID;
        WriteLine("Employee object {0} created", IdNumber);
    }
    ~Employee()
    {
        WriteLine("Employee object {0} destroyed!", IdNumber);
    }
}
```

Figure 9-44 Employee class with destructor

```
using static System.Console;
class DemoEmployeeDestructor
{
    static void Main()
    {
        Employee aWorker = new Employee(101);
        Employee anotherWorker = new Employee(202);
    }
}
```

Figure 9-45 The DemoEmployeeDestructor program

```
Employee object 101 created
Employee object 202 created
Employee object 202 destroyed!
Employee object 101 destroyed!
```

Figure 9-46 Output of DemoEmployeeDestructor program

The program in Figure 9-45 never explicitly calls the Employee class destructor, yet you can see from the output that the destructor executes twice. Destructors are invoked automatically; you cannot explicitly call one. Interestingly, the last object created is the first object destroyed; the same relationship would hold true no matter how many objects the program instantiated.

An instance of a class becomes eligible for destruction when it is no longer possible for any code to use it—that is, when it goes out of scope. The actual execution of an object's destructor might occur at any time after the object becomes eligible for destruction.

For now, you have little reason to create a destructor except to demonstrate how it is called automatically. Later, when you write more sophisticated C# programs that work with files, databases, or large quantities of computer memory, you might want to perform specific cleanup or close-down tasks when an object goes out of scope. Then you will place appropriate instructions within a destructor.

TWO TRUTHS & A LIE

Understanding Destructors

1. To explicitly declare a destructor, you use an identifier that consists of a tilde (~) followed by the class name.

2. You cannot provide any parameters to a destructor; it must have an empty argument list.

3. The return type for a destructor is always void.

The false statement is #3. Like a constructor, a destructor has no return type.

Understanding GUI Application Objects

The objects you have been using in GUI applications, such as Forms, Buttons, and Labels, are objects just like others you have studied in this chapter. That is, they encapsulate properties and methods. When you start a Windows Forms application in the IDE and drag a Button onto a Form, a statement is automatically created to instantiate a Button object.

CHAPTER 9 Using Classes and Objects

Figure 9-47 shows the code behind a new GUI application that a programmer started simply by dragging one **Button** onto a **Form**. If you click on Form1.Designer.cs in the Solution Explorer and scroll down, you can display the code where the **Button** is declared. See Figure 9-47.

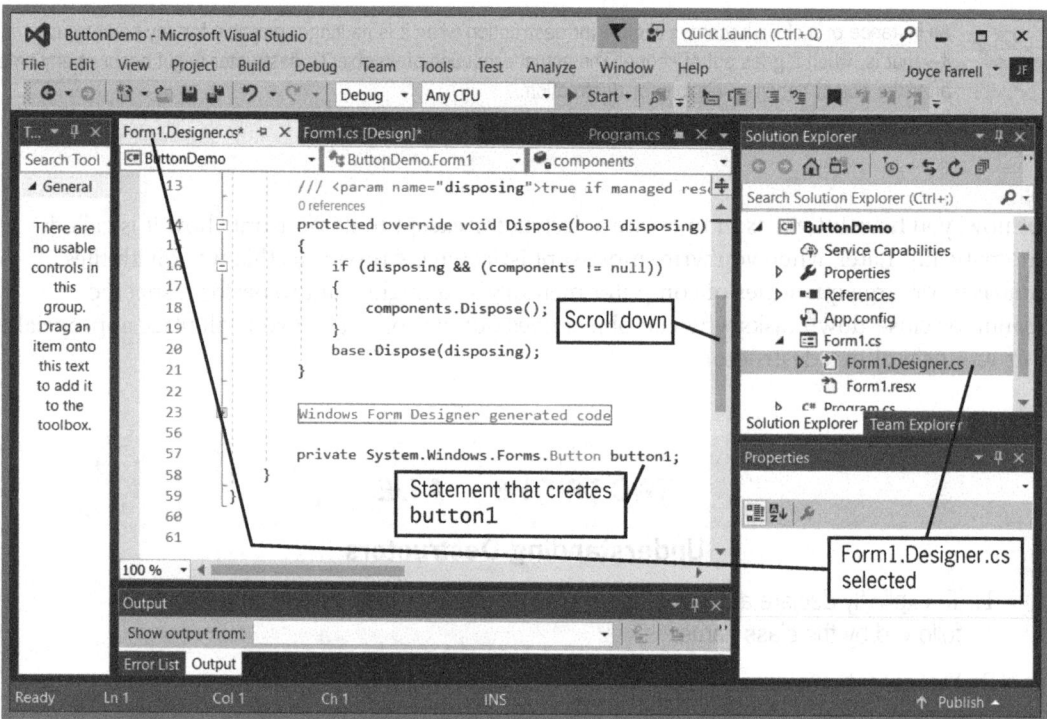

Figure 9-47 The automatically generated statement that declares **button1**

If you right-click **button1** in the code and select Find All References from the menu that appears, a list of every reference to **button1** in the project is displayed in the Find Symbol Results area at the bottom of the IDE. (You might need to resize the window to see the references clearly.) You can double-click each entry in the list in turn to locate all the places where code has been generated for **button1**. For example, several instances of **button1** are in a method named **InitializeComponent()**, as shown in Figure 9-48. The first reference to **button1** calls its constructor. You can also see how the **Button**'s **Name**, **Location**, **Size**, and other properties are set. You could have written these statements yourself, especially now that you know more about objects and how they are constructed, but it is easier to develop an application visually by dragging a **Button** onto a **Form** and allowing the IDE to create these statements for you.

```
private void InitializeComponent()
{
    this.button1 = new System.Windows.Forms.Button();   ─── Button constructor
    this.SuspendLayout();
    //
    // button1
    //
    this.button1.Location = new System.Drawing.Point(69, 60);   ─── setting Location
    this.button1.Name = "button1";   ─── setting Name
    this.button1.Size = new System.Drawing.Size(75, 23);   ─── setting Size
    this.button1.TabIndex = 0;
    this.button1.Text = "button1";   ─── setting Text
    this.button1.UseVisualStyleBackColor = true;
    //
    // Form1
    //
    this.AutoScaleDimensions = new System.Drawing.SizeF(8F, 16F);
    this.AutoScaleMode = System.Windows.Forms.AutoScaleMode.Font;
    this.ClientSize = new System.Drawing.Size(282, 253);
    this.Controls.Add(this.button1);
    this.Name = "Form1";
    this.Text = "Form1";
    this.ResumeLayout(false);

}
```

Figure 9-48 Some automatically generated `button1` references in the IDE

In Figure 9-48, the this reference preceding each occurrence of `button1` refers to the class (`Form1`) that contains these statements.

Now that you understand how to create properties in your own classes, you can understand the properties of GUI objects and how they were created for your use.

Chapter Summary

- Application classes contain a `Main()` method. You also can create classes from which you instantiate objects; these classes need not have a `Main()` method. The data components of a class are its instance variables (or fields) and methods. A program or class that instantiates objects of another prewritten class is a class client or class user.

- When you create a class, you must assign a name to it and determine what data and methods will be part of the class. A class header or class definition contains an optional access modifier, the keyword `class`, and an identifier. A class body is enclosed between curly braces. When you create a class, you usually declare instance variables to be `private` and instance methods to be `public`.

CHAPTER 9 — Using Classes and Objects

- When you create an object that is an instance of a class, you supply a type and an identifier, and you allocate computer memory for that object using the `new` operator. After an object has been instantiated, its `public` methods can be accessed using the object's identifier, a dot, and a method call. You can pass objects to methods just as you can pass simple data types.

- A property is a member of a class that provides access to a field. Properties have `set` accessors for setting an object's fields and `get` accessors for retrieving the stored values. As a shortcut, you can create an auto-implemented property when a field's `set` accessor should simply assign a value to the appropriate field, and when its `get` accessor should simply return the field.

- In most classes, fields are `private` and methods are `public`. This technique ensures that data will be used and changed only in the ways provided in the class's accessors. Occasionally, however, you need to create `public` fields or `private` methods.

- The `this` reference is passed to every instance method and property accessor in a class. You can explicitly refer to the `this` reference within an instance method or property, but usually you are not required to do so.

- A constructor is a method that instantiates an object. If you do not write a constructor, then each class is automatically supplied with a `public` constructor with no parameters. You can write your own constructor to replace the automatically supplied version. Any constructor you write must have the same name as its class, and constructors cannot have a return type. You can overload constructors and pass arguments to a constructor.

- An object initializer allows you to assign values to any accessible members or properties of a class at the time of instantiation without calling a constructor with parameters. Using object initializers allows you to create multiple objects with different initial assignments without having to provide multiple constructors to cover every possible situation. Additionally, using object initializers allows you to create objects with different starting values for different properties of the same data type.

- You can overload an operator by writing a method whose identifier is `operator`, followed by the operator being overloaded—for example, `operator+()` or `operator*()`. When you overload an operator, you should write statements that intuitively have the same meaning as the common use of the operator.

- You can declare arrays of references to objects. After doing so, you must call a constructor to instantiate each object. To use a method that belongs to an object that is part of an array, you insert the appropriate subscript notation after the array name and before the dot-method. The `IComparable` interface contains the definition for the `CompareTo()` method; you override this method to tell the compiler how to compare objects.

- A destructor contains the actions you require when an instance of a class is destroyed. If you do not explicitly create a destructor for a class, C# automatically provides one. To explicitly declare a destructor, you use an identifier that consists of a tilde (~) followed by the class name. You cannot provide any parameters to a destructor; a class can have one destructor at most.

- GUI objects such as `Forms`, `Buttons`, and `Labels` are typical C# objects that encapsulate properties and methods. When you start a Windows Forms application and drag a component onto a `Form`, statements are automatically created by the IDE to instantiate the object and assign values to some of its properties.

Key Terms

To **instantiate** an object is to create it.

An **instantiation** of a class is a created object.

An **instance** of a class is one object, or one instantiation.

The **instance variables** of a class are the data components that exist separately for each instantiation.

Fields are instance variables within a class.

Instance methods are methods that are used with object instantiations.

A **class client** or **class user** is a program or class that instantiates objects of another prewritten class.

A **class header** or **class definition** describes a class; it contains an optional access modifier, the keyword `class`, and any legal identifier for the name of the class.

A **class access modifier** describes access to a class.

The **public** class access modifier means access to the class is not limited.

The **protected** class access modifier means access to the class is limited to the class and to any classes derived from the class.

The **internal** class access modifier means access is limited to the assembly to which the class belongs.

The **private** class access modifier means access is limited to another class to which the class belongs. In other words, a class can be `private` if it is contained within another class, and only the containing class should have access to the `private` class.

An **assembly** is a group of code modules compiled together to create an executable program.

Information hiding is a feature found in all object-oriented languages, in which a class's data is private and changed or manipulated only by its own methods.

Composition is the technique of using an object within another object.

A **has-a relationship** is the relationship created using composition, so-called because one class "has an" instance of another.

A **reference type** is a type that holds a memory address.

Value types hold a value; they include predefined types such as `int`, `double`, and `char`.

An **invoking object** is an object that calls an instance method.

A **property** is a member of a class that provides access to a field of a class; properties define how fields will be set and retrieved.

Accessors in properties specify how a class's fields are accessed.

The **set accessors** of a class allow assignment of values to fields using a property name.

The **get accessors** of a class allow retrieval of a field value by using a property name.

A **backing field** is a field that has a property coded for it.

A **read-only property** has only a `get` accessor, and not a `set` accessor.

The **getter** is another term for a class property's `get` accessor.

The **setter** is another term for a class property's `set` accessor.

Contextual keywords are identifiers that act like keywords in specific circumstances.

An **implicit parameter** is undeclared and gets its value automatically.

An **auto-implemented property** is one in which the code within the accessors is created automatically. The only action in the `set` accessor is to assign a value to the associated field, and the only action in the `get` accessor is to return the associated field value.

Automatic properties are auto-implemented properties.

The `this` **reference** is the reference to an object that is implicitly passed to an instance method of its class.

A **constructor** is a method that instantiates (creates an instance of) an object.

A **default constructor** is a parameterless constructor.

The **default value of an object** is the value initialized with a default constructor.

A **parameterless constructor** is one that takes no arguments.

A **constructor initializer** is a clause that indicates another instance of a class constructor should be executed before any statements in the current constructor body.

An **object initializer** allows you to assign values to any accessible members or properties of a class at the time of instantiation without calling a constructor with parameters.

An **abstract method** has no method statements.

An **interface** is a collection of abstract methods (and perhaps other members) that can be used by any class, as long as the class provides a definition to override the interface's do-nothing, or abstract, method definitions.

To **override** a method is to take precedence over another method version.

A **destructor** contains the actions required when an instance of a class is destroyed.

Review Questions

1. An object is a(n) _____ of a class.
   a. instantiation
   b. institution
   c. child
   d. relative

2. A class header or class definition can contain all of the following *except* _____.
   a. an optional access modifier
   b. the keyword `class`
   c. an identifier
   d. initial field values

3. Most fields in a class are created with the _____ modifier.
   a. `public`
   b. `private`
   c. `new`
   d. `protected`

4. Most methods in a class are created with the _____ modifier.
   a. `public`
   b. `private`
   c. `new`
   d. `protected`

5. Instance methods that belong to individual objects are _____ `static` methods.
   a. always
   b. usually
   c. occasionally
   d. never

6. To allocate memory for an object instantiation, you must use the _____ operator.
   a. `mem`
   b. `alloc`
   c. `instant`
   d. `new`

7. Assume that you have created a class named `MyClass`. The header of the `MyClass` constructor can be _____.
   a. `public void MyClass()`
   b. `public MyClassConstructor()`
   c. Either of these can be the constructor header.
   d. Neither of these can be the constructor header.

8. Assume that you have created a class named MyClass. The header of the MyClass constructor can be _____.

   a. public MyClass()
   b. public MyClass(double d)
   c. Either of these can be the constructor header.
   d. Neither of these can be the constructor header.

9. Assume that you have created a class named DemoCar. Within the Main() method of this class, you instantiate a Car object named myCar and the following statement executes correctly:

   WriteLine("The Car gets {0} miles per gallon",
      myCar.ComputeMpg());

   Within the Car class, the ComputeMpg() method can be _____.

   a. public and static
   b. public and nonstatic
   c. private and static
   d. private and nonstatic

10. Assume that you have created a class named TermPaper that contains a character field named letterGrade. You also have created a property for the field. Which of the following cannot be true?

    a. The property name is letterGrade.
    b. The property is read-only.
    c. The property contains a set accessor that does not allow a grade lower than 'C'.
    d. The property does not contain a get accessor.

11. A this reference is _____.

    a. implicitly passed to nonstatic methods
    b. implicitly passed to static methods
    c. explicitly passed to nonstatic methods
    d. explicitly passed to static methods

12. When you use an instance variable within a class's nonstatic methods, you _____ explicitly refer to the method's this reference.

    a. must
    b. can
    c. cannot
    d. should (even though it is not required)

Review Questions

13. A class's default constructor _____.

    a. sets numeric fields to 0
    b. is parameterless
    c. is both of these
    d. is none of these

14. Assume that you have created a class named Chair with a constructor defined as Chair(int height). Which of the following overloaded constructors could coexist with the Chair constructor without ambiguity?

    a. Chair(int legs)
    b. Chair(int height, int legs)
    c. Both of these
    d. None of these

15. Which of the following statements correctly instantiates a House object if the House class contains a single constructor with the declaration House(int bedrooms, double price)?

    a. House myHouse = new House();
    b. House myHouse = new House(3, 125000.00);
    c. House myHouse = House(4, 200000.00);
    d. Two of these

16. You explicitly call a destructor _____.

    a. when you are finished using an object
    b. when an object goes out of scope
    c. when a class is destroyed
    d. You cannot explicitly call a destructor.

17. In a program that creates five object instances of a class, the constructor executes _____ time(s) and the destructor executes _____ time(s).

    a. one; one
    b. one; five
    c. five; one
    d. five; five

18. Suppose that you declare a class named Furniture that contains a string field named woodType and a conventionally named property with a get accessor. When you declare an array of 200 Furniture objects named myChairs, which of the following accesses the last Furniture object's wood type?

   a. Furniture.Get(woodType[199])
   b. myChairs[199].WoodType
   c. myChairs.WoodType[199]
   d. myChairs[199].WoodType()

19. A collection of methods that can be used by any class, as long as the class provides a definition to override the collection's abstract definitions, is _____.

   a. an interface
   b. a polymorph
   c. a perimeter
   d. a superclass

20. When you create a class and want to include the capability to compare its objects so they can use the Array.Sort() or Array.BinarySearch() method, you must _____.

   a. include at least one numeric field within the class
   b. write a CompareTo() method for the class
   c. be careful not to override the existing IComparable.CompareTo() method
   d. Two of these are true.

Exercises

Programming Exercises

1. Create an application named **TestSoccerPlayer** that instantiates and displays a SoccerPlayer object. The SoccerPlayer class contains properties that hold a player's name (a string), jersey number (an integer), goals scored (an integer), and assists (an integer).

Exercises

2. Create an application named **TestClassifiedAd** that instantiates and displays at least two ClassifiedAd objects. A ClassifiedAd has fields for a category (for example, *Used Cars*), a number of words, and a price. Include properties that contain get and set accessors for the category and number of words, but only a get accessor for the price. The price is calculated at nine cents per word.

3. Create an application named **SalesTransactionDemo** that declares several SalesTransaction objects and displays their values and their sum. The SalesTransaction class contains fields for a salesperson name, sales amount, and commission and a readonly field that stores the commission rate. Include three constructors for the class. One constructor accepts values for the name, sales amount, and rate, and when the sales value is set, the constructor computes the commission as sales value times commission rate. The second constructor accepts a name and sales amount, but sets the commission rate to 0. The third constructor accepts a name and sets all the other fields to 0. An overloaded + operator adds the sales values for two SalesTransaction objects.

4. Create a program named **PaintingDemo** that instantiates an array of eight Room objects and demonstrates the Room methods. The Room constructor requires parameters for length, width, and height fields; use a variety of values when constructing the objects. The Room class also contains a field for wall area of the Room and number of gallons of paint needed to paint the room. Both of these values are computed by calling private methods. Include read-only properties to get a Room's values. A room is assumed to have four walls, and you do not need to allow for windows and doors, and you do not need to allow for painting the ceiling. A room requires one gallon of paint for every 350 square feet (plus an extra gallon for any square feet greater than 350). In other words, a 12 × 10 room with 9-foot ceilings has 396 square feet of wall space, and so requires two gallons of paint.

5. Create an application named **CarDemo** that declares at least two Car objects and demonstrates how they can be incremented using an overloaded ++ operator. Create a Car class that contains a model and a value for miles per gallon. Include two overloaded constructors. One accepts parameters for the model and miles per gallon; the other accepts a model and sets the miles per gallon to 20. Overload a ++ operator that increases the miles per gallon value by 1. The CarDemo application creates at least one Car using each constructor and displays the Car values both before and after incrementation.

6. a. Create a program named **SalesTaxDemo** that declares an array of 10 Sale objects. Prompt the user for data for each object and display the 10 objects. Data fields for Sale objects include an inventory number, amount of the sale, and tax owed. Include a property with get and set accessors for the first two data fields, but make

the tax owed a read-only property. The tax should be calculated whenever the amount of the sale is set. Assume that the tax rate is 8 percent for the first $100 and 6 percent for any amount greater than $100.

b. Create a program named **SalesTaxDemo2** so that after the 10 Sale objects are displayed, they are sorted in order by the amount of tax owed and displayed again. Modify the Sale class so its objects are comparable to each other based on tax owed.

7. Create an application named **ShirtDemo** that declares several Shirt objects and includes a display method to which you can pass different numbers of Shirt objects in successive method calls. The Shirt class contains auto-implemented properties for a material, color, and size.

8. Create a program named **ConferencesDemo** for a hotel that hosts business conferences. Allows a user to enter data about five Conference objects and then displays them in order of attendance from smallest to largest. The Conference class contains fields for the Conference group name, starting date (as a string), and number of attendees. Include properties for each field. Also, include an IComparable.CompareTo() method so that Conference objects can be sorted.

9. a. Create a program named **RelativesList** that declares an array of at least 12 relative objects and prompts the user to enter data about them. The Relative class includes auto-implemented properties for the Relative's name, relationship to you (for example, *aunt*), and three integers that together represent the Relative's birthday—month, day, and year. Display the Relative objects in alphabetical order by first name.

b. Create a **RelativesBirthday** program that modifies the RelativesList program so that after the alphabetical list is displayed, the program prompts the user for a specific Relative's name and the program returns the Relative's relationship and birthday. Display an appropriate message if the relative requested by the user is not found.

10. a. Write a program named **DemoJobs** for Harold's Home Services. The program should instantiate several Job objects and demonstrate their methods. The Job class contains four data fields—description (for example, "wash windows"), time in hours to complete (for example, 3.5), per-hour rate charged (for example, $25.00), and total fee (hourly rate times hours). Include properties to get and set each field except the total fee—that field will be read-only, and its value is calculated each time either the hourly fee or the number of hours is set. Overload the + operator so that two Jobs can be added. The sum of two Jobs is a new Job containing the descriptions of both original Jobs (joined by *and*), the sum of the time in hours for the original Jobs, and the average of the hourly rate for the original Jobs.

b. Harold has realized that his method for computing the fee for combined jobs is not fair. For example, consider the following:

- His fee for painting a house is $100 per hour. If a job takes 10 hours, he earns $1000.
- His fee for dog walking is $10 per hour. If a job takes 1 hour, he earns $10.
- If he combines the two jobs and works a total of 11 hours, he earns only the average rate of $55 per hour, or $605.

Devise an improved, weighted method for calculating Harold's fees for combined Jobs and include it in the overloaded operator+() method. Write a program named **DemoJobs2** that demonstrates all the methods in the class work correctly.

11. a. Write a **FractionDemo** program that instantiates several Fraction objects and demonstrates that their methods work correctly. Create a Fraction class with fields that hold a whole number, a numerator, and a denominator. In addition:

- Create properties for each field. The set accessor for the denominator should not allow a 0 value; the value defaults to 1.

- Add three constructors. One takes three parameters for a whole number, numerator, and denominator. Another accepts two parameters for the numerator and denominator; when this constructor is used, the whole number value is 0. The last constructor is parameterless; it sets the whole number and numerator to 0 and the denominator to 1. (After construction, Fractions do not have to be reduced to proper form. For example, even though 3/9 could be reduced to 1/3, your constructors do not have to perform this task.)

- Add a Reduce() method that reduces a Fraction if it is in improper form. For example, 2/4 should be reduced to 1/2.

- Add an operator+() method that adds two Fractions. To add two fractions, first eliminate any whole number part of the value. For example, 2 1/4 becomes 9/4 and 1 3/5 becomes 8/5. Find a common denominator and convert the fractions to it. For example, when adding 9/4 and 8/5, you can convert them to 45/20 and 32/20. Then you can add the numerators, giving 77/20. Finally, call the Reduce() method to reduce the result, restoring any whole number value so the fractional part of the number is less than 1. For example, 77/20 becomes 3 17/20.

- Include a function that returns a string that contains a Fraction in the usual display format—the whole number, a space, the numerator, a slash (/), and a denominator. When the whole number is 0, just the Fraction part of the value should be displayed (for example, 1/2 instead of 0 1/2). If the numerator is 0, just the whole number should be displayed (for example, 2 instead of 2 0/3).

b. Add an operator*() method to the Fraction class created in Exercise 11a so that it correctly multiplies two Fractions. The result should be in proper, reduced format. Demonstrate that the method works correctly in a program named **FractionDemo2**.

c. Write a program named **FractionDemo3** that includes an array of four Fractions. Prompt the user for values for each. Display every possible combination of addition results and every possible combination of multiplication results for each Fraction pair (that is, each type will have 16 results).

Debugging Exercises

1. Each of the following files in the Chapter.09 folder of your downloadable student files has syntax and/or logical errors. In each case, determine the problem and fix the program. After you correct the errors, save each file using the same filename preceded with *Fixed*. For example, DebugNine1.cs will become FixedDebugNine1.cs.

   a. DebugNine1.cs
   b. DebugNine2.cs
   c. DebugNine3.cs
   d. DebugNine4.cs

Case Problems

1. In previous chapters, you have created programs for the Greenville Idol competition. Now create a Contestant class with the following characteristics:

   - The Contestant class contains public static arrays that hold talent codes and descriptions. Recall that the talent categories are *Singing*, *Dancing*, *Musical instrument*, and *Other*.
   - The class contains an auto-implemented property that holds a contestant's name.
   - The class contains fields for a talent code and description. The set accessor for the code assigns a code only if it is valid. Otherwise, it assigns *I* for *Invalid*. The talent description is a read-only property that is assigned a value when the code is set.

   Modify the **GreenvilleRevenue** program so that it uses the Contestant class and performs the following tasks:

   - The program prompts the user for the number of contestants in this year's competition; the number must be between 0 and 30. The program continues to prompt the user until a valid value is entered.

- The expected revenue is calculated and displayed. The revenue is $25 per contestant.
- The program prompts the user for names and talent codes for each contestant entered. Along with the prompt for a talent code, display a list of the valid categories.
- After data entry is complete, the program displays the valid talent categories and then continuously prompts the user for talent codes and displays the names of all contestants in the category. Appropriate messages are displayed if the entered code is not a character or a valid code.

2. In previous chapters, you have created programs for Marshall's Murals. Now create a `Mural` class with the following characteristics:

   - The `Mural` class contains public static arrays that hold mural codes and descriptions. Recall that the mural categories are *Landscape, Seascape, Abstract, Children's,* and *Other*.
   - The class contains an auto-implemented property that holds a mural customer's name.
   - The class contains fields for a mural code and description. The `set` accessor for the code assigns a code only if it is valid. Otherwise, it assigns *I* for *Invalid*. The mural description is a read-only property that is assigned a value when the code is set.

   Modify the **MarshallsRevenue** program so that it uses the `Mural` class and performs the following tasks:

   - The program prompts the user for the month, the number of interior murals scheduled, and the number of exterior murals scheduled. In each case, the program continues to prompt the user until valid entries are made.
   - The expected revenue is calculated and displayed. Recall that exterior murals cannot be painted in December through February. Also recall that exterior murals are $750 in all months except April, May, September, and October, when they are $699. Interior murals are $500 except during July and August, when they are $450.
   - The program prompts the user for names and mural codes for interior and exterior murals. Along with the prompt for a mural code, display a list of the valid categories.
   - After data entry is complete, the program displays the valid mural categories and then continuously prompts the user for codes and displays the names of all customers ordering murals in the category. Appropriate messages are displayed if the entered code is not a character or a valid code.

CHAPTER 10

Introduction to Inheritance

Upon completion of this chapter, you will be able to:

- ◎ Describe inheritance
- ◎ Extend classes
- ◎ Use the `protected` access specifier
- ◎ Override base class members
- ◎ Describe how a derived class object "is an" instance of the base class
- ◎ Understand the `Object` class
- ◎ Work with base class constructors
- ◎ Create and use abstract classes
- ◎ Create and use interfaces
- ◎ Use extension methods
- ◎ Recognize inheritance in GUI applications

Understanding classes helps you organize objects. Understanding inheritance helps you organize them more precisely. If you have never heard of a *Braford*, for example, you would have a hard time forming a picture of one in your mind. When you learn that a Braford is an animal, you gain some understanding of what it must be like. That understanding grows when you learn it is a mammal, and the understanding is almost complete when you learn it is a cow. When you learn that a Braford is a cow, you understand it has many characteristics that are common to all cows. To identify a Braford, you must learn only relatively minor details—its color or markings, for example. Most of a Braford's characteristics, however, derive from its membership in a particular hierarchy of classes: animal, mammal, and cow.

All object-oriented programming languages make use of inheritance for the same reasons—to organize the objects used by programs, and to make new objects easier to understand based on your knowledge about their inherited traits. In this chapter, you will learn to make use of inheritance with your C# objects.

Understanding Inheritance

Inheritance is the principle that you can apply your knowledge of a general category to more specific objects. You are familiar with the concept of inheritance from all sorts of situations. When you use the term *inheritance*, you might think of genetic inheritance. You know from biology that your blood type and eye color are the products of inherited genes. You can say that many other facts about you (your attributes) are inherited. Similarly, you often can attribute your behaviors to inheritance; for example, the way you handle money might be similar to the way your grandmother handles it, and your gait might be the same as your father's—so your methods are inherited, too.

You also might choose to own plants and animals based on their inherited attributes. You plant impatiens next to your house because they thrive in the shade; you adopt a poodle because you know poodles don't shed. Every plant and pet has slightly different characteristics, but within a species, you can count on many consistent inherited attributes and behaviors. In other words, you can reuse the knowledge you gain about general categories and apply it to more specific categories. Similarly, the classes you create in object-oriented programming languages can inherit data and methods from existing classes. When you create a class by making it inherit from another class, you are provided with data fields and methods automatically; you can reuse fields and methods that are already written and tested.

You already know how to create classes and how to instantiate objects from those classes. For example, consider the `Employee` class in Figure 10-1. The class contains a field for the employee's salary as well as two properties, `IdNum` and `Salary`. The `IdNum` property is an auto-implemented property, but the `Salary` property is not auto-implemented—it is created manually to ensure that an `Employee`'s salary cannot be less than a specified limit. The class also contains a method that creates an `Employee` greeting.

```
class Employee
{
   private double salary;
   public int IdNum {get; set;}
   public double Salary
   {
      get
      {
         return salary;
      }
      set
      {
         const double MIN = 15_000;
         if(value < MIN)
            salary = MIN;
         else
            salary = value;
      }
   }
   public string GetGreeting()
   {
      string greeting = "Hello. I am employee #" + IdNum;
      return greeting;
   }
}
```

Figure 10-1 The Employee class

After you create the Employee class, you can create specific Employee objects, as in the following:

```
Employee receptionist = new Employee();
Employee deliveryPerson = new Employee();
```

These Employee objects can eventually possess different numbers and salaries, but because they are Employee objects, you know that each possesses *some* ID number and salary.

Suppose that you hire a new type of Employee who earns a commission as well as a salary. You can create a class with a name such as CommissionEmployee, and provide this class with three properties (IdNum, Salary, and CommissionRate) and a greeting method. However, this work would duplicate much of the work that you already have done for the Employee class. The wise and efficient alternative is to create the class CommissionEmployee so it inherits all the attributes and methods of Employee. Then, you can add just the new property that is an addition within CommissionEmployee objects.

When you use inheritance to create the `CommissionEmployee` class, you acquire the following benefits:

- You save time, because you need not re-create any fields, properties, or methods already defined in the `Employee` class.
- You reduce the chance of errors, because the `Employee` properties and method have already been used and tested.
- You make it easier for anyone who has used the `Employee` class to understand the `CommissionEmployee` class because such users can concentrate on the new features only.

The ability to use inheritance makes programs easier to write, easier to understand, and less prone to errors. Imagine that besides `CommissionEmployee`, you want to create several other specific `Employee` classes (perhaps `PartTimeEmployee`, including a property for hours worked, or `DismissedEmployee`, including a reason for dismissal). By using inheritance, you can develop each new class correctly and more quickly.

In part, the concept of class inheritance is useful because it makes class code reusable and development faster. However, you do not use inheritance simply to save work. When properly used, inheritance always involves a general-to-specific relationship.

Understanding Inheritance Terminology

A class that is used as a basis for inheritance, such as `Employee`, is called a **base class**. When you create a class that inherits from a base class (such as `CommissionEmployee`), it is a **derived class** or **extended class**. When presented with two classes that have a parent-child relationship, you can tell which class is the base class and which is the derived class by using the two classes in a sentence with the phrase "is a." A derived class always "is a" case or instance of the more general base class. For example, a `Tree` class might be a base class to an `Evergreen` class. Every `Evergreen` "is a" `Tree`; however, it is not true that every `Tree` is an `Evergreen`. Thus, `Tree` is the base class, and `Evergreen` is the derived class. Similarly, a `CommissionEmployee` "is an" `Employee`—not always the other way around—so `Employee` is the base class and `CommissionEmployee` is derived.

You can use the terms **superclass** and **subclass** as synonyms for base class and derived class. Thus, `Evergreen` can be called a subclass of the `Tree` superclass. You also can use the terms **parent class** and **child class**. A `CommissionEmployee` is a child to the `Employee` parent. Use the pair of terms with which you are most comfortable; all of these terms will be used interchangeably in this book.

As an alternative way to discover which of two classes is the base class and which is the derived class, you can try saying the two class names together (although this technique might not work with every superclass-subclass pair). When people say their names together in the English language, they state the more specific name before the all-encompassing family name, such as *Ginny Kroening*. Similarly, with classes, the order that "makes more sense" is the child-parent order. Thus, because *Evergreen Tree* makes more sense than *Tree Evergreen*, you can deduce that Evergreen is the child class. It also is convenient to think of a derived class as building upon its base class by providing the "adjectives" or additional descriptive terms for the "noun." Frequently, the names of derived classes are formed in this way, as in CommissionEmployee.

Finally, you usually can distinguish base classes from their derived classes by size. A derived class is larger than a base class, in the sense that it usually has additional fields, properties, and methods. A derived class description might look small, but any subclass contains all the fields, properties, and methods of its superclass as well as its own more specific ones. Do not think of a subclass as a "subset" of another class—in other words, possessing only parts of its superclass. In fact, a derived class contains everything in the superclass, plus any new attributes and methods.

A derived class can be extended further. In other words, a subclass can have a child of its own. For example, after you create a Tree class and derive Evergreen, you might derive a Spruce class from Evergreen. Similarly, a Poodle class might derive from Dog, Dog from DomesticPet, and DomesticPet from Animal. The entire list of parent classes from which a child class is derived constitutes the **ancestors** of the subclass.

After you create the Spruce class, you might be ready to create Spruce objects. For example, you might create theTreeInMyBackYard, or you might create an array of 1000 Spruce objects for a tree farm. Similarly, one Poodle object might be myPetDogFifi.

Inheritance is **transitive**, which means a child inherits all the members of all its ancestors. In other words, when you declare a Spruce object, it contains all the attributes and methods of both an Evergreen and a Tree. As you work with C#, you will encounter many examples of such transitive chains of inheritance.

When you create your own transitive inheritance chains, you want to place fields and methods at their most general level. In other words, a method named Grow() rightfully belongs in a Tree class, whereas LeavesTurnColor() does not, because the method applies to only some of the Tree child classes. Similarly, a LeavesTurnColor() method would be better located in a Deciduous class than separately within the Oak or Maple child class.

> **TWO TRUTHS & A LIE**
>
> **Understanding Inheritance**
>
> 1. When you use inheritance to create a class, you save time because you can copy and paste fields, properties, and methods that have already been created for the original class.
>
> 2. When you use inheritance to create a class, you reduce the chance of errors because the original class's properties and methods have already been used and tested.
>
> 3. When you use inheritance to create a class, you make it easier for anyone who has used the original class to understand the new class because such users can concentrate on the new features.
>
> The false statement is #1. When you use inheritance to create a class, you save time because you need not re-create the fields, properties, and methods that have already been created for the original class. You do not copy these class members; you inherit them.

Extending Classes

When you create a class that is an extension or child of another class, you use a single colon between the derived class name and its base class name. For example, the following class header creates a subclass-superclass relationship between `CommissionEmployee` and `Employee`.

```
class CommissionEmployee : Employee
```

Each `CommissionEmployee` object automatically contains all the fields, properties, and methods of the base class; you then can add new components to the new, derived class. Figure 10-2 shows a `CommissionEmployee` class.

```
class CommissionEmployee : Employee
{
    public double CommissionRate {get; set;}
}
```

Figure 10-2 The `CommissionEmployee` class

Although you see only one property defined in the CommissionEmployee class in Figure 10-3, it contains three properties: IdNum and Salary, inherited from Employee, and CommissionRate, which is defined within the CommissionEmployee class. Similarly, although you do not see any fields or methods in the CommissionEmployee class, it inherits the salary field and greeting method of Employee.

Figure 10-3 shows a program with a Main() method that declares several Employee and CommissionEmployee objects and shows all the properties and methods that can be used

```
using static System.Console;
class DemoEmployees
{
   static void Main()
   {
      Employee accountant = new Employee();
      Employee programmer = new Employee();
      CommissionEmployee salesperson1 = new CommissionEmployee();
      CommissionEmployee salesperson2 = new CommissionEmployee();
      accountant.IdNum = 123;
      accountant.Salary = 30_000.00;
      programmer.IdNum = 234;
      programmer.Salary = 300_000;
      salesperson1.IdNum = 345;
      salesperson1.Salary = 22_500.00;
      salesperson1.CommissionRate = 0.07;
      salesperson2.IdNum = 456;
      salesperson2.Salary = 229_500.00;
      salesperson2.CommissionRate = 0.04;
      WriteLine("\n" + accountant.GetGreeting());
      WriteLine("   Accountant #{0} salary: {1} per year",
         accountant.IdNum, accountant.Salary.ToString("C"));
      WriteLine("\n" + programmer.GetGreeting());
      WriteLine("   Programmer #{0} salary: {1} per year",
         programmer.IdNum, programmer.Salary.ToString("C"));
      WriteLine("\n" + salesperson1.GetGreeting());
      WriteLine("   Salesperson 1 #{0} salary: {1} per year",
         salesperson1.IdNum, salesperson1.Salary.ToString("C"));
      WriteLine("...plus {0} commission on all sales",
         salesperson1.CommissionRate.ToString("P"));
      WriteLine("\n" + salesperson2.GetGreeting());
      WriteLine("   Salesperson 2 #{0} salary: {1} per year",
         salesperson2.IdNum, salesperson2.Salary.ToString("C"));
      WriteLine("...plus {0} commission on all sales",
         salesperson2.CommissionRate.ToString("P"));
   }
}
```

Note in the output in Figure 10-4 that these high salaries are restricted

Figure 10-3 The DemoEmployees program that declares Employee and CommissionEmployee objects

CHAPTER 10 Introduction to Inheritance

with each. Figure 10-4 shows the program output. Notice that the salary limit is enforced for both object types.

```
Hello. I am employee #123
   Accountant #123 salary: $30,000.00 per year

Hello. I am employee #234
   Programmer #234 salary: $15,000.00 per year

Hello. I am employee #345
   Salesperson 1 #345 salary: $22,500.00 per year
...plus 7.00 % commission on all sales

Hello. I am employee #456
   Salesperson 2 #456 salary: $15,000.00 per year
...plus 4.00 % commission on all sales
```

Figure 10-4 Output of the DemoEmployees program

Inheritance works only in one direction: A child inherits from a parent—not the other way around. If a program instantiates an `Employee` object as in the following statement, the `Employee` object does *not* have access to the `CommissionEmployee` properties or methods.

```
Employee clerk = new Employee();
clerk.CommissionRate = 0.1;
```

Don't Do It
This statement is invalid—`Employee` objects don't have a `CommissionRate`.

`Employee` is the parent class, and `clerk` is an object of the parent class. It makes sense that a parent class object does not have access to its child's data and methods. When you create the parent class, you do not know how many future child classes might be created, or what their data or methods might look like. In addition, child classes are more specific. A `HeartSurgeon` class and an `Obstetrician` class are children of a `Doctor` class. You do not expect all members of the general parent class `Doctor` to have the `HeartSurgeon`'s `RepairValve()` method or the `Obstetrician`'s `DeliverBaby()` method. However, `HeartSurgeon` and `Obstetrician` objects have access to the more general `Doctor` methods `TakeBloodPressure()` and `BillPatients()`. As with doctors, it is convenient to think of derived classes as *specialists*. That is, their fields and methods are more specialized than those of the base class.

 Watch the video *Inheritance*.

TWO TRUTHS & A LIE

Extending Classes

1. The following class header indicates that Dog is a subclass of Pet:
   `public class Pet : Dog`

2. If class X has four fields and class Y derives from it, then class Y also contains at least four fields.

3. Inheritance works only in one direction: A child inherits from a parent—not the other way around.

The false statement is #1. The following class header indicates that Dog is a subclass of Pet:
`public class Dog : Pet`

You Do It

In this section, you create a working example of inheritance. You create this example in four parts:

1. You create a general Loan class that holds data pertaining to a bank loan—a loan number, a customer name, and the amount borrowed.

2. After you create the general Loan class, you write a program to instantiate and use a Loan object.

3. You create a more specific CarLoan derived class that inherits the attributes of the Loan class but adds information about the automobile that serves as collateral for the loan.

4. You modify the Loan demonstration program to add a CarLoan object and demonstrate its use.

(continues)

(continued)

Creating the Loan Class and a Program That Uses It

1. Open a new project named **DemoLoan**, and then enter the following first few lines for a Loan class. The class contains three auto-implemented properties for the loan number, the last name of the customer, and the value of the loan.

   ```
   class Loan
   {
      public int LoanNumber {get; set;}
      public string LastName {get; set;}
      public double LoanAmount {get; set;}
   }
   ```

2. At the top of the file, enter the following code to add a DemoLoan class that contains a Main() method. The class declares a Loan object and shows how to set each field and display the results.

   ```
   using static System.Console;
   class DemoLoan
   {
      static void Main()
      {
         Loan aLoan = new Loan();
         aLoan.LoanNumber = 2239;
         aLoan.LastName = "Mitchell";
         aLoan.LoanAmount = 1_000.00;
         WriteLine("Loan #{0} for {1} is for {2}",
            aLoan.LoanNumber, aLoan.LastName,
            aLoan.LoanAmount.ToString("C2"));
      }
   }
   ```

3. Save the file, and then compile and execute the program. The output looks like Figure 10-5. There is nothing unusual about this class or how it operates; it is similar to many you saw in the last chapter before you learned about inheritance.

   ```
   Loan #2239 for Mitchell is for $1,000.00
   ```

   Figure 10-5 Output of the DemoLoan program

(continues)

(continued)

Extending a Class

Next, you create a class named CarLoan. A CarLoan "is a" type of Loan. As such, it has all the attributes of a Loan, but it also has the year and make of the car that the customer is using as collateral for the loan. Therefore, CarLoan is a subclass of Loan.

1. Save the DemoLoan file as **DemoCarLoan**. Change the DemoLoan class name to **DemoCarLoan**. Begin the definition of the CarLoan class after the closing curly brace for the Loan class. CarLoan extends Loan and contains two properties that hold the year and make of the car.

   ```
   class CarLoan : Loan
   {
       public int Year {get; set;}
       public string Make {get; set;}
   }
   ```

2. Within the Main() method of the DemoCarLoan class, just after the declaration of the Loan object, declare a CarLoan as follows:

   ```
   CarLoan aCarLoan = new CarLoan();
   ```

3. After the three property assignments for the Loan object, insert five assignment statements for the CarLoan object.

   ```
   aCarLoan.LoanNumber = 3358;
   aCarLoan.LastName = "Jansen";
   aCarLoan.LoanAmount = 20_000.00;
   aCarLoan.Make = "Ford";
   aCarLoan.Year = 2007;
   ```

4. Following the WriteLine() statement that displays the Loan object data, insert two WriteLine() statements that display the CarLoan object's data.

   ```
   WriteLine("Loan #{0} for {1} is for {2}",
       aCarLoan.LoanNumber, aCarLoan.LastName,
       aCarLoan.LoanAmount.ToString("C2"));
   WriteLine(" Loan #{0} is for a {1} {2}",
       aCarLoan.LoanNumber, aCarLoan.Year,
       aCarLoan.Make);
   ```

(continues)

> (continued)
>
> 5. Save the program, and then compile and execute it. The output looks like Figure 10-6. The `CarLoan` object correctly uses its own properties as well as those of the parent `Loan` class.
>
> ```
> Loan #2239 for Mitchell is for $1,000.00
> Loan #3358 for Jansen is for $20,000.00
>    Loan #3358 is for a 2007 Ford
> ```
>
> **Figure 10-6** Output of the DemoCarLoan program

Using the protected Access Specifier

In typical C# classes, data fields are `private`, and properties and methods are `public`. In the chapter "Using Classes and Objects," you learned that this scheme provides for information hiding—protecting your `private` data from alteration by methods outside the data's own class. When a program is a client of the `Employee` class in Figure 10-1 (that is, it instantiates an `Employee` object), the client cannot alter the data in the `private salary` field directly. For example, when you write a `Main()` method that creates an `Employee` named `clerk`, you cannot change the `Employee`'s `salary` directly using a statement such as `clerk.salary = 20_000;`. Instead, you must use the `public Salary` property.

When you use information hiding, you are assured that your data will be altered only by the properties and methods you choose and only in ways that you can control. If outside classes could alter an `Employee`'s `private` fields, then the fields could be assigned values that the `Employee` class couldn't control. In such a case, the principle of information hiding would be destroyed, causing the behavior of the object to be unpredictable.

Any derived class you create, such as `CommissionEmployee`, inherits all the data and methods of its base class. However, even though a child of `Employee` has `idNum` (implicitly) and `salary` (explicitly) fields, the `CommissionEmployee` methods cannot alter or use those `private` fields directly. If a new class could simply extend your `Employee` class and "get to" its data fields without "going through the proper channels," then information hiding would not be operating.

On some occasions, you do want to access parent class data from a child class.

For example, assume that a `CommissionEmployee` draws commission only and no regular salary; that is, when you set a `CommissionEmployee`'s `commissionRate` field, the `salary` should become 0. You could write the `CommissionEmployee` class `CommissionRate` property `set` accessor as follows:

```
set
{
   commissionRate = value;
   Salary = 0;
}
```

Using this implementation, when you create a `CommissionEmployee` object and set its `CommissionRate`, 0 is sent to the `Employee` class `Salary` property. Because the value of the salary is less than 15000, the `Salary` property code forces the salary to 15000, even though you want it to be 0.

A possible alternative would be to rewrite the `set` accessor for the `CommissionRate` property in the `CommissionEmployee` class using the field `salary` instead of the property `Salary`, as follows:

```
set
{
   commissionRate = value;
   salary = 0;
}
```

In this `set` accessor, you bypass the parent class's `Salary set` accessor and directly use the `salary` field. However, when you include this accessor in a program and compile it, you receive an error message: *Employee.salary is inaccessible due to its protection level*. In other words, `Employee.salary` is `private`, and no other class can access it, even a child class of `Employee`.

So, in summary:

- Using the `public set` accessor in the parent class does not work because of the minimum salary requirement.

- Using the `private` field in the parent class does not work because it is inaccessible.

- Making the parent class field `public` would work, but doing so would violate the principle of information hiding.

Fortunately, there is a fourth option. The solution is to create the `salary` field with **protected access**, which provides you with an intermediate level of security between `public` and `private` access. A `protected` data field or method can be used within its own class or in any classes extended from that class, but it cannot be used by "outside" classes. In other words, `protected` members can be used "within the family"—by a class and its descendants.

Some sources say that `private`, `public`, and `protected` are *access specifiers*, while other class designations, such as `static`, are *access modifiers*. However, Microsoft developers, who created C#, use the terms interchangeably in their documentation.

Figure 10-7 shows how you can declare `salary` as `protected` within the `Employee` class so that it becomes legal to access it directly within the `CommissionRate set` accessor of the `CommissionEmployee` derived class. Figure 10-8 contains a `CommissionEmployee` class

```
class Employee
{
   protected double salary;
   public int IdNum {get; set;}
   public double Salary
   {
      get
      {
         return salary;
      }
      set
      {
         const double MIN = 15_000;
         if(value < MIN)
            salary = MIN;
         else
            salary = value;
      }
   }
   public string GetGreeting()
   {
      string greeting = "Hello. I am employee #" + IdNum;
      return greeting;
   }
}
```
Notice the salary field is protected

Figure 10-7 The Employee class with a protected field

```
class CommissionEmployee : Employee
{
   private double commissionRate;
   public double CommissionRate
   {
      get
      {
         return commissionRate;
      }
      set
      {
         commissionRate = value;
         salary = 0;
      }
   }
}
```
CommissionEmployee can use Employee's protected salary field

Figure 10-8 The CommissionEmployee class that uses its parent's protected field

Using the protected Access Specifier

that inherits from the new Employee class and uses the protected field. Figure 10-9 shows a program that instantiates a CommissionEmployee object, and Figure 10-10 shows the output. Notice that the CommissionEmployee's salary initially is set to 20_000 in the program, but the salary becomes 0 when the CommissionRate is set later.

```
using static System.Console;
class DemoCommissionEmployee
{
    static void Main()
    {
        CommissionEmployee salesperson = new CommissionEmployee();
        salesperson.IdNum = 567;
        salesperson.Salary = 20_000.00;
        salesperson.CommissionRate = 0.06;
        WriteLine("   Salesperson #{0} salary: {1} per year",
            salesperson.IdNum, salesperson.Salary.ToString("C"));
        WriteLine("...plus {0} commission on all sales",
            salesperson.CommissionRate.ToString("P"));
    }
}
```

Figure 10-9   The DemoCommissionEmployee program

```
Salesperson #567 salary: $0.00 per year
...plus 6.00 % commission on all sales
```

Figure 10-10   Output of the DemoCommissionEmployee program

If you set the salesperson's CommissionRate first in the DemoCommissionEmployee program, then set Salary to a nonzero value, the commissioned employee's salary will not be reduced to 0. If your intention is to always create CommissionEmployees with salaries of 0, then the Salary property should also be overridden in the derived class. You will learn about overriding parent class members in the next section.

Using the protected access specifier for a field can be convenient, and it also slightly improves program performance by using a field directly instead of "going through" property accessors. Also, using the protected access specifier is occasionally necessary. However, protected data members should be used sparingly. Whenever possible, the principle of information hiding should be observed, and even child classes should have to go through accessors to "get to" their parent's private data. When child classes are allowed direct access to a parent's fields, the likelihood of future errors increases. Classes that depend on field names from parent classes are said to be **fragile** because they are prone to errors—that is, they are easy to "break."

> **TWO TRUTHS & A LIE**
>
> **Using the protected Access Specifier**
>
> 1. A child class does not contain the `private` members of its parent.
> 2. A child class cannot use the `private` members of its parent.
> 3. A child class can use the `protected` members of its parent, but outside classes cannot.
>
> The false statement is #1. A child class contains the `private` members of its parent, but cannot use them directly.

Overriding Base Class Members

When you create a derived class by extending an existing class, the new derived class contains properties and methods that were defined in the original base class. Sometimes, the superclass features are not entirely appropriate for the subclass objects. Using the same method or property name to indicate different implementations is called polymorphism. You first learned the term *polymorphism* in Chapter 1; it means "many forms." In programming, it means that many forms of action take place, even though you use the same method name. The specific method executed depends on the object.

Everyday cases provide many examples of polymorphism:

- Although both are musical instruments and have a `Play()` method, a guitar is played differently than a drum.
- Although both are vehicles and have an `Operate()` method, a bicycle is operated differently than a truck.
- Although both are schools and have a `SatisfyGraduationRequirements()` method, a preschool's requirements are different from those of a college.

You understand each of these methods based on the context in which it is used. In a similar way, C# understands your use of the same method name based on the type of object associated with it.

For example, suppose that you have created a `Student` class as shown in Figure 10-11. `Students` have `names`, `credits` for which they are enrolled, and `tuition` amounts. You can set a `Student`'s `name` and `credits` by using the `set` accessors in the `Name` and `Credits` properties, but you cannot set a `Student`'s `tuition` directly because the `Tuition` property has no `set` accessor. Instead, `tuition` is calculated based on a standard RATE (of $55.75) for each `credit` that the `Student` takes. (In Figure 10-11, the `Student` fields that hold `credits` and `tuition` are declared as `protected` because a child class will use them.)

```
class Student
{
    private const double RATE = 55.75;
    protected int credits;
    protected double tuition;
    public string Name {get; set;}
    public virtual int Credits
    {
        get
        {
            return credits;
        }
        set
        {
            credits = value;
            tuition = credits * RATE;
        }
    }
    public double Tuition
    {
        get
        {
            return tuition;
        }
    }
}
```

Figure 10-11 The Student class

In Figure 10-11, `Credits` is declared to be virtual (see shading). A **virtual method** (or property) is one that can be overridden by a method with the same signature in a child class. In Chapter 9, you learned that when a method overrides another, it takes precedence over the method.

Suppose that you derive a subclass from `Student` called `ScholarshipStudent`, as shown in Figure 10-12. A `ScholarshipStudent` has a `name`, `credits`, and `tuition`, but the tuition is not calculated in the same way as it is for a `Student`; instead, `tuition` for a `ScholarshipStudent` should be set to 0. You want to use the `Credits` property to set a `ScholarshipStudent`'s `credits`, but you want the property to behave differently than the parent class `Student`'s `Credits` property. As a child of `Student`, a `ScholarshipStudent` possesses all the attributes, properties, and methods of a `Student`, but its `Credits` property behaves differently.

```
class ScholarshipStudent : Student
{
    public override int Credits
    {
        set
        {
            credits = value;
            tuition = 0;
        }
    }
}
```

Figure 10-12 The ScholarshipStudent class

In C#, you can use either new or override when defining a derived class member that has the same name as a base class member, but you cannot use both together. When you write a statement such as ScholarshipStudent s1 = new ScholarshipStudent();, you won't notice the difference. However, if you use new when defining the derived class Credits property and write a statement such as Student s2 = new ScholarshipStudent(); (using Student as the type), then s2.Credits accesses the base class property. On the other hand, if you use override when defining Credits in the derived class, then s2.Credits uses the derived class property.

In the child ScholarshipStudent class in Figure 10-12, the Credits property is declared with the override modifier (see shading) because it has the same header (that is, the same signature—the same name and parameter list) as a property in its parent class. The Credits property overrides and **hides** its counterpart in the parent class. (You could do the same thing with methods.) If you omit override, the program still will operate correctly, but you will receive a warning that you are hiding an inherited member with the same name in the base class. Using the keyword override eliminates the warning and makes your intentions clear. When you use the Name property with a ScholarshipStudent object, a program uses the parent class property Name; it is not hidden. However, when you use Credits to set a value for a ScholarshipStudent object, the program uses the new, overriding property from its own class.

If credits and tuition had been declared as private within the Student class, then ScholarshipStudent would not be able to use them.

You are not required to override a virtual method or property in a derived class; a derived class can simply use the base class version. A base class member that is not hidden by the derived class is **visible** in the derived class.

Figure 10-13 shows a program that uses Student and ScholarshipStudent objects. Even though each object assigns the Credits property with the same number of credit hours (in the

Overriding Base Class Members

```
using static System.Console;
class DemoStudents
{
   static void Main()
   {
      Student payingStudent = new Student();
      ScholarshipStudent freeStudent = new ScholarshipStudent();
      payingStudent.Name = "Megan";
      payingStudent.Credits = 15;
      freeStudent.Name = "Luke";
      freeStudent.Credits = 15;
      WriteLine("{0}'s tuition for {1} credits is {2}",
         payingStudent.Name, payingStudent.Credits,
            payingStudent.Tuition.ToString("C"));
      WriteLine("{0}'s tuition for {1} credits is {2}",
         freeStudent.Name, freeStudent.Credits,
            freeStudent.Tuition.ToString("C"));
   }
}
```

Figure 10-13 The DemoStudents program

two shaded statements), the calculated `tuition` values are different because each object uses a different version of the `Credits` property. Figure 10-14 shows the execution of the program.

If a base class and a derived class have methods with the same names but different parameter lists, then the derived class method does not override the base class method; instead, it *overloads* the base class method. For example, if a base class contains a method with the header `public void Display()`, and its child contains a method with the header `public void Display(string s)`, then the child class would have access to both methods. (You learned about overloading methods in the chapter "Advanced Method Concepts.")

```
Megan's tuition for 15 credits is $836.25
Luke's tuition for 15 credits is $0.00
```

Figure 10-14 Output of the DemoStudents program

Accessing Base Class Methods and Properties from a Derived Class

When a derived class contains a method or property that overrides a parent class method or property, you might have occasion to use the parent class version within the subclass. If so, you can use the keyword **base** to access the parent class method or property.

For example, recall the `GetGreeting()` method that appears in the `Employee` class in Figure 10-7. If its child, `CommissionEmployee`, also contains a `GetGreeting()` method, as shown in Figure 10-15, then within the `CommissionEmployee` class you can call

CHAPTER 10 Introduction to Inheritance

```
class CommissionEmployee : Employee
{
    private double commissionRate;
    public double CommissionRate
    {
        get
        {
            return commissionRate;
        }
        set
        {
            commissionRate = value;
            salary = 0;
        }
    }
    new public string GetGreeting()
    {
        string greeting = base.GetGreeting();
        greeting += "\nI work on commission.";
        return greeting;
    }
}
```

Keyword **new** in method header eliminates compiler warning when base class method is overridden

This statement calls parent's version of method

Figure 10-15 The CommissionEmployee class with a GetGreeting() method

base.GetGreeting() to access the base class version of the method. Figure 10-16 shows an application that uses the method with a CommissionEmployee object. Figure 10-17 shows the output.

```
using static System.Console;
class DemoCommissionEmployee2
{
    static void Main()
    {
        CommissionEmployee salesperson = new CommissionEmployee();
        salesperson.IdNum = 345;
        WriteLine(salesperson.GetGreeting());
    }
}
```

Figure 10-16 The DemoCommissionEmployee2 program

Figure 10-17 Output of the DemoCommissionEmployee2 program

In Figure 10-15, the child class, the GetGreeting() method uses the keyword new in its header to eliminate a compiler warning. Then, within the method, the parent's version of the GetGreeting() method is called. The returned string is stored in the greeting variable, and then an *I work on commission.* statement is concatenated before the complete message is returned to the calling program. By overriding the base class method in the child class, the duplicate typing to create the first part of the message is eliminated. Additionally, if the first part of the message is altered in the future, it will be altered in only one place—in the base class.

 Watch the video *Handling Methods and Inheritance*.

TWO TRUTHS & A LIE

Overriding Base Class Members

1. When you override a parent class method in a child class, the methods have the same name.

2. When you override a parent class method in a child class, the methods have the same parameter list.

3. When you override a parent class method in a child class and then use the child class method, the parent class method executes first, followed by the child class method.

The false statement is #3. When you override a parent class method in a child class and then use the child class method, the child class method executes instead of the parent class version.

 You Do It

In the previous sections, you created Loan and CarLoan classes and objects. Suppose that the bank adopts new rules as follows:

- No regular loan will be made for less than $5,000.
- No car loan will be made for any car older than model year 2008.
- Although Loans might have larger loan numbers, CarLoans will have loan numbers that are no more than three digits. If a larger loan number is provided, the program will use only the last three digits for the loan number.

(continued)

Using Base Class Members in a Derived Class

1. Open the DemoCarLoan file, and immediately save it as **DemoCarLoan2**. Also, change the class name from DemoCarLoan to **DemoCarLoan2**.

2. Within the Loan class, add a new constant that represents the minimum loan value:

   ```
   public const double MINIMUM_LOAN = 5_000;
   ```

3. Add a field for the loanAmount because the LoanAmount property, which was previously an auto-implemented property, will need to use it:

   ```
   protected double loanAmount;
   ```

   The field is protected so that CarLoan objects will be able to access it as well as Loan objects.

4. Replace the auto-implemented property for LoanAmount in the Loan class with get and set accessors as follows. This change ensures that no loan is made for less than the minimum allowed value.

   ```
   public double LoanAmount
   {
      set
      {
         if(value < MINIMUM_LOAN)
            loanAmount = MINIMUM_LOAN;
         else
            loanAmount = value;
      }
      get
      {
         return loanAmount;
      }
   }
   ```

5. Within the CarLoan class, add two new constants to hold the earliest year for which car loans will be given and the lowest allowed loan number:

   ```
   private const int EARLIEST_YEAR = 2008;
   private const int LOWEST_INVALID_NUM = 1000;
   ```

6. Also within the CarLoan class, add a field for the year of the car, and replace the existing auto-implemented Year property with one that contains coded get

(continues)

(continued)

and set accessors. The Year property set accessor not only sets the year field, it sets loanAmount to 0 when a car's year is less than 2008.

```
private int year;
public int Year
{
    set
    {
        if(value < EARLIEST_YEAR)
        {
            year = value;
            loanAmount = 0;
        }
        else
            year = value;
    }
    get
    {
        return year;
    }
}
```

If loanAmount were private in the parent Loan class, you would not be able to set its value in the child CarLoan class, as you do here. You could use the public property LoanAmount to set the value, but the parent class set accessor would force the value to 5000.

7. Suppose that unique rules apply for issuing loan numbers for cars. Within the CarLoan class, just before the closing curly brace, change the inherited LoanNumber property to accommodate the new rules. If a car loan number is three digits or fewer, pass it on to the base class property. If not, obtain the last three digits by calculating the remainder when the loan number is divided by 1000, and pass the new number to the base class property. Add the following property after the definition of the Make property.

```
public new int LoanNumber
{
    get
    {
        return base.LoanNumber;
    }
```

(continues)

(continued)

```
    set
    {
        if(value < LOWEST_INVALID_NUM)
            base.LoanNumber = value;
        else
            base.LoanNumber = value % LOWEST_INVALID_NUM;
    }
}
```

If you did not use the keyword base to access the LoanNumber property within the CarLoan class, you would be telling this version of the LoanNumber property to call itself. Although the program would compile, it would run continuously in an infinite loop until it ran out of memory and issued an error message.

 A method that calls itself is a **recursive** method. Recursive methods are sometimes useful, but they require specialized code to avoid infinite loops and are not appropriate in this case.

8. Save the file. Compile it, and correct any errors. When you execute the program, the output looks like Figure 10-18. Compare the output to Figure 10-7. Notice that the $1,000 bank loan has been forced to $5,000. Also, notice that the car loan number has been shortened to three digits and the value of the loan is $0 because of the age of the car.

```
Loan #2239 for Mitchell is for $5,000.00
Loan #358 for Jansen is for $0.00
   Loan #358 is for a 2007 Ford
```

Figure 10-18 Output of the DemoCarLoan2 program

9. Change the assigned values within the DemoCarLoan2 class to combinations of early and late years and valid and invalid loan numbers. After each change, save the program, compile and execute it, and confirm that the program operates as expected.

Understanding Implicit Reference Conversions

Every derived object "is a" specific instance of both the derived class and the base class. In other words, myCar "is a" Car as well as a Vehicle, and myDog "is a" Dog as well as a Mammal. You can assign a derived class object to an object of any of its superclass types. When you do, C# makes an **implicit conversion** from derived class to base class.

You have already learned that C# also makes implicit conversions when casting one data type to another. For example, in the statement double money = 10;, the integer value 10 is implicitly converted (or cast) to a double. When a derived class object is assigned to its ancestor's data type, the conversion can more specifically be called an **implicit reference conversion**. This term is more accurate because it emphasizes the difference between numerical conversions and reference objects. When you assign a derived class object to a base class type, the object is treated as though it had only the characteristics defined in the base class and not those added in the child class definition.

For example, when a CommissionEmployee class inherits from Employee, an object of either type can be passed to a method that accepts an Employee parameter. In Figure 10-19, an Employee is passed to DisplayGreeting() in the first shaded statement, and a CommissionEmployee is passed in the second shaded statement. Each is referred to as emp within the method, and each is used correctly, as shown in Figure 10-20.

```
using static System.Console;
class DemoCommissionEmployee3
{
   static void Main()
   {
      Employee clerk = new Employee();
      CommissionEmployee salesperson = new CommissionEmployee();
      clerk.IdNum = 234;
      salesperson.IdNum = 345;
      DisplayGreeting(clerk);
      DisplayGreeting(salesperson);
   }
   public static void DisplayGreeting(Employee emp)
   {
      WriteLine("Hi there from #" + emp.IdNum);
      WriteLine(emp.GetGreeting());
   }
}
```

Both an Employee and a CommissionEmployee can be passed to this method

Figure 10-19 The DemoCommissionEmployee3 program

```
Hi there from #234
Hello. I am employee #234
Hi there from #345
Hello. I am employee #345
```

Figure 10-20 Output of the DemoCommissionEmployee3 program

TWO TRUTHS & A LIE

Understanding Implicit Reference Conversions

1. You can assign a derived class object to an object of any of its superclass types.
2. You can assign a base class object to an object of any of its derived types.
3. An implicit conversion from one type to another is an automatic conversion.

The false statement is #2. You can assign a derived class object to an object of any of its superclass types but not the other way around.

Using the `Object` Class

Every class you create in C# derives from a single class named `System.Object`. In other words, the **object** (or `Object`) class type in the `System` namespace is the ultimate base class, or **root class**, for all other types. When you create a class such as `Employee`, you usually use the header `class Employee`, which implicitly, or automatically, descends from the `Object` class. Alternatively, you could use the header `class Employee : Object` to explicitly show the name of the base class, but it would be extremely unusual to see such a format in a C# program.

The keyword `object` is an alias for the `System.Object` class. You can use the lowercase and uppercase versions of the class interchangeably. The fact that `object` is an alias for `System.Object` should not surprise you. You already know, for example, that `int` is an alias for `Int32` and that `double` is an alias for `Double`.

Because every class descends from `Object`, every object "is an" `Object`. As proof, you can write a method that accepts an argument of type `Object`, and it will accept arguments of any type. Figure 10-21 shows a program that declares three objects using classes created earlier in this chapter—a `Student`, a `ScholarshipStudent`, and an `Employee`. Even though these types possess different attributes and methods (and one type, `Employee`, has nothing in common with the other two), each type can serve as an argument to the `DisplayObjectMessage()` because each type "is an" `Object`. Figure 10-22 shows the execution of the program.

Using the Object Class

```
using System;
using static System.Console;
class DiverseObjects
{
    static void Main()
    {
        Student payingStudent = new Student();
        ScholarshipStudent freeStudent = new ScholarshipStudent();
        Employee clerk = new Employee();
        Write("Using Student: ");
        DisplayObjectMessage(payingStudent);
        Write("Using ScholarshipStudent: ");
        DisplayObjectMessage(freeStudent);
        Write("Using Employee: ");
        DisplayObjectMessage(clerk);
    }
    public static void DisplayObjectMessage(Object o)
    {
        WriteLine("Method successfully called");
    }
}
```
Any type of object can be passed to this method

Figure 10-21 The DiverseObjects program

```
Using Student: Method successfully called
Using ScholarshipStudent: Method successfully called
Using Employee: Method successfully called
```

Figure 10-22 Output of the DiverseObjects program

When you create any child class, it inherits all the methods of all of its ancestors. Because all classes inherit from the Object class, all classes inherit the Object class methods. The Object class contains a constructor, a destructor, and four public instance methods, as summarized in Table 10-1.

Method	Explanation
Equals()	Determines whether two Object instances are equal
GetHashCode()	Gets a unique code for each object; useful in certain sorting and data management tasks
GetType()	Returns the type, or class, of an object
ToString()	Returns a String that represents the object

Table 10-1 The four public instance methods of the Object class

The Object class contains other nonpublic and noninstance (static) methods in addition to the four methods listed in Table 10-1. The C# documentation provides more details on these methods.

Using the Object Class's GetType() Method

The GetType() method returns an object's type, or class. For example, if you have created an Employee object named someWorker, then the following statement displays *Employee:*

WriteLine(someWorker.GetType());

If an object's class is defined in a namespace, then GetType() returns a string composed of the namespace, a dot, and the class name.

Using the Object Class's ToString() Method

The Object class methods are not very useful as they stand. For example, when you use the Object class's ToString() method with an object you create, it simply returns a string that holds the name of the class, just as GetType() does. That is, if someWorker is an Employee, then the following statement displays *Employee:*

WriteLine(someWorker.ToString());

When you create a class such as Employee, you often want to override the Object class's ToString() method with your own, more useful version—perhaps one that returns an Employee's ID number, name, or combination of the two. Of course, you could create a differently named method to do the same thing—perhaps GetEmployeeIdentification() or ConvertEmployeeToString(). However, by naming your class method ToString(), you make the class easier for others to understand and use. Programmers know the ToString() method works with every object; when they use it with your objects, you can provide a useful set of information. A class's ToString() method is often a useful debugging aid.

For example, you might create an Employee class ToString() method, as shown in Figure 10-23. This method assumes that IdNum and Name are Employee properties with get accessors. The returned string will have a value such as *Employee: 234 Johnson*.

```
public override string ToString()
{
    return(getType() + ": " + IdNum + " " + Name);
}
```

Figure 10-23 An Employee class ToString() method

You have been using an overloaded version of the ToString() method since Chapter 2. There, you learned that you can format numeric output when you pass a string such as "F3" or "C2" to the ToString() method.

Using the Object Class's Equals() Method

The Equals() method compares objects for reference equality. **Reference equality** occurs when two reference type objects refer to the same object. The Equals() method returns true if two Objects have the same memory address—that is, if one object is a reference to the other and both are literally the same object. For example, you might write the following:

if(oneObject.Equals(anotherObject))...

Like the ToString() method, this method might not be useful to you in its original form. For example, you might prefer to think of two Employee objects at unique memory addresses as equal if their ID numbers or first and last names are equal. You might want to override the Equals() method for any class you create if you anticipate that class clients will want to compare objects based on any of their field values.

If you overload the Equals() method, it should meet the following requirements by convention:

- Its header should be as follows (you can use any identifier for the Object parameter):

    public override bool Equals(Object o)

- It should return false if the argument is null.

- It should return true if an object is compared to itself.

- It should return true only if both of the following are true:

    oneObject.Equals(anotherObject)
    anotherObject.Equals(oneObject)

- If oneObject.Equals(anotherObject) returns true and oneObject.Equals(aThirdObject) returns true, then anotherObject.Equals(aThirdObject) should also be true.

You first used the Equals() method to compare String objects in Chapter 2. When you use Equals() with Strings, you use the String class's Equals() method that compares String contents as opposed to String addresses. In other words, the Object class's Equals() method has already been overridden in the String class.

When you create an Equals() method to override the one in the Object class, the parameter must be an Object. For example, if you consider Employee objects equal when their IdNum properties are equal, then an Employee class Equals() method might be created as follows:

```
public override bool Equals(Object e)
{
   bool isEqual;
   Employee temp = (Employee)e;
   if(IdNum == temp.IdNum)
      isEqual = true;
   else
      isEqual = false;
   return isEqual;
}
```

In the shaded statement in the method, the `Object` parameter is cast to an `Employee` so the `Employee`'s `IdNum` can be compared. If you did not perform the cast and tried to make the comparison with `e.IdNum`, the method would not compile because an `Object` does not have an `IdNum` property.

An even better alternative is to ensure that compared objects are the same type before making any other decisions. For example, the `Equals()` method in Figure 10-24 uses the `GetType()` method with both the `this` object and the parameter before proceeding. If compared objects are not the same type, then the `Equals()` method should return `false`.

```
public override bool Equals(Object e)
{
   bool isEqual = true;
   if(this.GetType() != e.GetType())
      isEqual = false;
   else
   {
      Employee temp = (Employee)e;
      if(IdNum == temp.IdNum)
         isEqual = true;
      else
         isEqual = false;
   }
   return isEqual;
}
```

Figure 10-24 An `Equals()` method for the `Employee` class

Using the `Object` Class's `GetHashCode()` Method

When you override the `Equals()` method, you should also override the `GetHashCode()` method, because `Equals()` uses `GetHashCode()`, and two objects considered equal should have the same hash code. A **hash code** is a number that should uniquely identify an object; you might use hash codes in some advanced C# applications. For example, Figure 10-25 shows an application that declares two `Employees` from a class in which the `GetHashCode()` method has not been overridden. The output in Figure 10-26 shows a unique number for each object. (The number, however, is meaningless to you.) If you choose to override the `GetHashCode()` method, you should write this method so it returns a unique integer for every object—an `Employee` ID number, for example.

```
using static System.Console;
class TestHashCode
{
   static void Main()
   {
      Employee first = new Employee();
      Employee second = new Employee();
      WriteLine("First hash code " + first.GetHashCode());
      WriteLine("Second hash code " + second.GetHashCode());
   }
}
```

Figure 10-25 The TestHashCode program

```
First hash code 21083178
Second hash code 55530882
```

Figure 10-26 Output of the TestHashCode program

A hash code is sometimes called a *fingerprint* for an object because it uniquely identifies the object. In C#, the default implementation of the GetHashCode() method does not guarantee unique return values for different objects. However, if GetHashCode() is explicitly implemented in a derived class, it must return a unique hash code.

In cooking, hash is a dish that is created by combining ingredients. The term hash code derives from the fact that the code is sometimes created by mixing some of an object's data.

Although you can write an Equals() method for a class without overriding GetHashCode(), you receive a warning message. Additionally, if you overload == or != for a class, you will receive warning messages if you do not also override both the Equals() and GetHashCode() methods.

> **TWO TRUTHS & A LIE**
>
> **Using the Object Class**
>
> 1. The `Object` class contains a method named `GetType()` that returns an object's type, or class.
>
> 2. If you do not override the `ToString()` method for a class, it returns the value of the first string declared within the class, if any.
>
> 3. The `Object` class's `Equals()` method returns `true` if two `Object`s have the same memory address—that is, if one object is a reference to the other and both are literally the same object.
>
> The false statement is #2. If you do not override the `ToString()` method for a class, it returns a string that holds the name of the class.

Working with Base Class Constructors

When you create any object, you call a constructor that has the same name as the class itself. Consider the following example:

```
SomeClass anObject = new SomeClass();
```

When you instantiate an object that is a member of a derived class, the constructor for the base class executes first, and then the derived class constructor executes. In other words, when you create any object, you always implicitly call the `Object` constructor because all classes are derived from `Object`. So, when you create a base class and a derived class, and instantiate a derived class object, you call three constructors: one from the `Object` class, one from the base class, and one from the derived class.

In the examples of inheritance you have seen so far in this chapter, each class contained only default constructors, so their executions were transparent. However, you should realize that when you create a subclass instance, both the base and derived constructors execute. For example, consider the abbreviated `Employee` and `CommissionEmployee` classes in Figure 10-27. `Employee` contains just two fields and a constructor; `CommissionEmployee` descends from `Employee` and contains a constructor as well. The DemoCommissionEmployee4 program in Figure 10-28 contains just one statement; it instantiates a `CommissionEmployee`. The output in Figure 10-29 shows that this one statement causes both constructors to execute.

Of course, most constructors perform many more tasks than displaying a message to inform you that they exist. When constructors initialize variables, you usually want the base class constructor to initialize the data fields that originate in the base class. The derived class constructor needs to initialize only the data fields that are specific to the derived class.

Working with Base Class Constructors

```
class Employee
{
    private int idNum;
    protected double salary;
    public Employee()
    {
        WriteLine("Employee constructed");
    }
}
class CommissionEmployee : Employee
{
    private double commissionRate;
    public CommissionEmployee()
    {
        WriteLine("CommissionEmployee constructed");
    }
}
```

Figure 10-27 The Employee and CommissionEmployee classes with parameterless constructors

```
using static System.Console;
class DemoCommissionEmployee4
{
    static void Main()
    {
        CommissionEmployee salesperson = new CommissionEmployee();
    }
}
```

Figure 10-28 The DemoCommissionEmployee4 program

Figure 10-29 Output of the DemoCommissionEmployee4 program

Using Base Class Constructors That Require Arguments

When you create a class and do not provide a constructor, C# automatically supplies one that never requires arguments. When you write your own constructor for a class, you replace the automatically supplied version. Depending on your needs, the constructor you create for a class might require arguments. When you use a class as a base class and the class only has constructors that require arguments, you must make sure that any derived classes provide arguments so that one of the base class constructors can execute.

When all base class constructors require arguments, you must include a constructor for each derived class you create. Your derived class constructor can contain any number of statements; however, within the header of the constructor, you must provide values for any arguments required by the base class constructor that you use. Even if you have no other reason for creating a derived class constructor, you must write the derived class constructor so it can call its parent's constructor.

The header for a derived class constructor that calls a base class constructor includes a colon, the keyword **base**, and a list of arguments within parentheses. The keyword **base** always refers to the superclass of the class in which you use it. Although it seems that you should be able to use the base class constructor name to call the base class constructor, C# does not allow you to do so—you must use the keyword **base**.

For example, if you create an Employee class with a constructor that requires two arguments—an integer and a string—and you create a CommissionEmployee class that is a subclass of Employee, then the following code shows a valid constructor for CommissionEmployee:

```
public CommissionEmployee() : base(1234, "XXXX")
{
    // Other statements can go here
}
```

In this example, the CommissionEmployee constructor requires no arguments for its own execution, but it passes two arguments to its base class constructor. Every CommissionEmployee instantiation passes *1234* and *XXXX* to the Employee constructor. A different CommissionEmployee constructor might accept arguments; then it could pass the appropriate arguments on to the base class constructor, as in the following example:

```
public CommissionEmployee(int id, string name) : base(id, name)
{
    // Other statements can go here
}
```

Yet another CommissionEmployee constructor might require that some arguments be passed to the base class constructor and that some be used within CommissionEmployee. Consider the following example:

```
public CommissionEmployee(int id, string name, double rate) :
    base(id, name) // two parameters passed to base constructor
{
    CommissionRate = rate;
    // rate is used within child constructor
    // Other statements can go here
}
```

 Watch the video *Constructors and Inheritance*.

Working with Base Class Constructors

TWO TRUTHS & A LIE

Working with Base Class Constructors

1. When you create any derived class object, the base class constructor executes first, followed by the derived class constructor.

2. When a base class constructor requires arguments, you must include a constructor for each derived class you create.

3. When a derived class's constructor requires arguments, all of the arguments must be passed to the base class constructor.

The false statement is #3. When a derived class's constructor requires arguments, all of the arguments might be needed in the derived class, or perhaps all must be passed to the base class constructor. It also might be possible that some arguments are passed to the base class constructor and others are used within the derived class constructor.

You Do It

Adding Constructors to Base and Derived Classes

When a base class contains only constructors that require parameters, then any derived classes must provide for the base class constructor. In the next steps, you add constructors to the Loan and CarLoan classes and demonstrate that they work as expected.

1. Open the DemoCarLoan2 program, and change the class name to **DemoCarLoan3**. Save the file as **DemoCarLoan3**.

2. In the Loan class, just after the declaration of the loanAmount field, add a constructor that requires values for all the Loan's properties:

```
public Loan(int num, string name, double amount)
{
    LoanNumber = num;
    LastName = name;
    LoanAmount = amount;
}
```

(continues)

(continued)

3. In the CarLoan class, just after the declaration of the year field, add a constructor that takes five parameters. It passes three of the parameters to the base class constructor and uses the other two to assign values to the properties that are unique to the child class.

   ```
   public CarLoan(int num, string name, double amount,
       int year, string make) : base(num, name, amount)
   {
       Year = year;
       Make = make;
   }
   ```

4. In the Main() method of the DemoCarLoan3 class, remove the existing declarations for aLoan and aCarLoan, and replace them with two declarations that use the arguments passed to the constructors.

   ```
   Loan aLoan = new Loan(333, "Hanson", 7_000.00);
   CarLoan aCarLoan = new CarLoan(444, "Carlisle",
       30_000.00, 2014, "BMW");
   ```

5. Remove the eight statements that assigned values to Loan and CarLoan, but retain the WriteLine() statements that display the values.

6. Save the program, and then compile and execute it. The output looks like Figure 10-30. Both constructors work as expected. The CarLoan constructor has called its parent's constructor to set the necessary fields before executing its own unique statements.

   ```
   Loan #333 for Hanson is for $7,000.00
   Loan #444 for Carlisle is for $30,000.00
       Loan #444 is for a 2014 BMW
   ```

   Figure 10-30 Output of the DemoCarLoan3 program

Creating and Using Abstract Classes

Creating classes can become easier after you understand the concept of inheritance. When you create a child class, it inherits all the general attributes you need; you must create only the new, more specific attributes required by the child class. For example, a Painter and a Sculptor are more specific than an Artist. They inherit all the general attributes of Artists, but you must add the attributes and methods that are specific to Painter and Sculptor.

Creating and Using Abstract Classes

Another way to think about a superclass is to notice that it contains the features shared by its subclasses. The derived classes are more specific examples of the base class type; they add features to the shared, general features. Conversely, when you examine a derived class, you notice that its parent is more general.

Sometimes you create a parent class to be so general that you never intend to create any specific instances of the class. For example, you might never create "just" an `Artist`; each `Artist` is more specifically a `Painter`, `Sculptor`, `Illustrator`, and so on. A class that is used to instantiate objects is a **concrete class**. A class that you create only to extend from, but not to instantiate from, is an abstract class. An **abstract class** is one from which you cannot create concrete objects but from which you can inherit. You use the keyword `abstract` when you declare an abstract class. If you attempt to instantiate an object from an abstract class, you will receive a compiler error message.

Abstract classes are like regular classes in that they can contain data fields and methods. The difference is that you cannot create instances of abstract classes by using the `new` operator. Rather, you create abstract classes simply to provide a base class from which other objects can be derived.

Abstract classes usually contain abstract methods, and they also can contain nonabstract methods. However, they are not required to contain any methods. Recall from Chapter 9 that an abstract method has no statements. Any class derived from a class that contains an abstract method must override the abstract method by providing a body (an implementation) for it. (Alternatively, the derived class can declare the method to be abstract; in that case, the derived class's children must implement the method.) You can create an `abstract` class with no `abstract` methods, but you cannot create an `abstract` method outside of an `abstract` class.

A method that is declared `virtual` is not required to be overridden in a child class, but a method declared `abstract` must be overridden.

When you create an abstract method, you provide the keyword `abstract` and the intended method type, name, and parameters, but you do not provide statements within the method; you do not even supply curly braces. When you create a derived class that inherits an abstract method from a parent, you must use the keyword **override** in the method header and provide the actions, or implementation, for the inherited method within the derived class. In other words, you are required to code a derived class method to override any empty base class methods that are inherited.

For example, suppose that you want to create classes to represent different animals. You can create a generic, abstract class named `Animal` so you can provide generic data fields, such as the animal's name, only once. An `Animal` is generic, but each specific `Animal`, such as `Dog` or `Cat`, makes a unique sound. If you code an abstract `Speak()` method in the abstract `Animal` class, then you require all future `Animal` derived classes to override the `Speak()` method and provide an implementation that is specific to the derived class. Figure 10-31 shows an abstract `Animal` class that contains a data field for the name, a constructor that assigns a name, a `Name` property, and an abstract `Speak()` method.

CHAPTER 10 Introduction to Inheritance

```
abstract class Animal
{
   private string name;
   public Animal (string name)
   {
      this.name = name;
   }
   public string Name
   {
      get
      {
         return name;
      }
   }
   public abstract string Speak();
}
```

Figure 10-31 The Animal class

The Animal class in Figure 10-31 is declared to be abstract. (The keyword is shaded.) You cannot place a statement such as Animal myPet = new Animal("Murphy"); within a program, because the program will not compile. Because Animal is an abstract class, no Animal objects can exist.

You create an abstract class like Animal so that you can extend it. For example, you can create Dog and Cat classes as shown in Figure 10-32. Because the Animal class contains a constructor that requires a string argument, both Dog and Cat must contain constructors that provide string arguments for their base class.

```
class Dog : Animal
{
   public Dog(string name) : base(name)
   {
   }
   public override string Speak()
   {
      return "woof";
   }
}
class Cat : Animal
{
   public Cat(string name) : base(name)
   {
   }
   public override string Speak()
   {
      return "meow";
   }
}
```

Figure 10-32 The Dog and Cat classes

Creating and Using Abstract Classes

 If a method that should be overridden in a child class has its own implementation, you declare the base class method to be `virtual`. If it does not have its own implementation, you declare the base class and the method to be `abstract`.

The `Dog` and `Cat` constructors perform no tasks other than passing out the name to the `Animal` constructor. The overriding `Speak()` methods within `Dog` and `Cat` are required because the `abstract` parent `Animal` class contains an `abstract Speak()` method. The keyword `override` (shaded) is required in each `Speak()` method header. You can code any statements you want within the `Dog` and `Cat` class `Speak()` methods, but the methods must exist.

Figure 10-33 shows a program that implements `Dog` and `Cat` objects. Figure 10-34 shows the output, in which `Speak()` operates correctly for each animal type.

```
using static System.Console;
class DemoAnimals
{
   static void Main()
   {
      Dog spot = new Dog("Spot");
      Cat puff = new Cat("Puff");
      WriteLine(spot.Name + " says " + spot.Speak());
      WriteLine(puff.Name + " says " + puff.Speak());
   }
}
```

Figure 10-33 The DemoAnimals program

Figure 10-34 Output of the DemoAnimals program

Figure 10-35 shows an alternate way to create the DemoAnimals program. In this version, the `Dog` and `Cat` objects are passed to a method that accepts an `Animal` parameter. The output is the same as in Figure 10-34. The `Name` property and `Speak()` method operate polymorphically, acting appropriately for each object type.

CHAPTER 10 Introduction to Inheritance

```
using static System.Console;
class DemoAnimals2
{
    static void Main()
    {
        Dog Spot = new Dog("Spot");
        Cat puff = new Cat("Puff");
        DisplayAnimal(spot);
        DisplayAnimal(puff);
    }
    public static void DisplayAnimal(Animal creature)
    {
        WriteLine(creature.Name + " says " + creature.Speak());
    }
}
```

Figure 10-35 The DemoAnimals2 program

TWO TRUTHS & A LIE

Creating and Using Abstract Classes

1. An abstract class is one from which you cannot create concrete objects.

2. Unlike regular classes, abstract classes cannot contain methods.

3. When a base class contains an abstract method, the descendants of the base class must override the abstract method or declare the overriding method to be abstract.

The false statement is #2. Abstract classes are like regular classes in that they can contain data fields and methods. The difference is that you cannot create instances of abstract classes by using the new operator. Rather, you create abstract classes simply to provide a base class from which other objects may be derived.

Creating and Using Interfaces

Some object-oriented programming languages, notably C++, allow a subclass to inherit from more than one parent class. For example, you might create an Employee class that contains data fields pertaining to each employee in your organization. You also might create a Product class that holds information about each product your organization manufactures. When you create a Patent class for each product for which your company holds a patent, you might want to include product information as well as information about the employee who was responsible for the invention. In this situation, it would be convenient to inherit fields and methods from both the Product and Employee classes. The ability to inherit from more than one class is called **multiple inheritance**.

Multiple inheritance is a difficult concept, and programmers encounter many problems when they use it. For example, variables and methods in the parent classes might have identical names, creating a conflict when the child class uses one of the names. Additionally, as you already have learned, a child class constructor must call its parent class constructor. When two or more parents exist, this becomes a more complicated task: To which class should base refer when a child class has multiple parents?

For all of these reasons, multiple inheritance is prohibited in C#. However, C# does provide an alternative to multiple inheritance, known as an interface. Much like an abstract class, an **interface** is a collection of methods (and perhaps other members) that can be used by any class as long as the class provides a definition to override the interface's abstract definitions. Within an abstract class, some methods can be abstract, while others need not be. Within an interface, all methods are abstract.

You first learned about interfaces in the chapter "Using Classes and Objects" when you used the IComparable interface.

You create an interface much as you create an abstract class definition, except that you use the keyword interface instead of abstract class. For example, suppose that you create an IWorkable interface as shown in Figure 10-36. For simplicity, the IWorkable interface contains a single method named Work().

```
public interface IWorkable
{
    string Work();
}
```

Figure 10-36 The IWorkable interface

Although not required, in C# it is customary to start interface names with an uppercase *I*. Other languages follow different conventions. Interface names frequently end with *able*.

When any class implements IWorkable, it also must include a Work() method that returns a string. Figure 10-37 shows two classes that implement IWorkable: the Employee class and the Animal class. Because each implements IWorkable, each must declare a Work() method. The Employee class implements Work() to return the *I do my job* string. The abstract Animal class defines Work() as an abstract method, meaning that descendants of Animal must implement Work(). Figure 10-37 also shows two child classes of Animal: Dog and Cat. Note how Work() is defined differently for each.

```
class Employee : IWorkable
{
    public Employee(string name)
    {
        Name = name;
    }
    public string Name {get; set;}
    public string Work()
    {
        return "I do my job";
    }
}
abstract class Animal : IWorkable
{
    public Animal(string name)
    {
        Name = name;
    }
    public string Name {get; set;}
    public abstract string Work();
}
class Dog : Animal
{
    public Dog(string name) : base(name)
    {
    }
    public override string Work()
    {
        return "I watch the house";
    }
}
class Cat : Animal
{
    public Cat(string name) : base(name)
    {
    }
    public override string Work()
    {
        return "I catch mice";
    }
}
```

Figure 10-37 The Employee, Animal, Cat, and Dog classes with the IWorkable interface

When you create a program that instantiates an Employee, a Dog, or a Cat, as in the DemoWorking program in Figure 10-38, each object type knows how to "Work()" appropriately. Figure 10-39 shows the output.

```
using static System.Console;
class DemoWorking
{
    static void Main()
    {
        Employee bob = new Employee("Bob");
        Dog spot = new Dog("Spot");
        Cat puff = new Cat("Puff");
        WriteLine(bob.Name + " says " + bob.Work());
        WriteLine(spot.Name + " says " + spot.Work());
        WriteLine(puff.Name + " says " + puff.Work());
    }
}
```

Figure 10-38 The DemoWorking program

```
Bob says I do my job
Spot says I watch the house
Puff says I catch mice
```

Figure 10-39 Output of the DemoWorking program

Abstract classes and interfaces are similar in that you cannot instantiate concrete objects from either one. Abstract classes differ from interfaces in that abstract classes can contain nonabstract methods, but all methods within an interface must be abstract. A class can inherit from only one base class (whether abstract or not), but it can implement any number of interfaces. For example, if you want to create a Child that inherits from a Parent class and implements two interfaces, IWorkable and IPlayable, you would define the class name and list the base class and interfaces separated by commas:

`class Child : Parent, IWorkable, IPlayable`

You implement an existing interface because you want a class to be able to use a method that already exists in other applications. For example, suppose that you have created a Payroll application that uses the Work() method in the interface class. Also suppose that you create a new class named BusDriver. If BusDriver implements the IWorkable interface, then BusDriver objects can be used by the existing Payroll program. As another example, suppose that you have written a game program that uses an IAttackable interface with methods that determine how and when an object can attack. When you create new classes such as MarsAlien, Vampire, and CivilWarSoldier, and each implements the IAttackable interface, you must define how each one attacks and how each type of object can be added to the game. If you use these IAttackable classes, you are guaranteed that they can all determine how and when to attack.

You can think of an interface as a contract. A class that implements an interface must abide by the rules of the contract.

Beginning programmers sometimes find it difficult to decide when to create an abstract base class and when to create an interface. You can follow these guidelines:

- Typically, you create an abstract class when you want to provide some data or methods that derived classes can inherit, but you want the subclasses to override some specific methods that you declare to be `abstract`.
- You create an interface when you want derived classes to override every method.

In other words, you inherit from an abstract base class when the class you want to create "is a" subtype, and you use an interface when the class you want to create will act like the interface.

Interfaces provide you with a way to exhibit polymorphic behavior. If diverse classes implement the same interface in unique ways, then you can treat each class type in the same way using the same language. When various classes use the same interface, you know the names of the methods that are available with those classes, and C# classes adopt a more uniform functionality; this consistency helps you to understand new classes you encounter more easily. If you know, for example, the method names contained in the `IWorkable` interface, and you see that a class implements `IWorkable`, you have a head start in understanding how the class functions.

Now that you understand how to construct your own interfaces, you will benefit from rereading the section describing the `IComparable` interface in the chapter "Using Classes and Objects."

TWO TRUTHS & A LIE

Creating and Using Interfaces

1. An interface is a collection of methods (and perhaps other members) that can be used by any class as long as the class provides a definition to override the interface's abstract definitions.

2. Abstract classes and interfaces differ in that all methods in abstract classes must be abstract, but interfaces can contain nonabstract methods.

3. A class can inherit from only one base class, but it can implement any number of interfaces.

The false statement is #2. Abstract classes and interfaces are similar in that you cannot instantiate concrete objects from either one. However, they differ in that abstract classes can contain nonabstract methods, but all methods within an interface must be abstract.

Using Extension Methods

When you write a C# program, sometimes you might wish a class had an additional method that would be useful to you. If you created the original class, you have two options:

- You could revise the existing class, including the new useful method.
- You could derive a child class from the existing class and provide it with a new method.

Sometimes, however, classes you use were created by others, and you might not be allowed to either revise or extend them. Of course, you could create an entirely new class that includes your new method, but that would duplicate a lot of the work already done when the first class was created. In these cases, the best option is to write an extension method. **Extension methods** are methods you can write to add to any type. Extension methods were introduced in C# 3.0.

Programmers sometimes define classes as sealed within the class header, as in `sealed class InventoryItem`. A **sealed class** cannot be extended. For example, the built-in `String` class is a sealed class.

For example, you have used the prewritten `Int32` class throughout this book to declare integers. Suppose that you work for a company that frequently uses customer account numbers, and that the company has decided to add an extra digit to each account number. For simplicity, assume that all account numbers are two digits and that the new, third digit should be the rightmost digit in the sum of the first two digits. You could handle this problem by creating a class named `AccountNumber`, including a method to produce the extra digit, and redefining every instance of a customer's account number in your applications as an `AccountNumber` object. However, if you already have many applications that define the account number as an integer, you might prefer to create an extension method that extends the `Int32` class.

In Chapter 2 you learned that each C# intrinsic type, such as `int`, is an alias for a class in the `System` namespace, such as `Int32`.

When organizations append extra digits to account numbers, the extra digits are called check digits. *Check digits* help assure that all the digits in account numbers and other numbers are entered correctly. Check digits are calculated using different formulas. If a digit used to calculate the check digit is incorrect, then the resulting check digit is probably incorrect as well.

Figure 10-40 contains a method that extends the `Int32` class. The first parameter in an extension method specifies the type extended and must begin with the keyword `this`. For example, the first (and in this case, only) parameter in the `AddCheckDigit()` method is `this int num`, as shown in the shaded portion of the figure. Within the `AddCheckDigit()` method in Figure 10-40, the first digit is extracted from the two-digit account number by dividing by 10 and taking the resulting whole number, and the second digit is extracted by taking the remainder. Those two digits are added, and the last digit of that sum is returned from the

```
public static int AddCheckDigit(this int num)
{
   int first = num / 10;
   int second = num % 10;
   int third = (first + second) % 10;
   int result = num * 10 + third;
   return result;
}
```

Figure 10-40 The AddCheckDigit() extension method

method. For example, if 49 is passed into the method, `first` becomes 4, `second` becomes 9, and `third` becomes the last digit of 13, or 3. Then the original number (49) is multiplied by 10 and added to the third digit, resulting in 493.

An extension method must be static and must be stored in a static class. For example, the DemoExtensionMethod program in Figure 10-41 shows an application that is declared `static` in the shaded portion of the class header and uses the extension method in the second shaded statement. The static method `AddCheckDigit()` is used as if it were an instance method of the `Int32` class; in other words, it is attached to an `Int32` object with a dot, just as instance methods are when used with objects. No arguments are passed to the `AddCheckDigit()`

```
using static System.Console;
static class DemoExtensionMethod
{
   static void Main()
   {
      int acctNum = 49;
      int revisedAcctNum = acctNum.AddCheckDigit();
      WriteLine("Original account number was {0}", acctNum);
      WriteLine("Revised account number is {0}", revisedAcctNum);
   }
   public static int AddCheckDigit(this int num)
   {
      int first = num / 10;
      int second = num % 10;
      int third = (first + second) % 10;
      int result = num * 10 + third;
      return result;
   }
}
```

Figure 10-41 The DemoExtensionMethod program

method explicitly from the DemoExtensionMethod class. The parameter in the method is implied, just as these references are always implied in instance methods. Figure 10-42 shows the execution of the program.

```
Original account number was 49
Revised account number is 493
```

Figure 10-42 Execution of the DemoExtensionMethod program

You can create extension methods for your own classes in the same way one was created for the Int32 class in this example. Just like other outside methods, and unlike ordinary class instance methods, extension methods cannot access any private members of classes they extend. Furthermore, if a class contains an instance method with the same signature as an extension method, the instance method takes priority and will be the one that executes.

> **TWO TRUTHS & A LIE**
>
> **Using Extension Methods**
>
> 1. The first parameter in an extension method specifies the type extended and must be preceded by the keyword this.
> 2. Extension methods must be static methods.
> 3. When you write an extension method, it must be stored within the class to which it refers, along with the class's other instance methods.
>
> The false statement is #3. Although you use an extension method like an instance method, any extension method you write must be stored in a static class.

Recognizing Inheritance in GUI Applications

When you create a Windows Forms application using Visual Studio's IDE, you automatically use inheritance. Every Form you create is a descendent of the Form class. Figure 10-43 shows a just-started project in which the programmer has double-clicked the automatically generated Form to expose the code. You can see that the automatically generated Form1 class extends Form.

CHAPTER 10 Introduction to Inheritance

Figure 10-43   Automatically generated Form code in the IDE

The Form class descends from the Object class like all other C# classes but not directly. It is six generations removed from the Object class in the following line of descent:

- Object
- MarshalByRefObject
- Component
- Control
- ScrollableControl
- ContainerControl
- Form

Other GUI objects such as Labels and Buttons follow similar lengthy ancestry lines. You might guess that certain universal properties of GUI controls such as Text and Visible are inherited from ancestors. You will learn more about these hierarchies in the chapter

Recognizing Inheritance in GUI Applications

"Using Controls," but even though you have worked with only a few controls so far, you can understand the benefits inheritance provides, for both GUI and non-GUI classes.

When an automobile company designs a new car model, it does not build every component from scratch. The car might include a new feature—for example, some model contained the first air bag—but many of a new car's features are simply modifications of existing features. The manufacturer might create a larger gas tank or a more comfortable seat, but these new features still possess many of the properties of their predecessors from older models. Most features of new car models are not even modified; instead, existing components, such as air filters and windshield wipers, are included on the new model without any changes.

Similarly, you can create many computer programs more easily if many of their components are used either "as is" or with slight modifications. Inheritance does not enable you to write any programs that you could not write if inheritance did not exist; you *could* create every part of a program from scratch, but reusing existing classes and interfaces makes your job easier.

You already have used many "as is" classes, such as `Console`, `Int32`, and `String`. Using these classes made it easier to write programs than if you had to invent the classes yourself. Now that you have learned about inheritance, you can extend existing classes as well as just use them. When you create a useful, extendable base class, you and other future programmers gain several advantages:

- Derived class creators save development time because much of the code that is needed for the class already has been written.
- Derived class creators save testing time because the base class code already has been tested and probably used in a variety of situations. In other words, the base class code is reliable.
- Programmers who create or use new derived classes already understand how the base class works, so the time it takes to learn the new class features is reduced.
- When you create a derived class in C#, the base class source code is not changed. Thus, the base class maintains its integrity.

Classes that are not intended to be instantiated and that contain only `static` members are declared as `static` classes. You cannot extend `static` classes. For example, `System.Console` is a static class.

When you think about classes, you need to think about the commonalities between them, and then you can create base classes from which to inherit. You might even be rewarded professionally when you see your own superclasses extended by others in the future.

> **TWO TRUTHS & A LIE**
>
> **Recognizing Inheritance in GUI Applications**
>
> 1. Inheritance enables you to create powerful computer programs more easily.
>
> 2. Without inheritance, you could create every part of a program from scratch, but reusing existing classes and interfaces makes your job easier.
>
> 3. Inheritance is frequently inefficient because base class code is seldom reliable when extended to a derived class.
>
> The false statement is #3. Derived class creators save testing time because the base class code already has been tested and probably used in a variety of situations. In other words, the base class code is reliable.

Chapter Summary

- The classes you create in object-oriented programming languages can inherit data and methods from existing classes. The ability to use inheritance makes programs easier to write, easier to understand, and less prone to errors. A class that is used as a basis for inheritance is called a base class, superclass, or parent class. When you create a class that inherits from a base class, it is called a derived class, extended class, subclass, or child class.

- When you create a class that is an extension or child of another class, you use a single colon between the derived class name and its base class name. The child class inherits all the methods, properties, and fields of its parent. Inheritance works only in one direction—a child inherits from a parent, but not the other way around.

- If you could use private data outside of its class, the principle of information hiding would be destroyed. However, when you must access parent class data from a derived class, you declare parent class fields using the keyword `protected`, which provides you with an intermediate level of security between `public` and `private` access.

- When you declare a child class method with the same name and parameter list as a method within its parent class, you override the parent class method and allow your class objects to exhibit polymorphic behavior. You can use the keyword `new` or `override` with the derived class method. When a derived class overrides a parent class member but you want to access the parent class version, you can use the keyword `base`.

- Every derived class object "is a" specific instance of both the derived class and the base class. Therefore, you can assign a derived class object to an object of any of its base class types. When you do so, C# makes an implicit conversion from derived class to base class.
- Every class you create in C# derives from a single class named `System.Object`. Because all classes inherit from the `Object` class, all classes inherit the four `Object` class `public` instance methods: `Equals()`, `GetHashCode()`, `GetType()`, and `ToString()`.
- When you instantiate an object that is a member of a subclass, the base class constructor executes first, and then the derived class constructor executes.
- An abstract class is one from which you cannot create concrete objects but from which you can inherit. Usually, abstract classes contain abstract methods; an abstract method has no method statements. Any class derived from a class that contains an abstract method must override the abstract method by providing a body (an implementation) for it.
- An interface provides an alternative to multiple inheritance. Much like an abstract class, an interface is a collection of methods (and perhaps other members) that can be used by any class as long as the class provides a definition to override the interface's abstract definitions. Within an abstract class, some methods can be abstract, while others need not be. Within an interface, all methods are abstract. A class can inherit from only one abstract base class, but it can implement any number of interfaces.
- Extension methods are methods you can write to add to any type. They are static methods, but they operate like instance methods. Their parameter lists begin with the keyword `this` and the data type being extended.
- GUI classes such as `Button` and `Form` descend from several ancestors. You can create many computer programs more easily using inheritance because it saves development and testing time.

Key Terms

Inheritance is the application of your knowledge of a general category to more specific objects.

A **base class** is a class that is used as a basis for inheritance.

A **derived class** or **extended class** is one that has inherited from a base class.

A **superclass** is a base class.

A **subclass** is a derived class.

A **parent class** is a base class.

A **child class** is a derived class.

The **ancestors** of a derived class are all the superclasses from which the subclass is derived.

Transitive describes the feature of inheritance in which a child inherits all the members of all its ancestors.

Protected access provides an intermediate level of security between public and private access; a `protected` data field or method can be used within its own class or in any classes extended from that class, but it cannot be used by "outside" classes.

Fragile describes classes that depend on field names from parent classes because they are prone to errors—that is, they are easy to "break."

A **virtual method** is one whose behavior is determined by the implementation in a child class.

To **hide** a parent class member is to override it in a derived class.

Visible describes a base class member that is not hidden by a derived class.

Recursive describes a method that calls itself.

An **implicit conversion** occurs when a type is automatically converted to another upon assignment.

An **implicit reference conversion** occurs when a derived class object is assigned to its ancestor's data type.

The **object** (or Object) class type in the `System` namespace is the root base class for all other types.

A **root class** is the first base class in a hierarchal ancestry tree.

Reference equality occurs when two reference type objects refer to the same object.

A **hash code** is a number that should uniquely identify an object.

A **concrete class** is a nonabstract class from which objects can be instantiated.

An **abstract class** is one from which you cannot create concrete objects but from which you can inherit.

The keyword **override** is used in method headers when you create a derived class that inherits an abstract method from a parent.

Multiple inheritance is the ability to inherit from more than one class.

An **interface** is a collection of abstract methods (and perhaps other members) that can be used by any class as long as the class provides a definition to override the interface's abstract definitions.

Extension methods are static methods that act like instance methods. You can write extension methods to add to any type.

A **sealed class** cannot be extended.

Review Questions

1. Specific types of objects assume features of more general classes through _____.
   - a. polymorphism
   - b. inheritance
   - c. encapsulation
   - d. structure

2. Which of the following is *not* a benefit of using inheritance when creating a new class?
   - a. You save computer memory because when you create objects of the new class, storage is not required for parent class fields.
   - b. You reduce the chance of errors, because the parent class methods have already been used and tested.
   - c. You make it easier for anyone who has used the parent class to understand the new class because the programmer can concentrate on the new features.
   - d. You save time, because you need not create fields and methods that already exist in a parent class.

3. A child class is also called a(n) _____.
   - a. extended class
   - b. base class
   - c. superclass
   - d. delineated class

4. Assuming that the following classes are well named, which of the following is a parent class of `House`?
   - a. `Apartment`
   - b. `VictorianHouse`
   - c. `Building`
   - d. `myHouse`

5. A derived class usually contains _____ than its parent.
   - a. more fields and methods
   - b. the same number of fields but fewer methods
   - c. fewer fields but more methods
   - d. fewer fields and methods

6. When you create a class that is an extension or child of another class, you use a(n) _____ between the derived class name and its base class name.
   - a. ampersand
   - b. hyphen
   - c. dot
   - d. colon

CHAPTER 10 Introduction to Inheritance

7. A base class named `Garden` contains a private field `width` and a property `public int Width` that contains `get` and `set` accessors. A child class named `VegetableGarden` does not contain a `Width` property. When you write a class in which you declare an object as follows, what statement can you use to access the `VegetableGarden`'s `width`?

   `VegetableGarden myGarden = new VegetableGarden();`

   a. `myGarden.Width`

   b. `myGarden.base.Width`

   c. `VegetableGarden.Width`

   d. You cannot use `Width` with a `VegetableGarden` object.

8. When a parent class contains a `private` data field, the field is _____ the child class.

   a. hidden in
   b. not a member of
   c. directly accessible in
   d. `public` in

9. When a base class and a derived class contain a method with the same name and parameter list, and you call the method using a derived class object, _____.

   a. you receive an error message
   b. the base class version overrides the derived class version
   c. the derived class version overrides the base class version
   d. both method versions execute

10. Which of the following is an English-language form of polymorphism?

    a. seeing a therapist and seeing the point
    b. moving friends with a compelling story and moving friends to a new apartment
    c. both of these
    d. neither of these

11. When base and derived classes contain a method with the same name and parameter list, you can use the base class method within the derived class by using the keyword _____ before the method name.

    a. `new`
    b. `override`
    c. `base`
    d. `super`

Review Questions

12. In a program that declares a derived class object, you _____ assign it to an object of its base class type.

    a. can
    b. cannot
    c. must
    d. should not

13. The root base class for all other class types is _____.

    a. `Base`
    b. `Super`
    c. `Parent`
    d. `Object`

14. All of the following are `Object` class methods *except* _____.

    a. `ToString()`
    b. `Equals()`
    c. `Print()`
    d. `GetHashCode()`

15. When you create any derived class object, _____.

    a. the base class and derived class constructors execute simultaneously
    b. the base class constructor must execute first, and then the derived class constructor executes
    c. the derived class constructor must execute first, and then the base class constructor executes
    d. neither the base class constructor nor the derived class constructor executes

16. When a base class constructor requires arguments, then each derived class _____.

    a. must include a constructor
    b. must include a constructor that requires arguments
    c. must include two or more constructors
    d. must not include a constructor

17. When you create an abstract class, _____.

    a. you can inherit from it
    b. you can create concrete objects from it
    c. Both of these are true.
    d. None of these is true.

18. When you create an abstract method, you provide _____.

    a. the keyword `abstract`
    b. curly braces
    c. method statements
    d. all of these

19. Within an interface, _____ .

    a. no methods can be abstract
    b. some methods might be abstract
    c. some, but not all, methods must be abstract
    d. all methods must be abstract

20. Abstract classes and interfaces are similar in that _____ .

    a. you can instantiate concrete objects from both
    b. you cannot instantiate concrete objects from either one
    c. all methods in both must be abstract
    d. neither can contain nonabstract methods

Exercises

Programming Exercises

1. Create an application class named **LetterDemo** that instantiates objects of two classes named Letter and CertifiedLetter and that demonstrates all their methods. The classes are used by a company to keep track of letters they mail to clients. The Letter class includes auto-implemented properties for the name of the recipient and the date mailed. Also, include a ToString() method that overrides the Object class's ToString() method and returns a string that contains the name of the class (using GetType()) and the Letter's data field values. Create a child class named CertifiedLetter that includes an auto-implemented property that holds a tracking number for the letter.

2. Create an application class named **PhotoDemo** that demonstrates the methods of three related classes for a company that develops photographs. Create a class named Photo that includes fields for width and height in inches and properties for each field. Include a protected price field, and set it to $3.99 for an 8-inch by 10-inch photo, $5.99 for a 10-inch by 12-inch photo, and $9.99 for any other size (because custom cutting is required). The price field requires a get accessor but no set accessor. Also include a ToString() method that returns a string constructed from the return value of the object's GetType() method and the values of the fields. Derive two subclasses—MattedPhoto and FramedPhoto. The MattedPhoto class includes a string field to hold a color, and the FramedPhoto class includes two string fields that hold the frame's material (such as *silver*) and style (such as *modern*). The price for a MattedPhoto increases by $10 over its base cost, and the price for a FramedPhoto increases by $25 over its base cost. Each subclass should include a ToString() method that overrides the parent class version.

3. a. Create an application named **JobDemo** that declares and uses Job objects. The Job class holds job information for a home repair service. The class has five properties that include a job number, customer name, job description, estimated hours, and price for the job. Create a constructor that requires parameters for all the data except price. Include auto-implemented properties for the job number, customer name, and job description, but not for hours or price; the price field value is calculated as estimated hours times $45.00 whenever the hours value is set. Also create the following for the class:

   - An Equals() method that determines two Jobs are equal if they have the same job number
   - A GetHashCode() method that returns the job number
   - A ToString() method that returns a string containing all job information

   The JobDemo application declares a few Job objects, sets their values, and demonstrates that all the methods work as expected.

   b. Using the Job class you created in Exercise 3a, write a new application named **JobDemo2** that creates an array of five Job objects. Prompt the user for values for each Job. Do not allow duplicate job numbers; force the user to reenter the job when a duplicate job number is entered. When five valid objects have been entered, display them all, plus a total of all prices.

   c. Create a RushJob class that derives from Job. A RushJob has a $150.00 premium that is added to the normal price of the job. Override any methods in the parent class as necessary. Write a new application named **JobDemo3** that creates an array of five RushJobs. Prompt the user for values for each, and do not allow duplicate job numbers. When five valid RushJob objects have been entered, display them all, plus a total of all prices.

   d. Make any necessary modifications to the RushJob class so that it can be sorted by job number. Modify the JobDemo3 application so the displayed orders have been sorted. Save the application as **JobDemo4**.

4. a. Create an application for Nina's Cookie Emporium named **CookieDemo** that declares and demonstrates objects of the CookieOrder class and its descendants. The CookieOrder class includes auto-implemented properties for an order number, recipient's name, and cookie type (for example, *chocolate chip*), and fields for number of dozens ordered and price. When the field value for number of dozens ordered is set, the price field is set as $15 per dozen for the first two dozen and $13 per dozen for each dozen over two.

   b. Create a child class named SpecialCookieOrder, which includes a field with a description as to why the order is special (for example, *gluten-free*). Override the method that sets a CookieOrder's price as described in part a, but also to include special handling, which is $10 for orders up to $40 and $8 for higher-priced orders. Create an application named **CookieDemo2** that demonstrates using several SpecialCookieOrder objects.

5. a. Create an application named **AutomobileDemo** that prompts a user for data for eight Automobile objects. The Automobile class includes auto-implemented properties for ID number, make, year, and price. Override the ToString() method to return all the details for an Automobile. During data entry, reprompt the user if any ID number is a duplicate. Sort the objects in ID number order, and display all their data as well as a total of all their prices.

   b. Using the Automobile class as a base, derive a FinancedAutomobile class that contains all the data of an Automobile, plus fields to hold the amount financed and interest rate. Override the parent class ToString() method to include the child class's additional data. Create a program named **AutomobileDemo2** that contains an array of four FinancedAutomobile objects. Prompt the user for all the necessary data, and do not allow duplicate ID numbers and do not allow the amount financed to be greater than the price of the automobile. Sort all the records in ID number order and display them with a total price for all FinancedAutomobiles and a total amount financed.

   c. Write an application named **AutomobileDemo3** that uses an extension method for the FinancedAutomobile class. The method computes and returns a FinancedAutomobile's monthly payment due (1/24 of the amount financed). The application should allow the user to enter data for four objects and then display all the data for each.

6. Create an application named **ShapesDemo** that creates several objects that descend from an abstract class called GeometricFigure. Each GeometricFigure includes a height, a width, and an area. Provide get and set accessors for each field except area; the area is computed and is read-only. Include an abstract method called ComputeArea() that computes the area of the GeometricFigure. Create three additional classes:

   - A Rectangle is a GeometricFigure whose area is determined by multiplying width by height.
   - A Square is a Rectangle in which the width and height are the same. Provide a constructor that accepts both height and width, forcing them to be equal if they are not. Provide a second constructor that accepts just one dimension and uses it for both height and width. The Square class uses the Rectangle's ComputeArea() method.
   - A Triangle is a GeometricFigure whose area is determined by multiplying the width by half the height.

   In the ShapesDemo class, after each object is created, pass it to a method that accepts a GeometricFigure argument in which the figure's data is displayed. Change some dimensions of some of the figures, and pass each to the display method again.

7. Create an application named **RecoveringDemo** that declares objects of three types: Patient, Upholsterer, and FootballPlayer. Create an interface named IRecoverable that contains a single method named Recover(). Create the classes named Patient, Upholsterer, and FootballPlayer so that each implements IRecoverable. Create each class's Recover() method to display an appropriate message. For example, the Patient's Recover() method might display "I am getting better."

8. Create an application named **TurningDemo** that creates instances of four classes: Page, Corner, Pancake, and Leaf. Create an interface named ITurnable that contains a single method named Turn(). The classes named Page, Corner, Pancake, and Leaf implement ITurnable. Create each class's Turn() method to display an appropriate message. For example, the Page's Turn() method might display "You turn a page in a book."

9. Write a program named **SalespersonDemo** that instantiates objects using classes named RealEstateSalesperson and GirlScout. Demonstrate that each object can use a SalesSpeech() method appropriately. Also, use a MakeSale() method two or three times with each object, and display the final contents of each object's data fields. First, create an abstract class named Salesperson. Fields include first and last names; the Salesperson constructor requires both these values. Include properties for the fields. Include a method that returns a string that holds the Salesperson's full name—the first and last names separated by a space. Then perform the following tasks:

   - Create two child classes of Salesperson: RealEstateSalesperson and GirlScout. The RealEstateSalesperson class contains fields for total value sold in dollars and total commission earned (both of which are initialized to 0), and a commission rate field required by the class constructor. The GirlScout class includes a field to hold the number of boxes of cookies sold, which is initialized to 0. Include properties for every field.

   - Create an interface named ISellable that contains two methods: SalesSpeech() and MakeSale(). In each RealEstateSalesperson and GirlScout class, implement SalesSpeech() to display an appropriate one- or two-sentence sales speech that the objects of the class could use.

   In the RealEstateSalesperson class, implement the MakeSale() method to accept an integer dollar value for a house, add the value to the RealEstateSalesperson's total value sold, and compute the total commission earned. In the GirlScout class, implement the MakeSale() method to accept an integer representing the number of boxes of cookies sold and add it to the total field.

CHAPTER 10 Introduction to Inheritance

Debugging Exercises

1. Each of the following files in the Chapter.10 folder of your downloadable student files has syntax and/or logical errors. In each case, determine the problem and fix the program. After you correct the errors, save each file using the same filename preceded with *Fixed*. For example, DebugTen01.cs will become FixedDebugTen01.cs.

   a. DebugTen01.cs
   b. DebugTen02.cs
   c. DebugTen03.cs
   d. DebugTen04.cs

Case Problems

1. In Chapter 9, you created a `Contestant` class for the Greenville Idol competition. The class includes a contestant's name, talent code, and talent description. The competition has become so popular that separate contests with differing entry fees have been established for children, teenagers, and adults. Modify the `Contestant` class to contain a field that holds the entry fee for each category, and add `get` and `set` accessors.

   Extend the `Contestant` class to create three subclasses: `ChildContestant`, `TeenContestant`, and `AdultContestant`. Child contestants are 12 years old and younger, and their entry fee is $15. Teen contestants are between 13 and 17 years old, inclusive, and their entry fee is $20. Adult contestants are 18 years old and older, and their entry fee is $30. In each subclass, set the entry fee field to the correct value, and override the `ToString()` method to return a string that includes all the contestant data, including the age category and the entry fee.

   Modify the **GreenvilleRevenue** program so that it performs the following tasks:

   - The program prompts the user for the number of contestants in this year's competition, which must be between 0 and 30. The program continues to prompt the user until a valid value is entered.
   - The program prompts the user for names, ages, and talent codes for the contestants entered. Along with the prompt for a talent code, display a list of valid categories. Based on the age entered for each contestant, create an object of the correct type (adult, teen, or child), and store it in an array of `Contestant` objects.
   - After data entry is complete, display the total expected revenue, which is the sum of the entry fees for the contestants.
   - After data entry is complete, display the valid talent categories and then continuously prompt the user for talent codes, and display all the data for all the contestants in each category. Display an appropriate message if the entered code is not a character or a valid code.

2. In Chapter 9, you created a `Mural` class for Marshall's Murals. The class holds a customer's name, a mural code, and a description. Now, add a field to the `Mural` class that holds a price. Extend the `Mural` class to create subclasses named `InteriorMural` and `ExteriorMural`, and place statements that determine a mural's price within these classes. (A mural's price depends on the month, as described in the case problem in Chapter 9.) Also create `ToString()` methods for these subclasses that return a string containing all the pertinent data for a mural.

   Modify the **MarshallsRevenue** program so that it performs the following tasks:

   - The program prompts the user for the month, the number of interior murals scheduled, and the number of exterior murals scheduled. In each case, the program continues to prompt the user until valid entries are made.
   - The program prompts the user for customer names and mural codes for interior and exterior murals. Along with the prompt for a mural code, display a list of valid categories.
   - After data entry is complete, display the total revenue of interior murals, exterior murals, and all murals.
   - After data entry is complete, the program displays the valid mural categories and then continuously prompts the user for codes and uses the `ToString()` method to display all the details for the murals in each category. Appropriate messages are displayed if the entered code is not a character or a valid code.

CHAPTER 11

Exception Handling

Upon completion of this chapter, you will be able to:

- ◎ Describe exceptions, the Exception class, and SystemExceptions

- ◎ Compare traditional and object-oriented error-handling methods

- ◎ Use the Exception class's ToString() method and Message property

- ◎ Catch multiple exceptions

- ◎ Describe the structure of the TryParse() methods

- ◎ Use the finally block

- ◎ Handle exceptions thrown from outside methods

- ◎ Trace Exception objects through the call stack

- ◎ Create your own Exception classes

- ◎ Rethrow Exceptions

CHAPTER 11 Exception Handling

While visiting websites, you probably have seen an unexpected and cryptic message that announces an error and then shuts down your browser immediately. Perhaps something similar has happened to you while using a piece of application software. Certainly, if you have worked your way through all of the programming exercises in this book, you have encountered such errors while running your own programs. A program that just stops is aggravating, especially when you lose data, and the error message seems to indicate that the program "knows" what is causing the problem. You might grumble, "If the program knows what is wrong, why doesn't it just fix the problem?" In this chapter, you will learn how to handle these unexpected error conditions so your programs can be more user-friendly than those that simply shut down in the face of errors.

Understanding Exceptions

An **exception** is any error condition or unexpected behavior in an executing program. Exceptions are caused by errors in program logic or insufficient system resources. The programs you write can generate many types of potential exceptions, including when:

- Your program asks for user input, but the user enters invalid data.
- The program attempts to divide an integer by zero.
- You attempt to access an array with a subscript that is too large or too small.
- You calculate a value that is out of range for the answer's variable type.

These errors are called exceptions because presumably they are not usual occurrences; they are "exceptional." The object-oriented techniques used to manage such errors make up the group of methods known as **exception handling**. If you do not handle an exception, the running program terminates abruptly.

Managing exceptions involves an oxymoron; you must expect the unexpected.

Errors you discover when compiling a program are not exceptions; they are compiler errors. Only execution-time (also called *runtime*) errors are called exceptions.

In C#, all exceptions are objects that are instances of the Exception class or one of its derived classes. An exception condition generates an object that encapsulates information about the error. Like all other classes in the C# programming language, the Exception class is a descendant of the Object class. The Exception class has several descendant classes of its own, many with unusual names such as CodeDomSerializerException, SUDSParserException, and SoapException. Others have names that are more easily understood, such as IOException (for input and output errors), InvalidPrinterException (for when a user requests an invalid printer), and PathTooLongException (used when the path to a file contains more characters than a system allows). C# has more than 100 defined Exception subclasses; Table 11-1 lists just a few to give you an idea of the wide variety of circumstances they cover.

Class	Description
System.ArgumentException	Thrown when one of the arguments provided to a method is not valid
System.ArithmeticException	Thrown for errors in an arithmetic, casting, or conversion operation
System.ArrayTypeMismatchException	Thrown when an attempt is made to store an element of the wrong type within an array
System.Data.OperationAbortedException	Thrown when an ongoing operation is aborted by the user
System.Drawing.Printing.InvalidPrinterException	Thrown when you try to access a printer using printer settings that are not valid
System.FormatException	Thrown when the format of an argument does not meet the parameter specifications of the invoked method
System.IndexOutOfRangeException	Thrown when an attempt is made to access an element of an array with an index that is outside the bounds of the array; this class cannot be inherited
System.InvalidCastException	Thrown for an invalid casting or explicit conversion
System.InvalidOperationException	Thrown when a method call is invalid for the object's current state
System.IO.InvalidDataException	Thrown when a data stream is in an invalid format
System.IO.IOException	Thrown when an I/O error occurs
System.MemberAccessException	Thrown when an attempt to access a class member fails
System.NotImplementedException	Thrown when a requested method or operation is not implemented
System.NullReferenceException	Thrown when there is an attempt to dereference a null object reference
System.OperationCanceledException	Thrown in a thread upon cancellation of an operation that the thread was executing
System.OutOfMemoryException	Thrown when there is not enough memory to continue the execution of a program
System.RankException	Thrown when an array with the wrong number of dimensions is passed to a method
System.StackOverflowException	Thrown when the execution stack overflows because it contains too many nested method calls; this class cannot be inherited

Table 11-1 Selected C# Exception subclasses

CHAPTER 11 Exception Handling

Table 11-1 uses the term *thrown*, which is explained later in this chapter.

Most exceptions you will use derive from three classes:

- The predefined Common Language Runtime exception classes derived from `SystemException`
- The user-defined application exception classes you derive from `ApplicationException`
- The `Exception` class, which is the parent of `SystemException` and `ApplicationException`

Microsoft previously advised that you should create your own custom exceptions from the `ApplicationException` class. The company has revised its thinking and now advise that you should use the `Exception` class as a base because in practice, it has not found the previous approach to be of significant value. For updates, visit *http://msdn.microsoft.com*.

Purposely Generating a `SystemException`

You can deliberately generate a `SystemException` by forcing a program to contain an error. As an example, in every programming language, it is illegal to divide an integer by zero because the operation is mathematically undefined. Consider the simple `MilesPerGallon` program in Figure 11-1, which prompts a user for two values and divides the first by the second. If the user enters nonzero integers, the program runs correctly and without incident. However, if the user enters 0 when prompted to enter gallons, division by 0 takes place, and an error is generated. Figure 11-2 shows two executions of the program.

When you divide a floating-point value by 0 in C#, no exception occurs. Instead, C# assigns the special value `Infinity` to the result. Because `float`s and `double`s are imprecise, dividing them by 0.000000 . . . to an infinite number of decimal places approaches infinity mathematically.

Understanding Exceptions

```
using System;
using static System.Console;
class MilesPerGallon
{
   static void Main()
   {
      int milesDriven;
      int gallonsOfGas;
      int mpg;
      Write("Enter miles driven ");
      milesDriven = Convert.ToInt32(ReadLine());
      Write("Enter gallons of gas purchased ");
      gallonsOfGas = Convert.ToInt32(ReadLine());
      mpg = milesDriven / gallonsOfGas;
      WriteLine("You got {0} miles per gallon", mpg);
   }
}
```

Figure 11-1 The MilesPerGallon program

```
Enter miles driven 300
Enter gallons of gas purchased 12
You got 25 miles per gallon
```

```
Enter miles driven 300
Enter gallons of gas purchased 0

Unhandled Exception: System.DivideByZeroException: Attempted to divide by zero.
   at MilesPerGallon.Main()
```

Figure 11-2 Two executions of the MilesPerGallon program

When the user enters a 0 for gallons in the MilesPerGallon program, a dialog box reports that the application has stopped working and needs to close. Because this error is intentional for demonstration purposes, you can ignore the message by clicking the Close program button in the lower-right corner of the dialog box.

In the first execution of the MilesPerGallon program in Figure 11-2, the user entered two usable integers, and division was carried out successfully. However, in the second execution, the user entered 0 for gallons of gas, and the error message indicates that an unhandled exception named System.DivideByZeroException was created. The message gives further information ("Attempted to divide by zero.") and shows the method where the exception occurred—in MilesPerGallon.Main().

The DiviseByZeroException object was generated automatically by C#. It is an instance of the DivideByZeroException class that has four ancestors. It is a child of the ArithmeticException class, which descends from the SystemException class. The SystemException class derives from the Exception class, which is a child of the Object class.

Just because an exception occurs and an Exception object is created, you don't necessarily have to deal with it. In the MilesPerGallon class, you simply let the offending program terminate; that's why the error message in Figure 11-2 indicates that the Exception is "Unhandled." However, the termination of the program is abrupt and unforgiving. When a program divides two numbers, or performs some other trivial task such as playing a game, the user might be annoyed if the program ends abruptly. If the program is used for air-traffic control or to monitor a patient's vital statistics during surgery, an abrupt conclusion could be disastrous. With exception handling, a program can continue after dealing with a problem. This is especially important in mission-critical applications. The term **mission critical** refers to any process that is crucial to an organization. Object-oriented error-handling techniques provide more elegant solutions than simply shutting down.

Programs that can handle exceptions appropriately are said to be more fault tolerant and robust than those that do not. **Fault-tolerant** applications are designed so that they continue to operate, possibly at a reduced level, when some part of the system fails. **Robustness** represents the degree to which a system is resilient to stress, maintaining correct functioning.

Watch the video *System Exceptions*.

TWO TRUTHS & A LIE

Understanding Exceptions

1. An exception is any error condition or unexpected behavior in an executing program.

2. In C#, all exceptions are objects that are members of the Exception class or one of its derived classes.

3. In C#, when an exception occurs and an Exception object is created, you must employ a specific set of exception-handling techniques in order to manage the problem.

The false statement is #3. Just because an exception occurs and an Exception object is created, you don't necessarily have to deal with it.

Understanding Exceptions

 You Do It

Purposely Causing Exceptions

C# generates SystemExceptions automatically under many circumstances. In the next steps, you purposely generate a SystemException by executing a program that provides multiple opportunities for Exceptions.

1. Start a new project named **ExceptionsOnPurpose**, and type the following program, which allows you to generate several different Exceptions.

   ```
   using System;
   using static System.Console;
   class ExceptionsOnPurpose
   {
      static void Main()
      {
         int answer;
         int result;
         int zero = 0;
         Write("Enter an integer >> ");
         answer = Convert.ToInt32(ReadLine());
         result = answer / zero;
         WriteLine("The answer is " + answer);
      }
   }
   ```

2. You cannot divide by the unnamed constant 0 (by changing the dividing statement to result = answer /0;), nor can you change the variable zero to a named constant (by inserting const at the start of the int zero declaration). If you made either of these changes, the program would not compile because the compiler can determine that division by zero will occur. Using a variable zero instead of either an unnamed or named constant, however, the compiler "trusts" that a legitimate value will be provided for the variable before division occurs (although in this case, the trust is not warranted). Save the program, and compile it.

3. Execute the program several times using different input values, and observe the results. Three windows appear with each execution. The first reports that Windows is checking for a solution to the problem, the second reports

(continues)

(continued)

that it is collecting more information about the problem. This window is soon replaced with a third window as shown in Figure 11-3, which repeats that ExceptionsOnPurpose.exe has stopped working. You would never write a program that purposely divides by zero; you do so here to demonstrate C#'s exception-generating capabilities. If you were executing a professional application, you might be notified about a solution. Because you created this exception on purpose, just click the **Close program** button.

Figure 11-3 The error report window generated by an unhandled exception

Figure 11-4 shows three executions of the program during which the user typed the following:

- **seven**—This generates a System.FormatException, which occurs when the program tries to convert the input value to an integer, because letters are not allowed in integers.
- **7.7**—This also generates a System.FormatException because the decimal point is not allowed in an integer.
- **7**—This does not generate a System.FormatException but instead causes a System.DivideByZeroException when the result is calculated.

(continues)

Comparing Traditional and Object-Oriented Error-Handling Methods

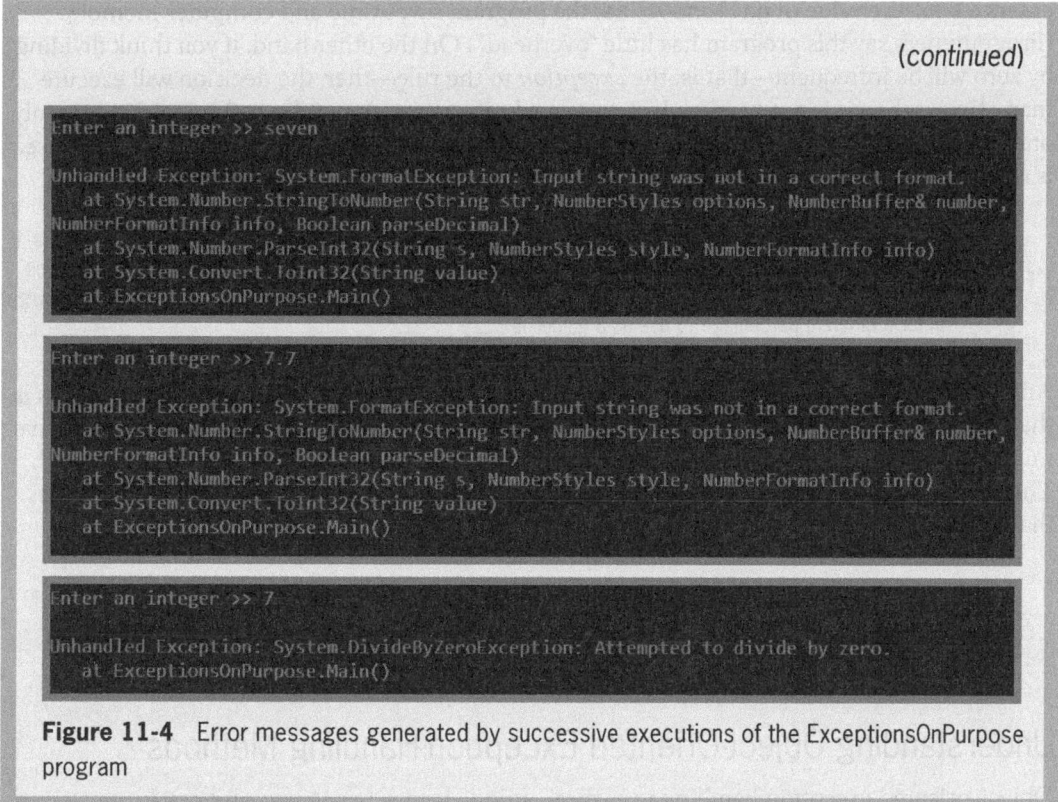

Figure 11-4 Error messages generated by successive executions of the ExceptionsOnPurpose program

Comparing Traditional and Object-Oriented Error-Handling Methods

Programmers had to deal with error conditions long before object-oriented methods were conceived. For example, dividing by zero is an avoidable error for which programmers always have had to plan. If you simply check a variable's value with an if statement before attempting to divide it into another number, you can prevent the creation of an Exception object. For example, the following code uses a traditional if statement to check a variable to prevent division by zero.

```
if(gallonsOfGas != 0)
   mpg = milesDriven / gallonsOfGas;
else
   mpg = 0;
```

This code successfully prevents division by zero, but it does not really "handle an exception" because no Exception class object is created. The example code illustrates a perfectly legal and reasonable method of preventing division by zero, and it represents the most efficient method of handling the error if you think it will be a frequent problem. Because a program that contains this code does not have to instantiate an Exception object every time the user enters a 0 for the value of `gallonsOfGas`, the program saves time and computer memory. (Programmers say this program has little "overhead.") On the other hand, if you think dividing by zero will be infrequent—that is, the *exception* to the rule—then the decision will execute many times when it is not needed. In other words, if a user enters 0 for `gallonsOfGas` in only one case out of 1,000, then the `if` statement is executed unnecessarily 999 times. In that case, it is more efficient to eliminate the `if` test and instantiate an `Exception` object when needed.

The creators of C# define "infrequent" as an event that happens less than 30 percent of the time. That is, if you think an error will occur in less than 30 percent of all program executions, create an exception; if you think the error will occur more often, use traditional error checking. Of course, your boss or instructor might prefer a different percentage to use as a guideline.

Another advantage to using exception handling instead of decision making to control errors is that when a program's main logic is interrupted by a series of `if` statements and decisions that might detect errors, the program can become more complicated and difficult to understand. The object-oriented approach to error handling separates a program's main tasks from code that deals with rare exceptions.

Programmers use the phrase *sunny day case* to describe a scenario in which everything goes well and no errors occur.

Understanding Object-Oriented Exception-Handling Methods

Object-oriented exception handling uses three unique terms: *try*, *throw*, and *catch*.

- You "try" a procedure that may not complete correctly.
- A method that detects an error condition "throws" an exception.
- The block of code that processes the error "catches" the exception.

When you write a block of code in which something can go wrong, you can place the code in a **try block**, which consists of the following elements:

- The keyword `try`
- A pair of curly braces containing statements that might cause exceptions

You must code at least one `catch` block or `finally` block immediately following a `try` block. (You will learn about `finally` blocks later in this chapter.) Each **catch block** can "catch" one type of exception—that is, an `Exception` object or an object of one of its child classes. Programmers sometimes refer to a `catch` block as a *catch clause*. You can create a `catch` block by typing the following elements:

- The keyword `catch`
- Parentheses containing an `Exception` type and, optionally, a name for an instance of the `Exception` type
- A pair of curly braces containing statements that deal with the error condition

Comparing Traditional and Object-Oriented Error-Handling Methods

You also can create a catch block omitting the parentheses and Exception type. If you do, the catch block will execute when any Exception type is thrown. In other words, catch and catch(Exception) are both correct ways to start a catch block to catch all Exceptions when you do not want to name the Exception object because you do not care about displaying its details.

Figure 11-5 shows the general format of a try...catch pair. The placeholder XxxException in the catch block represents the Exception class or any of its more specific subclasses. The placeholder XxxException is the data type of the anExceptionInstance object. A catch block looks a lot like a method named catch(), which takes an argument that is an instance of XxxException. However, it is not a method; you cannot call it directly. A method can accept multiple arguments, but a catch block can catch only one object, and, unlike a method, a catch block has no return type.

As XxxException implies, Exception classes typically are created using Exception as the second half of the name, as in SystemException and ApplicationException. The compiler does not require this naming convention, but the convention does make Exception descendants easier to identify.

```
try
{
   // Any number of statements;
   // some might cause an exception
}
catch(XxxException anExceptionInstance)
{
   // Do something about it
}
// Statements here execute whether there was an exception or not
```

Figure 11-5 General form of a try...catch pair

You can place any number of statements in a try block, including those you know will never throw an exception. However, if any one of the statements you place within a try block does throw an exception, then the statements in the catch block that catches the exception will execute. If no exception occurs within the try block, then the catch block does not execute. Either way, the statements following the catch block execute normally.

For example, Figure 11-6 contains a program in which the statements that prompt for, accept, and use gallonsOfGas are encased in a try block. (The three variable declarations are made before the try block by convention. In this case, mpg must be declared outside the try block to be recognized in the program's final output statement. Recall that a variable declared within a block is local to that block.)

CHAPTER 11 Exception Handling

```
using System;
using static System.Console;
class MilesPerGallon2
{
   static void Main( )
   {
      int milesDriven;
      int gallonsOfGas;
      int mpg;
      try
      {
         Write("Enter miles driven ");
         milesDriven = Convert.ToInt32(ReadLine( ));
         Write("Enter gallons of gas purchased ");
         gallonsOfGas = Convert.ToInt32(ReadLine( ));
         mpg = milesDriven / gallonsOfGas;
      }

      catch(Exception e)
      {
         mpg = 0;
         WriteLine("You attempted to divide by zero!");
      }
      WriteLine("You got {0} miles per gallon", mpg);
   }
}
```

Figure 11-6 The MilesPerGallon2 program

Figure 11-7 shows two executions of the program. In the first execution, a usable value is entered for gallonsOfGas, and the program operates normally, bypassing the catch block. In the second execution, however, the user enters 0 for gallonsOfGas. When division is attempted, an Exception object is automatically created and thrown. The catch block catches the Exception, where it becomes known as e. (The shaded arrow in Figure 11-6 extends from where the exception is created and thrown to where it is caught.) The statements in the catch block set mpg to 0 and display a message. Whether the catch block executes or not, the final WriteLine() statement that follows the catch block's closing curly brace executes.

```
Enter miles driven 250
Enter gallons of gas purchased 11
You got 22 miles per gallon
```

```
Enter miles driven 250
Enter gallons of gas purchased 0
You attempted to divide by zero!
You got 0 miles per gallon
```

Figure 11-7 Two executions of the MilesPerGallon2 program

Comparing Traditional and Object-Oriented Error-Handling Methods

When you compile the program in Figure 11-6, you receive a warning that e is declared but never used. You can declare a variable to hold the thrown Exception object, but you do not want to use it in this example, so you can safely ignore the warning. If you do not want to use the caught Exception object within a catch block, then you do not have to provide an instance name for it. For example, in Figure 11-6, the catch clause could begin as follows:

catch(Exception)

In later examples in this chapter, the Exception object will be used to provide information. In those cases, it is required to have an identifier.

In the MilesPerGallon2 program, you could catch a more specific DivideByZeroException object instead of catching an Exception object. You will employ this technique later in the chapter. Many programmers recommend that you never use the general Exception class in a catch block in a professional program because doing so can hide problems, but in your own programs, you might want to do so for simplicity.

In the application in Figure 11-6, the source of the exception and the catch block reside in the same method. Later in this chapter, you will learn that exceptions and their corresponding catch blocks frequently reside in separate methods.

Watch the video *Throwing and Catching Exceptions*.

TWO TRUTHS & A LIE

Comparing Traditional and Object-Oriented Error-Handling Methods

1. Before object-oriented methods were conceived, programmers had no way of handling unexpected conditions.

2. Using object-oriented techniques, when you write a block of code in which something can go wrong, you can place the code in a try block.

3. If a catch block executes, then an Exception must have been thrown.

The false statement is #1. Programmers had to deal with error conditions long before object-oriented methods were conceived. They typically used decision-making techniques to check for errors.

Using the Exception Class's ToString() Method and Message Property

When the MilesPerGallon2 program displays the error message ("You attempted to divide by zero!"), you actually cannot confirm from the message that division by zero was the source of the error. In reality, any Exception type generated within the try block of the program would be caught by the catch block in the method because the argument in the catch block is a general Exception, which is the parent class to all the Exception subtypes.

Instead of writing your own message, you can use the ToString() method that every Exception object inherits from the Object class. The Exception class overrides ToString() to provide a descriptive error message so a user can receive precise information about the nature of any Exception that is thrown. For example, Figure 11-8 shows a MilesPerGallon3 program. The shaded areas show the only changes from the MilesPerGallon2 program: the name of the class and the message that is displayed when an Exception is thrown. In this example, the ToString() method is used with the caught Exception e. Figure 11-9 shows an execution of the program in which the user enters 0 for gallonsOfGas. You can see in the output that the type of Exception caught is a System.DivideByZeroException.

 You learned about overriding the Object class ToString() method in the chapter "Introduction to Inheritance."

```
using System;
using static System.Console;
class MilesPerGallon3
{
   static void Main()
   {
      int milesDriven;
      int gallonsOfGas;
      int mpg;
      try
      {
         Write("Enter miles driven ");
         milesDriven = Convert.ToInt32(ReadLine());
         Write("Enter gallons of gas purchased ");
         gallonsOfGas = Convert.ToInt32(ReadLine());
         mpg = milesDriven / gallonsOfGas;
      }
```

Figure 11-8 The MilesPerGallon3 program *(continues)*

Using the Exception Class's ToString() Method and Message Property

(continued)

```
      catch(Exception e)
      {
         mpg = 0;
         WriteLine(e.ToString());
      }
      WriteLine("You got {0} miles per gallon", mpg);
   }
}
```

Figure 11-8 The MilesPerGallon3 program

```
Enter miles driven 250
Enter gallons of gas purchased 0
System.DivideByZeroException: Attempted to divide by zero.
   at MilesPerGallon3.Main()
You got 0 miles per gallon
```

Figure 11-9 Execution of the MilesPerGallon3 program

The error message displayed in Figure 11-9 (*System.DivideByZeroException: Attempted to divide by zero.*) is the same message that appeared in Figure 11-2 when you provided no exception handling. Therefore, you can assume that the operating system most likely uses the same ToString() method you can use when displaying information about an Exception object. In the program in which you provided no exception handling, execution simply stopped; in this one, execution continues, and the final output statement is displayed whether the user's input was usable or not. Programmers would say this new version of the program ends more "elegantly."

The Exception class also contains a read-only property named Message that contains useful information about an Exception object. For example, the program in Figure 11-10 contains just two shaded changes from the MilesPerGallon3 program: the class name and the use of the Message property in the statement that displays the error message in the catch block. The program produces the output shown in Figure 11-11. The value of e.Message is a string that is identical to the second part of the value returned by the ToString() method. You can guess that the DivideByZeroException class's ToString() method used in MilesPerGallon3 constructs its string from two parts: the return value of the getType() method (that indicates the name of the class) and the return value from the Message property.

```
using System;
using static System.Console;
class MilesPerGallon4
{
   static void Main()
   {
      int milesDriven;
      int gallonsOfGas;
      int mpg;
      try
      {
         Write("Enter miles driven ");
         milesDriven = Convert.ToInt32(ReadLine());
         Write("Enter gallons of gas purchased ");
         gallonsOfGas = Convert.ToInt32(ReadLine());
         mpg = milesDriven / gallonsOfGas;
      }
      catch(Exception e)
      {
         mpg = 0;
         WriteLine(e.Message);
      }
      WriteLine("You got {0} miles per gallon", mpg);
   }
}
```

Figure 11-10 The MilesPerGallon4 program

```
Enter miles driven 250
Enter gallons of gas purchased 0
Attempted to divide by zero.
You got 0 miles per gallon
```

Figure 11-11 Execution of the MilesPerGallon4 program

Using the Exception Class's ToString() Method and Message Property

TWO TRUTHS & A LIE

Using the Exception Class's ToString() Method and Message Property

1. Any Exception type generated within a try block in a program will be caught by a catch block that has an Exception type argument.

2. The Exception class overrides the Object class Description() method to provide a descriptive error message so a user can receive precise information about the nature of any Exception object that is thrown.

3. The Exception class contains a property named Message that contains useful information about an Exception.

The false statement is #2. The Exception class overrides the Object class ToString() method to provide a descriptive error message so a user can receive precise information about the nature of any Exception that is thrown.

You Do It

Handling Exceptions

You can handle exceptions by placing them in a try block and then catching any exceptions that are thrown from it.

1. Open the **ExceptionsOnPurpose** program if it is not still open. Change the class name to **ExceptionsOnPurpose2**, and immediately save the project as **ExceptionsOnPurpose2**.

2. In the Main() method, after the three variable declarations, enclose the next three statements in a try block as follows:

```
try
{
   Write("Enter an integer >> ");
   answer = Convert.ToInt32(ReadLine());
   result = answer / zero;
}
```

3. Following the try block (but before the WriteLine() statement that displays answer), add a catch block that catches any thrown Exception object and displays its Message property:

(continues)

(continued)

```
catch(Exception e)
{
    WriteLine(e.Message);
}
```

4. Save the program, and compile it. You should receive a compiler error indicating that answer is an unassigned local variable. This error occurs at the last line of the program where answer is displayed. In the first version of this program, no such message appeared. However, now that the assignment to answer is within the try block, the compiler understands that an exception might be thrown, terminating the block before a valid value is assigned to answer. To eliminate this problem, initialize answer at its declaration:

```
int answer = 0;
```

5. Compile and execute the program again. Figure 11-12 shows three executions. The values typed by the user are the same as in Figure 11-4 in the previous "You Do It" section. However, the results are different in several significant ways:

- No error message window appears (as in Figure 11-3).

- The error messages displayed are cleaner and "friendlier" than the automatically generated versions in Figure 11-4.

- The program ends normally in each case, with the answer value displayed in a user-friendly manner.

```
Enter an integer >> seven
Input string was not in a correct format.
The answer is 0
```

```
Enter an integer >> 7.7
Input string was not in a correct format.
The answer is 0
```

```
Enter an integer >> 7
Attempted to divide by zero.
The answer is 7
```

Figure 11-12 Error messages generated by successive executions of the ExceptionsOnPurpose2 program

Catching Multiple Exceptions

You can place as many statements as you need within a `try` block, and you can include as many `catch` blocks as you want to handle different `Exception` types. When a `try` block contains more than one statement, only the first error-generating statement throws an exception. As soon as the exception occurs, the logic transfers to the `catch` block, which leaves the rest of the statements in the `try` block unexecuted.

 The set of `catch` blocks following a `try` block should cover all possible exceptions that the code in the `try` block might encounter. Assuming there is at least one `catch` block, if an exception is thrown without a matching `catch` block, the program will terminate abruptly. (It's OK if there are no `catch` blocks at all if there is a `finally` block, as you will see shortly.)

When an `Exception` object is thrown and multiple `catch` blocks are present, the `catch` blocks are examined in sequence until a match is found. The matching `catch` block then executes, and each remaining `catch` block is bypassed.

For example, consider the program in Figure 11-13. The `Main()` method in the `TwoErrors` class potentially throws two types of `Exceptions`—a `DivideByZeroException` and an `IndexOutOfRangeException`. (An `IndexOutOfRangeException` occurs when an array subscript is not within the allowed range. In the `TwoErrors` program, the array has only three elements, but 13 is used as a subscript.)

```
using System;
using static System.Console;
class TwoErrors
{
   static void Main( )
   {
      int num = 13, denom = 0, result;
      int[ ] array = {22, 33, 44};
      try
      {
         result = num / denom;
         result = array[num];
      }
      catch(DivideByZeroException error)
      {
         WriteLine("In first catch block: ");
         WriteLine(error.Message);
      }
      catch(IndexOutOfRangeException error)
      {
         WriteLine("In second catch block: ");
         WriteLine(error.Message);
      }
   }
}
```

Figure 11-13 The TwoErrors program with two `catch` blocks

The TwoErrors class declares three integers and an integer array with three elements. In the Main() method, the try block executes, and at the first statement within the try block, an exception occurs because the denom in the division problem is zero. The try block is abandoned, and control transfers to the first catch block. Integer division by zero causes a DivideByZeroException, and because the first catch block receives that type of Exception, the message *In first catch block* appears along with the Message value of the Exception object. In this example, the second try statement is never attempted, and the second catch block is skipped. Figure 11-14 shows the output.

```
In first catch block:
Attempted to divide by zero.
```

Figure 11-14 Output of the TwoErrors program

If you reverse the two statements within the try block in the TwoErrors program, the process changes. If you use the try block in Figure 11-15, division by zero does not take place because the invalid array access throws an exception first.

```
using System;
using static System.Console;
class TwoErrors2
{
   static void Main( )
   {
      int num = 13, denom = 0, result;
      int[ ] array = {22, 33, 44};
      try
      {
         result = array[num];
         result = num / denom;
      }
      catch(DivideByZeroException error)
      {
         WriteLine("In first catch block: ");
         WriteLine(error.Message);
      }
      catch(IndexOutOfRangeException error)
      {
         WriteLine("In second catch block: ");
         WriteLine(error.Message);
      }
   }
}
```

Figure 11-15 The TwoErrors2 program

Catching Multiple Exceptions

The first statement within the try block in Figure 11-15 attempts to access element 13 of a three-element array, so the program throws an IndexOutOfRangeException. The try block is abandoned, and the first catch block is examined and found unsuitable because the Exception object is of the wrong type—it is not a DivideByZeroException object. The program logic proceeds to the second catch block, whose IndexOutOfRangeException argument type is a match for the thrown Exception type. The message *In second catch block* and the Exception's Message value are therefore displayed. Figure 11-16 shows the output.

```
In second catch block:
Index was outside the bounds of the array.
```

Figure 11-16 Output of the TwoErrors2 program

Sometimes you want to execute the same code, no matter which Exception type occurs. For example, in each version of the TwoErrors program, each of the two catch blocks displays a unique message. Instead, you might want both the DivideByZeroException catch block and the IndexOutOfRangeException catch block to use the thrown Exception's Message field. Because DivideByZeroException and IndexOutOfRangeException both are subclasses of Exception, you can rewrite the TwoErrors class as shown in Figure 11-17 and include only one Exception catch block that catches any type of Exception.

```csharp
using System;
using static System.Console;
class TwoErrors3
{
    static void Main()
    {
        int num = 13, denom = 0, result;
        int[] array = {22, 33, 44};
        try
        {
            result = array[num];
            result = num / denom;
        }
        catch(Exception error)
        {
            WriteLine(error.Message);
        }
    }
}
```

Figure 11-17 The TwoErrors3 program with one catch block

As an alternative to using a single `catch` block for multiple `Exception` types that require the same action, as in Figure 11-17, you could create the class to have separate `catch` blocks, each of which calls the same error-handling method.

The `catch` block in Figure 11-17 accepts a more generic `Exception` type than might be thrown by either statement in the `try` block, so the generic `catch` block can act as a "catch-all" block. That is, when either a division arithmetic error or an array error occurs, the thrown error is "promoted" to an `Exception` error in the `catch` block. Through inheritance, `DivideByZeroExceptions` and `IndexOutOfRangeExceptions` are `Exceptions`.

As stated earlier, some professional programmers recommend that a `catch` block should not handle general `Exceptions`. They say that if you cannot predict all possible causes of an exception, you should allow the application to terminate instead of handling the exception. Otherwise, it is easier for malicious code to exploit the resulting application state. However, many other professional programmers disagree with this policy. Programmers have called blocks that catch all exceptions *Pokemon blocks* because, like in the popular game, "you just gotta catch 'em all."

Although a block of code can throw any number of exceptions, many developers believe that it is poor style for a block or method to throw more than three or four types. If it does, one of the following conditions might be true:

- Perhaps the code block or method is trying to accomplish too many diverse tasks and should be broken up into smaller blocks or methods.

- Perhaps the `Exception` types thrown are too specific and should be generalized, as they are in the `TwoErrors3` program in Figure 11-17.

When you list multiple `catch` blocks following a `try` block, you must be careful that some `catch` blocks don't become unreachable. **Unreachable** blocks contain statements that can never execute under any circumstances because the program logic "can't get there." Programmers also call unreachable code **dead code**.

For example, if successive `catch` blocks catch an `Exception` followed by a `DivideByZeroException`, then even `DivideByZeroExceptions` will be caught by the `Exception` catch. The second `catch` block, (`DivideByZeroException`) is unreachable because the more general `Exception` catch block is first and in its way, and therefore the class will not compile.

TWO TRUTHS & A LIE

Catching Multiple Exceptions

1. If you try more than one statement in a block, each error-generating statement throws an Exception.

2. You can write catch blocks that catch multiple Exception types.

3. When you list multiple catch blocks following a try block, you must be careful that some catch blocks don't become unreachable.

The false statement is #1. If you try more than one statement in a block, only the first error-generating statement throws an Exception.

 You Do It

Catching Multiple Exception Types

In this section, you instigate multiple outcomes by providing multiple catch blocks for code in a try block.

1. Open the **ExceptionsOnPurpose2** program if it is not still open. Change the class name to **ExceptionsOnPurpose3**, and immediately save the project as **ExceptionsOnPurpose3**.

2. Replace the existing generic catch block with two catch blocks. (The statement that displays the answer still follows these catch blocks.) The first catches any FormatException and displays a short message. The second catches a DivideByZeroException and displays a much longer message.

```
catch(FormatException e)
{
    WriteLine("You did not enter an integer.");
}
catch(DivideByZeroException e)
{
    WriteLine("This is not your fault.");
    WriteLine("You entered the integer correctly.");
    WriteLine("The program divides by zero.");
}
```

(continues)

3. Save the program and compile it. When you execute the program and enter a value that is not an integer, the first catch block executes. When you enter an integer so that the program can proceed to the statement that divides by 0, the second catch block executes. Figure 11-18 shows two typical executions of the program.

```
Enter an integer >> four
You did not enter an integer.
The answer is 0
```

```
Enter an integer >> 4
This is not your fault.
You entered the integer correctly.
The program divides by zero.
The answer is 4
```

Figure 11-18 Error messages generated by successive executions of the ExceptionsOnPurpose3 program

Examining the Structure of the TryParse() Methods

In Chapter 8, you learned about the TryParse() methods that you can use to convert string data to another data type, such as int, double, or bool, without fear of generating an exception. A typical TryParse() statement might be as follows:

```
if(!int.TryParse(inputString, out number))
    number = DEFAULT_VALUE;
```

This statement uses the int version of the TryParse() method. The first argument is the string that you want to convert to a number, and the second argument is an out parameter that receives the result if the conversion is successful or 0 if it is not. Each of the TryParse() methods returns a Boolean value that indicates whether the conversion was successful. In the preceding example, the variable number is assigned a constant DEFAULT_VALUE if the method returns false—that is, if inputString is not an integer.

Suppose that no TryParse() method existed to convert a string to an integer safely. Using what you have learned so far in this chapter, you could now write your own method. The method handles the exception it might generate so that when a client uses the method, the client doesn't have to be concerned with exception handling. Figure 11-19 shows a usable method.

Examining the Structure of the TryParse() Methods

```
public static bool TryParse(string inputString, out int number)
{
   bool wasSuccessful = true;
   try
   {
      number = Convert.ToInt32(inputString);
   }
   catch(FormatException e)
   {
      wasSuccessful = false;
      number = 0;
   }
   return wasSuccessful;
}
```

Figure 11-19 A possible TryParse() method version

The TryParse() method in Figure 11-19 is public so that other classes can use it and static so that no object of its class needs to be instantiated. The method accepts a string and an out parameter that can hold the string's converted value. A bool variable named wasSuccessful is set to true, and then conversion is attempted. If the Convert.ToInt32() method works correctly, the variable number accepts the converted value. However, if a FormatException object is thrown, wasSuccessful is set to false and 0 is assigned to number. Whether an exception is thrown or not, the value of wasSuccessful is returned.

The creators of C# wrote code similar to that in Figure 11-19 when they created the TryParse() method for the Integer class. They may have included some differences—for example, they probably gave their variables different identifiers, and they might have reversed the positions of the statements in the catch block that set the Boolean value and the integer value, but the basic structure of the method must be similar. If no TryParse() method existed, you could write one for yourself, but the method is a convenience that already exists. As you continue to study programming, you might develop a method that would be convenient for others, and you might be rewarded in seeing your method used by other developers.

 Your downloadable Student Data Files contain a program named TestTryParse.cs that can be used to test the TryParse() method.

TWO TRUTHS & A LIE

Examining the Structure of the TryParse() Methods

1. The TryParse() method uses an out parameter.
2. The TryParse() method employs exception handling.
3. The TryParse() method must be used within a try block.

The false statement is #3. The TryParse() method contains a try block, but you don't need to use the method in a try block because it handles its own exception.

Using the finally Block

When you have actions to perform at the end of a try...catch sequence, you can use a **finally block**, which executes whether or not the try block identifies any exceptions. Typically, you use the finally block to perform clean-up tasks that must occur, regardless of whether any errors occurred or were caught. Figure 11-20 shows the format of a try...catch sequence that uses a finally block.

```
try
{
    // Statements that might cause an Exception
}
catch(SomeException anExceptionInstance)
{
    // What to do about it
}
finally
{
    // Statements here execute
    // whether an Exception occurred or not
}
```

Figure 11-20 General form of a try...catch block with a finally block

At first glance, it might seem as though the finally block serves no purpose. When a try block works without error, control passes to the statements that come after the catch block. Additionally, if the try code fails and throws an Exception object that is caught, then the catch block executes, and control again passes to any statements that are coded after the catch block. Therefore, it might seem as though the statements after the catch block always execute, so there is no need to place any statements within a special finally block. However, statements after the catch block might never execute for at least two reasons:

- An Exception for which you did not plan might occur, so it is not caught, and the program terminates.
- The try or catch block might contain a statement that terminates the application.

You can terminate an application with a statement such as Environment.Exit(0);. The Environment.Exit() method is part of the System namespace. It terminates a program and passes the argument (which can be any integer) to the operating system. You also might exit a catch block with a break statement or a return statement. You encountered break statements when you learned about the switch statement, and you learned about return statements when you studied methods.

It is easily possible that a try block might throw an Exception for which you did not provide a catch. After all, exceptions occur all the time without you handling them, as you saw in the first MilesPerGallon program at the beginning of this chapter. In the case of an unhandled exception, program execution stops immediately, sending the error to the operating system for handling and abandoning the current method. Likewise, if the try block contains an exit statement, execution stops immediately. When you include a finally block, you are assured that its enclosed statements will execute before the program is abandoned, even if the method concludes prematurely.

For example, the finally block is used frequently with file input and output to ensure that open files are closed. You will learn more about writing to and reading from data files in a later chapter. For now, however, consider the format shown in Figure 11-21, which represents part of the logic for a typical file-handling program. The catch block was written to catch an IOException, which is the type of Exception automatically generated if there is a problem opening a file, reading data from a file, or writing to a file.

```
try
{
   // Open the file
   // Read the file
   // Place the file data in an array
   // Calculate an average from the data
   // Display the average
}
catch(IOException e)
{
   // Issue an error message
   // Exit
}
finally
{
   // If the file is open, close it
}
```

Figure 11-21 Format of code that tries reading a file and handles an exception

The pseudocode in Figure 11-21 handles any file problems using the catch block. However, because the application uses an array (see the statement *Place the file data in an array*) and performs division (see the comment *Calculate an average...*), an uncaught exception could occur even though the file opened successfully. In such an event, you would want to close the file before proceeding. By using the finally block, you ensure that the file is closed, because the code in the finally block executes before the uncaught exception returns control to the operating system. The code in the finally block executes no matter which of the following outcomes of the try block occurs:

- The try ends normally.

- The try ends abnormally, and the catch executes.

- The try ends abnormally, and the catch does not execute. For example, an exception in the try block might cause the method to end prematurely—perhaps the array is not large enough to hold the data, or calculating the average results in division by 0. These exceptions do not allow the try block to finish, nor do they cause the catch block to execute because the catch block catches only IOExceptions.

- The try ends abnormally, the catch executes, but then the catch ends abnormally because an uncaught exception occurs.

If an application might throw several types of exceptions, you can try some code, catch the possible exception, try some more code, catch the possible exception, and so on. Usually, however, the superior approach is to try all the statements that might throw exceptions, then include all the needed catch blocks and an optional finally block. This is the approach shown in Figure 11-21, and it usually results in logic that is easier to follow.

You often can avoid using a finally block, but you would need repetitious code. For example, instead of using the finally block in the pseudocode in Figure 11-21, you could insert the statement *If the file is open, close it* as both the last statement in the try block and the second-to-last statement in the catch block, just before the program exits. However, writing code just once in a finally block is clearer and less prone to error.

Java, Visual Basic, and C++ provide try and catch blocks. Java and Visual Basic also provide a finally block, but C++ does not.

Many well-designed programs with one or more try blocks do not include catch blocks; instead, they contain only try-finally pairs. The finally block is used to release resources that other applications might be waiting for, such as database connections.

> **TWO TRUTHS & A LIE**
>
> **Using the `finally` Block**
>
> 1. When a `finally` block follows a `try` block, it executes whether or not the `try` block identifies any `Exceptions`.
> 2. Typically, you use a `finally` block to perform clean-up tasks that must occur after an `Exception` has been thrown and caught.
> 3. Statements that follow a `try...catch` pair might never execute because an unplanned `Exception` might occur, or the `try` or `catch` block might contain a statement that quits the application.
>
> The false statement is #2. Typically, you use a `finally` block to perform clean-up tasks that must occur, regardless of whether any errors occurred or were caught.

Handling Exceptions Thrown from Outside Methods

An advantage of using object-oriented exception-handling techniques is the ability to deal with exceptions appropriately as you decide how to handle them. When methods from other classes throw exceptions, the methods don't have to catch them; instead, your calling program can catch them, and you can decide what to do.

For example, suppose that you prompt a user to enter a value at the console and then call the `Convert.ToInt32()` method to convert the input to an integer with a statement such as the following:

```
int answer = Convert.ToInt32(ReadLine());
```

If the user enters a noninteger value, a `FormatException` is generated from the `Convert.ToInt32()` method, but it is not caught and handled there. Instead, your program can catch the exception, and you can take appropriate action for your specific application. For example, in one program you might want to force the user to reenter a value, but in a different program, you might want to force the value to a default value or you might want to display an error message and terminate the program. This flexibility is an advantage when you need to create specific reactions to thrown exceptions. In many cases, you want a method to check for errors, but you do not want to require the method to handle an error if it finds one. Just as a police officer can deal with a speeding driver differently depending on circumstances, you can react to exceptions specifically for your current purposes.

When you design classes containing methods that have statements that might throw exceptions, you most frequently should create the methods so they throw the `Exception` object but do not handle it. Handling an exception usually should be left to the client—the program that uses your class—so the exception can be handled in an appropriate way for the application.

For example, consider the very brief `PriceList` class in Figure 11-22. The class contains a list of prices and a single method that displays one price based on a parameter subscript value. Because the `DisplayPrice()` method uses an array, an `IndexOutOfRangeException` might be thrown. However, the `DisplayPrice()` method does not handle the potential exception.

```
class PriceList
{
   private static double[] price = {15.99, 27.88, 34.56, 45.89};
   public static void DisplayPrice(int item)
   {
      WriteLine("The price is " +
         price[item].ToString("C"));
   }
}
```

Figure 11-22 The `PriceList` class

Figure 11-23 shows an application that uses the `DisplayPrice()` method. It calls the method in a `try` block and handles an `IndexOutOfRangeException` by displaying a price of $0. Figure 11-24 shows the output when a user enters an invalid item number.

```
using System;
using static System.Console;
class PriceListApplication1
{
   static void Main()
   {
      int item;
      try
      {
         Write("Enter an item number >> ");
         item = Convert.ToInt32(ReadLine());
         PriceList.DisplayPrice(item);
      }
      catch(IndexOutOfRangeException e)
      {
         WriteLine(e.Message + " The price is $0");
      }
   }
}
```

Figure 11-23 The PriceListApplication1 program

Handling Exceptions Thrown from Outside Methods

```
Enter an item number >> 4
Index was outside the bounds of the array. The price is $0
```

Figure 11-24 Output of the PriceListApplication1 program when a user enters an invalid item number

Figure 11-25 shows a different application that uses the same `PriceList` class but handles the exception differently. In this case, the programmer wanted the user to keep responding until a correct entry was made. If an `IndexOutOfRangeException` is thrown from the `try` block, the `try` block is abandoned, `isGoodItem` is not set to `true`, and the `catch` block executes. Because `isGoodItem` remains `false`, the `while` loop continues to execute. Only when the first three statements in the `try` block are successful does the last statement execute, changing `isGoodItem` to `true` and ending the loop repetitions. Because the `DisplayPrice()` method in the `PriceList` class was written to throw an `Exception` but not handle it, the programmer of `PriceListApplication2` could handle the `Exception` in a totally different manner from the way it was handled in `PriceListApplication1`. Figure 11-26 shows a typical execution of this program.

```csharp
using System;
using static System.Console;
class PriceListApplication2
{
   static void Main()
   {
      int item = 0;
      bool isGoodItem = false;
      while(!isGoodItem)
      {
         try
         {
            Write("Enter an item number >> ");
            item = Convert.ToInt32(ReadLine());
            PriceList.DisplayPrice(item);
            isGoodItem = true;
         }
         catch(IndexOutOfRangeException e)
         {
            WriteLine("You must enter a number less " +
               "than 4.");
            WriteLine("Please reenter item number ");
         }
      }
      WriteLine("Thank you");
   }
}
```

Figure 11-25 The PriceListApplication2 program

```
Enter an item number >> 12
You must enter a number less than 4.
Please reenter item number
Enter an item number >> 4
You must enter a number less than 4.
Please reenter item number
Enter an item number >> 3
The price is $45.89
Thank you
```

Figure 11-26 Output of the PriceListApplication2 program when a user enters an invalid item number several times

TWO TRUTHS & A LIE

Handling Exceptions Thrown from Outside Methods

1. When methods from other classes throw exceptions, the methods don't have to catch them; instead, your calling program can catch them, and you can decide what to do.

2. Often, you don't want a called method to handle its own exception; in many cases, you want the calling program to handle any exception in the way most appropriate for the application.

3. When you design classes containing methods that have statements that might throw exceptions, you almost always should make sure your class handles each exception appropriately.

The false statement is #3. When you design classes containing methods that have statements that might throw Exceptions, you most frequently should create the methods so they throw the exception but do not handle it.

Tracing Exception Objects Through the Call Stack

When one method calls another, the computer's operating system must keep track of where the method call came from, and program control must return to the calling method when the called method is complete. For example, if MethodA() calls MethodB(), the operating system

Tracing Exception Objects Through the Call Stack

has to "remember" to return to MethodA() when MethodB() ends. Similarly, if MethodB() calls MethodC(), then while MethodC() is executing, the computer needs to "remember" that it will return to MethodB() and eventually to MethodA(). The memory location where the computer stores the list of locations to which the system must return is known as the **call stack**.

If a method throws an exception and does not catch it, then the exception is thrown to the next method "up" the call stack; in other words, it is thrown to the method that called the offending method. Consider this sequence of events:

- MethodA() calls MethodB().
- MethodB() calls MethodC().
- MethodC() throws an Exception.
- C# looks first for a catch block in MethodC().
- If none exists, then C# looks for the same thing in MethodB().
- If MethodB() does not have a catch block for the Exception, then C# looks to MethodA().
- If MethodA() doesn't catch the Exception, then the program terminates, and the operating system displays an error message.

This system of passing an exception through the chain of calling methods is called **propagating the exception**. It has great advantages because it allows your methods to handle exceptions more appropriately. However, a program that uses several classes makes it difficult for the programmer to locate the original source of an exception.

You already have used the Message property to obtain information about an Exception object. The StackTrace property is another useful Exception property. When you catch an Exception, you can display the value of StackTrace to provide a list of methods in the call stack so you can determine the location where the Exception object was created.

The StackTrace property can be a useful debugging tool. When your program stops abruptly, it is helpful to discover the method in which the exception occurred. Often, you do not want to display a StackTrace property in a finished program; the typical user has no interest in the cryptic messages that would appear. However, while you are developing a program, using StackTrace can help you diagnose problems.

A Case Study: Using StackTrace

As an example of when StackTrace can be useful, consider the Tax class in Figure 11-27. Suppose that your company has created or purchased this class to make it easy to calculate tax rates on products sold. For simplicity, assume that only two tax rates are in effect—6 percent for sales of $20 or less and 7 percent for sales greater than $20. The Tax class would be useful for anyone who wrote a program involving product sales, except for one flaw: in the shaded statement, the subscript is erroneously set to 2 instead of 1 for the higher tax rate. If this subscript is used with the `taxRate` array in the next statement, it will be out of bounds.

```
class Tax
{
   private static double[] taxRate = {0.06, 0.07};
   private static double CUTOFF = 20.00;
   public static double DetermineTaxRate(double price)
   {
      int subscript;
      double rate;
      if(price <= CUTOFF)
         subscript = 0;
      else
         subscript = 2;     ← Don't Do It
      rate = taxRate[subscript];   This mistake is intentional.
      return rate;
   }
}
```

Figure 11-27 The Tax class

Assume that your company has also created a revised `PriceList` class, as shown in Figure 11-28. This class is similar to the one in Figure 11-22, except that it includes a tax calculation and calls the `DetermineTaxRate()` method in the shaded statement.

```
class PriceList
{
   private static double[] price = {15.99, 27.88, 34.56, 45.89};
   public static void DisplayPrice(int item)
   {
      double tax;
      double total;
      double pr;
      pr = price[item];
      tax = pr * Tax.DetermineTaxRate(pr);
      total = pr + tax;
      WriteLine("The total price is " + total.ToString("C"));
   }
}
```

Figure 11-28 The `PriceList` class that includes a call to the Tax class method

Tracing Exception Objects Through the Call Stack

Suppose that you write the application shown in Figure 11-29. Your application is similar to the price list applications created earlier in this chapter, including a call to `PriceList.DisplayPrice()`. As in `PriceListApplication1` and `PriceListApplication2`, your new program tries the data entry and display statements and then catches an exception. When you run the program using what you know to be a good item number, as in Figure 11-30, you are surprised to see the shaded "Error!" message you have coded in the `catch` block. In the earlier examples that used `PriceList.DisplayPrice()`, using an item number 1 would have resulted in a successful program execution.

```
using System;
using static System.Console;
class PriceListApplication3
{
   static void Main()
   {
      int item;
      try
      {
         Write("Enter an item number >> ");
         item = Convert.ToInt32(ReadLine());
         PriceList.DisplayPrice(item);
      }
      catch(Exception e)
      {
         WriteLine("Error!");
      }
   }
}
```

Figure 11-29 The PriceListApplication3 program

 When you compile the program in Figure 11-29, you receive a warning that variable e is declared but never used. If you omit the name e from the catch block, the application will execute identically without displaying a warning.

Figure 11-30 Execution of the PriceListApplication3 program when a user enters 1 for the item number

To attempt to discover what caused the *Error!* message, you can replace the statement that writes it as follows:

WriteLine(e.Message);

When the statement to display e.Message is added to the price list program, a warning that e is never used no longer appears when the program is compiled.

However, when you execute the program to display e.Message, you receive the output in Figure 11-31, indicating that the index is out of the bounds of the array. You are puzzled because you know 1 is a valid item number for the price array, and it should not be considered out of bounds.

```
Enter an item number >> 1
Index was outside the bounds of the array.
```

Figure 11-31 Execution of the modified price list application in which e.Message is displayed in the catch block

Finally, you decide to replace the WriteLine() argument in the catch block statement with a StackTrace call, as follows:

WriteLine(e.StackTrace);

The output is shown in Figure 11-32. You can see from the list of methods that the error in your application came from Tax.DetermineTaxRate(), which was called by PriceList.DisplayPrice(), which was called by Main(). Notice that the last method executed is the first one displayed in the list. Before using StackTrace, you might have not even considered that the Tax class could have been the source of the problem. If you work in a small organization, you can look at the code yourself and fix it. If you work in a larger organization or you purchased the class from an outside vendor, you can contact the programmer who created the class for assistance.

```
Enter an item number >> 1
   at Tax.DetermineTaxRate(Double price)
   at PriceList.DisplayPrice(Int32 item)
   at PriceListApplication3.Main()
```

Figure 11-32 Execution of the modified price list application in which e.StackTrace is displayed in the catch block

The classes in this example were small to help you easily follow the discussion. However, a real-world application might have many more classes that contain many more methods, and so using StackTrace would become increasingly beneficial. In a large system of programs, you might find it useful to locate StackTrace calls strategically throughout the programs while testing them and then to remove them or comment them out when the programs are complete.

   Watch the video *Tracing Exceptions Through the Call Stack*.

TWO TRUTHS & A LIE

Tracing Exception Objects Through the Call Stack

1. The memory location where the computer stores the list of locations to which the system must return after a series of method calls is known as the stack trace.

2. If a method throws an exception and does not catch it, then the exception is thrown to the method that called the offending method.

3. When you catch an Exception object, you can output the value of StackTrace to display a list of methods in the call stack so you can determine the location of the error.

The false statement is #1. The memory location where the computer stores the list of locations to which the system must return after a series of method calls is known as the call stack.

Creating Your Own Exception Classes

C# provides more than 100 categories of Exceptions that you can throw in your programs. However, C#'s creators could not predict every condition that might be an exception in the programs you write. For example, you might want to declare an Exception when your bank balance is negative or when an outside party attempts to access your e-mail account. Most organizations have specific rules for exceptional data, such as "an employee number must not exceed three digits" or "an hourly salary must not be less than the legal minimum wage." Of course, you can handle these potential error situations with if statements, but you also can create your own Exception subclasses.

To create your own Exception type from which you can instantiate throwable objects, you can extend the ApplicationException class, which is a subclass of Exception, or you can extend Exception. Microsoft's advice on this matter has changed over time. Although you might see extensions of `ApplicationException` in classes written by others, the current advice is simply to derive your own classes from `Exception`. Either approach will produce workable programs.

Figure 11-33 shows a `NegativeBalanceException` class that extends `Exception`. This class passes an appropriate `string` message to its parent's constructor. If you create an `Exception` object and display its `Message` property, you will see the message *Error in the application.* When the `NegativeBalanceException` constructor passes the string *Bank balance is negative.* to its parent's constructor, the `Message` property will hold this more descriptive message. The C# documentation recommends that you create all `Exception` subclass messages to be grammatically correct, complete sentences ending in a period.

```
class NegativeBalanceException : Exception
{
   private static string msg = "Bank balance is negative. ";
   public NegativeBalanceException() : base(msg)
   {
   }
}
```

Figure 11-33 The `NegativeBalanceException` class

When you create a `BankAccount` class like the one shown in Figure 11-34, you can create the `Balance` property `set` accessor to throw a `NegativeBalanceException` when a client attempts to set the balance to be negative.

Instead of creating the nbe object in the `Balance` property in Figure 11-34, you could code the following statement, which creates and throws an anonymous `NegativeBalanceException` in a single step:
throw(new NegativeBalanceException());

The Microsoft documentation recommends creating three constructors for every exception class you create: the default constructor, a constructor that takes a string message, and a constructor that takes a string message and an inner exception. To keep this example simple, `NegativeBalanceException` in Figure 11-33 contains just one constructor.

Figure 11-35 shows a program that attempts to set a `BankAccount` balance to a negative value in the shaded statement. When the `BankAccount` class's `Balance set` accessor throws the `NegativeBalanceException`, the `catch` block in the `TryBankAccount` program executes, displaying both the `NegativeBalanceException Message` and the value of `StackTrace`. Figure 11-36 shows the output.

Creating Your Own Exception Classes

```
class BankAccount
{
   private double balance;
   public int AccountNum {get; set;}
   public double Balance
   {
      get
      {
         return balance;
      }
      set
      {
         if(value <0)
         {
            NegativeBalanceException nbe =
               new NegativeBalanceException();
            throw(nbe);
         }
         balance = value;
      }
   }
}
```

Figure 11-34 The BankAccount class

```
using System;
using static System.Console;
class TryBankAccount
{
   static void Main()
   {
      BankAccount acct = new BankAccount();
      try
      {
         acct.AccountNum = 1234;
         acct.Balance = -1000;
      }
      catch(NegativeBalanceException e)
      {
         WriteLine(e.Message);
         WriteLine(e.StackTrace);
      }
   }
}
```

Figure 11-35 The TryBankAccount program

```
Bank balance is negative.
   at BankAccount.set_Balance(Double value)
   at TryBankAccount.Main()
```

Figure 11-36 Output of the TryBankAccount program

In the error message in Figure 11-36, notice that the set accessor for the Balance property is known internally as set_Balance. You can guess that the set accessor for the AccountNum property is known as set_AccountNum.

The StackTrace begins at the point where an Exception is thrown, not where it is instantiated. This consideration makes a difference when you create an Exception in a class and throw it from multiple methods.

Exceptions can be particularly useful when you throw them from constructors. Constructors do not have a return type, so they have no other way to send information back to a calling method.

In C#, you can't throw an object unless it is an Exception or a descendent of the Exception class. In other words, you cannot throw a double or a BankAccount. However, you can throw any type of Exception at any time, not just Exceptions of your own creation. For example, within any program you can code any of the following:

```
throw(new ApplicationException());
throw(new IndexOutOfRangeException());
throw(new Exception());
```

Of course, you should throw appropriate Exception types. In other words, you should not throw an IndexOutOfRangeException when you encounter division by 0 or data of an incorrect type; you should use it only when an index (subscript) is too high or too low. However, if a built-in Exception type is appropriate and suits your needs, you should use it. You should not create an excessive number of special Exception types for your classes, especially if the C# development environment already contains an Exception type that accurately describes the error. Extra Exception types add a level of complexity for other programmers who will use your classes. Nevertheless, when appropriate, creating a specialized Exception class is an elegant way for you to take care of error situations. Exceptions allow you to separate your error code from the usual, nonexceptional sequence of events and allow for errors to be passed up the stack and traced.

> ### TWO TRUTHS & A LIE
> **Creating Your Own Exception Classes**
>
> 1. To create your own Exception types whose objects you can throw, you can extend the ApplicationException class or the Exception class.
> 2. In C#, you can throw any object that you create if it is appropriate for the application.
> 3. You can throw any type of Exception at any time—both those that are already created as part of C# and those of your own creation.
>
> The false statement is #2. In C#, you can't throw an object unless it is an Exception or a descendent of the Exception class.

Rethrowing an Exception

When you write a method that catches an exception, your method does not have to handle it. Instead, you might choose to **rethrow the exception** to the method that called your method. Then you can let the calling method handle the problem.

Within a catch block, you can rethrow an unnamed exception that was caught by using the keyword throw with no object after it. For example, Figure 11-37 shows a class that contains four methods. In this program, the following sequence of events takes place:

1. The Main() method calls MethodA().
2. MethodA() calls MethodB().
3. MethodB() calls MethodC().
4. MethodC() throws an Exception.
5. When MethodB() catches the Exception, it does not handle the Exception; instead, it throws the Exception back to MethodA().
6. MethodA() catches the Exception but does not handle it either. Instead, MethodA() throws the Exception back to the Main() method.
7. The Exception is caught in the Main() method, where the message that was created in MethodC() is finally displayed.

Figure 11-38 shows the execution of the program.

```csharp
using System;
using static System.Console;
class ReThrowDemo
{
   static void Main()
   {
      try
      {
         WriteLine("Trying in Main() method");
         MethodA();
      }
      catch(Exception ae)
      {
      WriteLine("Caught in Main() method --\n {0}",
         ae.Message);
      }
      WriteLine("Main() method is done");
   }
   private static void MethodA()
   {
      try
      {
         WriteLine("Trying in method A");
         MethodB();
      }
      catch(Exception)
      {
         WriteLine("Caught in method A");
         throw;
      }
   }
   private static void MethodB()
   {
      try
      {
         WriteLine("Trying in method B");
         MethodC();
      }
      catch(Exception)
      {
         WriteLine("Caught in method B");
         throw;
      }
   }
   private static void MethodC()
   {
      WriteLine("In method C");
      throw(new Exception("This came from method C"));
   }
}
```

Figure 11-37 The ReThrowDemo program

```
Trying in Main() method
Trying in method A
Trying in method B
In method C
Caught in method B
Caught in method A
Caught in Main() method --
   This came from method C
Main() method is done
```

Figure 11-38 Execution of the ReThrowDemo program

If you name the Exception argument in a catch block (for example, catch (Exception e)), then you should use that identifier when you use a throw statement in the block (for example, throw e;).

TWO TRUTHS & A LIE

Rethrowing an Exception

1. When you write a method that catches an exception, your method must handle it.

2. When a method catches an exception, you can rethrow it to a calling method.

3. Within a catch block, you can rethrow an unnamed caught Exception object by using the keyword throw with no object after it.

The false statement is #1. When you write a method that catches an Exception, your method does not have to handle the Exception.

Chapter Summary

- An exception is any error condition or unexpected behavior in an executing program. In C#, all exceptions are objects that are instances of the Exception class or one of its derived classes. Most exceptions you will use are derived from three classes: SystemException, ApplicationException, and their parent Exception. You can purposely generate a SystemException by forcing a program to contain an error. Although you are not required to handle exceptions, you can use object-oriented techniques to provide elegant error-handling solutions.

- When you think an error will occur frequently, the most efficient approach is to handle the error in the traditional way, with `if` statements. If an error will occur infrequently, instantiating an `Exception` object when needed is more efficient. In object-oriented terminology, you "try" a procedure that may not complete correctly. A method that detects an error condition or exception "throws" an exception, and the block of code that processes the error "catches" the exception. You must include at least one `catch` block or `finally` block immediately following a `try` block.

- Every `Exception` object contains a `ToString()` method and a `Message` property that contains useful information about the `Exception`.

- You can place as many statements as you need within a `try` block, and you can catch as many different exceptions as you want. If you try more than one statement, only the first error-generating statement throws an exception. When multiple `catch` blocks are present, they are examined in sequence until a match is found for the `Exception` type that occurred. When you list multiple `catch` blocks after a `try` block, you must be careful about their order, or some `catch` blocks might become unreachable.

- The `TryParse()` methods that you can use to convert strings to other data types without causing exceptions use exception-handling techniques internally.

- A `finally` block performs actions at the end of a `try...catch` sequence, whether an exception was thrown or not.

- Exceptions do not have to be caught by the methods that generate them. Instead, a program that calls a method that throws an exception can catch and handle it. Often, this approach produces the best software design.

- If a method throws an exception and does not catch it, then the `Exception` object is thrown to the calling method. When you catch an `Exception` object, you can display the value of the `StackTrace` property, which provides a list of methods in the call stack, allowing you to determine the location where the error occurred.

- To create your own `Exception` classes from which you create throwable objects, you can extend the `ApplicationException` class or the `Exception` class. The current advice is to extend `Exception`.

- When you write a method that catches an exception, your method does not have to handle it. Instead, you might choose to rethrow the exception to the method that called your method and let that method handle it.

Key Terms

An **exception** is any error condition or unexpected behavior in an executing program.

Exception handling is the set of object-oriented techniques used to manage unexpected errors in an executing program.

Mission critical describes any process that is crucial to an organization.

Fault-tolerant applications are designed so that they continue to operate, possibly at a reduced level, when some part of the system fails.

Robustness represents the degree to which a system is resilient to stress, maintaining correct functioning even in the presence of errors.

A **try block** contains code that might create exceptions you want to handle.

A **catch block** can catch one type of Exception.

Unreachable blocks contain statements that can never execute under any circumstances because the program logic "can't get there."

Dead code is unreachable code.

A **finally block** can follow a try block; code within a finally block executes whether the try block identifies any Exceptions or not.

The **call stack** is the memory location where the computer stores the list of locations to which the system must return after method calls.

Propagating an exception is the act of transmitting it unchanged through the call stack.

To **rethrow an exception** is to throw a caught exception to a calling method instead of handling it within the method that generated it.

Review Questions

1. Any error condition or unexpected behavior in an executing program is known as an _____.

    a. exclusion
    b. anomaly
    c. exception
    d. omission

2. Which of the following is *not* treated as a C# Exception?
    a. Your program asks the user to input a number, but the user enters a character.
    b. You calculate a value that is too large for the answer's variable type.
    c. You attempt to access an array with a subscript that is too large.
    d. You attempt to execute a C# program, but the C# compiler has not been installed.

3. Most exceptions you will use derive from three classes: _____.

    a. Object, ObjectException, and ObjectApplicationException
    b. Exception, SystemException, and ApplicationException
    c. FormatException, ApplicationException, and IOException
    d. SystemException, IOException, and FormatException

4. Exception objects can be _____.
   a. generated automatically by C#
   b. created by a program
   c. both of these
   d. none of these

5. When a program creates an Exception object, you _____.
   a. must handle it
   b. can handle it
   c. must not handle it
   d. none of these; programs cannot create Exceptions

6. If you do not use object-oriented techniques, _____.
   a. you can still manage error situations
   b. you cannot manage error situations
   c. you can manage error situations but with great difficulty
   d. error situations will seldom occur

7. In object-oriented terminology, you _____ a procedure that might not complete correctly.
   a. circumvent
   b. try
   c. catch
   d. throw

8. In object-oriented terminology, a method that detects an error condition _____ an exception.
   a. throws
   b. catches
   c. tries
   d. unearths

9. When you write a block of code in which something can go wrong, and you want to throw an exception if it does, you place the code in a _____ block.
   a. catch
   b. blind
   c. system
   d. try

10. A catch block executes when its try block _____.
    a. completes
    b. throws any Exception object
    c. throws an Exception of an acceptable type
    d. completes without throwing anything

Review Questions

11. Which of the following catch blocks will catch any Exception object?

    a. catch(Any e) {}
    b. catch(Exception e) {}
    c. catch(e) {}
    d. All of the above will catch any Exception.

12. Which of the following is valid within a catch block with the header catch(Exception error)?

    a. WriteLine(error.ToString());
    b. WriteLine(error.Message);
    c. return(error.ToString());
    d. two of these

13. You can place _____ statement(s) within a try block.

    a. zero
    b. one
    c. two
    d. any number of

14. How many catch blocks might follow a try block within the same method?

    a. only one
    b. any number as long as it is greater than zero
    c. any number as long as it is greater than one
    d. any number, including zero or one

15. Consider the following try block. If x is 15, what is the value of a when this code completes?

    ```
    try
    {
      a = 99;
      if(x > 10)
         throw(new Exception());
      a = 0;
      ++a;
    }
    ```

    a. 0
    b. 1
    c. 99
    d. undefined

CHAPTER 11 Exception Handling

16. Consider the following **catch** blocks. The variable b has been initialized to 0. If a **DivideByZeroException** occurs in a **try** block just before this **catch** block, what is the value of b when this code completes?

    ```
    catch(DivideByZeroException e)
    {
       ++b;
    }
    catch(Exception e)
    {
       ++b;
    }
    ```

    a. 0
    b. 1
    c. 2
    d. 3

17. Consider the following **catch** blocks. The variable c has been initialized to 0. If an **IndexOutOfRangeException** occurs in a **try** block just before this **catch** block, what is the value of c when this code completes?

    ```
    catch(IndexOutOfRangeException e)
    {
       ++c;
    }
    catch(Exception e)
    {
       ++c;
    }
    finally
    {
       ++c;
    }
    ```

    a. 0
    b. 1
    c. 2
    d. 3

18. If your program throws an **IndexOutOfRangeException**, and the only available **catch** block catches an **Exception**, _____.

    a. an **IndexOutOfRangeException catch** block is generated automatically
    b. the **Exception catch** block executes
    c. the **Exception catch** block is bypassed
    d. the **IndexOutOfRangeException** is thrown to the operating system

19. When you design your own classes that might cause exceptions, and other classes will use your classes as clients, you should usually create your methods to _____.

    a. neither throw nor handle exceptions
    b. throw exceptions but not handle them
    c. handle exceptions but not throw them
    d. both throw and handle exceptions

20. When you create an Exception subclass of your own, you should extend the _____ class.

    a. SystemException
    b. PersonalException
    c. OverloadedException
    d. Exception

Exercises

Programming Exercises

1. Write a program named **SubscriptExceptionTest** in which you declare an array of 10 doubles and store values in the array. Write a try block in which you place a loop that prompts the user for a subscript value and displays the value stored in the corresponding array position. Create a catch block that catches any IndexOutOfRangeException and displays an appropriate error message.

2. ArgumentException is an existing class that derives from Exception; you use it when one or more of a method's arguments do not fall within an expected range. Create an application named **SwimmingWaterTemperature** containing a variable that can hold a temperature expressed in degrees Fahrenheit. Within the class, create a method that accepts a parameter for a water temperature and returns true or false, indicating whether the water temperature is between 70 and 85 degrees and thus comfortable for swimming. If the temperature is not between 32 and 212 (the freezing and boiling points of water), it is invalid, and the method should throw an ArgumentException. In the Main() method, continuously prompt the user for data temperature, pass it to the method, and then display a message indicating whether the temperature is comfortable, not comfortable, or invalid.

3. Create a program named **FindSquareRoot** that finds the square root of a user's input value. The Math class contains a static method named Sqrt() that accepts a double and returns the parameter's square root. If the user's entry cannot be converted to a double, display an appropriate message, and set the square root value to 0. Otherwise, test the input number's value. If it is negative, throw a new ApplicationException to which you pass the message "Number can't be negative." and again set sqrt to 0. If the input value is a double and not negative, pass it to the Math.Sqrt() method, and display the returned value.

4. Create a program named **StudentGradeDemo** that attempts to create several valid and invalid ReportCard objects. Immediately after each instantiation attempt, handle any thrown exceptions by displaying an error message. Create a ReportCard class with four fields for a student name, a numeric midterm grade, a numeric final exam grade, and letter grade. The ReportCard constructor requires values for the name and two numeric grades and determines the letter grade. Upon construction, throw an ArgumentException if the midterm or final exam grade is less than 0 or more than 100. The letter grade is based on the arithmetic average of the midterm and final exams using a grading scale of A for an average of 90 to 100, B for 80 to 90, C for 70 to 80, D for 60 to 70, and F for an average below 60. Display all the data if the instantiation is successful.

5. a. Create a program named **BookExceptionDemo** for the Peterman Publishing Company. Create a BookException class that is instantiated when a Book's price exceeds 10 cents per page and whose constructor requires three arguments for title, price, and number of pages. Create an error message that is passed to the Exception class constructor for the Message property when a Book does not meet the price-to-pages ratio. For example, an error message might be:

   For Goodnight Moon, ratio is invalid.
   ...Price is $12.99 for 25 pages.

   b. Create a Book class that contains fields for title, author, price, and number of pages. Include properties for each field. Throw a BookException if a client program tries to construct a Book object for which the price is more than 10 cents per page. Create a program that creates at least four Book objects—some where the ratio is acceptable, and others where it is not. Catch any thrown exceptions, and display the BookException Message.

   c. Using the Book class, write an application named **BookExceptionDemo2** that creates an array of five Books. Prompt the user for values for each Book. To handle any exceptions that are thrown because of improper or invalid data entered by the user, set the Book's price to the maximum of 10 cents per page. At the end of the program, display all the entered, and possibly corrected, records.

6. Create a GUI application named **ExceptionHandlingDemoGUI** that prompts a user to enter an integer. When the user clicks a button, try to convert the user's entry to an integer using the `Convert.ToInt32()` method, and display a message indicating whether the user was successful.

7. In Chapter 6, you created a game named `GuessAWord` in which a player guesses letters to try to replicate a hidden word. Now create a modified version of the program named **GuessAWordWithExceptionHandling** that throws and catches an exception when the user enters a guess that is not a letter of the alphabet. Create a `NonLetterException` class that descends from `Exception`. The `Message` string for your new class should indicate the nonletter character that caused the `Exception`'s creation. When a `NonLetterException` is thrown and caught, the message should be displayed.

Debugging Exercises

1. Each of the following files in the Chapter.11 folder of your downloadable student files has syntax and/or logical errors. In each case, determine the problem and fix the program. After you correct the errors, save each file using the same filename preceded with *Fixed*. For example, DebugEleven1.cs will become FixedDebugEleven1.cs.

    a. DebugEleven1.cs

    b. DebugEleven2.cs

    c. DebugEleven3.cs

    d. DebugEleven4.cs

Case Problems

1. Modify the **GreenvilleRevenue** program created in the previous chapter so that it performs the following tasks:

    - The program prompts the user for the number of contestants in this year's competition; the number must be between 0 and 30. Use exception-handling techniques to ensure a valid value.

    - The program prompts the user for talent codes. Use exception-handling techniques to ensure a valid code.

    - After data entry is complete, the program prompts the user for codes so the user can view lists of appropriate contestants. Use exception-handling techniques for the code verification.

2. Modify the **MarshallsRevenue** program created in the previous chapter so that it performs the following tasks:

    - Modify the program to use exception-handling techniques to ensure valid values for the month, the number of interior murals scheduled, and the number of exterior murals scheduled. In each case, the program continues to prompt the user until valid entries are made.

    - Modify the program to use exception-handling techniques to ensure valid mural codes for the scheduled jobs.

    - After data entry is complete, the program continuously prompts the user for codes and displays associated jobs. Use exception-handling techniques to verify valid codes.

CHAPTER 12

Using Controls

Upon completion of this chapter, you will be able to:

◎ Use Controls

◎ Understand the IDE's automatically generated code

◎ Set a Control's Font

◎ Create a Form that contains LinkLabels

◎ Add color to a Form

◎ Add CheckBox and RadioButton objects to a Form

◎ Add a PictureBox to a Form

◎ Add ListBox, ComboBox, and CheckedListBox items to a Form

◎ Add a MonthCalendar and DateTimePicker to a Form

◎ Work with a Form's layout

◎ Add a MenuStrip to a Form

◎ Use other controls

CHAPTER 12 Using Controls

Throughout this book, you have created both console and GUI applications. Your GUI applications have used only a few Controls—Forms, Labels, TextBoxes, and Buttons. **Graphical control elements** are the components through which a user interacts with a GUI program. (Since Chapter 3, you have used the simpler name *controls* for these objects.)

If you have been creating mostly console applications while learning the concepts in this book, you might want to review the chapter "Using GUI Objects and the Visual Studio IDE." That chapter provides instruction in the basic procedures used to create GUI applications and describes Visual Studio Help.

When using programs or visiting Internet sites, you have encountered and used many other interactive controls such as scroll bars, check boxes, and radio buttons. C# has many classes that represent these GUI objects, and the Visual Studio IDE makes it easy to add them to your programs. (Controls are also often called **widgets**.) In this chapter, you will learn to incorporate some of the most common and useful widgets into your programs. Additionally, you will see how these components work in general so you can use other controls that are not covered in this book or that become available to programmers in future releases of C#.

GUI components are referred to as *widgets*, which some sources claim is a combination of the terms *window* and *gadgets*. Originally, *widget* comes from the 1924 play "Beggar on Horseback," by George Kaufman and Marc Connelly. In the play, a young composer gets engaged to the daughter of a rich businessman and foresees spending his life doing pointless work in a bureaucratic big business that manufactures widgets, which represent a useless item whose purpose is never explained.

Understanding Controls

When you design a Form, you can place Buttons and other controls on the Form surface. In C#, the Control class provides the definitions for these GUI objects. Control objects such as Forms and Buttons, like all other objects in C#, ultimately derive from the Object class. Figure 12-1 shows where the Control class fits into the inheritance hierarchy.

```
System.Object
    System.MarshalByRefObject
        System.ComponentModel.Component
            System.Windows.Forms.Control
                26 Derived classes
```

Figure 12-1 The Control class inheritance hierarchy

Figure 12-1 shows that all Controls are Objects, of course. They are also all MarshalByRefObjects. (A MarshalByRefObject is one you can instantiate on a remote computer so that you can manipulate a reference to the object rather than a local copy of the object.) Controls also descend from Component. (The Component class provides containment

Understanding Controls

and cleanup for other objects—inheriting from `Component` allows `Controls` to be contained in objects such as `Forms` and provides for disposal of `Controls` when they are destroyed. The `Control` class adds visual representation to `Components`.) The `Control` class implements very basic functionality required by classes that define the GUI objects the user sees on the screen. This class handles user input through the keyboard, pointing devices, and touch screens as well as message routing and security. It defines the bounds of a `Control` by determining its position and size.

Table 12-1 shows the 26 direct descendants of `Control` and some commonly used descendants of those classes. It does not show all the descendants that exist; rather, it shows only the descendants covered previously or in this chapter. For example, the `ButtonBase` class is the parent of `Button`, a class you have used throughout this book. In this chapter, you will use two other `ButtonBase` children—`CheckBox` and `RadioButton`. This chapter cannot cover every `Control` that has been invented; however, after you learn to use some `Controls`, you will find that others work in much the same way. You also can read more about them in the Visual Studio Help documentation.

Class	Commonly used descendents
Microsoft.WindowsCE.Forms.DocumentList	
System.Windows.Forms.AxHost	
System.Windows.Forms.ButtonBase	Button, CheckBox, RadioButton
System.Windows.Forms.DataGrid	
System.Windows.Forms.DataGridView	
System.Windows.Forms.DateTimePicker	
System.Windows.Forms.GroupBox	
System.Windows.Forms.Integration.ElementHost	
System.Windows.Forms.Label	LinkLabel
System.Windows.Forms.ListControl	ListBox, ComboBox, CheckedListBox
System.Windows.Forms.ListView	
System.Windows.Forms.MdiClient	
System.Windows.Forms.MonthCalendar	
System.Windows.Forms.PictureBox	

Table 12-1 Classes derived from `System.Windows.Forms.Control` *(continues)*

(continued)

Class	Commonly used descendents
System.Windows.Forms.PrintPreviewControl	
System.Windows.Forms.ProgressBar	
System.Windows.Forms.ScrollableControl	
System.Windows.Forms.ScrollBar	
System.Windows.Forms.Splitter	
System.Windows.Forms.StatusBar	
System.Windows.Forms.TabControl	
System.Windows.Forms.TextBoxBase	TextBox
System.Windows.Forms.ToolBar	
System.Windows.Forms.TrackBar	
System.Windows.Forms.TreeView	
System.Windows.Forms.WebBrowserBase	

Table 12-1 Classes derived from System.Windows.Forms.Control

Because Controls are all relatives, they share many of the same attributes. Each Control has more than 80 public properties and 20 protected properties. For example, each Control has a Font and a ForeColor that dictate how its text is displayed, and each Control has a Width and Height. Table 12-2 shows just some of the public properties associated with Controls in general; reading through them will give you an idea of the Control attributes that you can change.

Property	Description
AllowDrop	Gets or sets a value indicating whether the control can accept data that the user drags onto it
Anchor	Gets or sets the edges of the container to which a control is bound and determines how a control is resized with its parent
BackColor	Gets or sets the background color for the control
BackgroundImage	Gets or sets the background image displayed in the control

Table 12-2 Selected public Control properties *(continues)*

(continued)

Property	Description
Bottom	Gets the distance, in pixels, between the bottom edge of the control and the top edge of its container's client area
Bounds	Gets or sets the size and location of the control, including its nonclient elements, in pixels, relative to the parent control
CanFocus	Gets a value indicating whether the control can receive focus
CanSelect	Gets a value indicating whether the control can be selected
Capture	Gets or sets a value indicating whether the control has captured the mouse
Container	Gets the IContainer that contains the Component (inherited from Component)
ContainsFocus	Gets a value indicating whether the control or one of its child controls currently has the input focus
Cursor	Gets or sets the cursor that is displayed when the mouse pointer is over the control
Disposing	Gets a value indicating whether the base Control class is in the process of disposing
Dock	Gets or sets which control borders are docked to their parent control and determines how a control is resized with its parent
Enabled	Gets or sets a value indicating whether the control can respond to user interaction
Focused	Gets a value indicating whether the control has input focus
Font	Gets or sets the font of the text displayed by the control
ForeColor	Gets or sets the foreground color of the control
HasChildren	Gets a value indicating whether the control contains one or more child controls
Height	Gets or sets the height of the control
IsDisposed	Gets a value indicating whether the control has been disposed of
Left	Gets or sets the distance, in pixels, between the left edge of the control and the left edge of its container's client area
Location	Gets or sets the coordinates of the upper-left corner of the control relative to the upper-left corner of its container
Margin	Gets or sets the space between controls
ModifierKeys	Gets a value indicating which of the modifier keys (Shift, Ctrl, and Alt) is in a pressed state

Table 12-2 Selected public Control properties *(continues)*

(continued)

Property	Description
MouseButtons	Gets a value indicating which of the mouse buttons is in a pressed state
MousePosition	Gets the position of the mouse cursor in screen coordinates
Name	Gets or sets the name of the control
Parent	Gets or sets the parent container of the control
Right	Gets the distance, in pixels, between the right edge of the control and the left edge of its container's client area
Size	Gets or sets the height and width of the control
TabIndex	Gets or sets the tab order of the control within its container
TabStop	Gets or sets a value indicating whether the user can give focus to the control using the Tab key
Text	Gets or sets the text associated with this control
Top	Gets or sets the distance, in pixels, between the top edge of the control and the top edge of its container's client area
TopLevelControl	Gets the parent control that is not parented by another Windows Forms control; typically, this is the outermost Form in which the control is contained
Visible	Gets or sets a value indicating whether the control and all its parent controls are displayed
Width	Gets or sets the width of the control

Table 12-2 Selected public Control properties

The description of each property in Table 12-2 indicates whether the property is read-only; such properties only get values and do not set them.

You have altered Label, TextBox, and Button properties such as Text and Visible using the Properties window in Visual Studio. All the other Controls you learn about in this chapter can be manipulated in the same way.

A project can contain multiple Forms, each with its own Controls. You will learn how to add more Forms to a project in the "You Do It" exercises later in this chapter.

TWO TRUTHS & A LIE

Understanding Controls

1. The Control class implements basic functionality required by GUI objects that a user sees on the screen.
2. Most Controls have Font and ForeColor properties.
3. Every Control has Width and Height properties.

The false statement is #2. Every Control has Font and ForeColor properties.

Examining the IDE's Automatically Generated Code

Figure 12-2 shows a Form created in the IDE. The following actions have been performed:

1. A new Windows Forms App project has been started and given the name FormWithALabelAndAButton.
2. A Label has been dragged onto Form1. Using the Properties window in the IDE, the Label's Text property has been changed to *Click the button*, and its Font has been changed to Georgia, Bold, and size 16. Its Name has not been changed from the default name label1.
3. A Button has been dragged onto Form1. The Button's Text property has been changed to *OK*, and its Name has been changed from the default Name button1 to okButton.

Figure 12-2 A Form generated by the FormWithALabelAndAButton program

As you drag controls in the Form Designer or change properties in the Properties Window, Visual Studio automatically generates code in the file named Form1.Designer.cs. When you open the Form1.Designer.cs file for the FormWithALabelAndAButton project in Visual Studio, you can look for the method named InitializeComponent(), and you can see two lines of code generated within it near the bottom as follows:

```
private System.Windows.Forms.Label label1;
private System.Windows.Forms.Button okButton;
```

If you were to continue to drag additional components onto the Form, more declarations would be generated.

A grayed box containing Windows For Designer generated code appears above the declarations for label1 and okButton. If you expand this box by clicking on the small plus sign to its left, you see the following lines just before the method header for the InitializeComponent() method:

```
#region Windows Form Designer generated code
/// <summary>
/// Required method for Designer support - do not modify
/// the contents of this method with the code editor.
/// </summary>
```

Within the InitializeComponent() method, you can see automatically-generated statements that set the properties of the label, the button, and the form. Figure 12-3 shows the first part of this code that calls constructors for the Button and Label objects and sets a number of properties for the Label. Do not be intimidated by the amount of code automatically generated by the IDE. Based on what you have learned so far in this book, you can easily make sense of most of it.

```
private void InitializeComponent()
{
    this.label1 = new System.Windows.Forms.Label();
    this.okButton = new System.Windows.Forms.Button();
    this.SuspendLayout();
    //
    // label1
    //
    this.label1.AutoSize = true;
    this.label1.Font = new System.Drawing.Font("Georgia", 16.2F,
        System.Drawing.FontStyle.Bold, System.Drawing.GraphicsUnit.Point,
        ((byte)(0)));
    this.label1.Location = new System.Drawing.Point(12, 49);
    this.label1.Name = "label1";
    this.label1.Size = new System.Drawing.Size(244, 32);
    this.label1.TabIndex = 0;
    this.label1.Text = "Click the button";
```

Figure 12-3 Start of the code in the InitializeComponent() method for FormWithALabelAndAButton program

Examining the IDE's Automatically Generated Code

So much code is automatically generated by Visual Studio that it can be hard to find what you want. To locate a line of code, click Edit on the menu bar in the IDE, click Find and Replace, click Quick Find, type a key phrase to search for. Make sure that the drop down box correctly identifies the area in which you want to search—for example, the current selection or the current document.

Figure 12-3 contains the following:

- After the `InitializeComponent()` method header and opening brace, the next two statements call the constructor for each control that the programmer dragged onto the Form:

```
this.label1 = new System.Windows.Forms.Label();
this.okButton = new System.Windows.Forms.Button();
```

These statements create the actual objects.

- The next statement is a method call as follows:

```
this.SuspendLayout();
```

`SuspendLayout()` is a method that prevents conflicts when you are placing `Controls` on a form. Its counterparts, `ResumeLayout()` and `PerformLayout()`, appear at the bottom of the method. If you remove these method calls from small applications, you won't notice the difference. However, in large applications, suspending the layout logic while you adjust the appearance of components improves performance.

- Comments that start with forward slashes serve to separate the `label1` code from other code in the method. Following the `label1` comment lines, seven statements set properties of the Label as follows:

```
this.label1.AutoSize = true;
this.label1.Font = new System.Drawing.Font("Georgia",
    16.2F, System.Drawing.FontStyle.Bold,
    System.Drawing.GraphicsUnit.Point, ((byte)(0)));
this.label1.Location = new System.Drawing.Point(12, 49);
this.label1.Name = "label1";
this.label1.Size = new System.Drawing.Size(244, 32);
this.label1.TabIndex = 0;
this.label1.Text = "Click the button";
```

In the code in Figure 12-3 every instance of `this` means "this Form." You can see that the Font, Location, Name, Size, and Text have been assigned values based on the programmer's choices in the IDE. The TabIndex for `label1` is 0 by default; TabIndex values determine the order in which Controls receive focus when the user presses the Tab key. This property is typically more useful for selectable items such as Buttons.

If you return to the visual designer and make changes to the form or its components, for example, by relocating the label, when you next view the code, it will have been updated accordingly.

The statements that follow the Property settings for label1 are similar, but they define the properties of the Button on the Form. The TabIndex for the Button is set to 1 because it was dragged onto the Form after the Label. Additional Controls would receive consecutive TabIndex values.

- The InitializeComponent() method ends with statements that set the properties of the Form, such as its drawing size and text, and then, the following statements add the Label and Button to the Form:

```
this.Controls.Add(this.okButton);
this.Controls.Add(this.label1);
```

In this chapter, you will learn about several additional Controls. When designing a Form, you should use the drag-and-drop design features in the IDE to place components and use the Properties window in the IDE to set properties instead of typing statements in the code editor. However, this chapter also teaches you about the code behind these actions so you can troubleshoot problems in projects and write usable statements when necessary.

 Watch the video *Examining the IDE Code*.

TWO TRUTHS & A LIE

Examining the IDE's Automatically Generated Code

1. By using the Form Designer and the Properties window, you save time and eliminate many chances for error.

2. When you use the Form Designer to drag a Label onto a Form, no constructor call is needed for the Label.

3. You can use the Properties Window to set properties for a Label such as Font, Location, Size, and Text.

The false statement is #2. When you use the Form Designer to drag a Label onto a Form, you do not have to write a constructor call, but one is generated for you.

Setting a Control's Font

You use the Font class to change the appearance of printed text on your Forms. When designing a Label, Button, or other Control on a Form, it is easiest to select a Font from the Properties list. After you place a Control on a Form in the IDE, you can select the ellipsis (three dots) that follows the current Font property name in the Properties list. (See Figure 12-4.) Clicking the ellipsis displays a Font window in which you can choose a Font name, size, style, and other effects. (See Figure 12-5.)

Figure 12-4 Clicking the ellipsis following the Font property

CHAPTER 12 Using Controls

Figure 12-5 The Font window

However, if you wanted to change a Font later in a program—for example, after a user clicks a button—you might want to create your own instance of the Font class. As another example, suppose you want to create multiple controls that use the same Font. In that case, it makes sense to declare a named instance of the Font class. For example, you can declare the following Font:

```
System.Drawing.Font bigFont = new
   System.Drawing.Font("Courier New", 16.5f);
```

This version of the Font constructor requires two arguments—a string and a float. The string you pass to the Font constructor is the name of the font. If you use a font name that does not exist in your system, the font defaults to Microsoft Sans Serif. The second value is a float that represents the font size. Notice that you must use an F (or an f) following the Font size value constant when it contains a decimal point to ensure that the constant will be recognized as a float and not a double. (If you use an int as the font size, you do not need the f because the int will automatically be cast to a float.) An alternative would be to instantiate a float constant or variable and use its name as an argument to the Font constructor.

Setting a Control's Font

In Chapter 2, you learned to use an *f* following a floating-point constant to indicate the `float` type. Recall that a numeric constant with a decimal point is a `double` by default.

After a `Font` object named `bigFont` is instantiated, you can code statements similar to the following:

```
this.label1.Font = bigFont;
this.okButton.Font = bigFont;
```

If you want to change the properties of several objects at once in the IDE, you can drag your mouse around them to create a temporary group and then change the property for all of them with one entry in the Properties list.

The `Font` class includes a number of overloaded constructors. For example, you also can create a `Font` using three arguments, adding a `FontStyle`, as in the following declaration:

```
Font aFancyFont = new Font("Arial", 24, FontStyle.Italic);
```

Table 12-3 lists the available `FontStyle`s. You can combine multiple styles using the pipe (|), which is also called the *logical OR operator* or the *bitwise OR operator*. (You first learned about this operator in Chapter 4.) The word *or* indicates that bits are turned on in the result when either of the operands contains an on-bit in a given position. For example, the following code creates a `Font` that is bold and underlined because the bits that indicate bold and underlined are both turned on in the result:

```
Font boldAndUnderlined = new Font("Helvetica",
   10, FontStyle.Bold | FontStyle.Underline);
```

Member Name	Description
Bold	Bold text
Italic	Italic text
Regular	Normal text
Strikeout	Text with a line through the middle
Underline	Underlined text

Table 12-3 `FontStyle` enumeration

CHAPTER 12 Using Controls

Instead of instantiating a named Font object, you can create and assign an anonymous Font in one step. In other words, an identifier is not provided for the Font, as in this example:

```
this.label1.Font = new
   System.Drawing.Font("Courier New", 12.5F);
```

If you don't provide an identifier for a Font, you can't reuse it, and you would have to create it again to use it with additional Controls.

TWO TRUTHS & A LIE

Setting a Control's Font

1. You use the Font class to change the appearance of printed text on Controls in your Forms.

2. When designing a Control on a Form, you must select a Font from the Properties list in the IDE.

3. The Font class includes several overloaded constructors.

The false statement is #2. When designing a Control on a Form, a default font is selected. If you want to change the font, it is easiest to select a font from the Properties list, but you also can create your own instance of the Font class.

Using a LinkLabel

A **link label** is a control with a label that provides the user a way to link to other sources, such as Web pages or files. The C# class that creates a link label is LinkLabel; it is a child of Label. Table 12-4 summarizes the properties and lists the default event method for a LinkLabel. The **default event** for a Control is:

- The method whose shell is automatically created when you double-click the Control while designing a project in the IDE

- The method that you are most likely to alter when you use the Control

- The event that users most likely expect to generate when they encounter the Control in a working application

With many Controls, including a LinkLabel, a mouse click by the user triggers the default event. When designing a program, you can double-click a Control in the IDE to generate the default method shell, and then write any necessary statements within the shell.

Using a LinkLabel

Property or Method	Description
ActiveLinkColor	The color of the link when it is clicked
LinkColor	The original color of links before they have been visited; usually blue by default
LinkVisited	If true, the link's color is changed to the VisitedLinkColor
VisitedLinkColor	The color of a link after it has been visited; usually purple by default
LinkClicked()	Default event that is generated when the link is clicked by the user

Table 12-4 Commonly used LinkLabel properties and default event

The default event for many Controls, such as Buttons and LinkLabels, occurs when the user clicks the Control. However, the default event for a Form is the Load() method. In other words, if you double-click a Form in the IDE, you generate this method. In it, you can place statements that execute as soon as a Form is loaded.

When you create a LinkLabel, it appears as underlined text. The text is blue by default, but you can change the color in the LinkLabel Properties list in the IDE. When you pass the mouse pointer over a LinkLabel, the pointer changes to a hand; you have seen similar behavior while using hyperlinks in Web pages. When a user clicks a LinkLabel, it generates a click event, just as clicking a Button does. When a click event is fired from a LinkLabel, a LinkClicked() method is executed, similar to how clicking a Button can execute a Click() method.

You can create a program so that a user generates an event by clicking many types of objects. For example, for a Label named label1, you could write statements in a Label1_Click() method. However, users do not usually expect to click Labels; they do expect to click LinkLabels.

When you double-click a Label (as well as most other controls), the automatically generated method name ends with Click(), but when you double-click a LinkLabel, the corresponding method ends with Clicked().

Figure 12-6 shows a Form onto which two LinkLabels have been dragged from the Toolbox in the IDE. The default Frame size has been reduced, and the Text properties of the LinkLabels have been changed to *Cengage Website* and *Read our policy*.

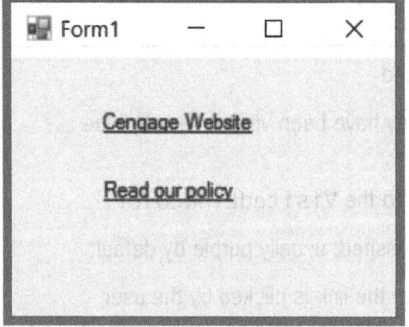

Figure 12-6 A Form with two LinkLabels

If you double-click a LinkLabel in the IDE, a method shell is created for you in the format xxx_LinkClicked(), where xxx is the value of the Name property assigned to the LinkLabel. (This corresponds to what happens when you double-click a Button in the IDE.) For example, double-clicking a linkLabel1 object generates a linkLabel1_LinkClicked() method shell. As with Button Click() methods, you usually want to rename LinkClicked() methods so they conventionally start with an uppercase letter. Figure 12-7 shows the two generated methods for the Form in Figure 12-6 when the automatically-created methods have been altered to start with uppercase letters. In Figure 12-7, the two shaded statements are the only parts of the code that were not generated automatically. The programmer added those lines to indicate which actions should occur when a user clicks the corresponding LinkLabel in a running application.

```
public partial class Form1 : Form
{
    public Form1()
    {
        InitializeComponent();
    }
    private void LinkLabel1_LinkClicked(object sender,
        LinkLabelLinkClickedEventArgs e)
    {
        System.Diagnostics.Process.Start("IExplore",
            "http://www.cengage.com");
    }
    private void LinkLabel2_LinkClicked(object sender,
        LinkLabelLinkClickedEventArgs e)
    {
        System.Diagnostics.Process.Start
            (@"C:\CSharp\Chapter12\Policy.txt");
    }
}
```

Figure 12-7 Two LinkClicked() methods

If you add using System.Diagnostics; at the top of your file, you can eliminate the references in Figure 12-7 and refer to the process simply as Process.Start.

When you view the code in the IDE, there will not be as many line breaks as you see in the code figures in this chapter. The line breaks have been inserted so the lines fit better on the pages of this book.

Using a LinkLabel

In each of the `LinkClicked()` methods in Figure 12-7, the programmer has added a call to `System.Diagnostics.Process.Start()`. This method allows you to run other programs within an application. The `Start()` method has two overloaded versions:

- When you use one `string` argument, you provide the name of the file to be opened.
- When you use two arguments, you provide the name of an application and its needed arguments.

In the `LinkLabel1_LinkClicked()` method, the two arguments open Internet Explorer ("IExplore") and pass it the address of the Cengage website. If an Internet connection is active, control transfers to the website.

In the `LinkLabel2_LinkClicked()` method, only one argument is provided. It opens a file stored on the local disk. The default application opens based on the file's application type, which is determined by its file extension. For example, Notepad is the default application for a file with a .txt extension. Alternatively, you could code the following, which explicitly names Notepad as the application:

```
System.Diagnostics.Process.Start("Notepad",
   @"C:\CSharp\Chapter12\Policy.txt");
```

In the `LinkLabel2_LinkClicked()` method, an at sign (@) appears in front of the filename to be opened. This symbol indicates that all characters in the string should be interpreted literally. Therefore, the backslashes in the path are not interpreted as escape sequence characters.

The `LinkVisited` property can be set to `true` when you determine that a user has clicked a link, as shown in the shaded statement in Figure 12-8. This setting indicates that the link should be displayed in a different color so the user can see the link has been visited. By default, the visited link color is purple, but you can change this setting in the Properties list for the `LinkLabel`.

```
private void LinkLabel1_LinkClicked(object sender,
    LinkLabelLinkClickedEventArgs e)
{
   System.Diagnostics.Process.Start("IExplore",
      "http://www.cengage.com");
   linkLabel1.LinkVisited = true;
}
```

Figure 12-8 Setting the `LinkVisited` property

CHAPTER 12 Using Controls

> **TWO TRUTHS & A LIE**
>
> **Using a LinkLabel**
>
> 1. A `LinkLabel` is a child class of `Label`, and it provides the additional capability to link the user to other sources.
>
> 2. The default event for a `Control` is the method whose shell is created automatically when you double-click the `Control` while designing a project in the IDE. Users most likely expect to generate this event when they encounter the `Control` in a working application.
>
> 3. When you create a `LinkLabel`, it appears as italicized underlined text, and when you pass the mouse pointer over a `LinkLabel`, the pointer changes to an hourglass.
>
> The false statement is #3. When you create a LinkLabel, it appears as underlined text, and when you pass the mouse pointer over a LinkLabel, the pointer changes to a hand.

Adding Color to a Form

The `Color` class contains a wide variety of predefined `Color`s that you can use with your `Control`s (see Table 12-5).

C# also allows you to create custom colors. If no color in Table 12-5 suits your needs, search for *custom color* in Visual Studio Help to obtain more information.

AliceBlue	DeepPink	Lime	RosyBrown
AntiqueWhite	DeepSkyBlue	LimeGreen	RoyalBlue
Aqua	DimGray	Linen	SaddleBrown
Aquamarine	DodgerBlue	Magenta	Salmon
Azure	Firebrick	Maroon	SandyBrown
Beige	FloralWhite	MediumAquamarine	SeaGreen
Bisque	ForestGreen	MediumBlue	SeaShell
Black	Fuchsia	MediumOrchid	Sienna

Table 12-5 Color properties *(continues)*

(continued)

BlanchedAlmond	Gainsboro	MediumPurple	Silver
Blue	GhostWhite	MediumSeaGreen	SkyBlue
BlueViolet	Gold	MediumSlateBlue	SlateBlue
Brown	Goldenrod	MediumSpringGreen	SlateGray
BurlyWood	Gray	MediumTurquoise	Snow
CadetBlue	Green	MediumVioletRed	SpringGreen
Chartreuse	GreenYellow	MidnightBlue	SteelBlue
Chocolate	Honeydew	MintCream	Tan
Coral	HotPink	MistyRose	Teal
CornflowerBlue	IndianRed	Moccasin	Thistle
Cornsilk	Indigo	NavajoWhite	Tomato
Crimson	Ivory	Navy	Transparent
Cyan	Khaki	OldLace	Turquoise
DarkBlue	Lavender	Olive	Violet
DarkCyan	LavenderBlush	OliveDrab	Wheat
DarkGoldenrod	LawnGreen	Orange	White
DarkGray	LemonChiffon	OrangeRed	WhiteSmoke
DarkGreen	LightBlue	Orchid	Yellow
DarkKhaki	LightCoral	PaleGoldenrod	YellowGreen
DarkMagenta	LightCyan	PaleGreen	
DarkOliveGreen	LightGoldenrodYellow	PaleTurquoise	
DarkOrange	LightGray	PaleVioletRed	
DarkOrchid	LightGreen	PapayaWhip	
DarkRed	LightPink	PeachPuff	
DarkSalmon	LightSalmon	Peru	
DarkSeaGreen	LightSeaGreen	Pink	
DarkSlateBlue	LightSkyBlue	Plum	
DarkSlateGray	LightSlateGray	PowderBlue	
DarkTurquoise	LightSteelBlue	Purple	
DarkViolet	LightYellow	Red	

Table 12-5 Color properties

CHAPTER 12 Using Controls

When you are designing a Form, you can choose colors from a list next to the BackColor and ForeColor properties in the IDE's Properties list. The statements created will be similar to the following:

```
this.label1.BackColor = System.Drawing.Color.Blue;
this.label1.ForeColor = System.Drawing.Color.Gold;
```

If you add using System.Drawing; at the top of your file, you can eliminate the references in the preceding lines and refer to the colors simply as Color.Blue and Color.Gold.

For professional-looking results when you prepare a resume or most other business documents, experts recommend that you use only one or two fonts and colors, even though your word-processing program allows many such selections. The same is true when you design GUI applications. Although many fonts and colors are available, you probably should stick with just a few choices in a single project.

TWO TRUTHS & A LIE

Adding Color to a Form

1. Because the choice of colors in C# is limited, you are required to create custom colors for many GUI applications.

2. When you are designing a Form, color choices appear in a list next to the BackColor and ForeColor properties in the IDE's Properties list.

3. The complete name of the color pink in C# is System.Drawing.Color.Pink.

The false statement is #1. The Color class contains a wide variety of predefined colors that you can use with your Controls.

You Do It

Adding Labels to a Form and Changing Their Properties

In the next steps, you begin to create an application for Bailey's Bed and Breakfast. (See Figure 12-9.) The main Form allows the user to select one of two suites and discover the amenities and price associated with each choice. You will start by placing two Labels on a Form and setting several of their properties.

(continues)

Adding Color to a Form

(continued)

 The screen images in the next steps represent a typical Visual Studio environment. Based on the version of Visual Studio you are using and the options selected during your installation, your screen might look different.

1. Open Microsoft Visual Studio, and then select **New**, **Project**, and **Windows Forms App**. Near the bottom of the New Project window, click in the **Name** text box, and replace the default name with **BedAndBreakfast**. Make sure that the Location field contains the folder where you want to store the project. See Figure 12-9.

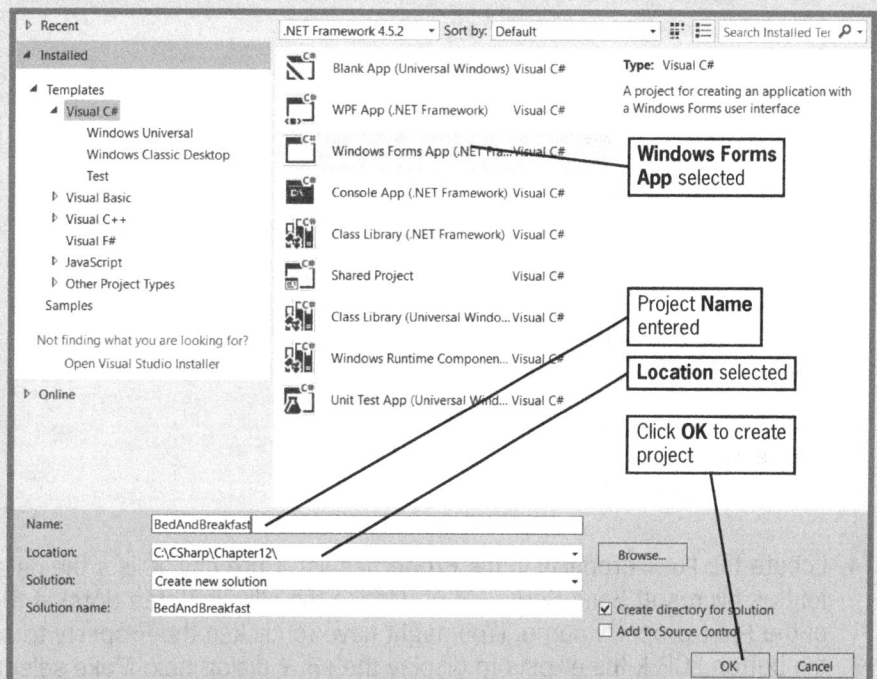

Figure 12-9 The New Project window for the BedAndBreakfast program

2. Click **OK**. The design screen opens. The blank Form in the center of the screen has an empty title bar. Click the Form. The lower-right corner of the screen contains a Properties window that lists the Form's properties. (If you do not see the Properties window, you can click **View** on the menu bar, and then click **Properties Window**.) In the Properties list, click the Name property and change the Name of the Form to **BaileysForm**. Click the Text property and change it to **Bailey's Bed and Breakfast**.

(continues)

(continued)

3. From the Toolbox at the left of the screen, drag a Label onto the Form. Change the Name of label1 to **welcomeLabel** and change the Text property to **Welcome to Bailey's**. Drag and resize the Label so it is close to the position of the Label in Figure 12-10.

 If you do not see the Toolbox, click the **Toolbox tab** at the left side of the screen and pin it to the screen by clicking the pushpin. Alternatively, you can select **View** from the menu bar, and then click **Toolbox**.

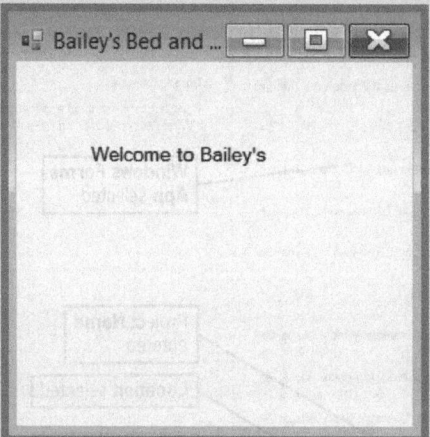

Figure 12-10 A Label placed on the Form in the BedAndBreakfast project

4. Locate the Font property in the Properties list. Currently, it lists the default font as Microsoft Sans Serif, 7.8 pt. Notice the ellipsis (three dots) at the right of the Font property name. (You might have to click in the Property to see the button.) Click the ellipsis to display the Font dialog box. Make selections to change the font to **Microsoft Sans Serif**, **18 point**, and **Bold**. Click **OK**. After you enlarge the Font for the Label, the Font appears larger. Drag the edge of the Form so the new, enlarged Label fits.

5. Drag a second Label onto the Form beneath the first one, and then set its Name property to rateLabel and its Text property to **Check our rates**. Change the Font for the new Label to **Microsoft Sans Serif**, **16 point**, **Regular**, and reposition the second Label so it is approximately centered under the first one.

(continues)

Adding Color to a Form

(continued)

6. Save the project, click **Debug** on the menu bar, and click **Start Without Debugging**, or use the shortcut keys listed in the menu. The Form appears, as shown in Figure 12-11.

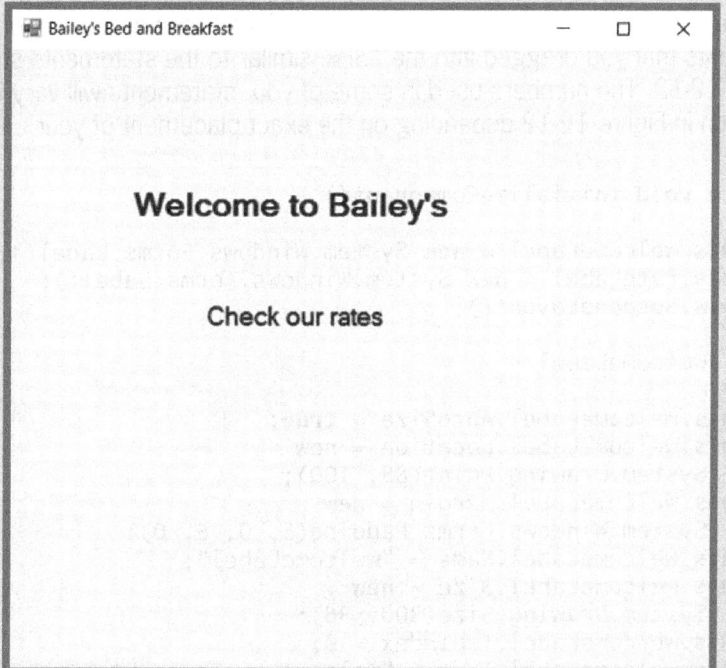

Figure 12-11 The BedAndBreakfast Form with two Labels

7. Dismiss the Form by clicking the **Close** button in its upper-right corner.

Examining the Code Generated by the IDE

In the next steps, you examine the code generated by the IDE for the following reasons:

- To gain an understanding of the types of statements created by the IDE.
- To lose any intimidation you might have about the code that is generated. You will recognize many of the C# statements from what you have already learned in this book.

(continues)

(continued)

1. In the Solution Explorer at the right side of the screen, double-click **Form1.Designer.cs**. Scroll down if necessary until you see the expandable box that contains *Windows Form designer generated code*, and expand it. If you can see only a few statements, you can drag the bottom and side borders of the code window to expose more of the code, or you can scroll to see all of it. You should be able to view statements that assign values to the properties of the components that you dragged into the Form, similar to the statements shown in Figure 12-12. The numbers used in some of your statements will vary from those seen in Figure 12-12 depending on the exact placement of your Labels.

```csharp
private void InitializeComponent()
{
    this.welcomeLabel = new System.Windows.Forms.Label();
    this.rateLabel = new System.Windows.Forms.Label();
    this.SuspendLayout();
    //
    // welcomeLabel
    //
    this.welcomeLabel.AutoSize = true;
    this.welcomeLabel.Location = new
       System.Drawing.Point(88, 100);
    this.welcomeLabel.Margin = new
       System.Windows.Forms.Padding(5, 0, 5, 0);
    this.welcomeLabel.Name = "welcomeLabel";
    this.welcomeLabel.Size = new
       System.Drawing.Size(300, 36);
    this.welcomeLabel.TabIndex = 0;
    this.welcomeLabel.Text = "Welcome to Bailey\'s";
    //
    // rateLabel
    //
    this.rateLabel.AutoSize = true;
    this.rateLabel.Font = new
       System.Drawing.Font("Microsoft Sans Serif",
       16.2F, System.Drawing.FontStyle.Regular,
       System.Drawing.GraphicsUnit.Point, ((byte)(0)));
    this.rateLabel.Location = new
       System.Drawing.Point(144, 185);
    this.rateLabel.Name = "rateLabel";
    this.rateLabel.Size = new
       System.Drawing.Size(181, 29);
    this.rateLabel.TabIndex = 1;
    this.rateLabel.Text = "Check our rates";
```

Figure 12-12 Part of the Form1.Designer.cs code

(continues)

> (continued)
>
> 2. Next, change the BackColor property of the Bailey's Bed and Breakfast Form. Click the **Form1.cs[Design]** tab and click the Form, or click the list box of components at the top of the Properties window and select **BaileysForm**. In the Properties list, click the BackColor property and click its down arrow to see its list of choices. Choose the **Custom** tab and select **Yellow** in the third row of available colors. Click the Form, notice the color change, and then view the code in the Form1.Designer.cs file. Locate the statement that changes the BackColor of the Form to Yellow. As you continue to design Forms, periodically check the code to confirm your changes and better learn C#.
> 3. Save the project.
> 4. If you want to take a break at this point, close Visual Studio. You return to this project in the "You Do It" section at the end of this chapter.

Using CheckBox and RadioButton Objects

A **checkbox** is a control that is a small rectangle that indicates whether a user has chosen an option. The C# class that allows you to create a checkbox is CheckBox. When a form contains multiple checkboxes, the user can select any number of them. When options are grouped so that only one can be checked at a time and selecting one deselects the others, they are called **radio buttons**. (You might also hear the term *option buttons*.) The C# class that creates a radio button is RadioButton. Like Button, both CheckBox and RadioButton descend from ButtonBase.

Table 12-6 contains commonly used CheckBox and RadioButton properties and the default event for which a method shell is generated when you double-click a CheckBox or RadioButton in the IDE.

Property or Method	Description
Checked	Indicates whether the CheckBox or RadioButton is checked
Text	The text displayed to the right of the CheckBox or RadioButton
CheckedChanged()	Default event that is generated when the Checked property changes

Table 12-6 Commonly used CheckBox and RadioButton properties and default event

CHAPTER 12 Using Controls

If you precede a letter with an ampersand (&) in the Text property value of a ButtonBase object, that letter acts as an access key. An **access key** provides a shortcut way for a user to make a selection using the keyboard. For example, if a Button's text is defined as &Press, then typing Alt + P has the same effect as clicking the Button. Access keys are also called *hot keys*.

You can place multiple groups of RadioButtons on a Form by using a GroupBox or Panel. You will learn more about GroupBoxes and Panels later in this chapter.

Figure 12-13 shows an example of a Form with which a user can select pizza options. It contains several Labels, four CheckBox objects, and three RadioButton objects. It makes sense for the pizza topping choices to be displayed using CheckBoxes because a user might select multiple toppings. However, options for delivery, pick-up, and dining in the restaurant are mutually exclusive, so they are presented using RadioButton objects.

Figure 12-13 A Form with Labels, CheckBoxes, and RadioButtons

When you add CheckBox and RadioButton objects to a form, they automatically are named using the same conventions you have seen with Buttons and Labels. That is, the first CheckBox without an explicitly assigned name is checkBox1 by default, the second is named checkBox2, and so on. Using the Properties list, you can assign more meaningful names such as sausageCheckBox and pepperoniCheckBox. Naming objects appropriately makes your code more understandable to others, and makes your programming job easier.

Both CheckBox and RadioButton objects have a Checked property whose value is true or false. For example, if you create a CheckBox named sausageCheckBox and you want to add $1.25 to a pizzaPrice value when the user checks the box, you can write the following:

```
if(sausageCheckBox.Checked)
    pizzaPrice = pizzaPrice + 1.25;
```

Using CheckBox and RadioButton Objects

The Checked property is a read/write property. That is, you can assign a value to it as well as access its value.

The default method that executes when a user clicks either a CheckBox or RadioButton is xxx_CheckedChanged(), where xxx represents the name of the invoking object. For example, suppose that the total price of a pizza should be altered based on a user's CheckBox selections. In this example, the base price for a pizza is $12.00, and $1.25 is added for each selected topping. You can declare constants for the BASE_PRICE and TOPPING_PRICE of a pizza and declare a variable that is initialized to the pizza base price as follows:

```
private const double BASE_PRICE = 12.00;
private const double TOPPING_PRICE = 1.25;
private double price = BASE_PRICE;
```

These declarations typically are placed in a Form's .cs file in the Form1 class, above both the constructor and other methods. Figure 12-14 shows the code you would add to the Form.cs file for the application. The SausageCheckBox_CheckedChanged() method changes the pizza price. The method shell was created by double-clicking the sausageCheckBox on the form. Then, the method name was changed to conventionally start with an uppercase letter, and the statements within the method were written by a programmer. If a change occurs because the sausageCheckBox was checked, then the TOPPING_PRICE is added to the price. If the change to the checkBox was to uncheck it, the TOPPING_PRICE is subtracted from the price. Either way, the Text property of a Label named outputLabel is changed to reflect the new price.

```
private void SausageCheckBox_CheckedChanged(object sender,
    EventArgs e)
{
    if (sausageCheckBox.Checked)
        price += TOPPING_PRICE;
    else
        price -= TOPPING_PRICE;
    outputLabel.Text = "Total is " + price.ToString("C");
}
```

Figure 12-14 The SausageCheckBox_CheckedChanged() method

In a similar fashion, you can add appropriate code for RadioButton objects. For example, assume that a $2.00 delivery charge is in effect, but there is no extra charge for customers who pick up a pizza or dine in. The code for DeliveryRadioButton_CheckedChanged() appears in Figure 12-15. When the user selects the deliveryRadioButton, $2.00 is added to the total. When the user selects either of the other RadioButtons, the deliveryRadioButton becomes unchecked and the $2.00 charge is removed from the total. Figure 12-16 shows a typical execution of the PizzaOrder program after it is complete.

CHAPTER 12 Using Controls

```
private void DeliveryRadioButton_CheckedChanged(object sender,
   EventArgs e)
{
   const double DELIVERY_CHARGE = 2.00;
   if (deliveryRadioButton.Checked)
      price += DELIVERY_CHARGE;
   else
      price -= DELIVERY_CHARGE;
   outputLabel.Text = "Total is " + price.ToString("C");
}
```

Figure 12-15 The DeliveryRadioButton_CheckedChanged() method

The entire PizzaOrderForm application can be found in the downloadable student files.

Figure 12-16 Typical execution of the PizzaOrderForm program

When an application starts, sometimes you want a specific CheckBox or RadioButton to be selected by default. If so, you can set the Control's Checked property to true in the Properties list in the IDE.

 Watch the video *CheckBoxes and RadioButtons*.

Adding a PictureBox to a Form

TWO TRUTHS & A LIE

Using CheckBox and RadioButton Objects

1. CheckBox objects are GUI widgets that the user can click to select or deselect an option; when a Form contains multiple CheckBoxes, any number of them can be checked or unchecked at the same time.

2. RadioButtons are similar to CheckBoxes, except that when they are placed on a Form, only one RadioButton can be selected at a time—selecting any RadioButton automatically deselects the others.

3. The default event for a CheckBox is xxx_CheckBoxChanged(), and the default event for a RadioButton is xxxRadioButtonChanged().

The false statement is #3. The default event for both CheckBox and RadioButton objects is xxx_CheckedChanged().

Adding a PictureBox to a Form

A **picture box** is a GUI element you use to display graphics. In C#, a PictureBox object can display graphics from a bitmap, icon, JPEG, GIF, or other image file type. Just as with a Button or a Label, you can easily drag a PictureBox Control onto a Form in the Visual Studio IDE. Table 12-7 shows the common properties and default event for a PictureBox.

Property or Method	Description
Image	Sets the image that appears in the PictureBox
SizeMode	Controls the size and position of the image in the PictureBox; values are Normal, StretchImage (which resizes the image to fit the PictureBox), AutoSize (which resizes the PictureBox to fit the image), and CenterImage (which centers the image in the PictureBox)
Click()	Default event that is generated when the user clicks the PictureBox

Table 12-7 Commonly used PictureBox properties and default event

Figure 12-17 shows a new project in the IDE. The following tasks have been completed:

- A project was started.
- The Form Text property was changed to *PictureBox Demo*.

CHAPTER 12 Using Controls

- The Form BackColor property was changed to White.
- A PictureBox was dragged onto the Form.

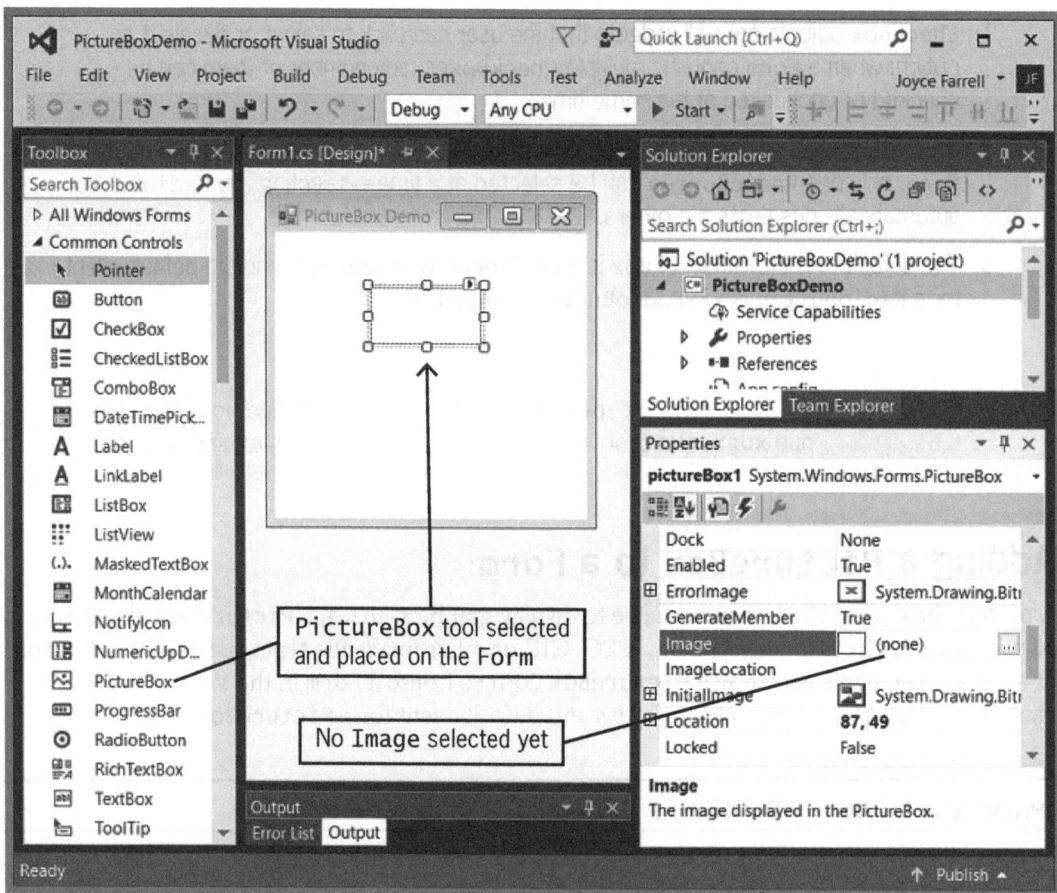

Figure 12-17 The IDE with a Form that contains a PictureBox

In Figure 12-17, in the Properties list at the right of the screen, the Image property is set to *(none)*. If you click the value, a button with an ellipsis appears. If you click it, a Select Resource window appears, as shown on the left in Figure 12-18. When you click the Import button, you can browse for stored images. When you select one, you see a preview in the Select Resource window, as shown on the right in Figure 12-18.

After you click OK, the image appears in the PictureBox, as in Figure 12-19. If the image does not fit the PictureBox, as in the left side of Figure 12-19), you can make a choice for the SizeMode property for the PictureBox. Table 12-8 Shows the possible choices for SizeMode for a PictureBox. For example, in the right side of Figure 12-19, the Zoom property has been selected before program execution.

Adding a PictureBox to a Form

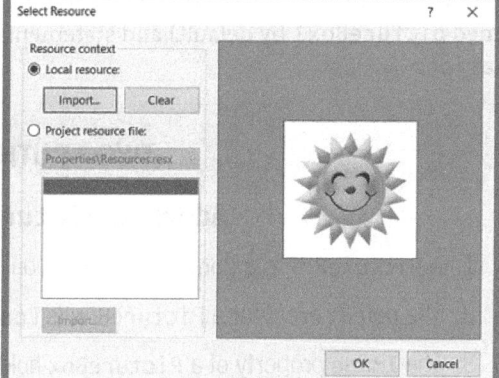

Figure 12-18 The Select Resource window before and after an image is selected

Figure 12-19 The PictureBoxDemo program with an inserted image

SizeMode value	Description
Normal	The image is positioned in the upper-left corner of the Picturebox; if the Image is too large, it is clipped.
StretchImage	The Image is stretched or shrunk to fit the PictureBox, but the aspect ratio is not maintained.
Zoom	The Image is stretched or shrunk to fit the PictureBox, but the aspect ratio is maintained.
AutoSize	The PictureBox is resized (rather than the Image).
CenterImage	The Image is centered in the PictureBox; if the Image is too large, it is clipped.

Table 12-8 PictureBox SizeMode properties

If you examine the generated code, you can find the statements that instantiate a `PictureBox` (named `pictureBox1` by default) and statements that set its properties, such as `Size` and `Location`.

> **TWO TRUTHS & A LIE**
>
> **Adding a PictureBox to a Form**
>
> 1. A `PictureBox` is a `Control` in which you can display graphics from an image file.
> 2. The default event for a `PictureBox` is `LoadImage()`.
> 3. The `Image` property of a `PictureBox` holds the name of a file that contains a picture.
>
> The false statement is #2. The default event for a `PictureBox` is `Click()`.

Adding `ListBox`, `CheckedListBox`, and `ComboBox` Controls to a Form

`ListBox`, `CheckedListBox`, and `ComboBox` objects all allow users to select choices from a list. The three classes descend from `ListControl`. Of course, they are also `Controls` and so inherit properties such as `Text` and `BackColor` from the `Control` class. Other properties are more specific to list-type objects. Table 12-9 describes some commonly used `ListBox` properties.

Property or Method	Description
Items	The collection of items in the `ListBox`; frequently, these are `strings`, but they can also be other types of objects
MultiColumn	Indicates whether display can be in multiple columns
SelectedIndex	Returns the index of the selected item. If no item has been selected, the value is –1. Otherwise, it is a value from 0 through $n-1$, where n is the number of items in the `ListBox`.
SelectedIndices	Returns a collection of all the selected indices (when `SelectionMode` is more than One)
SelectedItem	Returns a reference to the selected item
SelectedItems	Returns a collection of the selected items (when `SelectionMode` is more than One)
SelectionMode	Determines how many items can be selected (see Table 12-10)
Sorted	Sorts the items when set to `true`
SelectedIndexChanged()	Default event that is generated when the selected index changes

Table 12-9 Commonly used `ListBox` properties and default event

Adding `ListBox`, `CheckedListBox`, and `ComboBox` Controls to a Form

A **list box** displays a list of items from which the user can select by clicking. Figure 12-20 shows a typical `ListBox` on a `Form` before any strings have been added to it. After you drag a `ListBox` onto a `Form`, you can select its `Items` property and type a list into a String Collection Editor, as shown at the bottom of Figure 12-20.

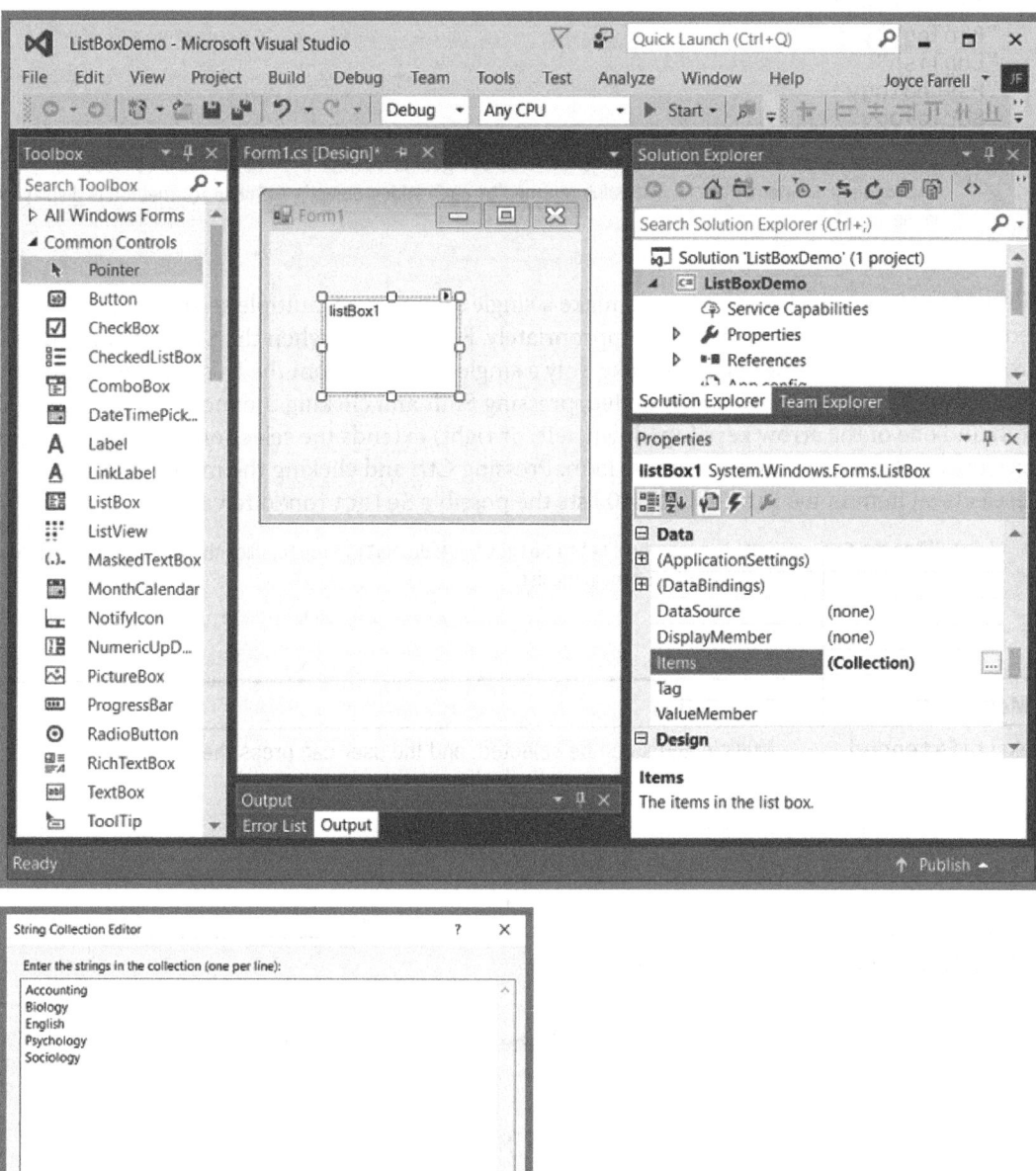

Figure 12-20 A `ListBox` on a Form and the String Collection Editor

Assuming the Name property of the ListBox is majorListBox, the following code is generated in the InitializeComponent() method when you fill the String Collection Editor with the strings in Figure 12-20:

```
this.majorListBox.Items.AddRange(new object[] {
    "Accounting",
    "Biology",
    "English",
    "Psychology",
    "Sociology" });
```

Objects added to a ListBox are not required to be strings. For example, you could add a collection of Employee or Student objects. The value returned by each added object's ToString() method is displayed in the ListBox.

With a ListBox, you allow the user to make a single selection or multiple selections by setting the SelectionMode property appropriately. For example, when the SelectionMode property is set to One, the user can make only a single selection from the ListBox. When the SelectionMode is set to MultiExtended, pressing Shift and clicking the mouse or pressing Shift and one of the arrow keys (up, down, left, or right) extends the selection to span from the previously selected item to the current item. Pressing Ctrl and clicking the mouse selects or deselects an item in the list. Table 12-10 lists the possible SelectionMode values.

When the SelectionMode property is set to SelectionMode.MultiSimple, click the mouse or press the spacebar to select or deselect an item in the list.

Member Name	Description
MultiExtended	Multiple items can be selected, and the user can press the Shift, Ctrl, and arrow keys to make selections.
MultiSimple	Multiple items can be selected.
None	No items can be selected.
One	Only one item can be selected.

Table 12-10 SelectionMode enumeration list

For example, within a Form's Load() method (the one that executes when a Form is first loaded), you could add the following:

```
this.majorListBox.SelectionMode =
    System.Windows.Forms.SelectionMode.MultiExtended;
```

As the example in Figure 12-21 shows, when you size a ListBox so that all the items cannot be displayed at the same time, a scroll bar is provided automatically on the side. The ListBox also provides the Boolean MultiColumn property, which you can set to display items in columns instead of a straight vertical list. This approach allows the control to display more items and can eliminate the need for the user to scroll down to an item. See Figure 12-22 which shows a multi-column list box to which 10 strings have been added.

Adding `ListBox`, `CheckedListBox`, and `ComboBox` Controls to a Form

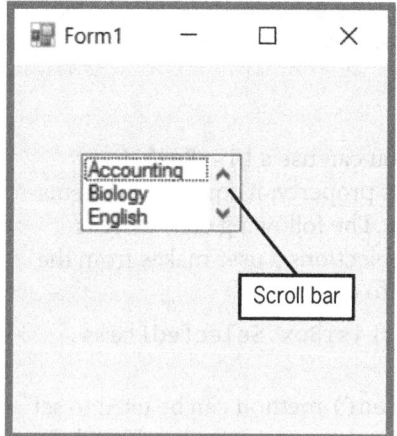

Figure 12-21 A `ListBox` with a scroll bar

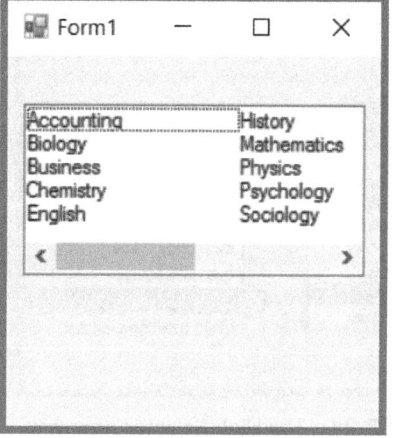

Figure 12-22 A multicolumn `ListBox`

The `SelectedItem` property of a `ListBox` contains a reference to the item a user has selected. For example, you can modify a `Label`'s `Text` property in the `MajorListBox_SelectedIndexChanged()` method with a statement such as the following, which appends the `SelectedItem` value to a label. Figure 12-23 shows a typical result.

```
private void MajorListBox_SelectedIndexChanged
   (object sender, EventArgs e)
{
   majorLabel.Text = "You selected " + majorListBox.SelectedItem;
}
```

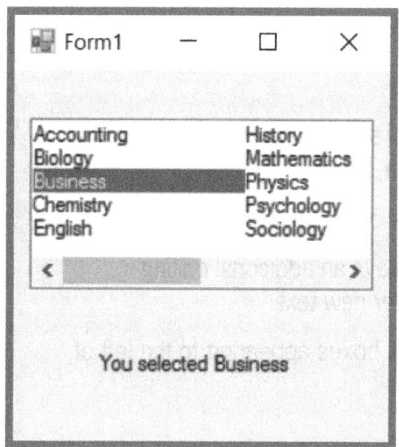

Figure 12-23 The ListBoxDemo application after a user has chosen *Business*

The `Items.Count` property of a `ListBox` object holds the number of items in the `ListBox`. The `GetSelected()` method accepts an integer argument representing the position of an item in the list. The method returns `true` if an item is selected and `false` if it is not. Therefore, code like the following could be used to count the number of selections a user makes from `majorListBox`:

```
int count = 0;
for(int x = 0; x < majorListBox.Items.Count; ++x)
   if(majorListBox.GetSelected(x))
      ++count;
```

CHAPTER 12 Using Controls

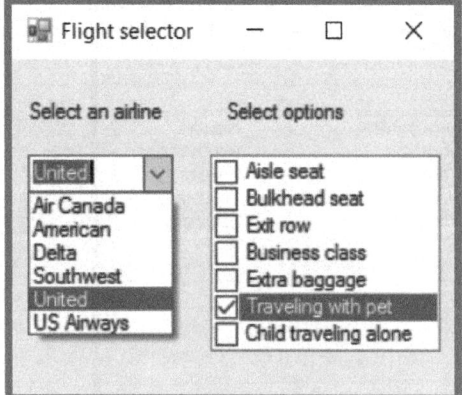

Figure 12-24 The FlightSelector program after the user has made some selections

 Recall that the first position in an array is position 0. The same is true in a `ListBox`.

Alternatively, you can use a `ListBox`'s `SelectedItems` property; it contains the items selected in a list. The following code assigns the number of selections a user makes from the `majorListBox` to count:

```
count = majorListBox.SelectedItems.
Count;
```

The `SetSelected()` method can be used to set a `ListBox` item to be automatically selected. For example, the following statement causes the first item in `majorListBox` to be selected:

```
majorListBox.SetSelected(0, true);
```

A **combo box** is a combination of a list box and and an editing control that allows a user to select from the list or to enter new text. The C# class is `ComboBox`, and the default `ComboBox` displays an editing area with a hidden list box. The application in Figure 12-24 contains a `ComboBox` for selecting an airline. A `CheckedListBox` is also similar to a `ListBox`, with check boxes appearing to the left of each desired item. The application in Figure 12-24 uses a `CheckedListBox` for flight options.

TWO TRUTHS & A LIE

Adding `ListBox`, `CheckedListBox`, and `ComboBox` Controls to a Form

1. With a `ListBox Control`, the user can select only one option at a time.

2. A `ComboBox` is similar to a `ListBox`, except that it displays an additional editing control that allows users to select from the list or to enter new text.

3. A `CheckedListBox` is similar to a `ListBox`, with check boxes appearing to the left of each desired item.

The false statement is #1. With a `ListBox`, you allow the user to make a single selection or multiple selections by setting the `SelectionMode` property appropriately.

Adding `MonthCalendar` and `DateTimePicker` Controls to a Form

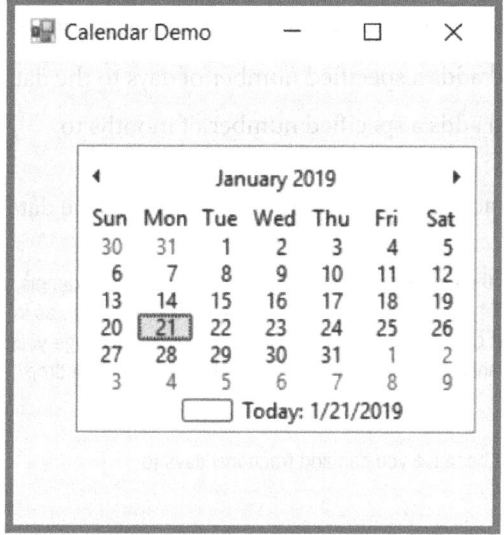

Figure 12-25 Typical execution of the MonthCalendarDemo application at startup

The `MonthCalendar` and `DateTimePicker` `Control`s allow you to retrieve date and time information. Figure 12-25 shows a `MonthCalendar` that has been placed on a `Form`. The current date is contained in a rectangle by default. When the user clicks a different date, it is shaded. `Control`s at the top of the calendar allow the user to go forward or back one month at a time, or the user can also move to a specific month or year by clicking the month and year title at the top of the calendar and then making a new month and year selection. Table 12-11 describes common `MonthCalendar` properties and the default event.

Property or Method	Description
`MaxDate`	Sets the last day that can be selected (the default is 12/31/9998)
`MaxSelectionCount`	Sets the maximum number of dates that can be selected at once (the default is 7)
`MinDate`	Sets the first day that can be selected (the default is 1/1/1753)
`MonthlyBoldedDates`	An array of dates that appear in boldface in the calendar (for example, holidays)
`SelectionEnd`	The last of a range of dates selected by the user
`SelectionRange`	The dates selected by the user
`SelectionStart`	The first of a range of dates selected by the user
`ShowToday`	If `true`, the date is displayed in text at the bottom of the calendar
`ShowTodayCircle`	If `true`, today's date is circled (the "circle" appears as a square)
`DateChanged()`	Default event that is generated when the user selects a date

Table 12-11 Commonly used `MonthCalendar` properties and default event

Several useful methods can be applied to the SelectionStart and SelectionEnd properties of MonthCalendar, including the following:

- ToShortDateString(), which displays the date in the format of *1/21/2019*
- ToLongDateString(), which displays the date in the format of *Monday, January 21, 2019*
- AddDays(), which takes a double argument and adds a specified number of days to the date
- AddMonths(), which takes an int argument and adds a specified number of months to the date
- AddYears(), which takes an int argument and adds a specified number of years to the date

The format in which dates are displayed depends on the operating system's regional settings. For example, using United Kingdom settings, the short string format would use the day first, followed by the month, as in *21/01/2019* for January 21. The examples in the list above assume United States settings. To change your regional setting in Windows, you can go to Control Panel, click Region, and choose a region from the drop down list.

The AddDays() method accepts a double argument because you can add fractional days to SelectionStart and SelectionEnd.

SelectionStart and SelectionEnd are structures of the DateTime type. The chapter "Files and Streams" contains additional information about using DateTime objects to determine when files were created, modified, or accessed.

Many business and financial applications use AddDays(), AddMonths(), and AddYears() to calculate dates for events, such as payment for a bill (perhaps due in 10 days from an order) or scheduling a salesperson's callback to a customer (perhaps two months after initial contact). The default event for MonthCalendar is DateChanged(). For example, Figure 12-26 shows a method that executes when the user clicks a MonthCalendar named monthCalendar1. Ten days are added to a selected date and the result is displayed on a Label that has been named messageLabel. Figure 12-27 shows the output when the user selects April 26, 2019. The date that is 10 days in the future is correctly calculated as May 6.

```
private void MonthCalendar1_DateChanged(object sender,
   DateRangeEventArgs e)
{
   const int DAYS_TO_ADD = 10;
   messageLabel.Text = "Date " + DAYS_TO_ADD +
      " days after selection is " +
      monthCalendar1.SelectionStart.AddDays
         (DAYS_TO_ADD).ToShortDateString();
}
```

Figure 12-26 The Calendar_DateChanged() method

Adding MonthCalendar and DateTimePicker Controls to a Form

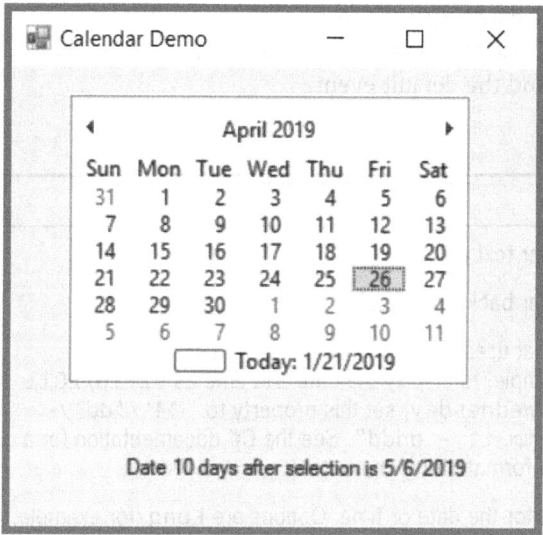

Figure 12-27 Typical execution of the MonthCalendarDemo program

 In Chapter 14, you will learn to use DateTime objects to hold data about dates and times.

If you set the MinDate value to the MonthCalendar's TodayDate property, the user cannot select a date before the date you select. For example, you cannot make appointments or schedule deliveries in the past, so you might code the following in a form's Load() method:

```
calendar1.MinDate =
   calendar1.TodayDate;
```

Conversely, you might want to prevent users from selecting a date in the future—for example, if the user is entering his birth date, it cannot be in the future. In that case, you could code a statement similar to the following:

```
calendar1.MaxDate = calendar1.TodayDate;
```

The DateTimePicker Control displays a month calendar when the down arrow is selected. This feature can be especially useful if you do not have much space available on a Form. Figure 12-28 shows a DateTimePicker before and after the user clicks the down arrow.

 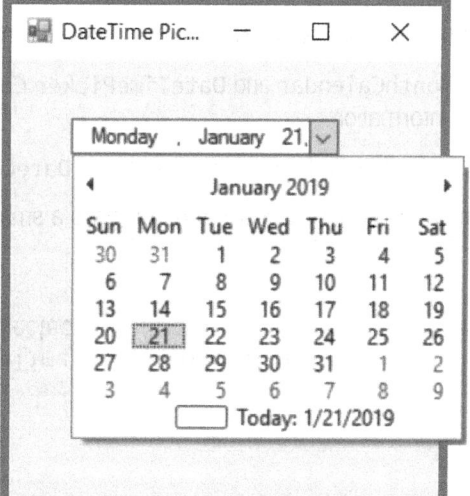

Figure 12-28 The DateTimePicker Control

CHAPTER 12 Using Controls

When you use the `CustomFormat` property, the date displayed in a `DateTimePicker` `Control` is more customizable than the one in a `MonthCalendar`. Table 12-12 describes some commonly used `DateTimePicker` properties and the default event.

Property or Method	Description
`CalendarForeColor`	Sets the calendar text color
`CalendarMonthBackground`	Sets the calendar background color
`CustomFormat`	A string value that uses codes to set a custom date and time format. For example, to display the date and time as 02/16/2011 12:00 PM - Wednesday, set this property to `"MM'/'dd'/'yyyy hh':'mm tt - dddd"`. See the C# documentation for a complete set of format string characters.
`Format`	Sets the format for the date or time. Options are `Long` (for example, Wednesday, February 16, 2011), `Short` (2/16/2011), and `Time` (for example, 3:15:01 PM). You can also create a `CustomFormat`.
`Value`	The data selected by the user
`ValueChanged()`	Default event that is generated when the `Value` property changes

Table 12-12 Commonly used `DateTimePicker` properties and default event

TWO TRUTHS & A LIE

Adding MonthCalendar and DateTimePicker Controls to a Form

1. The `MonthCalendar` and `DateTimePicker` `Controls` allow you to retrieve date and time information.
2. The default event for `MonthCalendar` is `DateChanged()`.
3. The `DateTimePicker` `Control` displays a small clock when you click it.

The false statement is #3. The `DateTimePicker` `Control` displays a month calendar when the down arrow is selected.

Working with a Form's Layout

Figure 12-29 Snap lines in the Visual Studio Designer

When you place Controls on a Form in the IDE, you can drag them to any location to achieve the effect you want.

When you drag multiple Controls onto a Form, blue **snap lines** appear and help you align new Controls with others already in place. Figure 12-29 shows two snap lines that you can use to align a second label below the first one. Snap lines also appear when you place a control closer to the edge of a container than is recommended.

You also can use the Location property in a Control's Properties list to specify a location. With either technique, code like the following is generated:

```
this.label1.Location = new System.Drawing.Point(23, 19);
```

Several other properties can help you to manage the appearance of a Form (or other ContainerControl). For example, setting the Anchor property causes a Control to remain at a fixed distance from the side of a container when the user resizes it. Figure 12-30 shows the Properties window for a Label that has been placed on a Form. The Anchor property has a drop-down window that lets you select or deselect the sides to which the label should be anchored. For most Controls, the default setting for Anchor is Top, Left.

Figure 12-30 Selecting an Anchor property

Figure 12-31 shows a Form with two Labels. On the Form, label1 has been anchored to the top left, and label2 has been anchored to the bottom right. The left side of the figure shows the Form as it first appears to the user, and the right side shows the Form after the user has resized it. Notice that in the resized Form, label1 is still the same distance from the top left as it originally was, and label2 is still the same distance from the bottom right as it originally was. Anchoring is useful when users expect a specific control to always be in the same general location in a container.

Figure 12-31 A Form with two Labels anchored to opposite corners

Setting the Dock property attaches a Control to the side of a container so that the Control stretches when the container's size is adjusted. Figure 12-32 shows the drop-down Dock Properties window for a Button. You can select any region in the window. Figure 12-33 shows a Button docked to the bottom of a Form before and after the Form has been resized.

Figure 12-32 The Dock Properties window

Figure 12-33 A Form with a docked Button before and after resizing

A Form also has a MinimumSize property and a MaximumSize property. Each has two values—Width and Height. If you set these properties, the user cannot make the Form smaller or larger than you have specified. If you do not want the user to be able to adjust a Form's size at all, set the MinimumSize and MaximumSize properties to be equal.

Understanding GroupBoxes and Panels

Many types of `ContainerControls` are available to hold `Controls`. For example, a group box or panel can be used to contain a group of other controls and to move them as a group. To create either of these `Controls`, you drag it from the Toolbox in the IDE and then drag the `Controls` you want on top of it. In C#, a **group box** and a **panel** differ in the following ways:

- A group box is created from the `GroupBox` class, and a panel is created from the `Panel` class.
- `GroupBoxes` can display a caption, but `Panels` cannot.
- `Panels` can include a scroll bar that the user can manipulate to view `Controls`; `GroupBoxes` do not have scroll bars.

You can anchor or dock `Controls` inside a `GroupBox` or `Panel`, and you can anchor or dock a `GroupBox` or `Panel` inside a `Form`. Doing this provides `Control` groups that can be arranged easily.

If you place several `GroupBox Controls` on a `Form` and several `RadioButtons` in each `GroupBox`, then a user can select one `RadioButton` from each `GroupBox` instead of being able to select just one `RadioButton` on a `Form`. In other words, each `GroupBox` operates independently.

When an application contains multiple `GroupBox` or `Panel Controls` on a `Form`, pressing Tab moves the focus to the next `GroupBox` or `Panel`. Then, within the `GroupBox` or `Panel`, you use arrow keys to progress to successive `RadioButtons`.

TWO TRUTHS & A LIE

Working with a Form's Layout

1. Setting the Anchor property causes a `Control` to remain at a fixed distance from the side of a container when the user resizes it.
2. Setting the Dock property attaches a `Control` to the side of a container so that the `Control`'s size does not change when the container's size is adjusted.
3. The `GroupBox` and `Panel` controls are `ContainerControls`.

The false statement is #2. Setting the Dock property attaches a `Control` to the side of a container so that the `Control` stretches when the container's size is adjusted.

Adding a `MenuStrip` to a Form

Many programs you use in a Windows environment contain a **menu strip**, which is a horizontal list of general options that appears under the title bar of a `Form` or `Window`. When you click an item in a menu strip, you might initiate an action. More frequently, you see a list box that contains more specific options. Each of these might initiate an action or lead to another menu. For example, the Visual Studio IDE contains a horizontal menu strip that begins with the options *File*, *Edit*, and *View*. You probably have used word-processing, spreadsheet, and game programs with similar menus.

You can add a `MenuStrip Control` object to any `Form` you create. Using the Visual Studio IDE, you can add a `MenuStrip` to a `Form` by dragging it from the Toolbox onto the `Form`. This creates a menu bar horizontally across the top of the `Form`, just below the title bar. The strip extends across the width of the `Form` and contains a *Type Here* text box. When you click the text box, you can enter a menu item. Each time you add a menu item, new boxes are created so you can see where your next options will go, as shown in Figure 12-34.

Figure 12-34 Creating a Form with a `MenuStrip`

If you do not see `MenuStrip` in your Toolbox, click the Menus & Toolbars group to expose it. You can click the `MenuStrip` icon at the bottom of the design screen to view and change the properties for the `MenuStrip`. For example, you might want to change the `Font` or `BackColor` for the `MenuStrip`.

Earlier in this chapter, you learned how to create an access key for a `Button`. Similarly, if you create each menu item with an ampersand (&) in front of a unique letter, then the letter becomes an access key, and the user can press Alt and the letter to activate the menu choice. For example, if two choices were Green and Gray, you might want to type &Green and G&ray so the user could type Alt+G to select Green and Alt+R to select Gray.

When you double-click an entry in the `MenuStrip`, a `Click()` method is generated. For example, if you double-click *Blue* under *Color* in the menu being created in Figure 12-34, the method generated is `blueToolStripMenuItem_Click()`. As with all the other controls you have learned about, you can rename the method to begin with an uppercase letter, and you can write any code statements within the method. For example, suppose that a `Label` named `helloLabel` has been dragged onto the `Form`. If choosing the *Blue* menu option should result in a blue forecolor for the label, you might code the method as follows:

```
private void BlueToolStripMenuItem_Click(object sender, EventArgs e)
{
    helloLabel.ForeColor = Color.Blue;
}
```

You can work with the other menu items in this program in an exercise at the end of this chapter.

If possible, your main horizontal menu selections should be single words. That way, a user will not mistakenly think that a single menu item represents multiple items. Most applications do not follow this single-word convention for submenus. Also, users expect menu options to appear in conventional order. For example, users expect the far-left option on the main menu bar to be *File*, and they expect the *Exit* option to appear under *File*. Similarly, if an application contains a *Help* option, users expect to find it at the right side of the main menu bar. You should follow these conventions when designing your own menus.

Watch the video *Using a MenuStrip*.

TWO TRUTHS & A LIE

Adding a MenuStrip to a Form

1. When you click an item in a menu strip, the most common result is to initiate an action.

2. When you drag a `MenuStrip Control` object onto a `Form` using the Visual Studio IDE, the `MenuStrip` is added horizontally across the top of the `Form`, just below the title bar.

3. The default event for `MenuStrip` is `Click()`.

The false statement is #1. When you click an item in a menu strip, you might initiate an action. More frequently, you see a list box that contains more specific options.

Using Other Controls

If you examine the Visual Studio IDE or search through the Visual Studio documentation, you will find many other Controls that are not covered in this chapter. If you click Project on the menu bar and click Add New Item, you can add extra Forms, Files, Controls, and other elements to your project. (In the next "You Do It" section, you create a project that adds new Forms that appear after selections are made from a primary Form.) New controls and containers will be developed in the future, and you might even design new controls of your own. Still, all controls will contain properties and methods, and your solid foundation in C# will prepare you to use new controls effectively.

You Do It

Adding CheckBoxes to a Form

In the next steps, you add two CheckBoxes to the BedAndBreakfast Form. These controls allow the user to select an available room and view information about it.

1. Open the BedAndBreakfast project in Visual Studio, if it is not still open on your screen.

2. In the Design view of the BedAndBreakfast project in the Visual Studio IDE, drag a CheckBox onto the Form below the *Check our rates* Label. (See Figure 12-35 for its approximate placement.) Change the Text property of the CheckBox to **Belle Aire Suite**. Change the Name of the property to belleAireCheckBox. Drag a second CheckBox onto the Form beneath the first one. Change its Text property to **Lincoln Room** and its Name to lincolnCheckBox. Change the Font property for both CheckBoxes to **Microsoft Sans Serif Bold 14**.

(continues)

Using Other Controls

(continued)

[Screenshot: Bailey's Bed and Breakfast form showing "Welcome to Bailey's", "Check our rates", and two checkboxes: "Belle Aire Suite" and "Lincoln Room"]

Figure 12-35 The BedAndBreakfast Form with two CheckBoxes

3. Next, you will create two new Forms: one that appears when the user selects the BelleAire CheckBox and one that appears when the user selects the Lincoln CheckBox. Click **Project** on the menu bar, and then click **Add New Item**. In the Add New Item window, click **Windows Form**. In the Name text box at the bottom of the window, type `BelleAireForm`. See Figure 12-36.

(continues)

(continued)

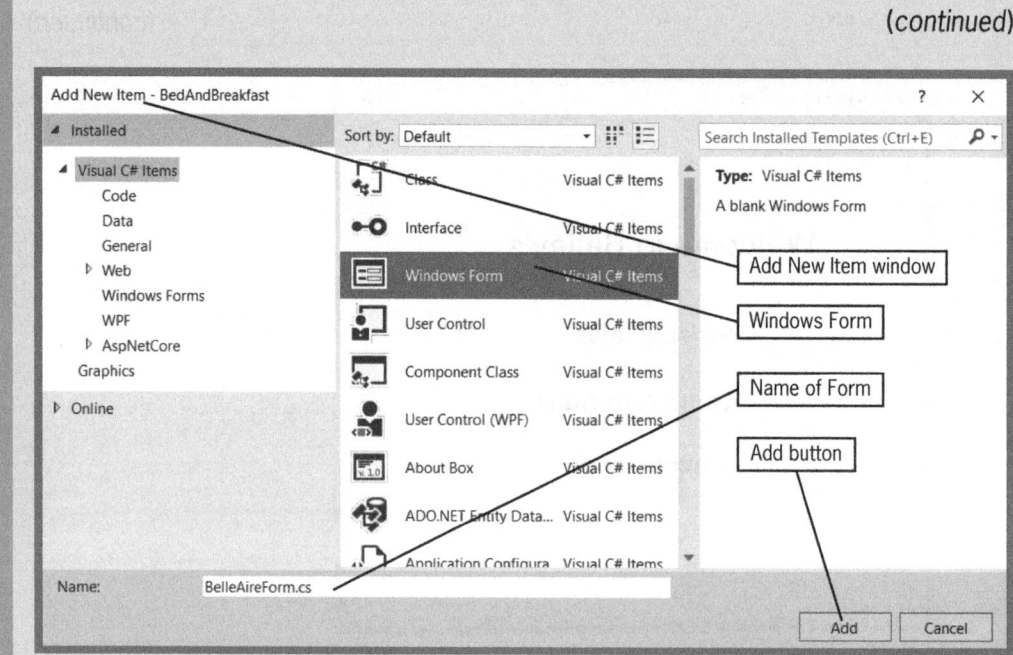

Figure 12-36 The Add New Item window

4. Click the **Add** button. A new Form is added to the project, and its Name and Text (title bar) properties contain *BelleAireForm*. Save the project (and continue to do so periodically).

5. Change the BackColor property of the Form to Yellow to match the color of BaileysForm.

6. Drag a Label onto the Form. Change the Name of the Label to **belleAireDescriptionLabel**. Change the Text property of the Label to contain the following: **The BelleAire suite has two bedrooms, two baths, and a private balcony**. Click the arrow on the text property to type the long label message on two lines. Drag a second Label onto the Form, name it **belleAirePriceLabel**, and type the price as the Text property: **$199 per night**. Adjust the sizes and positions of the Labels to resemble Figure 12-37.

(continues)

(continued)

Figure 12-37 The BelleAireForm with two Labels

7. Click the **Form1.cs[Design]** tab at the top of the Designer screen to view the original Bailey's Bed and Breakfast Form. Double-click the **BelleAire Suite CheckBox**. The program code (the method shell for the default event of a CheckBox) appears in the IDE main window. Rename the belleAireCheckBox_CheckedChanged() method to start with an uppercase letter, and within the method, add an if statement that determines whether the BelleAire CheckBox is checked. If it is checked, create a new instance of BelleAireForm and display it.

```
private void BelleAireCheckBox_CheckedChanged(object
   sender, EventArgs e)
{
   if (belleAireCheckBox.Checked)
   {
      BelleAireForm belleAireForm = new BelleAireForm();
      belleAireForm.ShowDialog();
   }
}
```

When a new Form (or other Windows class) is instantiated, it is not visible by default. ShowDialog() shows the window and disables all other windows in the application. The user must dismiss the new Form before proceeding. A secondary window that takes control of a program is a **modal window**; the user must deal with this window before proceeding.

(continues)

(continued)

8. Save and then execute the program by selecting **Debug** from the menu bar, and then select **Start Without Debugging**. The main BedAndBreakfast Form appears. Click the **BelleAire Suite** CheckBox. The BelleAire Form appears. Dismiss the Form. Click the **Lincoln Room** CheckBox. Nothing happens because you have not yet written event code for this CheckBox. When you uncheck and then check the **BelleAire Suite** CheckBox again, the BelleAire form reappears. Dismiss the BelleAire Form.

9. In the IDE adjust the size, position, or font of any controls if you think your adjustments would improve the program's appearance, and then test the program again.

10. When you dismiss the BelleAire Form, the BelleAire CheckBox on the Bed and Breakfast Form remains checked. To see it appear as unchecked after its Form is dismissed, dismiss the program's main form (Bailey's Bed and Breakfast) to end the program. Then, add a third statement within the if block in the CheckedChanged() message as follows:

    belleAireCheckBox.Checked = false;

    That way, whenever the CheckedChanged() method executes because the belleAireCheckBox was checked, it will become unchecked. Save the project, and then execute it again. When you select the BelleAire CheckBox, view the Form, and dismiss it, the CheckBox appears unchecked and is ready to check again. Dismiss the BedAndBreakfast Form.

11. Click **Project** on the menu bar, and then click **Add New Item**. Click **Windows Form**, and enter its Name: **LincolnForm**. Click the **Add** button, and when the new Form appears, its Name and Text properties will have been set to **LincolnForm**. Change the Text property to **Lincoln Room**. Then add two Labels to the Form, and provide appropriate Name properties for them. Change the Text on the first Label to **Return to the 1850s in this lovely room with private bath**. The second should be **$110 per night**. Change the Form's BackColor property to **White**. See Figure 12-38.

(continues)

(continued)

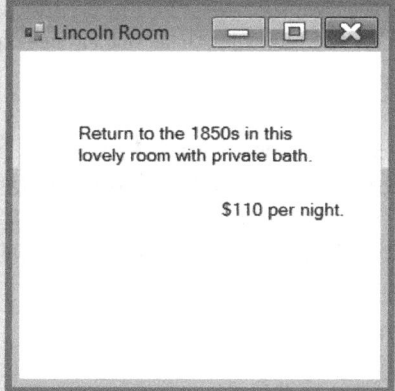

Figure 12-38 The LincolnForm

12. From the Toolbox, drag a PictureBox onto the Form. Select its **Image** property, and click the ellipsis. A dialog box allows you to select a resource. Click **Local resource**, and then click the **Import** button to browse for an image. Find the AbeLincoln file in the Chapter.12 folder of your downloadable student files, and double-click it. (Alternately, you can import another image you prefer.) After the image appears in the Select Resource dialog box, click **OK**. Part of the selected image appears in the PictureBox. Change the SizeMode property to **Zoom**. Adjust the size of the Form and the sizes and positions of the labels and picture box so that the picture is fully visible and everything looks attractive on the Form. See Figure 12-39.

Figure 12-39 The LincolnForm with an Image in a PictureBox

(continues)

CHAPTER 12 Using Controls

(continued)

 The AbeLincoln file was obtained at www.clipartkid.com. You can visit the site and download other images to use in your own applications. You also should search the Web for "free clip art" and similar phrases.

13. In the Solution Explorer, double-click **Form1.cs** or click the **Form1.cs[Design]** tab at the top of the design screen. On the BedAndBreakfast Form, double-click the Lincoln Room CheckBox, and rename the default method to start with an uppercase letter. Then add the following if statement to the LincolnCheckBox_CheckedChanged() method:

```
private void LincolnCheckBox_CheckedChanged(object
   sender, EventArgs e)
{
   if (lincolnCheckBox.Checked)
   {
      LincolnForm lincolnForm = new LincolnForm();
      lincolnForm.ShowDialog();
      lincolnCheckBox.Checked = false;
   }
}
```

14. Save the project and then execute it. When the BedAndBreakfast Form appears, click either CheckBox—the appropriate informational Form appears. Close it and then click the other CheckBox. Again, the appropriate Form appears.

15. Close all forms.

Adding RadioButtons to a Form

Next you add more Controls to the BedAndBreakfast Form. You generally use RadioButtons when a user must select from mutually exclusive options.

1. In the Design view of the main Form in the BedAndBreakfast project, add a Button near the bottom of the Form. Change the Button's Name property to **mealButton** and the Button's Text to **Click for meal options**. Adjust the size of the Button so that its text is fully visible.

2. From the menu bar, select **Project**, click **Add New Item**, and click **Windows Form**. Name the Form **BreakfastOptionForm**, and click **Add**. On the new Form, make the following changes:

   - Set the Form's BackColor to **Yellow**.
   - Drag a Label onto the Form. Name it appropriately, and set its Text to **Select your breakfast option**.

(continues)

(continued)

- Drag three RadioButtons onto the Form. Set their respective Text properties to **Continental, Full**, and **Deluxe**. Set their respective Names to **contRadioButton, fullRadioButton**, and **deluxeRadioButton**.
- Select an appropriate font for the Label and RadioButtons.
- Drag a Label onto the Form, and then set its Text to **Price:** and its Name to **priceLabel**. Make the Font property a little larger than for the other Form components, and also make it **Bold**.

See Figure 12-40 for approximate placement of all these Controls.

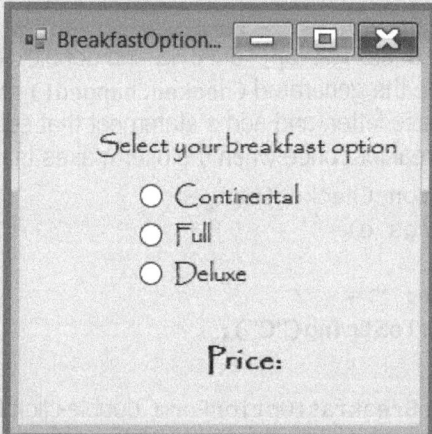

Figure 12-40 Developing the BreakfastOptionForm

3. Double-click the title bar of the BreakfastOptionForm to generate a method named BreakfastOptionForm_Load(). Within this method, you can type statements that execute each time the Form is created. Add the following statements within the BreakfastOptionForm class, which declare three constants representing prices for different breakfast options. Within the BreakfastOptionForm_Load() method, set the priceLabel Text property to the lowest price by default when the Form loads.

```
public partial class BreakfastOptionForm : Form
{
   private const double CONT_BREAKFAST_PRICE = 6.00;
   private const double FULL_BREAKFAST_PRICE = 9.95;
   private const double DELUXE_BREAKFAST_PRICE = 16.50;
```

(continues)

(continued)

```
    public BreakfastOptionForm()
    {
      InitializeComponent();
    }
    private void BreakfastOptionForm_Load (object sender,
       EventArgs e)
    {
      priceLabel.Text = "Price: " +
         CONT_BREAKFAST_PRICE.ToString("C");
    }
}
```

4. Return to the Design view for the BreakfastOptionForm, and double-click the **contRadioButton**. When you see the generated CheckedChanged() method, rename it to start with an uppercase letter, and add a statement that sets priceLabel to the continental breakfast price when the user makes that selection:

```
private void ContRadioButton_CheckedChanged
   (object sender, EventArgs e)
{
  priceLabel.Text = "Price: " +
     CONT_BREAKFAST_PRICE .ToString("C");
}
```

5. Return to the Design view for the BreakfastOptionForm, double-click the **fullRadioButton**, rename the generated method, and add a statement that sets the priceLabel to the full breakfast price when the user makes that selection:

```
private void FullRadioButton_CheckedChanged
   (object sender, EventArgs e)
{
  priceLabel.Text = "Price: " +
     FULL_BREAKFAST_PRICE.ToString("C");
}
```

6. Return to the Design view for the BreakfastOptionForm, double-click the **deluxeRadioButton**, rename the default method, and add a statement that sets the priceLabel to the deluxe breakfast price when the user makes that selection:

```
private void DeluxeRadioButton_CheckedChanged
   (object sender, EventArgs e)
{
  priceLabel.Text = "Price: " +
     DELUXE_BREAKFAST_PRICE.ToString("C");
}
```

(continues)

(continued)

7. In the Solution Explorer, double-click the **Form1.cs file** to view the original Form. Double-click the **mealButton Button**. When the Click() method is generated, rename its Click() method to start with an uppercase letter, and add the following code so that the BreakfastOptionForm is loaded when a user clicks the Button:

```
private void MealButton_Click(object sender,
   EventArgs e)
{
   BreakfastOptionForm breakfastForm = new
      BreakfastOptionForm();
   breakfastForm.ShowDialog();
}
```

8. Save the project and execute it. When the BedAndBreakfast Form appears, confirm that the BelleAire Suite and Lincoln Room CheckBoxes still work correctly, displaying their information Forms when they are clicked. Then click the **Click for meal options Button**. By default, the Continental breakfast option is chosen, as shown in Figure 12-41. Test the other radio buttons. Dismiss the Forms, return to the IDE, and adjust the sizes and positions of any components as needed, and then test the program again.

9. Dismiss all the Forms, and close Visual Studio.

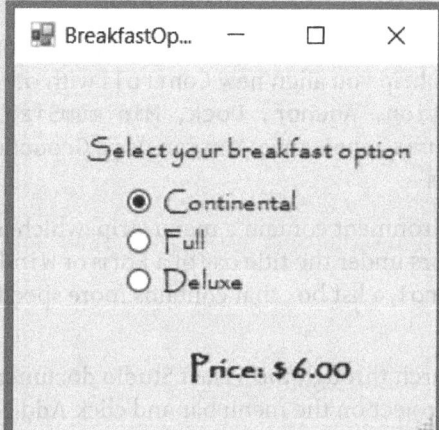

Figure 12-41 The BreakfastOptionForm with Continental breakfast RadioButton selected

CHAPTER 12 Using Controls

Chapter Summary

- The `Control` class provides definitions for GUI objects such as `Form`s and `Button`s. There are 26 direct descendants of `Control` and additional descendants of those classes. Each `Control` has more than 80 `public` properties and 20 `protected` ones.

- When you design GUI applications using the Visual Studio IDE, much of the code is generated automatically.

- You use the `Font` class to change the appearance of printed text on your `Form`s.

- A `LinkLabel` is similar to a `Label`; it is a child of `Label`, but it provides the additional capability to link the user to other sources, such as Web pages or files.

- The `Color` class contains a wide variety of predefined `Color`s that you can use with your `Control`s.

- `CheckBox` objects are GUI widgets the user can click to select or deselect an option. When a `Form` contains multiple `CheckBox`es, any number of them can be checked or unchecked at the same time. `RadioButton`s are similar to `CheckBox`es, except that when they are placed on a `Form`, only one `RadioButton` can be selected at a time.

- A `PictureBox` is a `Control` in which you can display graphics from a bitmap, icon, JPEG, GIF, or other image file type.

- `ListBox`, `ComboBox`, and `CheckedListBox` objects descend from `ListControl` and enable you to display lists of items that the user can select by clicking. The `MonthCalendar` and `DateTimePicker Control`s allow you to retrieve date and time information.

- When you place `Control`s on a `Form` in the IDE, you can drag them to any location to achieve the effect you want. Blue snap lines help you align new `Control`s with others already in place. You also can use the `Location, Anchor, Dock, MinimumSize,` and `MaximumSize` properties to customize a `Form`'s appearance. You can use a `GroupBox` or `Panel` to group related `Control`s on a `Form`.

- Many programs you use in a Windows environment contain a menu strip, which is a horizontal list of general options that appears under the title bar of a `Form` or `Window`. When a user clicks an item in a `MenuStrip Control`, a list box that contains more specific options is displayed frequently.

- If you examine the Visual Studio IDE or search through the Visual Studio documentation, you will find many `Control`s. If you click Project on the menu bar and click Add New Item, you can add extra `Form`s, `File`s, `Control`s, and other elements to a project.

Key Terms

Graphical control elements, or, more simply, **controls**, are the components through which a user interacts with a GUI program.

Widgets are GUI controls.

A **link label** is a control with text that links a user to other resources such as Web pages or files.

The **default event** for a `Control` is the one generated when you double-click the `Control` while designing it in the IDE and is the method you are most likely to alter when you use the `Control`, as well as the event that users most likely expect to generate when they encounter the `Control` in a working application.

A **check box** is a GUI widget the user can click to select or deselect an option.

A **radio button** is an option in a group in which only one can be selected at a time—selecting any radio button automatically deselects the others.

An **access key** provides a shortcut way to make a selection using the keyboard.

A **picture box** is a GUI element that can display graphics.

A **list box** is a GUI element that displays a list of items that the user can select by clicking.

A **combo box** is a GUI element that is a combination of a list box and an editing control that allows a user to select from the list or enter new text.

Snap lines appear in a design environment to help you align new `Controls` with others already in place.

A **group box** is a GUI element that contains other GUI elements; it is similar to a panel but does not have a scroll bar and can contain a caption.

A **panel** is a GUI element that contains other GUI elements; it is similar to a group box but does not have a caption and can contain a scroll bar.

A **menu strip** is a horizontal list of general options that appears under the title bar of a `Form` or `Window`.

A **modal window** is a secondary window that takes control from a primary window and that a user must deal with before proceeding.

Review Questions

1. `Labels`, `Buttons`, and `CheckBoxes` are all _____.

    a. GUI objects
    b. `Controls`
    c. widgets
    d. all of these

CHAPTER 12 Using Controls

2. All `Control` objects descend from _____.
   a. `Form`
   b. `Component`
   c. `ButtonBase`
   d. all of these

3. Which of the following is most like a `RadioButton`?
   a. `ListControl`
   b. `CheckedListBox`
   c. `PictureBox`
   d. `Button`

4. Which of the following is not a commonly used `Control` property?
   a. `BackColor`
   b. `Location`
   c. `Language`
   d. `Size`

5. The `Control` you frequently use to provide descriptive text for another `Control` object is a _____.
   a. `Label`
   b. `Form`
   c. `CheckBox`
   d. `MessageBox`

6. Which of the following creates a `Label` named `firstLabel`?
   a. `firstLabel = new firstLabel();`
   b. `Label = new firstLabel();`
   c. `Label firstLabel = new Label();`
   d. `Label firstLabel = Label();`

7. The property that determines what the user reads on a `Label` is the _____ property.
   a. `Setting`
   b. `Label`
   c. `Phrase`
   d. `Text`

8. Which of the following correctly creates a `Font`?
   a. `Font myFont = new Font("Arial", 14F, FontStyle.Bold);`
   b. `Font myFont = new Font("Courier", 13.6);`
   c. `myFont = Font new Font("TimesRoman", FontStyle.Italic);`
   d. `Font myFont = Font(20, "Helvetica", Underlined);`

9. The default event for a `Control` is the one that _____.
   a. occurs automatically whether or not a user manipulates the `Control`
   b. is generated when you double-click the `Control` while designing it in the IDE
   c. requires no parameters
   d. occurs when a user clicks the `Control` with a mouse

Review Questions

10. Assume that you have created a Label named myLabel. Which of the following sets myLabel's background color to green?

    a. myLabel = BackColor.System.Drawing.Color.Green;

    b. myLabel.BackColor = System.Drawing.Color.Green;

    c. myLabel.Green = System.DrawingColor;

    d. myLabel.Background = new Color.Green;

11. What is one difference between CheckBox and RadioButton objects?

    a. RadioButtons descend from ButtonBase; CheckBoxes do not.

    b. Only one RadioButton can be selected at a time.

    c. Only one CheckBox can appear on a Form at a time.

    d. RadioButtons cannot be placed in a GroupBox; CheckBoxes can.

12. The Checked property of a RadioButton can hold the values _____

    a. true and false

    b. Checked and Unchecked

    c. 0 and 1

    d. Yes, No, and Undetermined

13. The Control in which you can display a bitmap or JPEG image is a(n) _____.

    a. DisplayModule

    b. PictureBox

    c. BitmapControl

    d. ImageHolder

14. ListBox, ComboBox, and CheckedListBox objects all descend from which family?

    a. ListControl

    b. List

    c. ButtonBase

    d. ListBase

15. Which of the following properties is associated with a ListBox but not a Button?

    a. BackColor

    b. SelectedItem

    c. Location

    d. IsSelected

16. With a ListBox you can allow the user to choose _____.

    a. only a single option

    b. multiple selections

    c. either of these

    d. none of these

17. You can add items to a ListBox by using the _____ method.

    a. AddList()

    b. Append()

    c. List()

    d. AddRange()

18. A `ListBox`'s `SelectedItem` property contains _____.

    a. the position of the currently selected item
    b. the value of the currently selected item
    c. a Boolean value indicating whether an item is currently selected
    d. a count of the number of currently selected items

19. When you create a `ListBox`, by default its `SelectionMode` is _____.

    a. `Simple`
    b. `MultiExtended`
    c. `One`
    d. `false`

20. A horizontal list of general options that appears under the title bar of a `Form` or `Window` is a _____.

    a. task bar
    b. subtitle bar
    c. menu strip
    d. list box

Exercises

Programming Exercises

1. Create a project named **DayNight**. Include a `Form` that contains two `Buttons`, one labeled *Day* and one labeled *Night*. Add a `Label` telling the user to click a button. When the user clicks *Day*, change the `BackColor` of the `Form` to `Yellow`; when the user clicks *Night*, change the `BackColor` of the `Form` to `DarkBlue`.

2. Create a project named **FiveColors**. Its `Form` contains at least five `Button` objects, each labeled with a color. When the user clicks a `Button`, change the `BackColor` of the `Form` appropriately.

3. Create a project named **FiveColors2**. Its `Form` contains at least five `RadioButton` objects, each labeled with a color. When the user clicks a `RadioButton`, change the `BackColor` of the `Form` appropriately.

4. Create a project named **MyFlix**. Its `Form` contains a `ListBox` with the titles of at least six movies or TV shows available to purchase. Provide directions that tell users they can choose as many downloads as they want by holding down the Ctrl key while making selections. When the user clicks a `Button` to indicate the choices are final, display the number of selections made and total price, which is $1.99 per download. If the user selects or deselects items and clicks the button again, make sure the total is updated correctly.

Exercises

5. Create a project named **FontSelector**. Its Form contains two ListBoxes—one contains at least four Font names, and the other contains at least four Font sizes. Let the first item in each list be the default selection if the user fails to make a selection. Allow only one selection per ListBox. After the user clicks a Button, display *Hello* in the selected Font and size.

6. Create a project named **BreezyViewApartments** that contains a Form for an apartment rental service. Allow the user to choose a number of bedrooms, number of baths, and view—street or lake. After the user makes selections, display the monthly rent, which is calculated using a base price of $450, $550, or $700 per month for a one-, two-, or three-bedroom apartment, respectively. $75 is added to the base price for more than one bath, and $50 additional is added to the price for a lake view. Use the Controls that you think are best for each function. Label items appropriately, and use fonts and colors to achieve an attractive design.

7. Create a project named **VacationPlanner** for a tropical resort that offers all-inclusive vacation packages. The project contains a Form that allows the user to choose one option from at least three in each of the following categories—departure city, room type, and meal plan. Assign a different price to each selection, and display the total when the user clicks a Button. Use the Controls that you think are best for each function. Label items appropriately, and use fonts and colors to achieve an attractive design.

8. Create a project named **CarDealer** that contains a Form for an automobile dealer. Include options for at least three car models. After users make a selection, proceed to a new Form that contains information about the selected model. Use the Controls that you decide are best for each function. Label items on the Form appropriately, and use fonts and colors to achieve an attractive design.

9. Create a project named **AnnualBudget** that includes a Form with two LinkLabels One opens a spreadsheet for viewing, and the other visits your favorite Web site. Include Labels on the Form to explain each link. You can create a spreadsheet with a few numbers that represent an annual budget, or you can use the AnnualBudget.xls file in the Chapter.12 folder of the downloadable student files.

10. Create a project named **TinasCustomTees** that includes a Form for a company that produces T-shirts. Allow the user to select from at least four sizes, each with a different price, and from at least three colors. Adjust the final displayed price as the user chooses different sizes, and change the background color of the frame as the user chooses different colors. Also, allow the user to select an order date from a MonthCalendar, and display the shipping date, which is three days later. Include as many labels as necessary so the user understands how to use the Form.

11. Create a project named **MenuStripDemo2** that is based on the MenuStripDemo project in the Chapter.12 folder of your downloadable student files. (See Figure 12-34 earlier in this chapter). Add appropriate functionality to the currently unprogrammed menu options (the two options in the Font menu and the three options in the Color

menu). Add at least three other menu options to the program, either vertically, horizontally, or both.

12. Create a project named **LetsMakeADeal**. In this game, three prizes of varying value are assigned randomly to be hidden behind three "doors" that you can implement as `Buttons`. For example, the prizes might be a new car, a big-screen TV, and a live goat. The player chooses a `Button`, and then one of the two other prizes is revealed; the one revealed is never the most desirable prize. The user then has the option of changing the original selection to the remaining unseen choice. For example, consider these two game scenarios:

   - Suppose that the most valuable prize is randomly assigned to the first button. If the user chooses the first button, reveal either of the other two prizes, and ask the user if he wants to change his selection.
   - Suppose that the most valuable prize is assigned to the first button, but the user chooses the second button. Reveal the third prize so that the most valuable prize's location is still hidden, and then ask the user whether he wants to change his selection.

   After the user has chosen to retain his original selection or make a change, reveal what he has won.

Debugging Exercises

1. Each of the following projects in the Chapter.12 folder of your downloadable student files has syntax and/or logical errors. Immediately save the four project folders with their new names before starting to correct their errors. After you correct the errors, save each project using the same name preceded with *Fixed*. For example, DebugTwelve1 will become FixedDebugTwelve1.

   a. DebugTwelve1   c. DebugTwelve3
   b. DebugTwelve2   d. DebugTwelve4

Case Problems

1. Throughout this book, you have created programs for the Greenville Idol competition. Now create an interactive advertisement named **GreenvilleAdvertisement** that can be used to recruit contestants. Include at least three `Controls` that you studied in this chapter, and use at least two different `Fonts` and two different `Colors`.

2. Throughout this book, you have created programs for Marshall's Murals. Now create an interactive advertisement named **MarshallsAdvertisement** that can be used to advertise the available murals. Include at least three `Controls` that you studied in this chapter, and use at least two different `Fonts` and two different `Colors`.

CHAPTER 13

Handling Events

Upon completion of this chapter, you will be able to:

- Describe event handling
- Describe delegates
- Declare and use both custom and built-in event handlers
- Handle `Control` component events
- Handle mouse and keyboard events
- Manage multiple `Control`s
- Continue your exploration of `Control`s and events

CHAPTER 13 Handling Events

Throughout this book, you have learned how to create interactive GUI programs in which a user can manipulate a variety of Controls. You have worked with several Controls that respond to a user-initiated event, such as a mouse click, and you have provided actions for Control default events. In this chapter, you will expand your understanding of the event-handling process. You will learn more about the object that triggers an event and the object that captures and responds to that event. You also will learn about delegates—objects that act as intermediaries in transferring messages from senders to receivers. You will create delegates and manage interactive events. You will learn to manage multiple events for a single Control and to manage multiple Controls for a project.

Event Handling

In C#, an **event** is a reaction to an occurrence in a program; an event transpires when something interesting happens to an object. When you create a class, you decide exactly what is considered "interesting." For example, when you create a Form, you might decide to respond to a user clicking a Button but ignore a user who clicks a Label—clicking the Label is not "interesting" to the Form.

A program uses an event to notify a client when something happens to an object. Events are used frequently in GUI programs—for example, a program is notified when the user clicks a Button or chooses an option from a ListBox. In addition, you can use events with ordinary classes that do not represent GUI controls. When an object's client might want to know about any changes that occur in the object, events enable the object to signal the client.

The actions that occur during the execution of a program occur **at runtime**. The expression *at runtime* is used to distinguish execution-time activities from those that occur during development time and compile time. Events are runtime occurrences.

Because an event is generated when a user interacts with a GUI object, GUI programs are described as **event-driven**—an event such as a button click "drives" the program to perform a task. Programmers also say that an action like a button click **raises an event**, **fires an event**, or **triggers an event**.

For example, Figure 13-1 shows a Form that contains a Label and a Button. The following changes are the only ones that have been made to the default Form in the IDE:

- The Text on the Form has been changed to *Event Demo*.
- The Size property of the Form has been adjusted so the Form will be wide enough for the output it will eventually display.
- A Label has been dragged onto the Form, its Name property has been set to helloLabel, its Text property has been set to *Hello*, and its Font has been increased.

- A Button has been dragged onto the Form, its Name property has been set to changeButton, its Text property has been set to *Change the label*, and its size has been adjusted so the Text is fully visible.

Figure 13-1 A Form with a Label and a Button

When you double-click a button named changeButton, Visual Studio generates an empty method named changeButton_Click. After you rename the method so it conventionally starts with an uppercase letter, the method shell looks like the following:

```
private void ChangeButton_Click(object sender, EventArgs e)
{
}
```

A method that performs a task in response to an event is an **event handler**. The ChangeButton_Click() method is an event handler; it will handle clicks that generate from the Button.

Suppose that when a user clicks the button, you want the text on the label to change from *Hello* to *Goodbye*. You can write the following code for the event handler:

```
private void ChangeButton_Click(object sender, EventArgs e)
{
    helloLabel.Text = "Goodbye";
}
```

Then, when you run the application and click the button, the output appears as shown in Figure 13-2.

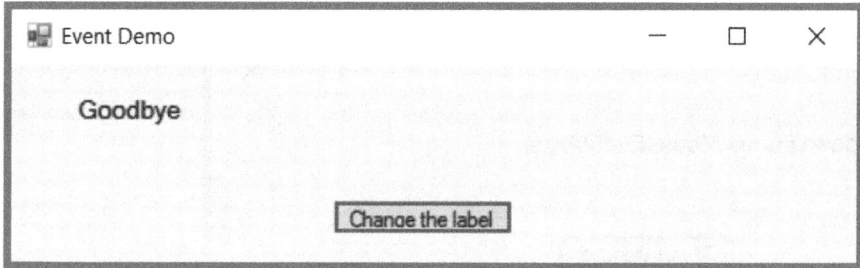

Figure 13-2 Output of the EventDemo application after the user clicks the button

The object that generates an event, such as a Button, is an **event sender**. The event-handling method is also known as an **event receiver**. The first parameter in the list for the event receiver method is an object named sender; it is a reference to the object that generated the event. For example, if you code the event handler to display sender's information as a string as in the following method version, the output after the user clicks the Button appears as shown in Figure 13-3.

```
private void ChangeButton_Click(object sender, EventArgs e)
{
    helloLabel.Text = sender.ToString();
}
```

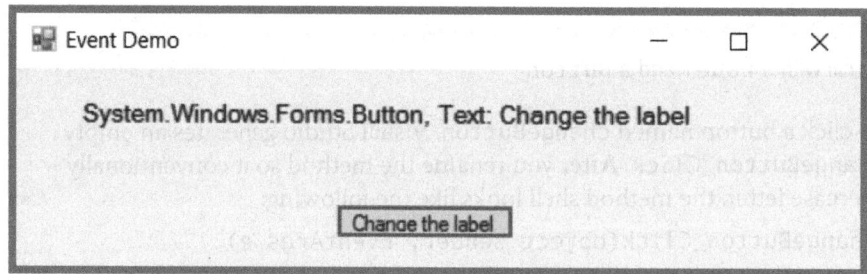

Figure 13-3 The EventDemo application modified to display sender information

The label in Figure 13-3 shows that the sender of the event is an instance of System.Windows.Forms.Button, whose Text property is *Change the label*.

The second parameter in the ChangeButton_Click() event handler's parameter list is a reference to an event arguments object of type EventArgs; in this method, the EventArgs argument is named e. EventArgs is a C# class designed for holding event information. If you change the code in the event handler to display the EventArgs ToString() value as in the following method version and then run the program and click the button, you see the output in Figure 13-4.

```
private void ChangeButton_Click(object sender, EventArgs e)
{
    helloLabel.Text = e.ToString();
}
```

Figure 13-4 The EventDemo application modified to display EventArgs information

Event Handling

In Figure 13-4, you can see that the **e** object is a `MouseEventArgs` object. That makes sense, because the user used the mouse to click the `Button`. (If the user has a touch screen, the user can also touch the `Button` to generate the event.)

When you open the Designer.cs file in the IDE, you can examine all the code generated for the application that creates the `Form` shown in Figure 13-4. Expanding the code generated by the Windows Form Designer lets you see comments as well as statements that set the `Controls`' properties. For example, the code generated for `changeButton` appears in Figure 13-5. You can recognize that such features as the button's `Location`, `Name`, and `Size` have been set.

```
// changeButton
//
this.changeButton.Location = new System.Drawing.Point(243, 92);
this.changeButton.Name = "changeButton";
this.changeButton.Size = new System.Drawing.Size(135, 23);
this.changeButton.TabIndex = 1;
this.changeButton.Text = "Change the label";
this.changeButton.UseVisualStyleBackColor = true;
this.changeButton.Click += new
    System.EventHandler(this.ChangeButton_Click);
```

Figure 13-5 Code involving `changeButton` generated by Visual Studio

The code generated in Design mode in the IDE is not meant to be altered by typing. You should modify `Control` properties through the Properties window in the IDE, not by typing in the Designer.cs file.

All the code in Figure 13-5 was created by Visual Studio. You have seen statements similar to most of the statements in Figure 13-5, including those that set the `Size`, `TabIndex`, and other properties of `changeButton`. (Recall that `this` that starts each statement refers to the `Form` that holds `changeButton`.) The most unusual statement in the section of `changeButton` code is shaded in Figure 13-5. This statement concerns a **click event**, which is an action fired when a user clicks a button during program execution. The shaded statement is necessary because `changeButton` does not automatically "know" what method will handle its events—C# and all other .NET languages allow you to choose your own names for event-handling methods for events generated by GUI objects. In other words, the event-handling method for `changeButton` is not required to be named `ChangeButton_Click()`; For example, you *could* create your program so that when the user clicks the button, the event-handling method is named `CalculatePayroll()`, `ChangeLabel()`, or any other identifier. Usually, however, you do not want to make such a change; using the name `ChangeButton_Click()` for the method that executes when `changeButton` is clicked is the clearest approach.

Connecting an event to its resulting actions is called **event wiring**. The event wiring for the `ChangeButton_Click()` method is accomplished in the shaded statement in Figure 13-5. The statement indicates that, for this program, the method named `ChangeButton_Click()` is the receiver for changeButton's Click event; the method executes when a user clicks the button and an event is fired. Programmers say the statement creates a *delegate* or, more specifically, a *composed delegate*. The delegate's type is EventHandler, and it takes a reference to the ChangeButton_Click() method. You will learn about delegates in the next two sections of this chapter, and you also will learn why the += operator is used in the statement.

> ### TWO TRUTHS & A LIE
> #### Event Handling
> 1. An action such as a key press or button click raises an event.
> 2. A method that performs a task in response to an event is an event handler.
> 3. The control that generates an event is an event receiver.
>
> The false statement is #3. The control that generates an event is an event sender.

Understanding Delegates

A **delegate** is an object that contains a reference to a method; object-oriented programmers would say that a delegate *encapsulates a method*. In government, a delegate is a representative that you authorize to make choices for you. For example, states send delegates to presidential nominating conventions. When human delegates arrive at a convention, they are free to make last-minute choices based on current conditions. Similarly, C# delegates provide a way for a program to take alternative courses that are not determined until runtime. When you write a method, you don't always know which actions will occur at runtime, so you give your delegates authority to run the correct methods.

In Chapter 1, you learned that encapsulation is a basic feature of object-oriented programming. Recall that encapsulation is the technique of packaging an object's attributes and methods into a cohesive unit that can then be used as an undivided entity.

After you have instantiated a C# delegate, you can pass this object to a method, which then can call the method referenced within the delegate. In other words, a delegate provides a way to pass a reference to a method as an argument to another method. Although you can't pass a method to a method, you *can* pass an object that is a reference to a method. For example, if del is a delegate that contains a reference to the method M1(), you can pass del to a new method named MyMethod(). Alternatively, you could create a delegate named del that contains a reference to a method named M2() and then pass this version to MyMethod(). When you write MyMethod(), you don't have to know whether it will call M1() or M2(); you only need to know that it will call whatever method is referenced within del. Perhaps the decision about which method will execute will be made as the result of user input, the date of execution, the result of a calculation, or some other factor.

A C# delegate is similar to a function pointer in the C++ programming language. A function pointer is a variable that holds a method's memory address. In C++, you pass a method's address to another method using a pointer variable. On the other hand, the Java programming language does not allow function pointers because they are dangerous—if the program alters the address, you might inadvertently execute the wrong method. C# provides a compromise between the dangers of C++ pointers and the Java ban on passing functions. Delegates allow flexible method calls, but they remain secure because you cannot alter the method addresses.

You declare a delegate using the keyword delegate, followed by an ordinary method declaration that includes a return type, method name, and parameter list. For example, by entering the following statement, you can declare a delegate named GreetingHandler(), which accepts a string argument and returns nothing:

```
delegate void GreetingHandler(string s);
```

Any delegate can encapsulate any method that has the same return type and parameter list as the delegate. So GreetingHandler can encapsulate any method as long as it has a void return type and a single string parameter. If you declare a delegate and then write a method with the same return type and parameter list, you can assign an instance of the delegate to represent it. For example, the following Hello() method is a void method that takes a string parameter:

```
public static void Hello(string s)
{
    WriteLine("Hello, {0}!", s);
}
```

Because the Hello() method matches the GreetingHandler definition, you can assign a reference to the Hello() method to a new instance of GreetingHandler, as follows:

```
GreetingHandler myDel = new GreetingHandler(Hello);
```

Once the reference to the Hello() method is encapsulated in the delegate myDel, each of the following statements will result in the same output: "Hello, Kim!".

```
Hello("Kim");
myDel("Kim");
```

In this example, the ability to use the delegate myDel does not seem to provide any benefits over using a regular method call to Hello(). If you have a program in which you pass the delegate to a method, however, the method becomes more flexible; you gain the ability to send a reference to an appropriate method you want to execute at the time.

For example, Figure 13-6 shows a Greeting class that contains Hello() and Goodbye() methods. The Main() method declares two delegates named firstDel and secondDel. One is instantiated using the Hello() method, and the other is instantiated using the Goodbye() method. When the Main() method calls GreetMethod() two times, it passes a different method and string each time. Figure 13-7 shows the output.

```
using static System.Console;
delegate void GreetingHandler(string s);
class Greeting
{
   public static void Hello(string s)
   {
      WriteLine("Hello, {0}!", s);
   }
   public static void Goodbye(string s)
   {
      WriteLine("Goodbye, {0}!", s);
   }
   static void Main()
   {
      GreetingHandler firstDel, secondDel;
      firstDel = new GreetingHandler(Hello);
      secondDel = new GreetingHandler(Goodbye);
      GreetMethod(firstDel, "Cathy");
      GreetMethod(secondDel, "Bob");
   }
   public static void GreetMethod(GreetingHandler gd,
      string name)
   {
      WriteLine("The greeting is:");
      gd(name);
   }
}
```

Figure 13-6 The Greeting program

Figure 13-7 Output of the Greeting program

 Delegates are useful in that a method reference can be passed to another method, so the receiving method can be customized. As with many other features of C# (and all other programming languages), you can use other techniques to accomplish the same result. For example, you certainly can produce simple output such as *Hello, Cathy* using other techniques. However, you are learning a little about delegates here because, as you will see later in this chapter, they are used in the code that responds to events in C#'s GUI environment.

Creating Composed Delegates

You can assign one delegate to another using the = operator. You also can use the + and += operators to combine delegates into a **composed delegate** that calls the delegates from which it is built. As an example, assume that you declare three delegates named del1, del2, and del3, and that you assign a reference to the method M1() to del1 and a reference to method M2() to del2. When the statement del3 = del1 + del2; executes, del3 becomes a delegate that executes both M1() and M2(), in that order. Only delegates with the same parameter list can be composed, and the delegates used must have a void return type. Additionally, you can use the - and -= operators to remove a delegate from a composed delegate. A composed delegate is a collection of delegates, and the += and -= operators add and remove items from the collection.

Figure 13-8 shows a program that contains a composed delegate. This program contains only two changes from the Greeting program in Figure 13-6: the class name (Greeting2) and the shaded statement that creates the composed delegate. The delegate firstDel now executes two methods, Hello() and Goodbye(), whereas secondDel still executes only Goodbye(). Figure 13-9 shows the output; *Cathy* is used with two methods, but *Bob* is used with only one.

```
using static System.Console;
delegate void GreetingHandler(string s);
class Greeting2
{
   public static void Hello(string s)
   {
      WriteLine("Hello, {0}!", s);
   }
   public static void Goodbye(string s)
   {
      WriteLine("Goodbye, {0}!", s);
   }
   static void Main()
   {
      GreetingHandler firstDel, secondDel;
      firstDel = new GreetingHandler(Hello);
      secondDel = new GreetingHandler(Goodbye);
      firstDel += secondDel;
      GreetMethod(firstDel, "Cathy");
      GreetMethod(secondDel, "Bob");
   }
   public static void GreetMethod(GreetingHandler gd,
      string name)
   {
      WriteLine("The greeting is:");
      gd(name);
   }
}
```

Figure 13-8 The Greeting2 program

CHAPTER 13 Handling Events

```
The greeting is:
Hello, Cathy!
Goodbye, Cathy!
The greeting is:
Goodbye, Bob!
```

Figure 13-9 Output of the Greeting2 program

 Watch the video *Event Handling*.

TWO TRUTHS & A LIE
Understanding Delegates

1. A delegate is an object that contains a reference to a method.
2. Once you have created a delegate, it can encapsulate any method with the same identifier as the delegate.
3. A composed delegate can be created using the += operator; it calls the delegates from which it is built.

The false statement is #2. Once you have created a delegate, it can encapsulate any method with the same return type and parameter list as the delegate.

 You Do It

Creating Delegates

To demonstrate how delegates work, you create two delegate instances in the next steps and assign different method references to them.

1. Open a new console project named **DiscountDelegateDemo**. Type the necessary using statements, and then create a delegate that encapsulates a void method that accepts a double argument:

   ```
   using System;
   using static System.Console;
   delegate void DiscountHandler(ref double saleAmount);
   ```

(continues)

(continued)

2. Begin creating a `DiscountDelegateDemo` class that contains a `StandardDiscount()` method. The method accepts a reference parameter that represents an amount of a sale. If the sale amount is at least $1,000, a discount of 5 percent is calculated and subtracted from the sale amount. If the sale amount is not at least $1,000, nothing is subtracted.

```
class DiscountDelegateDemo
{
   public static void StandardDiscount(ref double saleAmount)
   {
      const double DISCOUNT_RATE = 0.05;
      const double CUTOFF = 1000.00;
      double discount;
      if(saleAmount >= CUTOFF)
         discount = saleAmount * DISCOUNT_RATE;
      else
         discount = 0;
      saleAmount -= discount;
   }
```

3. Add a `PreferredDiscount()` method. The method also accepts a reference parameter that represents the amount of a sale and calculates a discount of 10 percent on every sale.

```
   public static void PreferredDiscount(ref double saleAmount)
   {
      const double SPECIAL_DISCOUNT = 0.10;
      double discount = saleAmount * SPECIAL_DISCOUNT;
      saleAmount -= discount;
   }
```

4. Start a `Main()` method that declares variables whose values (a sale amount and a code) will be supplied by the user. Declare two `DiscountHandler` objects named `firstDel` and `secondDel`. Assign a reference to the `StandardDiscount()` method to one `DiscountHandler` object and a reference to the `PreferredDiscount()` method to the other `DiscountHandler` object.

```
   static void Main()
   {
      double saleAmount;
      char code;
      DiscounHandler firstDel, secondDel;
      firstDel = new DiscountHandler(StandardDiscount);
      secondDel = new DiscountHandler(PreferredDiscount);
```

(continues)

(continued)

5. Continue the Main() method with prompts to the user to enter a sale amount and a code indicating whether the standard or preferred discount should apply. Then, depending on the code, use the appropriate delegate to calculate the correct new value for saleAmount. Display the value and add closing curly braces for the Main() method and the class.

```
Write("Enter amount of sale ");
saleAmount = Convert.ToDouble(ReadLine());
Write("Enter S for standard discount," +
   "or P for preferred discount ");
code = Convert.ToChar(ReadLine());
if(code == 'S')
   firstDel(ref saleAmount);
else
   secondDel(ref saleAmount);
WriteLine("New sale amount is {0}",
   saleAmount.ToString("C2"));
   }
}
```

6. Save the file, and then compile and execute it. Figure 13-10 shows the results when the program is executed several times.

```
Enter amount of sale 1000
Enter S for standard discount, or P for preferred discount S
New sale amount is $950.00


Enter amount of sale 1000
Enter S for standard discount, or P for preferred discount P
New sale amount is $900.00


Enter amount of sale 800
Enter S for standard discount, or P for preferred discount S
New sale amount is $800.00


Enter amount of sale 800
Enter S for standard discount, or P for preferred discount P
New sale amount is $720.00
```

Figure 13-10 Sample executions of the DiscountDelegateDemo program

(continues)

Creating a Composed Delegate

When you compose delegates, you can invoke multiple method calls using a single statement. In the next steps, you create a composed delegate to demonstrate how composition works.

1. Open the **DiscountDelegateDemo** file, and immediately save it as **DiscountDelegateDemo2**.

2. Within the Main() method, add a third DiscountDelegate object to the statement that declares the two existing versions, as follows:

   ```
   DiscountHandler firstDel, secondDel, thirdDel;
   ```

3. After the statements that assign values to the existing DiscountDelegate objects, add statements that assign the firstDel object to thirdDel, and then add secondDel to it through composition.

   ```
   thirdDel = firstDel;
   thirdDel += secondDel;
   ```

4. Change the prompt for the code, as follows, to reflect three options. The standard and preferred discounts remain the same, but the extreme discount (supposedly for special customers) provides both types of discounts, first subtracting 5 percent for any sale equal to or greater than $1,000, and then providing a discount of 10 percent more.

   ```
   Write("Enter S for standard discount, " +
      "P for preferred discount," +
      "\nor X for eXtreme discount ");
   ```

5. Change the if statement so that if the user does not enter *S* or *P*, then the extreme discount applies.

   ```
   if(code == 'S')
      firstDel(ref saleAmount);
   else
      if(code == 'P')
         secondDel(ref saleAmount);
      else
         thirdDel(ref saleAmount);
   ```

(continues)

CHAPTER 13 Handling Events

(continued)

6. Save the program, and then compile and execute it. Figure 13-11 shows the output when the program is executed several times. When the user enters a sale amount of $1,000 and an *S*, a 5 percent discount is applied. When the user enters a *P* for the same amount, a 10 percent discount is applied. When the user enters X with the same amount, a 5 percent discount is applied, followed by a 10 percent discount, which produces a net result of a 14.5 percent discount.

```
Enter amount of sale 1000
Enter S for standard discount, P for preferred discount
or X for eXtreme discount S
New sale amount is $950.00

Enter amount of sale 1000
Enter S for standard discount, P for preferred discount
or X for eXtreme discount P
New sale amount is $900.00

Enter amount of sale 1000
Enter S for standard discount, P for preferred discount
or X for eXtreme discount X
New sale amount is $855.00
```

Figure 13-11 Three executions of the DiscountDelegateDemo2 program

For `static` methods such as `StandardDiscount` and `PreferredDiscount`, a `delegate` object encapsulates the method to be called. When creating a class that contains instance methods, you create `delegate` objects that encapsulate both an instance of the class and a method of the instance. You will create this type of `delegate` in the next section.

Declaring and Using Both Custom and Built-in Event Handlers

To declare your own event, you use a delegate. An event provides a way for the clients of a class to dictate methods that should execute when an event occurs. The clients identify methods to execute by associating the delegate with the method that should execute when the event occurs. Just like the event handlers that are automatically created in the IDE, each of your own event handler delegates requires two arguments: the object where the event was initiated (the sender) and an EventArgs argument. You can create an EventArgs object that contains event information, or you can use the EventArgs class static field named Empty, which represents an event that contains no event data. In other words, using the EventArgs.Empty field simply tells the client that an event has occurred, without specifying details. For example, you can declare a delegate event handler named ChangedEventHandler, as follows:

```
public delegate void ChangedEventHandler(object sender, EventArgs e);
```

The identifier ChangedEventHandler can be any legal identifier you choose. This delegate defines the set of arguments that will be passed to the method that handles the event. The delegate ChangedEventHandler can be used in a client program that handles events.

For example, Figure 13-12 contains the ChangedEventHandler delegate and a simple Student class that is similar to many classes you already have created. The Student class contains just two data fields and will generate an event when the data in either field changes.

```
public delegate void ChangedEventHandler(object sender, EventArgs e);
class Student
{
   private int idNum;
   private double gpa;
   public event ChangedEventHandler Changed;
   public int IdNum
   {
      get
      {
         return idNum;
      }
      set
      {
         idNum = value;
         OnChanged(EventArgs.Empty);
      }
   }
}
```

Figure 13-12 The Student class *(continues)*

(continued)

```
    public double Gpa
    {
        get
        {
            return gpa;
        }
        set
        {
            gpa = value;
            OnChanged(EventArgs.Empty);
        }
    }
    private void OnChanged(EventArgs e)
    {
        Changed(this, e);
    }
}
```

Figure 13-12 The Student class

The class in Figure 13-12 contains fields that hold an ID number and grade point average for a Student. The first shaded statement in the figure defines a third attribute of the Student class—an event named Changed. The declaration for an event looks like a field, but instead of being an int or a double, it is a ChangedEventHandler. The event is declared as public, which is conventional, but you can use any accessibility modifier.

The Student class event (Changed) looks like an ordinary field. However, you cannot assign values to the event as easily as you can to ordinary data fields. You can take only two actions on an event: You can compose a new delegate onto it using the += operator, and you can remove a delegate from it using the -= operator. For example, to add StudentChanged to the Changed event of a Student object named stu, you would write the following:

stu.Changed += new ChangedEventHandler(StudentChanged);

In the Student class, each set accessor assigns a value to the appropriate class instance field. However, when either idNum or gpa changes, the method in the Student class named OnChanged() also is called, using EventArgs.Empty as the argument. The value of EventArgs.Empty is a read-only instance of EventArgs. You can pass it to any method that accepts an EventArgs parameter.

The OnChanged() method calls Changed() using two arguments: a reference to the Student object that was changed and the empty EventArgs object. Calling Changed() is also known as **invoking the event**.

If no client has wired a delegate to the event, the Changed field will be null, rather than referring to the delegate that should be called when the event is invoked. Therefore, programmers often check for null before invoking the event, as in the following example:

```
if(Changed != null)
    Changed(this, e);
```

For simplicity, the example in Figure 13-12 does not bother checking for null.

Figure 13-13 shows an EventListener class that listens for Student events. This class contains a Student object that is assigned a value using the parameter to the EventListener class constructor. The StudentChanged() method is added to the Student's event delegate using the += operator. The StudentChanged() method is the event-handling method that executes in response to a Changed event; it displays a message and Student data.

```
class EventListener
{
   private Student stu;
   public EventListener(Student student)
   {
      stu = student;
      stu.Changed += new ChangedEventHandler(StudentChanged);
   }
   private void StudentChanged(object sender, EventArgs e)
   {
      WriteLine("The student has changed.");
      WriteLine("ID# {0} GPA {1}",
         stu.IdNum, stu.Gpa);
   }
}
```

Figure 13-13 The EventListener class

Figure 13-14 shows a program that demonstrates using the Student and EventListener classes. The program contains a single Main() method, which declares a Student and an EventListener that listens for events from the Student class. Then three assignments are made. Because this program is registered to listen for events from the Student, each change in a data field triggers an event. That is, each field assignment not only changes the value of the data field, but it also executes the StudentChanged() method that displays two lines of explanation. In Figure 13-15, the program output shows that an event occurs three times— once when IdNum becomes 2345 (and Gpa is still 0), again when IdNum becomes 4567 (and Gpa still has not changed), and a third time when Gpa becomes 3.2.

```
using System;
using static System.Console;
class DemoStudentEvent
{
    static void Main()
    {
        Student oneStu = new Student();
        EventListener listener = new EventListener(oneStu);
        oneStu.IdNum = 2345;
        oneStu.IdNum = 4567;
        oneStu.Gpa = 3.2;
    }
}
```

Figure 13-14 The DemoStudentEvent program

```
The student has changed.
    ID# 2345   GPA 0
The student has changed.
    ID# 4567   GPA 0
The student has changed.
    ID# 4567   GPA 3.2
```

Figure 13-15 Output of the DemoStudentEvent program

Using the Built-in EventHandler

The C# language allows you to create events using any delegate type. However, the .NET Framework provides guidelines you should follow if you are developing a class that others will use. These guidelines indicate that the delegate type for an event should take exactly two parameters: a parameter indicating the source of the event, and an EventArgs parameter that encapsulates any additional information about the event. For events that do not use additional information, the .NET Framework already has defined an appropriate delegate type named EventHandler.

Figure 13-16 shows all the code necessary to demonstrate an EventHandler. Note the following changes from the classes used in the DemoStudentEvent program:

- No delegate is declared explicitly in the Student class.
- In the first statement with shading in the Student class, the event is associated with the built-in delegate EventHandler.
- In the second statement with shading, which appears in the EventListener class, the delegate composition uses EventHandler.

Declaring and Using Both Custom and Built-in Event Handlers

```csharp
using System;
using static System.Console;
class Student
{
   private int idNum;
   private double gpa;
   public event EventHandler Changed;
   public int IdNum
   {
      get
      {
         return idNum;
      }
      set
      {
         idNum = value;
         OnChanged(EventArgs.Empty);
      }
   }
   public double Gpa
   {
      get
      {
         return gpa;
      }
      set
      {
         gpa = value;
         OnChanged(EventArgs.Empty);
      }
   }
   private void OnChanged(EventArgs e)
   {
      Changed(this, e);
   }
}
class EventListener
{
   private Student stu;
   public EventListener(Student student)
   {
      stu = student;
      stu.Changed += new EventHandler(StudentChanged);
   }
```

Figure 13-16 The Student, EventListener, and DemoStudentEvent2 classes *(continues)*

(continued)

```
    private void StudentChanged(object sender, EventArgs e)
    {
        WriteLine("The student has changed.");
        WriteLine("  ID# {0} GPA {1}"
            stu.IdNum, stu.Gpa);
    }
}
class DemoStudentEvent2
{
    static void Main()
    {
        Student oneStu = new Student();
        EventListener listener = new EventListener(oneStu);
        oneStu.IdNum = 2345;
        oneStu.IdNum = 4567;
        oneStu.Gpa = 3.2;
    }
}
```

Figure 13-16 The `Student`, `EventListener`, and `DemoStudentEvent2` classes

When you compile and execute the program in Figure 13-16, the output is identical to that shown in Figure 13-15.

TWO TRUTHS & A LIE

Declaring and Using both Custom and Built-in Event Handlers

1. When an event occurs, any delegate that a client has given or passed to the event is invoked.
2. Built-in event handler delegates have two arguments, but those you create yourself have only one.
3. You can take only two actions on an event field: composing a new delegate onto the field using the += operator, and removing a delegate from the field using the -= operator.

The false statement is #2. Every event handler delegate requires two arguments—the object where the event was initiated (the sender) and an EventArgs argument.

Declaring and Using Both Custom and Built-in Event Handlers

  You Do It

Creating a Delegate That Encapsulates Instance Methods

In the next set of steps, you create a simple `BankAccount` class that contains just two data fields: an account number and a balance. It also contains methods to make withdrawals and deposits. An event is generated after any withdrawal or deposit.

1. Open a project named **DemoBankEvent**. Type the `using` statements you need, and then begin a class named `BankAccount`. The class contains an account number, a balance, and an event that executes when an account's balance is adjusted.

   ```
   using System
   using static System.Console;
   class BankAccount
   {
       private int acctNum;
       private double balance;
       public event EventHandler BalanceAdjusted;
   ```

2. Add a constructor that accepts an account number parameter and initializes the balance to 0.

   ```
   public BankAccount(int acct)
   {
       acctNum = acct;
       balance = 0;
   }
   ```

3. Add read-only properties for both the account number and the account balance.

   ```
   public int AcctNum
   {
       get
       {
           return acctNum;
       }
   }
   public double Balance
   {
       get
       {
           return balance;
       }
   }
   ```

(continues)

(continued)

4. Add two methods. One makes account deposits by adding the parameter to the account balance, and the other makes withdrawals by subtracting the parameter value from the bank balance. Each uses the `OnBalanceAdjusted` event handler that reacts to all deposit and withdrawal events by displaying the new balance.

   ```
   public void MakeDeposit(double amt)
   {
       balance += amt;
       OnBalanceAdjusted(EventArgs.Empty);
   }
   public void MakeWithdrawal(double amt)
   {
       balance -= amt;
       OnBalanceAdjusted(EventArgs.Empty);
   }
   ```

5. Add the `OnBalanceAdjusted()` method that accepts an `EventArgs` parameter and calls `BalanceAdjusted()`, passing it references to the newly adjusted `BankAccount` object and the `EventArgs` object. (Earlier in the chapter, you learned that calling a method such as `OnBalanceAdjusted()` is also known as *invoking the event*.) Include a closing curly brace for the class.

   ```
   public void OnBalanceAdjusted(EventArgs e)
   {
       BalanceAdjusted(this, e);
   }
   }
   ```

6. Save the file.

Creating an Event Listener

1. When you write an application that declares a `BankAccount`, you might want the client program to listen for `BankAccount` events. To do so, you create an `EventListener` class.

2. After the closing curly brace of the `BankAccount` class, type the following `EventListener` class that contains a `BankAccount` object. When the `EventListener` constructor executes, the `BankAccount` field is initialized with the constructor parameter. Using the `+=` operator, add the `BankAccountBalanceAdjusted()` method to the event delegate. Next, write the `BankAccountBalanceAdjusted()` method to display a message and information about the `BankAccount`.

(continues)

Declaring and Using Both Custom and Built-in Event Handlers

(continued)

```
class EventListener
{
   private BankAccount acct;
   public EventListener(BankAccount account)
   {
      acct = account;
      acct.BalanceAdjusted += new EventHandler
         (BankAccountBalanceAdjusted);
   }
   private void BankAccountBalanceAdjusted(object
      sender, EventArgs e)
   {
      WriteLine("The account balance has been adjusted.");
      WriteLine(" Account# {0} balance {1}", acct.AcctNum,
         acct.Balance.ToString("C2"));
   }
}
```

3. Create a class to test the `BankAccount` and `EventListener` classes. Below the closing curly brace for the `EventListener` class, start a `DemoBankAccountEvent` class that contains a `Main()` method. Declare an integer to hold the number of transactions that will occur in the demonstration program. Also declare two variables: one can hold a code that indicates whether a transaction is a deposit or withdrawal, and one is the amount of the transaction.

```
class DemoBankAccountEvent
{
   static void Main()
   {
      const int TRANSACTIONS = 5;
      char code;
      double amt;
```

4. Declare a `BankAccount` object that is assigned an arbitrary account number, and declare an `EventListener` object so this program is registered to listen for events from the `BankAccount`. Each change in the `BankAccount` balance will not only change the balance data field, it will execute the `BankAccountBalanceAdjusted()` method that displays two lines of explanation.

```
BankAccount acct = new BankAccount(334455);
EventListener listener = new EventListener(acct);
```

(continues)

(continued)

5. Add a loop that executes five times (the value of TRANSACTIONS). On each iteration, prompt the user to indicate whether the current transaction is a deposit or withdrawal and to enter the transaction amount. Call the MakeDeposit() or MakeWithdrawal() method accordingly.

```
for(int x = 0; x < TRANSACTIONS; ++x)
{
   Write("Enter D for deposit or W for withdrawal ");
   code = Convert.ToChar(ReadLine());
   Write("Enter dollar amount ");
   amt = Convert.ToDouble(ReadLine());
   if(code == 'D')
      acct.MakeDeposit(amt);
   else
      acct.MakeWithdrawal(amt);
}
```

6. At the end of the for loop, add a closing curly brace for the Main() method and another one for the class.

7. Save the file, and then compile and execute it. Figure 13-17 shows a typical execution in which five transactions modify the account. The output shows that an event occurs five times—twice for deposits and three times for withdrawals.

```
Enter D for deposit or W for withdrawal D
Enter dollar amount 2000
The account balance has been adjusted.
    Account# 334455   balance $2,000.00
Enter D for deposit or W for withdrawal W
Enter dollar amount 250
The account balance has been adjusted.
    Account# 334455   balance $1,750.00
Enter D for deposit or W for withdrawal W
Enter dollar amount 60
The account balance has been adjusted.
    Account# 334455   balance $1,690.00
Enter D for deposit or W for withdrawal D
Enter dollar amount 500
The account balance has been adjusted.
    Account# 334455   balance $2,190.00
Enter D for deposit or W for withdrawal W
Enter dollar amount 1005
The account balance has been adjusted.
    Account# 334455   balance $1,185.00
```

Figure 13-17 Typical execution of the DemoBankEvent program

Handling Control Component Events

Handling events requires understanding several difficult concepts. Fortunately, you most frequently will want to handle events in GUI environments when the user will manipulate Controls, and the good news is that these events already have been defined for you. When you want to handle events generated by GUI Controls, you use the same techniques as when you handle any other events. The major difference is that when you create your own classes, such as Student, you must define both the data fields and events you want to manage. However, existing Control components, such as Buttons and ListBoxes, already contain events with names, such as Click. Table 13-1 lists just some of the more commonly used Control events. You can consult the Visual Studio Help feature to discover additional Control events as well as more specific events assigned to individual Control child classes.

Event	Description
BackColorChanged	Occurs when the value of the BackColor property has changed
Click	Occurs when a control is clicked
ControlAdded	Occurs when a new control is added
ControlRemoved	Occurs when a control is removed
CursorChanged	Occurs when the Cursor property value has changed
DragDrop	Occurs when a drag-and-drop operation is completed
DragEnter	Occurs when an object is dragged into a control's bounds
DragLeave	Occurs when an object has been dragged into and out of a control's bounds
DragOver	Occurs when an object has been dragged over a control's bounds
EnabledChanged	Occurs when the Enabled property value has changed
Enter	Occurs when a control is entered
FontChanged	Occurs when the Font property value has changed
ForeColorChanged	Occurs when the ForeColor property value has changed
GotFocus	Occurs when a control receives focus
HelpRequested	Occurs when a user requests help for a control
KeyDown	Occurs when a key is pressed while a control has focus; event is followed immediately by KeyPress
KeyPress	Occurs when a key is pressed while a control has focus; event occurs just after KeyDown
KeyUp	Occurs when a key is released while a control has focus

Table 13-1 Some Control class public instance events (*continues*)

CHAPTER 13 Handling Events

(continued)

Event	Description
Leave	Occurs when a control is left
LocationChanged	Occurs when the Location property value has changed
LostFocus	Occurs when a control loses focus
MouseDown	Occurs when the mouse pointer hovers over a control and a mouse button is pressed
MouseEnter	Occurs when the mouse pointer enters a control
MouseHover	Occurs when the mouse pointer hovers over a control
MouseLeave	Occurs when the mouse pointer leaves a control
MouseMove	Occurs when the mouse pointer moves over a control
MouseUp	Occurs when the mouse pointer hovers over a control and a mouse button is released
MouseWheel	Occurs when the mouse wheel moves while a control has focus
Move	Occurs when a control is moved
Resize	Occurs when a control is resized
TextChanged	Occurs when the Text property value has changed
VisibleChanged	Occurs when the Visible property value has changed

Table 13-1 Some Control class public instance events

You already have used the IDE to create some event-handling methods. These methods have been the default events generated when you double-click a Control in the IDE. For example, you have created a Click() method for a Button and a LinkClicked() method for a LinkLabel. A Form can contain any number of Controls that might have events associated with them. Additionally, a single Control might be able to raise any number of events. For example, in addition to creating a Button's default Click event, you might want to define various actions when the user's mouse rolls over the button. Table 13-1 lists only a few of the many events available with Controls; any Control conceivably could raise many of the available events.

Suppose you want to create a project that takes a different set of actions when the mouse is over a Button than when the mouse is clicked. Figure 13-18 shows a project that has been started in the IDE. The following actions have been taken:

- The Form was resized.
- The Form's Text property was changed.
- A Button was dragged onto the Form, and its Text was set to *Click me*.
- A Label was added to the Form, its Text was set to *Hello*, and its Font was increased.

Handling Control Component Events

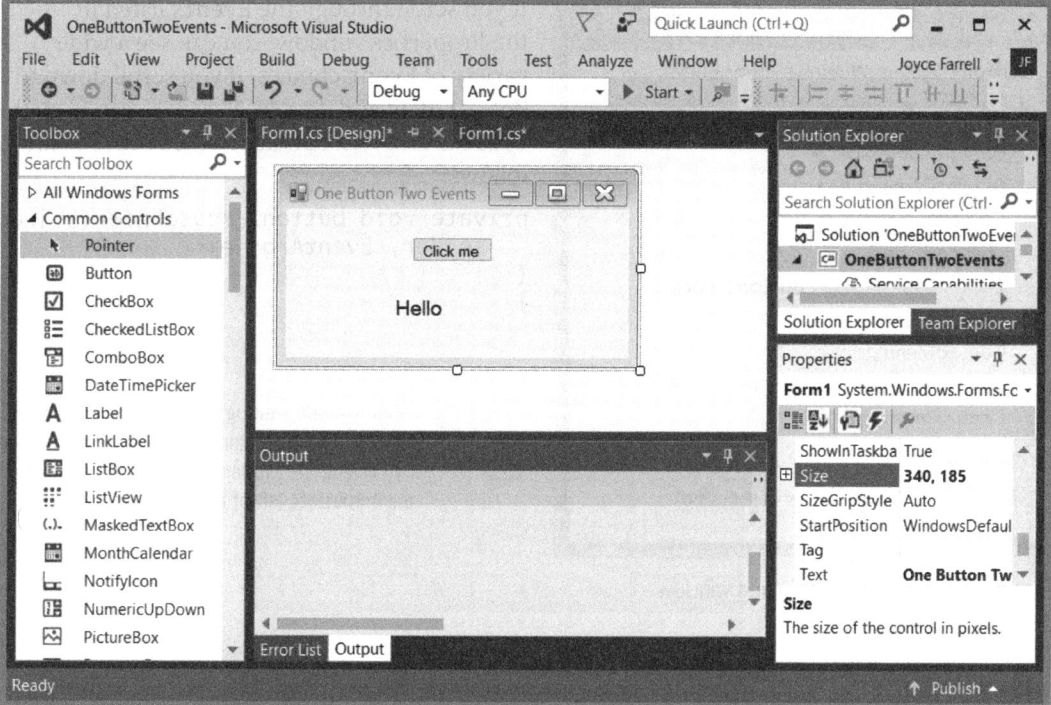

Figure 13-18 Start of the OneButtonTwoEvents project in the IDE

When you double-click the Button on the Form in the IDE, you generate the shell of a Click() method. You can change the method's identifier to start with an uppercase letter, and then you can add statements to change the Label's text and color when the user clicks the Button, as follows:

```
private void Button1_Click(object sender, EventArgs e)
{
   label1.Text = "Button was clicked";
   label1.BackColor = Color.CornflowerBlue;
}
```

 Color.CornflowerBlue is one of C#'s predefined Color properties. A complete list appears in Table 12-5 in Chapter 12.

With the Button selected on the design Form, you can click the Events icon in the Properties window at the right side of the screen. The Events icon looks like a lightning bolt. Figure 13-19 shows that the Properties window displays events instead of properties and that the Click event has an associated method.

CHAPTER 13 Handling Events

If you scroll through the Events listed in the Properties window, you can see a wide variety of Event choices. If you scroll down to MouseEnter and double-click, you can view the code for an event handler in the Form1.cs file as follows:

```
private void button1_MouseEnter(object
   sender, EventArgs e)
{
}
```

 When you are viewing events in the Properties window, you can return to the list of properties by clicking the Properties icon. This icon is to the immediate left of the Events icon.

Figure 13-19 The Properties window displaying events

You can rename the method to start with an uppercase letter, and you can type any statements you want within this method. For example, you might write the following method:

```
private void Button1_MouseEnter(object sender, EventArgs e)
{
   label1.Text = "Go ahead";
   button1.BackColor = Color.Red;
}
```

When you run the program with the two new methods, two different events can occur:

- When you enter the button with the mouse (that is, pass the mouse over it), the Label's Text changes to *Go ahead*, and the button turns red, as shown on the left in Figure 13-20.

- After the button is clicked, the Label's Text changes again to *Button was clicked*, and the Label becomes blue, as shown on the right in Figure 13-20.

Figure 13-20 The OneButtonTwoEvents program when the mouse enters the button and after the button is clicked

Handling Control Component Events

If you examine the code generated by the Windows Form Designer, you will find the following two statements:

```
this.button1.Click += new
   System.EventHandler(this.button1_Click);
this.button1.MouseEnter += new
   System.EventHandler(this.button1_MouseEnter);
```

These `EventHandler` statements are similar to those in the `Student` class in Figure 13-16. The `Click` and `MouseEnter` delegates have been set to handle events appropriately for this application. You could have used the IDE to create these events just by selecting them from the Properties list and writing the action statements you want. The IDE saves you time by automatically entering the needed statement correctly. However, by knowing how to manually create a GUI program that contains events, you gain a greater understanding of how event handling works. This knowledge helps you troubleshoot problems and helps you create your own new events and handlers when necessary.

 Watch the video *Handling Control Component Events*.

TWO TRUTHS & A LIE

Handling Control Component Events

1. The default methods generated when you double-click a `Control` in the IDE are known as procedures.

2. A `Form` can contain any number of `Control`s that might have events associated with them, and a single `Control` might be able to raise any number of events.

3. You can type any statements you want within an automatically generated event method.

The false statement is #1. The default methods generated when you double-click a Control in the IDE are known as event handlers.

Handling Mouse and Keyboard Events

Users can interact with GUI applications in multiple ways. Two common tactics are to use a mouse or to type on a keyboard. Mouse and keyboard events are similar in that every mouse or key event-handling method must have two parameters: an object representing the sender and an object that holds information about the event.

Handling Mouse Events

Mouse events include all the actions a user takes with a mouse, including clicking, pointing, and dragging. Mouse events can be handled for any Control through an object of the class MouseEventArgs, which descends from EventArgs. The delegate used to create mouse event handlers is MouseEventHandler. Depending on the event, the type of the second parameter in the event-handling method is EventArgs or MouseEventArgs. Table 13-2 describes several common mouse events, and Table 13-3 lists some properties of the MouseEventArgs class.

Mouse event	Description	Event argument type
MouseClick	Occurs when the user clicks the mouse within the Control's boundaries	MouseEventArgs
MouseDoubleClick	Occurs when the user double-clicks the mouse within the Control's boundaries	MouseEventArgs
MouseEnter	Occurs when the mouse cursor enters the Control's boundaries	EventArgs
MouseLeave	Occurs when the mouse cursor leaves the Control's boundaries	EventArgs
MouseDown	Occurs when a mouse button is pressed while the mouse is within the Control's boundaries	MouseEventArgs
MouseHover	Occurs when the mouse cursor is within the Control's boundaries	MouseEventArgs
MouseMove	Occurs when the mouse is moved while within the Control's boundaries	MouseEventArgs
MouseUp	Occurs when a mouse button is released while the mouse is within the Control's boundaries	MouseEventArgs

Table 13-2 Common mouse events

A MouseDown event can occur without a corresponding MouseUp if the user presses the mouse but switches focus to another control or application before releasing the mouse button.

MouseEventArgs property	Description
Button	Specifies which mouse button triggered the event; the value can be Left, Right, Middle, or none
Clicks	Specifies the number of times the mouse was clicked
X	The x-coordinate where the event occurred on the control that generated the event
Y	The y-coordinate where the event occurred on the control that generated the event

Table 13-3 Properties of the MouseEventArgs class

MouseClick and Click are separate events. The Click event takes an EventArgs parameter, but MouseClick takes a MouseEventArgs parameter. For example, if you define a Click event, you do not have the MouseEventArgs class properties.

Figure 13-21 contains a Form with a single Label named locationLabel that changes as the user continues to click the mouse on it. The figure shows how the Label changes in response to a series of user clicks. Initially, the Label is empty (that is, the default Text property has been deleted and not replaced), but the following code was added to the Form1.cs file:

```
private void Form1_MouseClick(object sender, MouseEventArgs e)
{
    locationLabel.Text += "\nClicked at " + e.X + ", " + e.Y;
}
```

Every time the mouse is clicked on the Form, the Label is appended with a new line that contains "Clicked at" and the x- and y-coordinate position where the click occurred on the Form. Figure 13-21 shows the Form after the user has clicked nearer the top left, top right, bottom right, and bottom left areas of the Form.

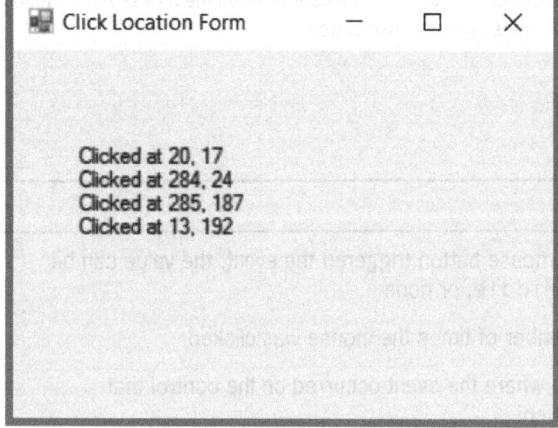

Figure 13-21 A Form that responds to clicks

When the programmer selects the MouseClick() event for Form1 from the Event list in the IDE, the following code is generated in the Designer.cs file. This code instantiates the MouseClick delegate.

```
this.MouseClick += new System.Windows.Forms.MouseEventHandler
    (this.Form1_MouseClicked);
```

Handling Keyboard Events

Keyboard events, also known as **key events**, occur when a user presses and releases keyboard keys. Table 13-4 lists some common keyboard events. Similar to the way mouse events work, every keyboard event-handling method must have two parameters. Depending on the event, the delegate used to create the keyboard event handler is either KeyEventHandler or KeyPressEventHandler and the type of the second parameter is KeyEventArgs or KeyPressEventArgs.

Keyboard event	Description	Event argument type
KeyDown	Occurs when a key is first pressed	KeyEventArgs
KeyUp	Occurs when a key is released	KeyEventArgs
KeyPress	Occurs when a key is pressed	KeyPressEventArgs

Table 13-4 Keyboard events

Handling Mouse and Keyboard Events

Table 13-5 describes `KeyEventArgs` properties, and Table 13-6 describes `KeyPressEventArgs` properties. An important difference is that `KeyEventArgs` objects include data about helper keys or modifier keys that are pressed with another key. For example, if you need to distinguish between a user pressing *A* and pressing *Alt+A* in your application, then you must use a keyboard event that uses an argument of type `KeyEventArgs`.

Property	Description
Alt	Indicates whether the Alt key was pressed
Control	Indicates whether the Control (Ctrl) key was pressed
Shift	Indicates whether the Shift key was pressed
KeyCode	Returns the code for the key
KeyData	Returns the key code along with any modifier key
KeyValue	Returns a numeric representation of the key (this number is known as the Windows virtual key code)

Table 13-5 Some properties of `KeyEventArgs` class

Property	Description
KeyChar	Returns the ASCII character for the key pressed

Table 13-6 A property of `KeyPressEventArgs` class

For example, suppose that you create a Form with a Label, and, from the Properties window for the Form, you double-click the KeyUp event to generate the shell for a method named Form1_KeyUp(). Suppose you then insert the statements into the method in the Form1.cs file, as shown in Figure 13-22. When the user runs the program and presses and releases a keyboard key, the Label is filled with information about the key. Figure 13-23 shows three executions of this program. During the first execution, the user typed *a*. You can see on the form that the KeyCode is *A* (uppercase), but you also can see that the user did not press the Shift key.

```
private void Form1_KeyUp(object sender, KeyEventArgs e)
{
   label1.Text += "Key Code " + e.KeyCode;
   label1.Text += "\nAlt " + e.Alt;
   label1.Text += "\nShift " + e.Shift;
   label1.Text += "\nControl " + e.Control;
   label1.Text += "\nKey Data " + e.KeyData;
   label1.Text += "\nKey Value " + e.KeyValue + "\n\n";
}
```

Figure 13-22 The Form1_KeyUp() method in the KeyDemo program

CHAPTER 13 Handling Events

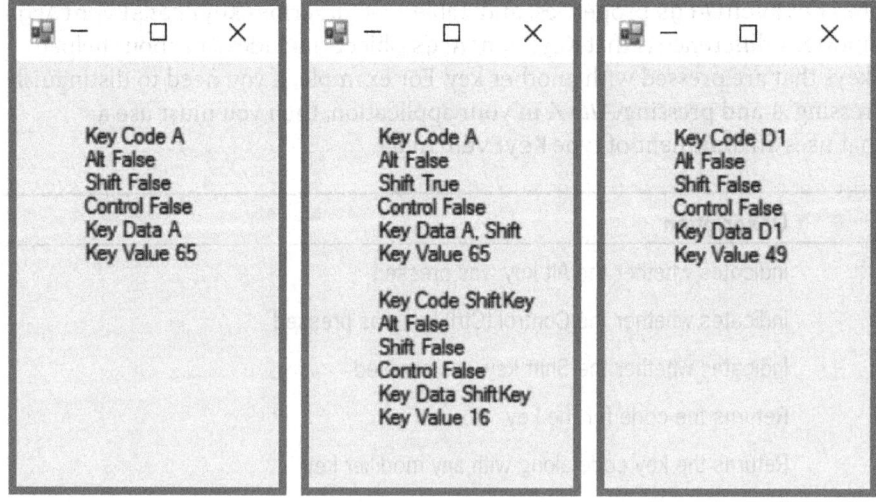

Figure 13-23   Three executions of the KeyDemo program

In the second execution in Figure 13-23, the user held down Shift, pressed *a*, and then released the Shift key. This causes two separate KeyUp events. The first has KeyCode A with Shift true, and the second has KeyCode ShiftKey. Notice that the Key values generated after typing *a* and *A* are the same, but the value after typing Shift is different.

In the third execution in Figure 13-23, the user pressed the number *1*, whose code is D1.

When you view the Form1.Designer.cs file for the KeyDemo program, you see the following automatically created statement, which defines the composed delegate:

```
this.KeyUp += new System.Windows.Forms.KeyEventHandler
   (this.Form1_KeyUp);
```

TWO TRUTHS & A LIE

Handling Mouse and Keyboard Events

1. The delegate used to create mouse event handlers is MouseEventHandler.
2. Keyboard events, also known as key events, occur when a user presses and releases keyboard keys.
3. Unlike mouse events, every keyboard event-handling method must be parameterless.

The false statement is #3. Like mouse events, every keyboard event-handling method must have two parameters: an object representing the sender, and an object that holds information about the event.

Managing Multiple Controls

When Forms contain multiple Controls, you often want one to have focus. You also might want several actions to have a single, shared consequence. For example, you might want the same action to occur whether the user clicks a button or presses the Enter key, or you might want multiple buttons to generate the same event when they are clicked.

Defining Focus

When users encounter multiple GUI Controls on a Form, usually one Control has **focus**. For example, when a Button has focus, a user expects that clicking the button or pressing the Enter key will raise an event.

TabStop is a Boolean property of a Control that identifies whether the Control will serve as a stopping place—that is, a place that will receive focus—in a sequence of Tab key presses. The default value for TabStop for a Button is true, but the default value for a Label is false because Labels are not expected to be part of a tabbing sequence. TabIndex is a numeric property that indicates the order in which the Control will receive focus when the user presses the Tab key. Programmers typically use small numbers for TabIndex values, beginning with 0. When a Control's TabStop value is true and the Control has the lowest TabIndex of a Form's Controls, it receives focus when the Form is initialized.

Setting the TabIndex values of two or more Controls to 0 does not cause an error. Only one Control will receive focus, however.

Figure 13-24 shows a Form that contains three Buttons and a Label. Each Button has been associated with a Click() event such as the following:

```
private void Button1_Click(object sender, EventArgs e)
{
    buttonInfoLabel.Text = "Button 1 selected";
}
```

In the program shown running in Figure 13-24, each Button has been assigned a TabIndex value in ascending order. When the application starts, the first Button (labeled *1*) has focus. Whether the user clicks that button or presses Enter, the message appears as shown on the left in the figure. In the next part of the figure, the user has pressed Tab and Enter to select button2, so it has focus, and the Label's Text property has changed. Alternatively, the user could have clicked button2 to achieve the same result. The user then could select either of the other Buttons by clicking them as usual or by pressing Tab until the desired button has focus and then pressing Enter.

CHAPTER 13 Handling Events

Figure 13-24 Execution of the FocusDemo application

Handling Multiple Events with a Single Handler

When a `Form` contains multiple `Control`s, you can create a separate event handler for each `Control`. However, you also can associate the same event handler with multiple `Control`s. For example, suppose you create a `Form` that contains three `Button`s and a `Label`. The buttons have been labeled *A*, *B*, and *1*. Further suppose you want to display one message when the user clicks a letter button and a different message when the user clicks a number button. In the IDE, you can double-click the first `Button` and create an associated method such as the following:

```
private void Button1_Click(object sender, EventArgs e)
{
    buttonInfoLabel.Text = "You clicked a letter button";
}
```

If you click the second button so its properties are displayed in the IDE's Properties list, you can click the Events icon to see a list of events associated with the second button. If no `Click` event has been chosen yet, a list box is available. This list contains all the existing events that have the correct signature to be the event handler for the event. Because the `Button1_Click()` handler also can handle a `Button2_Click()` event, you can select it as the event for `button2`. When you run the program, clicking either letter button produces the output shown in Figure 13-25.

Figure 13-25 Output of the SingleHandler program after a letter button is clicked

Until you associate an event with the *1* button, nothing happens when the user clicks it. To complete the application that is running in Figure 13-25, you would want to associate an event with the *3* button to modify the `Label`'s `Text` to *You clicked a number button*.

 When two or more `Control`s generate the same event, many programmers prefer to generalize the event method name. For example, if `button1` and `button2` call the same method when clicked, it makes sense to name the event method `LetterButton_Click()` instead of `Button1_Click()`.

Perhaps you have shopped online at a site that offers multiple ways to "buy now." For example, you might click a grocery cart icon, choose *Place order now* from a menu, or click a button. Often, *Place order now* buttons are displayed at several locations on the page. If you want to encourage a user's behavior, you should provide multiple ways to accommodate it.

 Watch the video *Managing Multiple Controls*.

> ### TWO TRUTHS & A LIE
> **Managing Multiple Controls**
>
> 1. The Control TabStop property can be set to true or false; it identifies whether the Control will serve as a stopping place in a sequence of Tab key presses.
>
> 2. On a Form with multiple Controls, one Control must have a TabIndex value of 0.
>
> 3. When a Form contains multiple Controls, you can associate the same event with all of them.
>
> The false statement is #2. TabIndex is a numeric property that indicates the order in which the control will receive focus when the user presses the Tab key. Programmers typically use small numbers for TabIndex values, beginning with 0. However, you might choose not to use any TabIndex values, or if you do, you might choose not to start with 0.

Continuing to Learn about Controls and Events

If you examine the Visual Studio IDE, you will discover many additional Controls that contain hundreds of properties and events. No single book or programming course can demonstrate all of them for you. However, if you understand good programming principles and the syntax and structure of C# programs, learning about each new C# feature becomes progressively easier. When you encounter a new control in the IDE, you probably can use it without understanding all the code generated in the background, but when you do understand the background, your knowledge of C# is more complete.

Continue to explore the Help facility in the Visual Studio IDE. Particularly, read the brief tutorials there. Also, you should search the Internet for C# discussion groups. C# is a new, dynamic language, and programmers pose many questions to each other online. Reading these discussions can provide you with valuable information and suggest new approaches to resolving problems.

You Do It

Using `TabIndex`

In the next steps, you create a `Form` in the Visual Studio IDE and add four `Buttons` so you can demonstrate how to manipulate their `TabIndex` properties.

1. Open the Visual Studio IDE and start a new project. Define it to be a **Windows Forms Application** named **ManyButtons**.

2. Change the `Size` of the `Form` so it is wider and shorter, and change the `Text` property of `Form1` to **Many Buttons**.

3. Drag four `Buttons` onto the `Form`, and place them so that they are similar to the layout shown in Figure 13-26. Change the Name properties of the buttons to `redButton`, `whiteButton`, `blueButton`, and `favoriteButton`. Change the `Text` on the `Buttons` to **Red**, **White**, **Blue**, and **My favorite color**, respectively. Adjust the size of the last button so its longer `Text` is fully displayed.

Figure 13-26 Four `Buttons` on the Many Buttons `Form`

4. Examine the Properties list for the Red button. The `TabIndex` is 0. Examine the properties for the White, Blue, and My favorite color buttons. The IDE has set their `TabIndex` values to 1, 2, and 3, respectively.

5. Click the **Save All** button, and then run the program. When the `Form` appears, the Red button has focus. Press the **Tab** key, and notice that focus changes to the White button. When you press **Tab** again, focus changes to the Blue button. Press **Tab** several more times, and observe that the focus rotates among the four `Buttons`.

6. Dismiss the `Form`.

7. Change the `TabIndex` property of the Blue button to **0**, and change the `TabIndex` of the Red button to **2**. (The `TabIndex` of the White button remains 1,

(continues)

(continued)

and the `TabIndex` of the My favorite color button remains 3.) Save the program again, and then run it. This time, the Blue button begins with focus. When you press Tab, the order in which the `Buttons` receive focus is Blue, then White, then Red, then My favorite color. (Clicking the `Buttons` or pressing Enter raises no event because you have not assigned events to the `Buttons`.)

8. Change the `TabIndex` property for the Red button back to **0** and the `TabIndex` property for the Blue button back to **2**. Click the **Save All** button.

Associating One Method with Multiple Events

In the next steps, you add three methods to the Many Buttons `Form` and cause one of the methods to execute each time the user clicks one of the four `Buttons`.

1. If it is not still open, open the **ManyButtons** project in the Visual Studio IDE.
2. Double-click the **Red** button on the `Form` to view the code for the shell of a `redButton_Click()` method. Rename the method to start with an uppercase letter, and then, between the method's curly braces, insert a statement that will change the `Form`'s background color to red as follows:

   `this.BackColor = Color.Red;`

At first glance, you might think `this` refers to the `Button` that is clicked. However, if you examine the `RedButton_Click()` code in the Form1.cs file in the IDE, you will discover that the method is part of the Form1 class. Therefore, `this.BackColor` refers to the Form's `BackColor` property.

3. Select the **Form1.cs [Design]** tab, and then double-click the **White** button. Rename the generated method, and add the following code to the `WhiteButton_Click()` method:

   `this.BackColor = Color.White;`

4. On the `Form`, double-click the **Blue** button. Rename its `Click()` method, and add the following statement:

   `this.BackColor = Color.Blue;`

5. On the form, click the **My favorite color** button. In its Properties list, click the **Events** button (the lightning bolt). Select the `Click` event. From the list box next to the `Click` event, select one of the three events to correspond to your favorite color of the three.

(continues)

> *(continued)*
>
> When you double-click a component on a Form in Design View, you move to the default method code. By clicking the component, however, you remain in Design View, and the correct set of properties appears in the Properties list.
>
> 6. Click the **Save All** button, and then execute the program. As you click Buttons, the Form's background color changes appropriately.
> 7. Dismiss the form, and exit Visual Studio.

Chapter Summary

- GUI programs are event-driven—an event such as a button click "drives" the program to perform a task. Programmers also say a button click *raises an event, fires an event, or triggers an event*. A method that performs a task in response to an event is an event handler. The Click event is the event generated when a button is clicked.

- A delegate is an object that contains a reference to a method. C# delegates provide a way for a program to take alternative courses that are not predetermined; a delegate provides a way to pass a reference to a method as an argument to another method. You can assign one delegate to another using the = operator. You also can use the + and += operators to combine delegates into a composed delegate that calls the delegates from which it is built.

- To declare your own event, you use a delegate. A client identifies methods to execute by associating the delegate with the method that should execute when the event occurs. The delegate type for an event should take exactly two parameters: a parameter indicating the source of the event, and an EventArgs parameter that encapsulates any additional information about the event. For events that do not use additional information, the .NET Framework already has defined an appropriate type named EventHandler.

- When you use existing Control components such as Buttons and ListBoxes, they contain events with names such as Click. A Form can contain any number of Controls that might have events associated with them, and a single control might be able to raise any number of events.

- Every mouse or keyboard event-handling method must have two parameters: an object representing the sender, and an object that holds event information. Mouse events include all the actions a user takes with a mouse, including clicking, pointing, and dragging. Mouse events can be handled for any Control through an object of the class MouseEventArgs.

The delegate used to create mouse event handlers is `MouseEventHandler`. Depending on the event, the type of the second parameter is `EventArgs` or `MouseEventArgs`. Keyboard events, also known as key events, occur when a user presses and releases keyboard keys. Depending on the event, the type of the second parameter is `KeyEventArgs` or `KeyPressEventArgs`.

- When users encounter multiple GUI `Control`s on a `Form`, usually one `Control` has focus. That is, if the user presses Enter, the `Control` will raise an event. When a `Form` contains multiple `Control`s, you can create a separate event for each `Control`, or you can associate the same event with multiple `Control`s.

- When you encounter a new control in the IDE, you probably can use it without understanding all the code generated in the background. However, when you learn about the background code, your knowledge of C# is more complete.

Key Terms

An **event** is a reaction to an occurrence in a program.

At runtime describes actions that occur during a program's execution.

Event-driven programs contain code that causes an event such as a button click to drive the program to perform a task.

A button click **raises an event, fires an event,** or **triggers an event.**

An **event handler** is a method that performs a task in response to an event.

An **event sender** is the object that generates an event.

An **event receiver** is another name for an event handler.

A **click event** is an action fired when a user clicks a button in a GUI environment.

Event wiring is the act of connecting an event to its resulting actions.

A **delegate** is an object that contains a reference to a method.

A **composed delegate** calls the delegates from which it is built.

Invoking the event occurs when you call an event method.

Key events are keyboard events that occur when a user presses and releases keyboard keys.

Focus is the property of a `Control` that causes an event to be raised when the user presses Enter.

CHAPTER 13 Handling Events

Review Questions

1. In C#, events are _____.
   a. Boolean objects
   b. handled by `catch` blocks
   c. triggered by actions
   d. only used in GUI programs

2. A delegate is an object that contains a reference to a(n) _____.
   a. object
   b. method
   c. class
   d. `Control`

3. C# delegates provide a way for a program to _____.
   a. take alternative courses that are not determined until runtime
   b. include multiple methods
   c. include methods from other classes
   d. include multiple `Control`s that use the same method

4. Which of the following correctly declares a `delegate` type?
   a. `void aDelegate(int num);`
   b. `delegate void aDelegate(num);`
   c. `delegate void aDelegate(int num);`
   d. `delegate aDelegate(int num);`

5. If you have declared a `delegate` instance, you can assign it a reference to a method as long as the method has the same _____ as the `delegate`.
   a. return type
   b. identifier
   c. parameter list
   d. two of the above

6. You can combine two delegates to create a(n) _____ delegate.
   a. assembled
   b. classified
   c. artificial
   d. composed

7. To combine two delegates using the + operator, the `delegate` objects must have _____.
   a. the same parameter list
   b. the same return type
   c. both of these
   d. neither of these

Review Questions

8. In C#, a(n) _____ is triggered when specific changes to an object occur.
   a. event
   b. delegate
   c. notification
   d. instantiation

9. An event handler delegate requires _____ argument(s).
   a. zero
   b. one
   c. two
   d. at least one

10. In an event-handling method, the sender is the _____ .
    a. delegate associated with the event
    b. method called by the event
    c. object where the event was initiated
    d. class containing the method that the event invokes

11. The `EventArgs` class contains a static field named _____.
    a. `Empty`
    b. `Text`
    c. `Location`
    d. `Source`

12. When creating events, you can use a predefined delegate type named _____ that is provided automatically by the .NET Framework.
    a. `EventArgs`
    b. `EventHandler`
    c. `EventType`
    d. `Event`

13. Which of the following is not a predefined `Control` event?
    a. `MouseEnter`
    b. `Click`
    c. `Destroy`
    d. `TextChanged`

14. A single `Control` can raise _____ event(s).
    a. one
    b. two
    c. five
    d. any number of

15. When you create `Forms` with `Controls` that raise events, an advantage to creating the code by hand over using the Visual Studio IDE is _____.
    a. you are less likely to make typing errors
    b. you save a lot of repetitious typing
    c. you are less likely to forget to set a property
    d. you gain a clearer understanding of the C# language

16. When a Form contains three Controls and one has focus, you can raise an event by _____.
    a. clicking any Control
    b. pressing Enter
    c. either of these
    d. none of these

17. The TabStop property of a Control is a(n) _____.
    a. integer value indicating the tab order
    b. Boolean value indicating whether the Control has a position in the tab sequence
    c. string value indicating the name of the method executed when the Control raises an event
    d. delegate name indicating the event raised when the user tabs to the Control

18. The TabIndex property of a Control is a(n) _____.
    a. integer value indicating the tab order
    b. Boolean value indicating whether the Control has a position in the tab sequence
    c. string value indicating the name of the method executed when the Control raises an event
    d. delegate name indicating the event raised when the user tabs to the Control

19. The Control that causes an event is the _____ argument to an event method.
    a. first
    b. second
    c. third
    d. fourth

20. Which of the following is true?
    a. A single event can be generated from multiple Controls.
    b. Multiple events can be generated from a single Control.
    c. Both of the above are true.
    d. None of the above are true.

Exercises

 Programming Exercises

1. Create a project named **WordsOfWisdom** with a Form containing at least four Labels that hold "wise" quotes of your choice. When the program starts, the background color of the Form and each Label should be black. When the user passes a mouse over a Label, change its BackColor to white, revealing the text of the quote.

2. Create a project named **RecentlyVisitedSites** that contains a Form with a list of three LinkLabels that link to any three Web sites you choose. When a user clicks a LinkLabel, link to that site. When a user's mouse hovers over a LinkLabel, display a brief message that explains the site's purpose. After a user clicks a link, move the most recently selected link to the top of the list, and move the other two links down, making sure to retain the correct explanation with each link.

3. Create a project named **ClassicBookSelector** that contains a Form with a ListBox that lists at least five classic books that you think all educated people should have read. When the user places the mouse over the ListBox, display a Label that contains a general statement about the benefits of reading. The Label disappears when the user's mouse leaves the ListBox area. When the user clicks a book title in the ListBox, display another Label that contains a brief synopsis of the specific book. Also, change the BackColor of the Form to a different color for each book.

4. Locate an animated .gif file on the Web. Create a project named **Animated** with a Form that contains a PictureBox. Display three different messages on a Label—one when the user's mouse is over the PictureBox, one when the mouse is not over the PictureBox, and one when the user clicks the PictureBox.

5. Create a project for a sandwich shop. The project, named **SalsSandwiches**, allows a user to use a ListBox to choose a type of sandwich from at least four choices (for example, *Roast beef*). When the user selects a sandwich type, the program should display a second ListBox that contains at least three types of bread (for example, *Whole wheat*). After the user selects a bread type, the program should display a third ListBox with at least three choices for additions (for example, *Lettuce*). Display a message on a Label that lists all the chosen options, and make the bread and additions ListBoxes invisible. If the user makes a new selection from the first ListBox with the main sandwich choices, the bread option becomes available again, and if a new bread selection is chosen, the additions option becomes available again.

6. Create a project named **GuessANumber** with a Form that contains a guessing game with five RadioButtons numbered 1 through 5. Randomly choose one of the RadioButtons as the winning button. When the user clicks a RadioButton, display a message indicating whether the user is right.

   Add a Label to the Form that provides a hint. When the user's mouse hovers over the label, notify the user of one RadioButton that is incorrect. After the user makes a selection, disable all the RadioButtons.

   You can create a random number that is at least min but less than max using the following statements:

   ```
   Random ran = new Random();
   int randomNumber;
   randomNumber = ran.Next(min, max);
   ```

7. Create a project named **PickLarger** with a Form that contains two randomly generated arrays, each containing 100 numbers. Include two Buttons labeled *1* and *2*. Starting with position 0 in each array, ask the user to guess which of the two arrays contains the higher number and to click one of the two buttons to indicate the guess. After each button click, the program displays the values of the two compared numbers, as well as running counts of the number of correct and incorrect guesses. After the user makes a guess, disable the Buttons while the user views the results. After clicking a Next Button, the user can make another guess using the next two array values. If the user makes more than 100 guesses, the program should reset the array subscript to 0 so the comparisons start over but continue to keep a running score.

Debugging Exercises

1. Each of the following files or projects in the Chapter.13 folder of your downloadable student files has syntax and/or logical errors. Immediately save the two project folders with their new names before starting to correct their errors. After you correct the errors, save each file or project using the same filename preceded with *Fixed*. For example, the file DebugThirteen1.cs will become FixedDebugThirteen1.cs and the project folder for DebugThirteen3 will become FixedDebugThirteen3.

   a. DebugThirteen1.cs

   b. DebugThirteen2.cs

   c. DebugThirteen3

   d. DebugThirteen4

Exercises

 Case Problems

1. In Chapter 12, you created an interactive advertisement named **GreenvilleAdvertisement** that can be used to recruit contestants for the Greenville Idol competition. Now, modify that program to include at least one handled event using the techniques you learned in this chapter.

2. In Chapter 12, you created an interactive advertisement named **MarshallsAdvertisement** that can be used to advertise the available murals painted by Marshall's Murals. Now, modify that program to include at least one handled event using the techniques you learned in this chapter.

CHAPTER 14

Files and Streams

Upon completion of this chapter, you will be able to:

- ◎ Describe computer files and the `File` and `Directory` classes
- ◎ Describe file data organization
- ◎ Describe streams
- ◎ Write to and read from a sequential access text file
- ◎ Search a sequential access text file
- ◎ Appreciate serialization and deserialization

CHAPTER 14 Files and Streams

In the early chapters of this book, you learned that using variables to store values in computer memory provides programs with flexibility; a program that uses variables to replace constants can manipulate different values each time the program executes. However, when data values in a program are stored in memory, they are lost when the program ends. To retain data values for future use, you must store them in files. In this chapter, you will learn to create and manage files in C#.

Files and the `File` and `Directory` Classes

Data items can be stored in a computer system either temporarily or permanently.

Temporary storage is usually called computer memory, or **random access memory** (RAM). When you write a C# program that stores a value in a variable, you are using temporary storage; the value you store is lost when the program ends or the computer loses power. This type of storage is **volatile**.

Permanent storage, on the other hand, is not lost when a computer loses power; it is **nonvolatile**. When you write a program and save it to a disk, you are using permanent storage. Likewise, you use permanent storage when you write a program that saves data to a file.

When discussing computer storage, *temporary* and *permanent* refer to volatility, not length of time. For example, a *temporary* variable might exist for several hours in a large program or one that the user forgets to end, but a *permanent* piece of data in a file might be saved and then deleted within a few seconds.

A **computer file** is a collection of data stored on a nonvolatile device in a computer system. Files exist on **permanent storage devices**, such as hard disks, USB drives, reels of magnetic tape, and optical discs, which include CDs and DVDs.

You can categorize files by the way they store data:

- **Text files** contain data that can be read in a text editor because the data has been encoded using a scheme such as ASCII or Unicode. Text files might include facts and figures used by business programs; when they do, they are also called **data files**. The C# source programs you have written (with .cs extensions) are stored in text files.

- **Binary files** contain data that has not been encoded as text. Their contents are in binary format, which means that you cannot understand them by viewing them in a text editor. Examples include images, music, videos, and the compiled program files with an .exe extension that you have created using this book.

Files and the `File` and `Directory` Classes

Although their contents vary, text and binary files have many common characteristics:

- Each has a name. The name often includes a dot and a file extension that describes the type of the file. For example, MyNotes.txt is a plain text file, and MyPicture.jpg is an image file in Joint Pictures Expert Group format.
- Each file has a specific time of creation.
- Each file occupies space on a section of a storage device; that is, each file has a size. Sizes are measured in bytes. A **byte** is a small unit of storage; for example, in a simple text file, a byte holds only one character. Because a byte is so small, file sizes usually are expressed in **kilobytes** (thousands of bytes), **megabytes** (millions of bytes), or **gigabytes** (billions of bytes).

When you use data, you never directly use the copy that is stored in a file. Instead, you use a copy that has been loaded into memory. Especially when data items are stored on a hard disk, their locations might not be clear to you—data just seems to be "in the computer." However, when you work with stored data, you must transfer copies from the storage device into memory. When you copy data from a file on a storage device into RAM, you **read from the file**. When you store data in a computer file on a persistent storage device, you **write to the file**. This means you copy data from RAM to the storage device.

Because you can erase data from files, some programmers prefer the term *persistent* storage to permanent storage. In other words, you can remove data from a file stored on a device such as a disk drive, so it is not technically permanent. However, the data remains in the file even when the computer loses power, so, unlike RAM, the data persists, or perseveres.

Computer files are the electronic equivalent of paper documents stored in file cabinets. In a physical file cabinet, the easiest way to store a document is to toss it into a drawer without a folder. When storing computer files, this is the equivalent of placing a file in the main or **root directory** of your storage device. However, for better organization, most office clerks place documents in folders; most computer users also organize their files into **folders** or **directories**. Users also can place folders within folders to form a hierarchy. The combination of the disk drive plus the complete hierarchy of directories in which a file resides is its **path**. For example, in the Windows operating system, the following line would be the complete path for a file named Data.txt on the C drive in a folder named Chapter14 within the CSharp folder:

`C:\CSharp\Chapter14\Data.txt`

The terms *directory* and *folder* are used synonymously to mean an entity that is used to organize files. *Directory* is the more general term; the term *folder* came into popular use in graphical systems. For example, Microsoft began calling directories *folders* with the introduction of Windows 95 in 1995. The term *folder* was first used in the 1950s with the Electronic Recording Machine, Accounting (ERMA).

C# provides built-in classes named `File` and `Directory` that contain methods to help you manipulate files and their directories, respectively.

CHAPTER 14 Files and Streams

Using the `File` and `Directory` Classes

The `File` class contains methods that allow you to access information about files. Some of the methods are listed in Table 14-1.

Method	Description
Create()	Creates a file
CreateText()	Creates a text file
Delete()	Deletes a file
Exists()	Returns `true` if the specified file exists
GetCreationTime()	Returns a `DateTime` object specifying when a file was created
GetLastWriteTime()	Returns a `DateTime` object specifying when a file was last modified
Move()	Moves a file to the specified location

Table 14-1 Selected `File` class methods

`DateTime` is a structure that contains data about a date and time. In the chapter "Using Controls," you used the data from `DateTime` structures with `MonthCalendar` and `DateTimePicker` GUI objects. `DateTime` values can be expressed using Coordinated Universal Time (UTC), which is the internationally recognized name for Greenwich Mean Time (GMT). By default, `DateTime` values are expressed using the local time set on your computer. The property `DateTime.Now` returns the current local time. The property `DateTime.UtcNow` returns the current UTC time.

The `File` class is contained in the `System.IO` namespace. So, to use the `File` class, you can use its fully qualified name, `System.IO.File`, or you can just use `File` if you include the statement `using System.IO;` at the top of your program file as shown in the first shaded statement in Figure 14-1.

Figure 14-1 shows a program that demonstrates several `File` class methods. The program prompts the user for a filename and then tests the file's existence in the second shaded statement. If the file exists, the creation time and last write time are displayed. If the file does not exist, a message is displayed. Figure 14-2 shows two executions of the program. In the first execution, the user enters a filename that is not found. In the second execution, the file is found, and the significant dates and times are displayed.

The `System.IO.FileInfo` class also allows you to access information about a file. See the Microsoft documentation at http://msdn.microsoft.com for more information.

Files and the File and Directory Classes

```
using static System.Console;
using System.IO;
class FileStatistics
{
   static void Main()
   {
      string fileName;
      Write("Enter a filename >> ");
      fileName = ReadLine();
      if(File.Exists(fileName))
      {
         WriteLine("File exists");
         WriteLine("File was created " +
            File.GetCreationTime(fileName));
         WriteLine("File was last written to " +
            File.GetLastWriteTime(fileName));
      }
      else
      {
         WriteLine("File does not exist");
      }
   }
}
```

Figure 14-1 The FileStatistics program

In the FileStatistics program in Figure 14-1, the file must be in the same directory as the program that is running.

```
Enter a filename >> MyLetter.txt
File does not exist
```

```
Enter a filename >> BusinessLetter.txt
File exists
File was created 2/22/2017 8:09:46 AM
File was last written to 2/22/2017 8:38:24 AM
```

Figure 14-2 Two typical executions of the FileStatistics program

CHAPTER 14 Files and Streams

The `Directory` class provides you with information about directories or folders. Table 14-2 lists some available methods in the `Directory` class.

Method	Description
`CreateDirectory()`	Creates a directory
`Delete()`	Deletes a directory
`Exists()`	Returns `true` if the specified directory exists
`GetCreationTime()`	Returns a `DateTime` object specifying when a directory was created
`GetDirectories()`	Returns a `string` array that contains the names of the subdirectories in the specified directory
`GetFiles()`	Returns a `string` array that contains the names of the files in the specified directory
`GetLastWriteTime()`	Returns a `DateTime` object specifying when a directory was last modified
`Move()`	Moves a directory to the specified location

Table 14-2 Selected `Directory` class methods

Figure 14-3 contains a program that declares an array of strings where filenames can be stored. (See the first shaded statement.) The program prompts a user for a directory and then fills the string array with a list of filenames using the `GetFiles()` method. (See the second shaded statement.) Then a `for` loop is used to display the list of files. Figure 14-4 shows two typical executions of the program.

```
using static System.Console;
using System.IO;
class DirectoryInformation
{
   static void Main()
   {
      string directoryName;
      string[] listOfFiles;
      Write("Enter a folder >> ");
      directoryName = ReadLine();
      if(Directory.Exists(directoryName))
      {
         WriteLine("Directory exists, " +
            "and it contains the following: ");
```

Figure 14-3 The DirectoryInformation program *(continues)*

Files and the File and Directory Classes

(continued)

```
        listOfFiles = Directory.GetFiles(directoryName);
        for(int x = 0; x < listOfFiles.Length; ++x)
           WriteLine("   {0}", listOfFiles[x]);
      }
      else
      {
         WriteLine("Directory does not exist");
      }
   }
}
```

Figure 14-3 The DirectoryInformation program

```
Enter a folder >> ClientMemos
Directory exists, and it contains the following:
   ClientMemos\ClientBillingWorksheet.xlsx
   ClientMemos\JohnsonMemo.txt
   ClientMemos\SmithMemo.txt
```

```
Enter a folder >> OtherMemos
Directory does not exist
```

Figure 14-4 Two typical executions of the DirectoryInformation program

 Watch the video *File Handling*.

TWO TRUTHS & A LIE

Files and the File and Directory Classes

1. Temporary storage is nonvolatile; permanent storage is volatile.

2. When you write to a file, you copy data from RAM to a permanent storage device.

3. Most computer users organize their files into directories; the complete hierarchy of directories in which a file resides is its path.

The false statement is #1. Temporary storage is volatile; permanent storage is nonvolatile.

Understanding File Data Organization

Businesses store data in a relationship known as the **data hierarchy**, as described in Figure 14-5. For most users, the smallest useful piece of data is the character. A **character** is any one of the letters, numbers, or other special symbols (such as punctuation marks and arithmetic symbols) that constitute data. Characters are made up of bits (the zeros and ones that represent computer circuitry), but people who use data do not care whether the internal representation for an *A* is 01000001 or 10111110; rather, they are concerned with the meaning of *A*. For example, it might represent a grade in a course, a person's initial, or a company code.

C# uses Unicode to represent its characters. You first learned about Unicode in Chapter 1. The set of all the characters used to represent data on a particular computer is that computer's **character set**.

Figure 14-5 Hierarchical relationships of data components

You can think of a character as a unit of information instead of data with a particular appearance. For example, the mathematical character *pi* (π) and the Greek letter *pi* look the same, but have two different Unicode values.

In computer terminology, a character can be any group of bits, and it does not necessarily represent a letter or number. Some characters do not correspond to those in natural language. Some "characters" produce a sound or control your display. For example, you have used the `'\n'` character to start a new line.

Understanding File Data Organization

When businesses use data, they group characters into fields. A **field** is a character or group of characters that has some meaning. For example, the characters *T*, *o*, and *m* might represent your first name. Other data fields might represent items such as last name, Social Security number, zip code, and salary.

Fields are grouped together to form records. A **record** is a collection of fields that contain data about an entity. For example, the fields that hold a person's first and last names, Social Security number, zip code, and salary collectively are that person's record. When programming in C#, you have created many classes, such as an `Employee` class or a `Student` class. You can think of the data typically stored in each object that is an instance of these classes as a record. In other words, classes contain individual variables that represent data fields. A business's data records often represent a person, item, sales transaction, or some other concrete object or event.

Records are grouped to create files. Data files consist of related records. For example, a company's personnel file contains many related records—one record for each company employee. Some files have only a few records; perhaps your professor maintains a file for your class with 25 records—one record for each student. Other files contain thousands or even millions of records. For example, a large insurance company maintains a file of policyholders, and a mail-order catalog company maintains a file of available items.

A data file is a **sequential access file** when each record is read in order from first to last in the file. Usually, the records are stored in order based on the value in some field; for example, employees might be stored in Social Security number order, or inventory items might be stored in item number order. The field used to uniquely identify each record in a sequential file is the **key field**. Frequently, records are sorted based on the key field. When records are not used in sequence, the file is used as a **random access file**, in which records can be accessed in any order.

Before an application can use a data file, it must open the file. A C# application **opens a file** by creating an object and associating a stream of bytes with that object. When you finish using a file, the program should **close the file**—that is, make the file no longer available to your application. Failing to close an input file (a file from which you are reading data) usually does not result in serious consequences; the data still exists in the file. However, if you fail to close an output file (a file to which you are writing data), the data might become inaccessible. You should always close every file you open, and you should close the file as soon as you no longer need it. Leaving a file open for no reason uses computer resources, and your computer's performance will suffer. Also, within a network, another program might be waiting to use the file. For example, if your program leaves the company's inventory file open after adding a new item, the program that fills orders for customers might fail to work correctly.

TWO TRUTHS & A LIE

Understanding File Data Organization

1. A field is a character or group of characters that has some meaning.
2. A record is a collection of data files that contain information about an entity.
3. A sequential access data file frequently contains records stored in order based on the value in some field.

The false statement is #2. A record is a collection of fields that contain data about an entity. Data files consist of related records.

Understanding Streams

Whereas people view files as a series of records, with each record containing data fields, C# views files as just a series of bytes. When you perform an input operation in an application, you can picture bytes flowing into your program from an input device through a **stream**, which functions as a pipeline or channel. When you perform output, some bytes flow out of your application through another stream to an output device, as shown in Figure 14-6. A stream is an object, and like all objects, streams have data and methods. The methods allow you to perform actions such as opening, closing, and flushing (clearing) the stream.

Figure 14-6 File streams

When you produce screen output and accept keyboard input, you use the `Console` class, which provides access to several standard streams:

- `Console.In` refers to the standard input stream object, which accepts data from the keyboard.
- `Console.Out` refers to the standard output stream object, which allows a program to produce output on the screen.
- `Console.Error` refers to the standard error stream object, which allows a program to write error messages to the screen.

Understanding Streams

You have been using `Console.Out` and its `WriteLine()` and `Write()` methods throughout this book. However, you might not have realized it because you do not need to refer explicitly to `Out`, so you have been writing the instruction as `WriteLine()`. Likewise, you have used `Console.In` with the `ReadLine()` and `Read()` methods.

Most streams flow in only one direction; each stream is either an input or output stream. You might open several streams at once within an application. For example, an application that reads a data disk and separates valid records from invalid ones might require three streams: the data arrives via an input stream, and as the program checks the data for invalid values, one output stream writes some records to a file of valid records, and another output stream writes other records to a file of invalid records.

When you read from or write to a file, you use a file-processing class instead of `Console`. Many file-processing classes are available in C#, including:

- `StreamReader`, for text input from a file
- `StreamWriter`, for text output to a file
- `FileStream` (which is used alone for bytes and with either `StreamReader` and `StreamWriter` for text), for either input from and output to a file.

`StreamReader` and `StreamWriter` inherit from `TextReader` and `TextWriter`, respectively. `Console.In` and `Console.Out` are properties of `TextReader` and `TextWriter`, respectively.

When you write a program that stores data in a file, you create a `FileStream` object that defines a file's characteristics and abilities. Programmers say `FileStream` **exposes** a stream around a file. Table 14-3 lists some `FileStream` properties.

Property	Description
CanRead	Gets a value indicating whether current `FileStream` supports reading
CanSeek	Gets a value indicating whether current `FileStream` supports seeking
CanWrite	Gets a value indicating whether current `FileStream` supports writing
Length	Gets the length of the `FileStream` in bytes
Name	Gets the name of the `FileStream`
Position	Gets or sets the current position of the `FileStream`

Table 14-3 Selected `FileStream` properties

The `FileStream` class has 15 overloaded constructors. One frequently-used constructor version includes the filename (which might include the complete path), mode, and type of access. For example, you might construct a `FileStream` object using the following statement:

```
FileStream outFile = new FileStream("SomeText.txt",
   FileMode.Create, FileAccess.Write);
```

In this example, the filename is *SomeText.txt*. Because no path is indicated, the file is assumed to be in the current directory. The mode is `Create`, which means a new file will be created even if one with the same name already exists. The access is `Write`, which means you can write data to the file but not read from it.

Another of `FileStream`'s overloaded constructors requires only a filename and mode. If you use this version and the mode is set to `Append`, then the default access is `Write`; otherwise, the access is set to `ReadWrite`.

Table 14-4 describes the available file modes, and Table 14-5 describes the access types.

Member	Description
Append	Opens the file if it exists and seeks the end of the file to append new data
Create	Creates a new file; if the file already exists, it is overwritten
CreateNew	Creates a new file; if the file already exists, an `IOException` is thrown
Open	Opens an existing file; if the file does not exist, a `System.IO.FileNotFoundException` is thrown
OpenOrCreate	Opens an existing file; if the file does not exist, it is created
Truncate	Opens an existing file; once opended, the file is truncated so its size is zero bytes

Table 14-4 The `FileMode` enumeration

Member	Description
Read	Data can be read from the file.
ReadWrite	Data can be read from and written to the file.
Write	Data can be written to the file.

Table 14-5 The `FileAccess` enumeration

You can use a `FileStream` object as an argument to the `StreamWriter` constructor. Then you use `WriteLine()` or `Write()` with the `StreamWriter` object in much the same way you use it with `Console.Out`. The `FileStream` object must be created first, followed by the `StreamWriter`. At the end of the application, they must be closed in reverse order.

For example, Figure 14-7 shows an application in which a `FileStream` object named `outFile` is created, then associated with a `StreamWriter` named `writer` in the first shaded line. The `writer` object then uses `WriteLine()` to send a `string` to the `FileStream` file instead of sending it to the `Console`. Figure 14-8 shows a typical execution of the program, and Figure 14-9 shows the file as it appears in Notepad.

```
using static System.Console;
using System.IO;
class WriteSomeText
{
   static void Main()
   {
      FileStream outFile = new
         FileStream("SomeText.txt", FileMode.Create,
            FileAccess.Write);
      StreamWriter writer = new StreamWriter(outFile);
      Write("Enter some text >> ");
      string text = ReadLine();
      writer.WriteLine(text);
      // Error occurs if the next two statements are reversed
      writer.Close();
      outFile.Close();
   }
}
```

Figure 14-7 The WriteSomeText program

Although the WriteSomeText application uses `ReadLine()` to accept user input, you could also create a GUI Form to accept input. You will create an application that writes to and reads from files using a GUI environment in a "You Do It" exercise at the end of this chapter.

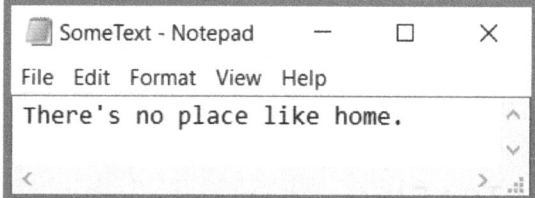

Figure 14-8 Typical execution of the WriteSomeText program

Figure 14-9 File created by the WriteSomeText program

In most applications that use files, you will want to place all the statements that open, write to, read from, and close files in a `try` block and then catch any `IOExceptions` that are thrown. Exception handling is eliminated from many examples in this chapter so that you can concentrate on the details of handling files without extra statements. In the "You Do It" section at the end of this chapter, you will add exception handling to an application.

CHAPTER 14 Files and Streams

The classes `BinaryReader` and `BinaryWriter` exist for working with binary files, which can store any of the 256 combinations of bits in any byte instead of just those combinations that form readable text. For example, photographs and music are stored in binary files.

The classes `XmlTextReader` and `XmlTextWriter` exist for working with XML files. **XML** is an abbreviation of eXtensible Markup Language, which is a standard for exchanging data over the Internet.

TWO TRUTHS & A LIE

Understanding Streams

1. When a file is opened in C#, an object is created, and a stream is associated with that object.

2. Most streams flow in only one direction; each stream is either an input or output stream.

3. You can open only one stream at a time within a C# application.

The false statement is #3. You might open several streams at once within an application.

Writing and Reading a Sequential Access File

Although people think of data files as consisting of records that contain fields, C# uses files only as streams of bytes. Therefore, when you write a program to store a data file or write a program to retrieve data from a file that already has been created, you must dictate the form in which the program will handle the file. Additionally, whether you are writing data to a file or reading data from one, you create a `FileStream` object.

Writing Data to a Sequential Access Text File

For example, suppose that you want to store `Employee` data in a file. Assume that an `Employee` contains an ID number, a name, and a salary that are respectively an `int`, a `string`, and a `double`. You could write standalone data for each of the three data types

Writing and Reading a Sequential Access File

to a file, or you could create an `Employee` class that is similar to many you have seen throughout this book. Figure 14-10 shows a typical `Employee` class that contains three fields and properties for each.

```
class Employee
{
   public int EmpNum {get; set;}
   public string Name {get; set;}
   public double Salary {get; set;}
}
```

Figure 14-10 An `Employee` class

To store `Employee` data to a persistent storage device, you declare a `FileStream` object to define the characteristics of the stored file. For example:

```
FileStream outFile = new FileStream(FILENAME,
   FileMode.Create, FileAccess.Write);
```

The `FileStream` object is then passed to the constructor of a `StreamWriter` object so that text can be written. For example:

```
StreamWriter writer = new StreamWriter(outFile);
```

You can then use the `writer` object's `WriteLine()` method to write `Employee` data to the output stream. You can compose strings to write using text fields and commas. A block of text within a string that represents an entity or field is a **token**. Each comma that separates tokens is a **delimiter**, which is a character used to specify the boundary between data items in text files. Without a delimiter, the process of separating and interpreting tokens is more difficult. For example, suppose you define a delimiter as a comma using the following statement:

```
const string DELIM = ",";
```

Then, when you write data to a file, you can separate the fields with the comma delimiter using a statement such as the following:

```
writer.WriteLine(emp.EmpNum + DELIM + emp.Name + DELIM + emp.Salary);
```

A delimiter can be any character that is not needed as part of the data in a file, but a comma is commonly used. A file that contains comma-separated values is often called a **CSV file**. When a comma cannot be used as a delimiter because commas are needed as characters within the data, sometimes either the Tab character, the pipe character (|), or a comma within quotation marks is used as a delimiter.

The `WriteLine()` method ends output with a carriage return. When you use this method to create file output, the automatically appended carriage return becomes the *record delimiter*.

Figure 14-11 contains a complete program that opens a file and continuously prompts the user for Employee data. The first shaded statement in the figure is a **priming read**—an input statement that gets a first data item or record. In this case, the first item is an employee number. If the first input is the END value, the `while` loop is never entered. If a valid employee number value is entered, the rest of the record's data is retrieved within the loop, and the next employee number is entered in the second shaded statement at the bottom of the loop. When all three fields have been entered for an employee, the fields are written to the file, separated by commas. When the user enters the sentinel value 999 for an Employee ID number, the data entry loop ends, and the file is closed. Figure 14-12 shows a typical execution, and Figure 14-13 shows the contents of the sequential data file that is created.

```
using System;
using static System.Console;
using System.IO;
class WriteSequentialFile
{
   static void Main()
   {
      const int END = 999;
      const string DELIM = ",";
      const string FILENAME = "EmployeeData.txt";
      Employee emp = new Employee();
      FileStream outFile = new FileStream(FILENAME,
         FileMode.Create, FileAccess.Write);
      StreamWriter writer = new StreamWriter(outFile);
      Write("Enter employee number or " + END +
         " to quit >> ");
      emp.EmpNum = Convert.ToInt32(ReadLine());
      while(emp.EmpNum != END)
      {
         Write("Enter last name >> ");
         emp.Name = ReadLine();
         Write("Enter salary >> ");
         emp.Salary = Convert.ToDouble(ReadLine());
         writer.WriteLine(emp.EmpNum + DELIM + emp.Name +
            DELIM + emp.Salary);
         Write("Enter next employee number or " +
            END + " to quit >> ");
         emp.EmpNum = Convert.ToInt32(ReadLine());
      }
      writer.Close();
      outFile.Close();
   }
}
```

Figure 14-11 The WriteSequentialFile program

Writing and Reading a Sequential Access File

In the WriteSequentialFile program in Figure 14-11, the delimiter is defined to be a string instead of a char to force the composed argument to WriteLine() to be a string. If the first data field sent to WriteLine() was a string, then DELIM could have been declared as a char.

In the WriteSequentialFile program in Figure 14-11, the constant END is defined to be 999 so it can be used to check for the sentinel value. You first learned to use named constants in Chapter 2. Defining a named constant eliminates using a magic number in a program. The term **magic number** refers to the bad programming practice of hard-coding numbers (unnamed, literal constants) in code without explanation. In most cases, this makes programs harder to read, understand, and maintain.

```
Enter employee number or 999 to quit >> 217
Enter last name >> Santini
Enter salary >> 42000
Enter next employee number or 999 to quit >> 344
Enter last name >> Perez
Enter salary >> 51500
Enter next employee number or 999 to quit >> 510
Enter last name >> Schmidt
Enter salary >> 61000
Enter next employee number or 999 to quit >> 999
```

Figure 14-12 Typical execution of the WriteSequentialFile program

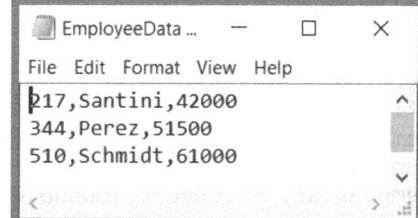

Figure 14-13 Contents of file created by the WriteSequentialFile program

Reading from a Sequential Access Text File

A program that reads from a sequential access data file contains many similar components to one that writes to a file. For example, a `FileStream` object is created, as in a program that writes a file. However, the access must be `FileAccess.Read` (or `ReadWrite`), as in the following statement:

```
FileStream inFile = new FileStream(FILENAME,
   FileMode.Open, FileAccess.Read);
```

Then, as data is being written, the `FileStream` object is passed to a `StreamReader` object's constructor, as in the following statement:

```
StreamReader reader = new StreamReader(inFile);
```

After the `StreamReader` has been defined, the `ReadLine()` method can be used to retrieve one line at a time from the data file. For example, the following statement gets one line of data from the file and stores it in a string named `recordIn`:

```
string recordIn = reader.ReadLine();
```

Using `ReadLine()` assumes a carriage return is the record delimiter, which is true, for example, if the records were created using `WriteLine()`.

If the value of `recordIn` is `null`, then no more data exists in the file. Therefore, a loop that begins `while(recordIn != null)` can be used to control the data entry loop.

After a record (line of data) is read in, the `Split()` method can be used to separate the data fields into an array of strings. The `Split()` method is a member of the `String` class; it takes a character delimiter parameter and separates a string into substrings at each occurrence of the delimiter. For example, the following code splits `recordIn` into the `fields` array at each `DELIM` occurrence. Then the three array elements can be stored as an `int`, `string`, and `double`, respectively.

```
string[] fields;
fields = recordIn.Split(DELIM);
emp.EmpNum = Convert.ToInt32(fields[0]);
emp.Name = fields[1];
emp.Salary = Convert.ToDouble(fields[2]);
```

Figure 14-14 contains a complete ReadSequentialFile application that uses the data file created in Figure 14-12. The records stored in the EmployeeData.txt file are read in one at a time, split into their `Employee` record components, and displayed. The first shaded statement is the priming read, and all subsequent records are input using the second shaded statement. Figure 14-15 shows the output.

```
using System;
using static System.Console;
using System.IO;
class ReadSequentialFile
{
   static void Main()
   {
      const char DELIM = ',';
      const string FILENAME = "EmployeeData.txt";
      Employee emp = new Employee();
```

Figure 14-14 The ReadSequentialFile program *(continues)*

Writing and Reading a Sequential Access File

(continued)

```
      FileStream inFile = new FileStream(FILENAME,
         FileMode.Open, FileAccess.Read);
      StreamReader reader = new StreamReader(inFile);
      string recordIn;
      string[] fields;
      WriteLine("\n{0,-5}{1,-12}{2,8}\n",
         "Num", "Name", "Salary");
      recordIn = reader.ReadLine();
      while(recordIn != null)
      {
         fields = recordIn.Split(DELIM);
         emp.EmpNum = Convert.ToInt32(fields[0]);
         emp.Name = fields[1];
         emp.Salary = Convert.ToDouble(fields[2]);
         WriteLine("{0,-5}{1,-12}{2,8}",
             emp.EmpNum, emp.Name, emp.Salary.ToString("C"));
         recordIn = reader.ReadLine();
      }
      reader.Close();
      inFile.Close();
   }
}
```

Figure 14-14 The ReadSequentialFile program

```
Num  Name          Salary

217  Santini    $42,000.00
344  Perez      $51,500.00
510  Schmidt    $61,000.00
```

Figure 14-15 Output of the ReadSequentialFile program

 Watch the video *Sequential Access Files*.

TWO TRUTHS & A LIE

Writing and Reading a Sequential Access File

1. Although people think of data files as consisting of records that contain fields, C# uses files only as streams of bytes.

2. A comma is the default C# delimiter.

3. The `Split()` method can be used to separate data fields into an array of strings based on the placement of the designated delimiter.

The false statement is #2. A delimiter is any character used to specify the boundary between characters in text files. Although a comma is commonly used for this purpose, there is no default C# delimiter, and any character could be used.

You Do It

Creating a File

In the next steps, you create a file that contains a list of names.

1. Open a new file named **CreateNameFile**, and write the first lines needed for a program that creates a file of names.

   ```
   using System;
   using System.IO;
   class CreateNameFile
   {
   ```

2. Start a `Main()` method that declares a `FileStream` you can use to create a file named Names.txt that is open for writing. Also create a `StreamWriter` to which you associate the file.

   ```
   static void Main()
   {
      FileStream file = new FileStream("Names.txt",
         FileMode.Create, FileAccess.Write);
      StreamWriter writer = new StreamWriter(file);
   ```

(continues)

(continued)

3. Add an array of names as follows. Each name is padded with spaces to make it 10 characters long so that you can easily demonstrate the Seek() method in a later exercise.

   ```
   string[] names = {"Anthony   ",
                     "Belle     ",
                     "Carolyn   ",
                     "David     ",
                     "Edwin     ",
                     "Frannie   ",
                     "Gina      ",
                     "Hannah    ",
                     "Inez      ",
                     "Juan      "};
   ```

4. Declare a variable to use as an array subscript, then write each name to the output file.

   ```
   int x;
   for(x = 0; x < names.Length; ++x)
      writer.WriteLine(names[x]);
   ```

5. Close the StreamWriter and the FileStream. Also add two closing curly braces—one for the Main() method and one for the class.

   ```
        writer.Close();
        file.Close();
      }
   }
   ```

6. Save the file, and then compile and execute it. Open the newly created **Names.txt** file in a text editor. The file contents appear in Figure 14-16.

Figure 14-16 File created by the CreateNameFile program

(continues)

(continued)

Reading from a File

In the next steps, you read the text from the file created by the CreateNameFile program.

1. Start a new file named **ReadNameFile** as follows:

   ```
   using static System.Console;
   using System.IO;
   class ReadNameFile
   {
   ```

2. Start a `Main()` method that declares a `FileStream` that uses the same filename as the one created by the `CreateNameFile` program. Declare the file mode to be `Open` and the access to be `Read`. Declare a `StreamReader` with which to associate the file. Also declare an integer that counts the names read and a `string` that holds the names.

   ```
   static void Main()
   {
      FileStream file = new FileStream("Names.txt",
         FileMode.Open, FileAccess.Read);
      StreamReader reader = new StreamReader(file);
      int count = 1;
      string name;
   ```

3. Display a heading, and read the first line from the file. While a name is not `null`, display a count and a name, and increment the count.

   ```
   WriteLine("Displaying all names");
   name = reader.ReadLine();
   while(name != null)
   {
      WriteLine("" + count + " " + name);
      name = reader.ReadLine();
      ++count;
   }
   ```

4. Close the `StreamReader` and the `File`, and add closing curly braces for the method and the class.

   ```
         reader.Close();
         file.Close();
      }
   }
   ```

(continues)

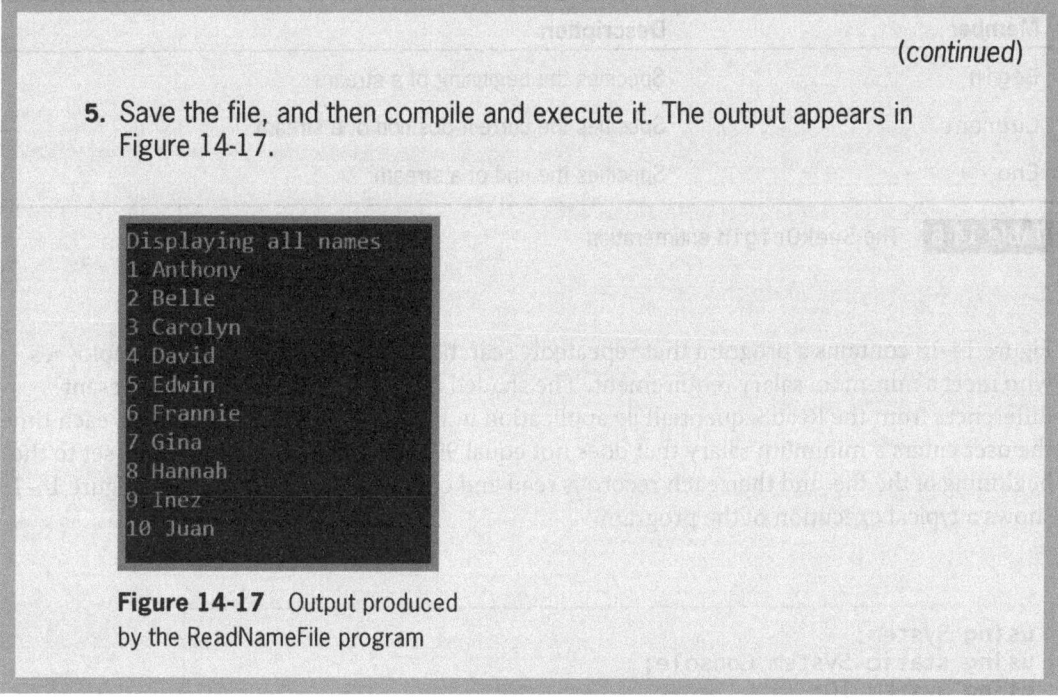

(continued)

5. Save the file, and then compile and execute it. The output appears in Figure 14-17.

Figure 14-17 Output produced by the ReadNameFile program

Searching a Sequential Text File

When you read data from a sequential text file, as in the ReadSequentialFile program in Figure 14-14, the program starts at the beginning of the file and reads each record in turn until all the records have been read. Subsequent records are read in order because a file's **file position pointer** holds the byte number of the next byte to be read. For example, if each record in a file is 32 bytes long, then the file position pointer holds 0, 32, 64, and so on in sequence during the execution of the program.

Sometimes it is necessary to process a file multiple times from the beginning during a program's execution. For example, suppose you want to continue to prompt a user for a minimum salary and then search through a file for Employees who make at least that salary. You can compare the user's entered minimum with each salary in the data file and list those employees who meet the requirement. However, after one list is produced, the file pointer is at the end of the file, and no more records can be read. To reread the file, you could close it and reopen it, but that requires unnecessary overhead. Instead, you can just reposition the file pointer using the Seek() method and the SeekOrigin enumeration. For example, the following statement repositions the pointer of a file named inFile to 0 bytes away from the Begin position of the file:

```
inFile.Seek(0, SeekOrigin.Begin);
```

Table 14-6 lists the values in the SeekOrigin enumeration that you can use.

Member	Description
Begin	Specifies the beginning of a stream
Current	Specifies the current position of a stream
End	Specifies the end of a stream

Table 14-6 The SeekOrigin enumeration

Figure 14-18 contains a program that repeatedly searches a file to produce lists of employees who meet a minimum salary requirement. The shaded portions of the program represent differences from the ReadSequentialFile application in Figure 14-14. In this program, each time the user enters a minimum salary that does not equal 999, the file position pointer is set to the beginning of the file, and then each record is read and compared to the minimum. Figure 14-19 shows a typical execution of the program.

```
using System;
using static System.Console;
using System.IO;
class FindEmployees
{
   static void Main()
   {
      const char DELIM = ',';
      const int END = 999;
      const string FILENAME = "EmployeeData.txt";
      Employee emp = new Employee();
      FileStream inFile = new FileStream(FILENAME,
         FileMode.Open, FileAccess.Read);
      StreamReader reader = new StreamReader(inFile);
      string recordIn;
      string[] fields;
      double minSalary;
      Write("Enter minimum salary to find or " +
         END + " to quit >> ");
      minSalary = Convert.ToDouble(ReadLine());
      while(minSalary != END)
      {
         WriteLine("\n{0,-5}{1,-12}{2,8}\n",
            "Num", "Name", "Salary");
         inFile.Seek(0, SeekOrigin.Begin);
         recordIn = reader.ReadLine();
```

Figure 14-18 The FindEmployees program *(continues)*

(continued)

```
        while(recordIn != null)
        {
           fields = recordIn.Split(DELIM);
           emp.EmpNum = Convert.ToInt32(fields[0]);
           emp.Name = fields[1];
           emp.Salary = Convert.ToDouble(fields[2]);
           if(emp.Salary >= minSalary)
              WriteLine("{0,-5}{1,-12}{2,8}", emp.EmpNum,
                 emp.Name, emp.Salary.ToString("C"));
           recordIn = reader.ReadLine();
        }
        Write("\nEnter minimum salary to find or " +
           END + " to quit >> ");
        minSalary = Convert.ToDouble(ReadLine());
     }
     reader.Close(); // Error occurs if
     inFile.Close(); // these two statements are reversed
  }
}
```

Figure 14-18 The FindEmployees program

```
Enter minimum salary to find or 999 to quit >> 50000

Num  Name         Salary

344  Perez        $51,500.00
510  Schmidt      $61,000.00

Enter minimum salary to find or 999 to quit >> 55000

Num  Name         Salary

510  Schmidt      $61,000.00

Enter minimum salary to find or 999 to quit >> 0

Num  Name         Salary

217  Santini      $42,000.00
344  Perez        $51,500.00
510  Schmidt      $61,000.00

Enter minimum salary to find or 999 to quit >> 999
```

Figure 14-19 Typical execution of the FindEmployees program

The program in Figure 14-18 is intended to demonstrate using the Seek() method. In a business setting, you might prefer to not leave a file open in one application if other users might be waiting for it. As an alternative, you could load all the records into an array and then search the array for desired records. Problems also exist with this approach because you would have to overestimate the number of records in the file to create an array large enough to hold them.

When you seek beyond the length of the file, you do not cause an error. Instead, the file size grows. In Microsoft Windows NT and later, any data added to the end of a file is set to zero. In Microsoft Windows 98 or earlier, any data added to the end of the file is not set to zero. This means that previously deleted data might become visible to the stream.

TWO TRUTHS & A LIE
Searching a Sequential Text File

1. When you read data from a sequential file, the program starts at the beginning of the file and reads each record in turn until all the records have been read.

2. When you read from a sequential file, its file position pointer holds the number of the record to be read.

3. To reread a file, you can close it and reopen it, or you can reposition the file pointer to the beginning of the file.

The false statement is #2. When you read from a sequential file, its file position pointer holds the byte number of the next byte to be read.

You Do It

Using the Seek() Method

In the next steps, you use the Seek() method to reposition a file pointer so you can access a file from any location. The user will be prompted to enter a number representing a starting point to list the names in the Names.txt file. Names from that point forward will be listed, and then the user will be prompted for another selection.

1. Start a new program named **AccessSomeNames** that demonstrates how to access requested names from the Names.txt file you created in the CreateNameFile application.

(continues)

(continued)

```
using System;
using static System.Console;
using System.IO;
class AccessSomeNames
{
   static void Main()
   {
      FileStream file = new FileStream("Names.txt",
         FileMode.Open, FileAccess.Read);
      StreamReader reader = new StreamReader(file);
```

2. Declare a constant named END that represents an input value that allows the user to exit the program. Then declare other variables that the program will use.

```
const int END = 999;
int count = 0;
int num;
int size;
string name;
```

3. Read a line from the input file. While names are available, continue to read and count them. Then compute the size of each name by dividing the file length by the number of strings stored in it.

```
name = reader.ReadLine();
while(name != null)
{
   ++count;
   name = reader.ReadLine();
}
size = (int)file.Length / count;
```

4. Prompt the user for the number of the first record to read, and read the value from the Console.

```
Write("\nWith which number do you want to start? >> ");
num = Convert.ToInt32(ReadLine());
```

5. Start a loop that continues as long as the user does not enter the sentinel END value. Within the loop, display the user's number, and then use the Seek() method to position the file pointer at the correct file location. Because users enter numbers starting with 1 and file positions start with 0, you calculate the

(continues)

(continued)

file position by first subtracting 1 from the user's entry. The calculated record number is then multiplied by the size of each name in the file. For example, if each name is 10 bytes long, then the calculated starting position should be 0, 10, 20, 30, or some other multiple of the name size.

```
while(num != END)
{
   WriteLine("Starting with name " + num +": ");
   file.Seek((num - 1) * size, SeekOrigin.Begin);
```

6. Read and write the name at the calculated location. Then, in a nested loop, read and write all the remaining names until the end of the file.

```
name = reader.ReadLine();
WriteLine("   " + name);
while(name != null)
{
   name = reader.ReadLine();
   WriteLine("   " + name);
}
```

7. Finally, prompt the user for the next starting value for a new list, inform the user how to quit the application, and accept the next input value. Add a closing brace for the outer `while` loop.

```
   WriteLine("\nWith which number do you " +
      "want to start?");
   Write("     (Enter " + END + " to quit) >> ");
   num = Convert.ToInt32(ReadLine());
}
```

8. Close the `StreamReader` and `File` objects, and add closing braces for the method and the class.

```
      reader.Close();
      file.Close();
   }
}
```

9. Save the file, and then compile and execute it. Figure 14-20 shows a typical execution during which the user displays three sets of names starting at a different point each time.

(continues)

Understanding Serialization and Deserialization

(continued)

```
With which number do you want to start? >> 7
Starting with name 7:
   Gina
   Hannah
   Inez
   Juan

With which number do you want to start?
   (Enter 999 to quit) >> 2
Starting with name 2:
   Belle
   Carolyn
   David
   Edwin
   Frannie
   Gina
   Hannah
   Inez
   Juan

With which number do you want to start?
   (Enter 999 to quit) >> 9
Starting with name 9:
   Inez
   Juan

With which number do you want to start?
   (Enter 999 to quit) >> 999
```

Figure 14-20 Typical execution of the AccessSomeNames program

Understanding Serialization and Deserialization

Writing to a text file allows you to store data for later use. However, writing to a text file does present two disadvantages:

- Data in a text file are easily readable in a text editor such as Notepad. Although this feature is useful to developers when they test programs, it is not a very secure way to store data.

- When a record in a data file contains many fields, it is cumbersome to convert each field to text and combine the fields with delimiters before storing the record on a disk. Similarly, when you read a text file, it is somewhat unwieldy to eliminate the delimiters, split the text into tokens, and convert each token to the proper data type. Writing an entire object to a file at once would be more convenient.

CHAPTER 14 Files and Streams

C# provides a technique called serialization that can be used for writing objects to and reading objects from data files. **Serialization** is the process of converting objects into streams of bytes. **Deserialization** is the reverse process; it converts streams of bytes back into objects.

To create a class that can be serialized, you mark it with the [Serializable] attribute, as shown in the shaded statement in Figure 14-21. The Employee class in the figure is identical to the one in Figure 14-10 except for the [Serializable] attribute.

```
[Serializable]
class Employee
{
   public int EmpNum {get; set;}
   public string Name {get; set;}
   public double Salary {get; set;}
}
```

Figure 14-21 The serializable Employee class

Attributes provide a method of associating information with C# code. They are always contained in square brackets. Search for *C# attributes* at *http://msdn.microsoft.com* for more details.

In a class marked with the [Serializable] attribute, every instance variable must also be serializable. By default, all C# simple data types are serializable, including strings. However, if your class contains fields that are more complex data types, you must check the declaration of those classes to ensure they are serializable. By default, array objects are serializable. However, if the array contains references to other objects, such as Dates or Students, those objects must be serializable.

If you create a class and want to be able to write its objects to a file, you can implement the ISerializable interface instead of marking a class with the [Serializable] attribute. When you use this approach, you must write a method named GetObjectData(). Marking the class with the attribute is simpler.

Two namespaces are included in programs that employ serialization:

- System.Runtime.Serialization.Formatters.Binary;
- System.Runtime.Serialization;

When you create a program that writes objects to files, you declare an instance of the BinaryFormatter class with a statement such as the following:

BinaryFormatter bFormatter = new BinaryFormatter();

Then, after you fill a class object with data, you can write it to the output file stream named outFile with a statement such as the following:

bFormatter.Serialize(outFile, objectFilledWithData);

Understanding Serialization and Deserialization

The `Serialize()` method takes two arguments—a reference to the output file and a reference to a serializable object that might contain any number of data fields. The entire object is written to the data file with this single statement.

Similarly, when you read an object from a data file, you use a statement like the following:

`objectInstance = (TypeOfObject)bFormatter.Deserialize(inFile);`

This statement uses the `Deserialize()` method with a `BinaryFormatter` object to read in one object from the file. The object is cast to the appropriate type and can be assigned to an instance of the object. Then you can access individual fields. An entire object is read with this single statement, no matter how many data fields it contains.

Figure 14-22 shows a program that writes `Employee` class objects to a file and later reads them from the file into the program. After the `FileStream` is declared for an output file, a `BinaryFormatter` is declared in the first shaded statement. The user enters an ID number, name, and salary for an `Employee`, and the completed object is written to a file in the second shaded statement. When the user enters 999, the output file is closed.

```
using System;
using static System.Console;
using System.IO;
using System.Runtime.Serialization.Formatters.Binary;
using System.Runtime.Serialization;
class SerializableDemonstration
{
   static void Main()
   {
      const int END = 999;
      const string FILENAME = "Data.ser";
      Employee emp = new Employee();
      FileStream outFile = new FileStream(FILENAME,
         FileMode.Create, FileAccess.Write);
      BinaryFormatter bFormatter = new BinaryFormatter();
      Write("Enter employee number or " + END +
         " to quit >> ");
      emp.EmpNum = Convert.ToInt32(ReadLine());
      while(emp.EmpNum != END)
      {
         Write("Enter last name >> ");
         emp.Name = ReadLine();
         Write("Enter salary >> ");
         emp.Salary = Convert.ToDouble(ReadLine());
         bFormatter.Serialize(outFile, emp);
         Write("Enter employee number or " + END +
            " to quit >> ");
         emp.EmpNum = Convert.ToInt32(ReadLine());
      }
```

Figure 14-22 The SerializableDemonstration program *(continues)*

(continued)

```
        outFile.Close();
        FileStream inFile = new FileStream(FILENAME,
            FileMode.Open, FileAccess.Read);
        WriteLine("\n{0,-5}{1,-12}{2,8}\n",
            "Num", "Name", "Salary");
        while(inFile.Position < inFile.Length)
        {
            emp = (Employee)bFormatter.Deserialize(inFile);
            WriteLine("{0,-5}{1,-12}{2,8}",
                emp.EmpNum, emp.Name, emp.Salary.ToString("C"));
        }
        inFile.Close();
    }
}
```

Figure 14-22 The SerializableDemonstration program

After the output file closes in the SerializableDemonstration program in Figure 14-22, it is reopened for reading. A loop is executed while the `Position` property of the input file is less than its `Length` property. In other words, the loop executes while there is more data in the file. The last shaded statement in the figure deserializes data from the file and casts it to an `Employee` object, where the individual fields can be accessed. Figure 14-23 shows a typical execution of the program.

```
Enter employee number or 999 to quit >> 189
Enter last name >> West
Enter salary >> 45500
Enter employee number or 999 to quit >> 272
Enter last name >> Palmer
Enter salary >> 51200
Enter employee number or 999 to quit >> 387
Enter last name >> Wong
Enter salary >> 55000
Enter employee number or 999 to quit >> 426
Enter last name >> Lopez
Enter salary >> 61250
Enter employee number or 999 to quit >> 999

Num  Name         Salary

189  West         $45,500.00
272  Palmer       $51,200.00
387  Wong         $55,000.00
426  Lopez        $61,250.00
```

Figure 14-23 Typical execution of the SerializableDemonstration program

Understanding Serialization and Deserialization

The file created by the SerializableDemonstration program is not as easy to read as the text file created by the WriteSequentialFile program discussed earlier in the chapter (in Figure 14-11). Figure 14-24 shows the file contents displayed in Notepad (with some newline characters inserted so the output can fit on this page). If you examine the file carefully, you can discern the string names and some `Employee` class information, but the rest of the file is not easy to read.

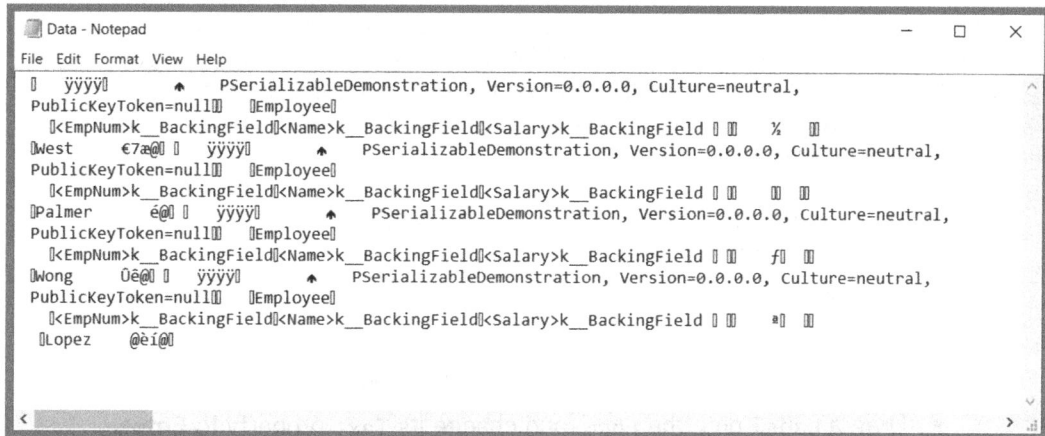

Figure 14-24 Data file created using the SerializableDemonstration program

   Watch the video *Understanding Serialization and Deserialization*.

TWO TRUTHS & A LIE

Understanding Serialization and Deserialization

1. An advantage of writing data to a text file is that the data is easily readable in a text editor such as Notepad.

2. Serialization is the process of converting objects into streams of bytes. Deserialization is the reverse process; it converts streams of bytes back into objects.

3. By default, all C# classes are serializable.

The false statement is #3. By default, all C# simple data types are serializable, including `strings`. However, if your class contains fields that are more complex data types, you must check the declaration of those classes to ensure they are serializable.

CHAPTER 14 Files and Streams

You Do It

Creating a Text File in a GUI Environment

The file writing and reading examples in this chapter have used console applications so that you could concentrate on the features of files in the simplest environment. However, you can write and read files in GUI environments as well. In the next steps, you create two applications. The first allows a user to enter invoice records using a Form and to store them in a file. The second application allows a user to view stored records using a Form.

1. Open the Visual Studio IDE, and start a new Windows Forms Application project named **EnterInvoices**.

2. Create a Form like the one shown in Figure 14-25 by making the following changes:

    - Change the Text property of the Form to **Invoice Data.**

    - Drag a Label onto the Form, and change its Text property to **Enter invoice data**. Increase the Label's Font to 12.

    - Drag three more Labels onto the Form, and change their Text properties to **Invoice number**, **Last name**, and **Amount**, respectively.

    - Drag three TextBoxes onto the Form next to the three descriptive Labels. Change the Name properties of the three TextBoxes to **invoiceBox**, **nameBox**, and **amountBox**, respectively.

    - Drag a Button onto the Form, change its Name to **enterButton**, and change its Text to **Enter record**. If necessary, resize **enterButton** so all of its text is visible.

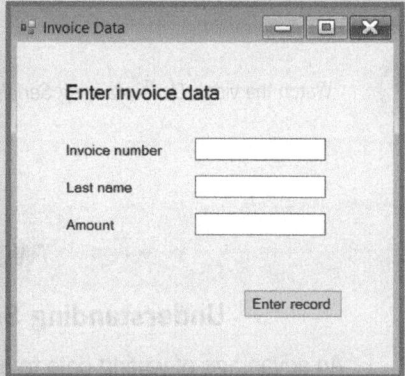

Figure 14-25 Designing the EnterInvoices Form

3. View the code for the Form. At the start of the class, before the Form1() constructor, add the shaded code shown in Figure 14-26. The new code contains statements that perform the following:

    - Declare a delimiter that will be used to separate records in the output file.

    - Declare a path and filename. You can change the path if you want to store the file in a different location on your system.

(continues)

(continued)

- Declare variables for the number, name, and amount of each invoice.
- Open the file, and associate it with a `StreamWriter`.

```
namespace EnterInvoices
{
    public partial class Form1 : Form
    {
        const string DELIM = ",";
        const string FILENAME =
            @"C:\CSharp\Chapter14\Invoices.txt";
        int num;
        string name;
        double amount;
        static FileStream outFile = new
            FileStream(FILENAME, FileMode.Create,
            FileAccess.Write);
        StreamWriter writer = new StreamWriter(outFile);
        public Form1()
        {
            InitializeComponent();
        }
```

Figure 14-26 Partial code for the EnterInvoices program with typed statements shaded

Remember that placing an at sign (@) in front of a string indicates that its characters should be interpreted literally. The @ sign is used with the filename so that the backslashes in the path will not be interpreted as escape sequence characters.

4. At the top of the file, with the other `using` statements, add the following so that the `FileStream` can be declared:

   using System.IO;

5. Click **Save All** (and continue to do so periodically as you work). Return to Design view, and double-click the **Enter record** button. Rename the `enterButton_Click()` method to start with an uppercase E. Then, as shown in the shaded portions of Figure 14-27, add statements within the method to accept data from each of the three `TextBoxes`, and convert each field to the appropriate type. Write each field to a text file, separated by delimiting commas. Finally, clear the `TextBox` fields to be ready for the user to enter a new set of data.

(continues)

(continued)

```
private void EnterButton_Click(object sender, EventArgs e)
{
    num = Convert.ToInt32(invoiceBox.Text);
    name = nameBox.Text;
    amount = Convert.ToDouble(amountBox.Text);
    writer.WriteLine(num + DELIM + name + DELIM + amount);
    invoiceBox.Clear();
    nameBox.Clear();
    amountBox.Clear();
}
```

Figure 14-27 Code for the `EnterButton_Click()` method of the EnterInvoices program

6. Locate the `Dispose()` method, which executes when the user clicks the Close button to dismiss the `Form`. A quick way to locate the method in the Visual Studio IDE is to select **Edit** from the main menu, click **Find and Replace**, click **Quick Find**, and type **Dispose** in the dialog box. (The Look in: setting can be either Entire Solution or Current Project.) The method appears on the screen. Add two statements to close `writer` and `outFile`, as shown in the shaded statements in Figure 14-28.

```
protected override void Dispose(bool disposing)
{
    writer.Close();
    outFile.Close();
    if (disposing && (components != null))
    {
        components.Dispose();
    }
    base.Dispose(disposing);
}
```

Figure 14-28 The `Dispose()` method in the EnterInvoices program

7. Click **Save All**. Execute the program. When the `Form` appears, enter data in each `TextBox`, and then click the **Enter record** button when you finish.

(continues)

(continued)

The `TextBoxes` clear in preparation for you to enter another record. Enter at least three records before dismissing the `Form`. Figure 14-29 shows data entry in progress.

Reading Data from a Text File into a Form

In the next steps, you create a `Form` that you can use to read records from a `File`.

1. Open a new Windows project in Visual Studio, and name it **ViewInvoices**.

2. Create a `Form` like the one shown in Figure 14-30 by making the following changes:

   - Change the `Text` of `Form1` to **Invoice Data**.
   - Add four `Labels` with the text, font size, and approximate locations shown in Figure 14-30. (You can click the down arrow next to the `Text` property of a component to get a box into which you can type multiline text.)
   - Add a `Button` with the `Text` **View records**. Resize the `Button` if necessary. Name the `Button` `viewButton`.
   - Add three `TextBoxes`. Name them `invoiceBox`, `nameBox`, and `amountBox`, respectively.

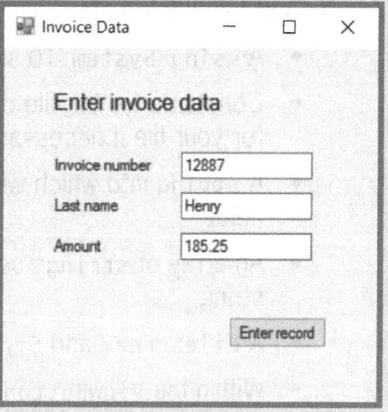

Figure 14-29 Entering data in the EnterInvoices application

Figure 14-30 The ViewInvoices Form

3. In the IDE, double-click the **View records** `Button` to view the code. Rename the `Click()` method to start with an uppercase letter.

(continues)

(continued)

4. Add the shaded statements shown in Figure 14-31. They include:
   - A using System.IO statement
   - Constants for the file delimiter character and the filename (change the path for your file if necessary)
   - A string into which whole records can be read before they are split into fields
   - An array of strings used to hold the separate, split fields of the entered string
   - A FileStream and StreamReader to handle the input file
   - Within the ViewButton_Click() method, statements to read in a line from the file and split it into three components

```csharp
using System;
using System.Collections.Generic;
using System.ComponentModel;
using System.Data;
using System.Drawing;
using System.Linq;
using System.Text;
using System.Windows.Forms;
using System.IO;
namespace ViewInvoices
{
    public partial class Form1 : Form
    {
        const char DELIM = ',';
        const string FILENAME = @"C:\CSharp\Chapter14\Invoices.txt";
        string recordIn;
        string[] fields;
        static FileStream file = new FileStream(FILENAME,
            FileMode.Open, FileAccess.Read);
        StreamReader reader = new StreamReader(file);
        public Form1()
        {
            InitializeComponent();
        }
```

Figure 14-31 Partial code for the ViewInvoices application *(continues)*

(continues)

Understanding Serialization and Deserialization

(continued)

```
        private void ViewButton_Click(object sender, EventArgs e)
        {
            recordIn = reader.ReadLine();
            fields = recordIn.Split(DELIM);
            invoiceBox.Text = fields[0];
            nameBox.Text = fields[1];
            amountBox.Text = fields[2];
        }
    }
}
```

Figure 14-31 Partial code for the ViewInvoices application

5. Add two `Close()` statements to the `Dispose()` method in the Form1Designer.cs file, as shown in Figure 14-32.

```
protected override void Dispose(bool disposing)
{
    reader.Close();
    file.Close();
    if (disposing && (components != null))
    {
        components.Dispose();
    }
    base.Dispose(disposing);
}
```

Figure 14-32 The `Dispose()` method for the ViewInvoices program

6. Save the project, and then execute it. When the Form appears, click the Button to view records. You see the data for the first record you entered when you ran the EnterInvoices application; your Form should look like the one in Figure 14-33. Click the Button again to display the next record.

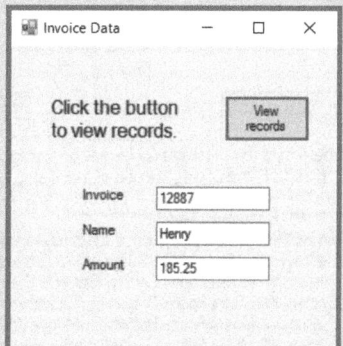

Figure 14-33 Typical execution of the ViewInvoices program

(continues)

CHAPTER 14 Files and Streams

(continued)

7. Continue to click the Button to view each record. After you view the last record you entered, click the Button again. An unhandled exception is generated, as shown in Figure 14-34, because you attempted to read data past the end of the input file.

Figure 14-34 Error message window displayed after user attempts to read past the end of the file

Your error message might look different than the one in Figure 14-34 depending on the version of Visual Studio you are using.

8. Click the **Details** button in the UnhandledException window to view details of the error. Figure 14-35 shows that a System.NullReferenceException was thrown and not handled.

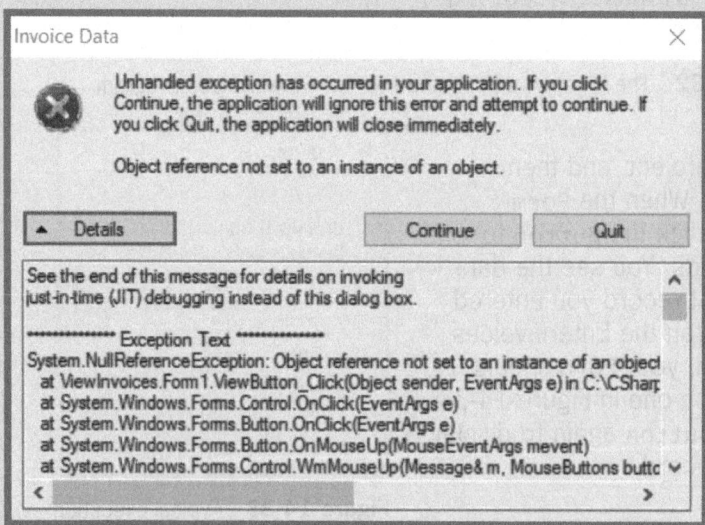

Figure 14-35 Details displayed by the unhandled exception window

(continues)

Understanding Serialization and Deserialization

(continued)

9. Click **Quit** to close the unhandled exception window.

10. To remedy the unhandled NullReferenceException problem, you could take any number of actions. Depending on the application, you might want to do one or more of the following:
    - Display a message.
    - Disallow any more button clicks.
    - End the program.
    - Reposition the file pointer to the file's beginning so the user can view the records again.

    For this example, you take the first two actions: display a message and disallow further button clicks. Return to Visual Studio, and locate the code for the ViewButton_Click() method. Add a try...catch block, as shown in Figure 14-36. Place all the record-handling code in a try block, and if a NullReferenceException is thrown, change the Text in label1 and disable the View records Button.

```
private void ViewButton_Click(object sender, EventArgs e)
{
   try
   {
      recordIn = reader.ReadLine();
      fields = recordIn.Split(DELIM);
      invoiceBox.Text = fields[0];
      nameBox.Text = fields[1];
      amountBox.Text = fields[2];
   }
   catch (NullReferenceException)
   {
      label1.Text = "You have viewed\nall the records";
      viewButton.Enabled = false;
   }
}
```

Figure 14-36 The ViewButton_Click() method modified to handle an exception

(continued)

11. Save the project, and then execute it. This time, after you have viewed all the available records, the last record remains on the Form, an appropriate message is displayed, and the button is disabled, as shown in Figure 14-37.

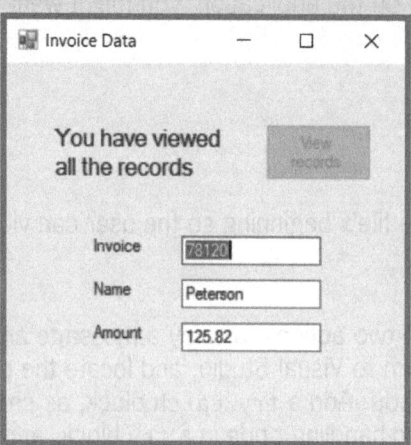

Figure 14-37 The ViewInvoices Form after user has viewed the last record

12. Dismiss the Form. Close Visual Studio.

Chapter Summary

- A computer file is a collection of information stored on a nonvolatile, permanent storage device in a computer system. Computer users organize their files into folders or directories. In C#, the File class contains methods that allow you to access information about files, and the Directory class provides you with information about directories or folders.

- Data items are stored in a hierarchy of character, field, record, and file. A data file is a sequential access file when each record is read in order from first to last. Usually, the records are stored in order based on the value in a key field. Before an application can use a data file, it must open the file by creating an object and associating a stream of bytes with that object. When you close a file, it is no longer available to your application.

- Bytes flow into and out of applications through streams. When you use the Console class, you have access to several standard streams: Console.In, Console.Out, and Console.Error.

When you read from or write to a file, you use a file-processing class instead of `Console`. Many file-processing classes are available in C#, including `StreamReader` for text input from a file, `StreamWriter` for text output to a file, and `FileStream` for both input and output.

- You can use a `StreamWriter` object to write objects to a file using the `WriteLine()` method. Fields should be separated by a delimiter. Data can be read from a file using a `StreamReader` object and the `ReadLine()` method. If the value of the returned string from `ReadLine()` is null, then no more data exists in the file. After a record (line of data) is read in, the `String` class `Split()` method can be used to separate the data fields into an array of strings.

- When you read data from a sequential file, subsequent records are read in order because a file's position pointer holds the byte number of the next byte to be read. To reread a file, you could close it and reopen it, or you can just reposition the file pointer using the `Seek()` method and the `SeekOrigin` enumeration.

- Serialization is the process of converting objects into streams of bytes. Deserialization is the reverse process; it converts streams of bytes back into objects. To create a class that can be serialized, you mark it with the `[Serializable]` attribute. A serializable object can be written to or read from a data file with a single statement.

Key Terms

Random access memory (RAM) is temporary storage in a computer.

Volatile describes storage in which data is lost when power is interrupted.

Nonvolatile storage is permanent storage; data is not lost when a computer loses power.

A **computer file** is a collection of information stored on a nonvolatile device in a computer system.

Permanent storage devices, such as hard disks, USB drives, reels of magnetic tape, and optical discs, are used to store files.

Text files contain data that can be read in a text editor because the data has been encoded using a scheme such as ASCII or Unicode.

Data files contain facts and figures.

Binary files contain data that has been encoded in binary format.

A **byte** is a small unit of storage; in a simple text file, a byte holds only one character.

A **kilobyte** is approximately one thousand bytes.

A **megabyte** is approximately one million bytes.

A **gigabyte** is approximately one billion bytes.

To **read from a file** is to copy data from a file on a storage device into RAM.

To **write to a file** is to store data in a computer file on a permanent storage device.

Persistent storage is nonvolatile storage.

The **root directory** is the main directory of a storage device.

Folders or **directories** are structures used to organize files on a storage device.

A **path** is composed of the disk drive in which a file resides plus the complete hierarchy of directories.

The **data hierarchy** is the relationship of characters, fields, records, and files.

A **character** is any one of the letters, numbers, or other special symbols (such as punctuation marks) that constitute data.

A **character set** is the group of all the characters used to represent data on a particular computer.

A **field** is a character or group of characters that has some meaning.

A **record** is a collection of fields that contain data about an entity.

A **sequential access file** is a data file in which each record is read in order based on its position in the file; usually the records are stored in order based on the value in some field.

The **key field** is the field used to control the order of records in a sequential file.

A **random access file** is one for which records can be accessed in any order.

Opening a file involves creating an object and associating a stream of bytes with it.

Closing a file means it is no longer available to an application.

A **stream** is a pipeline or channel through which bytes are input from and output to a file.

Programmers say `FileStream` **exposes** a stream around a file.

XML is an abbreviation of eXtensible Markup Language, which is a standard for exchanging data over the Internet.

A **token** is a block of text within a string that represents an entity or field.

A **delimiter** is a character used to specify the boundary between characters in text files.

A **CSV file** is one that contains comma-separated values.

A **priming read** is an input statement that gets a first data item or record.

The term **magic number** refers to the bad programming practice of hard-coding numbers in code without explanation.

A file's **file position pointer** holds the byte number of the next byte to be read.

Serialization is the process of converting objects into streams of bytes.

Deserialization is the process of converting streams of bytes back into objects.

Review Questions

1. Random access memory is _____.
   a. volatile
   b. persistent
   c. permanent
   d. sequential

2. A collection of data stored on a nonvolatile device in a computer system is a(n) _____.
   a. application
   b. operating system
   c. computer file
   d. memory map

3. Which of the following is not considered to be permanent storage?
   a. a USB drive
   b. a hard disk
   c. RAM
   d. None of these is permanent storage.

4. When you store data in a computer file on a persistent storage device, you are _____.
   a. reading
   b. writing
   c. directing
   d. rooting

5. Which of the following is not a `File` class method?
   a. `Create()`
   b. `Delete()`
   c. `Exists()`
   d. `End()`

6. In the data hierarchy, a group of characters that has some meaning, such as a last name or ID number, is a _____.
   a. byte
   b. field
   c. file
   d. record

7. When each record in a file is stored in order based on the value in some field, the file is a(n) _____ file.
   a. random access
   b. sequential
   c. formatted
   d. application

CHAPTER 14 — Files and Streams

8. A channel through which data flows between a program and storage is a _____.

    a. path
    b. folder
    c. directory
    d. stream

9. Which of the following is not part of a `FileStream` constructor?

    a. the file size
    b. the file mode
    c. the filename
    d. the type of access

10. When a file's mode is `Create`, a new file will be created _____.

    a. even if one with the same name already exists
    b. only if one with the same name does not already exist
    c. only if one with the same name already exists
    d. only if the access is `Read`

11. Which of the following is not a `FileStream` property?

    a. `CanRead`
    b. `CanExist`
    c. `CanSeek`
    d. `CanWrite`

12. Which of the following is not a file `Access` enumeration?

    a. `Read`
    b. `Write`
    c. `WriteRead`
    d. `ReadWrite`

13. A character used to specify the boundary between data items in text files is a _____.

    a. sentinel
    b. stopgap
    c. delimiter
    d. margin

14. Which character can be used to specify a boundary between characters in text files?

    a. a comma
    b. a semicolon
    c. either of these
    d. neither of these

Review Questions

15. After a `StreamReader` has been created, the `ReadLine()` method can be used to _____.

    a. retrieve one line at a time from the file
    b. retrieve one character at a time from the file
    c. store one line at a time in a file
    d. split a `string` into tokens

16. The argument to the `String` class `Split()` method is _____.

    a. `void`
    b. the number of fields into which to split a record
    c. the character that identifies a new field in a `string`
    d. a `string` that can be split into tokens

17. The `String` class `Split()` method stores its results in _____.

    a. a `string`
    b. an array of `strings`
    c. an appropriate data type for each token
    d. an array of bytes

18. A file's _____ holds the byte number of the next byte to be read.

    a. index indicator
    b. position pointer
    c. header file
    d. key field

19. The process of converting objects into streams of bytes is _____.

    a. extrication
    b. splitting
    c. mapping
    d. serialization

20. Which of the following is serializable?

    a. an `int`
    b. an array of `ints`
    c. a `string`
    d. all of the above

Exercises

Programming Exercises

1. Create a program named **DirectoryInformation** that allows a user to continually enter directory names until the user types *end*. If the directory name exists, display a list of the files in it; otherwise, display a message indicating the directory does not exist. Create as many test directories and files as necessary to test your program.

2. Create a program named **FileComparison** that compares two files. First, use a text editor such as Notepad to save your favorite movie quote. Next, copy the file contents, and paste them into a word-processing program such as Word. Then, write the file-comparison application that displays the sizes of the two files as well as the ratio of their sizes to each other. To discover a file's size, you can create a System.IO.FileInfo object using statements such as the following, where FILE_NAME is a string that contains the name of the file, and size has been declared as an integer:

   ```
   FileInfo fileInfo = new FileInfo(FILE_NAME);
   size = fileInfo.Length;
   ```

3. Using Visual Studio, create a project named **ShowFileInfo** that contains a Form like the one in Figure 14-38. Specify a directory on your system, and when the Form loads, list the files the directory contains in a ListBox Allow the user to click a file name, and then display the file's creation date and time. (Each time the user checks a new filename, display its creation date in place of the original selection.) Create as many files as necessary to test your program.

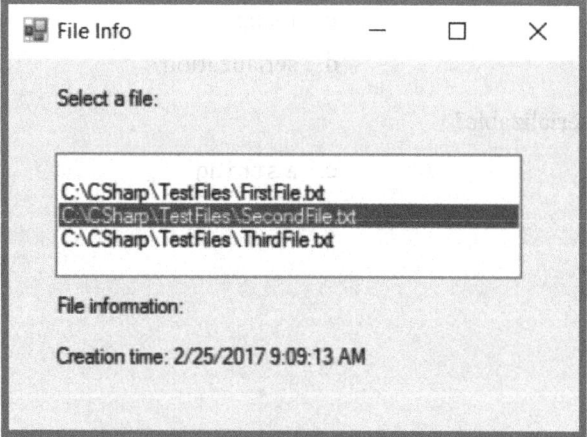

Figure 14-38 Typical execution of the ShowFileInfo program

4. a. Create a program named **WritePatientRecords** that allows a doctor's staff to enter data about patients and saves the data to a file. Create a `Patient` class that contains fields for ID number, name, and current balance owed to the doctor's office.

   b. Create a program named **ReadPatientRecords** that reads the file created in Exercise 4a and displays each patient's data on the screen.

   c. Create a program named **FindPatientRecords** that prompts the user for an ID number, reads the file created in Exercise 4a, and displays data for the specified record.

   d. Create a program named **FindPatientRecords2** that prompts the user for a minimum balance due, reads the file created in Exercise 4a, and displays all the records containing a balance greater than or equal to the entered value.

5. Create a program named **CustomizeAForm** that includes a `Form` for which a user can select options for the background color, size, and title. Change each feature of the `Form` as the user makes selections. After the user clicks a button to save the form settings, save the color, size, and title as strings to a file, and disable the button.

6. Design a program named **RetrieveCustomizedForm** that includes a `Form` with a `Button`. When the user clicks the `Button`, the settings saved to the file in the CustomizeAForm project in Exercise 5 are retrieved, and the new `Form`'s color, size, and title are set appropriately.

7. Create a program named **HighScore** containing a `Form` that hosts a game in which the computer randomly selects one of three letters (A, B, or C) and the user tries to guess which letter was selected. At the start of the game, read in the previous high score from a data file. (Create this file to hold *0* the first time the game is played.) Display the previous high score on the `Form` to show the player the score to try to beat. Play continues for 10 rounds. As the player makes each guess, show the player's guess and the computer's choice, and award a point if the player correctly guesses the computer's choice. Keep a running count of the number of correct guesses. After 10 rounds, disable the game controls, and create a file that holds the new high score, which might be the same as before the game or a new higher number. When the player begins a new game, the high score will be displayed on the `Form` as the new score to beat.

CHAPTER 14 Files and Streams

Debugging Exercises

1. Each of the following files in the Chapter.14 folder of your downloadable student files has syntax and/or logical errors. In each case, determine the problem, and fix the program. After you correct the errors, save each file using the same filename preceded with *Fixed*. For example, save DebugFourteen1.cs as **FixedDebugFourteen.cs**.

    a. DebugFourteen1.cs

    b. DebugFourteen2.cs

    c. DebugFourteen3.cs

    d. DebugFourteen4.cs

Case Problems

1. In Chapter 11, you created the most recent version of the **GreenvilleRevenue** program, which prompts the user for contestant data for this year's Greenville Idol competition. Now, save all the entered data to a file that is closed when data entry is complete and then reopened and read in, allowing the user to view lists of contestants with requested talent types.

2. In Chapter 11, you created the most recent version of the **MarshallsRevenue** program, which prompts the user for customer data for scheduled mural painting. Now, save all the entered data to a file that is closed when data entry is complete and then reopened and read in, allowing the user to view lists of customer orders for mural types.

APPENDIX A

Operator Precedence and Associativity

When an expression contains multiple operators, their **precedence** controls the order in which the individual operators are evaluated. For example, multiplication has a higher precedence than addition, so the expression 2 + 3 * 4 evaluates as 14 because the value of 3 * 4 is calculated before adding 2. Table A-1 summarizes all operators in order of precedence from highest to lowest.

When you use two operators with the same precedence, the **associativity** of the operators controls the order in which the operations are performed.

- Except for the assignment and conditional operators, all binary operators (those that take two arguments) are **left-associative**, meaning that operations are performed from left to right. For example, 5 + 6 + 7 is evaluated first as 5 + 6, or 11; then 7 is added, bringing the value to 18.

- The assignment operators and the conditional operator (?:) are **right-associative**, meaning that operations are performed from right to left. For example, x = y = z is evaluated as y = z first, the result is then assigned to x.

- All unary operators (those that take one argument) are right-associative. If b is 5, the value of -++b is determined by evaluating ++b first (6), then taking its negative value (-6).

You can control precedence and associativity by using parentheses. For example, a + b * c first multiplies b by c and then adds the result to a. The expression (a + b) * c, however, forces the sum of a and b to be calculated first; then the result is multiplied by c.

APPENDIX A — Operator Precedence and Associativity

Category	Operators	Associativity
Primary	x.y f(x) a[x] x++ x-- new typeof checked unchecked	left
Unary	+ - ! ~ ++x --x (T)x	right
Multiplicative	* / %	left
Additive	+ -	left
Shift	<< >>	right
Relational and type testing	< > <= >= is as	left
Equality	== !=	left
Logical AND	&	left
Logical XOR	^	left
Logical OR	|	left
Conditional AND	&&	left
Conditional OR	||	left
Conditional	?:	right
Assignment	= *= /= %= += -= <<= >>= &= ^= |=	right

Table A-1 Operator precedence

Key Terms

The **precedence** of operators controls the order in which individual operators are evaluated in an expression.

The **associativity** of operators controls the order in which operations of equal precedence are performed in an expression.

With **left-associative** operators, operations are performed from left to right.

With **right-associative** operators, operations are performed from right to left.

APPENDIX B

Understanding Numbering Systems and Computer Codes

The numbering system you know best is the **decimal numbering system**, which is based on 10 digits, 0 through 9. Mathematicians call decimal system numbers *base 10 numbers*. When you use the decimal system to express positive whole numbers, no other symbols are available; if you want to express a value larger than 9, you must resort to using multiple digits from the same pool of 10, placing them in columns.

When you use the decimal system, you analyze a multicolumn number by mentally assigning place values to each column. The value of the rightmost column is 1, the value of the next column to the left is 10, the next column is 100, and so on, multiplying the column value by 10 as you move to the left. There is no limit to the number of columns you can use; you simply keep adding columns to the left as you need to express higher values. For example, Figure B-1 shows how the value 305 is represented in the decimal system. You simply sum the value of the digit in each column after it has been multiplied by the value of its column.

```
    Column value
  100    10    1
 ┌─────┬─────┬─────┐
 │  3  │  0  │  5  │
 └─────┴─────┴─────┘
 ┌─────────────────┐
 │ 3 * 100 = 300   │
 │ 0 *  10 =   0   │
 │ 5 *   1 =   5   │
 │             305 │
 └─────────────────┘
```

Figure B-1   Representing 305 in the decimal system

APPENDIX B: Understanding Numbering Systems and Computer Codes

The **binary numbering system** works in the same way as the decimal numbering system, except that it uses only two digits, 0 and 1. Mathematicians call these numbers *base 2 numbers*. When you use the binary system, if you want to express a value greater than 1, you must resort to using multiple columns, because no single symbol is available that represents any value other than 0 or 1. However, instead of each new column to the left being 10 times greater than the previous column, when you use the binary system, each new column is only two times the value of the previous column. For example, Figure B-2 shows how the numbers 9 and 305 are represented in the binary system. Notice that in both the binary and decimal systems, it is perfectly acceptable—and often necessary—to create numbers with 0 in one or more columns. As with the decimal system, the binary system has no limit to the number of columns; you can use as many as it takes to express a value.

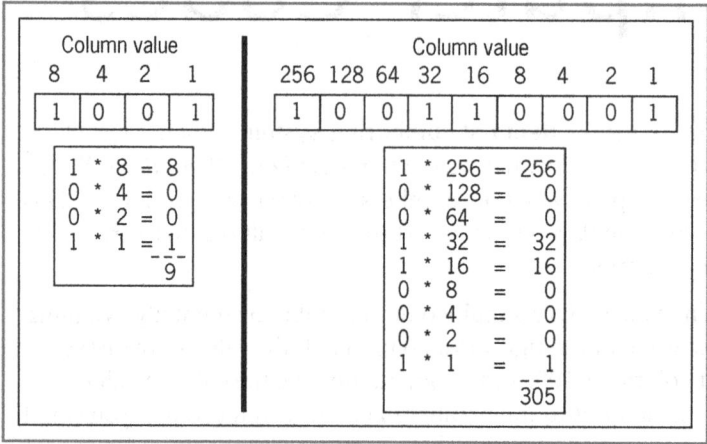

Figure B-2 Representing decimal values 9 and 305 in the binary system

A computer stores every piece of data it uses as a set of 0s and 1s. Each 0 or 1 is known as a **bit**, which is short for *binary digit*. Every computer uses 0s and 1s because all values in a computer are stored as electronic signals that are either on or off. This two-state system is most easily represented using just two digits.

Computers use a set of binary digits to represent stored characters. If computers used only one binary digit to represent characters, then only two different characters could be represented, because the single bit could be only 0 or 1. If computers used only two digits, then only four characters could be represented—the four codes 00, 01, 10, and 11, which in decimal values are 0, 1, 2, and 3, respectively. Many computers use sets of eight binary digits to represent each character they store, because using eight binary digits provides 256 different combinations. One combination can represent an *A*, another a *B*, still others *a* and *b*, and so on. Two hundred fifty-six combinations are enough so that each capital letter, small letter, digit, and punctuation mark used in English has its own code; even a space has a code. For example, in some computers 01000001 represents the character *A*. The binary number 01000001 has a decimal

Understanding Numbering Systems and Computer Codes — APPENDIX B

value of 65, but this numeric value is not important to ordinary computer users; it is simply a code that stands for *A*. The code that uses 01000001 to mean *A* is the **American Standard Code for Information Interchange (ASCII)**.

 A set of eight bits is called a **byte**. Half a byte, or four bits, is a **nibble**. You will learn more about bytes later in this appendix.

ASCII is not the only computer code, but it is typical and is the one used in most personal computers. The **Extended Binary Coded Decimal Interchange Code (EBCDIC)** is an eight-bit code that is used in IBM mainframe computers. In these computers, the principle is the same—every character is stored as a series of binary digits. However, the actual values used are different. For example, in EBCDIC, an *A* is 11000001, or 193. **Unicode** is another code used by languages such as Java and C#; with this code, 16 bits are used to represent each character. The character *A* in Unicode has the same decimal value (65) as the ASCII *A*, but it is stored as 0000000001000001. Using 16 bits provides many more possible combinations than using only eight bits—65,536 to be exact. Unicode has enough available codes for all English letters and digits and for characters from many international alphabets.

Ordinary computer users seldom think about the numeric codes behind the letters, numbers, and punctuation marks they enter from their keyboards or see displayed on a monitor. However, they see the consequence of the values behind letters when they see data sorted in alphabetical order. When you sort a list of names, *Andrea* comes before *Brian*, and *Caroline* comes after *Brian* because the numeric code for *A* is lower than the code for *B*, and the numeric code for *C* is higher than the code for *B*, no matter whether you are using ASCII, EBCDIC, or Unicode.

Table B-1 shows the decimal and binary values behind the most commonly used characters in the ASCII character set—the letters, numbers, and punctuation marks you can enter from your keyboard using a single key press. Most of the values not included in Table B-1 have a purpose. For example, the decimal value 7 represents a bell—a dinging sound your computer can make, often used to notify you of an error or some other unusual condition. Each binary number in Table B-1 is shown containing two sets of four digits; this convention makes the long eight-digit numbers easier to read.

APPENDIX B Understanding Numbering Systems and Computer Codes

Decimal number	Binary number	ASCII character		Decimal number	Binary number	ASCII character	
32	0010 0000		Space	51	0011 0011	3	
33	0010 0001	!	Exclamation point	52	0011 0100	4	
34	0010 0010	"	Quotation mark, or double quote	53	0011 0101	5	
35	0010 0011	#	Number sign, octothorpe, pound sign, or hash	54	0011 0110	6	
36	0010 0100	$	Dollar sign	55	0011 0111	7	
37	0010 0101	%	Percent	56	0011 1000	8	
38	0010 0110	&	Ampersand	57	0011 1001	9	
39	0010 0111	'	Apostrophe, single quote	58	0011 1010	:	Colon
40	0010 1000	(	Left parenthesis	59	0011 1011	;	Semicolon
41	0010 1001	)	Right parenthesis	60	0011 1100	<	Less-than sign
42	0010 1010	*	Asterisk	61	0011 1101	=	Equal sign
43	0010 1011	+	Plus sign	62	0011 1110	>	Greater-than sign
44	0010 1100	,	Comma	63	0011 1111	?	Question mark
45	0010 1101	-	Hyphen or minus sign	64	0100 0000	@	At sign
46	0010 1110	.	Period or decimal point	65	0100 0001	A	
47	0010 1111	/	Slash or front slash	66	0100 0010	B	
48	0011 0000	0		67	0100 0011	C	
49	0011 0001	1		68	0100 0100	D	
50	0011 0010	2		69	0100 0101	E	

Table B-1 Decimal and binary values for common ASCII characters *(continues)*

Understanding Numbering Systems and Computer Codes **APPENDIX B**

(continued)

Decimal number	Binary number	ASCII character	Decimal number	Binary number	ASCII character
70	0100 0110	F	89	0101 1001	Y
71	0100 0111	G	90	0101 1010	Z
72	0100 1000	H	91	0101 1011	[Opening or left bracket
73	0100 1001	I	92	0101 1100	\ Backslash
74	0100 1010	J	93	0101 1101	] Closing or right bracket
75	0100 1011	K	94	0101 1110	^ Caret
76	0100 1100	L	95	0101 1111	_ Underline or underscore
77	0100 1101	M	96	0110 0000	` Grave accent
78	0100 1110	N	97	0110 0001	a
79	0100 1111	O	98	0110 0010	b
80	0101 0000	P	99	0110 0011	c
81	0101 0001	Q	100	0110 0100	d
82	0101 0010	R	101	0110 0101	e
83	0101 0011	S	102	0110 0110	f
84	0101 0100	T	103	0110 0111	g
85	0101 0101	U	104	0110 1000	h
86	0101 0110	V	105	0110 1001	i
87	0101 0111	W	106	0110 1010	j
88	0101 1000	X	107	0110 1011	k

Table B-1 Decimal and binary values for common ASCII characters *(continues)*

(continued)

Decimal number	Binary number	ASCII character	Decimal number	Binary number	ASCII character
108	0110 1100	l	118	0111 0110	v
109	0110 1101	m	119	0111 0111	w
110	0110 1110	n	120	0111 1000	x
111	0110 1111	o	121	0111 1001	y
112	0111 0000	p	122	0111 1010	z
113	0111 0001	q	123	0111 1011	{ Opening or left brace
114	0111 0010	r	124	0111 1100	| Vertical line or pipe
115	0111 0011	s	125	0111 1101	} Closing or right brace
116	0111 0100	t	126	0111 1110	~ Tilde
117	0111 0101	u			

Table B-1 Decimal and binary values for common ASCII characters

Understanding Numbering Systems and Computer Codes   APPENDIX B

The Hexadecimal System

The **hexadecimal numbering system** is a **base 16 system** because it uses 16 digits. As shown in Table B-2, the digits are 0 through 9 and A through F. Computer professionals often use the hexadecimal system to express addresses and instructions as they are stored in computer memory because hexadecimal provides convenient shorthand expressions for groups of binary values. In Table B-2, each hexadecimal value represents one of the 16 possible combinations of four-digit binary values. Therefore, instead of referencing memory contents as a 16-digit binary value, for example, programmers can use a 4-digit hexadecimal value.

Decimal value	Hexadecimal value	Binary value (shown using four digits)
0	0	0000
1	1	0001
2	2	0010
3	3	0011
4	4	0100
5	5	0101
6	6	0110
7	7	0111
8	8	1000
9	9	1001
10	A	1010
11	B	1011
12	C	1100
13	D	1101
14	E	1110
15	F	1111

Table B-2   Values in the decimal and hexadecimal systems

In the hexadecimal system, each column is 16 times the value of the column to its right. Therefore, column values from right to left are 1, 16, 256, 4096, and so on. Figure B-3 shows how 171 and 305 are expressed in hexadecimal.

Figure B-3 Representing decimal values 171 and 305 in the hexadecimal system

Measuring Storage

In computer systems, both internal memory and external storage are measured in bits and bytes. Eight bits make a byte, and a byte frequently holds a single character (in ASCII or EBCDIC) or half a character (in Unicode). Because a byte is such a small unit of storage, the size of memory and files is often expressed in thousands or millions of bytes. Table B-3 describes some commonly used terms for storage measurement.

Understanding Numbering Systems and Computer Codes — APPENDIX B

Term	Abbreviation	Number of bytes using binary system	Number of bytes using decimal system	Example
Kilobyte	KB or kb	1024	one thousand	This appendix occupies about 85 kilobytes on a hard disk.
Megabyte	MB	1,048,576 (1024 × 1024 kilobytes)	one million	One megabyte can hold an average book in text format. A 3½-inch diskette you might have used a few years ago held 1.44 megabytes.
Gigabyte	GB	1,073,741,824 (1,024 megabytes)	one billion	The hard drive on a fairly new laptop computer might be 500 gigabytes. An hour of HDTV video is about 4 gigabytes.
Terabyte	TB	1024 gigabytes	one trillion	The entire Library of Congress can be stored in 10 terabytes.
Petabyte	PB	1024 terabytes	one quadrillion	Popular Web sites such as Google have 20 to 30 petabytes of activity per day.
Exabyte	EB	1024 petabytes	one quintillion	A popular expression claims that all words ever spoken by humans could be stored in text form in 5 exabytes.
Zettabyte	ZB	1024 exabytes	one sextillion	A popular expression claims that all words ever spoken by humans could be stored in audio form in 42 zettabytes.
Yottabyte	YB	1024 zettabytes	one septillion (a 1 followed by 24 zeros)	All data accessible on the Internet and in corporate networks is estimated to be 1 yottabyte.

Table B-3 Commonly used terms for computer storage

APPENDIX B — Understanding Numbering Systems and Computer Codes

In the metric system, "kilo" means 1000. However, in Table B-3, notice that a kilobyte is 1024 bytes. The discrepancy occurs because everything stored in a computer is based on the binary system, so multiples of two are used in most measurements. If you multiply 2 by itself 10 times, the result is 1024, which is a little more than 1000. Similarly, a gigabyte is 1,073,741,624 bytes, which is more than a billion.

Confusion arises because many hard-drive manufacturers use the decimal system instead of the binary system to describe storage. For example, if you buy a hard drive that holds 10 gigabytes, it actually holds exactly 10 billion bytes. However, in the binary system, 10 GB is 10,737,418,240 bytes, so when you check your hard drive's capacity, your computer will report that you don't quite have 10 GB, but only 9.31 GB.

Key Terms

The **decimal numbering system** is a numbering system that uses 10 digits, 0 through 9, arranged in columns to represent numbers.

The **binary numbering system** is a numbering system that uses two digits, 0 and 1, arranged in columns to represent numbers.

A **bit** is a binary digit.

The **American Standard Code for Information Interchange (ASCII)** is an eight-bit code that represents characters.

A **byte** is eight bits.

A **nibble** is four bits.

The **Extended Binary Coded Decimal Interchange Code (EBCDIC)** is an eight-bit code used in IBM mainframe computers.

Unicode is a 16-bit code used with languages such as C# and Java.

The **hexadecimal numbering system** is a numbering system that uses 16 digits, 0 through 9 and A through F, arranged in columns to represent numbers.

The **base 16 system** is the hexadecimal system.

APPENDIX C

Using the IDE Editor

The Visual C# Code Editor is like a word processor for writing source code. Just as a word-processing program provides support for spelling and grammar, the C# Code Editor helps ensure that your C# syntax is free from spelling and grammar errors. This support can be grouped into several categories that are described in this appendix.

IntelliSense

IntelliSense is Microsoft's name for the set of features designed to minimize the time you spend looking for help and to help you enter code more accurately and efficiently. The IntelliSense features provide basic information about C# language keywords, .NET Framework types, and method signatures as you type them in the editor. The information is displayed in ToolTips, list boxes, and Smart Tags. Features of IntelliSense include:

- Providing completion lists
- Providing quick information
- Providing parameter information
- Adding using statements

Providing Completion Lists

As you enter source code in the editor, IntelliSense displays a list box that contains all of the C# keywords, .NET Framework classes, and names you have defined in your program that fit the current circumstances. This feature is called **completion mode**. For example, Figure C-1 shows a list box that makes suggestions based on what the programmer has typed in the Code Editor. If you find a match in the list box for the name you intend to type, you can select the item. Alternatively, you can press the Tab key to have IntelliSense finish entering the name or keyword for you.

APPENDIX C Using the IDE Editor

Figure C-1 A list displayed by IntelliSense

IntelliSense also supports a **suggestion mode**. In this mode, IntelliSense does not automatically complete identifiers, which makes it easier for you to type variable or method names without the completion list appearing. You can toggle between completion mode and suggestion mode by pressing Ctrl+Alt+Spacebar or by pointing to IntelliSense on the Edit menu and clicking Toggle Completion Mode.

Similarly, when you enter a .NET Framework type or an identifier of a specific type into the Code Editor and then type the dot operator (.), IntelliSense displays a list box that contains the members of that type. When you don't know what method or property you want for an object, typing its identifier and a dot can direct you to the appropriate choice. This technique sometimes teaches you about features you did not even realize were available.

Providing Quick Information

When you hover the cursor over a .NET Framework type, IntelliSense displays a Quick Info ToolTip that contains basic documentation about that type.

Providing Parameter Information

When you enter a method name in the Code Editor and then type an opening parenthesis, IntelliSense displays a Parameter Info ToolTip that shows the method's parameter list. If the method is overloaded, multiple method signatures are displayed, and you can scroll through them.

Adding using Statements

If you attempt to create an instance of a .NET Framework class without a sufficiently qualified name, IntelliSense displays a Smart Tag after the unresolved identifier. When you click the Smart Tag, IntelliSense displays a list of using statements to help you resolve the identifier. When you select a statement from the list, IntelliSense adds the using directive to the top of your source code file, and you can continue to write code at your current location.

Code Snippets

Code snippets are small units of commonly used C# source code that you can enter accurately and quickly with only a couple of keystrokes. To access the code snippet menu, right-click in the Code Editor, select Insert Snippet, and select Visual C#. Then, you can browse from the many available snippets, or you can create your own.

Squiggles and Lightbulbs

Squiggles, which are wavy underlines, give you instant feedback about errors in your code as you type. A red squiggle underline identifies a syntax error, such as a missing semicolon or mismatched braces. You also see a lightbulb in the left margin if Visual Studio has a suggestion on how to fix the problem. In Figure C-2, a squiggle appears under a partially-completed statement.

Figure C-2 Squiggle and lightbulb in Code Editor

Readability Aids

The editor assigns different colors to various categories of identifiers in a C# source code file to make the code easier to read. For example, C# keywords are bright blue, classes are blue-green, and comments are green.

Key Terms

IntelliSense is Microsoft's name for the set of features designed to minimize the time you spend looking for help and to help you enter code more accurately and efficiently.

Completion mode is an IDE editing mode in which suggestions are automatically provided for your code based on context.

Suggestion mode is an IDE editing mode in which completion mode is turned off.

Code snippets are small units of commonly used C# source code that you can enter accurately and quickly with only a couple of keystrokes.

Glossary

A

abstract class—A class from which concrete objects cannot be instantiated but can serve as a basis for inheritance. Contrast with *concrete class*.

abstract method—A method that contains no statements and must be implemented by classes that derive from its class.

access key—A shortcut way to make a menu selection using the keyboard.

access specifier—A keyword that dictates which outside classes can use a method.

accessibility—Describes limitations about how a method can be used.

accessors—Methods in properties that specify how a class's fields are accessed. See *get accessors* and *set accessors*.

accumulated—Describes totals that are added into a final sum by processing individual records one at a time in a loop.

actual parameters—Arguments within a method call.

add and assign operator (+=)—An operator that adds the operand on the right to the operand on the left and assigns the results to the operand on the left in one step.

alias—An alternative name or pseudonym.

ambiguous—Describes overloaded methods between which the compiler cannot distinguish.

American Standard Code for Information Interchange (ASCII)—An eight-bit code that represents characters.

ancestors—All the superclasses from which a subclass is derived.

AND operator—An operator that determines whether two expressions are both true; it is written using two ampersands (&&). Also called the *conditional AND operator*. Contrast with *Boolean logical AND operator*.

applicable methods—The collection of potential methods that could be used by a method call.

application classes—Classes that contain a `Main()` method and are executable programs.

application software—Programs that allow users to complete tasks, in contrast with

GLOSSARY

system software that the computer needs to complete tasks.

argument—An expression passed to a method.

arithmetic operators—Used to perform arithmetic; they include +, -, *, /, and %.

array—A list of data items that all have the same data type and the same name, but are distinguished from each other by a subscript or index.

array element—One object in an array.

assembly—A group of code modules compiled together to create an executable program.

assignment—A statement that provides a variable with a value.

assignment operator—The equal sign (=); any value to the right of the assignment operator is assigned to, or taken on by, the variable or constant to the left.

associativity—Specifies the order in which a sequence of operations with the same precedence are evaluated.

at runtime—A phrase describing actions that occur during a program's execution.

attributes of an object—The characteristics of an object.

auto-implemented property—A property in which the code within the accessors is created automatically. The only action in the set accessor is to assign a value to the associated field, and the only action in the get accessor is to return the associated field value.

automatic properties—Auto-implemented properties.

B

backing field—A field that has a property coded for it.

base 2 numbers—Binary system numbers.

base 10 numbers—Decimal system numbers.

base 16 system—A mathematical system that uses 16 symbols to represent numbers; hexadecimal.

base class—A class that is used as a basis for inheritance.

behaviors of an object—The methods associated with an object.

betterness rules—The rules that determine the best overloaded method to execute based on the arguments in a method call.

binary files—Files that can store any of the 256 combinations of bits in any byte instead of just those combinations that form readable text.

binary numbering system—A numbering system that uses two digits, 0 and 1, arranged in columns to represent numbers.

binary operators—Operators that use two operands: one value to the left of the operator and another value to the right of it.

binary search—An algorithm that attempts to find an item in a list by splitting the sorted list of objects in half repeatedly as the search gets closer to a match.

bit—A binary digit.

bitwise operators—Operators that are used to manipulate the individual bits of values.

black box—Any device that can be used without knowing how it works internally.

GLOSSARY

block—A collection of one or more statements contained within a pair of curly braces.

block comments—Comments that start with a forward slash and an asterisk (/*) and end with an asterisk and a forward slash (*/). Block comments can appear on a line by themselves, on a line before executable code, or after executable code. They also can extend across as many lines as needed. Compare with *line comments*.

bool—A data type that holds a Boolean value.

Boolean logical AND operator—An operator that determines whether two expressions are both true; it is written using a single ampersand (&), but, unlike the conditional AND operator, it does not use short-circuit evaluation.

Boolean logical inclusive OR operator—An operator that determines whether at least one of two conditions is true; it is written using a single pipe (|), but, unlike the conditional OR operator, it does not use short-circuit evaluation.

Boolean variable—A variable that can hold only one of two values: true or false.

bugs—Program errors.

byte—An integral data type that can hold an unsigned numeric value from 0 through 255.

C

C# programming language—A computer programming language developed as an object-oriented and component-oriented language. It exists as part of Visual Studio, a package used for developing applications for the Windows family of operating systems.

call—To invoke a method.

call stack—The memory location where the computer stores the list of locations to which the system must return after method calls.

called—Describes a method that has been invoked.

called method—A method that has been invoked by another method.

calling method—A method that calls another method.

camel casing—A style of creating identifiers in which the first letter is not capitalized, but each new word is. Contrast with *Pascal casing*.

case label—Identifies a course of action in a switch structure.

catch block—A block of code that can catch one type of Exception.

char—An integral data type that can store a character such as 'A', '4', or '$'; char values are written between single quotation marks.

character—Any one of the letters, numbers, or other special symbols (such as punctuation marks) that comprise data.

character set—The group of all the characters used to represent data on a particular computer.

check box—A GUI widget that a user can click to select or deselect an option.

child class—A derived class; a subclass; a class that has inherited from a base class.

class—A category of objects or a type of object.

class access specifier—Describes access to a class.

class client—A program or class that instantiates objects of another prewritten class. Also called a *class user*.

GLOSSARY

class definition—The first class line that describes a class; it contains an optional access specifier, the keyword `class`, and any legal identifier for the name of the class. Also known as *class header*.

class header—The first class line that describes a class; it contains an optional access specifier, the keyword `class`, and any legal identifier for the name of the class. Also known as *class definition*.

class user—A program or class that instantiates objects of another prewritten class. Also called a *class client*.

click event—An action fired when a user clicks a button in a GUI environment.

client—A method that uses another method.

closing a file—The process of making a file no longer available to an application.

code bloat—Describes unnecessarily long or repetitive program statements.

code refactoring—The process of changing a program's internal structure without changing the way the program works.

code snippets—Small units of commonly used C# source code that are generated in the IDE using a few keystrokes.

combo box—A GUI element that is a combination of a list box and an editing control that allows a user to select from the list or enter new text.

command line—The operating system's text interface.

command prompt—A request for input that appears at the beginning of the command line.

comment out—To turn a statement into a comment so that the compiler will not execute its command.

comparison operator—An operator that compares two values.

compiler—A computer program that translates high-level language statements into machine code.

completion mode—An IDE editing mode in which suggestions are provided automatically based on context.

composed delegate—A delegate that calls the delegates from which it is built.

composition—The technique of using an object within another object.

computer file—A collection of information stored on a nonvolatile device in a computer system.

computer simulations—Programs that attempt to mimic real-world activities to foster a better understanding of them.

concatenate—To join strings together in a chain.

concrete class—A nonabstract class from which objects can be instantiated. Contrast with *abstract class*.

conditional AND operator—An operator that determines whether two expressions are both true; it is written using two ampersands (&&). Also called the *AND operator*. Contrast with *Boolean logical AND operator*.

conditional operator—A ternary operator that is used as an abbreviated version of the `if-else` statement; it requires three expressions separated by a question mark and a colon.

conditional OR operator—An operator that determines whether at least one of two conditions is true; it is written using two pipes (||). Also called the *OR operator*.

Contrast with *Boolean logical inclusive OR operator*.

constant—Describes a data item when it cannot be changed after a program is compiled; in other words, when it cannot vary.

constructor—A method that instantiates (creates an instance of) an object.

constructor initializer—A clause that indicates another instance of a class constructor should be executed before any statements in the current constructor body.

contextual keywords—Identifiers that act like keywords in specific circumstances.

control—A GUI component such as a text field, button, or check box that users can manipulate to interact with a program.

control statement—The part of a structure that determines whether the subsequent block of statements executes.

counted loop—A definite loop.

CSV file—A file that contains comma-separated values.

culture—A set of rules that determines how culturally dependent values such as money and dates are formatted.

D

data files—Files that contain facts and figures; persistent collections of related records.

data hierarchy—The relationship of characters, fields, records, and files.

data type—A description of the format and size of a data item as well as the operations that can be performed on it.

dead code—Statements that can never execute under any circumstances because the program logic "can't get there." Also see *unreachable*.

debugging—The process of removing all syntax and logical errors from a program.

decimal—A floating-point data type that has a greater precision and a smaller range than a `float` or `double`, which makes it suitable for financial and monetary calculations.

decimal numbering system—The system that uses 10 digits, 0 through 9, arranged in columns to represent numbers.

decision structure—A unit of program logic that involves choosing between alternative courses of action based on some value.

decrement operator (- -)—An operator that consists of two minus signs and that reduces a variable's value by 1; there is a prefix and a postfix version.

decrementing—The act of decreasing the value of a variable, often by 1.

default constructor—A constructor that requires no parameters; it can be automatically supplied or written by a programmer.

default event for a `Control`—The event or method generated when it is double-clicked in the IDE, as well as the event that users expect to generate when they encounter the `Control` in a working application.

default value of an object—The value initialized with a default constructor.

definite loop—A loop in which the number of iterations is predetermined. Also a *counted loop*. Contrast with *indefinite loop*.

delegate—An object that contains a reference to a method.

GLOSSARY

delimiter—A character used to specify the boundary between characters in text files.

derived class—A subclass; a class that has inherited from a base class.

deserialization—The process of converting streams of bytes back into objects.

design time—The period of time during which a programmer designs a program's interface and writes the code.

destructor—A method that contains the actions performed when an instance of a class is destroyed.

Developer Command Prompt—A special version of the command prompt for which specific settings have been enabled so that you can easily compile and run C# programs.

digit separators—Symbols used to separate the digits in a long number for readability; in C# the underscore (_) is the digit separator.

directories—Structures used to organize files on a storage device; folders.

do loop—A type of posttest loop; a loop that is tested at the bottom of the loop after one repetition has occurred.

double—A data type that can hold a floating-point number with 15 or 16 significant digits of accuracy.

dual-alternative decisions—Decisions that have two possible outcomes.

E

empty body—A block that has no statements in it.

encapsulation—The technique of packaging an object's attributes and methods into a cohesive unit that can be used as an undivided entity.

enhanced for loop—A version of the for loop that cycles through an array without specifying the starting and ending points for the loop control variable.

enumeration—A list of values in which names are substituted for numeric values.

Equals()—A method that determines equivalency. In the String class, it is the method that determines if two strings have the same value.

escape sequence—A single character composed of two symbols beginning with a backslash that represents a nonprinting character such as a tab.

event—An object generated when a user interacts with a GUI object, causing the program to perform a task.

event-driven programs—Programs that contain code that causes an event such as a button click to perform a task.

event handler—A method that performs a task in response to an event; an event receiver.

event receiver—A method that performs a task in response to an event; an event handler.

event sender—The object, such as a control, that generates an event.

event wiring—The act of connecting an event to its resulting actions.

exception—An error condition or unexpected behavior in an executing program.

exception handling—The set of object-oriented techniques used to manage unexpected errors.

explicit cast—Purposefully assigns a value to a different data type; it involves placing the desired result type in parentheses followed by the variable or constant to be cast.

GLOSSARY

explicitly—Purposefully. Contrast with *implicitly*.

exposes—Associates a `FileStream` with a file.

Extended Binary Coded Decimal Interchange Code (EBCDIC)—An eight-bit code that is used in IBM mainframe computers.

extended class—A derived class; a child class; a subclass; a class that has inherited from a base class.

extension methods—Static methods that act like instance methods.

F

fault-tolerant—Describes applications that are designed so that they continue to operate, possibly at a reduced level, when some part of the system fails.

field—In a class, an instance variable. In a file or database, a character or group of characters that has some meaning.

file position pointer—A variable that holds the byte number of the next byte to be read from a file.

finally block—A block of code that optionally follows a `try` block; the code within a `finally` block executes whether the preceding `try` block identifies any `Exceptions` or not.

fires an event—Causes an event to occur. Also see *raises an event* and *triggers an event*.

fixed-pitch font—A font in which each character occupies the same width.

float—A data type that can hold a floating-point number with as many as seven significant digits of accuracy.

floating-point—Describes a number that contains decimal positions.

flowchart—A tool that helps programmers plan a program's logic by writing program steps in diagram form, as a series of shapes connected by arrows.

focus—The state of a GUI component when the user's attention is drawn to it visually. When a component has focus, its action can be executed by pressing the Enter key.

folders—Structures used to organize files on a storage device; directories.

for loop—A loop that contains the starting value for the loop control variable, the test condition that controls loop entry, and the expression that alters the loop control variable, all in one statement.

form—A GUI interface for collecting, displaying, and delivering information.

formal parameter—A parameter within a method header that accepts a value.

format specifier—One of nine built-in format characters in a format string that defines the most commonly used numeric format types.

format string—A string of characters that controls the appearance of output.

fragile—Describes classes that depend on field names from parent classes because they are prone to errors; that is, they are easy to "break."

fully qualified—Describes a name that includes the class name as well as the identifier.

G

garbage—An unknown memory value.

get accessors—Methods in properties that allow retrieval of a field value by using a property name.

GLOSSARY

getter—Another term for a class property's get accessor.

gigabyte—Approximately one billion bytes.

governing type—In a `switch` statement, the type that is established by the `switch` expression.

graphical control elements—The components through which user interacts with a GUI program.

graphical user interface (GUI)—An interface that employs graphical images representing controls the user manipulates.

group box—A GUI element that can be used to group controls on a form, it is similar to a panel but it can contain a caption and does not have a scroll bar.

H

hardware—The physical devices associated with a computer.

has-a relationship—The relationship created using composition, so called because one class "has an" instance of another.

hash code—A number that should uniquely identify an object.

hexadecimal numbering system—A mathematical system that uses 16 symbols to represent numbers; base 16.

hide—To override a parent class member in a child class, making the parent class member invisible.

high-level programming language—A language that uses a vocabulary of reasonable terms such as *read*, *write*, or *add* instead of referencing the sequence of on/off switches that perform these tasks.

I

identifier—The name of a program component such as a variable, class, or method.

`if` statement—A program statement used to make a single-alternative decision.

`if-else` statement—A statement that performs a dual-alternative decision.

immutable—Unchangeable.

implementation hiding—The technique of keeping the details of a method's operations hidden.

implicit cast—The automatic transformation that occurs when a value is assigned to a type with higher precedence.

implicit conversion—The conversion that occurs when a type is automatically changed to another upon assignment.

implicit parameter—An undeclared parameter that gets its value automatically.

implicit reference conversion—The type of conversion that occurs when a derived class object is assigned to its ancestor's data type.

implicitly—Automatically. Contrast with *explicitly*.

incrementing—The act of increasing the value of a variable, often by 1.

indefinite loop—A loop in which the number of iterations is not predetermined. Contrast with *definite loop*.

index—An integer contained within square brackets that indicates the position of one of an array's elements. Also see *subscript*.

infinite loop—A loop that (theoretically) never ends.

information hiding—A feature found in all object-oriented languages, in which a class's data items are private and changed or manipulated only by their own methods.

inheritance—The ability to extend a class so as to create a more specific class that contains all the attributes and methods of a more general class; the extended class usually contains new attributes or methods as well.

initialization—An assignment made when a variable is declared.

initializer list—The list of values provided for an array.

inner loop—The loop in a pair of nested loops that is entirely contained within another loop.

instance methods—Methods that are used with object instantiations.

instance of a class—An object; a tangible example of a class.

instance variables—Data components of a class that exist separately for each instantiation. Also called *fields*.

instantiate—To create an object.

instantiation—A created object.

`int`—An integral data type that can hold a signed numeric value in four bytes.

integer—A whole number without a fractional part.

integral data types—Data types that store whole numbers; the nine integral types are `byte`, `sbyte`, `short`, `ushort`, `int`, `uint`, `long`, `ulong`, and `char`.

Integrated Development Environment (IDE)—A program development environment in which programmers select options from menus or by clicking buttons; an IDE provides helpful features such as color coding and automatic statement completion.

IntelliSense—Microsoft's name for the set of features designed to minimize program development time in the IDE.

interactive program—A program that allows user input.

interface—A collection of abstract methods (and perhaps other members) that can be used by any class as long as the class provides a definition to override the interface's abstract definitions.

intermediate language (IL)—The language into which source code statements are compiled.

`internal`—A class access modifier that means access is limited to the assembly to which the class belongs.

`internal` **access**—A level of method accessibility that limits method access to the containing program.

intrinsic types—Basic, built-in data types; C# provides 15 intrinsic types.

invoke—To call a method.

invoking object—The object referenced by `this` in an instance method.

invoking the event—Calling an event method.

iteration—One execution of any loop.

iteration variable—A temporary variable that holds each array value in turn in a `foreach` statement.

J

jagged array—A one-dimensional array in which each element is another array.

GLOSSARY

just in time (JIT)—The C# compiler that translates intermediate code into executable code.

K

key—A value that uniquely identifies a record.

key events—Keyboard events that occur when a user presses and releases keyboard keys.

key field—The field used to uniquely identify records and to control the order of records in a sequential file.

keywords—Predefined and reserved identifiers that have special meaning to the compiler.

kilobyte—Approximately one thousand bytes.

L

label—A control that typically provides descriptive text for another control or displays other text information on a Form.

left-associative—Describes operators whose operations are performed from left to right.

length field—A field that contains the number of elements in an array.

lexically—Alphabetically.

line comments—Comments that start with two forward slashes (//) and continue to the end of the current line. Line comments can appear on a line by themselves, or at the end of a line following executable code. Compare with *block comments*.

link label—A GUI control with text and that links the user to other sources, such as Web pages or files.

list box—A GUI element that displays a list of items the user can select by clicking.

literal constant—A value that is taken literally at each use.

literal string—A series of characters that is used exactly as entered.

local function—A method that resides within another method and can be called only from the containing method.

local variable—A variable that is declared in the current method.

logic—The sequence of statements and methods that produce the desired results in a computer program.

long—An integral data type that can hold a signed numeric value in eight bytes.

loop—A structure that allows repeated execution of a block of statements.

loop body—The block of statements executed in a loop.

loop control variable—A variable that determines whether loop execution will continue on each iteration.

loop fusion—The technique of combining two loops into one.

lower camel casing—A style of creating identifiers in which the first letter is not capitalized, but each new word is. Also called *camel casing*. Contrast with *Pascal casing*.

M

machine language—The most basic circuitry-level language.

magic number—A hard-coded number.

mandatory parameters—Method parameters for which an argument is required in every method call.

GLOSSARY

megabyte—Approximately one million bytes.

menu bar—In the Visual Studio IDE, the list of choices that run horizontally across the top of the screen.

menu strip—A horizontal list of general options that appears under the title bar of a `Form` or `Window`.

method—An encapsulated series of statements that carry out a task.

method body—All the instructions contained within a pair of curly braces ({ }) following a method header.

method declaration—A method header or definition; it precedes a method and includes a return type, identifier, and an optional parameter list.

method definition—A method header or declaration; it precedes a method and includes a return type, identifier, and an optional parameter list.

method header—The first line of a method, which includes the method name and information about what will pass into and be returned from a method.

method's type—A method's `return` type.

mission critical—Describes any process that is crucial to an organization.

modal window—A secondary window that takes control from a primary window and that a user must deal with before proceeding.

multidimensional arrays—Arrays that require multiple subscripts to access the array elements.

multifile assembly—A group of files containing methods that work together to create an application.

multiple inheritance—The ability to inherit from more than one class.

N

named argument—A method argument that is preceded with the name of the called method's parameter to which it will be assigned.

named constant—An identifier whose contents cannot change.

namespace—A scheme that provides a way to group similar classes.

nested if—A statement in which one decision structure is contained within another.

nested method calls—Method calls placed inside other method calls.

nibble—Four bits; half a byte.

node—In the Visual Studio IDE, a box that appears on a vertical tree to the left of a list or a section of code and that can be expanded or condensed.

non-application classes—Classes that do not contain a `Main()` method and therefore are not runnable programs; they provide support for other classes.

nonstatic—Describes a method that requires an object reference.

nonvolatile—The type of computer storage that is permanent; it is not lost when a computer loses power.

NOT operator (!)—An operator that negates the result of any Boolean expression.

O

object—A concrete entity that has attributes and behaviors; an object is an instance of a class.

GLOSSARY

Object (or object)—A class type in the System namespace that is the ultimate base class for all other types.

object initializer—A clause that assigns values to any accessible members or properties of a class at the time of instantiation without calling a constructor with parameters.

object-oriented approach—An approach to a problem that involves defining the objects needed to accomplish a task and developing classes that describe the objects so that each maintains its own data and carries out tasks when another object requests them.

object-oriented programming (OOP)—A programming technique that features objects, classes, encapsulation, interfaces, polymorphism, and inheritance.

one-dimensional array—An array whose elements are accessed using a single subscript. Also see *single-dimensional array*.

opening a file—The process of creating an object and associating a stream of bytes with it.

operands—The values that operators use in expressions.

operator precedence—Rules that determine the order in which parts of a mathematical expression are evaluated. Also called *order of operation*.

optional parameter—A parameter to a method for which a default value is supplied automatically when no argument is sent explicitly; a parameter is optional when it is given a value in the method declaration.

OR operator—An operator that determines whether at least one of two conditions is true; it is written using two pipes (||). Also called the *conditional OR operator*. Contrast with *Boolean logical inclusive OR operator*.

order of operation—Rules that determine the order in which parts of a mathematical expression are evaluated. Also called *operator precedence*.

orphaned method—A method that never executes in an application, and thus serves no purpose.

out of bounds—Describes a subscript that is not within the allowed range for an array.

out of scope—Describes a variable or named constant that is not usable because it has ceased to exist.

out variable—A variable declared at the point where it is passed to a method as an out argument.

outer loop—The loop in a pair of nested loops that contains another loop.

output parameter—A parameter to a method that receives the argument's address; it is not required to have an initial value. Contrast with *value parameter* and *reference parameter*.

overload resolution—The process of determining which of multiple applicable methods is the best match for a method call.

overloading—Using one term to indicate diverse meanings. In C#, methods are overloaded when there are multiple versions with the same name but different parameter lists.

override—A keyword used in method headers when a derived class inherits an abstract method from a parent.

override—To take precedence over another method version.

P

panel—A GUI element that can be used to group controls on a Form; similar to a group box, but it does not have a caption and can have a scroll bar.

parallel array—An array that has the same number of elements as another array and holds corresponding data.

parameter array—A local array declared within a method header that can accept any number of elements of the same data type.

parameter list—The data types and parameter names that appear between parentheses in a method header.

parameter to a method—An object or reference that is declared in a method definition.

parameterless constructor—A constructor that takes no parameters; one that is called using no arguments.

parent class—A base class; a superclass; a class that is used as a basis for inheritance.

parse—To break an item into component parts.

Pascal casing—A style of creating identifiers in which the first letter of all new words in a variable name, even the first one, is capitalized. Contrast with *camel casing*.

passed by reference—Describes how an argument is passed to a method when the method receives its memory address.

passed by value—Describes how data is passed to a method when the method receives a copy of the argument passed to it.

path—The disk drive in which a file resides plus the complete hierarchy of directories.

permanent storage devices—Hardware such as hard disks, USB drives, and compact discs that are used to store files.

persistent—Describes storage that is nonvolatile.

picture box—A GUI element that displays graphics.

place holder—A number within curly braces that holds a position for a variable value within a string.

polymorphism—The ability to create methods that act appropriately depending on the context.

populating an array—The act of providing values for all the elements in an array.

positional argument—An unnamed method argument that is assigned to a parameter list based on its position in the method call.

postfix increment operator—An operator that evaluates a variable and then adds 1 to it. This operator is represented by two plus signs (++) after a variable.

posttest loop—A loop in which the loop control variable is tested after the loop body executes. Contrast with *pretest loop*.

precedence—A feature of operators that controls the order in which they are evaluated in an expression.

precision specifier—A specifier that controls the number of significant digits or zeros to the right of the decimal point in a format string.

prefix increment operator—An operator that increases the variable's value by 1 and then evaluates it. This operator is represented by two plus signs (++) before a variable.

pretest loop—A loop in which the loop control variable is tested before the loop body executes. Contrast with *posttest loop*.

GLOSSARY

priming read—An input statement that gets a first data item or record.

private—An access specifier that indicates other classes cannot use the method or variable that it modifies. When used as a class access specifier, it means access is limited to another class to which the class belongs.

private access—A level of method accessibility that limits method access to the containing class.

procedural program—A program created by writing a series of steps or operations to manipulate values.

program—A set of written computer instructions.

program comments—Nonexecuting statements that document a program.

prompt—An instruction to the user to enter data.

propagating an exception—The act of transmitting an exception object unchanged through the call stack.

property—A member of a class that provides access to a field of a class; properties define how fields will be set and retrieved. The value of an object.

proportional font—A font in which different characters have different pitches or widths.

protected—A keyword that provides an intermediate level of security between `public` and `private` access.

protected access—A level of method accessibility that limits method access to the containing class or types derived from the containing class.

pseudocode—A tool that helps programmers plan a program's logic by writing plain English statements.

public—An access specifier that indicates other classes can use the method or variable it modifies.

public access—A level of method accessibility that allows unlimited access to a method by any class.

R

radio buttons—GUI widgets, similar to check boxes, except that when they are placed on a form, only one can be selected at a time and selecting any one automatically deselects the others.

raises an event—Causes an event to occur. Also see *fires an event* and *triggers an event*.

random access file—A file from which records can be accessed in any order.

random access memory (RAM)—Temporary storage in a computer.

range check—A series of statements in which each statement determines whether a value falls within a specified range.

range match—A process that determines whether a value falls between a pair of limiting values.

read from the file—To copy data from a file on a storage device into RAM.

read-only—Describes a value, property, or file that can be accessed but not altered.

read-only property—A property that has only a get accessor, and not a set accessor.

record—A collection of fields that contains data about an entity.

rectangular array—An array in which each row has the same number of columns.

recursive—Describes a method that calls itself.

GLOSSARY

reference—A memory address.

reference equality—The type of equality that occurs when two reference type objects refer to the same object.

reference parameter—A parameter to a method that receives the argument's address; it is required to have an initial value. Contrast with *value parameter* and *output parameter*.

reference type—A data type that holds a memory address. Contrast with *value types*.

rethrow an Exception—To throw a caught Exception instead of handling it.

return statement—A method statement that causes a value to be sent back from a method to its calling method.

return type—The type of value a method will return to any other method that calls it.

right-associative—Describes operators whose operations are performed from right to left.

robustness—Describes the degree to which a system is resilient to stress, maintaining correct functioning even in the presence of errors.

root class—The ultimate or first base class in a hierarchical ancestry tree.

root directory—The main directory of a storage device.

run time—The period of time during which a program executes.

runnable—Describes files that are executable.

S

sbyte—An integral data type that can hold a signed numeric value from −128 through 127.

scientific notation—A numeric expression format that includes an *E* (for exponent) and that specifies a number of implied decimal places.

scope—The area where a variable or constant is known and can be used.

screaming caps—A naming style that uses all uppercase letters and underscores; often used for named constants.

sealed class—A class that cannot be extended.

searching an array—The process of comparing a value to a list of values in an array, looking for a match.

self-documenting—Describes a program element that is self-explanatory.

sentinel value—A value that a user must supply to stop a loop.

sequence structure—A unit of program logic in which one step follows another unconditionally.

sequential access file—A data file in which each record is stored in order based on the value in some field.

sequential search—A search that is conducted by examining a list item-by-item in sequence.

serialization—The process of converting objects into streams of bytes.

set accessors—Methods in properties that allow use of the assignment operator with a property name.

setter—Another term for a class property's set accessor.

short—An integral data type that can hold a signed numeric value in two bytes.

short-circuit evaluation—The C# feature in which parts of an AND or OR expression are evaluated only as far as necessary to determine whether the entire expression is true or false.

GLOSSARY

side effect—An unintended consequence of an operation.

signature—A method's name and parameter list.

significant digits—Specify the mathematical accuracy of a value.

simple type—Describes one of the following in C#: `byte`, `sbyte`, `short`, `ushort`, `int`, `uint`, `long`, `ulong`, `float`, `double`, `decimal`, `char`, and `bool`.

single-dimensional array—An array whose elements are accessed using a single subscript. Also see *one-dimensional array*.

snap lines—Lines that appear in a design environment to help designers align new `Control`s with others that are already in place.

software—Computer programs.

source code—Program statements.

standard numeric format strings—Strings of characters expressed within double quotation marks that indicate a format for output.

state of an object—The collective value of all of an object's attributes at any point in time.

`static`—A keyword that indicates that a method will be executed through a class and not by an object.

step value—The amount by which a loop control variable is altered on each iteration, especially in a `for` loop.

stream—A pipeline or channel through which bytes are input from and output to a file.

string—A data type that can hold a series of characters.

string interpolation—The process of replacing string place holders with values; also called *variable substitution*.

subclass—A derived class; a child class; a class that has inherited from a base class.

subscript—An integer contained within square brackets that indicates the position of one of an array's elements. Also see *index*.

suggestion mode—An IDE editing mode in which completion mode is turned off.

superclass—A base class; a parent class; a class that is the basis for inheritance.

`switch` **structure**—A structure that tests a single variable against a series of exact matches.

syntax—The set of grammar rules in a programming language.

syntax error—An error that occurs when a programming language is used incorrectly.

T

tab order—Describes the sequence of controls selected when the user presses the Tab key in a program with a GUI interface.

ternary—Describes an operator that requires three arguments.

`TextBoxes`—Controls through which a user can enter input data in a GUI application.

text files—Files that contain data that can be read in a text editor because the data has been encoded using a scheme such as ASCII or Unicode.

`this` **reference**—The reference to an object that is implicitly passed to an instance method of its class.

GLOSSARY

token—A block of text within a string that represents an entity or field.

transitive—Inheriting all the members of one's ancestors.

triggers an event—Causes an event to occur. Also see *fires an event* and *raises an event*.

truth tables—Diagrams used in mathematics and logic to help describe the truth of an entire expression based on the truth of its parts.

try block—A block of code that might create exceptions that will be handled.

two-dimensional arrays—Multidimensional arrays that have two or more columns of values for each row.

type precedence—A hierarchy of data types used to determine the unifying type in arithmetic expressions containing dissimilar data types.

U

uint—An integral data type that can hold an unsigned numeric value in four bytes.

ulong—An integral data type that can hold an unsigned numeric value in eight bytes.

unary operators—Operators used with one operand.

Unicode—a 16-bit coding scheme for characters.

unifying type—The type chosen for an arithmetic result when operands are of dissimilar types.

unreachable—Describes program statements that can never execute under any circumstances because the program logic "can't get there." Also see *dead code*.

upper camel casing—A style of creating identifiers in which the first letter of all new words in a name is capitalized, even the first one; Pascal casing.

ushort—An integral data type that can hold an unsigned numeric value in two bytes.

using clause, or using directive—code that declares a `namespace`.

V

value parameter—A parameter to a method that receives a copy of the value passed to it. Contrast with *reference parameter* and *output parameter*.

value types—Data types that hold a value; they are predefined types such as `int`, `double`, and `char`. Contrast with *reference type*.

variable—A named location in computer memory that can hold different values at different points in time during program execution.

variable declaration—The statement that names a variable; it includes a data type, an identifier, an optional assignment operator and assigned value, and an ending semicolon.

verbatim identifier—An identifier with an @ prefix.

virtual method—A method whose behavior is determined by the implementation in a child class.

visible—Describes a program element that is in scope; also describes a base class member that has not been hidden by a derived class.

void—A keyword that indicates that a method does not return any value when called.

volatile—The type of computer storage that is lost when power is lost.

GLOSSARY

W

while loop—A structure that executes a body of statements continuously while some condition continues to be true; it uses the keyword `while`.

whitespace—Any combination of spaces, tabs, and carriage returns (blank lines) in a program.

widgets—Interactive controls such as labels, scroll bars, check boxes, and radio buttons.

write to a file—To store data in a computer file on a permanent storage device.

X

XML—An abbreviation of eXtensible Markup Language, which is a standard for exchanging data over the Internet.

XML-documentation format comments—Comments that use a special set of tags within angle brackets to create documentation within a program.

Index

Note: Bold page numbers indicate definitions.

A

aBackspaceChar variable, 74
AbeLincoln file, 585
abstract classes, **456**–460, 472, **711**
   abstract methods, 457, 463
   data or methods for derived classes, 464
   nonabstract methods, 457, 463
abstract keyword, 457
abstract methods, **396**, 410, **711**
   abstract classes, 457, 463
   interfaces, 460–464
   overriding, 457
AcceptButton property, 103
accessibility, **269**–270, 299, **711**
access keys, **560**, 578, 591, **711**
access modifiers
   classes, 354
   properties, 363
accessors, **362**, 410, **711**
AccessSomeNames program, 670–672
access specifiers, **108**, 126, 355, **711**
ACCOUNTING constant, 162–163
AccountNumber class, 465
AccountNumber objects, 465
AccountNum property, 522
accumulated totals, 206–208, 216, **711**
ActiveLinkColor property, 549
actual parameters, **278**, 299, 309, **711**
add and assign shortcut operator (+=), **65**, 91, 605, 613, 618, **711**
AddBooks program, 393
AddCheckDigit() method, 465
AddDays() method, 572
add identifier, 15
addition operator (+), 63, 390, 605
AddMonths() method, 572
AddRangeObjectsDemo program, 568
AddYears() method, 572
AdvertisingMessage() method, 376
ageOverMinimum variable, 166

age variable, 154–156
alert escape sequence (\a), 75
aliases, **48**, 50, 90, **711**
   memory, 310
   variables, 310, 311
alias identifier, 15
AllowDrop property, 538
Alt property, 629
ambiguous methods, **330**–331, 342, **711**
American Standard Code for Information Interchange (ASCII), **699**, 706, **711**
AMethod() method, 331, 339–340
ancestors, **425**, 471, **711**
Anchor property, 538, 575
AND operator (&&), **150**–152, 167, 169, 176, 233, **711**
   combining with OR operator (||), 154–158
anExceptionInstance object, 493
Animal class, 352, 425, 457–458, 461–462
Animal parameter, 459
anInt variable, 59
annualIncome variable, 69–70
annualSalary variable, 57
anotherValue variable, 65
answer variable, 500
anUnsignedInt variable, 59
AnyLegalClassName identifier, 17
Append file mode, 656
applicable methods, **326**, 342, **711**
application classes, **13**, **711**
ApplicationException class, 486, 519
applications
   See also programs
   classes, 352
   runnable, **13**
application software, **2**, **711**–**712**
area field, 373
Area property, 374
args variable, 293
ArgumentException class, 485

INDEX

arguments, 11, **11**, 241–247, 266, 276–280, **712**
   constructors, 453–454
   data types, 279–280
   default, 281
   method call, 272
   named, **335**–340
   passing by reference, 308
   passing by value, 308
   positional, **335**
   strings, 11
   unnamed, 334–335
arithmetic
   array elements, 229
   numeric type conversion, 71–73
   parentheses ( ) in expressions, 64
ArithmeticException class, 485, 488
arithmetic operators, **63**–64, 91, 390, **712**
   shortcut arithmetic operators, 64–66
ArrayDemo1 program, 232
ArrayDemo2 program, 245–247
array elements, **224**, 255, **712**
array of references, 395
arrays, 29, **224**, 255, 650, 665, 670, 674, 682, **712**
   accessing elements, 228–231
   arithmetic on elements, 229
   automatically altering value, 230
   bool fields, 227
   character field, 227
   comparing value to valid values in, 233
   creation, 232
   cycling through elements, 230–231
   declaring, 224–228
   default values, 227
   descending order elements, 396
   duplicate values, 243
   GUI programs, 253–254
   identifiers, 225
   increasing value of elements, 228
   index, **224**
   initializer list, **227**
   initializing, 226–228
   iteration variable, **230**
   jagged, **251**–252
   length, 229–230, 241
   matching values in, 396
   methods for manipulating, 241–244
   multidimensional, 247–251, **248**
   naming, 225
   navigating, 230–231
   nondefault values for elements, 227
   numbering elements, 225, 226
   numeric fields, 227
   one-dimensional, **247**
   parallel arrays, **234**
   passed by reference, **290**
   passing to methods, 289–292
   range match, 243
   rectangular, **248**
   reserving memory locations for, 225
   resizing, 225, 230
   reversing order of items, 244–245
   searching with loops, 233–241
   separating fields into strings, 662
   serializable, 674
   single-dimensional, **247**
   size, 227
   sorting, 241–244
   subscripts, 224, **224**, 226
   three-dimensional, 251
   two-dimensional, **248**
   usage, 232
   values for elements, 224–228
   variables, 224
   zeroth element, 226
arrays of objects, 395–403
   searching, 396–400
   sorting, 396–400
Array.Sort() method, 401
ArrayTypeMismatchException class, 485
Artist class, 457
ASCII (American Standard Code for Information Interchange), 699
   decimal and binary values for characters, 700–702
assemblers, 3
assemblies, **354**, 409, **712**
assembly language, 3
assignment, **50**, 90, **712**
assignment operator (=), **50**, 90, 143–148, 167, 358, 605, **712**
   right-associative, **695**
associativity, 64, 91, **695**, **712**
aTabChar variable, 74
at runtime, **712**
   See also runtime
attributes, **5**, 7, 353, **712**
   associating information with code, 674
auto-implemented property, **366**–367, 371, 410, **712**
automatically generated code, 541–544
automatic properties, **366**–367, 410, **712**
Automobile class, 7–9
a variable, 274
aWorker object, 379, 387

B

BackColorChanged event, 621
BackColor property, 103, 106, 124, 538, 554, 559, 564, 566, 578, 582, 584, 586, 635
BackgroundImage property, 538
backing field, **363**, 410, **712**
backslash escape sequence (\\ ), 75
backspace escape sequence (\b), 75

INDEX

Bad command or file name error message, 24
`BaileysForm` form, 555
`balanceDue` variable, 65
`Balance` property, 521–522
`BankAccountBalanceAdjusted()` method, 618–619
`BankAccount` class, 8, 521–522, 617–620
`BankAccount` object, 618–619
`BankBalance` form, 214
`bankBalance` variable, 73, 192
`bankBal` variable, 65
base class, **424**, 469, 471, **712**
    abstract classes, 457
    constructors, 452–456
    derived classes, 439–444
    implicit conversion, **445**
    overriding members, 436–441
    size, 424
`base` keyword, 453–454
base 2 numbers, 698, **712**
base 10 numbers, 697, **712**
`BASE_PRICE` constant, 561
base 16 shorthand notation, **74**, 92
base 16 system, **703**, **712**
BASIC
    array elements, 226
    interpreter, 3
`BedAndBreakfast` form, 586, 589
`BedAndBreakfast` program, 555–559
    check boxes, 580–586
`bedrooms` variable, 249, 251
`Begin` member, 668
behaviors, **5**, 7, **712**
`bellAireCheckBox` object, 580
`belleAireCheckBox_CheckedChanged()` method, 583
`BelleAire CheckBox` object, 581
`belleAireDescriptionLabel` label, 582
`BelleAireForm`, 581–583
`belleAirePriceLabel` label, 582
`BelleAire Suite` check box, 583, 589
betterness rules, **326**, 342, **712**
`bigFont` object, 547
`biggerNum` variable, 164
`BillPatients()` method, 428
binary digit, 698
binary files, **646**, 647, 658, **712**
binary form, 390
`BinaryFormatter` class, 674
`BinaryFormatter` objects, 675
binary numbering system, **698**, 698–699, 706, **712**
binary operators, **63**, 91, 164, **712**
    left-associative, **695**
    overloaded, 390–391
`BinaryReader` class, 658
binary search, **241**–243, 256, **712**
`BinarySearchDemo` program, 242

`BinarySearch()` method, 241–243, 245, 266
    array of objects, 396–400
`BinaryWriter` class, 658
bin folder, 36
bit, **698**, **712**
bits (binary digits), 698, 704, 706
bitwise operators, **154**, 176, **712**
bitwise OR operator (|), 547
black box, **8**, **267**, 298, **712**
block comments (/* */), **18**, **713**
blocks, **140**, 176, **713**
    aligning braces ({}), 141
    exiting immediately, 237
    `if-else` statements, 145
    K & R style, 141
    multiple statements, 140
    single statement, 141
    unreachable, 504
`blueButton` button, 634
`blueToolStripMenuItem_Click()` method, 578–579
`BMethod()` method, 340
`Bold` property, 547
`bonus` parameter, 338
`bonus` variable, 153
`Book` class, 375–377, 391–394
`Book` objects, 375–376, 394
`Book` parameter, 394
`Book` return type, 392
`bool` data type, 48–49, 68–70, 92, 138, 284–285
Boole, George, 69
Boolean expressions, 137–138
    combining AND operator (&&) and OR operator (||), 154–158
    compound, 150–152
    negating, 165–166
    side effects, **153**–154
`Boolean` fields, 379
Boolean logical AND operator (&), **153**–154, 176, **713**
Boolean logical inclusive OR operator (|), **153**–154, 176, **713**
`boolean.Parse()` method, 86
Boolean values, 136–137, 284–285
Boolean variables, **68**, 70, 92, **713**
    comparison operators, **69**
    naming, 68
`BorderDemo1` program, 322–323
`BorderDemo2` program, 324, 325
`Bottom` property, 539
`Bounds` property, 539
`Box` class, 388
`BreakfastOptionForm` class, 587
`BreakfastOptionForm` form, 586–589
`BreakfastOptionForm_Load()` method, 587
`break` keyword, 160–161
`break` statements, 161, 237, 509
`Budget2016` class, 16
`BudgetForm` form, 104

INDEX

bugs, **3**, **713**
Build, `Build Solution` command, 28, 35
Build failed error message, 116
`building` variable, 251
Build Solution (Ctrl + Shift + B) keyboard shortcut, 27, 28
built-in methods, 285
   `out` parameter, 314–316
   overloaded, 327
`BusDriver` class, 463
`BusinessOffice` class, 357
`ButtonBase` class, 559
`button1` button, 106–108, 406–407, 541, 547, 709
`button2` button, 631
`button1_Click()` event handler, 632
`button2_Click()` event, 632
`button1_Click()` method, 108–110, 115, 270
`button2_Click()` method, 108
`Button()` constructor, 542
`Button` control, 105–106, 110, 545
   focus, 112–113
   properties, 122
`button1` object, 109
`Button` objects, 405–407, 468, 536–537, 542, 576, 598, 621–623, 631, 634
`Button` property, 627
buttons, 105, 121–125, 172, 598–599
   adding functionality, 107–109
   click event, **601**
   `Click()` event, 631
   clicking, 107–108
   default event, 107
   double-clicking, 623
   focus, 634
   functionality, 123–124
   method executing when pressed, 107
   naming, 114
   positioning, 122
   properties, 106
   renaming, 115
   resizing, 122, 586
   summing numbers, 110
   text, 541
`b` variable, 274
`byte` data type, **56**–57, 59, 72
   automatic conversions, 279
bytes, **647**, 654, 658, 699, **699**, 704, 706, **713**

C

C++, 5
   compared to C# programming language, 10
   declaring array variable, 224
   function pointers, 613
`CalcArea()` method, 374
`CalcPay()` method, 282–284
`CalcPay` program, 283

`CalcPhoneCallPrice()` method, 286–288
`calculatePayroll()` method, 601
`CalculateWithholdingTax()` method, 5
`CalendarForeColor` property, 574
`CalendarMonthBackground` property, 574
`calendar` object, 572
called method, **266**, 298, **713**
calling method, **5**, 12, **266**, 298, **713**
`callLength` variable, 288
call stack, 515, 527, **713**
   listing methods in, 514–519
   tracing Exception objects through, 514–519
camel casing, **3**, **713**
`CancelButton` property, 103
`CanFocus` property, 539
`CanRead` property, 655
`CanSeek` property, 655
`CanSelect` property, 539
`CanWrite` property, 655
`Capture` property, 539
`Car` class, 445
`CarLoan` class, 429–431, 442–443, 456
`CarLoan()` constructor, 456
`CarLoan` objects, 429, 442
`Carpet` class, 372, 374
`Carpet` objects, 373
carriage return escape sequence (\r), 75
`case` keyword, 160
`case` labels, **160**–161, 176, **713**
case sensitivity, 3
case structure. *See* switch structure
`catch` block, **492**–495, 499–506, 508–510, 513, 527, 685, **713**
   `break` statement, 509
   displaying information about exception, 497
   `e.Message`, 518
   `Exception` type, 492, 493
   multiple, 501, 504
   rethrowing exceptions, **523**–525
   `return` statement, 509
   unreachable, 504
   `WriteLine()` method, 518
   `XxxException` placeholder, 492
catch clause, 492
catching exceptions, 492–497, 499–500
   multiple exceptions, 501–505
`catch` keyword, 492
`Cat` class, 457–458, 461–462
C# Code Editor, 707–710
   code snippets, **709**
   readability aids, 710
   squiggles and lightbulbs, 709
C# compiler, 25–26
cd (change directory) command, 32, 36
`changeButton` button, 599, 601
`ChangeButton_Click()` method, 599–602

INDEX

Changed event, 612, 613
ChangedEventHandler delegate, 611–613
ChangedEventHandler event handler, 611
Changed field, 613
Changed() method, 612
changeLabel() method, 601
changeOutputButton button, 124–125
changeOutputButton_Click() method, 124
changing properties of multiple objects, 547
character fields, initial values, 379
characters, 56, 74–75, **652**, 653, 659, **713**
   array with subscripts, 228
   assigning array to string, 227
   bits (binary digits), 698–699
   case sensitivity, 192
   character set, **652**
   char variables, 74
   EBCDIC (Extended Binary Coded Decimal Interchange Code), 699
   hexadecimal shorthand notation, **74**
   nonprinting, **74**
   numbers as, 74
   sorting, 396
   strings, 74
   Unicode, 74–75, 699
character set, **652**, **713**
char data type, 48, **56**, 72, 74–75, 92, 661
   automatic conversions, 279
char variables, 74
CheckBox control, 105
check boxes, **559**–562, 580–586, 591, **713**
checkBox1 object, 560
checkBox2 object, 560
CheckBox objects, 537, 559–563, 580–586
check digits, 465
CheckedChanged() method, 559, 583, 588
checked list boxes, 566–570
CheckedListBox objects, 537, 566–570
Checked property, 559–563
Child class, **424**, 463, 471, **713**
   accessing parent class data, 432–433
   inheriting from parent class, 428, 447
CIS constant, 162–163
CivilWarSoldier class, 463
class access modifier, **354**, 409, **713**
class body, 354–355
class client, **353**, 409, **713**
class definition, **354**, 409
classes, 7, 12, 352, **713**
   abstract classes, **456**–460
   access modifiers, 354
   application classes, **13**
   application programs, 352
   class body, 354–355
   class definition, **354**
   class headers, 14, **354**

concrete class, **457**
constructors, 359, 379, 388, 452
conventional names, 16
creation, 354–357, 368–371
curly braces ({}), 14, 21
declaring, 354
destructors, **403**–405
enumerations, 81
extending, 426–429, 431–432
fields that are objects of other classes, 357
fragile, **435**
grouping, 12
identifiers, 14–17, 354
illegal names, 16
implementing interfaces, 397, 463
inheritance, **8**, **422**–424, 456
instances, **7**, **352**, 403–405
instance variables, 354–357
instantiating objects, 352, 422
instantiation, **352**
methods, **266**, 272–273, 355–356
named behaviors for, 397
naming, 8, 14
non-application classes, **13**
objects, 375
overloaded constructors, 385–386
overloaded operators, 391
parameterless constructor, 380–381
private data fields, 355–356
repeatedly using from same namespace, 19–20
return type, 282
sealed classes, **465**
static classes, 469
string holding name of, 448
unconventional names, 16
using an within another object, 357
class headers, 14, **354**, 409, **714**
class keyword, 17, 354
class user, **353**, 409, **714**
clerk object, 428, 432
Click delegate, 625
Click event, **108**, 126, **601**, 621–623, 627, 631–632, 635, 637, **714**
Click() method, 109, 119, 171–172, 266, 270, 295–296, 563, 578, 589, 622, 635
ClickParameterInfo program, 295
Clicks property, 627
clients, **267**, **298**, **714**
closing files, 654, **714**
Closing() method, 336–337
COBOL, referring to array elements, 226
code
   attributes associating information with, 674
   automatically generated, 541–544
   catch block, **492**–493
   correcting errors, 116–117

733

INDEX

code (*continued*)
   expanding or condensing, 102
   line numbers, 117
   locating line of, 543
   reusable, 424
   try block, **492**–493
code bloat, **268**, 298, **714**
CodeDomSerializerException class, 484
code refactoring, **115**, 127, **714**
code snippets, **709**, **714**
code window, 107
color
   background, 559
   forms, 552–554
   GUI applications, 554
   source code, 709
Color class, 552–554
ComboBox class, 570
combo boxes, 566–**570**, 591, **714**
ComboBox objects, 537, 566–570
command line, **23**, 30–31, **714**
   compiling and executing programs, 32–33
   incorrect subdirectory or folder, 24
   namespaces, 29
   program comments, 37
   running programs, 26
   using statements, 29
command prompt, **23**–26, **714**
commenting out statements, **18**, **714**
comments, 543
   block comments (/* */), **18**
   line comments (//), **18**
   programs, 37
   XML-documentation format contents (< >), **18**
CommissionEmployee class, 423–426, 433–435, 439, 445, 452–454
CommissionEmployee() constructor, 454
CommissionEmployee objects, 427, 433
commissionRate field, 423, 432–433
CommissionRate property, 433
commissionRate variable, 167–168
Common Language Runtime exception classes, 486
ComparableEmployeeArray program, 399–400
Compare() method, 78–79
CompareThreeNumbers project, 148–149
CompareTo() method, 77–78, 396–400, 402
comparison operators, **69**, 92, **714**
compiler errors, 484
compilers, **3**, **714**
   just in time (JIT), **23**
compiling programs, 23–31
   command prompt, 24–26
   high-level programming languages, 3
   IDE (Integrated Development Environment), 26–29
   intermediate language (IL), **23**
completion mode, **707**–708, 710, **714**

Component class, 468, 536–537
composed delegates, 602, **605**–610, 637, **714**
composition, **357**, 409, **714**
compound Boolean expressions, 150–152
   short-circuit evaluation, **152**–153
compound expressions and if statements, 150–156
ComputeGross() method, 338–339
ComputePaycheck() method, 276
computer files, **646**, 647, **714**
computers
   hardware, **2**
   measuring storage, 704–706
computer simulations, **6**, **714**
ComputeTotalPay() method, 338–339
concatenating strings, **53**, 55, 90, 390, **714**
concrete class, **457**, 472, **714**
conditional AND operator (&&), **150**–152, 176, **714**
conditional operator (?:), **164**–165, 176, **714**
   right-associative, **695**
conditional OR operator (||), **152**–153, 176, **714**–**715**
Connelly, Marc, 536
Consolas, 114
console applications, 119–120
Console class, 12, 20, 270, 469, 654
Console.Error class, 654
Console.In class, 654
console input, 84
Console.Out class, 654, 655
constants, **48**, 90, **715**
   assigning value to, 81, 162
   base 16 shorthand notation, **74**
   character values, 74
   enumerations, **81**–83
   floating-point constants, 547
   floating-point numbers, 60
   int data type, 57
   int data type and implicit conversion, 72
   methods, 273–274, 296
   naming, 80–81
   public access modifiers, 373
   scope, **273**
   subscripts, 229
   unnamed, 48
const field, 384
const keyword, 80, 373
const modifier, 384
constructor initializer, **383**, 410, **715**
constructors, **378**–384, 410, **715**
   automatically generated, 359, 453–454
   base class, 452–456
   constructor initializer, **383**
   default constructor, 359, 379
   derived class, 452–456
   initial field values, 379
   initializing variables, 452
   objects, 452

INDEX

overloading, 380–382
parameterless constructor, **380**
passing parameters to, 379–380
readonly modifier, 384
requiring arguments, 453–454
throwing exceptions, 522
user-created, 379
`ContainerControl` class, 468
`ContainerControl` objects, 577
`Container` property, 539
`ContainsFocus` property, 539
contextual keywords, **363**, 410, **715**
contRadioButton, 587
`ControlAdded` event, 621
`Control` class, 468, 536–537, 566
`Control` objects, 536–537, 548
`Control` property, 629
`ControlRemoved` event, 621
controls, **100**, 536–540, 580, 591, **715**
  aligning, 575
  check boxes, **559**–563, 580–586
  checked list boxes, 566–570
  combo boxes, 566–570
  constructors, 542
  dates and time, 571–574
  default event, **548**–549, 591
  default font, 114
  default names, 115
  deleting, 106
  double-clicking, 549
  event handling, 621–625
  focus, **112**, 543, 631
  fonts, 545–548
  group boxes, **577**
  handling multiple events with single handler, 632–633
  layout on form, 575–577
  link label, **548**–549
  listing, 105
  locating, 575
  managing multiple, 631–633
  menu strips, 578–579
  monthly calendar, 571–574
  mouse events, 626–628
  multiple, 111
  naming, 114–116
  panels, **577**
  picture boxes, **563**–565
  predefined colors, 552–554
  preventing conflicts, 543
  properties, 601
  protected properties, 538
  public properties, 538–540
  radio buttons, **559**–562, 586–589
  relocating, 106
  renaming, 115–116
  snap lines, 575
  tab order, **113**
  universal properties, 468
control statement, **140**, 176, **715**
`ConversionWithParse` program, 314
`ConversionWithTryParse` program, 315
`Convert` class, 84–86, 314
`ConvertEmployeeToString()` method, 448
`Convert.ToInt32()` method, 85, 284, 327, 511
`CountContributions` program, 253–254
counted loops, **191**, 216, **715**
`counter` variable, 64–65
Courier New, 114
C# programming language, 4, 5, **9**–11, **713**
  compiling and executing, 23–31
  features, 10
  OOPs, 4–9
  programming process of, 2–4
  selecting identifiers, 14–17
  system namespace, 18–20
  writing produces output, 11–14
`CreateDirectory()` method, 650
`CreateEmployee` class, 359
`CreateEmployee` program, 359–360
`CreateEmployee2` program, 364
Create file mode, 653, 659
`Create()` method, 648
`CreateNameFile` program, 664–665
`CreateNew` file mode, 656
`CreateSomeEmployees` program, 381–382
`CreateStudents2` class, 386
`CreateStudents.cs` file, 370–371
`CreateStudents3 program`, 401–403
`CreateText()` method, 648
`CreateTwoBooks` program, 377
credits field, 436–438
`Credits` property, 436–439
csc (C Sharp compiler) command, 24–25, 36
cs file extension, 22, 24, 683
CSV (comma-separated values) files, 659, **715**
culture, **62**, 91, **715**
`CultureInfoClass` class, 62
Currency format specifier, 61
currency values, 62
`Current` member, 668
`CursorChanged` event, 621
`Cursor` property, 539
`CustomFormat` property, 574
custStatus variable, 69

D

DailySpecial program, 173–174
data, 646
  characters, **652**
  data hierarchy, **652**
  fields, **653**

INDEX

data (*continued*)
    files, 653
    formatting in GUI applications, 113
    organization, 652–654
    records, **653**
    sequential access files, **653**, 658–673
data files, **715**
data hierarchy, **715**
`Data.txt` file, 662
data types, **48**, 90, **715**
    arguments, 279–280
    betterness rules for conversion, 326
    `bool` data type, 68–70
    enumerations, 81–83
    explicitly overriding, **73**
    floating-point data types, 59–62
    fully qualified name, 50
    implicit numeric conversions, 71–73
    integral data types, **56**–57
    intrinsic types, **48**
    largest and smallest values, 48–49
    method names, 323
    numeric type conversion, 71–73
    objects, 357–358
    one-dimensional arrays, 248
    overloading operators, 390
    parameters, 277
    properties, 363
    return type, 282
    serializable, 674
    simple types, **48**
    strings, 85–86
    two-dimensional arrays, 248
    type precedence, **72**
    type-safe, **83**
    unifying type, **72**
    variables, 50, 57
`DateChanged()` method, 571–574
Date class, 357
Date fields, 357
dates, 571–574, 648–649, 674
`DateTime` objects, 572, 648
`DateTimePicker` objects, 571–574, 648
dayBox text box, 173
`DayOfWeek` enumeration, 81–82
de Morgan, Augustus, 166
dead code, 504, 527, **715**
Debug folder, 36
debugging programs, 3, **715**
debugging tools in IDE (Integrated Development Environment), 26
Debug, Start Without Debugging command, 28, 29, 35
`Deciduous` class, 425
`decimal` data type, 48, **60**, 72, 91, **715**
Decimal format specifier, 61

decimal numbering system, **697**, **715**
    base 10 numbers, 697
decision making
    assignment operator (=), 167
    common errors, 167–170
    conditional operator (?), **164**–165
    dual-alternative decisions, **145**–147
    equal to operator (==), 167
    event-driven programs, 172
    flowcharts, 135
    GUI applications, 171–172
    `if-else` statements, **145**–147
    `if` statements, **137**–143
    logic-planning tools, 134–137
    NOT operator (!), 169–170
    AND operator (&&), 169
    OR operator (||), 169
    range checks, **167**–168
    `switch` structure, **159**–163
decision structure, **135**, 176, **715**
    control statement, **140**
decrementing, **190**, 216, **715**
decrement operator (--), **66**, 92, **715**
`DeductTax()` method, 271
`DeductUnionDues()` method, 271
default arguments, 281
default case, 161
default constructor, 359, **379**, 388, 395, 410, 452, **715**
default event for a Control, **715**
default font, 114
`default` keyword, 160
DEFAULT_VALUE constant, 506
default value of objects, **379**, 410, **715**
definite loops, **191**, 195, 216, **715**
`del` delegate, 602–603
`del1` delegate, 605
`del2` delegate, 605
`del3` delegate, 605
`delegate` keyword, 603
`delegate` objects, 610
delegates, **602**, 637, **715**
    assigning to another delegate, 605
    combining, 605
    creation, 606–608
    declaring, 603
    encapsulating instance methods, 617–618
    encapsulating methods, 603
    passing reference to methods, 602, 604
    removing delegate from, 605
    user-declared events, 611–616
`Delete()` method, 648
DELIM constant, 659
delimiters, **716**
`DeliverBaby()` method, 428
`deliverRadioButton_ CheckedChanged()` method, 561–562

INDEX

deluxeBreakfastButton RadioButton, 587, 588
DemoAnimals program, 459
DemoAnimals2 program, 460
DemoBankAccountEvent class, 619
DemoBankEvent program, 617–620
DemoCarLoan program, 431–432
DemoCarLoan2 program, 442–444
DemoCarLoan3 program, 455–456
DemoCommissionEmployee program, 435
DemoCommissionEmployee2 program, 440
DemoCommissionEmployee4 program, 452–453
DemoCommissionEmployee3 program, 445
DemoEmployeeDestructor program, 404
DemoEmployees class, 427
DemoEscapeSequences program, 76
DemoExtensionMethod program, 466–467
DemoLoan program, 429–431
DemoLogo program, 275
DemoObjectInitializer2 program, 389
DemoORAndAND file, 157–158
DemoProjectInitializer program, 387
DemoStudentEvent2 class, 615–616
DemoStudentEvent program, 614
DemoStudents program, 439
DemoVariables class, 58
DemoVariables.cs fil, 58–59
DemoVariables2 program, 67–68
DemoVariables3 program, 70–71
DemoVariables project, 58–59
DemoWorking program, 462–463
denom variable, 502
department variable, 169
Depth property, 388
derived class, **424**, 457, 469, 471, **716**
   abstract methods, 457
   accessing base class methods and properties, 439–441
   constructors, 452–456
   extending, 424–425
   implicit conversion to base class, **445**
   inheritance, 432
   overriding methods, 464
   overriding virtual methods or property, 438–439
   size, 425
   using base class members, 442–444
   visible methods or properties, **438**
deserialization, 673–675, **716**
Deserialize() method, 675
Designer.cs file, 102, 601, 628
Designer screen, 583
design time, **112**, 126, **716**
destructors, **403**–405, 410, **716**
DetermineTaxRate() method, 516
Developer Command Prompt command, **23**, **716**
digit separators, **57**, 91, **716**
dir (directory) command, 32, 36

directories, 646–651, **716**
Directory class, 646–651
discountButton_Click() method, 171
Discount class, 607
DiscountDelegateDemo program, 606–609
DiscountDelegateDemo2 program, 609–610
DiscountDelegate object, 609
discountRangeLowLimits array, 240
discounts array, 239
DismissedEmployee class, 424
DisplayArgs program, 293
DisplayCompanyLogo() method, 275–276
DisplayEmployeeData() method, 340, 360–361
DisplayEmployeeData() program, 360–361
DisplayGreeting() method, 445
Display() method, 370–371, 386, 401, 439
DisplayNetPay() method, 271
DisplayObjectMessage() method, 446
displayOutputButton button, 122, 125
displayOutputButton_Click() method, 125
DisplayPrice() method, 512
DisplayReferenceParameter() method, 311–312
DisplaySalesTax() method, 277–280
DisplaySize() method, 332–333
DisplaySomeMoney program, 52
DisplayValueParameter() method, 309
DisplayWithBorder() method, 323–324
DisplayWithBorderUsingInt() method, 323
Dispose() method, 680, 683
Disposing property, 539
DiverseObjects program, 447
divide and assign shortcut operator (/=), 65
DivideByZeroException class, 488, 490, 495–497, 501–505
DivideByZeroException object, 487–488
DivisionBasedOnMajor class, 163
division by zero, 489–492
division operator (/), 63
dockable or floating windows, 105
Dock property, 539, 576
Doctor class, 428
documenting programs, 18
doesEmployeeHaveDependents variable, 144
Dog class, 7–9, 425, 445, 457–458, 461–462
do keyword, 198
do loops, **198**–200, 206, 212, 216, **716**
DomesticPet class, 425
double array, 225, 247, **716**
Double class, 86, 352
double data type, 48, **59**–60, 72, 91, **225**, 282–285, 324, 326, 330–331, 445, 658
double quotation mark escape sequence (\"), 75
double variable, 283
do...while loop, **198**, 216
   See also do loops
DragDrop event, 621

INDEX

DragEnter event, 621
dragging onto forms, 106, 109
DragLeave event, 621
DragOver event, 621
dual-alternative decisions, 145–147, 176, **716**

E

EARLIEST_YEAR constant, 442–443
EBCDIC (Extended Binary Coded Decimal Interchange Code), 699
Ecma International web site, 10
elements, **224**, 255
    accessing, 228–231
    assigning values, 224–228
    cycling through, 230–231
    increasing value, 228
    numbering, 225–226
    passing single to method, 289–290
    performing arithmetic on, 229
else-if statements, 168
e.Message, 518
empArray array, 395
empID parameter, 383
Employee class, 16, 354–359, 361, 364–367, 378–379, 381, 383–384, 386, 395, 398, 400, 404, 422–424, 426–428, 432–435, 439, 445–450, 452–454, 460–463, 653, 659, 674, 675, 677
Employee() constructor, 359, 379, 381, 395
EmployeeData.txt file, 662
Employee() method, 378
Employee objects, 356, 360, 362, 379, 395, 397–399, 404, 423, 427, 432, 448–450, 676
Employee parameter, 361, 445
empty body, **190**, 216, **716**
Empty field, 611
EnabledChanged event, 621
Enabled property, 106, 125, 539
encapsulating methods, 602
encapsulation, **8**, 602, **716**
END constant, 660, 661, 671
End member, 668
enhanced for loop, **716**
Enter event, 621
EnterInvoices program, 678–681
entryID variable, 243
entryString variable, 315, 316
enumerations, 81–83, 93, **716**
    assigning values to constants or variables, 82
    data types, 81–83
    GUI applications, 173–174
    identifiers, 81
    switch structures, 162–163
    valid values, 82
enum keyword, 81
Environment.Exit() method, 509

e object, 599–600
Equals() method, 77–79, 447, **716**
    overloading, 449
    overriding, 449–451
equal to operator (==), 69, 77, 143–148, 167
equivalency, testing for, 143–148
Error list, 101, **117**
error messages and IDE (Integrated Development Environment), 26
escape characters, 113
escape sequences, **74**, 76, 92, **716**
event, **716**
EventArgs argument, 599–600, 611, 627
EventArgs class, 611
EventArgs.Empty instance, 611, 612
EventArgs object, 611, 612, 618
EventArgs parameter, 612, 614, 618, 627
EventArgs ToString(), 600
EventDemo program, 599–601
event-driven programs, **598**, 637, **716**
    decision making, 172
    loops, 213
    runtime, **172**
EventHandler delegate, 602, 614
event handlers, 599–601, 637, **716**
    associating with multiple controls, 632–633
    event receiver, **600**, 637
    event sender, **600**, 637
    user-declared, 611–616
EventHandler statements, 625
event handling, 598–602
    controls, 621–625
    handling multiple events, 632–633
    keyboard events, 628–630
    managing multiple controls, 631–633
    mouse events, 626–628
event-handling methods, 117–118, 296
EventListener class, 613–616, 618–620
EventListener object, 619
event listeners, 618–620
event receiver, **600**, 637, **716**
events, 108, 126, **598**, 637
    associating method with multiple, 635–636
    clicking objects and generating, 549
    connecting to actions, 601–602
    firing, **598**, 637
    generalizing method name, 632
    invoking, **612**, 637
    listing, 623–624
    raising, **598**, 637
    triggering, **598**, 637
    user-declared, 611–616
event sender, **600**, 637, **716**
event wiring, **601**, 637, **716**
Evergreen class, 424–425
exabytes, 705

INDEX

Exception class, 484, 486, 488, 493, 496–497, **716**
   extending, 519–521
   subclass messages, 520
   user-created, 519–522
exception handling, **484**–488, 499–500, 526, 657, **716**
   object-oriented, 492–495
   thrown from outside methods, 511–514
   traditional *versus* object-oriented, 491–492
Exception objects, 488, 491–492, 494–495, 499, 508–509, 511, 519, 520
   information about, 497, 515
   tracing through call stack, 514–519
exceptions, **484**–488, 526
   catching, 492–497, 499–500
   catching multiple, 501–505
   finally block, 508–510
   multiple, 504
   propagating, 515
   purposely causing, 489–491
   rethrowing, **523**–525
   throwing, 492–497, 499–500, 522–523
   unhandled, 314, 509–510
ExceptionsOnPurpose.exe file, 490
ExceptionsOnPurpose program, 489–491
ExceptionsOnPurpose2 program, 499–500
ExceptionsOnPurpose3 program, 505–506
Exception types, 492, 493, 496, 501, 503–504, 519–520, 522
executing programs, 23–31
execution-time errors, 484
.exe files, 26, 646
Exists() method, 648
explicit cast, 73, 92, **716**
explicitly overriding data types, 73, 92, **717**
exposing, 655, **717**
Extended Binary Coded Decimal Interchange Code (EBCDIC), **699**, 706, **717**
extended class, **424**, 471, **717**
eXtensible Markup Language. *See also* XMLextension
   methods, **465**–467, 472, **717**
external storage, 704

F

fault tolerant, **488**, 527, **717**
favoriteButton button, 634
fields, **353**, 409, 653, 659, 660, 675, **717**
   abstract classes, 457
   access specifiers, 355
   converting to text, 673
   delimiters, 659
   inheritance, 426
   initial values, 379
   private access, 365, 371–372
   protected access, **433**–435
   public access, 372–374
   retrieving values, 362

   separating into array of strings, 662
   setting, 362
   static, 373
fields array, 662
FileAccess enumeration, 656
FileAccess.Read member, 661
FileAccess.ReadWrite member, 661
File class, 648–653
File, Exit command, 36
FileInfo class, 648
filenames, 24, 648, 679
File objects, 672
file position pointer, 667, **717**
files, 646–654
   accessing information about, 648
   binary files, **646**–647
   closing, 509–510, 654
   creation, 653, 656
   creation time, 648
   CSV (comma-separated values) files, **659**
   data files, 653
   data organization, 652–654
   defining characteristics, 655
   directories, 646
   file position pointer, **667**
   folders, **647**
   key field, **653**
   last-modified time, 648, 650
   listing, 101, 102
   names, 647
   opening, **653**, 660
   path, **647**
   permanent storage devices, **646**
   priming read, **660**
   random access files, **646**
   reading from, 658–667
   record delimiter, 659
   sequential access files, **653**, 658–667
   size, 647
   storing, 647
   text files, **646**
   text input and output, 655
   writing to, 658–667
File, Save All command, 35
FileStatistics program, 649
FileStream class, 655
FileStream file, 655
FileStream objects, 655–659
finally block, 508–510, **527**, **717**
FindEmployees program, 668
FindItem() method, 320–321
FindPriceWithForLoop program, 235
FindPriceWithWhileLoop program, 238
findValue parameter, 320–321
fingerprints, 451
firing events, **598**, 637

INDEX

FirstClass class, 11–14, 16, 17
FirstClass console application, 11–13
firstDel delegate, 603, 605, 607, 609
firstName variable, 76
fixed-pitch fonts, **114**, 127, **717**
Fixed-point format specifier, 61
float, **717**
float argument, 546
Float class, 352
float data type, **59**, 72, 91, 279, 546
floating-point constants, 547, **717**
floating-point data types, 59–62, 91
    decimal data type, **60**
    double data type, **60**
    float data type, **59**
floating-point numbers, **59**–62, 90
    constants, 60
    dividing by zero, 486
    formatting, 60–62
    significant digits, **59**
    standard numeric format strings, **61**
floor variable, 249, 251
flowcharts, **134**, 175, **717**
    decision making, 135
    decision structure, **135**
    parallelograms, 138
    sequence structure, **134**
focus, **112**, 127, 543, **631**, 637, **717**
FocusDemo application, 632
Focused property, 539
folders, **647**, 688, **717**
FontChanged event, 621
Font class, 545–548
Font() constructor, 546
Font dialog box, 556
Font objects, 547–548
Font property, 103, 106, 114, 124, 538–539, 541, 542, 545, 556, 578, 587, 622
fonts
    bold, 547
    changing, 114
    controls, 545–548
    default, 114
    fixed-pitch, **114**, 127
    Font() constructor, 546
    GUI applications, 554
    labels, 583
    Microsoft Sans Serif, 546, 556
    monospaced, **114**, 127
    names, 546
    proportional, **114**, 127
    resizing, 556
    selecting, 545
    sizes, 546
    styles, 547
    underlined, 547

FontStyle enumeration, 81, 547
Font window, 545
forcing to contain error, 486–488
foreach statements, 230–231
ForeColorChanged event, 621
ForeColor property, 103, 106, 124, 538–539, 554
for keyword, 195
for loops, **195**–197, 212, 216, 650, **717**
    comparing value to valid values in array, 233
    displaying integers 1 through 10, 195
    exiting early, 237
    improving efficiency, 236–237
    loop body, 195, 196
    loop control variable, 195, 210
    navigating arrays, 230–231
    searching arrays, 234–236
formal parameters, **278**, 299, 309, **717**
FormatException class, 485, 490, 505, 511
FormatException object, 507
Format property, 574
format specifiers, **61**, 91, **717**
format strings, **53**–54, 90, 113, **717**
    alignment and field size, 55
    displaying number as, 62
    length, 55
Form class, 103, 253, 467–468
Form1 class, 407, 467, 541
Form1.cs[Design] tab, 125, 559, 583, 586, **635**
Form1.cs file, 101, 586, 589, 624, 627, 629, 635
Form1.cs node, 102
Form Designer, 101, 107, 110
    dragging controls, 541
    form name, 103
    unwanted event-handling methods, 117–118
Form1.Designer.cs file, 102, 406, 558, 630, 683
form feed escape sequence (\f), 75
Form1 file, 102
Form1 form, 103, 628
Form1_KeyUp() method, 629
Form objects, 405–406, 467–468, 536, 554–559, 563–564, 568, 571, 578, 582, 583, 598, 622, 629
    layout, 575–577
    properties, 544
forms, **100**, 126
    background color, 559
    buttons, 105–109, 121–125, **122**, 172, 598–599
    check boxes, **559**–562, 580–586
    checked list boxes, 566–570
    color, 552–554
    combo boxes, 566–570
    controls, **100**, 536–540, 622
    creation, 100–104
    date and time, 571–574
    default event, 549
    default names, 115

INDEX

dragging controls onto, 106, 109, 541, 544
failing to close before reexecuting
    program, 118
labels, **109**–112, 121, 124, 629
list boxes, 566, **567**–570
maximum and minimum size, 576
menu strips, 578–579
modifying, 103
monthly calendar, 571–574
multiple controls, 111
naming, 100, 102, 114–116, 122
nonstatic methods, 296
picture boxes, 563–565
properties, 103, 122
radio buttons, **559**–562, 586–589
reading data from text files, 681
relocating controls, 106
resizing, 622, 634
saving, **123**
strings, 104
text, 545–548
text boxes, **110**–112
`textboxes`, 172
`FormWithALabelAndAButton` program, 542–544
forward declarations, 10
fragile, **435**, 472, **717**
`Frame` property, 549
`fullBreakfastButton RadioButton`, 587, 588
fully qualified name, **270**, 299
function pointers, 603
functions, 5

G

`gallonsOfGas` variable, 493–494, 496
garbage, **717**
General format specifier, 61
`get` accessors, **362**–365, 371, 410, 433, 442,
    448, **717**
`GetCreationTime()` method, 648
`GetData()` method, 401–402
`GetDirectories()` method, 650
`GetEmployeeIndentification()` method, 448
`GetFiles()` method, 650
`GetGreeting()` method, 427, 439–440
`GetHashCode()` method, 447, 450–451
`get` identifier, 15
`GetLastAccessTime()` method, 648
`GetLastWriteTime()` method, 648
`GetLength()` method, 292
`GetPrice()` method, 284
`GetSelected()` method, 569
getter, **363**, 410, **718**
`GetType()` method, 447, 450, 497
`get` variable, 363
gigabytes, **647**, 705, **718**

`global` identifier, 15
`Goodbye()` method, 603, 605
`GotFocus` event, 621
governing type, **160**, 176, **718**
`gpa` field, 612
`Gpa` property, 612
`gradePointAverage` field, 369
`GradePointAverage` property, 370–371
graphical control elements, **536**, 591, **718**
graphical user interfaces. *See* GUIs
graphics, displaying, 563–565
Greater than operator (>), 69
Greater than or equal to operator (>=), 69
`Greeting` class, 603
`Greeting2` class, 605
`GreetingHandler()` delegate, 603
Greeting program, 603, 604
Greeting2 program, 605–606
`greeting` variable, 441
`GreetMethod()` method, 603
`gross` parameter, 338
`grossPay` variable, 283
`gross` variable, 283
group boxes, **577**, 591, **718**
`Grow()` method, 425
GUI applications
    arrays, 253–254
    automatically generated methods, 295–296
    closing, 112
    colors, 554
    controls, 536–540
    correcting errors, 116–117
    deciding to use, 119–120
    decision making, 171–172
    enumeration, 173–174
    event-driven, **598**, 637
    event handling, 621–625
    event-handling methods, 117–118
    executing, 112
    failing to close form before reexecuting, 118
    formatting data, 113
    `if-else` statements, 171
    `if` statements, 171
    inheritance, 467–470
    keyboard event handling, 628–630
    logical errors, 117
    `Main()` method, 108
    memory, 119
    methods, 295–296
    mouse event handling, 626–628
    objects, 405–407
    scope, 296
    `switch` structures, 171, 173–174
    text file creation, 678–681
GUI objects, 536
    events, **108**

INDEX

GUIs (graphical user interfaces), **6, 718**
  objects, 6, 100
  OOPs, 6
  switching between visual environment and code, 107

H

hardware, **2, 718**
has-a relationship, **357**, 409
`HasChildren` property, 539
hash codes, **450**, 472, **718**
`HeartSurgeon` class, 428
`heatingBill` variable, 48
`Height` property, 104, 388, 538–539
`Hello` class, 21–22
`HelloClass` program, 266, 273
Hello.cs program, 21–22, 32, 36
Hello.exe file, 32–33, 36
`HelloForm` form, 122
`helloLabel` label, 124, 579, 598
`Hello()` method, 603, 605
`Hello` namespace, 34
`Hello` project, 33
HelloVisualWorld project, 121–125
Help documentation, 118
`HelpRequested` event, 621
hexadecimal, **74**, 92
Hexadecimal format specifier, 61
hexadecimal numbering system, **703**–704, 706, **718**
  base 16 system, 703
hexadecimal shorthand notation, **74**
hidden or visible windows, 105
hide, **438**, 472, **718**
HIGH constant, 143
high-level programming language, **2–3, 718**
horizontal tab escape sequence (\t), 75
hot keys, 560
`hours` parameter, 338
`hoursWorked` variable, 4, 69

I

`IAttackable` interface, 463
`IComparable` interface, 397–398, 402
IDE (Integrated Development Environment), **23**, 30–31, **719**
  automatically generated code, 26, 30, 541–544, 557–558
  colors of code, 26, 31
  compiling and executing program, 33–36
  compiling code, 26–29
  correcting errors, 31
  debugging tools, 26
  double-clicking controls, 622
  error list, 101
  error messages, 26, 28
  executing program, 112
  Form Designer, 101
  forms, 100–104
  information about methods, 327
  menu bar, **26**, 100
  menu options, 28
  naming project, 26–27, 100
  New Project window, 101
  Properties window, 101
  shortcuts, 28
  Solution Explorer, 101
  syntax errors, 28
  text editors and, 29–30
  Toolbox tab, 101
  View menu, 100, 101
IDE Editor
  code snippets, **709**
  completion lists, 707–708
  IntelliSense, 707
  parameter information, 709
  quick information, 708
  readability aids, 711
  squiggles and lightbulbs, 710
  `using` statements, 709
identifiers, **4**, 29, **718**
  arrays, 225
  classes, 354
  enumerations, 81
  methods, 271–272
  names, 14–17
  objects, 358, 359
  parameters, 277
  @ prefix, 14
  properties, 363
  selecting, 14–17
  text editors, 29–30
  `using` statements, 30
  variables, 50
  verbatim identifiers, **14**
`idNumber` field, 355–356, 361–367, 369, 384, 398–400, 402, 404
`IdNumber` property, 361–365, 370–371, 383, 386–387, 402
`idNumbers` array, 242–243
`idNum` field, 422–423, 427, 432, 612
`IdNum` property, 432, 448–450, 612
`if-else` statements, **145**–149, 176, **718**
  blocks, 145
  failing to block set of statements, 167
  GUI applications, 171
  nested, 147, 168
`if` statements, **137**, 176, 284–285, 491, 583, 586, 609, **718**
  assignment operator (=), 143–144
  Boolean expressions, 137–138
  combining AND operator (&&) and OR operator (||), 154–158
  comparing variable to valid values, 233

INDEX

compound expressions, 150–156
conditional AND operator (&&), **150**–152
conditional OR operator (||), **152**–153
as control statement, **140**
equal to operator (==), 143–144
evaluated expression, 137
failing to block set of statements, 167
GUI applications, 171
indenting, 139–140
methods returning value, 138
nested, **141**–142, 151, 159
range checks, 167–168
semicolon (;) incorrectly placed in, 139, 167
IL. *See* intermediate language
`Illustrator` class, 457
`Image` property, 563–564, 585
immutable, **79**, 92, **718**
implementation hiding, **267**, 278, 298
  compromising, 337
implicit cast, **72**, 92, 326, **718**
implicit conversions, **72**–73, 92, 326, **445**, 472, **718**
implicitly, **72**, 92, **718**
implicit parameter, **364**, 410, **718**
implicit reference conversions, **445**, 472, **718**
INCHES_IN_A_FOOT constant, 81
`#include` files, 10
incrementing, **190**, 216
indefinite loops, **191**, 195, 216, **718**
indenting programs, 13
index, **224**, 255
`IndexOutOfRangeException` class, 229, 485, 501, 503–504, 512–513, 522
`inFile` file, 667
infinite loops, **187**, 190, 216, **718**
Infinity value, 486
information hiding, **355**, 409, 432, 435, **719**
inheritance, **8**, **422**–424, 456, 471, **719**
  ancestors, **425**
  base class, **424**
  child class, **424**
  derived class, **424**, 432
  extended class, **424**
  extending classes, 426–429, 431–432
  fields, 426
  GUI applications, 467–470
  implicit reference conversions, **445**
  methods, 426
  multiple inheritance, 10, **461**
  parent-child relationship, 424
  parent class, **424**
  reusable code, 424
  saving time, 424
  subclasses, **424**, 460
  superclass, **424**
  terminology, 424–425
  transitive, **425**

initialization, **50**, 90, **719**
`InitializeComponent()` method, 406, 542–544, 568
initializer list, **227**, 255, **719**
inner loop, **719**
`InputMethodDemo` program, 312
`InputMethod()` method, 312
input streams, 654, 655
instance methods, 78, **353**, 398, 409, **719**
  delegate encapsulating, 617–618
  objects, 359
  public access specifier, 355
  this reference, 376
instances, **7**, **352**, 409
  destroying, 403–405
instance variables, **353**, 375, 409, **719**
  serializable, 674
instantiate, **352**, 409, **719**
instantiation, **352**, 409, **719**
`Int32` class, 352, 465–467, 469
`int` data type, 48, **56**–57, 59, 72, 90, 324, 326, 330–331, 546, 658
  alias, 50
  automatic conversions, 279
integers, **56**, 90
  dividing by zero, 486–487, 502
  division, 63–64
  remainder operation, 63
  return type, 294
  sorting, 396
  subscripts, 226
`Integer.TryParse()` method, 507
integer variables, 67
integral data types, **56**–57, 91, **719**
Integrated Development Environment. *See* IDE
IntelliSense, **707**, 710, **719**
  completion mode, **707**–708, 710
  information about methods, 327
  parameter information, 709
  Quick Info ToolTip, 708
  suggestion mode, 708, **708**
  `using` statements, 709
`InteractiveAddition` file, 87–88
interactive programs, **84**, 93, **719**
`InteractiveSalesTax` program, 86
`interestRate` variable, 65
`interface` keyword, 461
interfaces, **8**, **100**, 126, **396**, 410, **461**, 472, **719**
  abstract methods, 460–464
  classes implementing, 463
  creation, 460–464
  deciding to use, 119–120
  methods, 397
  names, 397, 461
  polymorphism, 397, 464

INDEX

intermediate language (IL), **23**, **719**
internal, **719**
internal access modifier, 354, **719**
`internal` class, 409
internal field modifier, 355
`internal` keyword, 354
internal memory, 704
interpreters, 3
`int.Parse()` method, 86
intrinsic types, **48**, 90, 465, **719**
`int` variables, 68
`InvalidCastException` class, 485
`InvalidDataException` class, 485
`InvalidOperationException` class, 485
`InvalidPrinterException` class, 484
invoking, **5**, 12, **266**, 298, **719**
invoking events, **612**, 637, **719**
invoking object, **359**, 410, **719**
`IOException` class, 484–485, 509–510, 657
`IPlayable` interface, 463
`isDiscountProvided` variable, 69
`IsDisposed` property, 539
`isGoodItem` variable, 513
`isLocalCustomer()` method, 285
`isPreferredCustomer()` method, 284–285
`isProjectUnderBudget` variable, 145
`isSixMore` variable, 70–71
`IssueInvitations()` method, 353
`isValidIDNumber` variable, 137
`isValidItem` variable, 234, 238
`Italic` property, 547
`itemOrdered` variable, 233–234, 236–237
`itemPriceAsString` variable, 84–85
`itemPrice` variable, 236–237
`Items.Count` property, 569
`Items` property, 566–567
iterations, **186**, 216, **719**
iteration variable, **230**, 256, **719**
`IWorkable` interface, 461–464

J

jagged arrays, **251**–252, 256, 292, **719**
Java, 5, 10
   ban on passing functions, 603
   declaring array variable, 224
just in time (JIT) compiler, **23**, **719**

K

Kaufman, George, 536
Kernighan, Brian, 141
key, **720**
keyboard
   event handling, 628–630
   making selection from, 560
`KeyChar` property, 629

`KeyCode` property, 629, 630
`KeyData` property, 629
`KeyDemo` program, 629–630
`KeyDown` event, 621, 628
`KeyEventArgs` class, 629
`KeyEventArgs` parameter, 628
`KeyEventHandler` delegate, 628
key events, **628**, 637, **720**
key field, **653**, 688, **720**
`KeyPress` event, 621, 628
`KeyPressEventArgs` class, 629
`KeyPressEventArgs` parameter, 628
`KeyPressEventHandler` delegate, 628
`KeyUp` event, 621, 628–630
`KeyUp()` method, 629
`KeyValue` property, 629
keywords, **2**, 13, 39, **720**
   contextual, **363**
kilobytes, **647**, 705, **720**

L

`label1_Click()` method, 118, 549
`Label()` constructor, 543
Label control, 109, **109**–112, 541, 545
`label1` label, 109, 118, 541, 543
`label2` label, 575
Label objects, 468, 543, 554, 556–561, 569, 575, 582–583, 587, 598, 622, 624, 629, 631–633, 678
labels, **109**–112, 119, 121, 124, 125, 554–560, 582, 629, **720**
   adding to form, 554–560
   anchoring, 575, 576
   empty, 110, 111
   fonts, 114, 583
   multiple lines of text, 110
   names, 110
   positioning, 556
   properties, 554–560
   resizing, 110, 556
   responses to clicks, 627
   text, 109, 110
`lastName` field, 369
`LastName` property, 370–371
`Leave` event, 622
`LeavesTurnColor()` method, 425
left-associative, **695**–696, **720**
`leftOver` variable, 324
`Left` property, 539
`length` field, 373, **720**
`Length` property, **79**, 229–230, 237, 374, 676
Less than operator (<), 69
Less than or equal to operator (<=), 69
`letterButton_Click()` method, 632
lexically, **77**, 92
lightbulbs, 710

INDEX

LIMIT constant, 187–188, 190, 196
lincolnCheckBox_CheckChanged() method, 586
lincolnCheckBox object, 580, 581
LincolnForm form, 585
Lincoln Room check box, 584, 586, 589
line comments (//), 18, **720**
LinkClicked() method, 549–551, 622
LinkColor property, 549
link label, **548**–549, 591, **720**
LinkLabel class, 548–551
linklabel1_LinkClicked() method, 551
linklabel2_LinkClicked() method, 551
linkLabel1 object, 550
linkLabel2 object, 550
LinkLabel objects, 537, 549–550, 622
LinkVisited property, 549, 551
list boxes, 566, **568**, 591, **720**
    automatically selecting item, 566
    displaying items in columns, 568
    items selected in, 570
    number of items in, 569
    objects added to, 568
    position of item in list, 569
    resizing, 568
    selections, 568
    user-selected items, 569
ListBox event, 621
ListBox objects, 537, 566–570, 598
ListControl class, 566
literal characters, 74
literal constants, **48**, 90, **720**
literal strings, 11, **11**, 31, **720**
Load() method, 549, 568
loanAmount field, 442–443
LoanAmount property, 442–443
Loan class, 429–431, 442–444, 455–456
Loan() constructor, 455–456
Loan objects, 429–431
local function, **272**, 299, **720**
local variable, **273**, 299, **720**
LocalVariableDemo program, 274
LocationChanged event, 622
locationLabel label, 627
Location property, 122, 406, 539, 543, 555–557, 566, 575, 601
logic, **3**, **720**
logical errors, 3
    GUI applications, 117
logical operators, 390
logical OR operator (|), 547
logic-planning tools, 134–137
Logo, 4
long data type, **56**, 59, 72
    automatic conversions, 279
loop body, **186**, 216, **720**
    do loops, 198–199

executing at least one time, 198
for loops, 195–196
loop control variables, **187**, 192, 216, **720**
    altering by user input, 191
    decrementing, **190**
    incrementing, **190**, 210
    initializing, 195
    partially altering, 192
    starting value, 195
    step value, **195**
    testing, 195
    updating, 195
    while loops, 195
loop fusion, **206**, **720**
LoopingBankBalGUI program, 210
LoopingBankBal program, 191–192
LoopingBankBal2 program, 197
loops, **186**, 216, **720**
    accumulated totals, **206**–207
    arithmetic performed only once, 209
    avoiding unnecessary operations, 208–209
    combining, 210
    counted loops, **191**
    declaring variable outside, 209
    definite loops, **191**
    do loops, **198**–200
    empty body, **190**
    event-driven programs, 213
    expressions, 209–210
    GUI programs, 212–215
    improving efficiency, 236–237
    improving performance, 208–212
    indefinite loops, **191**
    infinite, **187**, 190
    iterations, **186**
    loop body, **186**
    loop fusion, **210**
    for loops, **195**–197
    nested, 200–205, 288, 292
    not executing, 198
    performing arithmetic on array elements, 229
    placing common items first in, 237
    posttest, **200**
    prefix and postfix incrementing, 210–212
    pretest, **200**
    repeating instructions, 186
    searching arrays, 233–241
    sentinel value, **192**
    short-circuit operators evaluation order, |209–210
    while loops, **186**–194
LostFocus event, 622
lower camel casing, **3**, **720**
LOWEST_INVALID_NUM constant, 442
LOW_QUANTITY constant, 157
LOWRATE constant, 200
lrateLabel label, 556

INDEX

M

machine language, 2–3, **720**
magic number, 661, **720**
`Main()` method, 12–13, 22, 27, 29, 34, 58, 68, 70, 87, 88, 108, 266, 268, 272–276, 287, 288, 290, 293–294, 311–312, 319, 321, 338–339, 352, 359, 370, 373, 381, 386, 401, 404, 427, 430, 501–502, 518, 523, 603, 607–609, 619
`majorListBox` object, 568
`majorListBox_SelectedIndexChanged()` method, 569
`MakeAppointment()` method, 11
`MakeDeposit()` method, 620
`Make` property, 443
`MakeWithdrawal()` method, 620
`Mammal` class, 445
mandatory parameters, **308**–310, 341, **720**
`ManyButtons` program, 634, 635
`ManyHellosGUI` program, 213
`Maple` class, 425
`Margin` property, 539
`MarsAlien` class, 463
`MarshalByRefObject` class, 468, 536
`Math` class, 285
`Math.PI` constant, 373
`Math.Pow()` method, 63
matrix, 248
`MaxDate` property, 571
`MAXDINNER` constant, 204
`MaximumSize` property, 576
`MAXRATE` constant, 204
`MaxSelectionCount` property, 571
`mealButton` button, 586, 589
measuring storage, 704–706
megabytes, **647**, 705, **721**
`MemberAccessException` class, 485
memory
 aliases, 310
 limited, 57
 measuring storage, 704–706
 random access memory (RAM), **653**
 volatile, 653
menu bar, **26**, **721**
`MenuStrip` objects, 578–579
menu strips, **578**–579, 591, **721**
`messageLabel` label, 572
`Message` property, 497, 499, 503, 515, 520
`MethodA()` method, 515, 523
`MethodB()` method, 515, 523
method body, 13, **13**, 272, 298, **721**
`MethodC()` method, 515, 523
method declaration, **268**, 298, **721**
method definition, **268**, 298, **721**
`MethodGetsArray()` method, 290–292
`MethodGetsOneInt()` method, 290
method header, **13**, **268**, 272, 293–294, 298, **721**

`Method1()` method, 334–335
`Method2()` method, 336
`MethodN()` method, 270
methods, 5, **266**, 302, 355–356
 abstract classes, 457
 abstract methods, **396**
 accessibility, **269**–270
 ambiguous, **330**–331
 applicable, **326**
 arguments, **11**, 241–247, 266, 272
 arrays, 289–292
 automatically generated, 295–296
 betterness rules, **326**
 built-in, 285
 called method, **266**
 calling, **5**, 13, 275–276
 calling method, **266**
 clients, **267**
 constants, 273–274, 296
 constructors, **378**–384
 curly braces ({}), 13
 default arguments, 281
 delegates, 602–603
 derived class accessing, 439–441
 encapsulating, 602
 event handlers, **599**–601
 event-handling, 117–118, 296
 event receiver, **600**
 exception handling thrown from outside methods, 511–514
 extension methods, 465–467
 fully qualified name, **270**
 GUI applications, 295–296
 identifiers, 271–272
 implementation hiding, **267**
 inheritance, 426
 instance methods, 78, **353**
 instructions executed by, 12
 interfaces, **8**, 397
 invoking, **5**, 12, **266**
 jagged arrays, 292
 listing in call stack, 514–519
 local variables, 273
 mandatory parameters, **308**–310
 manipulating arrays, 241–244
 method body, **13**
 method declaration, **268**
 method definition, **268**
 method header, **13**, **268**
 multidimensional arrays, 292
 multiple-argument, 280–281
 multiple events, 635–636
 named arguments, **335**–340
 names, 12–13, 271–272
 nested method calls, **284**
 nonstatic, **270**–271, 296

INDEX

no parameters, 268–274
no return value, 268–274
not returning value, 13
objects, 8, 353, 360–361, 602–610
optional parameters, **308**, 332–340
orphaned, **118**, 127
output parameters, **310**, 312
overloading, 322–329, 397
overload resolution, **326**
overriding, **397**, 437
parameter arrays, **310**, 316–317
parameter list, **272**
parameters, **272**, 276, 286–288, 308–310
Pascal casing, **5**
passing by reference, 313
passing single array element to, 289–290
placing in classes, 272–273
polymorphism, **9**
positional arguments, **335**
private access, 108, **269**–270
private access modifiers, 372–374
public access, **269**
public access modifiers, 371–372
recursive, **444**
reference parameters, **310**, 311–312, 318–319
returning Boolean value, 284–285
returning value, 138, 271, 282–288
return type, **271**, 282, 313
reusable, 268
signature, **322**
single argument, 276–280
static, 78, 108, **270**–271, 277
storing, 267, 376
`this` reference, 376–378
throwing exception and not catching it, 515
unnamed arguments, 334–335
valid and invalid declarations, 334
value parameters, **308**–310
variables, 273–274, 296
virtual methods, **437**
visible, **438**
void, 290
which outside classes can use, 108
MethodS() method, 270
method's type, **271**, 299
MethodThatAcceptsArray () method, 292
MethodWithItsOwnA() method, 274
metric system, 706
Microsoft Sans Serif, 114, 546, 556
Microsoft Visual Studio. *See* Visual Studio
Microsoft Web site, 9
Microsoft.WindowsCE.Forms.DocumentList class, 537
MilesPerGallon program, 486–487
MilesPerGallon2 program, 494–496
MilesPerGallon3 program, 496–497
MilesPerGallon4 program, 498

MinDate property, 571, 573
MINIMUM_LOAN constant, 442
MinimumSize property, 576
mission critical, **488**, 527, **721**
M1() method, 602, 605
M2() method, 602, 605
modal window, **583**, 591, **721**
ModifierKeys property, 539
modulus operator, 63
monetary values, 60
money variable, 72, 230
monospaced fonts, **114**, 127
MonthCalendar objects, 571–574, 648
MonthlyBoldedDates property, 571
monthly calendar, 571–574
MOTTO constant, 373
MouseButtons property, 540
MouseClick delegate, 628
MouseClick event, 626, 627
mouse click triggering default event, 548
MouseDoubleClick event, 626
MouseDown event, 622, 626–627
MouseEnter delegate, 625
MouseEnter event, 622, 624, 626
MouseEventArgs class, 626–627
MouseEventArgs object, 601
MouseEventArgs parameter, 626–627
MouseEventHandler delegate, 626
mouse events, 626–628
MouseHover event, 622, 626
MouseLeave event, 622, 626
MouseMove event, 622, 626
MousePosition property, 540
MouseUp event, 622, 626
MouseWheel event, 622
Move event, 622
Move() method, 648
Movie Discount form, 171
mpg variable, 493–494
MSDN library, 118
MultiColumn property, 566, 568
multidimensional arrays, 247–251, **248**, 256, 292, **721**
MultiExtended member, 568
multifile assembly, **267**, 298, **721**
multiple-argument methods, 280–281
multiple inheritance, 10, **461**, 472, **721**
multiply and assign shortcut operator (*=), 65
MultiSimple member, 568
myAge variable, 50–51
myAssistant object, 357–359, 362
myBook.AdvertisingMessage() method, 376
myCar class, 445
myChef object, 363–364
myDel delegate, 603
myDog class, 445
myGraduationParty identifier, 353

INDEX

myInteger class, 357
MyMethod() method, 326, 602–603
myMoney variable, 113
myPetDogFifi object, 425
myScores array, 227, 229–230
myString variable, 84

N

named arguments, **335**–340, 342, **721**
named constants, **80**–81, 92, 373, 661, **721**
named instances, 546
named variables, 59
name field, 436–439
Name property, 103, 106, 110, 114–116, 122, 406, 436–437, 448, 457, 459, 540–541, 543, 555, 568, 586, 598, 601
namespace-dot-class-dot-method format, 12
namespaces, 12, **12**, **721**
  built-in, 29
  curly braces ({}), 29
  declaration, 29
  repeatedly using class, 20–21
  user-created, 29
  using clause, **20**
  using directive, **20**
Names.txt file, 665, 670
NegativeBalanceException class, 520
nested
  if-else statements, 147, 168
  if statements, **141**–142, 151, 159, 176, **721**
nested loops, 200–206, 288
  inner loop, **200**
  outer loop, **200**, 202
nested method calls, **284**, 299, **721**
.NET framework culture settings, 62
new field modifier, 355
New Item window, 581
new keyword, 225, 438, 441
newline escape sequence (\n), 75
Newline in constant error message, 56
new line (\n), 652
new operator, **225**, 358
New Project command, 33
New Project window, 33, 100, 121, 555
nibbles, **699**, 706, **721**
nodes, **102**, 126, **721**
no fall-through rule, 161
nonabstract methods, 457, 463
non-application classes, **721**
None member, 568
nonprinting characters escape sequence, **74**
nonstatic methods, **270**–271, 299
nonstatic variables, 356
nonvolatile, **646**, **721**
Notepad, 21, 551

Not equal to operator (!=), 69, 77
NotImplementedException class, 485
NOT operator (!), **165**–166, 169–170, 177, **721**
null escape sequence (\0), 75
NullReferenceException class, 485, 684
Number format specifier, 61
numbering systems
  binary numbering system, **698**–699
  decimal numbering system, **697**
  hexadecimal numbering system, **703**–**704**
  measuring storage, 704–706
numberOfDependents variable, 57
number parameter, 311
numbers
  aligning, 114
  as characters, 74
  converting strings to, 86–87, 314–316
  converting to string, 61–62
  division, 63
  summing, 110
number variable, 143, 187–190, 312, 506–507
numDependents variable, 144
numeric fields, 379
numeric type conversion, 71–73
numeric variable, 57
numOfItems variable, 239, 240
numPages field, 375
num1 variable, 149
num2 variable, 149
num3 variable, 149

O

Oak class, 425
Object class, 397, 446–452, 468, 536
Object constructor, 452
object destructors, 10
object initializers, **386**–389, **722**
object keyword, 446
object-oriented approach, **6**, **722**
object-oriented exception-handling methods, 492–495
  versus traditional exceptionhandling methods, 491–492
object-oriented programming (OOP), **5**, **722**
  computer simulations, 6
  features of, 7–9
  GUIs, 6
  procedural and, 4–7
Object parameter, 397, 450
objects, **5**–6, 10, 352, 353, 375, 446–452, 472
  allocating memory, 358
  arithmetic symbols, 390
  arrays, 226
  attributes, **5**, 7, 353
  behaviors, **5**, 7

INDEX

comparing, 449–450
computer simulations, 6
constructors, 452
creation, 357–361, 368–371
data types, 357–361
default value, **379**
deserialization, 673–686
encapsulation, **8**
events, 549
fingerprints, 451
GUI applications, 405–407
GUIs (graphical user interfaces), 6
identifiers, 358, 359
instance methods, 359
instantiate, **352**, 422
interacting with, 598
interfaces, **8**
methods, 8, 353
names, 357, 358, 560
passing to methods, 360–361
properties, **7**
reading from text files, 674
reference equality, **449**–450
referencing methods, 602
serializable, 675
serialization, 673–677
state, **5**, 353
type or class, 448
uniquely identifying, 451
using within another object, 357
writing to text files, 674
obj folder, 36
`Obstetrician` class, 428
`okButton` button, 295, 542
`okButton_Click()` method, 111, 253, 295, 296
`oldEnough variable`, 166
`OnBalanceAdjusted` event handler, 618
`OnBalanceAdjusted()` method, 618
`OnChanged()` method, 612
`OneButtonTwoEvents` program, 624
one-dimensional arrays, **247**–248, 256, **722**
    jagged arrays, **251**–252
`One` member, 568
`oneVal` variable, 290
OOP. *See* Object-oriented programming
`Open` file mode, 656
opening files, **653**, **722**
`OpenOrCreate` file mode, 656
operands, **63**, 91, **722**
    implicitly converting, **71**
`Operate()` method, 436
operating system error message, 24–25
`OperationAbortedException class`, 485
`OperationCanceledException class`, 485
`operator*()` method, 394
`operator+()` method, 391–392

`operator-()` method, 394
operator precedence, **64**, 91, 695–696, **722**
operators
    associativity, **695**
    overloading, 390–394
    precedence, **64**, 91, **695**–696
`OptionalParameterDemo` program, 333
optional parameters, **308**, 332–341, **722**
    output parameters, **310**, 312
    parameter arrays, **310**, 316–317
    reference parameters, **310**–311
    unnamed arguments, 334–335
order of operation, **64**, 91, **722**
OR operator (||), **152**–153, 167, 169, 176, 233, **722**
    combining with AND operator (&&), 154–158
orphaned methods, **118**, 127, **722**
outer loop, **722**
`outFile` file, 656
`outFile` object, 656, 674
`out` keyword, 311, 315
out of bounds, **722**
`OutOfMemoryException` class, 485
out of scope, **196**, 216, **722**
`Out` parameters, 402, 506–507
output
    displaying onscreen, 11–12
    ending with carriage return, 659, 662
    programs producing, 11–13
`outputLabel` label, 561
output parameters, **310**, 312, 341, **722**
output streams, 654, 655, 659
`out` variable, **313**, 342, **722**
overloaded binary operators, 390
overloaded constructors, 385–386, 547, 656
overloaded operators, 391
`OverloadedTriples` program, 328–329
overloaded unary operators, 390
overloading, **322**, 342, **722**
    constructors, 380–382
    operators, 390–394
overloading methods, 322–329, 397
    ambiguous methods, **330**–331
    betterness rules, **326**
    overload resolution, **326**
    parameter lists, 324
overload resolution, **326**, 342, **722**
    named arguments, 339–340
    unnamed arguments, 339–340
`override` keyword, **457**, 459, 472
override modifier, 438
overrides, **397**, 410, **722**
overriding
    abstract methods, 457
    base class members, 436–441
    methods, 438

749

INDEX

P

Painter class, 457
panels, **577**, 591, **723**
parallel arrays, **234**, 239–240, 256, **723**
parameter arrays, **310**, 316–317, 341, **723**
ParameterDemo1 program, 310
Parameter Info ToolTip, **709**
parameterless constructor, **380**, 410, **723**
parameter lists, **272**, 299, **723**
    Main() method, 293–294
    optional parameters, 332–340
    overloading methods, 324
  parameters, **272**, 286–288, 299
    actual, **278**
    data types, 277
    formal, **278**
    identifiers, 277
    implicit parameter, **364**
    mandatory, **308**–310
    method header, 272
    methods, 299
    optional, **308**, 332–340
    passing to constructors, 379–380
    value, 278
ParamsDemo program, 316, 317
params keyword, 311, 316
Parent class, **424**, 463, 471, **723**
  child class, 428, 432–433
  hiding properties in, **438**
Parent property, 540
parse, **87**, 93, **723**
Parse() methods, 86–87, 314
Parse() variable, 84
partial identifier, 15
PartTimeEmployee class, 424
Party objects, 353
Pascal casing, **5**, **723**
PassArrayElement program, 289–290
passed by reference, **290**, 299, 308, 313, **723**
passed by value, 299, 308, **723**
PassEntireArray program, 290–291
Patent class, 460
path, **647**, 651, 656, 678, **723**
PathTooLongException class, 484
payment variable, 65
payRate array, 230
PayRate property, 379–380
payRate variable, 65, 169
PayrollApplication class, 271
payrollDay variable, 82
pay variable, 4
pepperoniCheckBox object, 560
Percent format specifier, 61
PerformLayout() method, 543
permanent storage, 646, 651
permanent storage devices, **646**, 651, **723**

persistent storage, **647**, **723**
petabytes, 705
PhoneCall program, 288
picture boxes, **563**–565, 591, **723**
PictureBox objects, 563–565, 585
pictureBox1 objects, 566
place holder, 53, 90, **723**
Play() method, 436
pointers, 10
polymorphism, **9**, 436–441, **723**
  interfaces, 397, 464
Poodle class, 425
Poodle object, 425
positional arguments, **335**, 342, **723**
Position property, **667**, 676
postfix decrement operator (−−), 66
postfix increment operator (++), **65**–66, 91, 189, **723**
  loops, 210–212
posttest loops, **723**
Pow() method, 285
precedence, **695**–696, **723**
precision specifier, **61**, 91, **723**
PreferredDiscount() method, 607, 610
prefix decrement operator (−−), 66
prefix increment operator (++), **65**–66, 91, 189, **723**
pretest loops, **723**
Preview Changes dialog box, 116
price field, 375
priceLabel label, 587–588
PriceListApplication1 program, 512–513
PriceListApplication2 program, 513–514
PriceListApplication3 program, 517
PriceList class, 512–513, 516
PriceList.DisplayPrice() method, 517–518
priceOfCall variable, 287, 288
price parameter, 377
prices array, 234, 238
price variable, 284
priming read, **660**, 662
private access, **269**–270, 299
private access modifiers, 354, 371–374
private class, 409
private field, 433
private keyword, 108
private methods, 111
private modifier, 269–270, 355
procedural programming, **4**–6, 39
procedures, 5, 8, 492
Product class, 460
Program class, 29, 34
program comments, **18**, 41
  See also comments
Program.cs file, 101, 108
programming
  high-level programming languages, **2**
  logic, **3**

object-oriented programming (OOP), 4–6
procedural, 4–6
programming languages
   assemblers, 3
   camel casing, **3**
   command prompt, 24–25
   high-level programming language, **2**–**3**
   IDE (Integrated Development Environment), 28–29
   interpreters, 3
   keywords, **2**
   lower camel casing, **3**
   semi-compiled, 23
   syntax, **3**
   syntax errors, **3**
   vocabulary, 3
programs, **2**, 38
   See also GUI applications
   alternative courses, 602
   blocks, **140**–141
   bugs, **3**
   code bloat, **268**
   code refactoring, **115**
   command line, 26
   command-line arguments, 293
   comments, 37
   compilers, **3**
   compiling, 23–31
   debugging, **3**
   deciding environment to use, 30–31
   decision making, 134–137
   design time, **112**
   documenting, 18
   events, **598**
   exceptions, **484**–488
   executing, 23–31
   failing to close form before reexecuting, 118
   fault tolerant, **488**
   flowcharts, **134**
   forcing to contain error, 486–488
   IDE (Integrated Development Environment), 23
   indenting, 13
   interactive, **84**
   interface, **100**
   intermediate language (IL), **23**
   keywords, 13
   logic, **3**
   logical errors, **3**
   logic-planning tools, 134–137
   machine language, 3
   magic number, **661**
   `Main()` method, 12–13
   multifile assembly, **267**
   namespace-dot-class-dot-method format, 12
   output, 11–13
   pseudocode, **134**

reusable modules, 6
robustness, **488**
running other programs in, 551
runtime, **112**, **598**
saving, 23
self-documenting, **337**
source code, **23**
starting point, 12
statements, 19
terminating, 509
text editors, 22
text editors *versus* IDE (Integrated Development Environment), 29–30
user input, 87–88
whitespace, **13**
projects
   closing, 123
   forms, 102
   listing files, 101, 102
   naming, 100
   saving, 100
prompt, **84**, 93
propagating execeptions, 515, 527
properties, **7**, **362**, 410, 541, 601
   access modifiers, 363
   accessors, **362**
   auto-implemented property, **366**–367
   automatic properties, **366**–367
   backing field, **363**
   buttons, 106, 122
   creation, 361–367
   curly braces ({}), 363
   data types, 363
   declaring, 363
   derived classes, 439–441
   description, 103
   expanding or condensing, 104
   forms, 122
   `get` accessors, **362**–365
   identifiers, 363
   listing of, 103
   naming, 363
   not passed as ref or out parameter, 365
   parent class, 438
   protecting private data, 362
   read from, 363
   readonly property, 363
   read/write, 561
   retrieving field values, 362
   `set` accessors, **362**–365
   setting fields, 362
   sorting, 104
   value acting like keyword, 363
   as variable, 364
   visible, **438**
   written to, 363

INDEX

Properties folder, 36
Properties window, 101, 106, 118, 122, 540–541, 545, 555
   form name, 103
      listing events, 623–624
      properties, 103, 104
   proportional fonts, **114**, 127
   protected access, **433**–435, 472
   `protected` access modifier, 354, 432–435
   `protected` field modifier, 355
pseudocode, **134**, 175
`public` access, **269**, 294, 299
`public` access modifiers, 354, 371–374
`public` class, 409
`public` keyword, 285
`public` modifier, 269, 355
`public set` accessor, 433
purchase variable, 208
`PushButtonControl` class, 16

Q

Quick Info ToolTip, 708
Quicksort algorithm, 244

R

`RadioButton` objects, 537, 559–563, 577, 586–589
radio buttons, **559**–562, 586–589, 591
   group boxes, 577
   selected by default, 562
raising events, **598**, 637
RAM. *See* random access memory
random access files, **653**
random access memory (RAM), **653**
range checks, **167**–168, 177
range match, **239**–241, 243, 256
`RankException` class, 485
RATE constant, 436–437
`rateLabel` label, 556
`rate` parameter, 338
`rate` variable, 65, 287, 288
rating variable, 154–156
Read access, 666
reading from files, 661–667
   sequential access files, 658–667
`ReadLine()` method, 84–85, 119, 266, 282, 284, 285, 314, 655, 662, 687
Read member, 656
`Read()` method, 84, 655
`ReadNameFile` program, 666–667
`readonly` field, 384
`readonly` modifier, 355, 384
readonly property, **363**, 367, 410
read-only variables, **231**, 256
`ReadSequentialFile` program, 662
`ReadWrite` member, 656
read/write properties, 561

record delimiter, 659, 662
`recordIn` string, 662
records, 663, 698, **653**, 655
rectangular arrays, **248**, 256
recursive, 472
recursive methods, **444**
`redButton_Click()` method, 635
`redButton` program, 634
reference, 299
reference equality, **449**–450, 472
reference parameters, **310**–319, 341
reference types, **358**, 409
`ref` keyword, 310–311, 313
`ref return` method, 319
`Regular` property, 547
remainder (modulus) operator (%), 63
remove identifier, 15
Rename command, 115–116
`RentFinder` program, 250
rents array, 249, 251
`RepairValve()` method, 428
`reportButton` button, 109
reserved keywords, 14–15, 30
`Resize` event, 622
response variable, 194, 198
`result` variable, 285
`ResumeLayout()` method, 543
`ReThrowDemo` program, 524–525
rethrowing exceptions, **523**–525, 527
returning value, 243
`ReturnRefDemo` program, 320
`return` statement, **282**, 299
   catch block, 509
   `switch` structure, 160
return type, **271**, 282, 299, 313
reusable code, 424
`ReverseArray` program, 244
`Reverse()` methods, 244–247, 266, 290
right-associative, **695**–696
`Right` property, 540
Ritchie, Dennis, 141
robustness, **488**, 527
`root` class, 446, 472
root directory, **647**
Round trip format specifier, 61
rules for betterness, 339
runnable, **13**
runtime, **112**, 126, **172**, 177, **598**, 602, 637
runtime errors, 484

S

`salary` field, 379, 422–423, 427, 432–435
`Salary` property, 379, 383, 387, 433
`saleAmount` variable, **141**–142, 151, 167–168, 277, 278, 281, 606–607

INDEX

sales array, 225–226, 248–249
salesArray array, 225
salesCode variable, 169–170
salesList array, 225
salesperson object, 427
salesTable array, 225
sal parameter, 383
SatisfyGraduationRequirements() method, 436
sausageCheckBox_CheckedChanged() method, 561
sausageCheckBox object, 560–561
Save All (Ctrl + Shift + S) keyboard shortcut, 35
SaveMoney frame, 566
saving programs, 22–23
sbyte data type, **56**–57, 59, 72
   automatic conversions, 279
ScholarshipStudent class, 438, 446–447
Scientific format specifier, 61
scientific notation, **60**, 91
scope, **273**
   GUI applications, 296
scores array, 245–247
score variable, 86, 315–316
screaming caps, **81**, 92
screen, displaying output, 11–12
ScrollableControl class, 468
Sculptor class, 457
sealed classes, **465**, 472
Search command, 24
searching arrays
   arrays of objects, 396–400
   binary search, **241**–243
   for loops, 234–236
   with loops, 233–241
   parallel arrays, 234
   range match, **239**–244
   sequential search, **234**
   while loops, 237–238
secondDel delegate, 603, 605, 607, 609
seekEmp object, 399–400
Seek() method, 665, 667, 670
SeekOrigin enumeration, 667–668
SelectedIndexChanged() method, 566
SelectedIndex property, 566
SelectedIndices property, 566
SelectedItems property, 566–567, 569, 570
SelectionEnd property, 571–574
SelectionMode enumeration, 568
SelectionMode property, 566, 568
SelectionRange property, 571
SelectionStart property, 571–572
Select Resource window, 564, 585
self-documenting, **337**, 342
self-documenting statements, **81**, 93
semicolon (;) expected error message, 117
sentinal value, **192**, 216, 660, 661
sequence structure, **134**, 176

sequential access files, 658–667
   reading from, 661–664
   rereading, 687
   searching, 667–670
   writing data to, 658–661
sequential search, **234**, 256
[Serializable] attribute, 674
SerializableDemonstration program, 675–677
serialization, 673–686
Serialize() method, 675
set accessors, **362**–365, 369, 371, 410, 426, 433, 437, 442–443, 521, 612
set_AccountNum set assessor, 522
set_Balance set assessor, 522
set identifier, 15
SetIdNumber() method, 361–362
SetPriceAndTax() method, 377
SetSelected() method, 570
setter, **363**, 410
Shift property, 629
short-circuit evaluation, **152**–153, 176, 285
shortcut arithmetic operators, 64–66
   add and assign shortcut operator (+=), **65**
   divide and assign shortcut operator (/=), 65
   multiply and assign shortcut operator (*=), 65
   postfix arithmetic operator (++), **65**–66
   postfix decrement operator (--), 66
   prefix decrement operator (--), 66
   prefix increment operator (++), **65**–66
   subtract and assign shortcut operator (-=), 65
shortcut operators, 189
short data type, **56**–57, 59, 72
   automatic conversions, 279
ShowDialog() method, 583
ShowDog class, 8–9
ShowTodayCircle property, 571
ShowToday property, 571
ShowWelcomeMessage() method, 272–273
side effects, **153**–154, 176
signature, **322**, 342
significant digits, 59, 91
simple data types, **48**, 90, 358
SimpleMethod() method, 330–331
single-argument methods, 276–280
single-dimensional arrays, **247**, 256
single quotation mark escape sequence (\'), 75
SizeMode property, 563
Size property, 103, 106, 110, 122, 406, 540, 543, 566, 598, 601, 634
snap lines, **575**, 591
SoapException class, 484
software, **2**
soldItem method, 320
Solution Explorer, 100, 406, 558, 586
   files part of current project, 101
   form name, 102

INDEX

Solution Explorer (*continued*)
   nodes, **102**
   project name, 100
`someMoney` variable, 52–54
`someNums` array, 289
`SomeOtherClass` class, 273
`someValue` variable, 65
`someWorker` object, 448
`SortArray` program, 243
`Sorted` property, 566
sorting
   arrays, 241–244
   arrays of objects, 396–400
   characters, 396
   integers, 396
   properties, 103, 104
`Sort()` methods, 243–247, 266, 290
source code, **23**
   colors, 710
   syntax errors, 25
source code editor. *See* IDE Editor
`Speak()` method, 457–459
`specialButton` button, 173–174
`specialButton_Click()` method, 174
`Split()` method, 662
`Spruce` class, 425
`Spruce` objects, 425
squiggles, 710
`StackOverflowException` class, 485
`StackTrace` property, 514–519, 522
`StandardDiscount()` method, 607, 610
standard numeric format strings, **61**, 91
`StartsWith()` method, **79**
state, **5**, 353
statements, 19
   commenting out, 18
   ending with semicolon (;), 11
   executing two or more conditionally, 140
   method body, 272
   self-documenting, **81**
static classes, 469
static field modifier, 355
`static` keyword, **13**, 20, 108, 274, 276, 285, 296, 373
`static` methods, 78, 108, **270**–271, 277, 299, 356, 392, 466, 610
static modifier, 356
static objects, 356
STEP keyword, 195
step value, **195**, 216
`StreamReader` class, 655
`StreamReader` objects, 661
streams, 654–658
   exposing, 655
   input, 655
   output, 655
`StreamWriter` class, 655

`StreamWriter` constructor, 656
`StreamWriter` object, 656, 659, 687
`Strikeout` property, 547
`string` argument, 546, 551, 603
`String` class, 77, 396, 449, 469, 662
String Collection Editor, 568
`string` data type, 48, **76**–80, 282, 659
`String.Format()` method, 53, 113
   formatting, 113
string interpolation, 53, 90
`string Length` property, 322
`String` objects, 449, 666, 674, 682
strings, **76**–80, 92, 322
   accessing character with subscripts, 228
   arguments, 11
   assigning array character to, 227
   characters, 74
   combining values, 53
   comparing, 77–79, 449
   concatenating, **53**, 390
   console input, 84
   converting, 84–88, 506–507
   converting integer to, 323
   converting numbers to, 61
   converting to number, 86–87, 314–316
   data types, 85–86
   delimiters, 659
   escape characters, 113
   format string, **53**–54
   formatting, 53–54, 113
   forms, 104
   holding name of class, 448
   immutable, **79**
   interpreting characters literally, 551
   largest and smallest values, 48
   `length`, 79, 230
   lexically, **77**
   placeholders for values, 53
   separating fields into array of, 662
   starting characters, 79
   `substrings`, 79
   text boxes, 111
   tokens, 659
   user input, 88
`struct`, 358
`StudentChanged()` method, 613
`Student` class, 368–371, 385, 437–439, 446–447, 611–616, 621, 653
`Student` constructor, 401
`Student` objects, 370–371, 401, 612, 613
`stu` object, 612
subclasses, **424**, 457, 460, 471
subroutines, 5
subscripts, **224**, 226, 255, 665
   accessing character in array, 228
   constants, 229

INDEX

integers, 226
range of, 229–230
two-dimensional arrays, 248
variables, 229
`Substring()` method, 79
subtract and assign shortcut operator (−=), 65, 605
subtraction operator (−), 63, 605
`sub` variable, 229
`SUDSParserException` class, 484
suggestion mode, **708**, 710
summing numbers, 110
`sum` property, 114
superclass, **424**, 457, 471
`SuspendLayout()` method, 543
`Swap()` method, 318–319
`SwapProgram` program, 318–319
switch-case structure. *See* switch structure
`switch` keyword, 160
switch structure, **159**
alternative courses of action, 162
`break` keyword, 160–165
`case` keyword, 160
`case` labels, **160**
`default` case, 161
`default` keyword, 160
enumerations, 162–163
governing type, **160**
GUI applications, 171, 173–174
`return` statement, 160
`switch` keyword, 160
`throw` statement, 160
syntax, **3**
syntax errors, **3**, 25, 116
IDE (Integrated Development Environment), 28
`System.Array` class, 226, 230, 241, 396
`System.Console` class, 275
`System.Diagnostics.Process.Start()` method, 551
`SystemException` class, 486–488
`SystemException` objects, 489–491
`System.IO` namespace, 682
`System` namespace, **12**, 19–20, 446, 465, 509
aliases, **48**
fully qualified data type name, 50
`System.Object` class, 446
`System.Runtime.Serialization.Formatters.Binary` namespace, 674, 675
`System.Runtime.Serialization` namespace, 674
system software, **2**
`System.Windows.Forms.AxHost` class, 537
`System.Windows.Forms.ButtonBase` class, 537
`System.Windows.Forms.Button` class, 600
`System.Windows.Forms.Control` class, 537–538
`System.Windows.Forms.DataGrid` class, 537
`System.Windows.Forms.DataGridView` class, 537
`System.Windows.Forms.DateTimePicker` class, 537
`System.Windows.Forms.GroupBox` class, 537
`System.Windows.Forms.Integration.ElementHost` class, 537
`System.Windows.Forms.Integration.Label` class, 537
`System.Windows.Forms.Integration.ListControl` class, 537
`System.Windows.Forms.Integration.ListView` class, 537
`System.Windows.Forms.Integration.MdiClient` class, 537
`System.Windows.Forms.Integration.MonthCalendar` class, 537
`System.Windows.Forms.Integration.PictureBox` class, 537
`System.Windows.Forms. PrintPreviewControl` class, 538
`System.Windows.Forms.ProgressBar` class, 538
`System.Windows.Forms. ScrollableControl` class, 538
`System.Windows.Forms.ScrollBar` class, 538
`System.Windows.Forms.Splitter` class, 538
`System.Windows.Forms.StatusBar` class, 538
`System.Windows.Forms.TabControl` class, 538
`System.Windows.Forms.TextBoxBase` class, 538
`System.Windows.Forms.ToolBar` class, 538
`System.Windows.Forms.TrackBar` class, 538
`System.Windows.Forms.TreeView` class, 538
`System.Windows.Forms.WebBrowserBase` class, 538

T

`TabIndex` property, 113, 540, 543, 634–635
`TabIndex` value, 631, 634–635
tables, 248
tab order, **113**, 127
`TabStop` property, 113, 631
`TakeBloodPressure()` method, 428
`Tax` class, 515–516, 518
`Tax.DetermineTaxRate()` method, 518
`taxRate` array, 516
`TAX_RATE` constant, 81
`taxRate` variable, 281
temporary variables, 319
`tempTotal` variable, 209
`temp` variable, 399
terabytes, 705
terminating programs, 509
ternary operators, 164, 176
`TestCarpet` class, 373–374
`testExpression` variable, 164
testing for equivalency, 143–144
`testScore` variable, 165
`TextBox` class, 110
`TextBox` control, **109**–114
text boxes, 109–112, **110**, 119, 126
`TextBox` objects, 538
`TextChanged` event, 622

INDEX

Text control, 468
text editors, 21
    filename extensions, 22
    find and replace feature, 230
    versus IDE (Integrated Development Environment) and, 29–30
    identifiers, 29
text files, 646, 661–673
    GUI application creation, 678–681
    reading data, 658–667
    reading data into form, 681–686
    reading objects from, 674
text in labels, 109–110
Text property, 102, 103, 106, 109–112, 122–124, 540–541, 543, 549, 555–556, 559, 561, 563–564, 566, 569, 598–600, 622, 624, 631–632, 634, 678, 681
TextReader class, 655
TextWriter class, 655
theTreeInMyBackYard object, 425
thirdDel delegate, 609
this keyword, 465–466, 542
this reference, **376**–378, 383, 398, 410
three-dimensional arrays, 251
ThreeLinesOutput class, 29
ThreeLinesOutput.cs file, 24–26
ThreeLinesOutput.exe file, 26
ThreeLinesOutput project, 28
throwing exceptions, 492–497, 499–500, 522–523
throw keyword, 523, 525
    switch structure, 160
tickets array, 252
ticketsUnderMinimum variable, 166
time, 571–574, 647–650
TIMES constant, 210
TippingTable program, 205, 206
TippingTable2 program, 206
tipRate variable, 203–205
TIPSTEP constant, 204
title field, 375
ToBoolean() method, 86
ToByte() method, 86
ToChar() method, 86
TodayDate property, 573
ToDecimal() method, 86
ToDouble() method, 84, 86
ToInt16() method, 86
ToInt32() method, 86, 507
ToInt64() method, 86
tokens, **659**, 673
ToLongDateString() method, 572
Toolbox, 122, 556
    adding button to form, 105–109
    listing controls, 105
    Menus & Toolbars group, 578
    pinning to screen, 105
TopLevelControl property, 540

TOPPING_PRICE constant, 561
Top property, 540
ToSbyte() method, 86
ToShortDateString() method, 572
ToSingle() method, 86
ToString() method, 86, 295, 370, 447, 496–497, 568, 600
    format specifiers, 61
    overriding, 448
total array, 253
totals
    accumulated, 206–207
    add and assign shortcut operator (+=), 207
total variable, 207–208
ToUInt16() method, 86
ToUInt32() method, 86
ToUInt64() method, 86
traditional exception-handling methods *versus* object-oriented exception-handling methods, 491–492
TRANSACTIONS constant, 620
transitive, **425**, 471
Tree class, 425
triggering events, **598**, 637
Triple() method, 328–329
true-or-false comparisons, 68–69, 136, 138, 176
Truncate file mode, 656
truth tables, **150**, 176
TryBankAccount program, 521–522
try block, **492**–493, 499–506, 508–510, 513, 527, 657, 685
try...catch block, 685
try keyword, 492
TryParse() method, 314–316, 365, 506–507
tuition field, 436–439
Tuition property, 437
two-dimensional arrays, **248**–249
TwoErrors class, 501–502
TwoErrors program, 501–502
TwoErrors2 program, 502–503
TwoErrors3 program, 503–504
.txt file extension, 551
type precedence, **72**, 92
type-safe data types, **83**, 93

U

uint data type, **56**, 72
    automatic conversions, 279
ulong data type, **56**, 72
    automatic conversions, 279
unary form, 390
unary operators, **65**, 92, 164
    overloaded, 390, 394
    right-associative, **695**
Underline property, 547
UnhandledException window, 684, 685
Unicode, **48**, 74–75, 90, 646, 652, **699**, 706
    characters represented as numbers, 56

INDEX

foreign alphabets, 75
letter values, 104
unifying type, **72**, 92
uninitialized variables, 51
uniquely identifying, 450
unnamed arguments, 334–335
  overload resolution, 339–340
unnamed constants, 48
unreachable, 504, 527
unsafe mode, 10
upper camel casing, **5**
user-created namespaces, 29
user-defined application exception classes, 486
`UseTaxMethod` program, 278, 279
`ushort` data type, **56**–57, 59, 72
  automatic conversions, 279
`using` clause, **20**
`using` directive, **20**
`using` statements, 21, 27, 29, 34, 606, **709**
`using static System.Console` statement, 20, 27, 29

V

`ValidID` project, 193–194
`validValues` array, 233–234, 236–237
`ValueChanged` property, 574
value identifier, 70
`value` keyword, 15, 364
value parameters, 278, **308**–310, 332, 341
`Value` property, 574
value-returning methods, 271, 282–285
values
  comparing to valid values in array, 233
  garbage, **207**
value types, **358**, 409
`Vampire` class, 463
variable declaration, **50**, 90
variables, **4**, 8, **48**
  aliases, 310, 311
  alignment, 55–56
  arrays, 224
  assigning values, 50–51
  camel casing, 3
  checking value, 491
  combining values, 53
  comparing to valid values, 233
  data types, 50, 57
  declaring, 48–51, 57–59
  displaying values, 52–56
  enumerations, 82
  fixed number of integral values for, 82
  identifiers, **4**, 50
  increasing value in, 64–66, 189
  initializing, **50**
  initial value, 50

instance variables, **353**
local, **273**
methods, 273–274, 296
naming, 49–50
nonstatic, 356
out of scope, **196**
postfix arithmetic operator (++), 65
prefix arithmetic operator (++), 65
read-only, **231**
reducing value in, 66
scope, **273**
subscripts, 229
uninitialized, 51
usage, 58–59
variable substitution, 53
verbatim identifiers, **14**
vertical tab escape sequence (\v), 75
`viewButton` button, 681
`viewButton_Click()` method, 682
`ViewInvoices` program, 681–683, 686
virtual methods, **437**, 457, 472
visible, **438**, 472
`VisibleChanged` event, 622
`Visible` control, 468
`Visible` property, 103, 106, 124, 540
`VisitedLinkColor` property, 549
Visual Basic, 5
Visual Studio, 9
  automatic completion, 30
  closing, 36
  compiling code with IDE (Integrated Development Environment), 26–29
  editor, 21
  enumerations, 82
  Help documentation, 118
  namespaces, 12, 29
  program comments, 37
  Properties window, 540
  using statements, 29
`Void` class, 16
`void` keyword, **13**, 272
`void` methods, 271, 290
`void` return type, 293, 603, 605
volatile, **646**
volatile field modifier, 355
volatile memory, 653

W

`wasSuccessful` variable, 507
WEDNESDAY constant, 83
`weeklyBudget` variable, 73
`welcomeLabel` label, 556
`WelcomeMessage()` method, 356, 359, 363
`where` identifier, 15
`while` keyword, 186

INDEX

`while` loops, **186**–194, 212, 513, 660
    comparing value to valid values in array, 233
    curly braces ({}), 189
    definite loops, 195
    displaying integers 1 through 10, 195
    empty body, **190**
    indefinite loops, 195
    loop body, 186–187
    loop control variable, **187**, 195
    navigating arrays, 230–231
    performing arithmetic, 229
    searching arrays, 237–238
`whiteButton` button, 634
whitespace, **13**
whole numbers, 56–57
widgets, **536**, 591
width field, 373
`Width` property, 104, 374, 388, 538, 540
`Width` value, 576
`Window` objects, 578
windows, 104
`WindowsFormsApp1`, 100
`worker1` object, 399
`worker2` object, 399
`Work()` method, 461–463
`WriteLine()` method, 11–12, 27, 34, 58, 61–62, 66–68, 76, 84, 119, 145, 266–267, 270, 276, 280, 284, 285, 322, 431, 456, 494, 518, 655, 659
    displaying variable values, 52–56
`WriteLine()` statement, 13
`Write` member, 656
`Write()` method, 12, 84, 655, 659
    displaying variable values, 52–56

`writer` objects, 656, 659
`WriteSequentialFile` class, 661
`WriteSomeText` program, 657
writing to files, 658–667

X

XML (eXtensible Markup Language), 18, 658, **728**
XML-documentation format contents (< >), **18**, 41
XML files, 658
`XmlTextReader` class, 658
`XmlTextWriter` class, 658
X property, 627
x variable, 309, 311, 312
`XxxException` placeholder, 492

Y

Year property, 443
`yearsOfService` variable, 153–154
year variable, 159, 161
`yield` identifier, 15
yottabytes, 705
`yourAge` variable, 51
`yourAnniversaryParty` identifier, 353
`yourBook.AdvertisingMessage()` method, 376
Y property, 627

Z

zeroth element, 226
`zero` variable, 489
zettabytes, 705
ZONE1 constant, 157
ZONE2 constant, 157